The War Beat, Europe

The War Beat, Europe

The American Media at War Against Nazi Germany

Steven Casey

OXFORD
UNIVERSITY PRESS

Oxford University Press is a department of the University of Oxford. It furthers the University's objective of excellence in research, scholarship, and education by publishing worldwide. Oxford is a registered trade mark of Oxford University Press in the UK and certain other countries.

Published in the United States of America by Oxford University Press
198 Madison Avenue, New York, NY 10016, United States of America.

Library of Congress Cataloging-in-Publication Data
Names: Casey, Steven, author.
Title: The war beat, Europe : the American media at war against
Nazi Germany / Steven Casey.
Description: New York, NY : Oxford University Press, [2017] |
Includes bibliographical references and index.
Identifiers: LCCN 2016041728 (print) | LCCN 2016058936 (ebook) |
ISBN 9780190660628 (hardback : acid-free paper) |
ISBN 9780190660635 (Updf) | ISBN 9780190660642 (Epub)
Subjects: LCSH: World War, 1939-1945—Press coverage—United States. |
World War, 1939-1945—Public opinion. | Mass media—Political
aspects—United States—History—20th century. |
War correspondents—United States—History—20th century. |
War correspondents—Europe—History—20th century. |
Censorship—United States—History—20th century. |
Civil-military relations—United States—History—20th century. | Public
opinion—United States—History—20th century. |
BISAC: HISTORY / Military / World War II. | HISTORY / Military / General. |
HISTORY / United States / 20th Century.
Classification: LCC D799.U6 C38 2017 (print) | LCC D799.U6 (ebook) |
DDC 940.53/112—dc23
LC record available at https://lccn.loc.gov/2016041728

1 3 5 7 9 8 6 4 2

Printed by Sheridan Books, Inc., United States of America

For my parents, Margaret and Terry

CONTENTS

ACKNOWLEDGMENTS

I began work on this book in 2008. Since then, a number of projects and a string of university administrative jobs have prevented me from finishing it as quickly as I would have liked. I want to begin by thanking the organizations that helped to fund this project and have waited patiently to see it finally appear in print, especially the US Military History Institute, which awarded me a Matthew Ridgway grant in 2009, the British Academy, which provided me with one its Small Grants in 2010, the Eisenhower Library, which gave me a research grant in 2013, and the International History department at the London School of Econmics, which provided me with two awards from its Research Infrastructure and Investment funds.

I owe a large debt to all the staff at so many archives, especially Valerie Comor and Francesca Pitaro at the AP Archives, Cynthia Young at the International Center for Photography, Art Miller at Lake Forest College, Eric Gillespie at the McCormick Archives, Richard Sommers at the US Military History Institute, David Gobel at the Citadel, Jeffrey Kozak at the Marshall Foundation, and Janet W. McKee at the Recorded Sound Research Center in the Library of Congress. I would also like to thank Yvonne Kincaid at Air Force Historical Research Agency, Diana Bachman at the Bentley Historical Library, Diane Jacob at the Virginia Military Institute, Roslyn Pachoca at the Library of Congress, and last but not least Dan Strieff, who all tracked down particular documents for me.

A number of colleagues have read earlier versions of the manuscript. I would like to thank Jim Hamilton, Ralph Levering, David Reynolds, and Philip Woods. I have been particularly fortunate to work for a fourth time with Susan Ferber at Oxford University Press, and I am extremely grateful for her continued support, advice, and editing expertise. I would also like to thank Ginny Faber for her excellent copyediting and Maya

Bringe who skillfully shepherded the book through the various production stages.

My final and most important thanks go to my family. My effervescent daughter, Lauren, always makes me laugh and smile. My parents, Terry and Margaret, have been particularly supportive in recent years. This book is dedicated to them.

The War Beat, Europe

Introduction

They were the men and women who braved bullets and bombs to report America's war against Nazi Germany, and over the decades they have acquired legendary status. Broadcasting pioneers like Edward R. Murrow and Walter Cronkite, unpretentious reporters like Ernie Pyle, dashing photographers like Robert Capa and Margaret Bourke-White: they are remembered for their courage in putting their lives on the line to record the sights and sounds of the World War II battlefield for a grateful home-front audience.[1]

Nor is theirs simply a tale of pure heroism. Often, these trailblazing correspondents are portrayed as key members of America's war-winning team. In return for their fervent loyalty to the anti-Nazi cause, so the argument goes, the military provided them with unprecedented access to all the major events of the war.[2] Thus, they hit the Normandy beaches on D-Day, flew on Flying Fortress missions over Germany, drove with George Patton's army into the heart of Germany—all without chaperones. As one major book claims, this generation of reporters "enjoyed a generous amount of freedom in pursuing their stories at the front."[3]

Small wonder that they apparently responded with patriotic generosity, telling a story that both the military and the home front wanted to hear. At one level, we are informed, these war correspondents wrote the first draft of a historical narrative that became the staple of subsequent books, movies, and TV shows—namely, that the GIs were basically unstoppable. After nervously boarding their landing crafts and climbing into transport planes on June 6, 1944, they drove relentlessly forward, breaking out of the Normandy beachhead within weeks, liberating Paris within months, and driving into the heart of Hitler's Reich by early 1945. As they did so, the war correspondents could tell a gripping morality tale of Americans as the good guys who freed Western Europe from the terrors of Nazi rule. They could also relate a triumphal victory, as American power swept aside almost every obstacle to force Germany to surrender unconditionally in May 1945.[4]

At another level, we are further told, these correspondents packaged battlefield news in a palatable form. When the air force insisted that its Flying Fortresses were only "precision bombing" German factories, not indiscriminately targeting German civilians, "few reporters were inclined to contest official claims. They saw themselves," argues one historian, "as enlisted in the war effort, their task that of establishing confidence in Allied virtue and victory and commanders." When the army got bogged down in a brutal stalemate in the Italian mountains, the correspondents again pulled their punches. "Had they accurately described the perils," according to another historian, "there would have been a public outcry to stop 'the senseless slaughter.'"[5]

Instead of having their words suppressed, World War II war correspondents engaged in self-censorship. As the dominant view puts it, these patriotic Americans did not need to be told what type of story would have a corrosive impact on home-front morale. They knew themselves. And so they willingly excised anything too gruesome from their daily dispatches, protecting loved ones back home from learning about the full horrors of war. Ernie Pyle led the way. As he followed GIs around the front line, Pyle quickly developed an eye for capturing the GIs' daily experiences, but without, apparently, ever crossing a line and providing his readers with images they could not stomach. Pyle, his biographer concludes, "gave Americans all the realism they wanted"—which was hardly any at all. The public much preferred to read about their citizen soldiers as team players, who looked out for each another but were often cynical about their officers, or as stoic survivors, whose daily needs were simple but who pined to return to their homes and families.[6]

The consequences of this kind of reporting are held to be critically important, too. According to conventional wisdom, the war correspondents played a pivotal role in forging a home-front consensus that enabled the United States to prevail: very few Americans, after all, were likely to oppose the fight against such an evil enemy, especially when the nasty battlefield scenes had been airbrushed. Subsequently, this record of apparent success has become a touchstone in broader discussions about the media coverage of war in an open society.

For those writers who believe that a healthy democracy requires an informed public, World War II marks a nadir: a time when excessive media deference served to hide everything except the genius of generals and the success of their soldiers. Phillip Knightley's classic *The First Casualty* exemplifies this line of attack. The war, according to Knightley, "could have been better reported. The main bar to this," he argues, "was the correspondent's excusable identification with the cause and his less excusable incorporation into the military machine."[7]

By contrast, those who sympathize with the military's need to restrict information have seen World War II as an experience to emulate—a halcyon age when both sides joined together to do what was necessary to keep the home front happy until victory was achieved.[8] The searing Vietnam experience has informed most of the work written from this perspective. After the US media disseminated vivid and emotive battlefield images during this "bad war," military officers and academic analysts alike harkened back to the so-called "good war," seeking to learn its apparent lessons. Substantive changes emerged slowly in the years after 1975; but by the time of the two Persian Gulf Wars, the military had overhauled its media relations. With a nod to the World War II era, officers attempted to make war correspondents a formal part of the military team, embedding them in units so that they would come to identify with the combat troops, and thereby understand the need to restrict the information emanating from a war zone.[9]

Whether they attack or applaud this close relationship, these works agree that it did indeed exist during World War II. The starting point of this book is very different. Utilizing a wealth of primary sources, *War Beat, Europe* reexamines the core assumption that World War II reporters fully enlisted in the military team. It also uncovers when and why these correspondents reported directly from the front. It assesses whether their dispatches told only a story of triumph and whether they repeatedly excised details that were too nasty. Above all, it explores the extent to which the American public was exposed to an upbeat and anodyne image of combat, which helped to ensure that domestic support remained durable and robust.

THE WAR REPORTERS

To address these issues, the book begins with the reporters themselves, although to write a comprehensive story of their actions presents a major challenge. Because war correspondents are generally so individualistic and competitive, they are difficult to write about as a group. On the battlefield, no obvious hierarchy exists. Sometimes reporters work together; on other occasions they are are rivals to get the scoop.

While earlier works have sidestepped this problem by focusing on the star names or on one particular branch of journalism, this book is organized around the news stories that mattered: the ones that got published, garnered the most attention, and exerted the biggest impact.[10] Sometimes this means treading a familiar path, given, for instance, the massive influence of Ernie Pyle's columns or Robert Capa's photographs. Frequently, though, it presents interesting new perspectives. The pages that follow showcase a number of highly influential correspondents who reached a huge national audience at the time, even though their names no longer resonate so powerfully. The dispatches of Wes Gallagher and Don Whitehead of the Associated Press (AP), Bill Stoneman of the *Chicago Daily News*, Homer Bigart of the *New York Herald Tribune*, and John Thompson of the *Chicago Tribune* were syndicated so widely that they frequently dominated the news pages of countless papers. Other reporters worked for mass-circulation outlets, such as Jack Belden and William Walton of *Time*, or wrote for highly prestigious titles like the *New York Times*, whose impressive Europe-based team included Pete Daniell, Harold Denny, Frank Kluckhohn, and Drew Middleton.[11]

Working back from their high-impact dispatches, the book seeks to understand why these reporters produced what they did by assessing their motives and recounting their experiences.[12] Comparing two or more reporters at various stages of the war reveals, among other things, why Middleton and Kluckhohn told clashing stories of Allied relations in the North African desert, Capa and Bourke-White produced very different photos of the Italian war, and Bigart became much more controversial than Stoneman or Pyle during the Anzio stalemate.

Although war reporters often responded to front-line conditions in their own idiosyncratic ways, or described what they saw in their own distinctive prose, they also shared a similar professional self-image that was rooted in the past. Indeed, the war correspondents of this era were heirs to a tradition dating back to the Crimean War and the colonial conflicts of the nineteenth century. It was a tradition that emphasized glamour, danger, and the prospect of fortune and fame. A war correspondent, as one of the most illustrious once observed, "was a more romantic figure, more dependent on his own resources, initiative, daring, imagination, and audacity" than any other type of journalist.[13]

At the start of World War II the vast of majority reporters headed for the front with images like these fixed firmly in their minds. Some, like Hal Boyle of the AP, had joined the profession in order to emulate legendary war correspondents, such as Richard Harding Davis, who at the turn of the twentieth century not merely had written the news but had made it. As one of his colleagues noted, he "seemed to have created a picture of himself and to be trying to live up to it." After leaving the battlefield, Davis wrote riveting books about his foreign adventures that made him even more money than his highly profitable war reports had. At first, these war reports contained an uplifting message. During America's "splendid little war" against Spain in 1898, they even exuded a Boys' Own quality that glorified combat. But, gradually, Davis's reporting changed. Before he died of a heart attack in 1916, the dean of American war correspondents was profoundly disillusioned with modern conflict. From World War I's horrific trenches, Davis had documented the tragedy of young soldiers broken by shells and bullets, as well as the gruesome battlefields that artillery and machine guns converted into "an endless grave."[14]

After World War I, few reporters would deny that war was a grisly, miserable business. But the image of the charismatic correspondent, such as Davis, was still so resonant that many remained deeply attracted to the prospect of covering it, often justifying their urge with a familiar cliché. Combat, they confessed, was like a drug: a dangerous addiction that could invigorate the mind while endangering the body.[15]

So as conflicts erupted around the globe during the late 1930s, a new generation of reporters hurried to the front. Often, they came in search of fame and glory. Usually, they left deeply disenchanted, even scarred, by the experience. But whatever the reality of their experiences, these new stars—an Ernest Hemingway during the Spanish Civil War or an Ed Murrow during the London blitz—did provide Americans back home with a sense of what modern combat had become. Equally, these big names inspired a new group of young journalists.[16]

By the time of Pearl Harbor, then, many of the correspondents angling to cover the American war against Nazi Germany had a clear expectation of what their professional role would be. They saw themselves as much more than chaperoned scribes who would merely jot down basic information on the latest battles. They were courageous danger seekers whose rightful place was in the midst of the action.

THE MILITARY AND THE MEDIA

Despite this heroic self-image, all war correspondents had to operate within two hierarchies: that of the military and that of their own news organizations.

Although their bosses back home were a distant presence, they invariably made made vital decisions about where to send which correspondents, and about the types of story they wanted them to write. At the front, the military exercised enormous power over what was reported, not just by overtly censoring dispatches, but also by providing access to transport and communications. In the following pages the focus therefore shifts between the battlefield and other places of power: the Allied command centers and local media offices in London, Algiers, Naples, and Paris, as well as the headquarters of the top bosses in Washington, DC, Chicago, and New York. In all of these locations, decisions were made that cast a long shadow over how the war was reported.

Presiding at the top of it all was President Franklin D. Roosevelt. In the immediate aftermath of Pearl Harbor, Roosevelt feared the war in Europe could become deeply contentious, especially since many Americans wanted to focus on defeating Japan. Against this backdrop, Roosevelt encouraged the military, when possible, to eschew simple suppression. He wanted—in the provocative words of General George C. Marshall, the army chief of staff—war news that would "entertain" the public so that it would feel it had a stake in the European war. A year later, after the German Wehrmacht had been defeated in North Africa and Sicily, the president worried that Americans had become too complacent about the prospect of a quick and easy victory. He therefore moved to relax censorship, so that the public would receive a more realistic view "of the dangers, sacrifices, and suffering endured by American fighting men."[17]

Roosevelt's actions were important because they helped to establish the broad parameters of permissible debate—what political scientists call "the sphere of legitimate controversy."[18] This "sphere" did not remain static throughout the war. Rather, the type of story deemed palatable for the home front fluctuated according to a number of variables. One was the progress of the war itself, for there were plenty of moments when the fighting went badly, particularly during the awful winter of 1943–44, when the Allied bombing campaign faltered and the fighting in Italy got bogged down in a gruesome stalemate. At such moments, the president—sometimes in conjunction with the War Department and the propagandists in the Office of War Information (OWI)—had to decide how much realism the public could stomach. Then officers near the front-lines had to implement the resulting policy, knowing full well that too grim a depiction of the fighting might lead to the termination of their careers.

In Europe, General Dwight D. Eisenhower was the senior American officer. As supreme commander during both the Mediterranean campaign of 1942–43 and the Western European campaign of 1944–45, Eisenhower played a major role in shaping how the military interacted with war correspondents. His press conferences set the tone, especially his repeated references to reporters being "quasi officers of my staff."[19] His headquarters provided crucial daily roundup briefings, which attempted to summarize all the disparate threads across a broad and often fast-moving battlefront. And his senior censors not only drafted and redrafted the basic censorship guidelines, but also worked to ensure that American and British news organizations were subjected to the same restrictions.[20]

As the war dragged on, responsibility for media relations increasingly devolved to generals who were closer to the fighting. From 1943, the army level commands bore the brunt of the job of housing, briefing, transporting, and censoring correspondents who wanted to observe the fighting firsthand. As these armies proliferated, some senior officers worried that the correspondents were identifying too strongly with the unit to which they had been allocated, which in turn gave the news reports a fragmented feel. General Omar N. Bradley, who as the commander of the Twelfth Army Group was situated between Eisenhower and these armies, repeatedly pressed for the strengthening of his own press relations to counter this problem, but to no avail. As a result, the American home front was bombarded with stories about the exploits of the First, Third, Fifth, or Ninth Armies. And the respective army commanders—especially Generals George Patton and Mark Clark—became, along with Eisenhower, some of the war's biggest stars.

Further down the chain of command, large support staffs helped to ensure that the media-military relationship steadily improved over the course of the war, albeit with a few savage setbacks. Many of the military's public relations officers (PROs) had been drafted from the media world. Knowing the profession inside out, they were often sensitive to the reporters' daily routines, regular demands, and intense pressures. They also facilitated a learning process that unfolded after the first chaotic fumbling during the North African campaign in 1942, so that by the time of the Normandy invasion in 1944, practical problems, such as when to ease censorship and how to ensure the rapid flow of news stories from the battlefront, were greatly improved, even if they were never totally resolved.

Equally importantly, these media-savvy PROs also expedited the introduction of new technologies that brought more vivid and dramatic versions of the war into the nation's living rooms. Radio was the most important of these. World War II erupted just as the main networks were finding their feet as purveyors of international news.[21] In the fall of 1940, Ed Murrow famously demonstrated radio's ability to grab the nation's attention with graphic battlefield reporting when he broadcast live commentaries of the German blitz on London. But for a long time after, Murrow's blitz broadcasts remained the exception rather than the norm. The reason was simple.

Radio equipment was too cumbersome to lug around a fluid, fast-moving battlefield. Not until late 1943, when the army provided radio correspondents with new, portable wire recorders, was this problem overcome. Until then, broadcasters had to make do with relating an insipid, second-hand version of the war, often merely regurgitating dry official communiqués into the microphone.

Which leads to a crucial point. Before the PROs worked out how to speed up the transmission of print copy from the battlefield or how to make it possible for radio correspondents to broadcast the sounds of combat, Americans were often exposed to nothing more exciting than the HQ version of the war—heavy on dull facts culled from the daily communiqués. Breaking news often came through on the radio first, but invariably amounted to little more than a bald announcement of a particular operation. The next edition of a newspaper might flesh out the story, but these initial articles tended to be written by reporters who were hundreds, if not thousands, of miles from the battle scene. Because of the poor communications links, eyewitness reports might not hit the front pages for days, sometimes weeks, after the event. On more than one occasion, the war correspondents risked their lives to report a story, only to find that their editors had spiked their dispatch as old news by the time it reached the stateside office.

As a result, even the most courageous correspondents sometimes decided to report a battle from a distant headquarters, rather than venture to the front. They knew that they were violating a key tenet of the war correspondent's heroic self-image, but they felt they had little choice. As one veteran remarked, "It was always fine and exciting to go in with the first assault wave, but not much use professionally since it was almost always impossible to get any copy out until a day or two later."[22] Meanwhile, their colleagues at the front were often far from happy. The military might have provided them with unprecedented access to great events, but it was little use if they could not get their stories back home. Some reporters became so angry at the communications snafus in North Africa, Sicily, Anzio, and the Bulge that they even insinuated a negative slant into their coverage of these key battles.

In short, the complex mechanics of military-media relations pushed in two directions. Often, Washington's keenness to use war news to educate the public, alongside the military's ability to learn from its mistakes, helped PROs to forge a close partnership with the media. But this partnership was always contingent. When the military allowed the war correspondents to report promptly and prolifically from the front, the reporters were generally happy to toe the official line. Because most of them were desperate to see the Nazis defeated, there were also times when they pulled their punches. The pages that follow, however, document plenty of occasions when neither appreciation for the military's practical help nor patriotic anti-Nazism proved strong enough to bind the war correspondents to their military. At these moments, the World War II reporters resembled their counterparts in other wars: demanding, questioning, even rebellious, with a strong desire to find any way to report the story, however embarrassing it might be for their country.

THE NATURE OF THE WAR

That this generation of heroic, patriotic, Nazi-hating correspondents could still cause their fair share of trouble also derived from the importance of the war itself in explaining their actions. Previous works have tended to treat the war as either an ideological inspiration for the reporters (who inevitably joined the military team because the Nazi enemy was so evil) or an arena for adventure (the only place where their heroics would lead to fame and fortune). In contrast, this book argues that the way this war unfolded is crucial to understanding when and why correspondents felt compelled to forge a close partnership with the military.

This dynamic operated in a variety of ways. When the United States finally became a full belligerent, in December 1941, a basic asymmetry existed between the military and the media. While the army was full of men new to the battle, their counterparts in the media tended to be war veterans. Many had been stationed in Europe since Hitler invaded Poland in September 1939, and they knew what it was like to experience modern war: the bewildering speed of the Nazi blitzkrieg, with massed tanks racing across open land and dive-bombers darting out of the sky, or the bludgeoning power of the Luftwaffe as it attempted to bomb Warsaw, Rotterdam, and especially London into submission. These seasoned correspondents had endured the sleepless nights; the shaky, sweaty hands; the stench of death; and the prospect that they might be next. And they were not about to become submissive junior partners to a bunch of officers who only knew about war from training manuals—or the reporters' own dispatches.

When the American offensive began, extreme peril quickly bound the media and military together. Quite simply, the challenges associated with defeating Nazi Germany created a series of danger-fueled incentives for the war correspondents to become active team players. By the time the United States fully entered the war, Adolf Hitler had already conquered a vast territory stretching from France in the west to the outskirts of Moscow in the east. To liberate the lands under Nazi yoke, the Americans and their British ally needed to launch a series of amphibious assaults in North Africa in 1942, Sicily and Italy in 1943, and France in 1944. At the same time, they undertook an intensive bombing campaign against targets in Germany and its neighboring satellites.

Because conquering the Nazi empire required a combination of amphibious assaults and sustained bombing missions, the war reporters had little choice but to cozy up to the military hierarchy: it was their only chance of getting a coveted spot on a landing craft or a Flying Fortress. Since the missions were invariably so dangerous, the chosen war correspondents rarely disputed the military's fierce determination to enforce total operational security. Faced with the prospect of landing on a hostile shore bristling with enemy guns, not even the bravest, most competitive, most reckless reporter wanted the enemy to be alerted ahead of time.

The problems tended to come after the acute danger had receded and the rationale for the restrictions no longer seemed so compelling. Then the reporters would revert to type, heading off on their own, digging for stories that spelled trouble, challenging the censors for blocking dispatches they thought were in the public interest, and attacking the briefing officers for trying to fob them off with an antiseptic version of the war.

The result was a series of war reports that were much more complex, nuanced, and realistic than they are often given credit for being. Over the years, this golden generation of journalists has become the stuff of legend, and the big names are still feted for their insights and prose, their patriotism and bravery. When the legend is stripped away, what remains are not heroes with clay feet, but courageous and determined reporters who knew when to cooperate and when to criticize. They were neither excessively submissive nor overly rebellious. Thrown together with the military in perilous and pivotal situations, they produced a corpus of compelling news stories that underpinned the home front's thinking about the critically important events unfolding in Europe—often reinforcing the public's desire to see the fight through to the bitter end, but sometimes raising real questions about the way the war was being waged.

This is their story.

CHAPTER 1

Going to War

SEASONED VETERANS

June 1942 was yet another dreary month for the large contingent of American correspondents based in London. As they walked to work each day, these reporters could scarcely miss the scars of war all around them. Indeed, along many streets lay the ruins of blitzed buildings, a cruel testament to the power of the German Luftwaffe during the long winter eighteen months earlier. Across the cloudy skyline floated a multitude of barrage balloons, intended to offer a modicum of protection if the German planes ever returned. But these days, as the reporters knew only too well, the German planes rarely returned. Like the rest of Hitler's formidable military, the Luftwaffe had been deployed elsewhere: to the distant Russian steppes, where Nazi forces were driving toward the key city of Stalingrad, or to the North African desert, where Erwin Rommel's famed Afrika Korps threatened Cairo and the Suez Canal.

The absence of a real war did not mean a lack of hard work. As America's European news hub, the British capital received a seemingly endless string of stories and communiqués from around the world, which the London-based reporters had to rewrite, condense, and route to New York or Chicago.[1] The trouble was that this work was unrelentingly dull. Young and ambitious reporters craved the fame and fortune that was supposed to accompany the danger and daring of battlefield journalism.[2] But these days, rather than having to brave incoming fire, the only real peril came from the sneezing and coughing of rival reporters in cramped and airless offices. Instead of an eyewitness story tapped out a short distance from the fighting, the end result tended to be a mere rewrite of a high command's handout or the paraphrasing of a military briefing.

It had been so different a couple of years earlier, when the United States had remained neutral, but Britain had been the front line in the battle against Nazi Germany. At the start of the war, London-based reporters had initially hated the strict, if erratic, British censorship regime, which placed too many stories out of bounds. They had also been impatient with Britain's inaction as Poland went down to defeat in September 1939—their exasperation turning to alarm when the mighty French army collapsed under the force of Hitler's blitzkrieg in May and June 1940. Then came the Battle of Britain, culminating in eight months of sustained bombing as Hitler tried to terrorize the British into submission.[3]

For the American reporters still in London two years later, the German bombing campaign had been pivotal in sharpening their attitudes toward the issues at stake in the war. It had also been the making of many of them as reporters, providing them with a record, a reputation, and a sense of self-confidence.

Drew Middleton typified this process. A round-faced pipe smoker who exuded an air of mellow affability, Middleton had been an AP cub reporter when the war began, still uneasily making the transition from covering New York sports to reporting Europe's descent into a new dark age. He got his first taste of conflict during France's rapid fall in the spring of 1940, before returning to London to witness the air battle that unfolded during that summer and fall.[4]

After a long shift, Middleton liked to visit one of Fleet Street's local pubs, where journalists rubbed shoulders in a profession in which alcohol-fueled bonhomie was as important to the self-image as the smoldering cigarette, crumpled suit, and fedora hat. One sweltering Saturday afternoon, in early September 1940, he quickly downed two brandies, before looking up at the azure sky. In the distance, he could hear the dull, low rumble of approaching planes. Thankful that the drink had fortified his courage, Middleton watched in horror as the aircraft moved closer. Then the bombs began to fall, followed rapidly by bursts of flame. After that came the sound of fire trucks and sirens, of women screaming about "the children," together with the studied calm of those doing their best to act normally, including a group of chorus girls from a West End show, who trooped into the street with their audience to see what all the fuss was about.

As the noise grew louder and the fires hotter, Middleton headed straight back to the AP office to receive his marching orders. His boss asked him, calmly and politely, if he would be willing to visit London's business district, where the bombing seemed especially bad. Middleton, who never shirked from danger, agreed. The story he wrote told readers across the United States what it was like to be in the midst of a Luftwaffe raid. "It is night now," he tapped on his typewriter, "and it will take daylight to ascertain the full effects of this evening's raid. But I can tell you what happened to the people who got bombed." Some, he explained, had undertaken "the frantic search for bodies in ruined houses." Others had returned home from work to find their loved ones dead. And many simply "had a look of horror and incredible bitterness on their faces."[5]

For Middleton, it was a transformative moment. Like many American reporters, he had initially confronted the war in a cautious frame of mind. Although instinctively anti-Nazi, he had no direct experience of Adolf Hitler's regime. He was also acutely aware that his editors back home demanded stories that were based on hard evidence, not pro-British bias. Indeed, since the United States was still neutral, their default position had been to call on correspondents to report only "the facts," leaving opinion pieces to be composed in the rarefied atmosphere of the stateside editorial office.[6]

As soon as the German bombs began to rain down, this sense of detachment proved impossible to maintain. "I was in it," declared one American reporter, "under it, part of it."[7] Middleton, for his part, soon began to evince the signs of a strong Anglophilia—and an equally strong Germanophobia—that would remain with him for years to come. The distressing scenes in London's streets played a large role. So did the intense fear—the cold and sweaty sensation when the planes appeared, and the temptation to take cover rather than go outside when the bombs fell—which, he later confessed, would never be equaled in another battle throughout the war.

Middleton's worst experience came when the AP offices were hit while he slept in the cellar. Jerked awake by the loud crash, he stumbled upstairs to help begin the task of relocating to the Reuters building, while also trying to keep the copy flowing to New York. At first light, he walked outside, where a crowd had gathered to inspect the damage. The story that he wrote the next day ended with the pithy remark of a cockney cabby, who summed up the sense that American reporters and British civilians were in this together. "Coo," the taxi driver observed. "They don't like you fellers neither."[8]

Back home, those who were braving these dangers were soon singled out for praise—and promotion. Middleton yearned to climb the journalistic ladder. "I'm extremely ambitious," he once confessed, "perhaps too much so, and I'm always concerned whenever I feel I am not doing enough of the sort of work that will lead to my advancement."[9] At this stage of his career, Middleton's goal was to get out of wire-service reporting, with its relentless pressures, especially the constant demands from editors for "new 'leads' for every edition of a running story." At an agency like the AP, one of his colleagues observed, a reporter like Middleton merely "did the spade work, while the other, 'special' writers for individual papers had time and leisure to select their material and take the long view."[10]

To move up required a stellar war record. Before the war, Middleton had known more about the Yankees' stats than the intricacies of European politics. After the blitz, he was one of the select band of AP correspondents "whose bylines appear frequently in the news." He was also a seasoned veteran—just the sort of man to impress the bureau chief of the *New York Times*, for whom the German bombing raids also remained a life-changing event.[11]

Inexhaustible if irascible, Raymond "Pete" Daniell's entire tenure as the *Times*' London bureau chief had been dominated by the war. Even before the blitz, he had confronted the vexed question of whether to find a safer haven somewhere in the south of London, where telephone communications might still be available in the event of a major Luftwaffe attack. Initially, he decided to move into a new building in the city center that had a steel and concrete structure and an "excellent subbasement shelter." But when the bombing began in September 1940, the *Times* reporters found working in this building "impossible." Daniell therefore supervised another search for new premises, ultimately plumping for the plush Savoy Hotel, which had an even stronger shelter.[12]

From the Savoy, he directed correspondents out on to London's perilous streets each night. While the reporters faced the dangers, Daniell shouldered the responsibility. Each morning, he would see the pain in his correspondents' tired eyes and the stress eating away at their nerves. When the tension became too much, Daniell gave them a couple of days off in a becalming countryside "rest billet." But he had little respite himself from "the mental strain of bombardment," together with "the dull routine of managing a large office and trying to be a reporter as well." And so, in January 1941, when his New York bosses offered him a chance to return home to rest, Daniell readily accepted.[13]

Like many returning veterans, Daniell found it difficult to adjust to a peacetime routine. Before long, he succumbed to a series of minor illnesses. He also became "despondent" when he was asked to cover mundane domestic stories, especially after the attack on Pearl Harbor. Increasingly, Daniell, like almost everyone else, was desperate to do his bit for the war effort. Nothing appealed to him more than a return to London, where, he realized, he had once held "one of the most challenging and fascinating jobs" in journalism. A year earlier, the war had been a stress to escape. Now it worked like a drug, luring this reporter—and many others—into its perilous clutches.[14]

Although the city that Daniell returned to in 1942 no longer faced persistent danger from the sky, London immediately triggered the old excitement and, especially, the need to take sides. "It is impossible to be neutral in thought," Daniell observed, "when a city one has grown to love is being smashed to bits wantonly, when one's friends are being killed and injured every day, when one's home has been wrecked. . . . Only an automaton, a journalistic robot," he concluded, "could remain neutral in such circumstances." For Daniell, thoughts of the blitz increasingly translated into a desire for retribution. He wanted, above all, the United States and Britain to strike back as decisively and as swiftly as possible—and he was determined to help out.[15]

In the meantime, he faced the more prosaic task of reorganizing his staff. Although the fighting had shifted elsewhere, Daniell felt constantly undermanned on his return to Britain, where his office was responsible for "backstopping" and "editing" all the copy from Europe, North Africa, and Russia, as well as "covering this country with its exiled governments [and] many American interests."[16] As he contemplated poaching another hand from the offices of rival newspapers and press agencies, one person quickly stood out from the rest. Pete Daniell had met Drew Middleton during the winter of the blitz. Since then, the AP man had enhanced his growing reputation with a series of scoops covering the Battle of the Atlantic. So, in the summer of 1942, Daniell snapped him up.[17]

Middleton, for his part, was elated to be hired by America's preeminent newspaper, although he also recognized the obvious drawbacks. Pay in the *Times*' London bureau was far from munificent: about $60 week even for blitz veterans, which was scarcely sufficient to cover the exorbitant costs of living and working out of the Savoy Hotel.[18] Nor was Daniell an easy boss. Often, the *Times* bureau chief came across as "brusque, impatient, and contentious." Even so, Middleton considered him the perfect mentor, who could make him an even better reporter.[19] And this, on balance, proved to be the crucial selling point. Middleton desperately wanted to learn and improve. A tireless worker, he would soon absorb so many lessons from his new colleagues that close observers would rank him as the *Times*' leading correspondent in Europe.[20]

After the blitz, however, Middleton, like Daniell, would always be more than just a prolific and well-respected reporter. Now he was also one of the many veterans who populated the American press corps in London. It proved to be a crucial distinction. Having been under fire, these veterans longed for more action. Having been targeted by German bombs, they could not wait to play a constructive part the minute the United States finally struck back. At the same time, having tasted the fear of battle, they believed they knew as much, if not more, about modern warfare than many in the military—including the smartly dressed American officers who were now slowly trickling into Britain.

On June 24, 1942, the most senior of these officers arrived in London to "command all US Army forces and personnel" in the newly established European Theater of Operations (ETO).[21] At first, seasoned reporters like Daniell and Middleton were decidedly unimpressed. Even the most cursory glance at the general's résumé revealed a glaring gap. The new man had absolutely no experience of commanding troops in battle and had merely held a series of training and staff jobs.

The contrast had been particularly stark in September 1940. When the correspondents were dodging German bombs, this officer had been stationed in faraway Washington state, as commander of the First Battalion of the Fifteenth Infantry of the Third Division. Since then, much of his time had been spent behind a desk, working feverishly to enhance America's sketchy war plans. The closest he had come to a battle had been during the large training maneuvers in the "steaming Louisiana bayous" nine months earlier, where he had received plaudits for devising a winning strategy. But in the eyes of the blitz-scarred correspondents, this scarcely counted as real combat experience.[22]

Nor, for that matter, had anyone really heard of this man before. Even the journalists who had singled him out for praise during the Louisiana maneuvers often got his name wrong, referring to him as "Lieutenant Colonel D. D. Ersenbeing." Perhaps it was the disturbingly German sound of his name or, possibly, the multiple vowel sounds. Whatever the reason, even the correspondents who could recall his name tended to refer to him as "Ike." It seemed much more appropriate than his full name: Lieutenant General Dwight David Eisenhower.[23]

Then, as they sat around in their smoke-filled offices, tapping away at the most recent communiqué rehash or swapping the latest rumors, reporters suddenly received a terse instruction from the ETO's public relations office. When the journalists wrote about American forces in Britain, the order read, they could only mention the top general in the theater. Everyone else was off limits.

To the battle-hardened cynics, this injunction made immediate sense. Clearly, the new commander was tired of being ignored. Like so many other

Figure 1.1 Drew Middleton and Dwight Eisenhower. When this photograph was taken in the spring of 1945, Ike was the senior commander. In the summer of 1942, however, he was still the war virgin, while Middleton was the veteran. Manuscripts and Archives Division, The New York Public Library, Astor, Lenox, and Tilden Foundations.

officers, he had caught the publicity bug the minute he rose in rank. Rather than spend his time in Britain working on a bold new military operation, he would concentrate, like all the rest, on burnishing his own reputation in order to climb even higher.

Adding to their anger, the reporters knew that they could scarcely appeal this draconian order to Eisenhower's public-relations team. Before Ike arrived in town, the US Army headquarters had managed to forge a spectacularly bad relationship with the local press corps. Daniell was an especially vociferous critic. "Certain personnel of the Public Relations Office," he believed, "looked upon newspapermen and their work with 'disdain.'" Lieutenant Colonel Harold Hinton, the chief PRO, was the central culprit. A professional officer, Hinton seemed to embody that class's instinctive hostility to the media. Rather than try to woo correspondents, he invariably adopted a "cold, austere attitude" toward them; instead of doling out information that could be turned into usable copy, he often seemed hell bent on blocking any story of interest.[24]

Days into his new job, Eisenhower was deeply perturbed when he heard about these discontented rumblings. Whatever the reporters might think, Ike knew that something big was afoot, possibly even a major new operation to strike back at Hitler before the end of the year. This made secrecy all the more essential. The Allies were already playing a desperate game of catch-up against the German Wehrmacht, which over the past three years had conquered most of Western and Eastern Europe. The last thing Eisenhower's new command needed was to give Hitler advance warning of an impending operation, providing him with time to plan and prepare—and to slaughter Allied troops on the invasion beaches.

Ike also bristled at the notion that he was yet another publicity-seeking prima donna who would eviscerate any story that did not extol his personal virtues. Nothing, in fact, was further from the truth. During his long years as a staff officer, Eisenhower had developed a profound personal dislike for the army's "glory hoppers." He had encountered far too many during his recent stint in Washington: fellow officers who tried to advance their careers through "phony or promoted stories" rather than real talent and achievement. "Every man likes publicity," he once remarked, "but the officer who indulges in it digs his own grave." So, even before he had fully come to grips with his new command, Eisenhower decided to convene a press conference to set the record straight.[25]

At four o'clock on July 14, about thirty reporters gathered at the US headquarters, housed in a large apartment block at 20 Grosvenor Square. Before long, the media would dub the building the "Eisenhower Platz," a moniker redolent with German efficiency. The reality could not have been more prosaic: creaky lifts, a range of cramped and noisy offices, and the ever-present "odor of boiled cabbage and Brussels sprouts" percolating up from the basement canteen.

With Daniell at the helm, the reporters arrived in a snarly, surly mood. Daniell had even drafted a detailed memorandum of complaint, outlining the main ills of the current censorship regime, which he thrust into Ike's hand the minute he entered the press-conference room. Eisenhower's response was telling. Immediately displaying a talent for defusing tricky situations, he listened carefully before making "it clear that he wanted to work with newspaper men and radio men on a basis of complete frankness and trust," recorded one observer. "He said he had been double-crossed by only one newspaperman in his life," and was therefore predisposed to view those in the profession as honorable men and women who would not betray confidences.

Then Eisenhower outlined some positive steps. He would revise the command's censorship rules, he assured everyone in the room, in order "to give newspapermen more freedom and clearer understanding." He would also recruit more censors, so that copy and photos could be processed more quickly. Perhaps, he concluded, he would even consider introducing "master" passes that would allow correspondents to escape the drudgery of the London beat and admit them "to all facilities of American forces."

To Ike's relief, the reporters reacted calmly and constructively. They wanted, as much as anybody, to see the American army strike back as soon as possible. They were, therefore, prepared to give Eisenhower the benefit of the doubt. Who knew, perhaps he might even become the commander of America's first offensive.[26]

WAR AS ENTERTAINMENT

On July 14, when Eisenhower was meeting with reporters, President Franklin D. Roosevelt was preparing to return to the White House after a short vacation. As he boarded his personal train for the long nighttime trip, Roosevelt recognized that the time had come to take crucial strategic steps.[27]

Until now, the United States had done little in the European theater except to provide materiel to its British and Soviet allies. And these allies, Roosevelt fretted, would not tolerate such a shameless lack of urgency from such a powerful country for much longer. Nor would the American public. As leading media commentators began issuing "feverish" demands for a second front, the domestic mood appeared to be dangerously fickle. Sometimes, Americans seemed brazenly overconfident that victory would be swift and easy; at other times, they were gripped by a panicky hysteria that all was lost. Periodically, some vocal groups demanded an immediate second front in Europe, but, more often than not, a majority of the nation preferred to focus on seeking revenge against Japan.[28]

Roosevelt had long been convinced that major events on the battlefield had a profound impact on popular opinion—certainly more profound than anything a president could achieve through speechmaking.[29] Based on this assumption, Roosevelt concluded that an early offensive would address the public's growing impatience with American inaction. In particular, he reasoned, news of GIs fighting the Germans would focus the nation's attention on the European war. And if a venue could be found that promised a relatively easy victory against the might of the German Wehrmacht, this would also buoy the nation's mood. It was "very important to morale," Roosevelt believed, "to give this country a feeling that they are in the war, . . . to have American troops fighting somewhere across the Atlantic."[30]

Yet for all the obvious logic behind such thinking, the president faced a formidable obstacle. After six months of war, the country simply lacked the troops, the air supremacy, and the experience to launch a successful invasion of France. Herein lay the nub: France, Roosevelt's senior military advisers repeatedly stressed, was the only viable venue for a decisive encounter with Hitler's army. Fighting anywhere else, insisted General George C. Marshall, would simply act as a "suction pump," draining men and materiel away from the one area that mattered.[31]

Marshall was a formidable opponent. Already, his integrity, studied reserve, and "rocklike constancy" had become legendary. So had his fierce temper, which he normally concealed beneath an icy countenance. A few years back, the president had tried to gain Marshall's support in one meeting by addressing him as "George." Irritated at Roosevelt's mannered intimacy, Marshall had shot back, "I'm sorry, Mr. President, but I don't agree with that at all." Startled, Roosevelt never again dared to use his first name.[32]

When the president met with his army chief on July 15, he firmly emphasized the importance of getting American troops into action in the European theater before the end of the year. As both men knew, this expedited timetable ruled out France. North Africa was the only viable location. Although Marshall predictably balked at what he considered a dangerous diversion of America's limited military resources, over the next week, Roosevelt made up his mind. On July 22 he instructed Marshall to reach an agreement with the British to launch an attack on Morocco and Tunisia. Three days later, he insisted that, if possible, the invasion should be launched before October 30, under the code name Operation Torch.[33]

The name was revealing: Roosevelt hoped the invasion would light the spark that would flare into a final victory over Hitler's Reich. But Marshall remained distinctly unimpressed, especially by the importance Roosevelt had accorded to public opinion in reaching this decision. "We failed to see," he later concluded, "that the leader in a democracy has to keep the people entertained. That may sound like the wrong word but it conveys the thought."[34]

Although Marshall was somewhat defensive about his description of Roosevelt's motives, he had made a shrewd observation with profound implications for the way the war would be reported to the home front. Indeed, if Roosevelt believed that the unstable nature of the domestic mood made it vital to keep the public "entertained," the president did not view himself as the star turn. Top billing would go to the battle itself, which meant that the media would play a major role in directing the public's attention toward the European theater.

This was where Eisenhower came in. Now that Torch had been given the go-ahead, Marshall decided that Ike should head this new operation, although neither man liked the proposed target. When Eisenhower heard that France would not be invaded in the near future, he had even complained that this decision could well go down as "the blackest day in history." Yet, as good soldiers, the two generals rapidly set about the task of overcoming the myriad problems involved in launching a large-scale amphibious assault, including working with the reporters who would have to produce stirring stories of American GIs fighting Nazi troops.

After contemplating how to deal with the media in the first major operation of his career, Eisenhower turned to Pete Daniell to ask him whether he would consider forming a small committee that would draw up a reporters' "plan for censorship." It was a shrewd move. On the one hand, it furthered Eisenhower's attempt to win over the press corps. On the other hand, Ike doubtless knew that reporters wanted to retain their independence and so would be leery of being directly coopted into drafting an official set of guidelines that they would scarcely be able to dissent from in the future. He was right. After deliberating with his colleagues, Daniell gracefully declined the chance to assume responsibility for a new censorship plan. Instead, he made "a number of useful suggestions," leaving Ike to turn elsewhere for more robust support.[35]

Luckily, the new commander did not have to look far. In the patriotic fervor generated by Pearl Harbor, scores of men from all corners of the media had swapped their notebooks, typewriters, or plush executive offices for life in the army and navy. Since Harold Hinton, the current PRO, was so unpopular with the London press corps, Ike could tap into that rich seam of talent. Already, he had personally recruited Harry Butcher, a close family friend, who had been a pioneer radio broadcaster, manager of the CBS's Washington office, and, most recently, a CBS vice president. Although Butcher was somewhat wary of having "a reputation as an expert in this lousy field," he soon began providing his boss with all sorts of practical help.

During his long radio career in Washington, Butcher had acquired a contact book that read like a who's who of the great and the good in the media world. Many of these powerful players were now in London, and before long he was meeting, drinking, or dining with such influential figures as Carroll Binder, the *Chicago Daily News*'s foreign-service editor, and Bill Paley, his old boss at CBS.[36] From these and other sessions, Butcher quickly discovered Hinton's shortcomings, so he helped Eisenhower pick a replacement.

Major Joseph B. Phillips was a trim, dapper forty-one-year-old, with degrees from the Virginia Military Institute and the Columbia School of Journalism and an established reputation in newspapers and magazines. As a foreign correspondent for the *New York Herald Tribune* between 1927 and 1937, he had reported from Paris, London, Rome, and Moscow, before switching to *Newsweek*, where he rose to the position of managing editor in 1941. By the time Ike arrived in London, Phillips had joined the army and had been posted as the executive officer under Hinton—a job in which he so clearly excelled that Eisenhower and Butcher soon decided to promote him.[37]

Phillips's most important quality was a basic sensitivity to reporters' needs. As a former journalist, he understood the numerous stresses they faced each day: the deadline pressures, the "rockets" from editors asking for a big story, the time-consuming rivalries and jealousies. Soon, Butcher found Phillips's knowledge and empathy so useful that he began to meet with him regularly to discuss the media's requirements for the Torch landings.

They started over lunch on September 18. After talking to the planners, Phillips learned that only two spaces could be reserved for reporters on each of the three invasion task forces, and a further single place would be available for a correspondent to accompany Eisenhower to his command post on Gibraltar.

Phillips did not like these paltry numbers. In a series of "troublesome" meetings with Daniell, he discovered that the media expected a far larger representation.[38] Luckily, Butcher and Eisenhower both agreed. They were particularly worried about the pressure that would be placed on the single reporter assigned to their command. Ike, recorded Butcher in his diary, "felt the responsibility for one man was terrorizing—what if he should become sick or be out of action."[39]

With the clear backing of the supreme commander, Phillips managed to acquire extra spaces for the press both in Gibraltar and on the invasion ships. He made sure that priority was given to the major press associations, the AP, the United Press (UP), and the smaller International News Service (INS). To ensure "basic coverage," he also worked hard to find places for the *New York Times, New York Herald Tribune, Chicago Daily News, Chicago Tribune, Time, Life*, and *Newsweek*, publications that either had a massive audience or syndicated their foreign reports to smaller newspapers across the country. Those excluded could pick up the wire services' spot dispatches before their own reporters made it to the battlefield. That only left the problem of which correspondents to choose for such an important job—and when to tell them without the secret leaking out.[40]

By September, Eisenhower felt he had established a good rapport with the London-based American reporters. The relationship, he told Marshall, was "of the very highest order." He even believed that 95 percent of them would cooperate wholeheartedly should he ask them to hold off on a particular story. Yet it would only take one reporter to blurt out information on the first American attack, and the whole invasion could well be doomed.[41]

Those in the know had no doubt that Torch was a risky proposition. The invasion ships had to make the long journey from either British or American ports through seas infested with German U-boats. Inexperienced troops then had to land on Moroccan and Algerian beaches that were guarded by Vichy French forces, who were not at war with the United States but who were allied with Nazi Germany—and no one knew whether they would hold their fire or pour down a deadly fusillade on the first invasion waves. Then, as soon as a bridgehead was established, the American and British troops would have to push rapidly toward Tunisia, where the formidable German Wehrmacht would doubtless lie in wait.

In the face of such dangers, secrecy was crucial. With D-Day looming, Eisenhower decided on two clear-cut media policies. He would censor any story that even mentioned the word "invasion." And he would not tell the reporters chosen to accompany the attack where they were heading until they were safely on board one of the invasion boats.

Since neither policy could stop the rumors that began sweeping through Fleet Street, Eisenhower also tried to throw journalists—and by extension the Germans—off the scent. Once again, Joe Phillips proved his worth. Whenever he invited reporters to his apartment for a quiet drink, Phillips made sure to leave a Russian dictionary lying in plain view. What it meant was anybody's guess, but a group of leading journalists soon began to surmise that somewhere to the north—perhaps Norway—might be the Allied target.[42]

Or, perhaps, the attack would have to wait until 1943. In late October, as Eisenhower and his senior staff prepared to leave London, the War Department "leaked" the story that Ike had been recalled to Washington for a conference. Even Roosevelt joined in the ruse. Although the president was hoping that Torch would direct the public's attention toward the German war, he knew full well that his public-opinion problems would be exacerbated by a military debacle. So when journalists asked him about Eisenhower's reported Washington trip, Roosevelt, adopting his most innocent tone, explained that he could never comment on the movement of army officers, acutely aware that his words would be enough to make front-page news.[43]

Still, Ike and his press officers knew that they would have to take the plunge soon. At some point, they needed to call in the chosen reporters and tell them what was about to happen. Until now, Eisenhower's increasingly warm relationship with journalists had remained at arm's length. He had sometimes revealed a few confidences, but mostly they had been kept out of the loop. Before long, however, both sides would have to become real partners, working in close proximity—if not complete tandem—until the invasion was well underway.

PARTNERS IN PERIL

The summons finally came shortly after lunch on Wednesday, October 21, 1942. Alerted by a cryptic telephone call, the reporters donned their fedoras, pulled on their macs, and left their Fleet Street offices for the short taxi ride to "Eisenhower Platz."

As they sat back in their taxis, few expected that the meeting would amount to much. True, they had heard the incessant rumors that something big was in the air, but seasoned veterans like Daniell and Middleton knew the importance of treating this kind of scuttlebutt with the caution, perhaps even the derision, it deserved. After all, a second front had been discussed for months, and now that winter was fast approaching, the campaigning season in much of the European theater seemed practically over. Probably just a typical dull afternoon ahead, they thought—another hour spent in a shabby, smoke-filled office, scribbling down a few notes while a low-ranking officer provided a few skimpy details about a distant operation or a pin-prick bombing raid.

When the reporters arrived at the imposing doorway of the red-brick American HQ, a stern-faced guard saluted smartly as they showed their passes and entered. For the first time, these men could see who else had received an invite, and the guest list immediately piqued their interest. The other correspondents represented major news organizations, including two each from the two main wire services, the AP and UP, and another two each from the big New York newspapers, the *Times* and the *Herald-Tribune*. The final person on the list was the odd one out. Bill Stoneman of the *Chicago Daily News* was the only correspondent from a Chicago-based newspaper. But none of the others saw anything unusual in his selection, since he was also one of America's most experienced foreign correspondents.

A native of Michigan, Stoneman had been working for the highly prestigious, staunchly anti-fascist *Chicago Daily News* for seventeen years.[44] He had first set foot in Europe more than a decade earlier, a tall, lean, soft-spoken man, fluent in French and already exuding gravitas. "He was a very proper gentleman," recalled one colleague. "He looked like and dressed like a diplomat, but he was famously blunt." Once he sniffed a good story, his sad eyes would come alive. Whenever he faced danger, he could yell profanities louder than anyone else. Middleton, who accompanied him around the crumbling French front in May 1940, always recalled him shouting, "For Christ's sake turn out that god-dammed light you bloody fool," when someone broke the strict blackout instructions during a German air raid.[45]

Stoneman's colleagues respected his aggressive style. They also valued his judgment and experience—the years he had spent suffering in the Soviet Union, dodging Italian bullets in the Abyssinian war, and being blackballed from Germany when the Nazis deemed his questions too blunt.[46] But the blitz had really established Stoneman's reputation. He had begun the war in London, railing against the stupidity of the overzealous British censors. A year later, he had produced a number of moving pieces on the German bombing, which the *Daily News* had syndicated widely.[47]

Once Stoneman and the other reporters were all assembled in the lobby, Joe Phillips, forgoing any formalities, ushered them into an office. As soon as they sat down, Brigadier General Robert W. McClure walked in. The more experienced reporters guessed that something big was afoot, for McClure, the head of American military intelligence, rarely deigned to meet the press. "This is it," McClure announced brusquely. "The Second Front. We will invade the Continent from six points."

To break the stunned tension in the room, McClure lit a cigarette. He then proceeded to announce the security measures he would take to keep the Germans from discovering this crucial secret. "I'm not telling you where you are going," he began. "Each of you will be told when you have reached marshaling points. You are well-known correspondents in London," he added.

> You get about. People see you every day. If you suddenly disappear people are going to start asking questions. You must leave London without causing suspicion. Just tell your wives and sweethearts that you are going on maneuvers. Don't even mention that to anyone else. You will be travelling with officers and soldiers. Many of them won't know where they are going either. Naturally, some of them will. So, please, just don't ask any questions. You will find out in due course. Just be patient.

McClure ended by telling the chosen correspondents to return before nine o'clock with all of their field equipment. Since it was already approaching four, and the shops closed in an hour, the men dashed to the door, only pausing to wonder precisely what they would need to take with them. Middleton and Stoneman both thought Norway the most likely destination. Stoneman, an expert skier, even wanted to rush home and grab his skis, until a colleague warned that this would make him too conspicuous. Others headed off to the nearby West End, where, like Victorian adventurers of old, they hurried about purchasing all manner of exotic clothing, from boots and field jackets to galoshes and fur-lined gloves.

Their shopping done, many reporters rendezvoused at the Savoy bar. The money left over immediately went on champagne at $14 a bottle. As the party became increasingly raucous, the more vocal among them shouted out toasts—albeit cautious toasts made with one drunken eye firmly on McClure's injunction not to give the game away. Then they downed "one last drink for the road" before it was time to head off to report the first American battle in the war against Nazi Germany.[48]

The next morning dawned damp and foggy, typical London fall weather, which only heightened the reporters' eagerness to be on their way. The long journey began on an old bus, followed by a ride on steam train north. On arriving at a grey, nondescript port, the reporters collected their luggage, waited for their names to be called, and then walked down the gangplank to their assigned boats.

Back in London, their bosses woke up that same misty morning to the humdrum task of sifting through communiqués about the distant fighting, only now they faced an additional burden: a sudden dearth of personnel. Not only had their offices been left cripplingly short staffed, protested Daniell, but they were forbidden from requesting reinforcements from the United States, lest it alert the Germans. Nor did the military's last-minute notification help matters. "So as not to attract too much attention here," Daniell added, "the selected correspondents notified their bureaus that they were going on the expedition only a few minutes before their departure, allowing them just enough time to pack." And that was all the information the harassed, overworked bureau chiefs received for almost three weeks. "After our men left," complained the UP head in London, "I heard nothing from them until they asked for collect filing privileges."[49]

On the high seas, the correspondents heading toward combat rapidly concluded that war reporting was not all glamor and excitement. Covering ration-book London, they had already adapted to a range of war-imposed inconveniences: tea instead of coffee, watered-down beer, stingy food portions, and inadequate heating. After a couple of days on board the ships, London suddenly seemed like a place of plenty. Some hated the unappetizing smell of cabbage and mutton that wafted up from the galleys. Others railed at selfish cabin mates who hogged the washbasins during the rare times when hot water was available. Many more went pale at "the ghastly news" that, because all ships were under the command of the teetotal US Navy, no alcohol would be served on board, just "orange, lemon, or grapefruit squash, ginger ale, tonic, or ginger beer." As days stretched into weeks, there was little to do, except read, tell tall tales, or play endless games of poker—anything to break what one reporter dubbed "the monotony of nothing but water."

Ever present, though rarely spoken about, was the deadly U-boat menace. Many reporters were self-confessed landlubbers who found the "corkscrew" motion of their ships torment enough. To contemplate the possibility that, at any moment, a U-boat attack might plunge them directly into the icy, grey sea was almost unbearable. By the second week of the tortuous voyage, most simply wanted to get off their boats as quickly as possible.

When the military officers finally revealed the convoy's true destination, the correspondents had an additional reason to crave dry land. Instead of the frigid winter climes of a Scandinavian coast, they would be attacking the balmy beaches of North Africa. This was the first piece of good news they had heard, even if it left many of them a little resentful about all the useless equipment they had lugged from London. The second positive was their likely reception. Morocco and Algeria remained part of the French empire. Although governed by a Vichy regime in thrall to Nazi Germany, no one thought that the Vichy forces would fight as ferociously as the German Wehrmacht, if they fought at all. Perhaps, everyone on board hoped, French soldiers might welcome them with white flags.

After more than two weeks at sea, the ships finally peeled off in different directions, taking their reporters to various parts of the invasion front—some to Algiers and Oran, where they would accompany the landing-craft assaults, others to Eisenhower's Gibraltar headquarters, where they could keep tabs on the operation as a whole.

Secrecy remained tight, but no one minded—especially when the convoy picked up speed to avoid U-boats as it slipped through the narrow straits into the Mediterranean. Until recently, many reporters had eyed the navy with the utmost suspicion. It was the "silent service," they grumbled, dark and mysterious, where the censor ruled and the briefing officer rarely dispensed information of any value. Now, such strict security appeared a highly laudable trait. When one correspondent joked that navy spokesmen "made the Sphinx look like the town gossip," his colleagues viewed it as a compliment. For the duration of the invasion, at least, these reporters had joined forces with the military. They had become, for a short while, truly partners in peril.[50]

PART I

North Africa

CHAPTER 2

Invasion, 1942

THE ROCK OF GIBRALTAR

Wes Gallagher first glimpsed Gibraltar on the evening of November 5, and he was immediately impressed. Clearly, he thought, this tiny British enclave perched on the southwestern tip of Spain would offer a welcome sanctuary. With his memories of the blitz still so vivid, Gallagher particularly appreciated the sheer size of Gibraltar's imposing mountain. "It was the safest air-raid shelter in the world," he observed. "With 1,400 feet of rock overhead, a tunnel had been bored through one side of the mountain to the other out of the limestone." In the middle sat a large number of small, squat offices, which would house Eisenhower's Allied Forces Headquarters Command (AFHQ). Connected to the outside world by ocean cables, these offices would allow everyone inside to stay in touch not only with the invasion forces but also with superiors in London, Washington, and New York.

Then the problems began. Because of a red-tape foul-up, Gallagher and the three other reporters slated to cover Ike remained cooped up on their boat for another frustrating day. When they finally disembarked the following afternoon, they quickly realized that Gibraltar's safe communications network came at a cost. Deep inside the rock, the air was stuffy and damp, the lighting gloomy and artificial. Fine cement dust floated in the air and tended to get in everyone's eyes. Rats scurried along the corridors, and the noisy ventilation system made it difficult to think straight, let alone hold a serious conversation. Even the most senior generals had only been allocated rooms sparsely decorated with a desk, upon which sat "a water carafe, a pen set, and an ancient telephone of the sort summoned with dual bells." The lowly accredited correspondents had to make do with much less. Small wonder that before long they began to pine, if not for the dangers of the ocean, then at least for some sun and fresh air.

Yet the four correspondents accredited to the AFHQ quickly came to appreciate their close proximity to the invasion's senior commanders. Issued a pass that allowed them to penetrate the rock's inner sanctum, Gallagher and his colleagues could talk to the top brass, striking up friendships and gaining a sense of the pressures faced by men at the top. Sometimes they could even watch Eisenhower jog around the long, wet tunnels, as he tried to keep his pre-invasion nerves in check.[1]

Ike summoned the reporters to his first Gibraltar press conference on Saturday, November 7, just hours before American troops were scheduled to hit the African beaches. As the men entered Ike's austere office, he tried hard to exude his normal sunny self-confidence. But, as he later admitted, he had found this to be the most excruciating period of the whole war, and his endless chain smoking—four packs of Camels a day—hinted at his subterranean edginess. Eisenhower's opening words were also tinged with tension. "I am going to consider you as quasi officers of my staff," he began. "You will have access to all our information but I don't expect you to spy on us nor do I want it to be necessary for us to spy on you. If you spy on us you will be shot."[2]

Figure 2.1 Eisenhower meets with his accredited reporters, November 10, 1942. Wes Gallagher is the second from the left. © PA Photos Limited.

The reporters' response was telling. They vividly recalled their own fears of a U-boat assault, especially when they were passing through the Gibraltar straits just a few days earlier. While Eisenhower spoke, their thoughts wandered to the fate of the USS *Thomas Stone*, a transport ship that had just been torpedoed more than 150 miles from the coast, with the loss of nine men. Ultimately, more than a thousand soldiers would survive the attack, after boarding their landing craft and making a slow, dangerous journey to shore, but their lucky escape was not yet known. And with hundreds more ships still on high alert to evade the lethal U-boats, Ike's blunt threat to shoot any leakers seemed eminently reasonable.[3]

Even Wes Gallagher agreed with the reasoning behind it. The thirty-one-year-old AP man was not known for his submissiveness. He had first come to prominence in 1935, when, as a student at Louisiana State, he had witnessed the shooting of Senator Huey Long. Demonstrating resourcefulness beyond his years, later that night he had located a nurse in uniform and, telling officers she was needed in the hospital, had slipped through the police cordon. Once inside, he had jotted down accurate details of Long's fatal injuries, and then immediately wired his major scoop to the world.

Since the start of the war, Gallagher had continued to display this tenacity and inventiveness. He had arrived in Western Europe in the early spring of 1940, as part of the AP's effort to beef up its coverage in anticipation of Hitler's next move. Like many other American war correspondents, Gallagher had become increasingly drawn to the British cause after the German bombs began falling on London. Still, with his jet-black hair, penetrating gaze, and booming voice, Gallagher quickly stood out from the press pack, whether dodging bombs during the blitz or covering the Nazi invasion of Greece.

He had also begun to sharpen his ideas of what made a good reporter. Possessing a self-confidence derived from more than two years of combat reporting, Gallagher did not view a war correspondent's job as merely paraphrasing daily communiqués or parroting officials' statements at press conferences. Correspondents, he firmly believed, should not act as servants for the government, even in wartime. Their central task was "to publish the truth as we see it."[4]

As well as a reluctance to toe the official line, Gallagher had to beat all comers, especially those from the UP, to breaking news. Single-minded in this pursuit—and "tough as hardtack," according to one PRO—he had developed into the ideal wire-service reporter. Even his bitterest rivals recognized his talent. Wes Gallagher, they respectfully muttered behind his back, was the one to watch, for he not only knew how to file the story first, but also how to frame the way a story would be covered. He was, many of them agreed, "the bellwether of American correspondents."[5]

Yet in the dank Gibraltar command post, even Gallagher was happy to curtail his normal competitive urge in favor of becoming a team player. He immediately struck up a close rapport with both Eisenhower and his deputy, Major General Mark Clark. He valued their readiness to take time out of a heavy schedule to talk to reporters as partners, not rivals. Because both men willingly explained many of the operation's complexities, he recognized the strains they were under, as well as the vast amount of work that had been expended to get so many troops to this point.

As the ships made their last turn toward the African shore, Gallagher also shared the military's overpowering sense of anticipation and fear—a sense that the war was at a turning point and that failure would have disastrous consequences. The night of November 7 passed slowly. Gallagher could not sleep. Instead, he sat down and tapped out his first invasion story, before pacing around the rock until H-Hour arrived and the news could, at long last, be released.[6]

A DEARTH OF DRAMATIC NEWS

Shortly after nine o'clock on the East Coast, American radio listeners suddenly lost their usual Saturday night shows. "Ladies and gentlemen," an announcer intoned, "we interrupt this program to bring you an important announcement. A powerful American force, equipped with adequate weapons of modern warfare and under American command, is landing on the Mediterranean and Atlantic coasts of Africa. It provides an effective second front."[7]

Inside the White House, the press corps was frantic. Stephen Early, the president's press secretary, had called the reporters into his office a few minutes earlier to tell them what was about to break. Then, in an unprecedented move, Early had dramatically locked the door, not allowing them to leave with a copy of Roosevelt's statement until after the clock had passed nine. At the appointed time, the reporters dashed to their desks to file their first copy, meeting up with colleagues who had been hastily roused from beds or bars to provide support. Ninety minutes later, Gallagher's story from Gibraltar came over the wires, adding a little more detail as editors finalized their Sunday editions. These would be emblazoned with the stark headline: "AEF INVADES AFRICA."[8]

An ex-newspaperman, Steve Early had been in charge of White House press relations for almost a decade, and he knew all about using a dash of suspense to squeeze every last ounce of drama out of a major news story. On the other side of the Atlantic, where American troops were currently landing around three separate North African cities, both the media and the military also had their fair share of veterans. But none of them knew much about how to strike exactly the right balance between censorship and publicity in the middle of an operation as complex as this one. Nor had anyone on the military side fully recognized the difficulties of getting stories out of the battle zone—which was a major shame because at all three invasion sites there were countless examples of heroism, tragedy, and pure theater. Just the sort of exploits that, had they been published, would have fulfilled Roosevelt's desire to fix the home front's attention firmly on the war against Nazi Germany.

Few had a more punishingly heroic tale to tell than Leo S. Disher Jr. of the UP. Disher had already caused quite a stir in London by marrying the Czech intelligence chief's daughter after a whirlwind romance. Previously, his main job had been to report on the US fleet patrolling European waters, so he was no stranger to the perils of the sea. But in the early hours of November 8, after the long voyage from Scotland to the Mediterranean, he could hardly wait to set foot in Africa.[9]

Disher's boat, the HMS *Walney*, was a two-hundred-and-fifty-foot cutter that had been charged with breaking in to Oran harbor, in a bold and daring attempt to capture it before French forces—if they remained hostile—could sabotage the port. Although it had been built to survive Atlantic storms, the *Walney* was packed so full of ammunition and depth charges that, as Disher described it, during the long voyage, "she wallowed as much as she sailed." She lurched even when the sea was calm. Within three days of leaving Britain, the ship's captain was seasick. Then Disher slipped on deck and broke his ankle.

Just after midnight, Disher made his way to the bridge. With one lifebelt tied around his ankle cast and another around his chest, he was in prime position to watch the show. Along with everyone else on board, he hoped the French would surrender Oran without a fight. Almost as soon as the *Walney* crashed into the harbor, though, the French rained murderous fire down on the boat. Amid explosions, flames, and machine-gun bullets, the casualties exceeded 90 percent.

Miraculously, Disher survived. Flinging himself into the water before the boat sank, he realized that the lifebelt around his chest had been torn by shrapnel. Worse, the belt around his broken ankle was still buoyant. It immediately pulled his leg to the surface, while his head and body were dragged down into the frigid water. Desperately, he ripped the ankle belt loose. Choking and shivering, he swam to the shore as bullets continued to splash the water around him. Then, just hours after Disher's war began, it was all over. The French picked him up and herded him into a prisoner compound, while his UP bosses back home listed him as the first media casualty of the invasion.[10]

For a war correspondent, the only possible upside in such a disaster was the chance to file an eyewitness scoop. As a prisoner, Disher initially lacked either a typewriter or access to a communications network. But even after the French agreed to a ceasefire and released him, Disher still found himself stymied in getting out his story.

Allied censorship was largely to blame. The *Walney* raid had been a risky proposition from its conception. Many senior officers had voiced qualms about a small cutter taking on the port's impressive defenses. Unwilling to spark public recriminations, the high command decided to clamp down hard on any story detailing the extent of the raid's bloody failure. "Silence," decreed the senior naval officer, "is the best policy."[11]

This was doubly frustrating to Disher because his UP colleagues thought he had a humdinger of a story that the folks back home needed to read. One even jotted down the salient details as Disher lay in a hospital bed recovering from no fewer than twenty-six wounds. But the censor ruthlessly blocked the dispatch. A week or so later, a few skimpy details about the raid dribbled out when Disher received a Purple Heart, before being flown to London for more intensive medical care. Still, neither the medal nor the belated column inches proved to be much consolation after his harrowing experience.[12]

A couple of hundred miles to the east of Oran, censorship proved less of an obstacle. Here, with French forces quickly laying down their arms, reporters enjoyed a series of eye-catching escapades, waged in close partnership with the military. But they still faced formidable problems when they tried to translate these adventures into page-one scoops. Even the redoubtable Bill Stoneman found himself partially thwarted.

The *Chicago Daily News* man was earmarked to participate in the assault on Algiers. The hub of the French empire in North Africa, the city was crucial to the success of Operation Torch. The most easterly invasion point, Algiers' early capture would allow the Anglo-American forces to make a dash into neighboring Tunisia, and hopefully wrap up the campaign within weeks.

Like other correspondents, Stoneman had first been told of his destination while at sea. Turning to Ned Russell of the UP, he immediately picked out Fort Sidi Ferruch as the best bet for a good story. A commando raid was scheduled to attack a French position at the fort, which was just fifteen miles west of Algiers. The UP man happily agreed. "Who was I to argue with Stoneman?" he thought. "This was old stuff to him. He is one of the top-notch reporters of all time." So Russell replied, "Sounds swell."

As the two reporters spent more time at sea, they not only struck up a close friendship, but also became active participants in the invasion's unfolding tactical plans. Because Stoneman spoke fluent French, he agreed to carry a heavy loudspeaker on his back so that he could urge the French defenders to give up without a fight. Russell, for his part, helped Stoneman by transporting enough extra chocolate, cigarettes, notebooks, and pencils for two.

In the early hours of November 8, both men joined their separate units. The navy dropped Russell in the wrong place. Wading chest deep in the icy Mediterranean water, he was so cold and exhausted when he made land that, on the rapid march toward the target, he soon abandoned his bag. Just in front of the imposing fort, as his comrades contemplated whether to cut the barbed wire, Russell was startled by a loud voice. "For Christ's sake, don't shoot," Stoneman boomed through his loudspeaker. With scarcely concealed joy, the veteran correspondent told Russell and the others that he had already liberated the fort.

As Russell stood shivering in his wet clothes, a grinning Stoneman explained what had happened. With fortune on his side, he had come ashore at precisely the right spot. Not long after, he had bumped into a French officer in charge of the fort who said, "*Amis, amis*. Welcome. We've been waiting for you. Come on in."

Having liberated Fort Sidi Ferruch without firing a shot, Stoneman headed east toward Algiers; Russell went inland to help capture the Blida airfield. Amid the initial postinvasion chaos, the Allied officers, lacking numbers and weapons, focused on trying to talk to the French rather than fight them. And they sometimes informally enlisted reporters into their ranks. At Blida, for instance, Russell briefly acted as adjutant to the commanding officer and, for the sake of appearances, felt obliged to address the man as "sir." The ruse worked. After three hours of anxious talks with the French soldiers, who aggressively brandished their rifles while angrily eyeing the damage caused by an Allied bombing raid, the officer and his journalist-assistant secured Blida airfield without any bloodshed.

As soon as the fighting subsided, the two reporters found themselves alone. They spent Sunday night trying to shelter from the freezing wind on the floor of an abandoned house. On Monday, they entered Algiers by electric trolley: "It wasn't very spectacular," Stoneman later told a friend, "but it was comfortable."[13]

After strolling along the waterfront, the reporters checked in to the Hotel Aletti. The week before it had been home to German and Italian officials, who had left in such a hurry that their belongings, including a couple of full liquor bottles, remained in the rooms given to Stoneman and Russell. Suitably refreshed, the reporters set up their typewriters and began tapping out their stories. Although neither man had seen much in the way of real fighting, they both knew they had a major scoop to file: the liberation of the most important invasion target. Unlike Disher's heroics on behalf of a controversial mission, they also knew that their story of a major bloodless success ought to have little problem getting through the censor.

On Monday evening Russell and Stoneman headed to the HMS *Bulolo*, the invasion force command ship. "After some argument," they prevailed on the naval officer in charge of the message center to send off their dispatch. Given their various adventures in recent days, it turned out to be an unusual document. In a major departure from the normal practice, their story carried both their bylines, side by side. Since the communications system was only able to take three hundred words, the two men had concluded that writing a single, joint story was the best, and fairest, way to provide the world with the barebones facts about their exploits.[14]

At least Stoneman and Russell got some sort of story out. Far to the west, at the other end of the elongated invasion area, US troops faced their stiffest test, and American reporters encountered the worst communications snafus.

The assault on Casablanca was quite different from the other two landings. The reporters bound for the Mediterranean had joined their boats in Britain. The Casablanca-bound Western Task Force, however, had departed from the United States, where the fight against Nazi Germany remained a distant affair. Unlike the veteran correspondents who had received the call in London, the five reporters assigned to accompany the Casablanca convoy were combat virgins. They only knew war from what they had read, so they tended to be nervier and more starry-eyed than their colleagues who had landed at Oran and Algiers, more excited about the prospect of going to war, but more prone to disappointment when the reality did not live up to their expectations.[15]

Hal Boyle was a case in point. Originally from Kansas City, Missouri, Boyle had been reporting for the AP since graduating from Columbia University. For the past five years, he had steadily worked his way up the agency's New York hierarchy, becoming the nighttime city-desk editor, but he had always hankered to be like Richard Harding Davis. So when he got the sudden call to join the invasion party, Boyle could scarcely wait to go, even if it meant leaving behind his wife and their "snug" Waverly Place apartment in Greenwich Village. Indeed, he gushed with gratitude at having grabbed "one of the best assignments of the war."[16]

Disillusion was not long in coming. For correspondents used to relative freedom, the transition to the bureaucratic regimentation of military life was tough. Some were bewildered and then irritated by the excessive red tape and apparent incompetence of those trying to administer it. Obtaining both a civilian passport and military credentials seemed, for some reason, to be particularly time-consuming. Others complained of a left arm as "sore as a boil" after thirteen jabs for yellow fever, smallpox, typhus, cholera, and seemingly countless other diseases. "You start out with visions of travel to romantic places," observed one of Boyle's close colleagues. "But before you've even moved off first base your nerves are quivering . . . your arms look like a dope fiend's from inoculations. And you're mumbling 'passport . . . visas . . . typhus . . . cholera . . . when-the-hell-am-I gonna-leave . . . typhoid . . . visas . . .' "[17]

Neither was the long sea voyage much fun. All the way across the Atlantic the invasion ships zigzagged so violently to avoid the U-boats that one observer likened their path to "a reeling drunk in the snow." Then, suddenly, almost everyone began reeling when, not far from their destination, the ships sailed into a major storm that rolled them as much as thirty degrees.[18]

Groggy by the time they finally arrived off the Moroccan coast, the men in the Western Task Force benefited when the storm suddenly subsided, turning the sea uncharacteristically calm along the invasion beaches. But the navy still made a hash of the landings. At Fedala, Boyle's destination, "indescribable confusion" reigned, according to an official account. While many of the landing craft headed off in the wrong direction, Boyle's armada struck a reef. The razor-sharp coral holed a number of boats, forcing men into the sea, where some floundered with too much equipment and others cut their arms and legs as they struggled toward land.[19]

Boyle, like many, clambered on to the beach, spluttering and shivering from this dunking in the sea. On getting his bearings, his first sensation was profound relief: the night was so dark, and the French were so surprised, that the landing had been virtually unopposed. But he soon realized that he had lost most of his clothes and equipment, including his portable typewriter, which, he ruefully informed his editor a few days later, "went to the bottom of the Atlantic with the jeep to which they were lashed."[20]

The loss made Boyle even more dependent on the army. Indeed, he had to hammer out his first dispatch on a typewriter borrowed from a PRO, who shared it with the reporter even though his own unit was short. For the officer, it proved to be a good trade. Boyle, in his first taste of combat, was an enthusiastic cheerleader. Relieved to be unscathed, thankful for the loan, and impressed by how quickly the GIs around him had recovered, he produced a story that emphasized their martial determination and resourcefulness. "When I could stand again," he wrote,

> I saw about me scores of dripping soldiers, their legs weary and wide-braced. . . . The way those soaked men, a few moments before so weary that they could barely stand, forgot their fatigue and set about their objectives was a never-to-be-forgotten example of soldierly fortitude. Forlorn, on a hostile coast with much of their heavy equipment fathoms under salt water, they quickly organized and turned to their assigned tasks.[21]

Like his fellow correspondents across North Africa, Boyle then faced the problem of getting his story out. On the Moroccan beaches, this problem was compounded by fierce fighting, as the French had rallied quickly and struck back hard. With officers expending all their energy on bringing sufficient order out of the beachhead chaos, no one had much time to think about setting up a robust communications network. Lieutenant General George S. Patton, the general in command, defended the situation with a rare admission of impotence. "I cannot control interstellar space," he explained, "and our radio simply would not work. The only person who lost by it was myself," he added sardonically, "since the press was probably unable to recount my heroic deeds."[22]

In fact, the press in Morocco initially found it impossible to record anyone's heroic deeds. While still at sea, PROs had told correspondents that they would be restricted to one daily two-hundred-word dispatch. Even after the fighting ended on November 11, this paltry number seemed beyond reach. Patton's PR team ultimately laid on a special courier plane to Gibraltar, but almost a week into the campaign the Casablanca-based correspondents were still complaining that there was "as yet no direct communication from here available to us." Not until November 15—eight days into the invasion—did they file their first stories. Even then, contact with the outside world was so sparse that they had no idea how their copy rated, especially compared to the reports about the ongoing Battle of Stalingrad, the British counterattack in the Egyptian desert at El Alamein, and the American stand on the Pacific island of Guadalcanal. The more pessimistic of them suspected that since their stories were "already old when we start to file it," they had doubtless been "crowded into distinctly secondary place."[23]

As the correspondents in Morocco quietly seethed at their inability to tell their stories to the world, those at Eisenhower's command readily stepped into the breach. Gallagher led the way. With regular access to Ike and a reliable communications network to the United States, his stories hit the front page day after day. The Americans were "pushing steadily forward" in Morocco, he wrote in a typical dispatch, "while the Mediterranean attack swept forward at an unprecedented pace." As for the fate of specific men or units, Gallagher had little to say—but a ready-made excuse at hand. "The scanty communications characteristic of all first days of fighting," he explained, "hid many tales of heroism in the widespread fighting."[24]

These Gibraltar-datelined dispatches also concealed a lot more: the fierceness of the fighting, the greenness of the American troops involved, and the blunders and disasters that befell a number of landing sites. Poor communications remained the public reason given for the lack of anything but the haziest updates about overall progress, but in private, senior officials admitted to other calculations. "The fighting and the casualties were much harder and greater than the public was purposely led by Allied Headquarters to believe," Butcher confided in his diary, "because we did not want the French to remain embittered for having to fight them into submission."[25]

As long as the fighting raged, the military emerged relatively unscathed from this conscious effort to sugarcoat the war news. In Gibraltar, Gallagher watched contentedly as each of his dispatches made a splash back home. In North Africa, meanwhile, exhausted or injured correspondents initially lacked the energy to press their complaints. Many also found the habit of collaborating with their partners in peril hard to break.

These war correspondents had been integrated into the military system for close to a month, during which they had shared almost everything, from the seasickness during the voyage to the gut-wrenching fear when they hit the beaches. As a result, many had come to sympathize with the soldiers' plight. Although they were frustrated at remaining incommunicado for so long or irritated that some of their carefully crafted copy had been cut, deep down they understood the causes and were willing to make allowances. These major irritants, they generally recognized, were inevitable consequences of the chaos that accompanies combat, especially in such a complex operation fought by such inexperienced troops.

Soon after the French agreed to a truce, on November 11, the dynamics of the media-military relationship started to change. The two sides were no longer active partners. Reporters invariably headed to one of the big hotels that doubled as a press camp. There, they quickly became exasperated with the continued delays in setting up a usable communications network and establishing a viable system for censorship and briefings.

The situation in Algiers summed it up. Everyone had looked forward to the city becoming a major base. If they were like Ike, they anticipated a balmy winter climate and "palm trees, banana and orange trees, lots of flowers and bougainvillea." The reality proved a disappointment. Next to the dockyards packed full of Allied boats stood workers huddling around fires for warmth or sheltering from the constant drizzle. Algiers's main thoroughfares had a reputation for embodying French chic, but veteran correspondents quickly saw in them the forlorn look so familiar from other Axis-occupied cities: the "empty, vacant eyes" of the population, alongside the shabby shop windows and unfilled grocery shelves.

The military had taken over three hotels, but in a way that made the reporters lives a misery. Daily briefings took place in the Regina, which also had a room where correspondents could write. The censors resided close by at the Hotel Central Touring, but once a piece of copy was approved, the reporter had to take it "three miles up the hill to the St. Georges message center to send it," complained one correspondent. "There it disappeared into a mess of flying paper and sometimes turned up three of four days later, never having been sent at all."[26]

Now that the perils of combat were no longer an excuse for such chaos, the reporters quickly lost patience. Irritated with the army, and with much more time on their hands, the prospect loomed that they would start to dig for stories that spelled trouble. So some senior officers believed the moment had come to encourage correspondents to begin entertaining the home front in earnest—not with upbeat overviews from headquarters or out-of-date dispatches from the front, but with something much more personal.

AN EXCESS OF ENTERTAINMENT

On November 10, Marshall had sent Eisenhower an important instruction. He told Ike to save up "color stories of exploits and personalities" for release during "dry spells." This initiative, Marshall believed, would give bored reporters something constructive to file. It might also satisfy readers back home, who had received only the haziest outlines of the invasion battles. Indeed, the type of story Marshall envisaged releasing during the lull would paint the landings more vividly on the canvas, with rosy tints and vigorous brush strokes animating the heroics of specific individuals and units.

Turning this notion into an effective policy proved to be surprisingly difficult. Marshall wanted stories to be "spread around so as not to overplay any one personality." But, he soon angrily conceded, the directive failed to factor in the oversized egos of a small number of generals who had arrived in Africa with either well-honed media skills or aggressive PR advisers—or both.

Take Patton. The commander at Casablanca embodied so many contradictions as to be almost impossible for reporters to characterize: hard, but emotional; a straight-talking, cussing man of action, who spoke in a "high squeaky voice" and liked nothing more than to study his books. Journeying across the Atlantic, he had read the Koran for inspiration and shown off his French fluency by spotting grammatical errors in propaganda leaflets. On the Moroccan beaches he had sworn at, manhandled, and even kicked his men to get them going.

Although Patton defied easy classification, he was a magnet to reporters. At this early stage of the war, descriptions of his more physical methods of inspiring GIs remained safely unprinted. The correspondents focused instead on his fighting language, especially the ghoulish phrase he often used to motivate his troops to annihilate the enemy: "When you stick your hand into the bunch of goo that a moment before was your best friend's face . . ." After hearing these words, many US soldiers not only began to hate the Germans, they also dubbed Patton "Ole Blood and Guts." This nickname, the reporters explained, embodied his whole approach to war, which was to confront its gruesome side head on while leading firmly, sometimes recklessly, from the front.[27]

Once an armistice had been signed in Morocco, even Patton's ability to hog the limelight dimmed. By the end of November, Morocco had become a rear base for American men and materiel being shipped across the Atlantic. Since these necessities of military life rarely preoccupied reporters, Patton largely dropped out of public view. Soon, his main relationship with the media became his somewhat sad perusal of the hundreds of press clippings on his Torch exploits that his wife sent him during his long, boring African winter.[28]

While Patton pined for the glory of combat, Ike faced a major press problem closer to home. In late October, Mark Clark had made a brief, incognito visit to Algiers to ascertain the likely French reaction to Operation Torch and the extent to which senior French figures could be persuaded to support the Allied cause. His subsequent escapades provided enough material to flood the driest of news spells. And after the invasion succeeded,

Clark wasted little time channeling the account of it in a direction that he thought placed him in the best possible light.[29]

Clark had given Gallagher the choicest details soon after the AP man arrived in Gibraltar. Ever cautious, Eisenhower held up publication of the story until after the French had signed the armistice. Ike wanted to portray Clark's mission as having been vital to ensuring the success of the landings without too much bloodshed. But he could not keep his number two from blabbing details to reporters. Clark even confessed that he had lost "practically everything" when, on one fraught occasion, his boat had capsized. "Everything" included his pants: Clark had scrambled ashore in his underwear and had to commandeer a pair of trousers from a subordinate. It also included $8,000 in gold, and he now joked that the Treasury Department might come after him for losing so much of Uncle Sam's money.[30]

As the story gathered momentum, Marshall failed to see the funny side. "American fathers and mothers want to feel that their boys are being led into battle by sober-minded, serious, conscientious, and forthright generals," the army chief lectured from afar. "They don't like cheap publicity, nor should the thinking ones, as indeed most of them are, be made to feel that their boys are being led by buffoons."

When the more colorful details of Clark's mission became known, Marshall's ire increased. What "newspapers have stressed," he cabled Eisenhower on November 21, was the "*loss of pants* and the fact that an enormous amount of money was carried." Some of the stories suggested that this money had fallen into enemy hands and that it was "going to be used by Axis propaganda to impugn the motives of every Frenchman that joins us. We will be called bribers," Marshall feared, "and the French takers thereof."[31]

Stories of seedy financial transactions with Vichy officials were particularly ill-timed. To conclude an armistice with the French, Eisenhower and Clark had struck a deal with Admiral Jean-François Darlan, the commander-in-chief of all Vichy forces and number two figure in the Vichy government, who happened to be in Algiers at the start of the invasion. The deal quickly became embroiled in controversy, as numerous reporters denounced Eisenhower for negotiating with a Nazi collaborator.[32]

Ike reacted with dismay. Already suffering from a hacking cough caused by chain-smoking in Gibraltar's damp and dark tunnels, "the storm of anxiety and bickering" over Darlan sent his mood plunging. "For two days," Eisenhower explained to Clark on November 19, "I thought I would simply have to go to a padded cell." As it was, he remained stuck inside the rock, where his small office felt ever more like a dungeon. But here, at least, he had "ready communications back to London and Washington" that allowed him to justify his actions.[33]

Eisenhower began by providing concrete evidence to sustain his claim that the Darlan deal had saved American lives. Two weeks into the invasion he authorized the release of the first casualty figures—a bold move because many of the next of kin had yet to be informed. This revealed a total of 1,800 losses, compared to estimates before the invasion that as many as 18,000 troops would be killed, wounded, or go missing in the battles for the beachheads. As Ike hastened to tell reporters, this low casualty total needed to be seen alongside the deal's other advantages, especially the relative peace and stability in Morocco and Algeria that would allow the Allies to launch an early drive into Tunisia.[34]

After Eisenhower finally moved to Algiers on November 23, he set in motion a major overhaul of media relations within his command. Communications naturally topped his list. Reporters still complained incessantly about the difficulty of getting their copy out of the theater, although many of them realized that Eisenhower's command was grappling with the problem with ingenuity and energy. The most eye-catching—and ill-fated—initiative came in late November, when Eisenhower sent a ship into the U-boat infested Mediterranean to dig up an old cable to Malta, splice it, and forge a new connection between Algiers and Gibraltar. Enemy submarines remained at bay throughout this delicate operation, but two hours after the job was finished, a storm dragged some boats that were anchored nearby over the new cable, and they "tore it to pieces." Small wonder that the officer in charge of communications soon took on the air of "the most harassed man in the army."[35]

Joe Phillips ran him a close second. In the first weeks of Torch, Ike's public relations chief had struggled to deal with reporters' growing complaints about the poor communications and censorship. But Phillips lacked the seniority, the clout with Washington, and a brief that stretched beyond military matters. So Eisenhower decided to place someone above Phillips, someone "thoroughly familiar with War Department problems in PR," Ike cabled the War Department on November 21, "as well as competent to judge what must be censored from viewpoint of security and who could anticipate public reaction to various stories." As the reporters' grievances multiplied, Phillips happily agreed. Only a general, he told Butcher, had the necessary authority to coordinate the military and political dimensions of PR and censorship. Phillips even suggested General McClure for the job, who was still stuck in London as intelligence chief.[36]

As soon as Ike "bought" the idea, McClure went to work. His main task was to coordinate the disparate threads of censorship, public relations, and psychological warfare. By making one key change, he became an immediate hit with reporters. In Algiers, noted Gallagher, "McClure pulled the monastic censors out of their hotel caves and put them, the press conferences, and censorship under one roof, along with a delivery system for stories. The so-called 'psychological warriors,' who were taking a none too bright hand in political censorship, also were captured and installed in the building henceforth known as the 'Tower of Babel.'"[37]

These important improvements immediately eased the daily lot of reporters working in and around Eisenhower's new command post. Only time would tell whether they would be sufficient to provide informative news when American troops finally encountered the German army.

CHAPTER 3

The Advent of Ernie

TO TÉBOURBA

Like many of his colleagues, Drew Middleton quickly learned to hate the Aletti Hotel. After coming ashore on November 8, he had seen little of the fighting. A few days later he had encountered a young GI from Georgia, whose gun was trained on a French position. "We've got orders to nootralize it," the boy had told him, "that is, if they start any trouble."[1] But there had been no trouble that day, just an early armistice. So Middleton had sauntered around town before checking in to the Aletti.

For a day or two, the hotel seemed a massive improvement on the ships' cabins and makeshift bivouacs of the invasion period. Middleton even thought that the Aletti might "become the kind of hotel about which people write books"—one of those crisis hotels where correspondents gathered amid the carnage of war to swap stories, trade rumors, and recharge their batteries.

Revelry was certainly rife at the Aletti. Stoneman, having checked in first, managed to liberate a case of Scotch, and each night in the bar, Middleton recalled, "you could hear the click of correspondents' typewriters rising above the click of glasses." Soon, though, even the revelry became dull, while the hotel rapidly lost its charm amid rising complaints of poor service, "thieving chambermaids," and the "occasional cockroach."[2]

Alongside the mounting frustrations with the Aletti came the strong pull of combat. The beachheads now secure, in the middle of November Eisenhower undertook an audacious gamble. Cobbling together four British brigades and a random assortment of American units, he struck east into

Tunisia. Acknowledging that this hodgepodge force, grandly named the First Army, would have to cover "almost stupendous" distances with limited transport, Ike hoped to get to the key cities of Tunis and Bizerte before the Germans poured in major reinforcements. As he told Marshall, these men would be "badly extended" and "operating by driblets," but he firmly believed that with "boldness rather than numbers," he could liberate the two cities and bring the North African campaign to a swift and successful conclusion.[3]

The First Army's march into Tunisia proved to be a major headache for the war correspondents. "Public relations," one noted privately on November 19, "being the Cinderella of the army, have failed to provide adequate transport, or staff." All reporters wishing to join the eastward expedition were on their own. Although some of them managed to cadge lifts in army jeeps, huddling under canvas covers to avoid the persistent, pelting hail, most of the reporters had dismissed this option as too unreliable and uncomfortable. Instead, the scroungers set about finding their own cars. Idle automobiles could be found everywhere in Algiers, but because of the gasoline shortage since the fall of France, most of them had seized-up engines and rotted tires. Whether they could make the 540-mile journey over steep, sometimes poorly drained roads remained to be seen.[4]

Stoneman, impatient to get going, took a chance on a 1934 Ford V-Eight sedan, for which he paid $450. To share the cost, he teamed up with Drew Middleton, Ned Russell, and Bill King of the AP. The four men rendezvoused in the Algerian coastal town of Bône on Saturday, November 21. After filling their new purchase with carefully chosen supplies—eight army blankets, four trench coats, three typewriters, and two boxes of army rations—they set off for the new Tunisian battlefront.[5]

For more than a week, the four reporters remained incommunicado. Back home, their editors therefore had little choice other than to fill their pages with Eisenhower's comments and communiqués, paraphrased by wire-service correspondents based at the Algiers HQ.

The resulting stories remained resolutely rose tinted. Eisenhower continued to put the best public gloss on his first foray into politics—going as far as to predict that the Darlan deal would speed up victory in North Africa by roughly ninety days. Unaware that as many as 25,000 Axis troops lay in wait around Tunis and Bizerte, Eisenhower's headquarters also encouraged reporters to write that the First Army was making great strides toward victory.[6]

The AP dispatches were typical. On November 20, Wes Gallagher reported that the "Allied forces having smashed one-third of a German armored column and crushed all Nazi tank attacks are closing in on all landward sides around the naval base of Bizerte and Tunis, the capital of Tunisia." His dispatch the next day was equally buoyant. "Allied armored forces streaming into Tunisia," Gallagher declared, "closed with German forces today in the opening phases of a full-scale assault on . . . [the] defenses within which the Axis has been herded with its back to the sea around Bizerte and Tunis."[7]

As the home front received daily bulletins predicting a major success, Stoneman, Middleton, and their two colleagues approached the town of Tébourba with a mounting sense of foreboding. The Luftwaffe dominated the skies. Although Allied armor and infantry seemed to be heading in the right direction, warning signs lurked everywhere. Not far from town, a group of British journalists, going the other way, warned the American reporters that "it's a little sticky at the front" and that the situation was "very fluid." Still, the Americans pressed on, reaching Tébourba just in time for the start of the big German counterattack on November 30.

At first, no one seemed to have a clear idea about how the battle was unfolding, but by early afternoon, German strength was obviously starting to tell. Just after dusk, a British officer invited Russell to peer through

Figure 3.1 Unidentified US war correspondents at an advanced position in North Africa, November 18, 1942. National Archives 111-SC-149965.

his field glasses. "Look along the line of trees on the top of the ridge," he guided him. "There are twenty-four German tanks among those trees. . . . It looks as if we're goners. If they don't come down and take us tonight, they'll come in the morning and there's not a bloody thing we can do to stop them."

Suddenly, the situation reverted to how it had been on the beaches: caught once more in a highly perilous situation, the correspondents willingly conceded their autonomy. They gratefully took cigarettes and swigs of whisky offered by an American liaison officer, recognizing, as Russell recalled later, that they "were fast ceasing to be independent war correspondents, who could roam where we pleased," but were effectively attached to the military, "at least for the duration of this crisis." Amid lame jokes about how the Germans would treat captured war correspondents, they obediently accepted terse orders neither to talk nor smoke, lest the noise or glowing embers attract the enemy's attention. Called to a conference with the commanding officer, they eagerly nodded their agreement when told of the plan to sneak through the German encirclement under cover of darkness.

Shortly before nine, the reporters crept inside their car, hoping that the noise of the Ford's engine would not alert the enemy. For four hours they inched along in low gear. The night was so dark that Russell drove by feel rather than sight; when the windscreen became so encrusted with dust that he could see nothing at all, he handed the wheel over to Stoneman and took up a position on the running board to give directions. Finally, they made it to relative safety. With only stray snipers to worry about, they dashed to divisional headquarters, desperate to file stories that diverged from the Algiers-written dispatches that had dominated the front pages.[8]

It ought to have been a moment of triumph. A major scoop beckoned: the first eyewitness account of Americans battling Germans; a stirring first-person narrative of a bold escape from an enemy encirclement; a chilling tale of setback that undermined the optimistic official account—or, as Stoneman put it, "a bitter purgatory ending in death, suffering, and disappointment." But to become a scoop, the story first had to leave Africa, and this proved as difficult as ever.[9]

The British correspondents who left Tébourba before the German counterattack had already encountered the chaos in the Allied rear. Radio communications remained erratic. The air force had not yet established regular courier flights to Algiers. Although friendly pilots took stories back on an impromptu basis, they did not always seem to know what to do with them. Those dispatches that did eventually make it to Algiers's "Tower of Babel" still had to pass muster with the censor. Some correspondents began to fret that even "guarded" pieces would be "massacred by the censor, as AFHQ are still on the optimistic tack." Others soon learned that the censors tended to delay any dispatch that made it to Algiers for around five days, so as not to divulge sensitive operational information to the enemy.[10]

Such delays called into question the value of reporting spot news from the front. As Stoneman recognized, war correspondents could only effectively recount their own narrow experiences. They had no real sense of what was happening elsewhere. "Occasionally," he added,

> we get tidbits of news from some headquarters or other, but none of it is very important and besides it will be on the BBC news program before we can even find a dispatch rider to take it back to the airdrome from which it can be flown to some place where the censor can operate on it and finally send it to the home offices.

In the privacy of his diary, one of Stoneman's colleagues reached an even more depressing conclusion. "Here, as a correspondent," he wrote from just outside Tébourba, "I am on the horns of a dilemma. I am where I ought to be, but my communications are bad; and if I can't get my articles home I ought not to be here."[11] Perhaps, the reporter mused, he should return to Algiers, where at least the overall picture was clearer, the censors closer, and the communications sturdier.

THE "HEROES AND GOATS" OF THE WAR

Editors and executives back home started to voice similar doubts. War correspondents cost a lot of money. Someone like Stoneman made more than $700 a month, plus a war separation allowance, and this soon added up. When his newspaper, the *Chicago Daily News*, offset all expenses against sales, it estimated that its foreign news service as a whole would lose more than $100,000 in 1942—much less than before the war, but still a tidy sum.[12]

What were these newspapers getting for their money? Because of unreliable communications and overzealous censorship, their expensive reporters sent spot news that tended to be old news by the time it reached the United States. Eyewitness invasion reports had only made it into print a week after American troops had hit the beaches; Tébourba battle stories had faced similar delays. Although these reports had added more color to the sketchy HQ-inspired dispatches, media bosses naturally started questioning whether they were worth the cost.

It was a knotty problem, because the obvious alternative hardly appealed. At a November meeting of AP members, some editors complained that America's biggest press agency "seemed to accept official news a 'bit too eagerly.'" As the conversation developed, a third course seemed to offer a better way of providing compelling war coverage. Rather than dated frontline dispatches or overoptimistic communiqué summaries, AP clients pressed for "more stories based on unofficial views," especially "feature stories on the 'heroes and goats' of the war."[13]

The top AP executives had already reached a similar conclusion, though they did not always find it easy to steer their huge organization in the desired direction. The AP was a non-profit, public-service cooperative that gathered news on an industrial scale. Every day, its 7,000 staff members generated more than a million words, all of which came hammering through 3,300 teletype machines. Before the war it had been stuck in a rut, exemplified by the uninspiring quality of its international news. Indeed, overly dependent on handouts from foreign news agencies, AP dispatches had a reputation for being dull or merely echoing the viewpoint of other governments.

Then general manager Kent Cooper gave the organization new direction. In 1940 he moved his head-office staff into a new purpose-built office at 50 Rockefeller Plaza, which, he declared, provided the AP with more fitting premises and epitomized its new ethos of "dignified showmanship."[14] He extended this same philosophy to international reporting. Slowly weaning the agency off its dependence on foreign news agencies, he prodded it to cater to an American audience that favored intimate human-interest stories. "I wanted it to be the day of the common soldier," he explained, "the 'jack-tar,' or combat pilot." Emphasizing tales of the lowly fighting man would minimize the problem of getting timely spot news from the front. It would also appeal to smaller AP clients dotted across the country—the hundreds of local newspapers that thrived on stories about the adventures and heroics of the boys next door. Cooper therefore began pressing his correspondents to send in dispatches "from someplace in some war area about a boy from each hometown where the Associated Press had a member paper."[15]

Of all the AP correspondents in North Africa, Hal Boyle relished this challenge the most. Having quickly recuperated from his invasion-day exploits, Boyle was enjoying himself in North Africa—perhaps a little too much. His most notorious escapade was to climb on a jeep that was first into an Arab town and begin yelling, "Vote for Boyle—son of toil! Vote for Hal, the Arab's pal." "Pretty soon," recalled a friend, "the Arabs caught on and were chanting the phrase in a paean of welcome to astonished American troops."[16]

Alongside such exuberant antics, Boyle had started to find his mark as a writer. He still focused on the staple of all wire-service reporting: trying to beat rivals to breaking news. But he also proved remarkably adept at turning Cooper's edict into effective copy. Whenever he encountered a new American unit, Boyle immediately took out his notebook and began "industriously getting the names" of everyone he met, in the hope of writing stories that would appeal to their hometown newspapers. Whenever he produced a piece that did not fit neatly into the AP's normal spot-news dispatches, he began to file it under the title, "Leaves from a War Correspondent's Notebook." The resulting little stories tackled an eclectic range of subjects—a Texas officer whose watch was wound daily to Texas time to remind him of home; a new supply policy that provided GIs with cigarettes, candy, and some toilet items as part of their daily ration; or the decision by some soldiers to pay Arabs four cigarettes to dig their foxholes for them.[17]

Back home, the AP bosses were delighted. "Boyle's copy," declared one, "has been exceptionally colorful and beautifully detailed for hometown delivery." In full agreement, numerous editors across the nation carved out precious space for Boyle's intriguing tidbits.[18]

As the AP moved consciously in the direction of reporting human-interest stories from the front, the Scripps-Howard press reached the same destination by a more fortuitous route.

Scripps-Howard had traditionally positioned itself partly as a foil to what it considered the staid dominance of the AP. As well as publishing more than twenty newspapers in most major cities, it controlled the UP, which had been created by Scripps-Howard president Roy W. Howard.

Diminutive and dapper, hard-driven and deeply ambitious, Howard had worked his way up the rungs of the newspaper business, from daily deliverer of the *Indianapolis Star*. Fast-talking his way into the job of heading the newly created UP in 1907, he had immediately challenged the AP by recruiting determined go-getters in his own image: reporters prepared to work for a low salary and often without the necessary equipment, but who could produce spot news without the dependence on official handouts that, he felt, so often marred AP dispatches.[19]

Although still keen to keep his hand in as a reporter, Howard's particular strength was in "the bargaining give and take accompanying the merging, selling, and purchasing [of] newspapers."[20] He held trenchant views on the layout of his titles, imploring his editors to produce "clean-cut and purposeful" front pages, especially for his tabloids.[21] He also knew what he wanted from his reporters: long hours and hard work, not philosophizing or pontificating. "I have never felt that brains are necessarily a handicap to a newspaperman," he once observed in his high-pitched Hoosier twang. But, he added, "a truly brilliant mind can be a complete washout in a newsroom unless associated with a will to work and a zest to do the same."[22]

Howard's own mind tended toward the practical. In December 1942, the UP hierarchy was in uproar about the AP's newfound emphasis on human-interest stories. Howard, by contrast, had a more prosaic view of what made good journalism: "The primary feature of a newspaper is to inform people accurately, quickly, succinctly. The ultimate distillation of news is 'what, where, when, and how.' "[23]

Yet even as Howard wrote, his organization was receiving combat dispatches from a fellow Hoosier who would do much more than write about what happened when. He would develop a distinctive brand of war reporting, and in the process make himself a major star—and the Scripps-Howard press a considerable sum of money.

ERNIE'S ARRIVAL

Ernest Taylor Pyle—or "Ernie" to his friends—first set foot in North Africa on November 25, 1942, unheralded, almost unnoticed, but already something of a hardened veteran.[24]

Like Middleton, Gallagher, and Stoneman, Pyle had been through the familiar wartime rite of passage. The London blitz two years earlier had been his first taste of modern war. He had endured it like the others, traipsing the cold, damp London streets at night as bombs fell and fires raged. But whereas the others had sometimes found exhilaration, even excitement, amid the chaos and destruction, for Pyle war was always to be endured, never enjoyed.

The blitz had therefore been a trial, but so had just about everything else in Ernie's life. His slow ascent from copyeditor to columnist had fulfilled his ambition to write clear, vivid portraits of his personal experiences, but it had been accompanied by growing doubts that he could keep up the pace of producing daily dispatches. His wife had initially provided stimulating company as he struggled to find new topics for his column, but, increasingly, she was consumed by alcoholism. Pyle himself had a tendency to drink too much, resulting in constant ailments and illnesses that sapped his strength and diminished his appearance. Often described as wiry, his weight invariably hovered below 110 pounds, dipping even lower at times of high stress or hard drinking.

Beset by all these tribulations, Ernie had become a restless soul. For the past five years, he had traveled for inspiration. He had traveled to build up a "cushion" of columns, so that he had something to send his editor if his concentration waned or his health collapsed. He had traveled in the hope of breaking out of a current routine that, he believed, was wearing him down. And he had traveled to escape his reality, initially the limited horizons of his native Indiana, and then his broken married life in Albuquerque. In the late 1930s he had stayed in more than 800 hotels as he drove relentlessly around America. A year after blitz, he had returned to Britain, where he began touring the American military camps that were dotted across the country.

His resulting columns had been successful, but not spectacularly so. In the late 1930s, Pyle did not even try to compete with the big names of the day—the likes of Walter Lippmann, who mused about democracy, war, and peace, or Drew Pearson, who engaged in good old-fashioned muckraking. Whereas these men syndicated their regular columns to hundreds of newspapers, Pyle's outpourings appeared only in Scripps-Howard's twenty-four titles.

Still, over the years Pyle had steadily built up a solid readership. Although his style of reporting was too personal, too quirky, and, for some, too humdrum to fit into any recognizable category of contemporaneous journalism, it had an obvious appeal. In the 1930s, the clarity of his descriptions, together with the almost-musical rhythm of his prose, had allowed readers to vicariously experience sights of Depression-era America. His style had worked particularly well during the blitz. While other reporters had watched the censors eviscerate their attempts to describe the number of bombs dropped or the places damaged, Ernie had focused on describing daily life, or, in his most famous blitz piece, producing a moving portrayal of "London stabbed with great fires, shaken by explosions, its dark regions along the Thames sparkling with pin points of white-hot bombs."

Ernie's blitz columns had not always reached such highs, but his more astute editors had started to feel that he had hit on something special. The average Pyle reader, concluded one, did not expect "something sensational every day. He looks on Ernie's columns as a sort of cross between a travelogue, a highly personalized and humanized diary, and a reporting job." When Pyle returned to the United States in 1941, he struggled for a time to produce anything sensational at all, and his column, complained the man in charge of its syndication, threatened to hit "an all-time low." Gripped by self-doubt, Ernie took a draft-board medical and contemplated going into the army. Meanwhile, some in the Scripps-Howard organization believed that he should be kept as far away from combat as possible. Perhaps, they pondered, if he returned to writing domestic-focused vignettes, his readers might view his more "whimsical" columns "as an antidote to the grimness of the war news."[25]

Fortunately, neither Pyle's slump nor his editors' doubts lasted very long. And when Ernie headed back to Britain in 1942 to tour American camps, his dispatches started to attract even more attention. "Folks with 'boys' over there," concluded one Scripps-Howard executive, "are a damned sight more interested in reading the homely, every day, what do they eat and how they live sort of stuff, than they are the heavy strategic stuff, as-I-predicted-in-my-analysis-back-in-1920 sort of stuff."[26]

Roy Howard, by contrast, viewed Pyle's output as a little dull, a little too "low altitude," but since a majority of his newspapers considered Pyle one of their most popular columnists, he did not protest too much.[27] And during the second half of 1942, Pyle, for once, was in a good frame of mind about his work. Gratified that so many of the troops he met in Britain carried around copies of his columns that relatives had sent them from the United States, he concluded that he was performing an important function—certainly more important than becoming a "104-pound typist soldier at Ft. Bragg or someplace." So in the fall, he successfully prevailed on his draft board to defer his call-up. His plan was to remain a full-time reporter for at least six more months, heading first to North Africa, before his normal restlessness drove him elsewhere.[28]

Pyle's African odyssey began in Oran, Algeria, a city still recovering from the short, vicious invasion a few weeks earlier. Unlike an ordinary war correspondent, who would have been tempted to strike out immediately for Tunisia in search of a scoop, Pyle decided to stay put and acclimatize. Besides, he lacked his customary "cushion" of columns, and, hearing the tales of woe about communications at the front, he wanted to build up plenty of copy before heading into the unknown.

It proved to be a shrewd decision. Oran was inundated with an array of Allied forces—sailors who had shepherded the invasion troops across the ocean, GIs who would soon be sent east into battle, pilots who were currently fighting the Luftwaffe, intelligence officers still grappling with former Vichy officials, and censors who were only just learning their trade. Pyle had always been adept at forging strong bonds with such people. "He had a gift for becoming a member of a group while retaining his ability to explain it to others," observed one biographer. Inherently shy, he was imbued with an impressive ability to make others feel at ease in his presence.[29]

As one of the few journalists left in a town the media had abandoned, Ernie quickly struck up a series of fruitful friendships. His most intriguing interlocutors were the merchant sailors convoying men and equipment from America. Blunt and outspoken, these men told him they were "astonished by the difference" between the overoptimistic media reports they had received stateside and the grim reality they witnessed in North Africa. "They say people at home," Pyle reported in his column on January 4, "think the North African campaign is a walkaway and will be over quickly. . . . If you think that, it is because we newspapermen here have failed at getting the finer points over to you." The time had come, Ernie believed, to set the record straight—to acknowledge the rawness of American forces, the tenacity of the German enemy, and the prospect that the Tunisian campaign would last for months, not weeks.[30]

Of course, it was not only newspapermen who had failed to get over the campaign's finer points. Eisenhower's command had been particularly guilty of encouraging reporters to do so. Ernie's dispatch, by directly challenging the official view, promised to cause quite a commotion—a prospect that delighted his bosses in New York. "No other newspaper account," enthused one senior Scripps-Howard executive, ". . . has approached Ernie's in revealing what the situation confronting us actually is." Consequently, he added, Scripps-Howard editors ought to give Pyle's "unusually clear presentation of conditions in North Africa . . . more than usual treatment."[31]

How had Ernie got such a discordant story past Ike's censorship office when so many others had failed in the past? Close observers posited various theories. Some suggested that Ernie had used his first weeks in Oran to construct a cozy, "chummy" relationship with all the censors, which had paid impressive dividends. Others insinuated that the average Pyle column tended to be so bland and harmless that the censor on duty simply saw his byline on the page, "yawned, and affixed his stamp of approval without reading the piece."[32]

Yet such theories ignored the changing mood inside Eisenhower's headquarters. During December, the Tunisian fighting bogged down in a depressing stalemate. As both sides settled into their winter positions, Eisenhower started to rethink his basic media message. He was particularly concerned that the press and the public had failed to grasp the new reality on the ground. "Columnists and newspaper writers," Ike complained, "have been leading the public to expect a quick and easy victory in the Tunisian area." To rectify this dangerous impression—which his own command had helped to engender—Eisenhower began considering a range of initiatives, including an informal press briefing that recounted why the Tunisian push had been such a gamble.[33]

Pyle's column therefore aligned neatly with the prevailing new mood at the top in the AFHQ in Algiers, which was starting to percolate down to those in Oran. Whether or not he knew of Ike's new attitude, Ernie's fortuitous timing ensured that he pulled off the astonishing feat of pleasing three conflicting audiences: his lowly military sources thought the story needed telling; his editors and readers considered it controversially compelling; and, at the very top, Eisenhower's command believed it to be opportunely enlightening.[34]

On the first day of 1943, Ernie left Oran, hoping that his luck would hold. His first destination was a major new American airbase at Biskra, situated in a desert oasis, with plentiful accommodation in rows of "pup tents" sitting "dry and neat in the crisp and breezy air."[35] Here again he struck up an important bond with military personnel of all ranks. He also struck commercial gold with a stirring story of ten men who had brought back their "crippled" Flying Fortress, having been given up for dead when both engines were hit.

This was a more characteristic Ernie column. Its appeal stemmed not from challenging conventional wisdom, but from a poignant frame and evocative prose. He began by telling of his euphoria at watching "the ten dead men coming home." Then he contrasted this joy with a heartbreaking description of war's grimmest aspect. "We had already seen death that afternoon," he wrote.

> For one of the returning Fortresses had released a red flare over the field, and I had stood with others beneath the great plane as they handed its dead pilot, head downward, thru the escape hatch onto a stretcher. The faces of the crew were grave, and nobody talked very loud. One man clutched a leather cap with blood on it. The pilot's hands were very white. Everybody knew the pilot. He was so young a couple of hours ago. The war came inside us then, and we felt it deeply.

This column, gasped one senior Scripps-Howard executive, was "a proper son-of-a-bitch." Although Pyle had demonstrated an uncanny ability to write about death in a moving manner that did not repel his readers, Scripps-Howard thought his upbeat tale of the Flying Fortress's unlikely resurrection was particularly saleable. America's professional marketers eagerly agreed. One Madison Avenue agency even "converted the story into a goodwill advertisement."[36]

Ernie, meanwhile, remained as restless as ever. In the last week of January he moved again, to the southern end of the Tunisian front to report on the US army's newly created II Corps. He drove hundreds of miles to cover these troops' experiences. He wore several layers of clothing as protection against the cold, eschewed the only baths on offer because the water was unheated, and began to acquire the look of an unkempt veteran.

His disheveled appearance immediately endeared him to the troops, as did his unhurried and attentive demeanor. In fact, Pyle's style of gathering stories quickly became marked by an interesting paradox: although he traveled constantly, he gave the impression of hanging around. Unlike the bulk of the press pack, he did not need to scurry off to a censor and a communications center to file regular copy. Instead, he had the luxury of staying put for days at a time, sharing the troops' discomforts and gaining an understanding of their hopes, fears, and grievances.[37]

Such a life could often be tough, but Ernie seemed energized by it. "I've been working very hard," he wrote to his family in late January, "and have in the past three weeks written thirty-five columns, which is just twice the number I produce ordinarily in that time."[38] He had also found his new subject: the birth of America's civilian army, especially its jarring transition

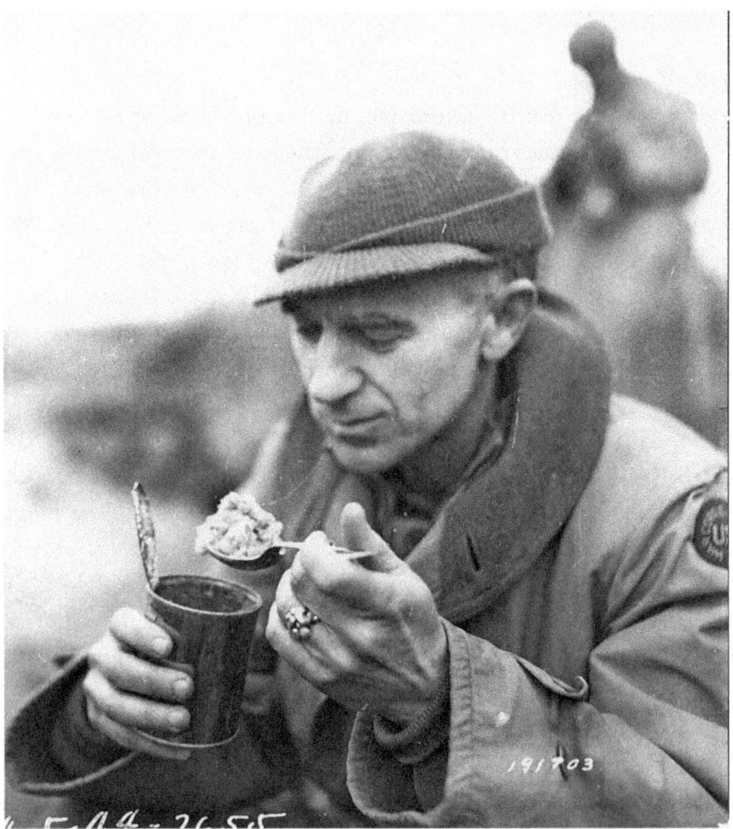

Figure 3.2 Ernie Pyle at the front. National Archives 111-SC-191703.

from training to combat. "From now on," he told American readers desperate to picture how their boys were living at the front,

> you sleep in bedrolls under little tents. You wash whenever and wherever you can. You carry your food on your back when you are fighting. You dig ditches for protection from bullets and from the chill wind off the Mediterranean. There are no more hot-water taps. There are no post exchanges where you can buy cigarettes. There are no movies.

Instead, there was plenty of fear. "The men are tense, and the danger is real," Ernie explained. "Every dusk brings its possibility of death, and any spot of light in this camp is likely to get a bullet through it." The experience of seeing friends and roommates killed, he believed, was teaching callow American soldiers to hate the enemy—which was a key prerequisite for forging them into an effective fighting force. It also kept morale surprisingly high, largely because "there is serious work to do—vital work, for you are working to preserve your life."[39]

As Pyle went into writing overdrive, his Scripps-Howard bosses realized that he was much easier to manage than other war correspondents. Because his columns were rarely time-sensitive, editors did not have to constantly worry whether they would arrive before the next deadline. He could send them by the wireless when it worked or by mail when it did not. "The contents aren't perishable," observed one editor. When communications were robust, Ernie's columns came flooding in at such a rate that there was "no prospect of a lapse in Pyle copy any time soon," the editor added. "He could fly to Calcutta and Chungking and back without filing a word and still leave us equipped to maintain the daily release."[40]

The Scripps-Howard bosses emitted a loud sigh of relief because they knew they had a major hit on their hands. Before long, *Time* magazine would informally crown Pyle "America's most widely read war correspondent." "Eight months ago," agreed *Look* magazine, "Ernie Pyle's column was published in 42 newspapers and nobody much gave a hoot. Today it appears in 149 papers (at last count) and is, to anyone who wants to be informed about the war, a must."

Despite the competitive nature of their work, few of Ernie's fellow war correspondents begrudged him this sudden success. Journalists at the National Press Club found his dispatches so gripping that they even held an impromptu collection. It netted $52, which they sent to Pyle's city editor, who in turn announced that he would invest it in cases of cigarettes to ship to the troops.

At the front, the reporter whose style tacked closest to Ernie's felt honored, rather than resentful, at the comparison. Hal Boyle finally met Pyle in an Oran hotel. Boyle immediately informed Pyle, in a jokey style, that he had won the title of America's human-interest columnist. "I'm writing for the people," Boyle admitted, "who look over the shoulders of the people reading Ernie Pyle's columns." Ernie laughed. Boyle then jested, without rancor or jealousy, that he styled himself as the "poor man's Ernie Pyle."[41]

The real deal was flattered by all the attention, but could never stand still for long. Big cities, he complained, gave him "the heebie-jeebies." Besides, Ernie knew full well that his place was living alongside the fighting man, for this was where he had found his ideal habitat as well as his perfect muse. So with spring fast approaching, Ernie Pyle returned to the front, where he hoped to witness a string of big battles that would finally break the stalemate in Tunisia.[42]

CHAPTER 4

Defeat at Kasserine

KASSERINE PASS

The German tanks lumbered out of the Faïd Pass in Tunsia at dawn on Sunday, February 14. Commanded by Rommel, they belonged to Wehrmacht units that had been at the forefront in defeating France in 1940; since then they had become, in the words of a leading historian, "perhaps the most experienced desert fighters on earth."[1] As they broke out into the open, the German panzers took the Americans totally by surprise. Worse, they caught thousands of GIs in the middle of an indefensible plain, between the mountains of the Eastern Dorsal and those of the Grand Dorsal.

The result was predictable. The Germans rapidly enveloped the small town of Sidi bou Zid, and easily repulsed an American counterattack the next day. By February 17, Rommel's tanks had made it halfway across the fifty-mile plain, taking Sbeïtla, where big, dark plumes of smoke were all that remained of a hastily detonated US ammunition dump. By February 21, exactly a week after the offensive had begun, Rommel's panzers had made it to the other side of the plain, taking the strategically important Kasserine Pass and standing ready to push into Algeria.

The scale of the catastrophe could be gleaned from a cursory glance at the map, which showed a menacing bulge in the center of the front that threatened the entire Allied position in North Africa. By the time Rommel's tanks finally halted their advance, the Americans had been forced to retreat eighty-five miles, losing 4,000 square miles, and suffering more than 6,000 casualties—or about 20 percent of the troops that had taken part—a sobering set of statistics in light of the many more battles to come before Germany would be forced to surrender.[2]

That this had been a disaster of the first magnitude was perfectly obvious to the large group of war correspondents who had rushed to the scene when the German attack began. Pyle's experience was typical. Ernie had been eighty-five miles to the north when he received word that Rommel was on the march. He headed straight to Sbeïtla, peering anxiously up at the blue sky as he drove for any signs of the deadly German dive bombers.

On arriving at the crumbling front line, Pyle, like other reporters, immediately recognized that the area resembled a "great natural amphitheater," with a range of ideal vantage points. Early on Monday morning, he joined a group heading for the most obvious of these: a stand-alone 2,000-foot ridge, about halfway between Sidi bou Zid and Sbeïtla. At first, a mirage shimmering across the desert plain hampered the reporters' view of that day's fight. Soon, graphic evidence of the defeat penetrated the haze, leaving a series of grim memories that no one present would ever forget: "The clank of a starting tank, the scream of a shell through the air, the ever-rising whine of fiendishness as a bomber dives."[3]

Nor would anyone present ever forget the extreme danger. Stoneman had already, a few weeks earlier, become the first US press casualty of the campaign. He had been driving around in his beat-up Ford sedan when he blundered into a vicious firefight. His car, which had survived so many miles over rocky roads, was no match for a marauding German tank, whose shell tore through its chassis "like buckshot through cardboard." Luckily, Stoneman had just enough time to throw himself into a ditch before the car burst into flames, but he suffered the further indignity of receiving a bullet in his behind—a painful and embarrassing wound that would make him, quite literally, the butt of his colleagues' jokes.[4]

As Rommel's offensive gathered pace, the risk to life and limb became no joking matter. On February 15, two wire-service reporters watched in horror as, just fifty yards away from them, a jeep carrying three soldiers took a direct hit, killing everyone inside. By the end of the week many more correspondents had their own tales of narrow escapes and brushes with death. Notebooks at the ready, they had all scribbled down the results of their harrowing interviews with dazed and haggard GIs who had seen buddies killed or maimed right in front of their eyes. Then came the long, depressing retreat. "This mass movement of engines," remembered one

Figure 4.1 Bill Stoneman and his battered Ford after running into a German tank. Stoneman Papers, Bentley Historical Library, University of Michigan.

correspondent, "the flames of tank exhausts, the roar of a vehicle stuck in a ditch at the side, the stench of petrol fumes, the dust that sometimes blinded us utterly so that even the shape of vehicles was lost, had in it all the grim brutality of a mechanized nightmare."[5]

Little of this grim nightmare made it into print. Pyle blamed the censors, charging them with spiking stories that were too "critical concerning the situation in Tunisia" lest this damage morale back home. [6] Historians have often blamed Pyle. As his most distinguished biographer points out, Ernie "didn't whitewash the defeat, which he called 'damned humiliating' and a 'complete melee.'"[7] But he did pull his punches in a more subtle way that was closely connected with his brand of war reporting.

By February, Pyle had spent many weeks at the front. Instead of dashing toward a battle, watching a few scenes, and rushing back to cable a story, he had lived and slept alongside the slogging infantrymen—sharing meals, trenches, and extreme danger. So it was scarcely surprising that he had begun to identify with the average GI, instead of writing about him with detachment.

Pyle's use of personal pronouns revealed just how far this bonding process had progressed by the time of Kasserine. "You folks at home must be disappointed at what happened to our American troops," Pyle cabled shortly after the battle had finished. "So are *we* over here." "*We* couldn't help feel a slight sense of humiliation," he added in another column.

> Yet, while it was happening, that humiliation was somewhat overcome by *our* pride in the orderliness and achievement. It simply could not have been done better. Military police patrolled the road with jeeps and motorcycles to see that there was no passing, no traffic jams, no loitering.

In Pyle's telling, such a well-ordered retreat meant that the American GIs, though they had headed in the wrong direction, had not been professionally embarrassed by Rommel's crack troops. "I don't believe their so-called greenness was the cause of *our* defeat," he contended. "One good man simply can't whip two good men. That's about the only way to put it."[8]

Hal Boyle largely agreed. Like Pyle, the AP man had spent most of the winter at various parts of the front. At the start of Rommel's offensive, he had headed straight for the action, where he found an upside in even the most dismal of defeats.[9] Boyle's standout story told of a lone Sherman tank fearlessly taking on ten German panzers in a running fight that saved three hundred American lives. In other dispatches, he further developed the notion that Kasserine had been a tale of bravery, which had also blooded the American fighting man and made him even more determined to come through in the end. "Here's the way one infantryman summed it up after plodding 15 miles cross-country at night," Boyle cabled on February 17. " 'That means it will take us another week more now to win the war. But every week I have spent away from the United States because of those kraut hounds makes me just that much sorer at them.' "

Neither Boyle—nor the troops to whom he gave a voice—doubted that the fight back would soon begin. In an evocative passage, he told of retreating American troops trudging through Kasserine pass, a light snow gathering on their helmets and tunics. While many smiled and waved, they all parted their fingers "in the 'V' signal for victory."[10]

"THE MADHOUSE"

As these battle-hardened troops prepared to turn around and drive the Germans into the sea, many battle-weary correspondents headed to the safe drudgery of Eisenhower's AFHQ.

Algiers was by now a major news hub. Like London, the big news organizations stationed large "rear-echelon" staffs here, charging them with piecing together broad overviews from HQ communiqués and PR office briefings. It was mind-numbing work, like that of 1942 London, albeit leavened by warmer weather and blooming bougainvillea.

The press room certainly lacked appeal. "Crude desks wedged together," noted one old hand,

> correspondents clutching precious typewriters and lugging them back and forth; bulletin boards containing handouts that no one ever reads plus a couple of mildly dirty cartoons; a peculiar kind of bored animation; everybody talking while everybody else works."[11]

The grinding routine created plenty of challenges, too. Impatient reporters resented having to wait beyond the scheduled time for their briefings—so much so that they coined a song, to the tune of "Oh, Come All Ye Faithful," with the words: "Oh! Why are we waiting? Always bloody well waiting!" Wire correspondents found the system for dispensing the communiqués even more exasperating. For much of the winter, Wes Gallagher had to race his UP rival across the press room "to be the first at the cable with the communiqués," until someone thought up the bright idea "of simply putting the communiqué on the cable addressed to all three agencies in turn." In the midst of all this mayhem, the "Tower of Babel" became "the Madhouse"—a place, one reporter observed, sometimes characterized by "engaging lunacy," but mostly infected with "exasperating" routines and petty intrigue.[12]

Yet this madhouse still held an obvious attraction for top-ranking reporters, especially after Kasserine. For those who had tagged along with the troops in Tunisia, it did not matter that the routine work could be chaotic as well as unglamorous or that the hotels were overcrowded and cockroach ridden. Nor did they even mind that the expensive booze—including a particularly "explosive" cocktail consisting of imitation brandy and Algerian champagne—consumed much of their back pay, while inflicting fierce hangovers. All that counted was the chance to recuperate for a brief period, away from the bullets, shells, and bombs of the battlefield. For this reason alone, the star reporters from the big organizations took it in turns to go back and forth between the front and the rear.

By February, that constant rotation generated another important phenomenon. The correspondents who returned to their Algiers offices after suffering in Tunisian trenches not only tended to be disheveled and sleep-deprived—and, in Stoneman's case, wounded. They also displayed a more assertive determination to get at the truth.

In Algiers, briefings and communiqués generally focused on the overall battlefield situation: what units were advancing and how far; who had sustained the most casualties and in what numbers; which side held the whip hand and how the next phase was likely to develop. Having just been at the front, the war-hardened correspondents approached these subjects with an air of assurance that sometimes bordered on arrogance. Wearing their tattered uniforms like badges of honor, they were in no mood to be given the runaround by impeccably dressed PROs whose daily routine merely took them from their offices to dinner in a lavish mess hall.[13]

The two *New York Times* reporters epitomized this aggressive, battle-scarred self-confidence. Athough he was "genial" on a good day, Frank L. Kluckhohn had already made his presence felt in North Africa with aggressive questioning and a tendency to bend the rules. By February, he had spent so long in the combat zone that his temper was starting to fray. The jaunty line pedaled by Ike's PROs particularly riled him. And within weeks, he would became so belligerent when challenging the censors that his relationship with Eisenhower's command was on the verge of breaking down completely.[14]

Drew Middleton was a more subtle operator. He, too, had spent the winter at the Tunisian front, and he had the worry lines and pale pallor to prove it. Week after week, he had experienced the grim reality of "sleeping on stone floors and in ditches, eating catch-as-can meals, having the gizzard scared out of you by bombers, living without baths or clean clothes and, worst of all, news of the outside world." About the only news that Middleton and his companions did receive had come from the AFHQ, and he almost shuddered whenever he heard its bland and "genial optimism." As anyone at the front knew, it was pure hogwash. "The Allies," he sighed with a war-weary air, "were committed to a long and bloody campaign."[15]

Despite his front-line exasperation, Middleton developed friendly relationships with both American and British PROs when he returned to Algiers. He particularly relished long chats with the more experienced among them, as they "dispensed liquor and wisdom in equal parts. Often it was cold and rainy outside," he recalled. "Inside there was a snug homeliness. We sat and talked and learned."[16]

One of the biggest lessons Middleton gleaned was that Ike's PROs had decided to tone down their excessive optimism. In fact, because Eisenhower was ready to accept personal responsibility for the Kasserine defeat, Joe Phillips wanted to paint a more "balanced" picture of the battle. He was even prepared to let reporters divulge the full extent of the "thorough shellacking," including the heavy casualties.[17]

Armed with this knowledge, Middleton spent his days in the Algiers press room tapping out a string of highly influential dispatches. At first, they were unrelentingly downbeat. American units had "suffered severe losses in men and tanks and other material," Middleton reported on February 17. "Because of the tank losses," he observed, "the possibilities of an American armored counterattack of any size are slight." "In Central Tunisia," he added four days later, the enemy "has won not only elbow room but space for a whole body. The American forces that might have formed the spearhead of a push to the sea have been driven sixty miles to the west, sixty more miles from the sea."[18]

With Phillips whispering in his ear, Middleton tried to place this local setback in a broader strategic perspective. Reinforcements would soon be arriving from the east, he stressed in an article published on February 18, from General Sir Bernard L. Montgomery's British Eighth Army, which had already "smashed" Rommel in Egypt and was closing in on the Mareth Line, the last major defensive position before Tunis. As a result, Middleton reported, however far west of Kasserine Rommel drove his tanks, he would soon be forced to retreat, for "his position becomes untenable once the Mareth Line has been broken or flanked by Montgomery's veterans."[19]

Although readers could almost sense the euphoria between the lines of Middleton's dispatch, his Anglophilia was by no means common among the American press corps. And the closer the British Eighth Army got to Tunisia, the more the majority of Middleton's colleagues began to believe that its impending arrival spelled real trouble for media relations in North Africa.

PERFIDIOUS ALBION

The problems began with the two nations' very different approaches to press operations. The reporters who had been at the front knew that the British tended to be much more hands-on. Once a campaign got underway, they would establish a forward press camp close to the action, as well as provide transport and conduct officers on well-regulated trips to the battle zone. This system placed reporters under a "considerable degree of subtle discipline," but even many of the American correspondents thought it "worked smoothly and well"—especially the advanced location, reliable communications, and steady flow of alcohol, which, as one reporter noted, were "the three major considerations in a war correspondent's life."

The British system certainly had obvious advantages over the free-for-all in the US sector. Correspondents who accompanied the GIs often lacked not just briefing officers to provide them with perspective about the battle but, more crucially, reliable connections to their home offices. "We were compelled," complained one, "after a hard day in the battle, after writing up our copy, often enough in a slit-trench, to drive back forty or fifty miles to a point where there was a teleprinter or to hand our copy over to the nearest dispatch rider and trust in the Lord."[20]

Since speed of transmission often meant the difference between grabbing a scoop or seeing a story spiked, the obvious disparity between the two front-line systems gave those working under the British an obvious advantage. But this was not how it looked to some editors sitting in the safety of their New York or Chicago offices, particularly those of an isolationist bent, whose suspicions of the British often reached epic proportions.

In the newspaper business, no one distrusted the British more than Robert McCormick, the proprietor of the *Chicago Tribune*. The Colonel, as he was known, spent his workdays in a twenty-fourth floor office of the Tribune Tower, surrounded by the smell of ink and paper and protected by a "cordon of feuding secretaries and armed guards." Although his newspaper had long been the mouthpiece of Midwesterners who felt geographically distant from the great events unfolding in Europe, McCormick's own brand of isolationism stemmed more from his previous encounters with the outside world. The Tribune Tower reflected this fact. Embedded with fragments from more than a hundred global landmarks, including places as diverse as the Taj Mahal, the Palace of Westminster, and the Great Wall of China, the Tower demonstrated the impressive reach of the *Tribune*'s "globe-straddling network." It also symbolized McCormick's firm conviction that bits of the world should come to Chicago, where he could fashion them into a structure that matched his own grand design.

Often, McCormick treated his highly paid foreign correspondents in the same lordly fashion. Each day, he would receive dozens of dispatches from his reporters around the world, which he would then tailor to conform to his own editorial line. For their part, these correspondents lived in an almost constant state of dread that they would receive a pithy cable from their idiosyncratic boss. Most ominous were those that could mean the start of a strange mission or the end of a promising career. Others could be highly revealing. Perhaps the most illuminating came when one reporter asked McCormick why he had chosen the only person who spoke no foreign languages to be his chief roving foreign correspondent. McCormick's response had been blunt: "I don't want my fine young American boys ruined by these damned foreigners."

McCormick reserved a special hatred for the British. The reasons were various. The Colonel recoiled from Britain's rigid class system. He blamed its wider political class for the pernicious Versailles Treaty. Not only did he think that the treaty had given Germany legitimate grievances, which Hitler's expansionism had aimed to address, but he also saw little difference between the Nazi regime and the British establishment. After the United States entered the fight, he constantly warned against spilling American blood to defend Albion's perfidious and anachronistic empire.[21]

Always on the lookout for fresh evidence of Albion's perfidy, McCormick avidly latched on to rumors that British battlefield stories enjoyed predominance over American ones. Perhaps, his *Chicago Tribune* alleged, copy cleared in North Africa had to be cleared again by a British censor in London. Or perhaps British officials in London fed stories to their own press agency, Reuters, while "holding out on stories sought by American correspondents." Whatever the cause, the *Tribune* claimed that too many battlefield dispatches had been written "by British newspapermen, whose journalistic standards, in the main, are not our own." The *Tribune*'s sister paper, the *New York Daily News*, went even further, charging British authorities with adopting a "discriminatory policy against American newspapermen."

Had these allegations remained on the American isolationist fringe, Eisenhower's command might have brushed them off. But within days, Berlin picked up on this spat. "A war has broken out between London and Washington," declared Joseph Goebbels's propagandists with glee, "a war for the predominance in the news system." General McClure responded by making a rare public statement to deny the existence of "a discriminatory policy against the American press." "If an occasional British dispatch has been cleared before an American story," McClure explained, "it was solely the good fortune in communications and there is no record of this occurring consistently."[22]

To make doubly sure that British and American dispatches from the front received roughly the same treatment, McClure decided to institute a US mobile press camp along the British lines. This not only provided reporters with a regular courier service to and from Algiers, but even hot meals and a place to sleep. "As a result," observed Hal Boyle happily, "reporters who used to have to hunt for a foxhole out of the wind to spread their blankets for a night's sleep now are quartered in a small tent city which can accommodate up to 50 correspondents with cots, good army food, [and] a place to work."[23]

Anglo-American tension was not confined to the media during that long, hard winter. Among rank-and-file troops on both sides, preexisting prejudices proliferated amid the stalemate and setback. The British, for their part, sneered at the Americans as "gifted amateurs" and referred to them as "our Italians." The Americans accused the British of lacking drive and innovation and claimed that the British liked to fight to the last American. Rather than discourage such talk, many senior officers encouraged it—much to the disgust of Eisenhower, who prioritized Anglo-American unity. "The great purpose of complete Allied teamwork must be achieved in this theater," Ike lectured subordinates on countless occasions. Problems, he conceded, were bound to occur, but they could best be resolved through "a friendly and personal conference with the man responsible," rather than public outbursts that immediately made it into print.[24]

As the fighting continued to go badly, even Ike did not always find it easy to practice what he preached. Just before the Kasserine battles, his bosses in London and Washington had decided to rejigger the command structure in North Africa. The British continued to worry about Eisenhower's lack of combat experience, and the campaign in Tunisia had done little to dispel their concerns. At the Casablanca Conference in January, they successfully prevailed on the Americans to accept three British commanders under Eisenhower, one each for land, air, and sea operations. Ike took the change badly. He "has been burning inside to the staff," noted Butcher. He also wrote directly to Marshall, protesting the prospect of having to run the war by committee. The American press, Joe Phillips added, would not like it, especially the Anglophobes at the *Chicago Tribune* and *New York Daily News*, who would claim that Ike had been "elevated to figurehead job."

When it came time to divulge the new arrangement to reporters, Eisenhower managed, as Butcher admiringly observed, to "put an excellent front on." "I've got the three stars of the British Empire," he told a press conference on February 11, "and I'm overjoyed to get them. Cooperation between the commanders has been excellent throughout the campaign," he added; "I know it will continue so." In the wake of Kasserine, Ike's prediction did not appear very prescient. It certainly bore little resemblance to what the troops had told many reporters after the searing defeat.[25]

In early March, Drew Middleton returned to Algiers after a brief trip to the front. Downcast by the anti-British sentiment in Tunisia, he went straight to Eisenhower's HQ in the St. Georges Hotel and asked brusquely to speak to a senior officer. Middleton began by telling Butcher of "the existence of bitter feeling of Americans against [the] British because of the recent American defeat." The main motive seemed to be bruised pride. Both officers and GIs, Middleton believed, wanted an "alibi" for defeat and found a ready-made one in the widespread belief that British forces had failed to offer "aggressive assistance" during the hardest phase of the fighting. Even worse, "certain members of the newspaper corps are taking up the criticism and the feeling generally is bad." Nonplussed, Butcher lamely replied that "his file of outgoing press stories did not indicate any such danger," only to have Middleton to educate him about the chilling effect of censorship. "Correspondents knew," the *New York Times* man pointed out, "that any story they wrote which reflected bad feeling between British and Americans, would not be passed by the censors and consequently, they had not written the story."[26]

This self-restraint did not extend to every member of the press corps. In fact, it did not even extend to Middleton's own colleague at the *Times*. Frank Kluckhohn had no love for the British. Working constantly in Middleton's shadow, he also had more incentive to share his Anglophobic findings with his editors than with Ike's command—especially when the "damn fool" censors proved ready to pass such a story.[27]

On March 2, Kluckhohn sent off a dispatch based on hundreds of interviews with front-line soldiers. Some GIs, he told his readers, expressed only a mild dislike of the British soldiers' customs, such as their mystifying obsession with a morning bath and afternoon tea, even at the height of battle. Other GIs frequently voiced concerns that went to the heart of front-line morale, especially the widespread belief among the American soldiers that the BBC typically referred "to American victories in Tunisia as 'Allied' and to United States setbacks as 'American.' "[28]

While Kluckhohn thought it better to air these tensions rather "than to bottle them up," Eisenhower's command vigorously dissented.[29] At a press conference on March 8, Ike felt compelled to issue a stern rebuke. He had "noticed an apparent effort on the part of one American correspondent to use the Kasserine battle as a means of starting a newspaper battle between British and Americans," and he was not prepared to tolerate a spat. After giving "the entire assembly a rather heated lecture," noted one observer, Ike warned that any attempt by any reporter to stir up "a British-American argument would be completely and invariably censored. As a matter of fact," Eisenhower added ominously, "if I found any reporter persisting in any such attempt, I would remove him from the theater."[30]

Reporters' careers were not the only ones on the line. Prodded by an irate Marshall, Ike reacted even more aggressively when the "screwy" censors permitted stories claiming that American troops had put in a "downright embarrassing" performance compared to the British. For a time, Eisenhower seriously considered firing McClure, whose only defense was never having seen the offending story. Fortunately—or perhaps shrewdly—McClure happened to be on a tour, inspecting the troops, at the height of the inquest. That helped to save his job, but no one in the Madhouse doubted that Anglo-American relations had become by far the most sensitive subject.[31]

McClure's censors therefore undertook a concerted effort to block any story that even hinted at Anglo-American discord, placing an especially alert eye on copy written by reporters for the Anglophobic *Chicago Tribune*.[32] At the same time, Joe Phillips's publicists encouraged dispatches that portrayed the alliance in upbeat terms. In this endeavor, the PROs deliberately reached out to rookie reporters who had not yet had a chance to talk to officers and soldiers at the front, feeding them an aggressively cheerful picture of Anglo-American relations. "Scarcely a day passes without a new example of the extraordinary cooperation existing between the United States and British Forces in French North Africa," wrote one correspondent on March 15.

> To a person fresh from the United States this is in some ways a most encouraging fact about the campaign.... It is no exaggeration to state that this tight Anglo-American unity will be worth several divisions before the fighting is over. To an almost unprecedented degree this cooperation derives not only from the determination of the Allied High Command that the two forces work as one but also from the deep respect held by the enlisted men and his line officers for their companions in arms.[33]

This benign portrait of front-line Anglo-American relations was doubly ironic given the impending arrival of Montgomery's Eighth Army. Few British commanders could match Monty's disdain for the Americans. The GIs "won't fight," he often remarked condescendingly to anyone who would listen. "They haven't got the light of battle in their eyes." Nor did Montgomery think their senior US commander would provide their men with the necessary edge. "Good chap, no soldier!" he had exclaimed after briefly meeting Eisenhower in Britain the previous year.

Approaching the Mareth Line fortifications in mid-March, Montgomery clearly intended to dominate the campaign's last act. In his eyes, the Eighth Army would simply brush aside the Germans before marching into Tunis, while the US forces played, at most, a small supporting role. Whatever happened, nobody who knew Monty expected him to be shy about claiming all the plaudits. As Churchill put it, the Eighth Army's commander was "indomitable in retreat, invincible in advance, insufferable in victory."[34]

For the American media, there was only one saving grace: the emergence of their own command hero—a man who could more than compete with Monty in terms of ego, charisma, and controversy.

CHAPTER 5

Victory in Tunisia

"TOP DOG"

Over the long, dismal winter of 1942–43, George Patton had felt as though he had been put out to pasture. Since commanding the invasion around Casablanca, he had successfully turned Morocco into one big supply dump, as well as a point of entry for new American units, but the work had bored him. He craved combat. "I want to be Top Dog," he mused plaintively, "and only battle can give me that."[1]

Patton finally got his chance after Kasserine, when Eisenhower turned to him to command II Corps. The two men had known each other since they had both served in the Tank Corps in 1919. Ike's only nagging concern was that his old friend tended to conflate aggression with "personal recklessness." "Don't forget," he cautioned Patton, "that in actual battle under present conditions a commander can really handle an outfit only from his command post," not the front line.[2]

Eisenhower probably knew that he was wasting his breath. As the war correspondents hastened to remind their readers, in Patton American troops now had a real fighting general leading them into battle. Just look at his uniform, they stressed: the steel helmet, brown leather jacket, ordinary pants, and tank boots, all adorned with "two cowboy model pearl-handed six-shooters," which swung at his hips as he marched around the battlefield "directing the fight." Patton's dictum, many reporters added, "is that officers should lead their men into battle and not direct from somewhere in the rear." Amid the din of battle, a number of correspondents reported, Patton could invariably be heard yelling at his officers to "go forward; always go forward! Go until the last shot is fired and the last drop of gasoline is gone and then go forward on foot!"[3]

Like many successful commanders, Patton also enjoyed his fair share of luck. Eisenhower's command released news of his appointment to the press on March 17, the very same day that US forces under Patton's command surged forty-five miles to liberate Gafsa. The stunning advance stemmed more from the German decision to evacuate the area than from any major turnaround in US fighting ability; but the correspondents portrayed the day's action as evidence of "a revitalized and reorganized American army. "Apparently the Nazis saw him [Patton] coming and ran," one reporter hypothesized.[4]

With Gafsa liberated, the corresponents constructed a pleasant press camp in a villa in the town's square. Whenever the sun appeared, they set up a desk in the paved courtyard, shaded "by a grapevine trained on wires overhead" and surrounded by "swaying palm trees with young clusters of golden dates." From this bucolic setting, they began pounding out a series of glowing reports on Patton's progress, although they did not always have to venture to the front to find their man.

Patton worried that his media honeymoon would be short. The forty-nine reporters who had swarmed into town, he believed, might soon start "sniping" at him if they became bored or disenchanted. So he quickly turned on his considerable charm. He began inviting the correspondents to his well-run mess, where they would listen intently to his enthralling monologues about past heroics, upcoming operations, and the bravery of his troops. As the new commander of II Corps spoke, the reporters enjoyed large portions of "Viennese steak, tinned apricots, and excellent coffee." At the meal's end, Patton made sure that everyone left with a packet of cigarettes and glucose sweets, which would prove useful in soothing the nerves once the fighting resumed, this time around El Guettar.[5]

Having taken over the *New York Times*' front-line responsibilities from Drew Middleton, Frank Kluckhohn could not wait to get back to the action. To him, Gafsa had been a gloomy reminder of the scars of war. He had expected the town's "sand-colored fort" to look "like a page out of Beau Geste," but what he actually found when he arrived there was a ruined fort and houses with smashed windows. Slit trenches "marred what had been the beauty of the palm-lined pool," and the threat of booby traps made it hard to relax.[6] So Kluckhohn hastened to join Patton's troops as they pushed eastward toward the coast. Catching up with them in front of a tough-looking German defensive position near El Guettar, all the bitterness he had felt in the recent weeks drained away.

The battle at El Guettar was a far cry from the dashing tank charge of Patton's dreams. While high winds whipped up dust storms that reduced visibility to a bare minimum, many units had to attack enemy troops that were dug into "tough mountain strong points," and the bare rock terrain afforded scarcely any cover against the retaliatory mortar fire. Patton often spoke about the Wehrmacht as being a "worthy" foe, "confident, brave, and ruthless." He now found, to his cost, that the enemy remained all those things.[7]

Still, Kluckhohn discovered an upbeat way to frame the fighting. In a series of eyewitness dispatches, he told his readers about the slow, grinding advance, as well as the vindication the US forces were finally enjoying after the galling defeat at Kasserine. In his dispatches Kluckhohn stressed that, at long last, an *American* army was pressing forward. It was "composed largely of Easterners," he explained, and equipped principally with "weapons produced at home." It was also a tough army, Kluckhohn elaborated after a particularly vicious confrontation on March 23, whose men were determined to fight rather than cede ground. As Rommel's crack troops launched a series of fierce counterattacks, Kluckhohn described "the courage of the common [US] soldier, standing by his weapons and positions, [to] block the tide and take a heavy toll." Even men who were cut off and encircled struck back hard, sometimes firing their guns while suffering from mortal wounds. "Apparently," he noted with pride, "the Americans had not been told that these select, all-German armored outfits were supposed to be invincible."[8]

Despite this upbeat reporting, many PROs considered Kluckhohn an awkward customer. Before the first week of April was out, Eisenhower's press office would even ban him from the front for ten days, after he had violated the censorship code.[9] Still, nothing could dampen Kluckhohn's enthusiasm for "Georgie" Patton. "He hit Tunisia like a whirlwind," Kluckhohn wrote in one *Times* feature, "amazing men who had never served under him, not to mention the Axis army he attacked." Once, Kluckhohn continued, Patton even shocked his own chief of staff by telling him, "We are going to attain our objectives if you have to drive a tank and I have to fire its gun."[10]

As March drew to a close, such bluster was increasingly unnecessary. Patton began to enjoy the rare luxury of setting the battlefield agenda, picking the location and the duration of the fighting, even if the dogged German resistance prevented him from dictating the outcome as rapidly as he would have liked. And this gave him another important advantage. During the El Guettar battle, Patton could brief reporters ahead of the day's engagement, and then make sure that they had "a ringside seat" at the fighting. "For perhaps the first time in the history of modern war," gushed one correspondent on March 30, "men today were able to watch a battle from beginning to end, to watch the forces gathering, deploying, attacking, and going through. I was one of those men, for I sat on a hill-top overlooking the wide plain and I could see everything that happened there."[11]

Hal Boyle was another. Often, the AP man would descend from his vantage point to jot down the names and hometowns of the GIs who were taking the war to the enemy. On one occasion, Boyle recorded the exploits of a group of US machine gunners who had halted a twenty-one-tank charge by turning captured Axis artillery on the enemy and firing the unfamiliar guns "until they were too hot to touch." His most eye-catching dispatch came when he encountered Patton in the midst of the action. The general calmly "studied the battle zone [for] almost an hour," Boyle reported, "poking jauntily at boulders with a silver-tipped cane presented to him by a friend." Although German shells fell all around, he refused to be hurried. He even paused to speak to some soldiers who were frying bacon over a handmade stove. "They know we are coming, general," one GI announced, while waving his hand toward the German lines. "Patton grinned, nodded, and walked to the waiting command car," Boyle wrote, in a tone that made his reverence plain.[12]

As the battle around El Guettar ground on, Patton's flamboyance stood out in even sharper relief, as reporters began to lose their autonomy. Even during the chaotic first phase of the invasion, Patton had often sought to keep his correspondents on a tight leash. Those, like Boyle, who had sailed with Patton's task force in October, had been obliged during the voyage to attend classes on "the fundamentals of soldierly conduct in action." Once they were ashore, a PRO accompanied them all the way to Casablanca, acting as their "aide and liaison man."[13]

Although the correspondents had largely been on their own once the North African beachheads were secured, by March the military was steadily encroaching on that freedom. The pressure on the American army to copy the more bureaucratized and efficient British PR system was one reason. Another was the growing number of staff officers in the theater, who inevitably seemed to generate more procedures, more paperwork, and more efforts to control the news reported from the front.

Over the winter of 1942–43, the size of Eisenhower's command in Algiers had ballooned out of recognition. Ike had hoped to limit it to 150 officers, but before long, more than 1,000 officers and 15,000 enlisted men were crammed into 2,000 houses, hostels, and hotels—prompting the joke,

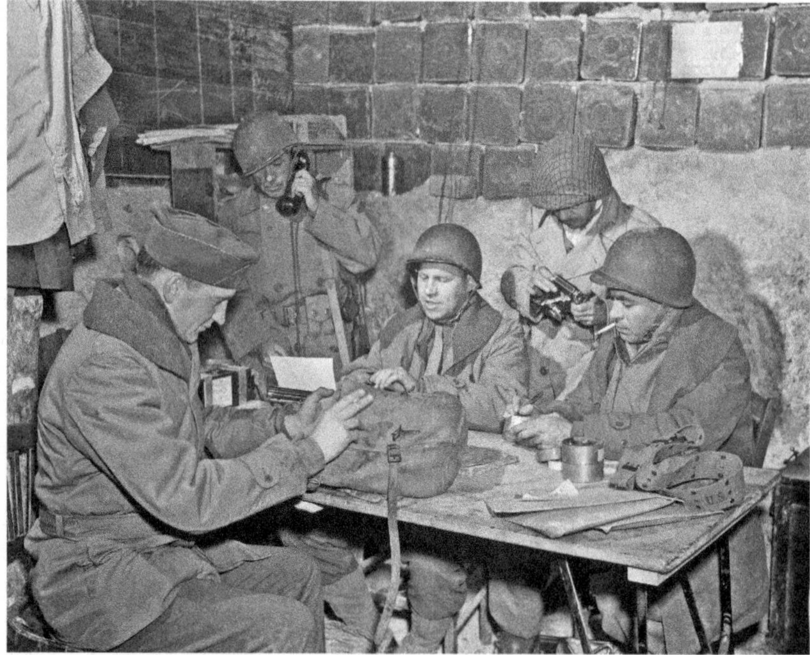

Figure 5.1 Hal Boyle (*center*) writing a story in a North African command post. On the left, one PRO puts copy into a dispatch bag and another checks air transport command on a field phone. AP photographer Irving Smith (*right*) prepares caption material for his film. © PA Photos Limited.

"Never were so few commanded by so many from so far."[14] Predictably, this burgeoning bureaucracy made some preposterous demands on its war correspondents. The edict that particularly rankled stipulated that all reporters flying to the front needed to take five copies of the same travel order, one for the PR office file, one for the general file, and three for themselves, which, as one journalist acidly noted, merely resulted in "five pieces of paper wasted."[15]

Not every initiative was so profligate or so pointless. Some catered to real journalistic needs. From the beginning of March, for instance, reporters heading to the American sector of the front had to be accompanied by a military conducting officer. They were also banned from using their own cars, because, as one officer explained, these "attract enemy attention from the ground and air." Naturally, few journalists relished the idea of being escorted around, but they also recognized that total freedom was no longer a viable option. Stoneman's continued inability to sit after his wound reminded everyone of the perils of driving around the front in a private car without a guide. Then there was the cautionary tale of a group of correspondents who, in the midst of the Kasserine battle, had asked a soldier how far east they could travel. "Oh, at least twenty-five miles," the GI had replied—advice that, had they followed it, would have taken them directly into the German lines.[16]

If chaperones promised to make the battlefield safer, they could not always guarantee that the correspondents would end up at the correct part of the front. Throughout March and early April, one prospective story dominated reporters' conversations: the impending juncture between Patton's II Corps and Montgomery's Eighth Army, which would unite the two Allies and doom the Axis forces huddling around Tunis and Bizerte.[17]

When the Brits and the Yanks finally met, on the afternoon of April 7, their greetings would have made priceless copy. "Hello, you bloody limey," shouted the GI. "Awfully glad to see you," replied the Tommy. Unfortunately, though, not a single reporter witnessed the scene. The meeting had been too unexpected—the result of a sudden German withdrawal from around El Guettar that allowed a US patrol to dash forward and meet men of the Eighth Army. As a result, Cyrus Sulzberger, the *New York Times* journalist who had been closest to the event, wrote, ruefully, that "no words of their historic meeting were recorded." Nor did reporters have much chance to catch up with the troops. "Forty-five minutes later," Sulzberger added, "the main bodies met and swung north on the enemy's heels."[18]

THE DANGEROUS ROAD TO VICTORY

Victory in Tunisia seemingly assured, Algiers suddenly emptied. Desperate to witness the endgame, all the top correspondents dragged themselves to the North African front for one last time.

Bill Stoneman led the way. Unlike many correspondents, he had put his time in Algiers to good use. As boredom in the press room had mounted, the bulk of reporters had taken to committing childish pranks, including drafting a comic communiqué that described "the alcoholic campaign of an army led by General Wes Gallagher." Stoneman, by contrast, had worked hard to add Arabic to his fluent French.[19]

On leaving Algiers in March, Stoneman initially found conditions at the front trying. At El Guettar, "a cold pelting rain . . . sent little rivers pouring along every ravine and chilled everybody to the bone." His temper souring, Stoneman began to wonder why the two sides were expending so many resources to capture "a worthless and desolate waste on which only camel scrub can thrive." Even the best American realtor, he jibed, "could not peddle 1,000 acres for $1,000. In today's rain, you couldn't give it away."[20]

A few weeks later, spring finally arrived. When Stoneman joined the Allied column closing on Bizerte, he was astounded by the transformation that had been wrought since the ill-fated advance through the same territory the previous December. In place of grim, gray hills, he found farmland "carpeted with wheat." Whereas then his car had gotten bogged down on muddy roads, now the soldier who chauffeured him in an army jeep passed smoothly over hard highways flanked with wild flowers.[21]

Then, suddenly, a covey of German planes darted toward Stoneman's jeep, their machine guns stuttering, and before he knew what had happened, he was again lying face down in a ditch. Dusting himself off, Stoneman was relieved to have escaped another nasty wound, but he emerged from the ordeal somewhat chastened: no longer full of springtime, he conceded, but even more desperate to witness payback for the German military.[22]

On the road to Bizerte, Stoneman felt that, for the first time in the war, the Allies really held the whip hand, although the Germans obviously remained a tough foe. "Our men are fighting beautifully against a vicious enemy and in terrain which would tear the heart out of a road engineer," he reported on April 28. "We all know that the Germans are on their way out of Africa. Yet it is going to be solid slugging most or all of the way."[23]

Even the final hard yards into Bizerte contained nasty hazards and ugly sights. For Stoneman, it began with the dizzying experience of dashing past the battlefields of November and December at thirty miles an hour. In warm sunshine, he watched Allied troops "swarming all over the flats below." It was almost a "perfect" sight, Stoneman wrote, but as he knew by now nothing in war could ever be perfect. On this occasion, he told his readers about the sight of "two shattered bodies by the roadside." The wounded survivors explained what had happened. "The Germans were hidden in caves," one GI recounted, "and didn't show their faces at all. We never did see them. Then when we got right into their positions they all opened up with machine guns fore and rear. They sure gave us hell."[24]

For Ernie Pyle war was always hell, but he found the slow march toward victory in Tunisia to be particularly brutish. Pyle spent it with the First Division, compiling his columns whenever the men stopped for a meal or a nap.[25]

Like the infantrymen he trudged alongside, the strain of this front-line grind gradually took its toll. Before long Pyle confessed to feeling "dead and crusty." He had acquired the depressing ability, he conceded, to look "on rows of fresh graves without a lump in my throat" or "on mutilated bodies without flinching deeply"—at least until it came time to sleep. Then, he would sit in his trench or tent, squeeze his eyes tightly shut, and attempt to come to terms with "the enormity of all these newly dead." It was "like a living nightmare," he admitted. "And there are times when I feel that I can't stand it and will have to leave." Yet Pyle had come to "love" the infantrymen, the slogging soldiers he memorably dubbed "the-mud-rain-frost-and-wind-boys." He planned to spend the last weeks of the campaign with them, before heading somewhere to relax his jaded mind and body and reconstruct his "cushion" of columns.[26]

First he had to survive. To do so, Pyle would exploit all the tricks he and his "boys" had learned over the winter, remembering that such tricks made great stories for home-front readers desperate to know every last detail of the GI experience. Thus, his final Tunisian tales focused not on who captured what when, but on the daily travails of life at the front with the First Division. He wrote of resting when the sun was up, and of the shells, snipers, and airplanes that remained a constant danger. He described the process of groping along at night, picking his way through minefields or bomb craters, on the slow, tortuous march to sea. He told of sharing three bars of D-ration chocolate, the only food men were allowed before combat. And he explained the recuperative effects of hot food, steaming coffee, and mail from home in the aftermath of a bloody battle.[27]

While Pyle's evocative prose gave the First Division's daily drag toward victory a poetic, if prosaic, slant, Wes Gallagher's punchy wire-service reports provided specific details of II Corps's slow but steady advance into Bizerte.

Gallagher finally escaped Eisenhower's headquarters in April, largely as a result of Montgomery's success in driving the German army all the way from Egypt to Tunisia. With Cairo now so distant from the fighting, the AP bosses decided to scale back that bureau and concentrate their operations in Algiers, which in turn raised the question of who should be in charge of this big consolidated operation. Ed Kennedy was the obvious choice. He had been covering Europe's wars since 1937, and as the AP publicists pointed out, he had "personally witnessed more hard fighting and endured more harrowing escapes than most professional soldiers in a lifetime of campaigning." More to the point, Kennedy had been in Egypt since 1940, and the AP hierarchy considered him the "able and conscientious stalwart of the Cairo hotspot," where his day-to-day work had been consistently "outstanding."[28]

Yet Kennedy also possessed a prickly character and volatile temper. Those who had worked with him in Egypt believed that he had been away from home so long that he was "slowly going to pieces from too much liquor." "One minute," noted one AP reporter, he could be "laughing and in top spirits. A few minutes later he may be moody and snappish."[29] To their credit, the AP bosses in New York recognized that both Kennedy and Gallagher had "somewhat volatile natures." They also fretted that Gallagher had done such a relentless job so "brilliantly" that he might bristle at being usurped by Kennedy. So they made the change with great care. While Kennedy settled into Villa AP, a plush two-story house set high on an Algiers hill, Gallagher grabbed the chance to head out to the front to witness the war at first hand.[30]

Gallagher avoided Pyle's trudge through the treeless terrain, but as he approached the bombed-out rubble of Bizerte, dangers still lurked everywhere. Some were relatively easy to navigate, especially the road signs marking where mines had been cleared. Others were more frightening because of their random nature—the shells that sporadically shrieked overhead or the frequent sniper bullets.

On May 7, Gallagher and his military escort drove slowly into the ruined remains of the city, meeting "a handful of combat engineers and a resting tank crew crouched in doorways, waiting for word to clean up the rest of the town." Unlike Pyle, who lingered with the troops, Gallagher had to dash straight back to file his story from the nearest PR camp, and this proved his undoing. As his jeep sped down a Bizerte side road, a French marine on a bicycle suddenly lurched into view, causing his driver to swerve so violently that the car overturned. Gallagher ended up "pinned under the car, with a fracture of the spine." It took the quick action of William Westmoreland, a lieutenant colonel in the Ninth Division, to drag him free from the wreckage.[31]

As a result of this nasty accident, the AP man who had told the nation of the campaign's start found himself in an Allied hospital at the campaign's end. It was left to his colleague, Hal Boyle, to record the details, helped by another modest easing of censorship, this time to allow correspondents to announce the names of the first units into Bizerte and Tunis.[32]

Boyle tackled the task with relish. He happily reported the downfall of the "once-invincible" German North African army. In his May 1943 dispatches, Boyle described dozens of victory vignettes: the weeping German general who surrendered unconditionally to the triumphant American commander; the thousands of prisoners rounded up and placed in vast bullpens in a Tunisian wheat field; the exultant GIs, who were not only pleased that the fight was over but "damned glad" to have gotten even for the "awful beating at Faïd and Kasserine."[33]

What type of soldiers had these victorious men become during the long, hard months of the North African campaign? This question inevitably dominated much of the writing throughout the battle's dying days, although the answers varied. Despite his growing reputation for masking the darker side of war, Pyle decided the time had come to accentuate the negative. "Our men can't make this change from normal civilians into warriors and remain the same people," he argued after the guns fell silent in Tunisia. "They are rougher than when you knew them," he warned his massive home-front audience. Their language was appalling, they yearned for female company, and they no longer had such a strong regard for the sanctity of property. "The stress of war," Ernie concluded, "puts old values in a changed light."[34]

Drew Middleton was not so sure. The North African campaign had been good to the *Times* man. Not only had he come through unscathed, but he had even found time to dash back to London to wed his fiancée.[35] Once there, he cut his honeymoon short to mull over the attitudes of the many GIs he had encountered during his months in North Africa, and he reached a much more upbeat assessment than Pyle. "Our troops have lost none of their cocky ways or their dash," Middleton concluded, "but there is a vein of iron underneath. They are growing up." At first, he continued, most men wondered out loud why they were fighting the Germans in Africa when they wanted to "go after the Japs" in the Pacific. But as Roosevelt had predicted, they changed their minds once the fighting began. "The realization that the fellow down the valley is going to kill you if he can," Middleton explained, "brushes away any doubts as to who is the enemy. The first sight of a town through which the Germans have passed also convinces many a soldier that he is fighting the right people in the right place. It is not a pretty sight."[36]

Nor was it pretty to gaze at the graves of the many Americans who would never return, although even here, Middleton managed to find something positive to say. Back in Tunisia for the campaign's final days, he movingly described the quiet peaceful American cemetery, where "poppies blow as red as any in Flanders and among them lie Americans who died as bravely and as grandly as any who fell in the Argonne, at Gettysburg, or at Bunker Hill."[37] In a longer piece for Memorial Day he told the story of a generic GI. Three years ago, Middleton wrote, this boy had been attending church, going to a ballgame, working in a factory, and dating his sweetheart. After being drafted into the army, he had received a crash-course in how to salute, drill, and fire a gun. He had seen the damage wrought on London and had witnessed how hard the British fought. He had learned the value of a foxhole and when to shoot or hold fire. Then, just before his unit marched into Bizerte, this emblematic GI had received a fatal wound. "He gave up everything freely," Middleton argued,

> without heroics, and crossed the seas to fight. He became a soldier, yet retained amid the grim horror of war the essential Americanism that made him offer cigarettes to his prisoners and perform conjuring tricks for French children. The day after he died his comrades stormed down the streets of Bizerte. It was his victory no less than theirs.[38]

THE WAR NEWS BALANCE SHEET

In one sense, the triumphant North African campaign was also a victory for Franklin Roosevelt, validating his conviction that this battle would focus the public's attention on the European war. At least, that was what the polls seemed to suggest.

Americans had certainly lost their fixation with the Pacific war. A year earlier, only 22 percent had advocated a Germany-first strategy, as opposed to 33 percent who wanted to concentrate on Japan. As the Tunisian campaign unfolded, these numbers decisively shifted, with 38 percent supporting Germany first and a mere 18 percent viewing Japan as the priority.[39] Popular morale appeared to have stabilized, too. In place of the unease eating away at the nation, which had sometimes descended into panicky hysteria, the North African invasion had immediately renewed the country's optimism. At the start of the campaign one government study of major headlines in twenty metropolitan centers indicated that "78 percent of them blazoned good news stories from one or another fighting fronts. Editorial comment was scarcely less buoyant." Bombarded with such headlines, the public dismissed any defeatist thoughts. In a poll taken just before the end of 1942, almost three-quarters of Americans believed the United States to be winning the war, compared to less than half a few months earlier.[40]

These figures also contained one critical danger sign. Throughout the North African campaign, reporters, editors, and many readers believed that the government had placed too much emphasis on trying to sugarcoat dispatches from the front. "Press and public," concluded one government report written on November 13, "are convinced that censorship is rigid beyond any requirements of security—that news which could not possibly aid the enemy is withheld."[41]

In the first weeks after the invasion these suspicions had been well founded: Eisenhower's command had indeed prodded the war correspondents to write the story as an upbeat narrative. By early 1943, however,

PROs newly educated in the hard school of combat had come to recognize the importance of not cutting every negative story, lest this generate an unrealistically complacent domestic mood. Unfortunately, none of their subsequent efforts to relax censorship had registered back home. According to one disturbing trend, the number of people believing in the accuracy of war news had actually declined during the first four months of the North African campaign, from more than half to about 40 percent; 39 percent were now convinced that official releases made "the situation look better than it really is." Nor did the darker stories in the run-up to victory improve the situation. In May 1943, another survey found many Americans still demanding "the truth about losses" or criticizing the "long delays, particularly of bad news." "Don't coddle the American people," demanded a typical respondent. "If the news is bad, tell us. We can take it, and we *need* it."[42]

For one day at least, even Eisenhower fully agreed with those who remained critical of excessively buoyant war news. That day was May 20, 1943, which saw the massive victory parade through Tunis, a triumphant spectacle, in scorching heat, as unit after unit, man after man, marched proudly past the assembled dignitaries.

Privately, Eisenhower abhorred the whole affair. Alongside his congenital dislike of flashy PR gestures, Ike believed that the effort to "puff up" the end to the campaign was particularly excessive. Besides, he grumbled to himself, a victory march was premature. North Africa might have been liberated, but Anglo-American troops still had to set foot on the Nazi-controlled continent of Europe, and that was likely to prove a much tougher proposition. Yet, along with all the other hard lessons Eisenhower had learned over the course of this long battle, he had discovered the importance of disguising his true feelings. So, at midday, as he took his place of honor to review the endless stream of conquering soldiers, Eisenhower appeared to reporters as "happy as a schoolboy," puffing away on his Camels, while laughing and joking with everyone around him.[43]

After the last troops had marched past, many of the reporters informally assessed how well Eisenhower's command had treated them and their copy over the past six months. As with the public back home, the scorecard was mixed. Many could not forget the early problems: the snafus over communications or the erratic and overly officious implementation of censorship. Those like Ernie Pyle who had grown to love the ordinary infantrymen continued to bristle whenever they recalled the "censorship policy exercised in North Africa of wanting to make the war 'nice.'"[44]

Yet these same correspondents could not be too critical. They had, after all, shared a great deal with the military, from boats and bivouacs during the invasion period to extreme vulnerability and ultimate victory during recent months. Those who had traveled with Eisenhower and his officers all the way from London recognized just how much had improved since then. Drew Middleton was a case in point. During the previous summer, he had been one of those war-correspondent veterans who had viewed Eisenhower's appointment with skepticism. Now he was an unabashed fan. "The job in North Africa," Middleton told Ike, had been made "easier by your understanding of the problems faced and your readiness to talk to us freely." A week after the victory parade, when he dropped in to see the general, his sense of gratitude could not have been plainer. On parting, Middleton even presented Eisenhower with the most treasured of all battlefield relics: a German Lugar.[45]

For many correspondents, the moment of departure was bittersweet. During the campaign's final weeks, almost everyone had craved the day of victory, fantasizing about clean clothes, crisp bed sheets, gallons of booze, and a break from the ceaseless deadline pressures. When the day finally came, euphoria was followed by a strong feeling of letdown and anticlimax. Ernie Pyle, as he did so often, summed up the prevailing mood best. "Staying in Tunisia," he concluded soon after the German surrender, "was like sitting on in the tent after the circus had finished its performance": an empty and enervating experience.[46]

Yet this mood was not destined to last too long. Shortly after the Tunis victory parade was over, the main performers began packing up in preparation for taking the show to its next destination—the continent of Europe, where the German military would have to be confronted before Hitler's Reich could be brought to its knees.

PART II

Bombing Germany

CHAPTER 6

How-I-Almost-Got-Killed-Today Stories

A DISTANT WAR

The American reporters working in London during the winter of 1942–43 experienced the frustrating sense of being left in a backwater, while their colleagues and rivals were making their names covering the real war in North Africa. Exacerbating their frustration was the knowledge that one battle was tantalizingly close. On many nights, the London-based correspondents could hear the dull drones of plane engines overhead, as squadrons of British Halifaxes, Lancasters, and Stirlings flew south to the English Channel and beyond to bomb sites across Nazi-occupied Europe.

Whenever a raid took place, the better-connected reporters would sit in their Fleet Street offices, anxiously awaiting a phone call relaying a cryptic message—something like "big poker game tonight." This would alert them as to which of the numerous airbases located north and east of London to head for. Once there, they could watch the planes return, count how many of them had made it back, and, as soon as the crews had been debriefed, interview the survivors. Afterward, they would have to return to London to file their censored stories, since the security-obsessed British officials refused to allow reporters to use the phones on the base. Back in Fleet Street, the more energetic reporters would grab a cup of ersatz coffee or milky tea—or something much stronger if the night had been particularly punishing—and then walk the few blocks to the Air Ministry building, where a briefing officer would provide bare-bones estimates of the damage the British bombers had inflicted on the enemy that night.[1]

To reporters who had spent years learning their trade at a big-city paper, this type of journalism differed little from what they normally did back home. Indeed, the careful cultivation of contacts, the frantic dash to reach a story, the painstaking interviewing of participants, and the jotting down of juicy quotes in a much-thumbed notebook: these activities reminded them of the drudgery of beat reporting. Small wonder, then, that many of them started to openly discuss an obvious way out of the routine tedium of covering a distant war. Why could they not experience a bombing mission themselves? They may have gulped nervously at the prospect; still, they asked, why could they not go on a raid, and observe the bombs fall, the explosions boom, and the fires rage?

Before heading to North Africa, Bill Stoneman, as president of the Association of American Correspondents in London, had led the first lobbying effort to get US reporters on board a British bombing mission to Germany. As early as March 1941, when the United States remained officially neutral in the war, he had sent a letter to senior British officers, making a powerful case. Reminding them that correspondents in other theaters had been allowed on British bombers, Stoneman pointed to the "injustice" of barring those based in London. At a time when the British government desperately wanted to bring the United States into the war, he also stressed that the Royal Air Force (RAF) would enjoy a "tremendous amount of excellent publicity" if American journalists were permitted to report on just one bombing mission.[2]

The RAF had previously been unyielding in its opposition. "There is very little space in bomber aircraft at the present time," senior British officers had told the press in late 1940, "and the responsibilities of our crews are already heavy enough without adding to them the necessity for looking after a press correspondent."[3] But Stoneman's timing was propitious. The RAF had just introduced a new generation of roomier heavy bombers, and few in the British government wanted to pass up the opportunity to reap a major PR coup in the United States. Even Sir Richard Peirse, the British bomber chief, reconsidered his earlier objections. Perhaps, Peirse conceded in May 1941, two American and two British reporters might be permitted to go on a raid, provided that, once airborne, they agreed "not [to] speak unless spoken to."[4]

Almost immediately, however, the plan collapsed. Even as British RAF officers in London began working with American reporters to decide who would accompany the mission, a number of the airbase commanders registered strong opposition. Some worried about the practicalities of sending reporters up at a time when plane losses were so high. Others doubted the propaganda value of the exercise, especially if reporters revealed "the poor serviceability" of many planes or the reality that "the accuracy of bombing under present day conditions is very largely a myth." "I can well imagine," added another skeptic, "the kind of melodramatic intensity with which some popular newspaper would announce the death or injury, or possibly the hairbreadth escape, of their own correspondent, and this would certainly not make for good propaganda, either with air crews, the British public, or in foreign countries."[5]

As word of the plan seeped out, other voices administered the coup de grace. Journalists working for British imperial newspapers complained of being excluded, especially since Australians and Canadians made up a sizeable contingent of RAF bomber crews. The US government, meanwhile, recoiled from the prospect of neutral American reporters taking part in such brazen acts of war. John G. Winant, the American ambassador in London, told Stoneman that "he regarded the risks as excessive." A few days later, Winant showed Stoneman a cable from the secretary of state, Cordell Hull, who brusquely refused to approve of "American correspondents bomber trip."[6]

There the matter rested—much to the frustration of the press corps—until the American Eighth Air Force began arriving in Britain in 1942. At first, it comprised of just a few planes and pilots, since the campaign in North Africa had priority, and it only undertook a limited number of raids, because bad weather restricted target visibility. Before long, though, even the small-scale presence of American planes exerted a big impact on British thinking about whether journalists ought to be allowed to fly on bombing missions.

Shortly after the first American bombers began attacking railroad-marshaling yards in France, the RAF commissioned a report to look into the Eighth Air Force's approach to media relations. The Americans, it discovered, instinctively adopted a much more open attitude toward the media. Whereas any British journalist wishing to visit an RAF station required a special permit, all US correspondents accredited to the European theater automatically had the right of admittance to any American base. Moreover, the RAF still refused to allow reporters to fly operational bombing missions, whereas the Eighth Air Force had already "granted authority to carry accredited correspondents in military aircraft," though it had yet to figure out a practical way of getting them on a bombing raid over Europe.[7]

This discovery immediately concentrated the RAF's mind. "Embarrassment [would] certainly be caused," concluded one RAF public-relations officer, if the British prohibited what the Americans allowed. Sir Arthur Harris, the new Bomber Command chief, agreed.[8] Harris decided to approve a plan in which both the British and American air forces would recruit, train, and then fly reporters on a bombing mission at roughly the same time. This would prevent inter-Allied jealousy. If stories on American and British raids appeared side by side, it would also emphasize the central point of the unfolding air campaign—its round-the-clock nature, with the Americans bombing by day and the British by night.

Yet there was one important snag. Once the decision was made, the RAF was keen to send up reporters as soon as the weather permitted. Reluctantly, the Eighth Air Force had to concede that it "could not provide facilities for the press in American bomber aircraft for some months to come." The North African campaign continued to siphon off its bombers. Although the Eighth Air Force had sufficient power to attack targets in France, the US officers believed that the reporters would only really be interested in observing a raid over the German Reich itself. Like the British a year before, they also doubted the wisdom of letting correspondents accompany missions that still resembled on-the-job training lessons in high-altitude bombing.[9]

Thus this experiment in propagandizing the air war began with a major irony: the RAF, which had for so long prevented reporters from witnessing bombing raids firsthand, would now lead the way.

BOMBING BERLIN

On December 16, 1942, senior newsmen got their second major summons in less than two months, this time from the British Air Ministry. Pete Daniell represented the American press, and he was excited by what he heard. Now that Britain was finally avenging the brutal blitz of 1940–41, he was enthralled by the prospect of witnessing the giving end of a bombing mission for once.[10]

At first, luck appeared to be on his side. When the London bureau chiefs drew lots, Daniell won the *New York Times* one of the two places allotted for American reporters—the other went to NBC. Exultant, he headed straight back to the office to announce the good news and ask who wanted to go on the mission. James MacDonald, a fifteen-year veteran on the paper, immediately expressed an interest. To decide who would get the job, Daniell and MacDonald stood in the center of the *Times*' recently refurbished offices in the swanky Savoy Hotel and tossed a coin. MacDonald won. "Disgusted with his luck," he recalled shortly afterward, "Daniell proposed that we make it two out of three. My luck held and I won the second time."[11]

Over the next three weeks, MacDonald had plenty of time to worry about the prudence of grabbing such a dangerous assignment from his irritable boss. Finally, on January 7, he got the call to head north to RAF Scampton in Lincolnshire, where he would receive basic training—"parachute adjustment, dinghy drill, ditching drill, and use of oxygen etc."—while living and eating with the bomber boys.

Because of persistently cloudy weather over the target site, MacDonald remained stuck at Scampton for a week after completing his training. He spent the time getting to know the British crews, although they were not allowed to ask him any questions in return—an edict they strictly adhered to. Then, all of a sudden, officers instructed MacDonald to get fitted out in full battledress: jacket, helmet, oxygen mask, boots, parachute straps, and life jacket. After clomping around in this unfamiliar gear, he headed for the large briefing room, immediately noticing a map on an easel. It showed Berlin. "As you can see," the briefing officer stated calmly, "the target for tonight is the big city." An audible whistle went around the room. The RAF had not hit the Nazi capital for more than a year.

After weeks of waiting, the last hour proved to be the worst. Since food was so scarce in Britain, the "operational tea" laid on for the crews seemed unsettlingly like a sumptuous last meal for condemned men, with a fried egg, thick slices of fried bread, and generous helpings of cake. Once again, MacDonald started to have second thoughts. "I rubbed my chin," he wrote the next day, "and wondered if maybe 'Pete' Daniell should not have won the toss after all."

Thankfully, there was not too much time for introspection. Along came the trucks that drove MacDonald and the seven airmen he would be flying with to their Lancaster bomber, named *Dee for Donald*. On board, MacDonald became so engrossed in watching the young fliers go efficiently about their assigned tasks that his "misgivings" started to ebb away—which was lucky, because the pilot had a tough time getting the large, lumbering plane airborne. Finally, MacDonald heard the reassuringly impersonal voice of the navigator over the intercom—"set course, Ronnie, 115 degrees"—and he realized he was on his way to Berlin.

The story he tapped out upon his safe return provoked a sensation. Its heroes were the quietly effective young crew members who had guided the plane all the way to Berlin, with only the odd intercom joke to break the tension and the "skipper's" occasional order instructing everyone to remain alert or carry out their next task. "Presently," he wrote about the minutes they spent above Berlin,

> it was our turn to bomb. Up to this moment we had been zigzagging, diving, climbing, and twisting our way through the enemy's frantic anti-aircraft fire. Now we leveled off on a straight course directly across the target area. In the

> middle of it the big Lancaster leaped upward like a surprised animal: we had released our two-ton bomb. We tore on across the conflagration and none of us saw the bomb burst.

MacDonald did see the damage wrought by the other planes, though. "Unaccustomed to gauging bombs from the air," he added, "I cannot estimate how big an area was on fire while I was there, but it looked plenty big. And still more fires were to follow because the raid was only at its half-way mark when we left the scene."[12]

For the next few weeks, the RAF basked in the publicity afterglow. "We have secured very vivid publicity," gushed one internal report. "The crews have been praised in a more outstanding way than ever before," and, to cap it all, "the American public was delighted with James MacDonald's story."[13] On a more practical level, all the reporters had returned safely. And in the process, both sides had discovered a newfound esteem for one another. "Good comradeship" had existed between the correspondents and crews throughout, noted another postmortem. The correspondents spoke "enthusiastically of the RAF men with whom they mixed on the stations," and the pilots "appeared to have enjoyed taking them" to Berlin and back.[14]

Even MacDonald's journalistic rivals scarcely begrudged him this stunning success. "What a night," recalled one of his *Times* colleagues a few days later,

> —the night he came back. We all stayed away from him until he'd written his story, and then—well, you can imagine how we all surrounded him until we'd dragged every last ounce out of his experiences. Jamie, of course, remained as modest and quiet as ever. But he'd apparently had a grand time, though he bruised his knee a bit when the plane bounced and threw him. Everyone said how glad he was that it was someone like Jamie who went, and not some "in-and-outer" . . . who are so apt to be let in on this sort of thing, and then write all about what brave boys they are. For once, there was no envy among the newspaper boys.[15]

Well, not quite all the newspaper boys. Those working for the *New York Herald Tribune*'s London bureau found it difficult to be quite so magnanimous.

For years, New York's two prestige papers had carried out a fierce, if unequal, battle. As the "*Trib*" reporters knew only too well, the *Times* always had more money, more reporters, more readers—even more pages, as an economy drive at the *Herald Tribune* had recently resulted in a six-page reduction in its daily edition. Most of the time, the *Trib* correspondents did not mind playing this perennial game of catch-up. Their paper might be smaller, they conceded. But, they were quick to boast, it adopted a much more streamlined and creative approach to the news than the larger, stodgier *Times*.[16]

Yet no one in the *Herald Tribune*'s London bureau considered January 18 to be a regular occasion. Instead, as MacDonald's report reverberated around London, New York, and beyond, the hurt ran deep. Not even the fact that the *Times* had only gotten the story by winning a lottery provided much balm: the scoop was simply too big.

Then, the day after MacDonald's article ran, someone walked in who would help to even out the odds between the two papers. Homer Bigart did not, at first glance, appear to be a likely star; indeed, he had a reserved, almost introverted, demeanor and a slender frame. But anyone who had heard his backstory knew that he had served a long and ultimately successful apprenticeship at the *Herald Tribune* and in the process had turned himself into a budding journalistic legend in New York.[17]

Bigart had begun on the *Trib* back in 1927, making a mere $12 a week as a humble copyboy while also studying literature and journalism at New York University. The Depression had brought an end to his studies, prodding him to take the copyboy job full-time. Five years later, he remained stuck in the same position. Some of the office wags joked that he must be the oldest, most experienced person ever to have held the menial post, whose main duties included "sharpening pencils, hauling copy paper, fetching coffee and cigarettes, and waiting to be noticed."

As a young man, getting noticed was Homer's big problem. Shy and somewhat solemn, he lacked the desire, as well as the funds, to schmooze his bosses after work. In their eyes, he appeared to be a mere plodder, especially compared to the dazzling Ivy League graduates that the distinguished *Trib* easily attracted. Moreover, Homer came across as slow in a business that valued speed. He also stuttered, which must have made more than one editor question his ability to interview newsmakers.

Yet Bigart loved the paper. And the paper, for its part, valued its employees. In 1932, the *Herald Tribune*'s bosses finally gave Homer his big chance. Promoted to reporter, at $25 a week, he was told to cover routine assignments throughout New York City: celebrities arriving on that day's ocean liner, local dignitaries delivering run-of-the-mill speeches, the St. Patrick's Day Parade, and, to begin with, church news.

What happened next was a revelation. The traits that had long held Bigart back turned out to be major strengths once he had stories to report. His rivals even came up with a name for his style: "Homer's All-American dummy act." "He would appear on the scene of a story," recalled one, "as a stuttering, bumbling incompetent, helpless and harmless, and approach his quarry, disarming him by the pitiable spectacle he presented. . . . And of course he would wind up with twice as much information from the sympathetic source as any other reporter." When he returned to the office and began tapping out his story, Bigart's editors recognized that he could write as well. The words might have come slowly, but they "flowed seamlessly and effortlessly," remarked a close observer. "He was literary on deadline."[18]

After a decade of steadily building and burnishing his reputation, in late 1942 Bigart finally earned one of the paper's plum assignments. With the enthusiastic backing of his bosses, he was sent across the Atlantic to become part of the *Herald Tribune*'s three-man London bureau.

On arriving in London on January 19, Bigart took over the bomber beat, which meant doing something akin to the routine reporting he had

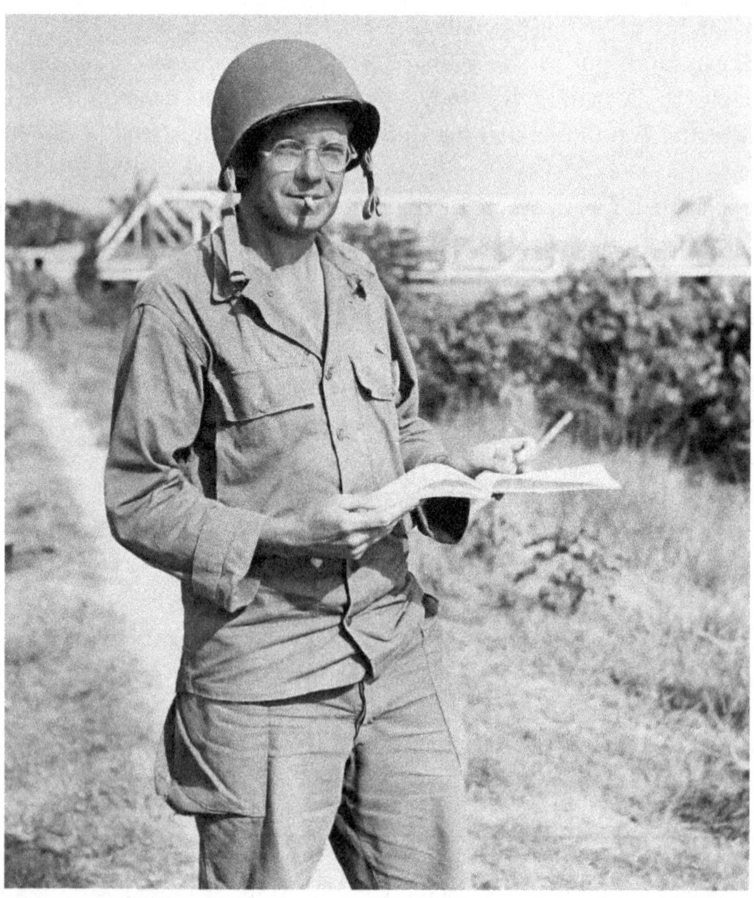

Figure 6.1 Homer Bigart. © PA Photos Limited.

learned so laboriously back in New York. A few weeks later, a colleague spotted him in the Ministry of Information press room, and later singled it out as a classic Bigart scene. "He was alone," the journalist recalled, "a slim, almost frail figure hunched over his Olivetti, slowly punching with two or three fingers, often pausing, often X-ing out words, often consulting notes, often looking out into space before resuming. . . . That late afternoon Bigart was the only reporter still writing his dispatch on the latest RAF raid on Germany."[19]

Had Bigart been a brooder, or a dashing danger seeker, he might have bristled at only landing this workaday job in London, especially after MacDonald's heroics over Berlin. But he was too busy trying to report the second-hand story in front of him—and he would not rest until he had reported it more conscientiously, exhaustively, and clearly than anyone else. Besides, Bigart would soon get his chance to emulate MacDonald.

By January 1943, the Eighth Air Force's PR team had long been primed to act. In fact, it had first outlined its plans to American reporters back on October 22. The idea at that stage had been to create a new journalistic category: "assigned," as opposed to "accredited," correspondents. They "would be the only newsmen allowed to make operational flights," explained one officer. "These men," he added, "would be required to learn first aid and certain other important duties before they would be allowed to fly." They would also "be permanently assigned to the Eighth Air Force by their respective offices," for a minimum of six months.[20]

Back in October, however, the air force's timing had been awry. On the one hand, the Eighth still lacked the capability to hit Germany. On the other, the London bureau chiefs had just learned that some of their star reporters would be heading off to cover the Eisenhower-led invasion of North Africa. Already desperately understaffed, they balked at the prospect of losing still more correspondents for at least six months.[21] So the plan remained on hold, until the day MacDonald's story hit the newsstands. Then, with the RAF success uppermost in their mind, senior Eighth Air Force officers instructed their PR men to begin making plans for a training course that would prepare American reporters to accompany an American bombing mission in the very near future.[22]

It took two weeks to finalize the plans. When they were ready, the Eighth's PROs contacted a range of news organizations. The bomber-beat correspondents were to assemble at Paddington Station early on Monday morning, February 1. From there, they would be taught how to go to war in the plane that captured all their imaginations: the B-17 Flying Fortress.

FLYING ON A FORTRESS

Seven correspondents, including Homer Bigart, milled around the station platform early that Monday morning: Robert P. Post from the *New York Times*, two wire-service reporters, Paul Manning of CBS, and two journalists from the military newspapers.[23] Then, at the very last moment, as the guard's whistle rang out and the steam engines began to hiss, the eighth man arrived. "In typical Cronkite style," he wrote to his wife later that week, "I damned nearly missed [the train] by failing to get a cab at the last minute out in front of the hotel. We were told to bring along our helmets and gas masks," he added, "and I'm sure I cut a very military figure in service pants, galoshes, mackinaw and helmet, and gas mask slung over shoulder. I felt pretty war-like too racing through Paddington Station to catch the train."[24]

Like Bigart, Walter Cronkite had only just arrived in London from the States and was finding life there tough. As a UP man, he faced the unrelenting pressure of trying to beat the much larger AP to spot news stories, day in and day out. He also struggled to adjust to the strict blackout and severe rationing, and in the privacy of his regular letters to his wife he confessed to feeling a little homesick. Yet, like Bigart, Cronkite threw himself with gusto into covering the air war, albeit in a very different way. Whereas Bigart was the model of a slow and methodical reporter, Cronkite, a committed lover of airplanes, personified a youthful and enthusiastic exuberance.

Although the two men were destined for great things, during the week-long training course they would both defer to Bob Post of the *Times*. A tall, thickset man, Post towered over the others, at least in a reputational sense. Harvard-educated, he had worked his way up at the *Times* from office boy to White House correspondent. He had been in London since 1938, had suffered during the long blitz nights of 1940–41, and had served as interim London bureau chief in Daniell's absence in 1941–42. After Daniell returned, Post was miffed at having to play second fiddle again. He also felt guilty that other men his age were fighting, while he held a safe office job. So the "boyish and irrepressible" Post had informed his local draft board that he wanted to join up, only to be thwarted when the *Times* hierarchy intervened and gained him a deferment.

In the wake of MacDonald's success on the RAF mission, Post's pining for action became acute. Daniell felt the same way, for only the vagaries of a coin toss had kept him off the earlier raid. But as the *Times*' bureau chief, Daniell needed, above all, to keep his team happy. He also knew about Post's resentment at being usurped from the top job six months earlier, and, partly to compensate, he decided to let his junior colleague have a shot at glory this time around.[25]

As their train pulled out of Paddington station for the short journey to Bovingdon airbase, Bigart, Cronkite, and Post knew that glory was one possible outcome of the impending mission. Extreme danger, even death, was the other. During the North African invasion, a similar prospect had helped to forge a close partnership between the military and reporters covering the story. As the eight correspondents arrived for their air-force training week, each one likewise evinced a strong determination to suppress his individualistic instincts and conform to the strict military routine. They knew that their lives might depend on it.

On the training course, each day started at 7:30, when a bugle blast jolted the reporters out of their "ultra-hard mattresses" in the officers' barracks. On the first morning, the eight men headed straight for a pressure chamber, which tested their adaptability to high-altitude flying.[26] Then they sat obediently in class, listening to a series of lectures on first-aid, aircraft identification, the use of oxygen, and, controversially, how to use a machine gun. "Apparently," Cronkite recalled many years later, "the air force considered, rationally enough, that once you bailed out of an airplane, the enemy could scarcely know whether you had fired a gun or not. And they figured that we might as well be able to take the place of wounded gunners." The only problem was international law. The Geneva Convention specified that correspondents should not carry guns. To prevent reporters from having to face a Nazi firing squad if they bailed out over enemy territory, the base censors told the eight men that, though they could discuss every other aspect of their training, no mention of machine guns would be permitted.[27]

The reporters reacted to the week's syllabus in their own idiosyncratic ways. Cronkite spent much of the time on a figurative, as well as literal, high. He reveled in going up in the plane, enthusing that he "felt like a real aviator in heavy flying suit and oxygen mask." When the aircraft took off, he experienced an even bigger "thrill," as he took up what he deemed the prized position, in the bombardier's glass enclosure, and watched with awe as a "beautiful picture" of the surrounding countryside unfolded before his eyes.[28]

Bigart focused less on the buzz of flying and more on the perils associated with the whole enterprise. He found the "ditching out" lecture particularly unsettling. It made him want to hop on "the next train back to Paddington Station," he confessed at the end of the course, because the subject "was a bit grim." Looking back at his notes, he discovered that his "shaky handwriting" had recorded the useful, if unnerving, advice that "the Channel and North Sea were dotted with rescue buoys and launches which might be reached by dinghy, if we were forced down over water." Mercifully,

Bigart was spared the harrowing statistic that 99 percent of American fliers who ditched into the sea during the Eighth Air Force's first year were never seen again. Had he known this, his stutter would doubtless have got worse. As it was, his fellow students voted him the "the least likely to return from a mission"—a joke, to be sure, but one that made passing the "very tough" examination a decidedly mixed blessing.[29]

Yet Bigart and his seven colleagues all passed the course. On February 5, they headed back to Fleet Street clutching an official letter that assigned each to the Eighth Air Force as a correspondent qualified to undertake operational flights. They had even acquired a name: the "Writing Sixty-Ninth," derived from the famous "Fighting Sixty-Ninth," which had fought with distinction in the last war. They could also proudly wear the much-valued accoutrements that identified them as members of the air force: a star with wings on their sleeves and a saggy hat with its wire stays removed.[30]

Thus attired, the eight members of the Writing Sixty-Ninth anxiously awaited their first mission. They all knew which base they would be heading to, for the air force trusted that the reporters had too much at stake to blurt out any secrets. Seven had been assigned to one of the glamorous B-17 Flying Fortresses, leaving one unfortunate soul to ride on a B-24 Liberator, which had such a poor reputation that the air force was keen to provide it

Figure 6.2 The Writing Sixty-Ninth getting ready to fly. From left to right Gladwin Hill, William Wade, Robert Post, Walter Cronkite, Homer Bigart, and Paul Manning. Private Collection.

with some positive publicity. At the end of the training week, an officer had explained to the eight reporters that a lottery would be held to pick the unlucky man. It had occasioned the first flash of journalistic independence; Cronkite and his AP colleague flatly refused to take part in a lottery, declaring that their offices had sent them "to cover the story of the B-17, Flying Fortresses, over Nazi Germany, and no other." It took Bob Post to break the impasse; although he was by far the most senior correspondent present, he gracefully volunteered to slum it with the Liberators.[31]

During the days before they took to the skies, all eight correspondents would learn the meaning of slumming it. Most airbases were far from opulent: "Nissen huts moored in a sea of mud," in the words of one historian. Bigart and Cronkite headed off to Molesworth in Cambridgeshire. Since the two men had little to do before the raid except compile background material on the crews, they spent much of their time "chopping, kindling, gathering up coal, or slaving (and worrying)" about the primitive coal stove, the only source of heating in their cold hut.[32]

A sudden call broke this base-camp routine, marking the disorientating shift from everyday matters of comfort to the extreme experience of air combat. The drill was familiar enough. After getting kitted out, they headed straight for the briefing room. Berlin, they heard, was off the American target list: it was too well defended to raid by day. For only the third time, though, US crews would be heading into Germany—to the northwest coast, where the aircraft factory at Bremen was the primary target and the submarine facilities at Wilhelmshaven were the backup. Different officers then filled them in with a bewildering array of different statistics—"on wind at varying altitudes; the rendezvous point for fighter escort; how far the fighters, with their limited fuel, could be expected to accompany the big bombers"—before the commander ended the session with an abrupt announcement: "Protestant chaplain on the right; padre here on the left."[33]

During the long, grim hours that followed, more than one correspondent had an occasion to reiterate the prayers they had said on the ground. Unlike in the North African desert, there were no foxholes at 25,000 feet, "no cover except occasional clouds, no retreat from faster German fighter planes in daylight." The extreme cold and high altitude made matters much worse. To fastidious reporters like Homer Bigart, used to noting down each and every observation, the big fleece gloves felt extremely cumbersome. One of Bigart's colleagues found that wearing an oxygen mask was even more awkward. Once, after accidentally unhooking it, he would have collapsed had one of the bomber boys not fixed him up to an emergency supply of oxygen.[34]

By the time the formation arrived over the target zone, the reporters were gradually acclimatizing, but nothing could prepare them for the terrors of combat: the flak shooting up from the ground, the Luftwaffe's Focke-Wulf fighters that seemingly appeared out of nowhere, the "long, black flag of smog" that followed the fuselage of a wounded plane, and the truly appalling sight of the somersaulting body of a bomber boy who had bailed out with his parachute on fire. With a thick bank of cloud over Bremen, the American planes headed for Wilhelmshaven, a small speck more than 25,000 feet below, on which they dropped 646 bombs before turning around and heading for home.[35]

Back in London, Harrison Salisbury, the new UP bureau chief, considered the Writing Sixty-Ninth a foolhardy enterprise. Left to his own devices he would have forbidden Walter Cronkite from taking part in such a monumentally risky operation. But he had arrived in Britain too late to call him back, and, as he recalled later, he knew full well that "a dozen elephants could not have kept Walter out of the B-17 Flying Fortress."[36]

That morning, Salisbury had woken up with a strong case of the jitters. Accompanied by two PROs, he drove up to Cambridgeshire, planning to meet the planes as they (hopefully) returned. Not far out of London, the three men got lost in the maze of winding country roads that still lacked signs, a quaint if confusing hangover from the days when the British government had feared a German invasion and wanted to flummox Hitler's troops.

Salisbury finally made it to Molesworth late in the afternoon. Thankfully, Cronkite and Bigart had already landed safely. The relieved UP boss found them sitting in a cold, windowless hut trying to psyche themselves up to write an eyewitness story of American bombers over Germany. It was only now that the huge drawbacks of this type of reporting were starting to dawn on the three men.[37]

Up in the sky, the reporters had managed to suppress their deepest fears, but on the ground they rapidly had to come to terms with the bloody brutality of a bomber raid. Five of the Fortresses had failed to return from the mission, as had two of the Liberators. Cronkite and Bigart had both seen one of the Liberators "go down in a dizzy spin, with two parachutes opening in its wake." As the debriefing officers pieced together information on the raid, they concluded that it had been Bob Post's plane, the Liberator he had so gallantly volunteered to fly on.[38]

As the reporters tried to digest this loss, they found it exceedingly difficult to write their story in any balanced way. "True perspective," recalled Bigart a few days later, "is rather hard to maintain in the hours immediately after an assignment in which your own neck was directly involved." First, he explained, he felt like he had just "had a ringside seat at the most crucial engagement since Waterloo or that final Yankee-Cardinal game." Soon after, came the inevitable comedown: the sense that it had all been "nothing really," just a routine raid, and not "worth setting down for posterity."[39]

While Bigart and Cronkite both suffered from the same post-raid ennui, they reacted to it in very different ways. As a wire-service reporter, Cronkite had the greater deadline pressure. Salisbury initially found him in an uncharacteristically downbeat mood. Having spent the day on pure oxygen, carrying fifty pounds of flying equipment, and trying to work the unwieldy machine guns, he felt physically, as well as emotionally, exhausted. To get him started, Salisbury threw out a few stock headline phrases. As Cronkite's cold fingers picked up speed on the typewriter, he quickly became "wound up like a top," and the words—many of them expressive or dramatic adjectives—began to flow. All the while, Salisbury "clucked" around him "like a hen," cajoling, encouraging, and urging him on. "That's right down the old groove, Cronkite," the UP boss reassured him, "now you're cooking."[40]

Unsurprisingly, Bigart's story came more slowly. His first instinct was to wander off to the base's intelligence library to immerse himself in as much detail as possible on Wilhelmshaven, although rather than glean anything useful, he merely scribbled sarcastic little notes in the margins of books. After a couple of hours, he snapped out of his daze and realized that "perhaps the boys on the cable desk might have an academic interest in my return." Hunting down a portable typewriter, Bigart sat down to read through his notes. Ever the professional, he immediately saw—to his intense chagrin—that up in the air he had largely abandoned his normal habit of compulsively jotting everything down, partly because the whole experience had been so alien and partly because the lead in his pencil had frozen. His fragmentary notes gave him only "enough material for two terse paragraphs of factual material." So with a "superhuman" effort, he forced himself to recollect the harrowing experience—the flak, the fighters, and the flames—and try to compile it in some sort of comprehensible order.[41]

It was dark by the time the weary reporters slumped into a command car that returned them to London. Long after, Cronkite told the famous story of what had happened when, during the journey back, Bigart asked him what his lead would be. "I think I'm going to say," Cronkite replied, "that I've just returned from an assignment to hell, a hell at 17,000 feet, a hell of bursting flak and screaming fighter planes, of burning Forts and hurtling bombs." "Homer," Cronkite recalled many years later, "whose Pulitzer Prize winning prose was never tinged with purple, looked at me a moment and finally said: 'You—you—you wouldn't.'"[42]

Bigart always challenged Cronkite's version of events, insisting that he had returned home by train that night, on his own.[43] Besides, as he conceded a few days later, his own post-raid story contained its fair share of colorful language—so much so that he soon dismissed it as mere "drivel." It began with an uncharacteristic air of heroic sangfroid. "The whole trip was so theatrical," Bigart told his *Herald Tribune* readers, "that you forgot to be scared. The Technicolor was excellent, the action fairly gripping, and the casting superb." The main problem, he conceded, had been trying to make sense of the actual bombing part of the mission. Bigart admitted that when his plane reached Wilhelmshaven, he had spent most of his time staring at the German flak coming from below or trying to spot the Luftwaffe's Focke-Wulf fighters, which kept darting in from the horizon at 400 miles an hour. Then he resorted to dramatic similes to describe the German planes that preyed on the Allied bombers as they headed back to England. They "hung around like vultures," Bigart observed, waiting to "pounce on a cripple."[44]

As soon as the reporters arrived in London, they handed their copy to the censor. For Cronkite, it was the start of a long, frustrating night. To begin with, an unexplained snafu meant that his story got held up, while the censor passed the dispatch from the rival AP. Luckily, Cronkite's "purple prose" provided some compensation; although the AP story hit the wires first, many editors preferred UP's zingy narrative of the raid's dangers. A short while later, Cronkite dashed to the BBC radio studios to make one of his first broadcasts for CBS, but once again, he was scooped. He was the first American to go on the air with the story, but the connection to New York was so poor that the broadcast was cut off after three minutes. "A half hour later," he grumbled, "NBC got through with an absolutely clear circuit," and won the day.[45]

Cronkite finally went to bed at 5:30 a.m., after an extremely long day of intense fear, unrelenting excitement, and hard work. Within a few hours, he was woken up by the telephone's shrill ring. The army censors had agreed that the loss of Bob Post's plane could now be divulged, along with the fact that Post had been listed as missing in action. Salisbury wanted Cronkite back at the office to write an eyewitness report of how the plane had gone down. Cronkite dutifully dashed back to Fleet Street, where for the first time on this story, he grabbed a scoop. Yet it was no time to rejoice. Although Post's death would not be confirmed until August, those who had seen the incident doubted that he had been one of the two men who had parachuted out of the plane. Everyone feared the worst.[46]

Daniell feared it more than most. Angry at the UP for breaking the story before he had notified New York, he phoned Salisbury and balled him out. "Pete was clogged with guilt," Salisbury recalled afterward. He "felt he should have flown the assignment; feared that people would say he pushed Post into it because he and Post didn't get along." Adding to the agony, Post's wife had just arrived in London and was staying at the Savoy. She had to be told and somehow comforted. The whole situation, Salisbury concluded, could not have been a bigger "mess."[47] It would, in fact, exert a profound effect over the future coverage of the air war.

Back home, the correspondents' bosses were already starting to assess the intense risks of war reporting.[48] In the wake of Bob Post's death, most of them issued stern warnings to their correspondents against undertaking such risky missions in the future. Fittingly, the *New York Times* led the way. Edwin L. James, the paper's managing editor, advised his overseas reporters that combat flights over enemy territory were " 'unwise' and not worth the risk to their necks." The *Herald Tribune* followed suit, instructing its reporters not to go on operational missions "except in extraordinary situations." But it was Cronkite's organization, the UP, which took the most categorical position. Aware of its reporter's great love of flying, Earl Johnson, the UP's general news manager, told Cronkite not to go on another mission without requesting specific permission from the New York office. "And I have in mind to turn it down," Johnson added. "There is not a dime-a-dozen's worth of difference in raids now so far as eyewitness material goes, and it would have to be one hell of a big undertaking before we risk a man's neck."[49]

Underpinning this rapid and firm stance was both an emotional and a hardheaded reaction. Post's death united the whole profession in grief, and no editor or executive wanted a casualty on his or her conscience. Furthermore, most newspaper bosses—and for that matter, many reporters—felt that copy based on experiencing such dire dangers had already reached the end of its very limited shelf-life. "Those stories have been overdone and the correspondents know it by now," remarked Ed Kennedy of the AP. The time had therefore come, he concluded, to mark the passing of the "how-I-almost-got-killed-today" story.[50]

For a reporter like Cronkite who loved the thrill of flying, it was a sad moment. For the Eighth Air Force, it represented a major opportunity. With the correspondents consigned to base, the air force PROs now possessed both the means and the motive to try to control how the media reported the ongoing battle to bludgeon the Nazi economy into submission.

CHAPTER 7

A High-Octane Outfit

A SUCCESSFUL EXPERIMENT

Major General Ira C. Eaker, the Eighth Air Force's forty-six-year-old commander, strode up to the press-conference podium on March 24, 1943. Handsome, athletic, and renowned for breaking the aviation endurance record fifteen years earlier, he remained something of an enigma to most of the correspondents in the room. Those who failed to see beyond his good looks, large cigar, and Texas drawl thought that he must have come straight out of central casting for the role of buccaneering and belligerent bomber leader. Those who knew him better recognized that Eaker did not easily fit the stereotype. He was "modest and retiring almost to the point of shyness," concluded one acute observer. He had "that unconsciously thoughtful courtesy usually associated with the antebellum South."[1]

Eaker kicked off the session in characteristically courtly fashion, even apologizing for waiting almost a year before holding his first press conference. The reason, he explained, was neither to snub reporters nor to deny them printable information. It was simply that the US bombing campaign had been at an experimental stage. "And people engaged in experiments do not like to have people looking over their shoulders. A doctor working on a cancer cure is not keen to call in newspapermen in the midst of an experiment," Eaker elaborated. "He waits until completion of the experiment before announcing the result. Those were my feelings."

Now, Eaker happily continued, this experimental stage had come to an end. Recent raids had demonstrated that American Fortresses and Liberators could defend themselves over enemy territory during daylight hours. Just look at the figures: no fewer than eighty confirmed Luftwaffe planes shot down in the past two missions over Vegesack and Wilhelmshaven. "Our losses have not been uneconomical," Eaker stressed. "Our loss ratio and the British night losses have been strikingly similar. So, in my opinion, the experiment has proved successful."[2]

After the high-profile loss of Bob Post's plane a month earlier, Eaker had good reason to be touchy about bomber casualties. But he also had much deeper motives for declaring that the daylight raids were succeeding at an acceptable cost.

For a start, Eaker needed to demonstrate the viability of his command, at a time when the insatiable appetites of other theaters threatened to consume so many of his planes. Eisenhower had grabbed almost 1,700 of them for the North African campaign, and Eaker knew he could ill afford to lose many more to battlefield attrition. "We were not going to see that force get smaller," he recalled after the war; "we were going to see it get bigger."[3] Crucially, too, Eaker wanted to prove the viability of the American air force doctrine. Like his superiors, he categorically rejected the RAF's indiscriminate nighttime area raids. Instead, he directed the Eighth to precision bomb during the day, when the bombardiers could see their targets.

Eaker believed that, because US planes were equipped with Nordern bombsights, his men could drop their bombs with pinpoint accuracy. He also thought that his Fortresses and Liberators, bristling with guns and flying in tight defensive formations, could complete their missions without suffering disabling losses. The British were deeply skeptical, however. As they knew from painful experience, the Germans had constructed impressive defenses. American bombers would have to make long journeys over enemy airspace, fully exposed to both ground flak and Luftwaffe fighters. "God knows, I hope you can do it," Sir Arthur Harris told Eaker, "but I don't think you can. Come and join us at night. Together we'll lick them."[4]

Eaker passionately defended daylight bombing, but his case was not helped when word of the British fears seeped into the American press. In February, Allan A. Michie, an American correspondent covering the British air war, penned a *Reader's Digest* article provocatively entitled "What's Holding Up the Air Offensive against Germany?", based on his conversations with RAF officers. Michie suggested that the American planes were overmatched against the German Focke-Wulf fighters. As a result, he insisted, the American losses were disproportionate, especially compared to those sustained by the British at night. Worse, he concluded, the Eighth

Air Force had obscured these facts from the American public by exaggerating the number of German planes it had shot out of the sky.[5]

In Washington, Henry "Hap" Arnold, the overall air chief, was incensed at Michie's "long series of charges, recriminations, and criticisms," which he pressed his subordinates to vigorously counter.[6] Eaker, having told the British that the first months of 1943 would demonstrate the feasibility of daylight raids, was equally troubled. He knew that his whole "experiment" depended on swiftly proving that daylight bombing could be "economically executed." He was therefore delighted when the Vegesack raid on March 18 turned out to be such a stunning success: just two US planes lost, compared to an estimated fifty German fighters downed, while "a very high percentage" of bombs had hit the small target.[7]

Eaker's press conference a few days later was just one attempt to flourish statistics to prove the viability of the Eighth Air Force. In mid-April, the War Department issued a press release that collated the figures on all the enemy aircraft shot down by US planes, including 235 over Europe, which, it claimed, conclusively demonstrated the Eighth's "devastating firepower." In mid-May, Eaker's command announced its first 150-bomber raid over Germany, which had struck the port at Emden. A few weeks later, his PROs drew the media's attention to the fact that the Eighth Air Force had doubled in size over the past year. Overall, Eaker added, it had "dispatched more than 4,000 aircraft against the enemy" in May, 1,600 of them heavy bombers.[8]

Although vital to the Eighth Air Force's continued existence, this relentless number-crunching raised an obvious problem. To date, bombing had been perhaps the most eye-catching story of the whole war. The London blitz, in particular, had turned many journalists into national stars. It had also shifted American popular opinion, as eyewitness reports of civilians coping under the severe stress of repeated bombings had engendered enormous sympathy for the British cause.

Herein lay the crux. Bombing was an attention-grabbing story when told from the victims' perspective. Now that the United States was dropping the bombs, the air campaign lacked the same sense of vivid drama. The Writing Sixty-Ninth had promised to rectify the situation, until newspaper editors decided that reporters participating in bombing missions was far too risky. That left the media with Eaker's numbers, but, as Arnold recognized, these hardly injected a sense of dash and glory into the Eighth's bombing campaign. Indeed, Arnold feared that just as the American effort began to take off, the bombing war threatened to become so dull that the news media might start to relegate it down the news agenda.

As spring turned to summer, Arnold spilled out his fears in a long letter to Eaker. At the start of the bombing experiment, he began, it had been fine to "confine reports to such statements as 'We sent out X-number of airplanes and shot down Y-number of enemy airplanes and we lost Z-number of our own planes.'" Now he firmly believed that the Eighth Air Force had to explain the rationale behind the campaign. It was "very important," he stressed,

> . . . that the people understand thoroughly our Air Forces [*sic*] precepts, principles, and purposes. It is important for them to know how we are destroying the enemy's air power. Still more, it is important for the people to understand that our prime purpose is the destruction of the enemy's ability to wage war. . . . And finally, it is important for them to realize that this takes time, as well as money and planes and planning and work—but that it will win the war and save perhaps millions of lives which otherwise would be sacrificed in bloody ground combat.[9]

For Arnold, the situation resembled what the president had faced a year earlier. Just as Roosevelt had hoped to use the North African invasion to fix the public's attention on the European war, Arnold wanted to use the Eighth's bombing campaign to cement the air force as, at the very least, a co-equal service with the army and navy.[10] In 1942 Roosevelt had been forced to rely on Eisenhower's PROs who, for the most part, had facilitated rather than controlled the media's efforts to cover the ground fighting. A year later Arnold could could turn to a much more dynamic and flamboyant set of characters who could exert a much greater dominance over what the media would publish.

Eaker led the way. Apart from his impressive flying record, the Eighth's commander held a journalism degree from the University of Southern California. He had also served as head of the PR section of the air force information division, where he had learned the practical skills of interacting with reporters. Once he arrived in Britain, Eaker did much of his PR work behind the scenes. Each Sunday, he would host a brunch, serving up food rarely available in ration-book Britain: chili con carne, chocolate, and ice cream. He would then quietly and succinctly outline his concept of the air war, as powerful media figures, such as Roy Howard, listened intently.[11]

While Eaker remained largely in the wings, many of his PR lieutenants took center stage in a series of dazzling efforts to cast the air force in the best possible light. Their brashness stemmed partly from the way they had been recruited. A year earlier Eaker's lieutenants had walked straight into the offices of major news organizations, approached handpicked targets, and encouraged them to join the air force.[12] Some were coaxed into uniform from prestigious Chicago newspapers; others came from the New York tabloids. At least one had worked for Henry Luce's *Time* magazine, while the résumé of Lieutenant Colonel John H. Whitney, who had headed the Eighth's PR operations since February 1943, included stints as executive committee member of the New York newspaper *PM*, director of *Newsweek*, and president of Selznick International Pictures, which had produced *Rebecca* and *Gone With the Wind*.[13]

As soon as this impressive, if eclectic, mixture of talent had settled into their new offices, they began to overawe many of the correspondents working the bomber beat. Harrison Salisbury summed up the prevailing mood. Eaker's command, he observed, was "a high-octane outfit. It was run by ambitious men and backed by an ambitious command in Washington. It . . . set up a large public-relations staff—men from newspaper, publicity firms, advertising agencies—and made use of Hollywood celebrities."[14]

Fueled by ambition and experience, Eaker's PR outfit soon reached a simple but key conclusion about its target audience. The media, it recognized, would handle news of the air war in two distinct ways. The press agencies and daily newspapers, facing tight deadlines, would concentrate on breaking news and the basic outlines of each battle: targets selected, numbers of planes sent up, numbers that returned, and the level of destruction inflicted on German industry. In contrast, the weekly magazines and the Hollywood movie studios enjoyed lavish resources and lacked the time constraints of the dailies. Offering the best prospects for jazzing up the coverage of the bombing campaign, they quickly became the major targets of the Eighth's pushy publicists.

But they would not be easy targets. Although the air force PROs hoped to concentrate on developing slick projects with the big magazines, in early 1943 they could only rely on receiving outright support from the agencies and dailies churning out the more mundane breaking news stories. The AP was a good example. Its London bureau, which provided most of the detailed information of daily raids to newspapers back home, soon began asking the Eighth's PROs for informal guidance on how to ensure that AP stories did not "run too much out of line" with the official statements.[15]

The big weekly magazines were nowhere near as malleable. At the start of 1943 the Eighth's PROs were particularly concerned about Henry Luce's two flagship magazines. "For a long time," recalled Whitney, "the Eighth Air Force received bad or inadequate handling from those two publications. . . . The Eighth Air Force," he elaborated, "was badly served when *Time* was digging up unfavorable stories and *Life* was ignoring us altogether."[16] Charged with turning the situation around, Whitney's team launched a somewhat frenzied courtship, relying on officers like James Parton, who had been a *Time* reporter and bureau chief before the war.

Fortunately, *Time* and *Life* chose to embrace these overtures. Henry Luce, the self-confident boss of both magazines, spent part of 1943 reassessing their war coverage. He concluded that his editors needed to take "risks" and to show "courage"—a mantra that the editors passed on to their reporters, who were encouraged to think about joining the type of mission that had killed Bob Post. Just as importantly, *Time* and *Life* had high advertising revenues. Unlike the overstretched dailies, they could afford to put a reporter into the now largely defunct role of "assigned" correspondent.[17]

In the summer of 1943, *Time* picked William Walton, one of its "best men," for the new job, much to the Eighth's surprised gratification. A native of Illinois, Walton possessed the ideal qualifications. Sociable and experienced, he turned out to be an intriguing mix of talented artist and intrepid danger seeker. Above all, he proved to be an enthusiastic team player. As Whitney noted, Walton left London to live on an airbase for several months, which "no representative of any other publication has done, magazine or newspaper. Naturally," Whitney added, "because he is an energetic and imaginative reporter, he fed excellent material into his organization."[18]

Walton's standout story came on the anniversary of the command's first raid. Throughout August, *Time*'s team worked intensively with Eaker to produce a cover article that glowingly depicted the Eighth's commander as the "man who had a long range plan and saw it through." Inside, the magazine told a tale of steadily improving successes. In only a year, *Time* declared, the Eighth had helped to cripple "the German U-boat weapon." It had also knocked out "20 percent of Germany's synthetic rubber production," while hitting "the sources of most of her airplane-tire and roller-bearing production."[19]

Eaker and Whitney were naturally delighted by *Time*'s front-cover treatment. They also valued the circulation figures *Time* and *Life* boasted—one million and four million a week, respectively—not to mention the large space both magazines reserved for photographs.[20]

For the air force, illustrations were crucial. Photos, the Eighth's publicists believed, provided the optimal means of grabbing attention on the home front. "People," Arnold explained, "believe more readily what they see than what they hear."[21] Because of their massive readerships, the Eighth decided to focus on *Time* and *Life*, but it did not entirely ignore other glossy magazines. *Collier's*, in particular, received so much attention that in September its London bureau chief gushed, in a letter of appreciation to a senior

Eighth PRO, "Not only have you personally bent every effort to arrange and to facilitate stories and pictures for us" but "you have many times voluntarily called us to suggest exclusive and quality picture possibilities for *Collier's*. You have given us intelligent, alert, whole-hearted, and industrious assistance. You have been unsparing of your own time. Nothing has been too much trouble." It was a telling testament to the Eighth's energetic cooperation with the photo-focused, mass-circulation part of the media market.[22]

IMAGES OF AN AIR WAR

The images that ultimately appeared in these magazines came from various sources. In the spring of 1943 the Eighth Air Force extended an open invitation to photographers from *Collier's* and *Life* to accompany flights in order take their own pictures. It was an offer that placed editors and bureau chiefs in a delicate position. *Collier's* responded with prudence. For many months, Joe Dearing, its main photographer, was unable to take advantage of the arrangement, largely because his bosses, chilled by Bob Post's death, blocked him. Frank Scherschel, by contrast, took to the skies with the enthusiastic endorsement of his superiors at *Life*. Less than three weeks after arriving in London from the Pacific, Scherschel accompanied a Fortress on a "tough" mission to Stuttgart "that ended with a crash landing."[23]

Life appreciated its photographers taking such risks, since it could then print exclusive pictures of the raid. But the Eighth understood that even the boldest news organizations did not want these risky flights to be a regular occurrence. So it began to train its own photographic officers, whose pictures would be pooled to all media outlets (that is, made freely available to all news organizations).

This training took place in a new photographic school, where officers were "indoctrinate[d] . . . in the specialized type of photographic coverage required for Public Relations." With the help of guest speakers, such as *Life*'s Scherschel, they were even taught how "to provide coverage of the 'feature' type suitable for magazine release," including how to light their images, what to focus on and what to avoid, and how to shoot a sequence of pictures that told the story of a particular mission.[24]

As soon as these officers passed the course, they reported to Major Richard R. "Tex" McCrary, a man who epitomized the flamboyance of the air force PR team. A native of Texas, McCrary had been editorial chief at the *New York Daily Mirror*, renowned for his popular columns in that tabloid.

Privately, many of his correspondent colleagues abhorred his style. Walter Cronkite, who encountered him during the Writing Sixty-Ninth's training week, dismissed McCrary as "loud and raucous," someone who "doesn't know what he's talking about and is pretty universally disliked." The air force viewed him in a much more positive light. In 1942, Arnold had personally ordered him to Britain, convinced that McCrary was "capable of writing up and presenting to the American people the true potentialities of air power."[25]

After a short time with the Eighth, McCrary begged to differ with his new boss. Although he had covered the London blitz for the *Mirror*, he found it "impossible" to capture the full drama of the American air war in press-release prose. Partly it was due to his journalistic background. "On a tabloid paper," he confessed, "I never learned the words you need to tell the story of the Eighth." Instead, he focused on photography, soon rising to chief of the Eighth Air Force Photographic Section.[26]

Restless and edgy, McCrary was constantly on the move, inspecting, briefing, and selling the air force. Sometimes he was even tempted to board a Fortress mission. Indeed, whenever he arrived on a base, McCrary would head straight for the ops room. Amid the blackboard scrawl outlining the upcoming missions, he would look for a big "C" next to the name of an aircraft. That meant it would carry a camera. If McCrary thought the prospective raid would produce some great shots—perhaps the chance to catch a dozen or more Fortresses in one frame or to picture the smoke billowing up from a destroyed synthetic rubber plant—he would nervously accept the good-natured challenge to eat some "fresh combat eggs" before getting kitted out in his flying gear.

Like the civilian correspondents who had gone up before him, McCrary's pre-combat jitters were intensified by the thought that he had *chosen* to fly. His mind frequently turned back to one occasion when he was about to board a plane. A fellow photographer had shouted, "Hold it." After the bulb flashed, McCrary had realized that the photo captured him standing next to a sign asking: "Is Your Journey Really Necessary?"

When his plane was preparing for take-off, McCrary often had his doubts. But as soon as he returned from the mission safely, the value of the trip was obvious in the reams of pictures showing the tense faces of American boys as they manned their combat stations, or in the images of distant German cities before and after the Fortress bombardier yelled "bombs away." The latter photos were often particularly difficult to take. McCrary found that he needed to brace himself "against the padded walls of the radio compartment, elbows against it, camera cocked against the side window" to steady his hand as flak burst outside.[27]

Because of these travails, even McCrary was grateful when technology took over that part of the photographers' jobs. Shortly after many missions, fighter planes flew at high altitude over the target sites, armed with automatic cameras that could capture images of the damage below. With the right safeguards in place to ensure that operational intelligence remained out of German hands, these photographs promised to become an eye-catching supplement to the press-release statistics that tended to emphasize the Eighth's losses. Arnold was particularly enthusiastic about their publication. He recognized that these pictures would allow the media to publish proof of how much damage the daylight bombers were inflicting on German factories—proof that, crucially, was taken from so high up that no one could detect whether German civilians had become collateral damage.[28]

Although the Eighth increasingly relied on photographs to sell the bombing war, experienced media hands like McCrary also believed they needed to provide the home front with personal narratives from individual airmen. As he toured the various bases, McCrary recognized that the Eighth had an almost limitless supply of material for such stories. After a raid, every airman who made it safely back to base went through an intensive debriefing. If a PRO was on the scene, he could decide which of the crew's experiences could best be turned into an effective press release.[29]

McCrary and his colleagues handled the interview material skillfully. At first, they simply used the airmen's words to emphasize the smoothness of the missions; but they were soon going much further. After all, the PROs with a tabloid past knew the value of an eye-catching news frame and big banner headline. They also recognized that sometimes these frames had to be teased out—perhaps even sexed up—in order to grab the biggest audience possible. With bomber losses still high during the spring of 1943, they even sought these striking angles in the most tragic of episodes.[30]

The story of the Mathis brothers exemplified the Eighth's publicity machine at work. A twenty-year-old farm boy from Texas, Jack Mathis had enlisted in the air force with his brother, Mark. They were desperate to serve together, but Jack got to England first and soon began flying the first of his fourteen missions. His brother arrived in early March 1943, in time to watch Jack take off on the Vegesack mission. As Mark waited anxiously in England, a flak burst struck his brother just before his plane reached the target, ripping off his right arm and filling his right side with shrapnel. Even so, Jack Mathis managed to crawl to his position and, in his final act, release the bombs and close the bomb bay.[31]

The bomber boys back at the base normally greeted news of such losses with a studied silence. "A dead crewman," historian David Reynolds has observed, "became a nonperson almost instantaneously. In some cases his belongings were cleared out of the hut before the other crew members came back from their debriefing."[32] Jack Mathis was different: he never became a nonperson. McCrary first became aware of Mathis's exploits from the citation for his posthumous Congressional Medal of Honor. In swashbuckling tabloid style, he immediately wanted to "shatter the restraint of official language and thunder the story through the pages of history that are reserved for heroes." The chance came at a Memorial Day service, where McCrary got Mark to pose for the newsreels. "Well, I figger it this a-way," Mark Mathis drawled when reporters asked him if this was a "gentleman's war": "You don't start hating till you've been hurt. Me, well, I've been hurt. So I hate the Germans. I wished we bombed their cities instead of just their factories."[33]

In this one remark, McCrary managed to both show how the pain of death was motivating the Eighth Air Force and emphasize how the American bombing campaign was continuing to operate with restraint despite the growing hatred of the enemy felt by many of the fighting men. Still, much to Eaker's frustration, the violent and tragic death of young American bomber boys remained at the heart of these stories. Soon after Jack's death, Mark was granted his desire, if not to bomb cities, then at least to go up in his brother's plane. The result was an even more gripping human-interest angle: an angry airman crouched over the equipment his brother had so valiantly operated during his last minutes. "It makes me mad every time I look at that bombsight," correspondents reported Mark as saying, "for I see the hole made by the bullet that killed Jack."[34]

Yet, as with so many of the Eighth's personal tales, this one was fated to end badly. A month later, one PRO recorded, Mark "followed Jack into the Bigger League. He, too, was killed in action over his Nordern bombsight."[35] With stories like this piling up, Eaker needed more than a positive twist. The Eighth's commander needed hope—and he soon found it.

THE MEMPHIS BELLE

On Monday, May 17, 1943, a Flying Fortress returned to its base at Bassingbourn without any casualties on board. Even better, this was the twenty-fifth time it had come through a mission unscathed. As the plane buzzed over the airfield, the large crowd waiting on the runway cheered;

many threw their hats in the air. As soon as each crew member stepped onto firm ground, he was almost overwhelmed with hugs. Then, someone propped a stepladder against the plane's nose. Captain Robert Morgan, the pilot, climbed up and placed a kiss on the painting of a sexy, leggy redhead that curved up the side of the plane. Beside it was etched the plane's name, the *Memphis Belle*.[36]

Before long, the home front would be swamped with stories about the *Memphis Belle* and its heroic survivors. A few months earlier, as the Eighth's losses grew and morale plummeted, Eaker had made twenty-five a magic number. After completing that many combat missions, the plane's combat crew would be free to return to the States. The day after the *Memphis Belle* had reached this milestone, Eaker decided to place it at the center of a publicity effort that fused all the main elements of Eighth's PR operations.

At first glance, the *Belle*'s central accomplishment harked back to the Eighth's initial publicity efforts—that is, with easy-to-understand numbers. But this time, instead of comparing the Allied and enemy losses, there was just one figure that mattered: twenty-five. To British-based crews and stateside relatives alike, it proved that young men could return home alive after taking part in a sustained effort to precision bomb Germany during the daytime.

By the summer of 1943, though, the Eighth's hard-hitting publicity outfit was no longer content simply to emphasize the basic figures. It had also learned the importance of working with all forms of media to generate a powerful narrative about the heroic aircrews, even if sometimes this narrative diverged from the facts.

Over the next few weeks, McCrary and his colleagues certainly wasted little time recasting the *Memphis Belle*'s exploits. First, they selected Morgan and nine other crew members from the much larger group who had flown on the *Belle*, with the aim of turning these men into stars. Then there was was the eye-catching redhead painted on to the plane's nose, which invariably provided the story's central frame. Although the artwork was inspired by the pilot's girlfriend, Margaret Polk, it was only a very approximate facsimile of the real thing: more of a racy poster-pinup girl than a straight-laced southern beauty.[37]

Still, this love story gave the *Memphis Belle* narrative its crucial human-interest angle when the ten crew members returned home in mid-June. Normally, Eaker was adamantly opposed to planes leaving the theater, but he made an exception for the *Memphis Belle*. At Bassingbourn, the Fortress and its crew received a rousing, newsreel-covered send-off, as Eaker proclaimed that Morgan and his men typified the "spirit of [the] air force to carry through to targets time and time again." After stopping in

Washington to meet Arnold, the plane and its crew embarked on a thirty-one-city tour, with parades and celebratory meals at each stop.[38]

Everywhere, the local newspapers looked for a local angle, radio broadcasters jostled for interviews, and photographers from national magazines snapped pictures of the handsome young warriors. As usual, *Life* published the best shot: Morgan and his bride-to-be in a tender embrace. Then it was on to Memphis, where the crowds surged and the crew almost got crushed. Journalists, recalled Morgan, "were yelling in our faces, in our ears, asking questions, yammering for a quote, already writing their stories in their heads about the two sweethearts of the *Memphis Belle*. Already they had us married and with children practically before we got inside the hangar."

As the clamor grew, the air-force publicists went too far. Morgan had planned to marry Margaret straight away. But, following the success of *Life*'s picture of the happy couple, one PRO decided that the tour would be a much bigger success "if the dashing *Belle* pilot and his sweetheart were *about* to be married, rather than *already* married." The couple therefore postponed their plans to get married in Memphis. And Morgan set off around the country, where his endless partying soon ended any prospect of marriage—though, as Morgan confessed, "neither of us bothered to inform *Life* magazine."[39]

So the public saw only happy images, and not just in the magazines. Hollywood got in on the act, too.

Back in the winter, at the start of the *Belle*'s successful string of combat missions, Morgan was asked to accommodate an eleventh crew member for a dangerous mission to Wilhelmshaven. The man was William Wyler, the Oscar-winning movie director, who would quickly become yet another cog in the air force publicity machine—though he made an unlikely airman. At the time, observes one historian, he was "forty years old, overweight, completely untrained, with a toddler and an expectant wife." When asked by a Pentagon official whether he wanted to be an air force major, Wyler's immediate thought was that he had been given "no training, nothing." "I was sent someplace to buy a uniform," he recalled. "Next thing, I put on this uniform that didn't fit and walk[ed] down the street with a cigarette, my briefcase, and here comes a general. Jeez, what do I do?" he asked himself. "Swallow the cigarette, throw the briefcase away[?] I threw away the cigarette and saluted. The general saw me and laughed."[40]

Charged with making a film about the Eighth's bombing campaign, Wyler headed to Los Angeles to handpick his camera crew. Then he flew to London, where he was already a celebrity because of his pro-British propaganda movie *Mrs. Miniver*. His fame got him accommodation at Claridge's and social calls from leading actors. When he spoke to Eaker's PR team, though, he soon discovered that even the most media-savvy officers had their rules and regulations. "I always ran into people saying, 'Come on now, this is not Hollywood,'" he recalled. The air war was real and highly dangerous, they emphasized, and Eighth officers insisted that no one could fly without airborne combat training. So Wyler headed off to Bovingdon to attend the training week, alongside the Writing Sixty-Ninth.

Once Wyler had been qualified to fly, he was keen to go on a raid as soon as possible. One of his first stops was the base at Bassingbourn. Wandering around the planes lined up neatly on the runway, he spotted the sexy picture that adorned the *Memphis Belle*'s nose and said to himself, "That's it." On tracking down the plane's pilot, Wyler wasted no time turning on his Hollywood charm. When Morgan asked Wyler why he had picked his plane, the director drawled, "That name of your plane. It has a mystique. Don't you think? Also, I have asked around, and I've heard that you're a magnificent pilot. . . . If I flew with you, I'd be right in the center of the action, Captain Morgan. And I'd have a pretty good chance of coming back."[41]

Wyler duly began hitching rides on the *Memphis Belle*. He was particularly keen to accompany the missions to Germany, where the Luftwaffe fighters were more numerous and the flak the most intense, for this would provide him with the best combat shots. Yet he realized the difficulty of filming the air battles. Not only did reloading a camera require taking off the heavy gloves and risking frostbite; just staying conscious entailed sucking oxygen from an uncomfortable mask. Recording a mission over Kiel in his diary, Wyler wrote that he had "passed out (bad show)." It proved a rare lapse. One of the *Belle*'s crew remembered a far more typical scene. "We could hear him cuss over the intercom," the airman recalled. "By the time he'd swing his camera over a flak burst, it was lost. Then he'd see another burst, try to get it, miss, see another, try that, miss, try, miss. Then we'd hear him over the intercom asking if [Morgan] couldn't possibly get the plane closer to the flak."[42]

By the time of the *Belle*'s final mission, Wyler had sufficiently mastered these conditions to get the footage he needed to make a movie. His timing was impeccable. For one thing, Eaker began fretting over the director's safety. "Because he was a Jew," noted one PRO, "and because he had made *Mrs. Miniver*," Eaker recognized that he "would not have an easy time if he were shot down on a mission." The commander therefore issued an order forbidding Wyler to fly.[43] For another, as Wyler began to think about an angle for his movie, he recognized that much of his footage told the tale of one of the Eighth's few surviving planes. If only the *Memphis Belle* could reach the magic number of twenty-five, Wyler knew that his film would basically write itself. Nevertheless, like any good director, he did not place the fate of his film entirely in the hands of providence. He had a plan B.

On the climactic day, Wyler left part of his camera crew at Bassingbourn to capture the mounting tension as everyone waited for the Fortresses to return. Although the strain on everyone's face was authentic, Wyler knew it would be even more dramatic if the *Memphis Belle* landed last. So he directed his cameras to record the rest of the squadron touching down, some of the planes badly damaged, some almost unscathed. Then he had the cameras zoom in on the faces of the officers and ground crews anxiously scanning the skies for the *Belle*, even though the base commander had already radioed to Morgan instructing him to come in last, "so that they could make a special scene out of [the] grand entrance."

After the *Belle* landed, Wyler pushed his way through the crowd and shouted, "I've got news for you, Morgan. We're naming the documentary *The Memphis Belle*." "What in the world would you have done if we'd got shot down today, and you hadn't been on board?" the pilot responded. "Oh, that wouldn't have been a problem," the director explained. "My backup film crew was working with another airplane that was about to finish its twenty-five missions."

Like the Eighth's full-time publicists, Wyler was not above strategic editing to improve a good story. When Morgan and his men arrived at the Los Angeles leg of their stateside tour, they spent a day dubbing dialogue over the combat images of the *Belle* fighting off Luftwaffe fighters. By that stage, Wyler had crafted the movie's basic narrative. Although he would use combat footage from each of his five flights, the film would revolve around just one mission, the famous last one. The narrator would introduce the different crew members, without making too much of their individual heroics. He would also gloss over the one major issue that the Eighth Air Force had carefully shied away from since the start of the campaign: were German civilians the real victims of all those bombs dropped by Flying Fortresses? Like the still photographs published in *Time* and *Life*, and the human-interest stories about the bloody derring-do of American bomber boys, Wyler's movie remained largely silent on German casualties, except to stress that the enemy deserved everything that came its way.[44]

The film was released in early 1944 and was an immediate smash hit with audiences nationwide. The air force was grateful, and not just because the movie reinforced the central themes of its own PR campaign. By the time *The Memphis Belle* was screened, the bombing campaign was in all sorts of trouble.

CHAPTER 8

Dark Days

SCHWEINFURT

By the fall of 1943, the day-to-day coverage of the air war had taken on a mind-numbing, mechanical quality. While the unvarying routine was partly to blame, since every raid generated similar stats and photographs, the crucial reason stemmed from a deepening gloom enveloping the air-bases, where death had become the dominant reality.

As each raid came to an end, the drill was always the same. Reporters would stand near the commanding officer at the top of the control tower. Binoculars at the ready, they would peer toward the horizon to get a glimpse of the first returning plane. Below, the ground crews would assemble the equipment they needed for the hours of repair ahead. At the edge of the runway, ambulance drivers would fire up their engines in anticipation of the frantic dash to rescue the wounded survivors. As the first planes appeared, the final phase of the waiting agony would unfold. Those with the best vantage point would begin totting up the number of planes in the sky, fervently hoping that the tally would not differ too much from the number that had taken off a few hours earlier. Others would watch for colored smoke, knowing that this signified a plane carrying wounded airmen.[1]

As the Eighth's daylight campaign gathered pace over the summer and fall, colored smoke, from a depleted number of planes, became a depressingly familiar sight. To cope, the bomber-beat reporters resorted to various techniques. Some simply drank too much on their return to London each night, intending to block out dark thoughts of the boys they had known who would never return. Others tried to acquire a tough exterior. "Don't make friends with the kids," Cronkite warned Salisbury on one occasion. "Don't get to know them too well. It's just too much when they are lost, and most of them, you know, will be."[2]

Against this solemn backdrop many reporters also took solace in their work. Mechanically pounding out a similar story each day helped take their minds off what was happening in the skies. War reporting, in other words, acted like a drug, but one that was very different from the war correspondents' normal metaphorical narcotic of choice. Whereas the prospect of adrenalin-inducing danger in other theaters often lured reporters toward combat, those working the bomber beat increasingly seemed to crave the repetitive, humdrum nature of the task, for it operated like an anesthetic, numbing them to the lengthening casualty lists at each base.

During much of that summer and early fall, the Eighth's hard-driving PROs could not have been happier. They had developed a way of selling the daily air war that they believed not only emphasized the positive aspects of what they were trying to achieve but had also found a receptive audience among the American press corps. Yet, just as all drugs have side-effects, so the numbing nature of this type of war reporting contained an inherent danger: what would happen if the reporters and PROs alike became so inured to the routine and the horror that they failed to place the story of a particularly large battle in its proper perspective?

The battle in question unfolded on October 14, and the Eighth's hierarchy should have been better prepared. Since the summer, the American bombing campaign had been targeted at the German air force, especially the factories that churned out its planes. Destroying the fighters that were making the skies over Europe so dangerous was not only an obvious prerequisite for launching a sustained daylight air attack on German industry as a whole. It would also facilitate any ground invasion of the European continent. So the Eighth began targeting synthetic rubber factories, oil refineries, and the plants that built the Focke-Wulfs and Messerschmitts.

The summer campaign had culminated, on August 17, in the Eighth Air Force's biggest mission to date: a double raid against the fighter factory at Regensburg and the ball-bearing plants at Schweinfurt. According to the official history, at Regensburg American bombers "blanketed the entire area with high explosives and incendiary bombs, damaging every important building in the plant and destroying a number of single-engine fighters in the field"; at Schweinfurt production was cut by more than half over the next two months. Yet success had come at a high cost. Both targets lay deep inside the Reich, giving German defenders plenty of time to organize and then maul the raiders. Although the planes directed to Regensburg had tricked the Luftwaffe by flying on to Allied bases in North Africa, the Eighth still lost thirty-six bombers over this target, and another twenty-four were downed at Schweinfurt, which translated into 16 percent of the force that had been dispatched.[3]

When Eaker next sent his bombers to Schweinfurt, on October 14, his command should have been ready for another bloody outcome. Recent raids had revealed the Luftwaffe to be experimenting with deadly new tactics and weapons, including rocket projectiles that could be fired from more than a thousand yards away—well out of the range of the Fortresses' guns. But whatever the command anticipated, the aircrews held few illusions about the task ahead. When they saw the map of their destination at the briefing session, a hush descended on the room, broken at the end only by the sounds of men praying even more fervently than usual.[4]

The Eighth Air Force sent 291 bombers to Schweinfurt that day. As the Fortresses neared the target, wave after wave of German fighters appeared. "Like good duck hunters," observed one historian, "they fired at the leading element, knowing that the normal spread of bursts would be likely to give them hits." Once the rocket attacks had torn into the bombers, breaking up their tightly organized formations, German fighters sped toward the isolated survivors. After sustaining more than two hours of lethal assaults, the bomber fleet that made it to the target was even more beleaguered than the one in August had been. Sixty Fortresses had been shot down, a loss ratio of more than 20 percent—not including "the major damage suffered by seventeen aircraft and the reparable damage sustained by 121."[5]

As the battered remnants limped home, those waiting at the Eighth's airbases experienced greater shock than usual. "Interrogation was grim and ghostly," observed an officer at one base, "the tin shacks where some twenty crews usually packed the place were now almost empty." Those who had survived the ordeal were "in pretty bad shape," but the PROs suffered in their own particular way. Acting automatically, almost unthinkingly, they put out a fifty-one-word communiqué that gave the barest outlines of the savage air battle, including the disturbing fact that "sixty bombers and two fighters are missing." The dazed reporters sent off equally terse dispatches. "Press dispatches," observed one official back in Washington, "apparently based on conversations with crews returning to base failed to give anything like a detailed, grandstand-seat, play-by-play description of the action. In both the communiqué and press association reports," the official added, "there is a serious lack of detail."[6]

These blunt and brief dispatches hit the cables and the airwaves so quickly that the air force hierarchy in Washington had no chance to place a positive spin on the battle. This was a significant and relatively new development. Unlike covering the ground war, when poor communications often made it difficult for correspondents to get their eyewitness accounts of the bloody battles out of the theater, the journalists reporting the air war were based in London, America's news hub. Because all the major media organizations had well-connected bureaus in the city center, any print story cleared by an airbase censor on the day of battle could be sent via a reliable cable in time to appear in the next morning's papers. A radio broadcast could reach a national audience that very same evening.

On October 14–15 these rapid transmission times combined with the scant information in the first dispatches to create a highly damaging story. Throughout that night, regular radio bulletins hammered away at the record number of bombers lost. The next morning, a typical headline announced: "60 US 'FORTS' SHOT DOWN." The story beneath added a few extra details that made the news even uglier. This loss, observed the AP account, "represented 600 American flyers killed or missing and perhaps $20,000,000 worth of precision bombing and fighting machinery."[7]

As media-savvy officials in Washington turned on their radios or picked up a daily paper, they could scarcely believe that the Eighth's much-vaunted PR outfit had been so dumb. "No newspaper story that day," complained one, "gave anything like an inning-by-inning . . . description of what apparently was the greatest air battle in history. No story gave the feeling of the combat. Any sports editor who got as cold and bare a report of a World Series ballgame would have fired his entire staff." Adding insult to injury, neither the PROs nor the bomber-beat reporters had tried to place the losses in any sort of context. No one had released the number of Nazi fighters shot down or the damage that had been inflicted on the ball-bearing factory. As a result, the alarmed official observed, "the American people took a pretty hard slap—the loss of 62 planes and 593 men—for about 16 hours."[8]

Senior figures in Washington scurried to respond. By chance, the president's weekly press conference was scheduled for Friday, October 15. When reporters questioned Roosevelt about the morning's grim headlines, he immediately tried to shift the focus to the "credit side of the picture. We haven't got the details of it yet," he explained, but "in all probability . . . we put out of commission a very, very large industrial plant, or plants, in Germany, thereby retarding their manufacture of the implements of war."[9] At the new Pentagon building, General Arnold frantically sought these details from Eaker before releasing his own account of the raid that afternoon. Even more than the president's press-conference comments, Arnold's statement concentrated on the German target, rather than the

American losses, stressing not only the importance of Schweinfurt's ball-bearing factories to the Nazi war effort but also the initial reports of "excellent" bombing results.[10]

Yet, as Arnold well knew, the air force was playing a desperate game of catch-up. The sheer scale of the American losses was now so fixed in the public's mind that it would take more than one or two high-ranking utterances to shift the conversation. Eaker ruefully agreed, though he was also working hard to defend his PR team. "Obviously," Eaker explained to Arnold, "our first flash on target attacks cannot give details of extent of damage. We must wait for development of strike photographs." When this information became available, Eaker believed that it showed "one of the best bombing missions yet," and his PROs duly incorporated this positive news into a new batch of press releases.[11]

Even so, Arnold remained unappeased. Over a fraught weekend the press continued to examine the ill-fated raid; most of the articles were still emphasizing the "record bomber loss."[12] Determined to reframe the story, Arnold decided to call a rare press conference, summoning all of Washington's big media names to his office first thing Monday morning. "Obviously feels heavily on defensive regarding losses," observed one of the reporters as Arnold entered the room. "I just want to talk," the general announced the minute everyone had settled in their seats, which he then proceeded to do for more than an hour. According to one account, Arnold stressed that it "was better to take a heavy loss in a saturation raid like this than to take little 5 percent losses over a period of minor raids which did relatively little damage." According to another, he declared the cost of 60 bombers and 593 men to be "incidental," adding, "You can't run a war on a dollar basis, but if you want to put it on that basis consider the dollars in what we have destroyed." "Regardless of our losses," the general concluded, "I'm ready to send over replacement crews for every one lost and at the same time keep building up our strength."[13]

Had Arnold ended here, his press-conference gambit might have been effective, but instead he decided to take questions. The most probing reporters picked up on a disturbing rumor swirling around the capital, suggesting that the Germans had received advance warning about the Schweinfurt raid, which explained their success in destroying so many Fortresses. Asked to comment, Arnold began by stating that he had "no information to substantiate" the rumor. Then he offered his own highly controversial opinion. As one observer noted, "he went on to say that the German opposition to our formations was so well organized that it indicated that they had been warned in advance."[14]

The censors were aghast. They rightly feared a spate of lurid stories about Nazi spies sabotaging air force missions. They also fretted about the effect Arnold's statement would have on the morale of airmen in Britain, especially if they became convinced that spies were further lowering their chances of survival. Arnold's press conference was on the record, however, so the censors could do little to block yet another media frenzy. Just as bad, the PROs faced the thankless task of refuting the basic premise of the spy story, which only distracted them from focusing press attention on the damage inflicted on the Schweinfurt factory.

Even the denial contained a nasty implication. In a series of briefings, officers of the Eighth conceded that base security had never been airtight. With so many people in the know, they admitted, "word could leak out to an enemy agent and be relayed in the interval before the bombers get across to the enemy targets." Yet, they insisted, this had definitely not happened on October 14. "The Nazis had mustered a defensive force of fewer than 300 fighters," explained one officer, "whereas if they really had had a tip-off they could have been expected to rally as many as a thousand to protect such a target."[15] Given the scale of the damage inflicted by those 300 planes, this was scarcely the most reassuring argument. By the second half of October, the Eighth's high-octane outfit was clearly struggling.

THE PERILS OF PUBLICITY

As the news about the Schweinfurt raid sank in, the bomber-beat correspondents found that a self-protective numbness was not the only possible response to the lengthening casualty lists. Many experienced alienation, outrage, even opposition to what the Eighth Air Force was doing, as well.

Still smarting at Bob Post's death, Harrison Salisbury was particularly angry. He had been in London eight months, and he confessed privately to having a "wobble." Drinking and partying too much at night, he was in no mood to accept what he considered the Eighth's PR "mush" during the day. "The command tried to justify daylight bombing in every possible way," he came to believe, "—by exaggerating results, by lying about losses, by long-winded theories of how the day-and-night pressures produced by round-the-clock British and American bombing were driving the Germans to the brink." And Salisbury increasingly refused to buy into any of it.[16] Nor was he was alone. One member of the ill-fated Writing Sixty-Ninth even called "Tex" McCrary not just "one of the greatest public-relations experts" but also one of the biggest "con artists of all time."[17]

If the whole image carefully constructed by the Eighth's PR team was indeed little more than a fraud, what did this mean for the daylight bombing campaign? Was it time to rethink, perhaps even to terminate, an experiment that was based on little more than a con artist's illusion? Allan Michie earlier in the year had challenged the veracity of some key air force claims. After Schweinfurt, other correspondents began to wonder if he had gone far enough.

Larry Rue, the *Chicago Tribune*'s bureau chief, was one. On October 15, he penned a letter to Colonel McCormick. Significantly, Rue was neither a neophyte nor a troublemaker; he had been reporting Europe's wars since resigning his air force commission following the 1918 armistice. After stints in the Soviet Union, Spain, and Western Europe, he had headed the *Tribune*'s London bureau since 1940, covering the blitz, and had acquired a reputation as a "quasi-staff officer" when American forces arrived two years later.[18] Now, the combination of the Eighth's excessive publicity operations and Schweinfurt's savage horror had put him a mutinous state of mind. "The pronounced policy of bombing the life out of Germany," he wrote to his boss the day after the raid, "is based upon the assumption that the Germans can invent no effective defence against this sort of thing." This was "a dangerous theory," Rue concluded, particularly if it took resources away from the ground troops, who would ultimately be the ones who would have to win the war.[19]

Such discontent threatened to have highly damaging consequences. The Eighth's good press had depended partly on the willingness of reporters and their bosses to believe in the air force mission. If this belief crumbled, then Schweinfurt might have a longer-term impact on the air war, especially as the bomber-beat correspondents began to nurse mounting personal and professional grievances.

Many of the reporters' problems were exacerbated by the damp and dreary London winter. Before they had arrived, the correspondents of a literary bent had anticipated the captivating city of Samuel Pepys and Charles Dickens. After a few months in situ, at least one of them believed that London retained a Dickensian feel, but he thought that outside the pages of a novel this lacked allure. "London is incredibly cramped and mean," the reporter wrote. The plumbing was poor, the heating inadequate, and the windows ill fitting. While the rationed food was often inedible, the warm beer was invariably watered down. Even getting clean could be an ordeal. Because heating water consumed precious coal, the British government exhorted everyone to restrict baths to just five inches of water.[20]

Reporting a bombing mission promised a welcome opportunity to escape the capital, but day trips to the bases rarely turned out to be glamorous. Sometimes a well-connected correspondent might cadge enough strictly rationed gasoline to travel by car, but more often than not, a journey to an Eighth Air Force base meant riding overcrowded and unpunctual trains. "Train travel was three times as expensive as before the war," one historian has observed, "yet it was probably three times as uncomfortable." Instead of gazing out the window at the pretty countryside, bomber-beat reporters often found themselves with scarcely enough space to breathe, let alone smoke, talk, or think.[21]

On returning to Fleet Street in the evening, the newspaper correspondents then had to write their stories. After the demise of the Writing Sixty-Ninth, they depended almost exclusively on second-hand information, which in turn tended to be either unrelentingly dismal or dull. Partly for that reason, bomber-beat correspondents rarely had the chance to make big names for themselves. In fact, most of them knew that if their stories ever got published, they would appear shrouded in a cloak of anonymity. Small wonder that they began to view themselves as B-teamers, denied the compelling eyewitness account of a gripping battle, the exhilaration of scoring a scoop, or the big byline on a front-page story.[22]

Increasingly embittered, ill, or jaded, by November the bolder reporters were airing their grievances in print. As well as revealing an overpowering sense of loss when the "guys" they had known suddenly disappeared, they openly expressed the fact that "we can't write all we hear and know and see." The bomber-beat correspondent, wrote one of them, "can only pass along the cold words of a communiqué."[23]

Had the Eighth's PROs been more attentive to the reporters of the daily print media, they might have detected this mounting sense of frustration fused with status insecurity and perhaps adopted some remedial measures. Instead, Eaker and his team took the support of the dailies and wire services for granted, while continuing to lavish attention on Henry Luce's big glossy magazines—a risky strategy that, by October, was clearly starting to backfire.

For a start, Eaker began to realize after the Schweinfurt raid that Luce could be a fair-weather friend. True, *Time*'s initial assessment of that battle had simply echoed the official view that "the price was not exorbitant." But the magazine had soon developed a more acerbic line as well. When one air force officer likened the Schweinfurt casualties to a family budget—explaining, somewhat tortuously, that "it's as though a family set aside $5 a week in their budget for pleasure, then decided to wait a month, save up $20 and blow the whole works on a damn good time"—*Time* retorted that the "U.S. crews would not appreciate the simile." "Empty barracks," the magazine added, "are hauntingly lonely. Morale always drops after heavy casualties."[24]

Eaker soon discovered that being jilted by a former partner was only one dimension of the problem he now faced. The other was having to deal with the jealousy of scorned suitors, who had come to hate the Eighth's blatant partiality. Even before Schweinfurt, Arnold had fretted that the Eighth was "playing *Life* and *Time* to the exclusion of other national magazines, and thereby incurring the risk of public censure for favoritism." In early October, Eaker's team made a "special effort" to feed exclusive stories to Luce's competitors. *Harpers* got one on the "reactions of a typical Eighth Air Force pilot," while *Cosmopolitan* published a piece on the Eighth's Photo Reconnaissance Unit. More importantly, the PROs handed the *Saturday Evening Post* a major article by Beirne Lay Jr., one of the air force's most talented writers, who had produced a harrowing eyewitness account of the August Regensburg mission, taking readers on a minute-by-minute journey aboard a Flying Fortress—the tense wait before takeoff, the German fighter attacks, the bomb release, and finally the safe return after traveling through "a high valley of the shadow of death."[25]

Although these stories went some way to calming the print media's discontent, almost immediately Eaker's PR team managed to destroy all this goodwill. The problems began when James Parton, an Eaker aide and former Luce employee, approached *Life* for advice on how to publish a book, *Target Germany*, whose aim was to provide yet another colorful description of the daylight bombing campaign. The *Life* editor, citing a paper shortage due to the government's rationing policies, passed up the opportunity to take on the project himself and instead contacted the book publisher Simon and Schuster. For its part in the brokering the deal, *Life* reserved for itself "first American serial rights," and then the problems began. When the terms of the deal leaked out, rivals were outraged that Luce's magazine was about to receive a batch of exciting new photographs for exclusive first publication.[26]

For some of the daily newspapers it was one snub too many. The *New York Times*' head office was particularly irate. An executive immediately cabled Eaker stating that he felt "strongly that newspapers should have had opportunity to print some of [this material] at same time inasmuch as it is [an] official document." When the War Department intervened to ensure that all the pictures would be released as part of the pool, not as an exclusive to *Life*, the *Times* continued to express its dissatisfaction. "We felt, and still feel that a grave injustice has been done to the newspapers in that an exclusive release was arranged for *Life*," complained owner Arthur Sulzberger. "Under present arrangements," he explained, "*Life* has these pictures for a period of from ten days to two weeks in advance of publication and so is able to publish them in their magazine, despite the slow printing process, the same day they appear in the newspapers."[27]

Inside the Pentagon, Arnold was fast losing patience with the Eighth's PR strategy. Eaker's failure to control the news cycle after a big battle had been bad enough. But his ability to antagonize powerful media players seemed almost perverse.

As Arnold mulled over the situation, he began to wonder if the two problems might in some way be linked. Perhaps, he mused, the Eighth's PR outfit had gotten the balance all wrong. Perhaps working with Luce's big, popular magazines on flashy projects had caused it to lose sight of the need to keep the public adequately informed about the more routine day-to-day nature of the bombing campaign. "It seems to me at least doubtful," Arnold wrote to Eaker in November, "whether the Eighth Air Force needs promotion." As a "national institution," he questioned whether it needed to be "sold" at all. "Specifically," Arnold continued, "I wonder if the public relations activities of the Eighth Air Force do not tend to be promotional in character, leading to undue reliance on organizations [like *Time* and *Life*] which can give widest notice and circulation, at the expense of good general relations with the entire press."[28]

The missive clearly worried Eaker. To try to shore up his position, his PR team began working with friendly correspondents to produce a series of sympathetic articles. A typical one by Lee McCardell of the *Baltimore Sun* described Eaker as "a good gambler" who liked to play his cards "close to his vest. His theories of aerial warfare follow the same general principle," insisted McCardell. "There's nothing rash or reckless in his makeup."[29]

In Arnold's eyes, however, such puffery paid a diminishing dividend. More to the point, with the Eighth's bombing campaign appearing to stall after Schweinfurt, Arnold increasingly demanded a commander for the Eighth who was, if anything, a little more "rash or reckless." He certainly evinced little sympathy for the practical problems Eaker kept mentioning: the need to build up his force, retain a sufficient number of pilots, and cope with the reality of bad weather over the target sites.[30]

Bombarded with Arnold's demands for vigorous action, during October and November Eaker began to send his planes out in dense cloud, assisted by new technology. A small number of Fortresses had recently been fitted with a radar device, the H2X, which, its boosters believed, would allow a crew to pinpoint a bombing target that it could not see. The H2X was crucial because it enabled Eaker to bomb in bad weather, while reinforcing the fiction that his Fortresses were still precisely targeting war industries, not indiscriminately bombing civilians. The reality, as the Eighth's intelligence officers knew, was that, even with radar, for each bomb dropped, there was an "average circular error of from one-half to one mile," lethal to many German civilians unfortunate enough to be within this radius.[31] Yet the Eighth's PROs also understood the importance of maintaining the fiction of precision bombing in order to differentiate the American air campaign from the savage German blitz.[32]

At least they thought they did. In the normal course of events, the H2X's supposed precision might have been a propaganda bonanza. Eaker, needing to demonstrate that he still had the courage and drive to hit the Germans hard, could have brandished this technological breakthrough, lauding the fact that it enabled him to fulfill the Eighth's core doctrine even in the bleakest weather months of the year. Behind the scenes, the intelligence officers were naturally leery about releasing any information on new technology. But after Schweinfurt, Eaker also faced two additional truths: on the one hand, the American home front exhibited an almost complete lack of interest in German civilian casualties; on the other, the press and public had become even more fixated with US bomber losses.

A series of blind-bombing missions to Wilhelmshaven and the Ruhr in early November demonstrated just how severely this fixation constrained Eaker's PR strategy. Because of incomplete photographic coverage of the obscured target, the Eighth's intelligence officers were unable to plot the bomb damage done during a bad-weather raid—and after Schweinfurt Eaker did not want to release a story that omitted an account of the destruction inflicted on the enemy. More importantly, because poor weather had prevented the German fighters from locating the attacking squadron, American losses in the Wilhelmshaven and Ruhr missions were much lower than they had been at Schweinfurt—a fact that Eaker fretted would be used by the air force's growing body of opponents to criticize the policy of sending bombers over Germany in clear weather. "It is difficult and would be misleading to compare losses on Wilhelmshaven with those on Schweinfurt," Eaker stressed to Arnold on November 7, "since one is shallow penetration with fighter cover and other deep penetration with but partial fighter cover. Suggest small losses of Wilhelmshaven and Ruhr raids be emphasized without comparison with earlier raids."[33]

Arnold continued to bristle at such suggestions. He did not want shallow penetrations. He wanted big, destructive raids deep into Hitler's Reich.

When the Eighth struggled to launch missions of this kind throughout November, Arnold began to wonder if he ought to have someone with a bit more fight at the helm of this critical command.

Still, Eaker's job would have probably been safe had it not been for the overall command shake-up in December 1943, as Allied leaders prepared for the massive invasion of France the following spring or summer. Eisenhower, who was slated to head the operation, naturally pushed for his own man to take over the strategic bombing of Germany from Britain. Lieutenant General Carl A. Spaatz had been with Ike since Operation Torch a year earlier, and the two men got on well. Since Arnold was also keen on a change, Eaker found himself "kicked upstairs" to the job of Mediterranean air chief. Spaatz became commander of the Strategic Air Force in Britain, bringing with him Major General James H. Doolittle as the new head of the Eighth Air Force. "I feel like a pitcher who has been sent to the showers during a World Series game," Eaker grumbled privately. His successors naturally viewed the situation differently. To extend the simile, Spaatz and Doolittle were determined to ensure that the media carried what one PR official called the "grandstand-seat, play-by-play description of the action"—the type of media description, in other words, that had been so conspicuously lacking at the time of the Schweinfurt raid.[34]

THE FIGHT BACK

When Spaatz and Doolittle took up their new commands at the start of 1944, they first had to grapple with the constraints that had recently held Eaker back. Even with radar, the winter weather remained a major obstacle to any effort to bomb German industry. The American airbases also continued to suffer massive casualties, the scale of which could be gleaned from the simplest of statistics: the loss of 64 out of every 100 crews over the last six months, or the fact that only 26 percent of crews could now expect to reach the magic figure of twenty-five missions. With the firm support of Arnold, "Spaatz and Doolittle," as one historian has observed, "hoped to surmount [this crisis] not by taking fewer casualties, but by building up their force fantastically so that the *percentage* of losses would drop. Such is the brutal logic of wars of attrition."[35]

Jimmy Doolittle, in particular, refused to hide from this brutality. He was a fearless, offensive-minded operator, who had been specifically tasked with intensifying the air war. He was also both shrewd and lucky in one of his first decisions, which would transform the nature of the air war in Europe.

For months, the Eighth's Fortresses had enjoyed fighter escorts for the first part of their missions. Yet the planes available to Eaker had lacked the range to accompany the bombers all the way to targets deep inside Germany. As Doolittle soon discovered, the fighters's mission was also limited to staying close to the bombers and fending off any attacks that the Germans threw at them—a defensive task that went against the grain of Doolittle's aggressive spirit. "The first duty of the Eighth Air Force," its new commander insisted, "is to destroy German fighters." If this meant American escorts abandoning the bombers and going after the Luftwaffe, so be it. "If it moved, could fly, or supported the German war effort," Doolittle declared, "I told my pilots to kill it in the place." Then, almost at the same time that the command of the Eighth changed hands, the air force acquired the P-51 Mustang, which would enable it to more effectively fulfill the aggressive new mission. Unlike other fighters, the Mustang carried enough fuel to fly deep into Germany and back. In enemy airspace, it also proved to be more than a match for the Luftwaffe's Focke-Wulfs and Messerschmitts.[36]

Anyone who knew the Eighth's new commander might have expected him to milk the publicity value of these brightening battlefield prospects. For Jimmy Doolittle was a born showman, who had become a household name for leading a daring bombing raid over Tokyo in April 1942. With only sixteen medium bombers at his disposal, Doolittle's first mission had inflicted little damage on Japan's war effort, but as a propaganda stunt, it had been a major success. Seven months later, Doolittle had arrived in North Africa at the start of Operation Torch, determined to burnish his already glowing image. And before long, he had acquired a reputation as one of the most flamboyant American airmen, quite an accomplishment in a service that seemed to attract so many charismatic newsmakers.[37]

Yet what the Eighth now required when dealing with reporters was something quite different. The Eighth, as Arnold had repeatedly cautioned, had placed far too much emphasis on flashy stunts. The time had come to produce solid and consistent information about each and every raid, with the first news frame emphasizing what the air force was trying to achieve.

Eaker's PR team, aware of the mess it had initially made of the Schweinfurt story, had already begun to move in that direction. In late October it had tried to coax reporters into using more positive language. "Aerial warfare," one PRO told reporters, "is so new that it has not yet developed its own particular nomenclature." Take the word "raid," which the press often used to describe a bombing mission. In ground warfare, the officer explained, raids were "operations conducted by small forces and usually implemented by stealth and the element of surprise," and so were quite unlike a 300-bomber mission against a German factory. The Eighth therefore called on reporters to use the more accurate word "attack." It also pressed them to banish words like "aborted," which correspondents often used as shorthand to describe all the planes that for personnel, mechanical, or weather reasons turned back before dropping their bombs. The Eighth wanted an alternative, although the suggested "fizzle" never caught on.[38]

Soon after Doolittle and Spaatz assumed their commands in Britain, the air force enacted a more significant change. It began to consider revamping the daily communiqués to emphasize the success of each mission, rather than the number of American planes downed. "Valuable information," Arnold argued, "is being given to the enemy by the immediate announcement in theaters of action of our combat losses." Worse, he lamented, was "the emphasis in the American press on Army Air Force losses," which "obscures the most important aspect of air operations—the damage done to enemy targets." After much discussion, Arnold's solution was a new style of communiqué that shifted the emphasis onto the effect of bombing on German targets. "Our own losses," the new policy guidance declared, "should be presented in the perspective of damage to targets—attainment of objective—instead of in ratio to enemy aircraft destroyed."[39]

This new focus was important because the weather finally cleared on February 20, paving the way for six days of intensive attacks that the air force PROs enthusiastically dubbed "Big Week." Whitney's men coined the term partly to differentiate Doolittle's new campaign from all those dark days in 1943, but they were not only motivated by spin. Although American losses remained high, the PROs could boast that in just one week the Eighth Air Force had dropped almost as many bombs as it had dropped during its entire first year in Britain.[40]

Reporters gleefully responded to the new communiqués brimming with such impressive numbers. Many of their ensuing dispatches led with references to the "smashing" or "ripping" blows that the bombers had unleashed on German aircraft production facilities. When the Eighth went back to hit the highly symbolic target of Schweinfurt, on February 22, the returning crews told the waiting reporters that this mission had actually been "much tougher" than the one the previous October. But these alarming comments were carefully counterbalanced by the reassuring news that losses had, in fact, been far lower. "We wiped out the whole target," added one veteran. "We've already got our strike pictures and they confirm that."[41]

As Doolittle's air campaign gathered momentum, the Eighth's immediate audience began to change. Part of the problem in 1943 had been the mounting frustration of the bomber-beat correspondents, combined with their lack of exposure to other battlefronts. By early 1944, a different breed of journalist began to arrive in London, in growing numbers, changing the mood on Fleet Street and on the bomber beat. Slowly, almost imperceptibly, London lost its status as a posting for those who had failed to get the golden ticket to cover a front-line battle in the Mediterranean. Instead, it became a welcome refuge for veterans who had had their fill of the realities of the ground war.

Bill Stoneman was typical. The *Chicago Daily News* man had a couple of spells in the British capital during 1943 and 1944, where he helped out his colleagues in the London bureau while recuperating from the rigors of front-line combat. Walking the city's streets, Stoneman was often struck by "the great gaps in the skyline, evidence of the terrific destruction and the property losses the British suffered from German bombs before they were able to turn the tables on the Nazis." His memories of the blitz still vivid, Stoneman found himself dwelling on the need to pay Germany back for its targeting of the British capital.[42]

In February and March of 1944, retribution tended to be on many minds after Germany responded to Big Week with a renewed bombing assault on London. For Drew Middleton, who had been in town as the *New York Times*' news editor since September, the new Luftwaffe raids were an opportunity to revive the narrative of the plucky Brit, which had been the staple of the blitz stories back in 1940. In one particularly emotive dispatch, Middleton introduced his readers to Mrs. Neame, the *Times*' charwoman, who had just been bombed out of her home for a third time. "Mrs. Neame is the sort of person American correspondents have in mind," Middleton wrote, "when, in discussing air attacks on London, they say, 'The British are wonderful.' She is wonderful," Middleton explained, "for all the familiar reasons—because she is frail and brave, underfed and enduring—but also because, although civilization has offered her so little and her children only a bit, she is willing to go on fighting for it."[43]

Significantly, Middleton gave little thought to whether there might be an equivalent Frau Neame suffering even worse torment under the intensifying American and British round-the-clock air attacks in Germany. On one occasion, Middleton revealed how the British government had "painstakingly" defended the RAF's nighttime area raids, stressing that the goal was to bring German war production to a standstill, not to indiscriminately target civilians, as some critics had suggested. On another, he divulged the existence of the H2X, which, he dutifully reported, enabled the Americans to precision bomb even through dense cloud. The photographs taken by the air force, Middleton disclosed, offered "proof that the targets were well hit with considerable damage" inflicted on military installations. "Accuracy," he added, "while not equal to that attained in high-altitude attacks when the target can be seen, is 'satisfactory' and will probably improve."[44]

This almost instinctive support for the Eighth's bombing campaign was common among the London-based veterans that winter, and it played an important role in how they covered Spaatz and Doolittle's air war. Hardened by witnessing tough land battles, these correspondents tended to approach the mechanical task of turning an air force communiqué into an publishable dispatch with much less squeamishness; they had, after all, seen far worse sights of death and destruction on their Mediterranean travels.

These seasoned correspondents also approached their task without the gnawing, almost debilitating, sense of frustration felt by their greener colleagues. They viewed their Fleet Street interlude as a welcome breather from war reporting, which, in turn, explained their most important reaction to the air campaign. Most of the veterans fully bought into the need to soften up the Hitler's Reich from the skies, whatever the cost in American bombers. Not only had these reporters been earmarked to take part in the massive invasion of Western Europe, which they believed would be the most dangerous operation of the entire war, but they had also experienced the true horror of fighting the German army in Sicily and Italy since the summer of 1943. These two Mediterranean campaigns had demonstrated just how hard it would be to defeat Adolf Hitler's Nazi regime.

PART III

Sicily and Italy

CHAPTER 9

Invasion, 1943

JUMPING INTO BATTLE

By July 1943, the heat of the Tunisian desert had become almost unbearable. At their base near Kairouan, just fifty miles to the east of February's Kasserine battlefields, men from the Eighty-Second Airborne Division sweated profusely as they busied themselves with last-minute preparations for Operation Husky, the long-awaited Allied invasion of Sicily.

Although they were nervous about what lay in store, many paratroopers could not wait to leave the North African desert. They had come to hate the flies that buzzed around them all day and, worse, the mosquitoes that tried to swarm under their nets at night. Although everyone had learned to tolerate the warm drinking water that was flavored with peppermint to mask its real taste, many had succumbed to bouts of dysentery that played havoc with their combat preparations. Every day, a fortunate few enjoyed a brief, cool respite when they stood under "ingenious showers rigged up by the engineers near some ice cold Arab well." But just before the invasion of Sicily, a stiff desert wind sent temperatures soaring as high as 146 degrees Farenheit, compelling everyone to swathe their heads in towels.[1]

Into this maelstrom of heat, insects, and swirling sand came a familiar face. Everyone who knew John Thompson of the *Chicago Tribune* considered him "gentle-mannered and considerate, and always willing to help a newcomer get onto the ropes." But his main claim to fame was as the paratrooper's biggest media friend. He certainly looked the part. A burly, well-built man, he had recently decided to cultivate "a terrific black beard" that made him appear almost as "ferocious" as the men with whom he now camped, ate, and mingled. Desperate to jump with the Eighty-Second, Thompson wanted to fit right into the paratroop team.[2]

Like most of the choices he had made in his career, Thompson's penchant for parachuting was no whim. He had grabbed his first reporting job in 1931, happily taking a 50 percent pay cut from his previous position at Montgomery Ward to trudge Chicago's depression-wracked streets for the City News Bureau. He had joined the *Chicago Tribune* two years later, working his way up from assistant city desk editor to rewrite man and then to general assignment reporter. When the American army started to grow after the outbreak of war in Europe, he became the paper's main expert on army camp life, covering no less than fourteen camps in the United States during 1941. He had sailed to Britain a year later, where he joined the first American parachute troops on British soil and immediately became hooked.[3]

It was not hard to see what drew Thompson to these men. Paratroopers prided themselves on being part of an elite unit. Each man had volunteered for the hazardous duty, which came with an extra $50 a month in danger money ($100 if they were officers). At the scorching desert camp in Tunsia, every trooper went through a rigorous physical training regime, which, according to the division's commander, had made them lean, mean, and tough.[4] "You will find no better physical specimens in the American army," Thompson agreed after a few days at Kairouan, "than these rugged young men from almost every state in the union. Their homeland garrisons know them as roistering crew, quick with their fists," he added admiringly. Now they would "prove the old adage that the poor garrison soldier is often the best fighter."[5]

As Thompson also recognized, key facets of the paratroopers' mission tapped into the national psyche. For a start, these men were an integral part of the technocratic way of war in which the United States excelled. Their mode of transport to the battlefield was the airplane, the era's archetypal symbol of modernity.[6] Although Germany had pioneered the use of airborne assaults, the Americans promised to take them to another level. "The Germans came in single planes," sneered Thompson, since to them formation flying "seemed too difficult." American planes, by contrast, planned to fly in a tight *V* formation, a task that "required the highest type of aerial skill."

Almost as soon as they jumped, however, the paratroopers would leave modernity behind, thereby appealing to another aspect of the American psyche. On the ground these men were effectively on their own. Fighting in small units, they would almost be like lone warriors, at a time when individualism was a rare commodity in the military. Surrounded by the enemy on all sides, they would also need all the heroism they could muster to seize the airfields and key hills that would allow the GIs wading ashore from landing craft to move rapidly inland.

Such a heady brew of modernism, individualism, and heroism held an obvious appeal for an ambitious correspondent seeking a front-page story, but that was not the only attraction. By jumping with the paratroopers, Thompson would be in the vanguard, beating every other American correspondent to Sicily. More than that, he would be the first reporter to set foot in Axis-dominated Europe since the Allied fight back had begun.[7]

Of course, the mission contained massive risks. Thompson had already made two jumps in North Africa. The first, on November 15, took place just a week after the 1942 invasion and had distinguished him as the first American correspondent to jump into combat. Three reporters had wanted to go on the operation that day, but there was only one parachute. Taking advantage of the close relationship he had developed with the troopers, Thompson grabbed it. Although his two rivals were sore at losing out, they were impressed when Thompson stood stoically by the door of the plane and waited for his signal to jump. He went out like a veteran, remarked Frank Kluckhohn of the *New York Times*. Although he weighed almost two hundred pounds, Thompson did not hesitate when the green light went on. He just jumped.[8]

If that mission had been hairy, the Sicilian operation promised to be far worse. It would take place at night, and no jump of its size had ever been attempted in the dark. To make matters worse, neither the planners nor the pilots had much experience with the task at hand, and the latter would somehow have to find the target zone, having made three sharp turns over water in an effort to avoid friendly fire from the nervous naval gunners below.[9]

On the afternoon of July 9, as the troopers smudged their faces black and rechecked their packs one last time, Thompson tapped out a story that would be released once the battle had started. "Future dispatches," he told his readers, "will be written on a typewriter dropped from a separate parachute, providing, of course, the machine is not broken in the fall." Unspoken but implied was the prospect that Thompson himself might not survive the fall. To relieve the tension before a mission, the paratroopers sometimes tried to reassure themselves with the maxim, "When you jump you've only got two things to worry about: whether your 'chute opens or whether it doesn't. If it doesn't you've got nothing to worry about. If it does you've only got to worry about landing." Yet Thompson knew he had much bigger worries than just hitting the ground in one piece. He would be accompanying a combat team that was expected to handle the "bulk of the fighting" as it tried to capture a key hill that dominated the main American invasion beach at Gela. If he made it out alive, he would have one hell of a story. But as dusk settled over the camp and the transport planes revved up their engines, this seemed a very big if indeed.[10]

After three hours of flying low over the sea to avoid enemy radar, Thompson's plane finally made it to Sicily. Before he had time to think, he saw the light turn green. Following the man in front, he hurled himself out of the door and felt the reassuring "snap of shoulders as the 'chute opened." As he floated down, a brilliant flare suddenly lit up the ground below, revealing an olive grove instead of the expected wheat field. At first, Thompson assumed the light was coming from a battle somewhere below, but looking to one side he realized "that the flare was from one our transports which had broken in two and had burst into flames."

Despite the brief light from the stricken plane, Thompson could not avoid hitting an olive tree. Thudding onto the hard ground, he emerged from the "tangled shroud" of his parachute "with a wrenched knee, skinned knuckles and bruises, and what was not to appear until later—a cracked rib." But at least he was alive. His heavy old typewriter had also landed, shepherded to the ground by a "sturdy sergeant major."

Trying hard to ignore the pain, Thompson set about getting his bearings and joining up with the other troopers. Not until morning did the men in his group realize that they had been dropped more than thirty miles to the east of the target. With little choice, they had to "march, march, march all afternoon and part of the night" to reach their target for the mission.

After traipsing fifteen miles in the scorching heat, Thompson's group had its first encounter with the enemy, near the town of Vittoria. As the men hastily sheltered from snipers' bullets, the senior officer decided that he lacked the numbers to stay and fight. So he hurried his men away so fast that Thompson's trusty typewriter got left behind.

Downbeat at the loss, Thompson took some solace in the Sicilian scenery. The yellows and greens seemed so lush after the months he had spent in the monochrome desert. The locals appeared friendly, too, proffering wine, bread, and water from the side of the rocky roads. Most encouragingly of all, as they marched, Thompson's men picked up more and more paratroopers, who had been scattered over a wide area by their planes but were now coalescing into a viable fighting force.

The next day, Thompson and the paratroopers finally reached their objective. Although the troopers were outnumbered three-to-one, the colonel in charge decided he had just about enough troops to chance an attack to take a key hill that lay about fifteen miles from the main American landing beach. It proved to be a tough fight. For one grim hour, the US paratroopers beat back huge German Tiger tanks with howitzers, while Thompson sheltered in a culvert a hundred yards behind the fighting. "Then," he wrote in a triumphant dispatch, "as in the last minutes of a Hollywood ending, came our General Sherman tanks and some half-tracks towing anti-tank guns. You could hear the parachute troopers' cheer even above the clutter of the tanks."[11]

Having secured their objective and joined forces with the GIs coming ashore from the invasion beaches, the paratroopers rested in a shady orchard. If one of Thompson's goals had been to become part of the fearsome paratroop team, he had succeeded almost too well. One PRO, who had just arrived by boat, spotted him covered in dust and sporting a seven-inch beard. "He had the appearance of an ancient when he walked down the road and I heard a battle-scarred soldier say, 'I'd hate to meet that man in the dark.'"[12]

But what of Thompson's goal to write a combat story on his exploits with the paratroopers? This was the question on the mind of Thompson's boss, Colonel McCormick, who sat brooding in his office in the Tribune Tower a few days later. The Colonel knew that Eisenhower's censors had released news of the airborne landings on July 11—he had read all the resulting dispatches in the newspapers, including his own. These stories carried an Algiers dateline, confirming that they were based on briefings and interviews, not firsthand experience. But they made such good copy nonetheless, with their details of "booted, toughly trained parachutists" who had beaten the "Axis with its own invention," that they were rapidly becoming *the* major story of the invasion.[13]

That same day, July 11, McCormick had received the dispatch that Thompson had written *before* he flew on the mission. The next day he received nothing at all—and the next, and the next, and the next. The Colonel, never known for his patience, had once cabled a reporter who had not filed for a week and asked sarcastically: "Are you a historian or a newspaperman?" His famous temper was only held in check now by concern for Thompson's safety. With each passing day, he received increasingly anxious inquiries from Thompson's distressed wife.[14]

To everyone's relief, Thompson's front-line dispatch finally arrived on July 15. As the first eyewitness account of America's first major airborne assault, it promised to create a major splash despite the time lag. Within hours, McCormick had a version of it broadcast over the WGN and Blue

Figure 9.1 John Thompson receiving a Purple Heart for the wound he sustained when jumping with the Eighty-Second Airborne in Sicily. National Archives 111-SC-181804.

radio networks. Within days, he also credited Thompson's bank account with a whopping $500 bonus as reward for "great work."[15]

Yet the Colonel had not relished the anxiety, bordering on anguish, when everyone had feared for Thompson's life. Nor had it escaped his beady editorial eye that Thompson's story had arrived too late on the fifteenth to place in that morning's *Tribune*. Even more galling, because all battlefield stories were pooled, and because the *Chicago Daily News* was an afternoon publication, with a later deadline, the Colonel could only watch hopelessly as his fiercest rival published Thompson's stunning scoop that day. The *Tribune*, which had funded the enterprise, did not carry it until the following morning.[16]

That final indignity decided matters for the Colonel. In a conscious echo of his fellow press bosses in the wake of Bob Post's death, McCormick determined that the risks of air combat were not worth the costs. Thompson, still soldiering on in Sicily with his bad knee and cracked rib, received a terse instruction from the Tribune Tower: "Jump no more."[17]

THE FRONT VERSUS THE REAR

Despite this abrupt end to his paratroop career, Thompson at least received a big bonus and a major byline. His colleagues who arrived in Sicily by sea mostly got neither.

Eighteen correspondents landed on the Sicilian beaches with George Patton's Seventh Army on July 10. The previous afternoon a strong storm had buffeted the massive invasion armada, churning up grey seas and nervous stomachs alike. The stiff winds, though gradually abating, made the task of getting to dry land particularly challenging. Jittery reporters with little naval experience had to navigate down sodden rope ladders and get into "bobbling assault boats." "We slid one by one down a rope," recorded *Time*'s Jack Belden, "and suddenly the boat was in the water, rocking sickeningly. . . . I was trying to hold the head of a soldier vomiting next to me when suddenly the craft shuddered violently once or twice, the engine raced and roared, there was a jerky bump, and the boat swerved and came to a halt." "Open ramp," roared an ensign, and Belden groped his way to shore alongside the combat troops, ducking and diving to avoid incoming bullets.[18]

Although "great confusion" reigned on the beach, the gritty American troops managed to push rapidly inland against wilting Italian opposition. In their wake came the bedraggled correspondents, unsteady from the choppy sea, wet from the surf, and desperately trying to get their bearings. Most paused to jot down their first impressions, before asking the same pertinent question: "How on earth are we going to get our copy out?"[19]

For the correspondents like Belden who landed near Gela with the First Division, the next day proved even worse. Woken up early by a strong sun that rapidly burned off the sea mist, Belden gazed down at the small beachhead won so far and muttered another thought often at the forefront of a war correspondent's mind: "Jeezus. What am I doing here?" That night, he had slept beside Don Whitehead of the AP and H. R. Knickerbocker of the *Chicago Sun*, bedding down on "flea-infested mattresses salvaged from an Italian beach barracks." The three reporters had gravitated to the First Division, knowing full well that the "Fighting First" was often at the heart of the really tough battles. Shortly after breakfast on July 11, they had no doubt that the day would be one of their toughest.

Overnight, the Germans had gathered more than a hundred tanks and were determined to drive the Americans back into the sea. As the enemy attack began, the correspondents set up their typewriters in an abandoned house and began tapping out their D-Day stories. Outside, the enemy's artillery barrage intensified. When an officer dropped in, he seemed "more startled by the sound of typewriters than shells." "That's wonderful," he replied after Whitehead explained what they were doing, "but by God you may have to swim back to Algiers with your stories. Right now the Germans are less than a mile away."

Gripped by a sense of danger, Belden, Knickerbocker, and Whitehead toured the trenches, meticulously jotting down the names and hometowns, and their overriding impressions, of the GIs under fire. With only three American tanks ashore, the infantrymen had to rely on antitank guns, howitzers, machine guns—any weapon at hand—as well as the naval guns of the vast armada at sea. On the beach, the reporters found a line of troops "digging in for a last-ditch stand." A few hundred yards inland, they discovered an officer recruiting an informal task force of "cooks, drivers, and clerks," as the division commander, the hell-raising Terry Allen, dashed around making morale-boosting pronouncements. "Send out an order," he instructed his senior officers at the worst moment. "We attack at ten o'clock!"

By the time Allen made his bold counterattack, it had become clear that the First would cling to its tenuous Sicilian foothold, and that no one would be jumping into the sea to avoid capture by the Germans. To the more sardonic correspondents, however, a swim back to Algiers still held some appeal, for it seemed to provide the best prospect of getting their graphic eyewitness stories back to the United States. Certainly, the two PROs who hastily constructed the Seventh Army's press camp had little else to offer, despite the futile assurance from one of them that his main goal was to get copy out "in [an] orderly fashion."

Receiving scant help from the military, the correspondents decided to gamble on giving their dispatches to any boat that was returning to Tunis or Algiers. But without designated couriers to ensure that the stories reached a communications hub, very few made it back to anxious editors during the first week of the campaign.

For Belden, who worked for a weekly magazine with more leisurely deadlines, this problem was frustrating rather than disastrous. And his stories did indeed appear in *Time* and *Life*, with much fanfare, a couple of weeks later. For correspondents like Knickerbocker and Whitehead employed by dailies or one of the news agencies, the situation was acute. The dispatches they were carrying in their packs covered a major landing and a desperate rearguard—and so, like Thompson's exploits, might have a slightly longer-than-usual shelf life. Nevertheless, the minute the fighting moved inland, any story delayed more than three or four days was likely to go "stale," and hence be spiked, by the time it arrived in a stateside newsroom.[20]

With putative scoops going stale in the Sicilian sun, a familiar vacuum opened up. During the Torch landings, Wes Gallagher had demonstrated how HQ-based reporters could steal the show if they had easy access to both reliable communications and the supreme commander's office. On the day of the Sicilian invasion, Eisenhower's headquarters was brimming with budding Gallaghers, all hoping to dominate the coverage while their colleagues at the front remained incommunicado.

Amazingly, most had known for almost a month that Sicily was the next target. That had been Eisenhower's doing. Over the course of the North African campaign, Ike had had his problems with reporters, but he had also learned to trust them not to spill the really big secrets. "Every once in a while I like to tell you fellows something [strictly off the record]," he grinned to one journalist that summer, "because you might hear it from somebody else, and if *I* tell you, it shuts you up!"[21]

On the basis of this shrewd maxim, Eisenhower had stunned the pressroom in June. At a background briefing, he suddenly announced that a new invasion would be launched within weeks. "The room became as still as a picture," noted one correspondent. "Nothing moved except Eisenhower's blue eyes which went slowly from face to face," before he divulged that Sicily was the target. "I almost wished he hadn't told us," groaned another correspondent. "I have never been so conscious of a responsibility."[22]

Given almost a month to prepare, most of the reporters decided to stay put in Algiers. At the Hotel Aletti, the veterans who frequented the bar were fond of repeating the same wisdom. "It was always fine and exciting to go in with the first assault wave, but not much use professionally since it was almost always impossible to get any copy out until a day or two later." At Eisenhower's PR center, where press officers were putting the finishing touches on the media plan for the invasion, Joe Phillips amended the press arrangements accordingly. The "only major change," he told the War Department on July 1, "is that the majority of correspondents at headquarters have now decided to remain at Algiers until forward communications improve."[23]

For those reporters, the Sicilian campaign began at four o'clock on the morning of July 10. As, bleary-eyed, they took their seats in the press room, one correspondent likened the situation to a "convention press-room on the eve of a presidential nomination." When a "stout, red-faced Scotsman" entered, the scene became particularly frantic, for he had the most important piece of information that morning: the priority list under which stories would be filed. Although a pooling system was in operation, wire-service reporters and radio correspondents still faced a fierce struggle to beat their rivals, even if only by seconds. So, almost immediately, the smoke-filled room erupted in a "bedlam of noise," as the reporters began banging away fiercely on their typewriters, almost falling over each other to get their copy to the filing room.[24]

As the briefers went to work, they were at pains "to impress the correspondents with the toughness of the Husky operation . . . on the principle that we don't want to have an over-built confidence at home such as arose during [the] . . . rapid rush to Tunisia in November." This emphasis found its way into the dispatches that sketched the early phase of the Sicily landings.[25] As soon as the beachhead was secured, however, the HQ-written reports became much more upbeat. A number of the stories even ignored the perils of combat altogether and focused instead on the vacation-like atmosphere in Sicily—the fact that for a single cigarette a GI could "buy a big juicy watermelon plus a half dozen equally luscious cantaloupe" or the comment of one "observer" that "our boys are bronzed and bearded and look very tough," while "our nurses [are] . . . knockout[s] in light blue uniforms."[26]

In the first days of the invasion, when the correspondents in Sicily remained largely out of touch, the HQ reporters in Algiers produced a vast corpus of similarly anodyne stories. According to one calculation, the filing room transmitted no less than 62,950 censored words on July 10, followed by 78,945 the next day and 65,991 the day after that. However insipid the content, the pace left everyone exhausted, from the operatives working the cables to the correspondents themselves. Dan De Luce, the AP man who had replaced Gallagher, sighed wearily as he told everyone that he had not worked so many consecutive hours since covering the 1936 Los Angeles earthquake.[27]

Before they could pat themselves too vigorously on the back, the reporters received a nasty shock. Reprising the Gallagher role, they all knew, not merely meant filing frequently through a reliable communications network. It also entailed sticking close to Eisenhower, who held the most authoritative, up-to-date battlefield information. The reporters soon learned, however, that Eisenhower was not at his Algiers HQ. He had left for Malta on July 8, to be nearer to the invasion, and had taken with him two hand-picked "super-coverage reporters."[28]

Joe Phillips had come up with the idea. His plan was for John Gunther, a famous writer accredited to the North American Newspaper Alliance, and Edward Gilling, a reporter with London's Exchange Telegraph Agency, to accompany Eisenhower to Malta. From there, they would file stories on HQ life, leaving the operational material to the correspondents in the field or in Algiers. Soon after the invasion began, however, Eisenhower's press office started to worry that a communications snafu might prevent Ike's daily communiqué from reaching Algiers or New York, so it decided to play safe. It would allow Gunther and Gilling to file stories about the battles. "In other words," noted a euphoric Gunther in his diary, "we have access to what the communiqué will say, and to hedge against breakdowns in transmission it now seems advisable that we should, independently, be permitted to cover the same material. What we are writing," he explained, "goes into the communiqué that is issued the next day; therefore, if our stuff gets through, we are twenty-four hours ahead on anything except eyewitness stories from the beaches."[29]

To the consternation of the Algiers-based correspondents, Gunther and Gilling were soon stealing the headlines. It was these two men who described how Eisenhower had dealt with the pressure in the hours before the assault. On July 13, they even filed an eyewitness account of the battlefront, grabbed when they had accompanied Eisenhower on "a quick, secret voyage" from Malta to Sicily.[30]

The reporters in Algiers were, naturally, miffed. One industry insider summed up the mood when he complained that American newspaper readers missed the familiar and famous names of the North African campaign and instead "had to be content with fare offered" by the likes of Gunther and Gilling—the latter not just relatively unknown but a Brit to boot. This last fact particularly rankled.[31]

If the reporters in Algiers were riled by Eisenhower feeding scoops to Gunther and Gilling, the correspondents in Sicily were angry about the randomness of what stories made it onto page one.

In the primitive press camp at Gela, the Seventh Army's PROs had still not devised a systematic way of getting copy off the island. Left to fend for themselves, the correspondents had little choice but to hand their hard-earned dispatches to someone leaving the island by boat or plane and to hope that this person knew where to take it in Algiers. But, as everyone recognized, success depended more on luck than skill. Most reporters handed their dispatches to press officers and never saw or heard anything about them again.

In this courier lottery, Ross Munro won the first jackpot on invasion day. An experienced reporter with the Canadian Press wire agency, Munro managed to get a detailed story of the successful Canadian attack in Sicily to North America seven-and-a-half hours before anybody else. He even mentioned the precise location of the Canadian landing, long before Eisenhower's headquarters released anything so specific. And, to compound his rivals' frustration, his dispatch hit the wires as an exclusive, not as part of the pool.[32]

Had this been a one-off, Munro's scoop might have been swiftly forgotten. But a week into the Sicilian campaign, a fresh bout of Anglo-American rivalry erupted at the front, causing many of the US reporters to question whether the lottery was loaded in favor of the Brits and their Canadian partners.

Montgomery, whose Eighth Army had invaded Sicily's southeastern corner, provided the spark. On July 13, Monty unilaterally grabbed a key road from the American-designated sector to sustain his push on the eastern side of the island, where the Germans, reinforced by two new divisions, were putting up a stiff defense. Patton, bristling at the prospect of being "relegated to the role of flank guard for the British," quickly sought authorization to occupy the west of Sicily, including the capital, Palermo, which was largely being defended by Italian troops. Soon, a race was underway. Patton took an early lead, capturing Palermo on July 23 and then shifting east to target the port city of Messina, the island's strategic prize.[33]

Patton had never suffered from publicity shyness, and now, with his blood up, he repeatedly trumpeted his army's achievements to any war correspondent within earshot. The drive to the Sicilian capital, he triumphantly declared on arriving in Palermo, was "the greatest blitz in history. . . . I am just a visiting fireman," he explained with studied humility. "The credit goes to the men who led the troops and armor on Sicily. They did a remarkable job."[34]

Yet if the American troops were moving faster than their British counterparts, many of the American correspondents suspected that the British were trying to compensate by providing their own reporters with speedier transmission from the battlefield. US correspondents, a worried press officer noted on July 21, are "indignant still over manner Canadian press copy got cleared hours ahead of others: Munro story in London within twelve hours of start of invasion," he added by way of explanation, "first American copy five days late."[35]

As Eisenhower knew, the situation would become toxic if these feelings bled into the frontline competition between the American and British forces. Ike's briefing officers therefore went into overdrive to explain to the correspondents the reasons for Patton's more rapid advance. "Equal accent," they insisted, "should be placed on stiff German resistance on Eighth Army front and almost total lack of organized resistance on [Patton's] Seventh Army front."[36]

At the same time, to mollify the American correspondents, the press office moved to equalize journalistic communications. As the battlefield rapidly fanned out to the west and north of the triangle-shaped island, the Seventh Army's press team recruited "cub" couriers, who flew between Sicily and Algiers with a pouch of dispatches added to their loads. It arranged a road courier service, comprising a quarter-ton truck and a motorcycle, which sometimes drove more than 200 miles a day, over steep, rocky roads, to pick up censored copy from the press camp and deliver it to the constantly shifting airfields. And it continued to use any means, from hospital ships to returning correspondents, to help the increasingly desperate reporters get their stories out of the battle zone. John Thompson was notable in this regard. A few weeks into the invasion, Thompson earned the gratitude of his fellow reporters by taking a large batch of their copy with him to Algiers, after McCormick had summoned him there to make a live radio broadcast.[37]

For the correspondents in the combat zone, the timing of these practical improvements was auspicious. By the start of August, the heady days of trying to keep up with Patton's advance had given way to a grimmer reality. Montgomery's troops were being held in a frustrating stalemate around the imposing slopes of Mount Etna. As soon as Patton's Seventh Army turned east from Palermo, it ground to a similar halt, for it now faced a tenacious German rearguard in the dusty foothills and steep mountains.[38]

The Seventh Army seemed prepared to publicize this grimmer campaign. Before the invasion, Eisenhower's HQ had instructed both senior officers and the press team to emphasize the "difficulty" of the operation. "If we get licked," Butcher had explained, "the public will know it was hard. If we win the public will give us credit for overcoming strenuous opposition."[39] As July turned to August, and the German opposition did indeed become strenuous, the military and the media had a perfect opportunity to join forces to convey a realistic picture of the war. And—with some significant exceptions—they grabbed it, with alacrity.

Take Richard Scott Mowrer of the *Chicago Daily News*, who had replaced the resting Bill Stoneman at the front. At the end of July, Mowrer focused on the "ridiculous, comic-opera atmosphere" of the Sicilian campaign. "The attitude of the population," he had reported, "and even of the Italian prisoners toward us is so friendly, so gay, that it is bewildering." Just over a week later, Mowrer was writing about an ugly, depressing battlefield reality as American infantrymen inched forward against a formidable enemy. "Here," he explained, "battles are fought in country too rough for tanks. The fighting consists of sniping with every arm from pistols to big 145's. The Germans are fighting a strong and expert delaying action. They have to be ferreted out almost individually from caves and rocks with mortars, automatic weapons, and artillery."[40]

For Allen's Fighting First, still toiling away three weeks after the invasion, the town of Troina proved to be the toughest place to ferret out the stubborn enemy troops, as Don Whitehead discovered when he rejoined the division halfway through a grueling six-day battle.

Long before the Sicily campaign, the "slim, angular AP correspondent" had acquired a reputation for fearlessness. Whitehead's first experience of covering violence had come during the bitter Kentucky labor disputes of the early 1930s. A decade later he had risen to a job in the AP's head office, but sitting behind a desk in New York held no appeal. He hankered to be like the reporters in Europe who, he observed, "were watching the greatest story of their lifetime unfold in an eruption of death and destruction on a scale of unbelievable proportions." "More and more," Whitehead confided in his diary, "I knew I could never be happy until I had a chance to report this war from a sideline seat. There would have been a gnawing frustration that would have poisoned me for years to come."

Whitehead's chance had come in the fall of 1942, when Middleton's move to the *New York Times* opened up a new overseas slot at the AP. Whitehead's bosses sent him first to Cairo, the site of British headquarters for the desert campaign against Rommel. But the restless reporter found this sideline seat too distant from the real event. He wanted to be in the thick of the battle, a recurring desire that now propelled him to follow the Fighting First, from its narrow escape at Gela to the vicious battle at Troina.[41]

After a couple of days, the bloody slogging match along Troina's slopes sated even Whitehead's desire for action. He could not help contrasting the sad sight of fatigued GIs dragging themselves toward the next ridge with the patriotic ads being run in slick magazines back home. In those glossy pictures, Madison Avenue executives showed handsome young soldiers, in immaculate uniforms, confidently declaring that they would never be scared in battle. The actual situation, Whitehead mused, could not have been more different. Real-life soldiers, he realized, had "faces caked with sweat and dust, unshaven and marked by lines of fatigue." Their uniforms bulged and sagged in all the wrong places. And none of them ever denied feeling fear, largely because they had all seen too much death and destruction in the past few weeks.

These thoughts made Whitehead want to weep. He also felt a strong urge to convey some sense of the bitter reality to his American audience. But as soon as he found a quiet moment to sit down with his typewriter, Whitehead felt the pull of a familiar instinct. Like his AP colleague Hal Boyle, Whitehead invariably wanted to hit at least one upbeat note in any battlefield story. In his Troina dispatch, he described the "bitterest and most savage fighting" on the island, the ground "literally one vast graveyard torn by shells, shrapnel, and bullets." But he managed to end on a high note, praising the men for their "dogged determination after twenty-four days of fighting and marching with hardly a break." He also correctly predicted the victory that would soon be achieved, as the Germans recognized that, ultimately, their position was "hopeless."[42]

The German evacuation of Troina on August 6 did indeed foreshadow the Wehrmacht's larger withdrawal from Sicily, which began a few days later. Now the race for Messina was well and truly on. Arriving in the city on August 17, Whitehead and Boyle were met with a "death-like silence," together with "about 50 Italian soldiers waiting to surrender."[43] Patton arrived a few hours later. Another correspondent described the scene.

> Commandos, smiling and shouting, sprawled over the exteriors of the tanks, and the little parade was made festive with many-colored flowers thrown by Sicilians. Some of the dirty-faced soldiers clutched huge bunches of grapes. . . . [Then] an American command car bearing the three silver stars of a lieutenant general rolled up. General Patton, dazzling in his smart gabardines, stepped out.

Almost immediately, a British officer approached. "It was a jolly good race," he told Patton. "I congratulate you."[44]

Back home, many news organizations were also in a congratulatory mood. Because Patton's PROs had invested so much time and effort in improving communications, editors received their war reporters' dispatches on the liberation of Messina in record time. On the evening of August 17, the army readied a series of cub planes to relay the correspondents' copy to Palermo. From there, Patton's personal aircraft was waiting to fly it to Algiers, where it arrived shortly after midnight. An hour later, radio correspondents began broadcasting it to the folks back home. "The result," declared one army report, "was eyewitness accounts in the United States of the occupation of Messina on the day of its occupation."[45]

PATTON AND THE PARATROOPERS

For Patton, the Sicilian victory could not have been more fleeting. As the Seventh Army commander triumphantly entered Messina on August 17, Eisenhower was back at his Algiers headquarters mulling over a report that Patton had struck two hospitalized soldiers, in separate incidents on August 3 and August 10. Neither man had any visible wounds, and when Patton approached, they both made similar comments, either "I guess I just can't take it" or "It's my nerves." On the first occasion, Patton, one observer noted, "immediately flared up, cussed the soldier, called him all types of coward, then slapped him across the face with his gloves." On the second, he struck the man twice before threatening to shoot him for being a "god-damned whimpering coward."[46]

The report stunned Eisenhower, though he dithered over his response. On the one hand, Ike was loath to lose his dazzling army commander. He saw Patton as his most pugnacious general, perhaps the only Allied officer who really knew how to fight. Yet he recognized that Patton had crossed an important line. An officer striking a soldier was clearly "a high offense." Besides, in Patton's case, this kind of behavior was scarcely out of character. As Eisenhower told Marshall, it was one of "those unfortunate personal traits" that had long marred Patton's record. In darker moments, Ike even suspected that Patton did not "mind sacrificing lives if by so doing he can gain greater fame."[47]

Even if Patton's craving for renown had not been the reason he had struck the soldiers, his celebrity status meant that news of the incidents was likely to precipitate an outcry powerful enough to destroy his career. On August 19, Eisenhower received an ominous report from Demaree Bess. The *Saturday Evening Post* reporter had gotten word of the second slapping incident almost as soon as it happened and found the story "so amazing" that he gave it "the closest possible investigation." Within hours, he had hurried to the hospital, quizzed fifteen eyewitnesses, and pieced together a set of events not very different from what Ike had already read. Within days, Bess's explosive findings were about the only subject of conversation among reporters in both Sicily and Algiers, many of whom had so decisively changed their minds about Patton that they now welcomed his comeuppance.[48]

This animosity had built up slowly throughout the Sicilian campaign. It stemmed partly from the obvious contrast between Patton and Lieutenant General Omar Bradley, the placid and unassuming II Corps commander.

Bradley, *Life* magazine told its readers, was a calm, quiet Missourian who came across "as unruffled as an Ozark lake on a dead-calm day." It was a trait that his men appreciated. In Sicily, in the private estimate of one correspondent, there were "at least 50,000 soldiers who would gladly shoot Patton if they had the slightest chance." Bradley, by contrast, quickly became known as the GI's general. "I don't believe that I have ever known a person to be so unanimously loved and respected by the men around and under him," Ernie Pyle wrote in an August column. "He has no idiosyncrasies, no superstitions, no hobbies. He laughs good-naturedly at small things and has an ordinary Middle Western sense of humor."[49] Unlike Patton, Pyle might well have added. "Ernie . . . hated Patton's guts," his friend Don Whitehead wrote privately. "Patton's bluster, show, and complete disregard for the dignity of the individual was the direct antithesis of Ernie's gentle character."[50]

At the end of the Sicilian campaign, a group of big-name reporters gathered in Algiers, including Demaree Bess and Quentin Reynolds of *Collier's*. They all agreed that Patton's deed needed to be punished with the utmost severity, perhaps even a court-martial: it would be the only way to demonstrate that no officer was above the law. To stiffen Eisenhower, the reporters descended on his HQ in the St. Georges Hotel, where they issued a veiled threat. Ike, they warned, had no chance of covering-up such a "colorful" incident. Too many reporters knew about it already, and someone was bound to try to publish a scoop.[51]

The meeting placed an already-stressed Eisenhower in a deep quandary. He barely slept over the next few nights as he considered his options. Still determined not to lose Patton, Ike decided to reject the Bess-Reynolds demand for a court-martial. Instead, he sent Patton a stiff reprimand, along with an order that he apologize to the soldiers he had hit. This created the possibility of a press-corps munity. If reporters like Bess or Reynolds did indeed write up the story, it would doubtless provoke a "howling for Patton's scalp." So Eisenhower resorted to blanket censorship.[52]

To enforce the ban on stories about the slapping incidents, the supreme commander relied on a number of strengths. For a start, not every reporter bought into the anti-Patton narrative. When Eisenhower began holding a series of candid, off-the-record briefings to explain his position, many reporters agreed that "Georgie" ought to be given a second chance to display his obvious gift for bashing the Germans. Even those who disagreed felt some sense of obligation to Ike—and not just because publishing a story that the censor had blocked would destroy their careers. As Eisenhower began justifying his decision, he recognized that he could tap into a large reservoir of media support. He had laid its foundations in London more than a year earlier and had constantly replenished it, especially when he chose to trust reporters and draw them into his team—the time, for instance, when he had been candid after Kasserine or had divulged secrets ahead of the Sicilian invasion, or even his recent attempts to adopt an "increasingly liberal" censorship regime that allowed the war's gorier side into print.[53]

This final factor proved crucial. Not only did the reporters generally trust Ike, but they also had a war to report—a war that Eisenhower's censors allowed, even encouraged, them to write about in an ever-more realistic manner. A year earlier, Roosevelt had shrewdly concluded that stories about battles could refocus the public's attention. Perhaps taking this cue from his commander-in-chief, Eisenhower calculated that the upcoming invasion of Italy would "build new headlines and occupy the minds of correspondents with other events."[54]

For the most part, the strategy worked. The war reporters in Italy became so preoccupied with the new battle that they quickly lost interest in Patton, whom Ike left to languish on Sicily. In November, Drew Pearson finally broke the embargo on the slapping incident, but he did so in a manner that did surprisingly little damage to Eisenhower's credibility. It certainly helped that Pearson broadcast the story from the United States—it meant that none of the correspondents in the Mediterranean felt scooped. It was also important that Pearson had been the one to speak out first, since his reputation as a shameless muckraker meant that Algiers-based correspondents could happily echo the HQ line that his story appeared to be "substantially incorrect in its details."[55]

Even so, Eisenhower left nothing to chance. Within days of Pearson's broadcast Ike sent a senior officer out to meet the press. Appearing beside the officer on the podium was NBC's Merrill Mueller, one of the reporters who had unearthed the story of the slappings back in August. The two men held an exhaustive session, lasting most of the morning, presenting a blow-by-blow account of the whole incident, which the censors immediately placed on the record. These moves helped to quiet what one reporter dubbed the "Patton tempest." Milton Bracker, who thoroughly investigated the matter in November, summed up the prevailing mood in the pages of the *New York Times*. "The reasons for the three-month delay in reporting the story are not vitally important," Bracker concluded. "As long as there are wars, there will be some episodes that may not be recorded as soon as they become known."[56]

Perhaps. But Eisenhower must have suspected that the media's deep well of support was not unlimited. Reporters had swallowed one cover-up. Whether they would respond in quite the same detached and measured manner when another one finally came to light was open to question, especially since it involved not merely the slapping of two soldiers but the deaths of hundreds of paratroopers.

The incident had occurred back in July, on the second day of the Sicilian invasion. The beachhead at Gela was still under intense German pressure, and Patton had decided to send in another wave of nighttime paratroop drops to reinforce Allen's hard-pressed First Division. Patton had given the order early in the morning, with the expressed instruction "that all subordinate units be cautioned not to fire on these friendly planes," but a communications foul-up meant that many of the Allied ships sitting just off the coast never received the notification of the attack.

The sailors on board these ships were already jumpy after two days of Luftwaffe attacks. Just before the Allied transports arrived, they had become positively trigger-happy when yet another German raid narrowly missed a cruiser and forced the fleet to scatter. Then came the first of 144 friendly planes carrying men from the Eighty-Second Airborne. Through the darkness, the navy gunners could just about discern the aircraft. But were they friendly planes? Few in the embattled ships either knew or could identify them as such. Perhaps they were the vanguard of another Luftwaffe raid. One gunner was taking no chances. All of a sudden, he opened fire; another gunner followed, and then another. Soon tracers were tearing into faltering planes and falling parachutists alike, downing twenty-three of the former and killing perhaps four hundred of the latter.[57]

As the military pieced together the scale of the disaster, no one in the top brass favored making it public. Paratroopers were fast becoming the invasion's major news frame. Why take the shine off such an eye-catching new form of warfare? Why divulge a story that might destroy public support for these airborne assaults forever? Besides, no one could be certain about the main facts. Almost a week later, Matthew B. Ridgway, the division's commander, estimated that he had lost 1,400 of the paratroopers sent to Sicily on July 9 and 11 but had no clear idea how many of them had been killed by friendly fire.[58] More to the point, no one in a position of authority was prepared to accept responsibility for the bloody debacle. Patton blithely wrote it off as "an unavoidable incident of combat"; neither the navy nor the air force volunteered when asked to shoulder the blame for the fatal communications snafu.[59]

Eisenhower privately seethed about the whole incident, but he saw no option other than to order blanket censorship. Interservice cooperation was vital for the future invasions of Italy and France, and he recognized that this cooperation would scarcely be fostered by an ongoing public investigation into which of the services had killed so many American soldiers.[60]

Yet, once again, blanket censorship also carried substantial risks. Most obviously in this case, too many people were privy to the secret. On the ill-fated night, the reporters in the beachhead had seen the horror for themselves. "We sat there and witnessed one of the most blood chilling sights I have ever seen," recalled Whitehead. "An awful hail of steel rolled up from the fleet to meet the paratroopers." One plane after another burst into flames and fell sickeningly to the ground. "Oh, God, no!" screamed Belden. "No! Stop, you bastards, stop! Stop shooting!" Before long, rumor and speculation about the precise scale of this catastrophe began seeping out of the beachhead. According to another correspondent, the "story was all over [the] ETO—and as high officers, couriers, and others poured back in a steady stream to Washington, it spread over the Pentagon Building. Every reporter knew it."[61]

Of course, everyone in the Mediterranean and at the Pentagon had also known about the Patton incident, but this was different. The other cover-up concerned a single general who, despite his darker side, had proved himself a fighter whose expertise would doubtless be useful in coming battles. This concealment effort centered on the Sicilian campaign's most newsworthy troops. It also belied all the talk in Eisenhower's headquarters about the military's determination to liberalize censorship policy and reveal the war's ugliness.

That talk had been rife in Sicily, but it would reach its height during the coming months when the Allied campaign bogged down in Italy. Time after time, officers claimed that they were allowing correspondents to reveal the horror as well as the glory of battlefield life. All the while, these same officers were still sitting on one of the most terrible episodes of the American war to date. The military, in other words, was setting itself up for a big fall, especially as so many people knew about the friendly-fire incident that someone was bound to blurt about it at some point.[62]

That point would come in March 1944, at the worst possible moment. Before then, though, Eisenhower and his officers had another campaign to wage, a campaign they wanted covered with more photographs than ever before—realistic photos, which would underline the war-is-hell message. Vitally, too, they had the ideal man to get those shots, a man so brave that he had accompanied the ill-fated parachute mission to Sicily and so lucky he had survived to tell the tale.

CHAPTER 10

An Antidote to Complacency

A MAN CALLED CAPA

Although the censors had clamped down hard on the friendly-fire story in July 1943, they had been more than happy to pass photographs of the paratroopers aboard their transport planes. The evocative images had shown tense young men clinging to their packs, their eyes closed as they tried desperately to think about something, anything, other than the jump and battle ahead. Adorning the first invasion stories, these photographs had whetted the public's appetite for John Thompson's gripping account of his exploits with the troopers, which appeared a few days later.

To the aficionados back home who wanted to know how the images had been taken, there were few obvious clues. The byline simply credited the photo pool, not the photographer. This was unsurprising. Almost all stories and photos were pooled in the first days of the invasion, to take the pressure off the limited communications network and to bring a degree of order to the coverage of a chaotic fight. In Algiers, however, the identity of the man who had snapped a stirring set of paratroop photos was the talk of the press room, and not just because of his already legendary reputation. As everyone soon discovered, he was about to lose his credentials to be in the theater because his news organization had fired him a few days earlier.

Anyone who knew the photographer in question knew that bending or breaking the rules was perfectly in character for him. For Robert Capa was the archetypal correspondent-adventurer, intent on braving any danger to make his name and, if not his fortune, then at least enough cash to buy

Figure 10.1 American paratroopers about to begin the Allied invasion of Sicily, on a plane en route from Kairouan, Tunisia, July 1943. Robert Capa. © International Center of Photography / Magnum Photos.

booze and poker chips, color film and paper, or, when the gambling winnings were particularly high, a fur coat for his mother.[1]

This adventurer had been born André Friedmann, a Hungarian Jew who had fled to Berlin and then Paris in the early 1930s to escape fascism in his country.[2] He had transformed himself into Robert Capa in 1936, inventing the persona of a famous American photographer to make more money from his trademark action shots.[3] The new name helped to launch his illustrious career; but, above all, he took extraordinary risks to capture the death and destruction of war. By the time he had covered the Spanish Civil War and the Sino-Japanese conflict, his reputation was firmly established. *Life* even dubbed him the "great War Photographer Robert Capa."

As well as ambition and money, Capa was driven by ideological enmity toward fascists and Nazis. "The world was never as sad as it is now," he remarked after Hitler conquered France and marched into Paris. When Britain held out against the German blitz in 1940, and the Soviets and Americans formally joined the anti-Nazi coalition a year later, Capa's world brightened. Only now he found it surprisingly tough to get close to the action.

Part of the problem was sheer bad luck. During the early years of World War II, Capa found it difficult to be in the right place at the right time. He went to London in the summer of 1941, but by then the blitz was over and his pictures merely captured working-class families struggling to survive amid the rubble. Although he returned to Britain a year later, employed by *Collier's* magazine, he was unable to get credentials to cover the fighting overseas and so missed out on the North African invasion. Like other London-bound reporters, he tried to compensate by concentrating on the bombing campaign over occupied Europe, but he found little joy in hanging around for days at a muddy airbase, and he actively hated the experience of vicariously covering an air raid. "This sort of photography," he wrote later, "was only for undertakers, and I didn't like being one. If I was to share the funeral, I swore, I would have to share the procession."[4]

Capa had made his first bid to cover the North African campaign in mid-December 1942. Knowing that Eisenhower was keen to limit the number of reporters in the theater, he stressed that he required neither accommodation close to headquarters nor "priority on communications." Even so, his application remained ensnared in PRO red tape for the next couple of months.[5]

Not until March did Capa receive permission to travel to North Africa. His departure from London was typical of the man. "His last day was frantic," complained the secretary who dealt with his business matters.

> We had a big party the night before, so everyone had [a] bad hangover in the morning. Capa still had his equipment (bed-roll, tent, etc.) to buy, he hadn't packed. . . . In the afternoon he bought his equipment, had last talks with the Army Public Relations people, finally came around to me about 6 o'c[lock] to announce that he still had to pack and he was supposed to be on the station platform at 7:30! So we chased off to his apartment, where a girl-friend was laying out things for packing, and we packed desperately till 7 o'c[lock]. Then we felt so weak we went to have a drink and finally all steered him to the station with nine pieces of luggage, a tripod, and a tin-hat. What a day!'[6]

Capa arrived in North Africa at an important moment. Before the Torch invasion the PROs had repeatedly bemoaned the lack of combat pictures appearing in the press.[7] To compensate, they had arranged for more than twenty-five camera crews to accompany the American troops during the initial assault, and, according to one estimate, these crews managed to produce about 6,000 feet of film. However, because of the poor communications network, two weeks later nothing had made it back to the United States. As one War Department official complained, this meant that there had been an almost criminal "lack of pictorial coverage" of a story of such "momentous impact." Over the winter the situation improved somewhat.

But not until the Gafsa and El Guettar battles in March did the Signal Corps institute a system that allowed "newspaper readers in the United States to see pictures of the fighting on the same day the battle occurs." Now that couriers were on hand to fly film from the front to Algiers, photographs could be sent from the AFHQ to Washington by land wires and radio in as little as seven minutes.[8]

Capa made it to the front just in time to benefit from this improvement. His main problem was trying to get a byline, for a pooling system remained in operation.[9] Because of this constraint, it took until June 19 before *Collier's* finally turned his gripping pictures into a three-page spread, replete with an explanation of how he had braved no less than thirteen German air raids to take them.[10]

Such lavish treatment provided another clear indication that Capa would ultimately enjoy a good war. The big photo magazines like *Collier's* and *Life* reached massive audiences, and, as weeklies, their editors could often afford to wait a long time after the event to publish the photos as part of an in-depth essay.

Often, but not always. At the start of July, *Collier's* bosses calculated that the upcoming Sicilian campaign would be so swift as to make Capa an expensive, and unnecessary, luxury. They therefore cabled him:

> YOUR NORTH AFRICA PICTURES WONDERFUL STOP WAR DEPARTMENT INSISTING ON POOL REGULATIONS STOP THEREFORE AVAILABLE TO ALL PAPERS STOP YOUR PICTURES USED BY EVERYONE BEFORE WE COULD PRINT THEM STOP REGRET HAVE TO RECALL YOU TO NEW YORK STOP.[11]

Capa received this missive in London, where he had repaired for a pre-invasion rest. Since his *Collier's* contract was due to expire on July 19, he would become unemployed and also lose the formal credentials of a war correspondent. His only hope was to find some way to the battlefield and to return with such an amazing set of photos that another organization—hopefully *Life*—would snap him up.[12]

Once again, fortune came to Capa's rescue. In Algiers, Eisenhower's command was no longer seeking to exclude photographers. On the contrary, Ike himself wanted more of them in the theater, but only those willing to take risks to shoot actual battles. "Photographers should be instructed before leaving the United States," Eisenhower told the War Department in June, "that action photos can only be made at front lines. If they are not willing to endure hardships and dangers thereof, they should not be sent here. We will provide every facility for frontline coverage but it will be the duty of the civilian assignment editor to force photographers to go forward."[13]

No one ever had to force Capa to "go forward." His professional ethos revolved around getting as close to the action as possible. And with his career on the line, he was prepared to take more risks than ever.

Landing in Algiers just before the invasion, Capa met a doleful colleague who had contracted such a bad case of "C-ration diarrhea" that he could no longer accompany the paratroop mission to which he had been assigned. Capa eagerly volunteered to replace him. Arriving at Kairouan, he quickly struck up a deal with a PRO from the Eighty-Second Airborne. Although Capa was not qualified to jump, he would join the second flight, photograph the men as they left the plane, and return to base by three in the morning, in time to ensure that the pictures hit the stateside presses the next day. The plan worked perfectly. Despite witnessing the heavy friendly fire that downed so many other planes, Capa returned with his photos intact. The only snag was the one that *Collier's* had predicted. The pictures went out as part of the pool, with no byline. And Capa had still failed to impress a potential employer in time to ensure his continued accreditation.

So with his gambler's instincts to the fore, he decided to up the ante. Grabbing a spot on a supply ship heading to Sicily, he immediately located his new friends in the Eighty-Second Airborne. "It was," his biographer points out, "a lucky move." These men had been slated to take part in the swift raid to capture Palermo, enabling Capa to take reels of film detailing the euphoric reception of many Sicilians. The Luce empire was suitably impressed. When Capa reached the battle at Troina soon afterward, the First Division's deputy commander said, "Capa, there's a message down at division headquarters saying you're working for *Life*."[14]

It was only now that Capa's luck took its decisive turn for the better, and for reasons that had little to do with either the vagaries of editorial calculations or the need to be in the right place at the right time. Rather, the main factor that ultimately cemented Capa's professional reputation was the government's decision to encourage a more realistic depiction of the war.

In Algiers, Eisenhower's command had long sought to dampen domestic complacency by stressing the toughness of the fight ahead. In Washington, Ike's bosses had likewise kept an eagle eye on any communiqué or briefing that obscured the reasons for, or reality of, a major setback.[15]

In Sicily, however, these good intentions had been difficult to sustain, and not merely because of the fateful decision to suppress news of both the Patton incident and the friendly-fire paratroop victims. Although the August fighting around Troina had been grueling, the media's overall coverage of the campaign had fostered the distinct impression in many American minds that the war might soon be over. The Seventh Army's rapid dash to Palermo, followed by US troops winning the race to Messina, had generated much of this new mood of triumphant complacency. But it was a major political development that really got America's hearts and minds racing about the prospect of an early end to the bloodshed.

On July 25, with the Allied foothold in Sicily secure, the Grand Council of Fascism forced Italian dictator Benito Mussolini to resign after twenty-one years in power. On the American home front many remembered how the last war had ended in 1918—not with a sweeping military drive into the enemy's capital but with internal revolution and an armistice with the new regime. Perhaps Mussolini's ouster foreshadowed a similar denouement to the current war. Perhaps it would prove infectious, spreading to the German capital where Hitler was reeling from both the Sicilian defeat and yet another massive failure against the Soviets on the Eastern Front.

In big-city editorial rooms, commentators hastened to draw the obvious parallel, insisting that "German fortunes have ebbed to a point where an internal break is a possibility which could develop at almost any moment." In European press bureaus, senior correspondents looked for concrete evidence to sustain this speculation. From London, Bill Stoneman reported on rumors that "Hitler has already been shelved by German generals." From Bern, Switzerland, his colleague Paul Ghali commented that across the continent, "pessimists say the end will not come until next summer," while "optimists say it will be this winter," but the "defeat of the Axis is doubted by no one."[16]

Avidly reading such reports, the American public reached the same conclusion. By July almost 60 percent of them thought Germany would be defeated within a year, a figure that had jumped 20 percent in just a few months. The government's correspondence panels—an early form of focus group—detected the reasons for this brimming confidence. According to one panelist, no one seemed prepared to believe anymore in the "long fight ahead," or at least if they did, this story lacked "vividness in the light of victories." The press was "partly to blame," added another, "because there is so much emphasis in the headlines on the victories we are winning now, and hardly any on the obstacles in the way." "There was great jubilation" at Mussolini's political demise, stressed a third, "and the general comment was that it was the beginning of the end and that the European theater of war should be over by the first of the new year."[17]

Across Washington, senior officials were deeply perturbed by this sudden change, since they knew that the war was far from won. Even in Italy the situation looked tough. Although Sicily had been conquered, many of the German defenders had escaped to fight another day. As soon as

Mussolini was forced out, Hitler's army had filled the resulting vacuum, securing control of most of the country, including Rome, on hearing that the Allies had concluded an armistice with Mussolini's successor.[18]

Given the likelihood that victory would only come after a long and bloody struggle, officials desperately needed a strong antidote to the popular complacency. Fortunately, they had an obvious tool to hand: they could encourage the media to focus on war's grim reality, with special accent on graphic photographic images.

This was the dominant view inside Roosevelt's civilian propaganda bureau, the OWI. Here, officials had long been convinced that overly sanitized images of the war had fueled the popular complacency. Censors, complained one OWI official, tended only to permit pictures in which "soldiers fight, . . . some of them get badly hurt and ride smiling in aerial ambulances, but . . . none of them get badly shot or spill any blood." Elmer Davis, the OWI chief, fully agreed. In his view, this misguided Hollywood approach to propaganda only intensified the public's persistent overconfidence. Davis therefore began lobbying for the release of more graphic footage of Americans fighting and dying on the battlefield.[19]

In the normal course of events, officers in the Pentagon tended to dismiss any suggestion emanating from the OWI as the product of naïve liberals who had little idea about the need for operational secrecy.[20] With the alarming rise in the public's complacency, however, the Pentagon was suddenly receptive to the OWI critique. On September 1, George Marshall wrote to subordinates in the field urging them to send him pictures for publication that would "vividly portray the dangers, horrors, and grimness of war." Three days later, Roosevelt added his powerful support for the new policy, calling for more visual images "of the dangers, sacrifices, and suffering endured by American fighting men." The president, one official told reporters, "believes not only that the people at home 'can take it' but that the lethargic elements should be aroused by pictorial proof that war abroad is not all beer and skittles for the country's soldiers, sailors, and airmen."[21]

"THE FAR-SPREADING CURTAIN OF A HUGE STAGE"

Robert Capa could scarcely believe his luck. As *Life*'s main man on the scene he now had a ready-made audience of around four million for his next batch of photos. All he had to do was get to the front, which again proved far from easy.

Capa missed out on the initial American invasion of Italy, lured by the prospect of a paratroop raid of Rome, which was aborted at the very last minute. Although he was crestfallen at having "missed the greatest scoop of anyone's life," Capa was fortunate not to have taken part in a mission that even the Eighty-Second Airborne's commander considered "harebrained." Yet Capa was never one to count his blessings over a danger avoided. Faced with having to cool his heels in the Sicilian sun, he complained of feeling "momentarily licked," a feeling that only intensified when he heard that the Allies had established a brittle beachhead around Salerno—a small port fifty miles south of Naples—on Thursday, September 9.[22]

While nowhere near as foolhardy as a one-division paratroop assault on Rome, Salerno was still a tough proposition. Just before the attack, Lieutenant General Mark Clark, the Fifth Army commander in charge of the assault, met with reporters. Clark was perhaps the military's most incorrigible publicist. When the press had revealed that he had lost his pants during a clandestine mission before Operation Torch, Marshall had sent him a stern rebuke, warning him against acting like a "buffoon" in front of reporters. Now, with the massive responsibilities of command resting heavily on his shoulders, Clark tried hard to adopt a "quiet air of confidence," although the more experienced reporters were not fooled. As one noted, Clark's outward bluster could not mask his obvious anxiety.[23]

The Fifth Army commander had plenty of reasons for his apprehension. As Allied ships approached Salerno, the radio blared news of the Italian surrender. Most of the men reacted with pure joy, convinced they would be landing to a welcome of white flags. "Speculation was rampant and it was all good," noted one disapproving officer, ". . . we would dock in Naples harbor unopposed, with an olive branch in one hand and an opera ticket in the other." The generals in charge disagreed. They thought it much more likely that the invasion would have to confront a typically tenacious German defense.[24]

Because of a landing craft shortage, just one division—the Thirty-Sixth (Texas National Guard)—would be wading ashore on D-Day. Its only company came from a group of war correspondents who had drawn lots to be by its side. Bill Stoneman was one.

With German shells whizzing overhead, the *Daily News* man managed to scurry inland, dodging in and out of foxholes, while the regiment he accompanied "was cut to pieces." Eventually, he arrived at "a rambling tobacco warehouse" where the division had established its headquarters. As more and more troops arrived to secure the beachhead, Stoneman and his fellow survivors quickly established a press camp in two buildings, turning one into an office and the other into living quarters. All day long Stoneman stoically refused to be cowered by the sounds of the battle and even took to running outside whenever the enemy's artillery started. As soon as the noise subsided, he would return inside to tap out his story, even though he had little chance of getting any copy off the bridgehead. As Lieutenant Colonel Kenneth W. Clark patiently explained to anyone who would listen, communications in the beachhead were as bad as anything experienced in the first days of Torch or Husky, with no designated courier service to Algiers and a radio transmitter that, infuriatingly, picked up interference from a frequency used by the air force.[25]

Ken Clark was a good PRO to have around in such a tricky situation. A "distinguished" alumnus of the Hearst organization, he had learned his trade in that "hard but tough school," where you either improved or "you didn't last." Yet even Clark could not work miracles. As well as the faulty radio, he had to make do with only one of his PR team's three designated jeeps, which eleven officers and correspondents somehow crammed into to tour the narrow slither of land captured at the end of the invasion's first day.[26]

When they returned from this claustrophobic jaunt, the reporters learned that Jack Belden of *Time* had been severely wounded. "His leg was shattered," a friend informed them, "and he lay between our fire and theirs for five hours." "I bet he got a hell of a story," responded one correspondent. "Sure," agreed the friend. "But it's only a good story if you can get it on the cable." And the closest cable was back in Sicily, which could only be reached by plane or boat.

For correspondents under ceaseless bombardment, this distance seemed almost unbridgeable—although some deadline-driven wire-service reporters did invent innovative methods. One UP reporter tried to send his copy in a sealed smoke-float container, throwing it onto a fast boat bound for Sicily. Only later did he discover that his unusual package "had been mistaken for German secret weapons and handed over to the bomb disposal squad at Palermo."[27]

Communications being so bad in Italy, Eisenhower's HQ in Algiers, predictably, stepped into the breach. Early briefings by Joe Phillips's team emphasized that "crack German armored units" had unleashed a series of "fierce counterattacks." Then, on September 11, Eisenhower appeared in person to tell reporters that the Allies faced "'a bitter battle' to drive the Germans out of Italy."[28]

That day the downbeat message from Ike's HQ did not fully reflect the reality on the ground, where the Allies had penetrated more than five miles inland and secured a number of key heights. All the next day, the omens grew steadily more disturbing, especially around the Sele River, which intersected the Allied front. Here, German resistance stiffened noticeably, setting the scene for the events of September 13—"Black Monday"—when a powerful panzer attack slammed into the hole around the Sele.[29]

The correspondents in the beachhead knew what was coming. Beforehand, an officer had warned the bedraggled group that the Germans were about to unleash a big push that could drive the Allies into the sea. As the reporters sat on a log to mull over the news, someone produced an emergency bottle of whisky and passed it around. Soon word came that enemy tanks had indeed broken through. So the reporters hunted around for a shelter from where they could watch cooks, clerks, and orderlies engage in the unfamiliar task of checking their rifles in preparation for a last-ditch effort to save the bridgehead.[30]

By evening the situation appeared bleak. One senior officer described it in a single word, "disaster." "I have no reserves," he informed Clark. "All I've got is a prayer." In a hastily convened conference the Fifth Army commander found the mood among his senior officers so downbeat that they even discussed the possibility of abandoning the Salerno beachhead altogether—although Clark quickly dismissed the idea, which in any case became moot the next day when a combination of plucky defense, brutal naval shelling, and the timely arrival of men from the Eighty-Second Airborne turned the tide.[31]

For Clark it proved to be a decisive moment. Ever conscious of his public image, he suddenly felt impatient with pedaling realistic stories to the home front. His career on the line, he was particularly keen to scotch any notion that he had contemplated abandoning Italy. This entailed mobilizing the censors. Communications had improved sufficiently in recent days to allow correspondents some chance of getting their stories off the beachhead. So Clark instructed his censors to cast an especially close eye on anything that might damage his reputation. The resulting copy scarcely enlightened the home front about the true state of the battle. One reporter merely noted that the German attack "didn't catch the Americans napping. They had expected it for some time and parried its full force with a quick side-stepping movement, pumping rifle fire and artillery shells into the enemy."[32] Even the fearless Stoneman had little choice but to go along. On September 13, Clark's men reduced his published reaction to that day's near disaster down to the anodyne statement that "at the present moment, the Americans are very hard pressed."[33]

In stark contrast, the reports emanating from Eisenhower's HQ continued to paint a far darker picture. On the basis of a high-command communiqué, the AP described Black Monday as "the most violent battle of the whole Mediterranean campaign," and the UP dubbed it "a battle to the death." Back home, many newspapers added to the sense of gloom by printing Nazi claims that the American retreat at Salerno "was as disastrous as that from Dunkerque."[34]

Outraged, Clark called reporters together for a conference. "From what I have heard on the radio during the past few nights," he began, "accounts published in America and England have given a rather black picture of what's happened here." That had no basis in reality, he insisted. "For every inch of ground gained, we have taken some blows but we've taken them well and I am proud of the way our men are already pushing the enemy back after securing our beachhead. We have had some hard going, but our situation was never desperate."[35]

While Allied troops struggled to retain the Salerno beachhead, Capa's run of bad luck returned with a vengeance. His Rome mission had been scratched. And with communications and equipment so scarce, Fifth Army had placed an embargo on new reporters coming into the beachhead. Despite his dogged persistence, Capa looked defeated. Hour after hour he would badger PROs in Sicily, pleading, cajoling, demanding a berth on one of the next boats, until at one point he even threatened to "swim across from Messina."

Then his fortunes suddenly turned. Capa discovered he could trade his designated berth on the Eighty-Second's aborted Rome mission for a place on the division's seaborne assault on Salerno. So on Black Monday, as the Fifth Army struggled to hang on to the beachhead, he joined a group of paratroopers assigned to a landing craft bound for Italy.[36]

After spending two frustrating days bobbing peacefully on the Mediterranean, the men on Capa's boat finally spotted land, late on the afternoon of September 15. From a distance, one reporter thought that the hulking Italian mountains "looked like the far-spreading curtain of a huge stage."[37] Capa finally strode onto this stage shortly after dark. Up close, the smoke laid to protect the beachhead from Luftwaffe raids obscured the moonlit vista. Through the mist, Capa could just about make out "the charred, half-submerged hulls of ships and barges, the flags waving over the white crosses of the first American cemetery on the European mainland." Now that the last German attempt to eradicate the beachhead had been beaten back, he found the press setup surprisingly orderly. But he remained so disoriented by the recent change in his own plans that, as he joked to one colleague, he could not make out if he was "air-borne, sea-borne, or still-born."[38]

In his memoirs, Capa insisted that as soon as he had gotten his bearings, he had headed straight to where a Rangers unit was engaged in a fierce fight to the north of the bridgehead, and calculated that these tough men would be the first to liberate Naples. The truth was more prosaic. On September 19, Mark Clark sent parts of the Eighty-Second Airborne north to reinforce the Rangers. Because Capa remained accredited to the Eighty-Second, the Fifth Army's PRO released a jeep that enabled him and two print reporters to travel with the paratroopers to witness this ongoing battle. It proved to be a chilling experience. Capa later recalled his visit to one of the Ranger first-aid stations, "I had been taking pictures of war and blood since Spain, but even after seven years the sight of torn flesh and fresh blood brought my stomach up close behind my eyes."[39]

Despite such horror, during the next two weeks Capa was in his element. He loved being with the Eighty-Second, who in turn appreciated "his professional competence, genial personality, and cheerful sharing of all dangers and hardships."[40] *Life* was paying him a guaranteed $600 a month, plus $100 for every page over six that it used for his pictures.[41] Crucially, the photos he sent back to New York pleased his *Life* bosses. They also chimed perfectly with the government's new determination to reveal a grittier side of the war—the broiling medics working without shirts, the uninviting foxholes carved into the cliffs beside a key road, and the anxious faces of officers as they directed naval guns on German positions.

Although photographing the protracted battle proved a grueling feat, Capa soon counted himself lucky in other ways. Since jeeps were still at a

Figure 10.2 Soldiers in and near foxholes, Chiunzi Pass, above Maiori, Italy, September 1943. Robert Capa. © International Center of Photography / Magnum Photos.

premium, communications sometimes unpredictable, and the press camp extremely primitive, Ken Clark refused to house any more correspondents in the theater.[42] As a result, Capa only had three rival photographers to worry about, one of whom was stuck with the unenviable task of snapping the image-obsessed Fifth Army commander. To Joe Phillips, who was monitoring the photo coverage from Algiers, the dearth of images was deeply troubling at a time when the Pentagon brass wanted pictorial coverage increased. "I would like to suggest that you do not have enough photographers," Phillips wrote to Ken Clark, "and that some of the ones you do have are not producing. . . . I do think your coverage is suffering."[43]

What Phillips lamented, Capa welcomed. He was, after all, in the midst of a big war without much competition. Nor did he much mind the paucity of all types of equipment. Indeed, rather than sit around grousing about the inadequate accommodations or parlous communications, he simply went out and took what he wanted. Transportation was a case in point. On one occasion in late September, Capa borrowed a jeep for several days—angering Ken Clark, who wanted to keep a tight rein on these precious vehicles. By the time Capa returned, he had taken all the shots he needed. Wearing his irrepressible grin, he managed to mute even Ken Clark as he tried to discipline the *Life* photographer.[44]

At the end of September, with Naples finally looming in the Fifth Army's sights, Capa swapped his jeep for a ride on a British tank. He arrived on liberation day, October 1, to find a grimy, starving city. The Germans might have left, but evidence of their recent presence lay everywhere: the destroyed port, the mined buildings, the graffiti daubed on grey walls. As Capa strolled the streets, he noticed a long line of Italians waiting outside a schoolhouse. Inside, he witnessed another horrific sight: "twenty primitive coffins, not well enough covered with flowers and too small to hide the dirty little feet of children—children old enough to fight the Germans and be killed, but just a little too old to fit in children's coffins." The scene made the next phase of the day seem particularly incongruous. Mark Clark was about to arrive to preside over a ceremony at the Royal Gardens. Already, his imperious air had earned him the nickname "Marcus Aurelius Clarkus." As Capa set up his camera, one of Clark's PR men came up and told him only to take photos of the general from his best side, the one showing the three stars on his cap.[45]

After briefly savoring this triumph, Clark and his army hit the road again. Capa eventually joined them near the Volturno River, where the fighting had settled down into a savage slugging match. "This was a job that pictures could do better than words," he wrote in his memoirs. "Here was a time for me to use my camera and like it." Capa certainly dragged himself "from mountain to mountain, from foxhole to foxhole, taking pictures of mud, misery, and death." But whether he liked it was another matter. As the temperatures plunged, the rain became icier by the day. "The winter at the front is not too agreeable," Capa wrote to his family, "but we don't always have to be there. I am well off," he added, "but a bit bored."[46]

"EISENHOWER SAYS HE DOES NOT RECOGNIZE SEX"

Then all of a sudden Capa had company. In mid-October Margaret Bourke-White appeared in Italy, ostensibly on assignment to cover the supply services for *Life*.[47]

In the hierarchy of the Luce empire the two photographers were surprisingly far apart. While Capa was the émigré arriviste—famous, but still needing to prove himself as a consistent performer for the organization—Bourke-White had been a Luce favorite for over a decade. In 1930 she had taken the first cover shot for *Fortune*; six years later she had done the same for *Life*. All the while she had compiled an illustrious overseas career, having become the first foreign photographer allowed into the Soviet Union, the first to photograph Stalin, and the first to take combat shots in Moscow and on the Eastern Front. On the back of these triumphs, Bourke-White had been the only *Life* photographer in the 1930s to have her own office, darkroom, and printer. With the war raging and his magazine sales high, Luce continued to indulge her. Whereas Capa liked to be on his own, armed just with a small, portable Leica, Bourke-White treated assignments like a full-blown expedition, arriving with no less than five cameras, "a battery of interchangeable lenses, various filters, film packs, flash guns, flash bulbs, a bedroll, and a typewriter."[48]

Yet for all their surface differences, these two great photographers shared many key attributes. Both were single-minded. Both were prepared to run huge risks to get their images. And both were hugely ambitious. Perhaps their greatest similarity, though, was to have good fortune at key moments. Italy was a prime example. Just as Capa's career was currently being boosted by the military's determination to depict the war more realistically, so Bourke-White suddenly became the beneficiary of the military's evolving attitude toward female correspondents.

Until now the ETO's response to women had been distinctly lukewarm, if not downright hostile. During the North African campaign Eisenhower had allowed female correspondents into the theater, but only to cover the

Women's Auxiliary Army Corps, which was charged mainly with clerical work and nursing. The AP's Ruth Cowan led the way in reporting this particular story, but she immediately encountered knee-jerk prejudice from Robert McClure, the chief PRO, and Wes Gallagher, her local bureau chief. Neither man viewed war as a suitable place for women, and left to their own devices they would have placed Cowan on the first boat back to the United States. As it was, Cowan and Inez Robb of the INS managed to spend a short spell with an evacuation hospital in Tunisia, but as soon as the German counterattack gathered pace in early 1943, their news organizations whisked them out of the theater.[49]

Bourke-White's overseas experiences proved quite different from Cowan's and Robb's. "*Life* photographers," observes her biographer, "were the princes then, performing the function and getting the money of anchormen now." By 1942 Bourke-White had become perhaps the biggest princess of all, and she quickly used the North African campaign to add to her almost-regal status.[50]

On the way to Algeria she survived a torpedo attack, spending hours in a sea-tossed lifeboat, a harrowing drama that she immediately turned into a compelling story for *Life*. Once on dry land, she traded on her fame, charisma, and charm, as well as the enormous clout of *Life* magazine. In Algiers, Jimmy Doolittle started her on her way. Aware that Bourke-White had been denied the chance to accompany a bombing mission to Germany, the media-savvy airman asked if she wanted to hitch a ride on a Flying Fortress raid over Tunisia. At the Biskra airbase, a close relationship with the commanding general quickly helped to seal the deal. The result was particularly striking. "*LIFE'S* BOURKE-WHITE GOES BOMBING," the magazine blared on March 1, "—First Woman to accompany US Air Force on combat mission photographs attack on Tunis."[51]

While Bourke-White's North African triumph had a profound impact on army officers, reactions varied in different theaters. In Britain, Eaker's pushy publicists wanted to build on her success, clarifying guidelines to ensure "that no discrimination . . . [was] made between men and women" unless the presence of a female reporter threatened to "interfere with crew performances." Perhaps the liberal attitude of the Eighth Air Force derived from its knowledge that most media bosses were reluctant to allow either men or women reporters to fly on bombing missions in the wake of Bob Post's death.[52] Whatever the cause, the Eighth's enlightened stance stood in stark contrast to the continued obstructionism at Eisenhower's headquarters. Here, Bourke-White's bombing escapade was viewed as an exception, and her presence in Algeria and Tunisia made officers even less likely to reassess their prejudices.

Many ETO officers, certainly, considered *Life*'s princess nothing but trouble. As a woman, they pointed out, she needed special facilities for dressing, washing, and so forth. To keep her safe and well briefed, the Pentagon assigned her a full colonel as a chaperone, but she still attracted far too much controversy. Everywhere she went rumor, gossip, and jealousy seemed to follow. Nor did Bourke-White's brash demeanor help her cause. Even many of her work colleagues considered her a prima donna, and the more misogynist officers were particularly glad when she left North Africa in March. As one of them hastened to inform *Life*, Bourke-White had "evaded PRO regulations, violated security, and broke the rules in other ways." It was scarcely a record likely to ease her passage back to the war—a fact confirmed by Eisenhower's suitably ambiguous parting comment that he would send her "to the right place" if she ever returned.[53]

In the late summer, as Bourke-White began angling for such a return, she shrewdly traded on a number of crucial assets that ultimately outweighed the military's mounting hostility. Apart from her fame and her position as the leading *Life* photographer, her timing was impeccable. Her bosses in New York fully supported her determination to get back to the front, perhaps to cover the engineers; more importantly, Joe Phillips in Algiers was under constant pressure to augment the photographic coverage of the Italian campaign. The head of the army supply services even came to Bourke-White, asking if she would head across the Atlantic again, this time to publicize his massive logistical operation in Algeria and Tunisia.[54]

Bourke-White's problems began when she pressed for permission to visit Italy. When Ike's deputy heard about this, he emphatically said no. All women at the front, he insisted, posed a nuisance. This particular woman, he added, would be a catastrophe. "No" did not deter Bourke-White, who reacted in a typically headstrong fashion. At the St. Georges Hotel, a harassed Joe Phillips bore the brunt of her persistent appeals. "Miss Bourke-White," he acerbically observed in the middle of October, "had brought her troubles to the attention of one full general, one lieutenant general, three major generals, uncounted brigadiers, and Christ knows how many colonels and lieutenant colonels," all of whom in turn had badgered him. This perseverance paid off. When Phillips finally briefed Ike on the subject, Eisenhower not only agreed to place "no obstructions" in Bourke-White's way, but also decided that the time had come to amend the ETO's overall policy. At a press conference on October 18, Ike announced that "he intended to give women correspondents exactly the same treatment [as] the men which means they can go anywhere with the approval of the commander on the spot." The more mischievous correspondents immediately saw that day's news frame. "EISENHOWER," they cabled in capitals, "SAYS HE DOES NOT RECOGNIZE SEX."

Even without this unhelpful headline, Eisenhower's press officers viewed their boss's announcement as a radical change. "I sit here today," Phillips wrote on October 19, "dowering [*sic*] at the thought of the army of women who probably will now besiege the War Department and the War Office for permission to come here." His British counterpart, Phillips added sardonically, was even more appalled, believing "that the foundations of Empire are truly shaken."[55]

It remained to be seen whether such a female army would ever lay siege to the Pentagon, let alone bring Britain's Empire to its knees. For the small battalion of women correspondents in the Mediterranean, though, there could be no doubt that they had won a major battle in the fight for equality. Doris Fleeson was the first to seize the fruits of victory. The forty-two-year-old former reporter for the *New York Daily News* had only recently arrived in the theater to a write a piece on the medical corps for *Women's Home Companion*. Somewhat to her surprise, she suddenly found that she had been granted permission "to join an evacuation hospital in Sicily, and go with it to Italy."[56]

Helen Kirkpatrick, the intrepid *Chicago Daily News* reporter, initially fared less well. Known for her expertise on political matters, Kirkpatrick had only just volunteered to cover the new Allied Military Government as it began trying to bring some order to the chaos of the rear, and so she dutifully headed off in that direction. Luckily, the men at headquarters viewed her as a reporter of "high repute and integrity." "In many ways," remarked Joe Phillips, "she was the best of the lot." On the basis of this judgment, Phillips happily angled to get her near to the front as soon as Fifth Army had sufficient space.[57]

Like Fleeson, Kirkpatrick found herself covering the medics, although her experiences proved far more harrowing. The field hospital where she lived for a few weeks was close to the front, and the Germans were "just over the hill on the other side." Because the carnage was so extensive, she often helped out the "terribly short-handed" nurses. "I did what errands I could do," she recalled after the war. "I found I could tolerate anything as long as I didn't see the face of the man. When they were operating on the head, that, I couldn't—I didn't care for that because the casualty became a person."[58]

Of course, showing the face of war's true horror was the main task of the photojournalists in Italy, including Margaret Bourke-White, who swiftly seized the opportunity created by Eisenhower's October 18 decree. She began in Naples, where she directed her camera at the tremendous destruction wrought by months of Allied bombing and weeks of German vandalism. Then she headed off to the front, where persistent rain often hampered her efforts to get decent shots. Undeterred, she slept in foxholes, flew over the frontline, and visited a field hospital, where a growing number of Texans from the ill-fated Thirty-Sixth Division lay suffering from severe wounds. She could just about take the nastiness that accompanied all these dimensions of the war. "But shelling," she wrote, "was different. Shelling was like a dentist with a drill. And with me, those shells found a nerve."[59]

Because of the grueling conditions, Bourke-White, like Capa, made regular trips back to Naples. The city might be half-destroyed and increasingly disease-ridden, but it at least provided some respite from the sights, sounds, and smells of combat. Besides, both photographers needed to post their packages of film back to the War Department. Although the Signal Corps developed some of their images in Naples, the remainder were sent straight to the Pentagon, where military censors checked both the pictures and the captions, before sending the acceptable ones on to New York. With Marshall's injunction to show more realism ringing in their ears, the censors increasingly passed grimmer photos, though how the two star photographers captured such scenes differed.[60]

Capa had long prided himself in getting close to the action. "If your pictures aren't good enough," he would declare, "then you aren't close enough." Bourke-White, by contrast, had always been happier snapping her subjects from on high, where she could explore a scene in its panoramic entirety. In Italy, Bourke-White's successful shots tended to be taken from mountaintop perches, where she recorded the drama of artillery duels. On one famous occasion, she even found a pilot who was willing to fly her over the front lines. The resulting photos revealed the war's unearthly quality: shell-induced pockmarks that left "Italy scarred like the face of the moon," or undulating patterns carved by tanks, heavy trucks, and artillery in the endless mud. Such sights caused Bourke-White's thoughts to wander, but as soon as the pilot reminded her that American infantrymen were "down there," she flinched. "The realization was almost more than I could bear," she wrote in a picture book that appeared a few months later, "—that our boys were trying to slog through that fatal square of earth being chewed up by high-explosive shells."[61]

Capa's pictures were grittier. They invariably showed GIs marching, crouching, and firing at the enemy; some even depicted the chilling sight of dead American soldiers lying prone in the mud. As a result, they were closer to what Roosevelt and Marshall had in mind for shaking domestic complacency. *Life* certainly thought so. Capa's latest images, the magazine observed at the start of 1944, "are grim and unsentimental, but they tell us something about what war is like in Italy. They prove it's a tough war."[62]

Yet it was also becoming a repetitive war: a series of intense artillery duels, followed by slow, short advances. Bourke-White's aerial shots provided a stunning new vision of the carnage wrought on this stalemated battlefield, but, as she knew only too well, her *Life* bosses would only publish one batch of such photos. Capa's up-close images showed a far more vivid side of the war than most of the home front had seen before, but even he quickly tired of photographing the same dismal sights. "The war is like an actress who is getting old," he told *Life* readers in early 1944. "It is less and less photogenic and more and more dangerous."[63]

Feeling that there were few camera-friendly images left to capture, Capa and Bourke-White both concluded that the time had come to head off—she home to write a book, he to London to prepare for the upcoming invasion of France.[64] The war in Italy continued to grind on, but it would increasingly be covered in a more traditional manner: by print correspondents, who had to confront the challenging task of warding off domestic complacency through words. Luckily for Roosevelt, Marshall, and the home front, the ideal man for this task was close at hand.

CHAPTER 11

Death in Winter

EXHAUSTED ERNIE

Ernie Pyle was a latecomer to the Italian battlefield, not arriving until November 1943. While Capa and Bourke-White were photographing the grim battles north of Salerno and Naples, Pyle had been enjoying two months' stateside leave. He desperately needed the rest.

The grueling months he had spent in the North African desert had gradually chipped away at Pyle's fragile constitution. Then came Sicily, with its tough terrain and scorching sun. Although Pyle began the campaign amid the unfamiliar luxury of a naval ship—sleeping soundly on a soft mattress, showering regularly under hot water, and dining splendidly with silver cutlery—he soon succumbed to "the worst exhaustion I've yet experienced."[1] Covering Patton's rapid dash to Palermo scarcely helped. So, a few days into the campaign, he checked himself into a medical clearing station complaining of "a burning fever and aching limbs." After a series of tests came back negative, the doctor diagnosed him as a victim of "too much dust, bad eating, exhaustion, and the unconscious nerve tension that comes to everybody in a front-line area."

Pyle had clearly needed a breather. He began by heading off to II Corps command, where he wrote a series of glowing stories about Omar Bradley—much to the amusement of John Thompson and Don Whitehead. "Forsaking the common soldier for a mess of general's pottage," joshed one. "Ernie Pyle sells out the GI not even for silver but for brass," ribbed the other.[2]

With these taunts ringing in his ears, Pyle did not let up for long, especially as there remained a war to cover—an increasingly grim, static war, in which his slogging GIs were battling slowly toward victory. Partially recovered, Pyle went off to report on the engineers, whose vital work not only rebuilt the bridges dynamited by the enemy but also provided the 50,000 gallons of water a division needed each day. Like most of the big-name reporters, he felt the inexorable pull of the tormenting thrust toward Troina, but by now, he could barely stand the pace. The next day, after walking just four miles with the infantry, he "had to lie down on the ground about half the time." "We were grimy, mentally as well as physically," he wrote soon after. "We'd drained our emotions until they cringed from being called out from hiding."[3]

Sick of war—sick, too, with the "terrific pressure" of finding new angles of writing about war—Pyle left Sicily once victory had been achieved. After a brief stop in Algiers, he boarded the Clipper flying boat, landing safely in New York on September 7.

Having spent so many weeks roughing it, Pyle hoped for a long sleep in a soft bed in the Algonquin Hotel. But within ten minutes of dozing off, the phone rang. A newspaper wanted an interview. So did one of the radio networks. Army intelligence needed to ask him questions. Pyle suddenly recognized what his editors had long known: he was now a major celebrity. Indeed, a reporter whose column appeared in 162 newspapers, with a total circulation of nine million each day, could scarcely expect much peace. Wherever he went, the phone would "never be silent"—as soon as he hung up, there would always be a new call waiting.[4]

One particularly intriguing telephone message came from Hollywood. At the behest of the War Department, producer Lester Cowan wanted to make a movie about the infantry. Keen to bolster the image of this unglamorous service, Cowan thought Pyle's columns would provide the perfect basis for a screenplay.

Flattered by the prospect, Ernie initially agreed. But he soon had second thoughts. Making wartime movies needed the Pentagon's full cooperation. And the more Pyle got to know about the Pentagon, the more he realized that its new policy of encouraging realistic war news had not permeated every corner of that sprawling building. "The hitch now," he remarked about the movie project toward the end of his leave, "is that the War Department, following the same censorship policy exercised in North Africa of wanting to make the war 'nice,' want the damn thing to be a flag-waving, war-is-glorious, nobody-gets-killed, happy ending sort of thing."[5]

On reflection, Pyle realized that the only way to counteract this dangerously sanitized view of the war would be to return to the front and produce a series of columns with a harsher, more realistic edge. He did not find the prospect terribly enticing. Indeed, he considered the "popular heroic myth" that returning warriors were soon itching to get back to the combat zone nothing more than "pap" and "tish." "I've never hated to do anything as badly in my life," Pyle explained to his readers, "as I hate to go back to the front. I dread it and am afraid of it." But at a time when the draft denied other men of his generation a choice in how they experienced the war, he felt unable to sit comfortably in New York, Washington, or Hollywood and enjoy the perks of fame.[6]

So after catching up with friends and family, fulfilling as many speaking engagements as possible, and trying to drink himself half to death in a vain effort to forget past and future battlefields, Pyle headed back across the Atlantic. His bosses were naturally delighted that his battlefield observations would again be appearing in almost two hundred newspapers.[7] Over a cordial lunch at Washington's plush Mayflower Hotel, Roy Howard did make a half-hearted attempt to direct Pyle to the Pacific, where he could work his magic on General Douglas MacArthur's island-hopping campaign against the Japanese. But Pyle demurred. Asia held no appeal, not compared to the men and units he knew so well from North Africa and Sicily. And Howard gracefully let Pyle have his own way, doubtless aware that his star columnist was such a draw that, if he were ever minded to leave, he could command at least $50,000 a year from competitors.[8]

Those in the military who wanted a more realistic edge to front-line reports were also happy. Indeed, if his past record was any guide, Pyle could be trusted to add a little more death and destruction to daily news coverage of the fighting without making it too unpalatable for squeamish newspaper readers.

"DEPRESSED BY THE WAR"

Pyle arrived in Italy in the second half of November. Somewhat to his surprise, he initially found the conditions tolerable, if not pleasant. On his first trip to the front he faced few moments of real hazard and even caught an occasional glimpse of the sun. Soon after, he headed to the capacious Caserta Palace, a building so big—and drafty—that one wag claimed it was "the only house where I've had my hat blown off indoors." The Fifth Army's PRO had established its new base in a small corner alongside the rest of Clark's staff, setting aside a series of rooms for correspondents.[9] Pyle shared his with Clark Lee of the INS and Reynolds Packard of the UP, and, at first, it lived up to its chilly billing. Then to Ernie's amazement, it suddenly became livable. Workmen came and replaced the blown-out windowpanes. An overattentive Italian boy appeared from nowhere and—unbidden—built a welcoming fire in the grate, decorated the table with flowers, and even washed the three reporters' dirty clothes. Only Packard was miffed, complaining that the boy "keeps everything so neat and regimented he can't find a thing." The other two thought that it would be "tough to leave" these unexpected comforts behind.

Yet Pyle soon found that he had been so ground down by his earlier war experiences that even such relative luxuries could not leaven his gloomy mood. On returning from an early sojourn to the Italian front, he recognized that he now got "touched" a little "too easily" by combat conditions. "It's hard to see and be part of the misery," he remarked privately, "and not be affected by it." After a few days of drinking too much by the fire, he even hankered for "mud and cold" in the hope that some real physical hardship might help obliterate the depressing thoughts that filled his mind.[10]

It was a wish that was easy to accommodate on the Italian front. After finally crossing the bending Volturno River, at the start of November, the Fifth Army now faced a series of sturdy German defensive positions. First there was the Bernard Line, which protected the Migano Gap, with the small village of San Pietro Infine to the right, sitting snugly in the shadow of the hulking Monte Sammurco. Beyond that lay the Gustav Line, based

Figure 11.1 Ernie Pyle (*center*) with the troops in Italy. National Archives 111-SC-191704.

on the Rapido River, with the Monte Cassino in front as an added protector. Even to the untrained eye, the task ahead looked daunting: a series of valleys shielded both by rivers and mountains, which German veterans had plowed with mines before retiring to well-camouflaged dugouts to ready their artillery and sniper fire. And then there was the weather. Not the famed Italian sunshine but an atypically harsh winter in which heavy rain fell on three-quarters of the days between mid-October and the end of the year. As the Allied troops inched northward, the fighting quickly began to resemble the muddy trench warfare of World War I. Shells and raindrops falling constantly from the sky left behind "a landscape that seemed almost lunar in its desolation," according to one soldier, "where men lived and died in so many unremembered ways."[11]

During his time at the front Pyle wanted to ensure that at least a fraction of those who had lived and died in this Italian wasteland were not forgotten. This, as ever, was the conscious task he set himself. Deep down, however, another process was at work. Consumed by increasingly dark thoughts, he could not help but convey some of the true horror that the soldiers were suffering. "I seem to become more and more depressed by the war," he confessed to his wife on New Year's Day 1944. "I'm low over it for days at a time and am sure it has affected my writings."[12] Pyle's writing had indeed been affected by the harsh conditions in Italy—most obviously during the fighting two weeks earlier.

In mid-December the bloody battle to capture San Pietro Infine produced a reunion of many of the reporters who had witnessed the equally vicious fight in Sicily four months before. Don Whitehead was there, having traipsed north with the troops from Naples. So was Homer Bigart, who had been assigned to the Mediterranean as reward for his strong coverage of the German bombing campaign. Now, during a lazy hour, both men sat and swapped stories with Pyle in a suitably lugubrious setting: a run-down cowshed at the foot of Monte Sammurco.[13]

The shed served as a base camp for the mule drivers who were taking supplies to the men from the Thirty-Sixth Division. Mule driving, though a crucial form of transport in the Italian hills, was the type of unspectacular work that rarely attracted the interest of A-list correspondents—and indeed Bigart and Whitehead soon headed off in the direction of San Pietro, hoping to get a sense of how the main assault was faring. But Pyle stayed put. He was intrigued by the vital, if unglamorous, aspects of military life, and watched in admiration as the men loaded up the mules by day and forced the stubborn creatures up steep, slippery paths by night. Pyle also knew that an important battle was being fought at the top of Monte Sammurco. Texans from the Thirty-Sixth Division had captured the peak almost a week before. Since then, they had suffered from the cold, a lack of sleep, and above all, a series of punishing German attempts to drive them off that key position. Perhaps, once that battle was over, the survivors would descend with some stirring stories for his column.

Late into the night, the mule drivers slowly made their way back down the mountain. Pyle emerged out of the cowshed as they approached. The moonlight was strong enough to cast shadows behind the soldiers who were trundling into camp, and Pyle could just about discern the gruesome cargo strapped on to the mules' backs: five dead American soldiers, "their heads hanging down on one side, their stiffened legs sticking out awkwardly from the other, bobbing up and down as the mules walked."[14]

One of the dead was Captain Henry T. Waskow, a company commander. "He was very young," Pyle wrote of Waskow, "only in his middle twenties, but he carried in him a sincerity and gentleness that made people want to be guided by him." When his comrades realized what had happened, Pyle explained, two of them bent over his body and tenderly offered their apologies. A third

> reached down and took the captain's hand, and he sat there for a full five minutes holding the dead hand in his own and looking intently into the dead face. And he never uttered a sound all the time he sat there. Finally he put the hand down. He reached over and gently straightened the points of the captain's shirt collar, and then sort of rearranged the tattered edges of the uniform around the wound, and then he got up and walked away down the road in the moonlight, all alone.[15]

Pyle's dispatch was not published for another month, until after Waskow's family had been notified of his death. But when it finally appeared, the public response was overwhelming. The *Washington Daily News*, Pyle's editor noted proudly, "devoted its entire first page to the column—not even a headline, just solid text." The paper sold out within hours. For the next few days, radio commentators read Pyle's moving story on air, as editorial writers discussed its deeper meanings. Some concluded that it signified the enlisted men's reverence for their commanders, while the *Washington Post* declared that the soldiers leaning over the captain's body had "silently dedicated themselves to fiercer opposition to oppression."[16]

For Pyle, the column simply underlined his new theme: death. A year earlier, he had emphasized the creation of the new civilian army. Now he was drawn to focus not on this army's destruction, but on the destruction of many—perhaps too many—individual lives.

DEATH EVERYWHERE

Pyle, however, was not unique. In one sense, writing about death was nothing more than a natural reaction to the reality that lay all around. The fighting at San Pietro proved so bloody that the area soon became known as "Purple Heart Valley." When Bigart and Whitehead had made their dash across the treacherous land around San Pietro, they were lucky not to have become victims themselves: only Bigart's sharp reactions and loud shout had saved Whitehead from a German mine. Many others were not so fortunate. As Bigart wrote in his dispatch of the battle, there were dead GIs everywhere. "One boy lay crumpled in a shallow slit trench beneath a rock," he told his *New York Herald Tribune* readers.

> Another, still grasping his rifle, peered from behind a tree, staring with sightless eyes toward the Liri plain. A third lay prone where he had fallen. He had heard the warning scream of a German shell. He had dropped flat on his stomach but on level ground affording no cover. Evidently some fragments had killed him instantly, for there had been no struggle. Generally there is no mistaking the dead—their strange contorted posture leaves no room for doubt. But this soldier, his steel helmet tilted over his face, seemed merely resting in the field. We did not know until we came within a few steps and saw a gray hand hanging limply from his sleeve.[17]

If death offered an obvious frame, witnessing, remembering, and writing about it clearly took a toll. Pyle spent much of the Christmas period enveloped in an alcoholic haze, working his way systematically through "a large supply of very good gin and very bad cognac" in a desperate effort to numb his angst-ridden thoughts. Soon after, he began complaining of a series of new aches and pains. Then he succumbed to a nasty cold, which plunged him so low that he headed to Naples for a rest—despite his hatred of cities. Pyle only really started to recover after he went to live with an infantry company for a brief period and could spend his days and nights in the open. But at the start of 1944 he began to encounter a major problem that greatly hampered his ability to record the war's true horror: he felt repelled by, rather than attracted to, the prospect of spending time at the front. "I seem more and more reluctant to go up," he wrote to his wife, "—I think it's as much a shying away from a consciousness of the misery of the kids up there, as it is fear of personal discomfort."

So instead of spending more time with the GIs, Pyle decided to report on the growing number of air crews stationed in Italy. Eaker was now in charge, having been shunted from Britain to the Mediterranean at the end of the year. As publicity conscious as ever, the air commander welcomed the famous columnist with open arms, putting him up in a big apartment with a wonderful view. Pyle's main ailments quickly abated, but he remained plagued by an enervating lethargy. "I just feel all the time like I'd like to lie down and sleep," he remarked privately. For a time, this lassitude even prevented him from keeping up to date with his column, but the change of scene helped, as did a chance to use the air force to push his new theme.[18]

Infantrymen, Pyle wrote in the middle of January, "live and die so miserably and they do it with such determined acceptance that your admiration for them blinds you to the rest of the war." But air men died, too, he reminded his readers, only in different circumstances. "You have to make some psychological adjustments when you switch from the infantry to the Air Forces," Pyle wrote. "The association with death is on a different basis. You approach death rather decently in the Air Forces. You die well-fed and clean-shaven, if that's any comfort."[19]

For those who could take scant comfort in American boys dying well-groomed and well-nourished, Pyle moved on to report on the work of the medics who saved so many lives. It ought to have been a more uplifting narrative, but Ernie was in no mood to highlight its positive aspect. Front-line hospitals, he reported, were often as grimy as the trenches soldiers had been rescued from. Doctors, he added, helped many of the wounded pull through; they also treated others who would never be the same again.

Pyle got his first experience of an Italian front-line hospital when visiting Dick Tregaskis at the end of December. Like Ernie, Tregaskis had become a media star during the past year, by turning his experiences with the marines on Guadalcanal into a bestselling book that Hollywood had just made into a hit movie. But if Pyle felt dejected every time he contemplated heading toward the fighting, Tregaskis was hooked. "The lure of the front is like an opiate," he jotted in his diary on November 21. "After abstinence and the tedium of workaday life, its attraction becomes more and more insistent. Perhaps the hazards of battle, perhaps the danger itself, stir the imagination and give transcendent meaning to things ordinarily taken for granted."

Keen to get a new fix, the next day Tregaskis accompanied a patrol to watch a battle unfolding at the top of one of the endless mountain peaks on the road to Rome. On his way up a rocky mule path, he saw that all the stones were covered in blood—the macabre detritus left by all the wounded who had retreated down over the past days. At the top, Tregaskis got a fabulous view of the unfolding battle, but also a sense of "how puny" the Allies' destructive efforts had been given the sheer vastness of the mountainous terrain they still had to subdue. Descending gingerly, he began to feel a sense of excitement as he contemplated writing up his story—the first time in a few weeks that he had grabbed "a bang-up eyewitness story of an action at a crucial sector of the front." The next thing he remembered was hearing a scream, followed by a series of massive explosions. When he came to, he realized he had been badly wounded: a piece of shell had penetrated his helmet and gouged a large hole in his skull. Luckily, a medic soon appeared to bandage his head and administer a shot of morphine. Although Tregaskis could barely walk or talk, he somehow made it down the hill to a tent hospital mired in mud, where a "crude scaffolding of board" served as an operating table.[20]

Pyle visited Tregaskis a few weeks later, and the resulting column was full of praise for his fellow reporter's quiet modesty, scholarly mien, and fierce determination to return to the front after recuperating. Tregaskis's chilling experience of trudging up that blood-stained path remained locked in a brain that still had trouble talking, let alone writing; but Pyle more than compensated with a graphic description of hospital life—from the overworked doctors who had extracted "more than a dozen pieces of bone and steel out of Dick's brain, along with some of the brain itself," to the intensive after-therapy treatment, whose the aim was readying such casualties for a return to the extreme hazards and harsh discomforts of front-line life.[21]

Like Pyle, the doctors who witnessed war's darkest side could not help but mull over its deeper meaning. Ernie was particularly interested in the thoughts of one medic who had been "touched by what he calls the 'mental wreckage' of war—the men whose spirits break under the unusual strain and incessant danger of the battlefield." Senior officials in Washington fretted that the public was too distant from the current war to understand its full dimensions; this medical officer believed that the problem ran far deeper. In another dark column, published in January, Pyle outlined the doctor's thinking: "He feels that American children in recent generations have had too much parental protection and too little opportunity for self-sufficiency," Pyle wrote, "and that the resulting weakness makes a man crumble when faced with something he feels he cannot bear." Americans therefore needed to toughen up—and the doctor thought that journalists had a crucial role to play in this vital process, albeit as role models whose life experiences equipped them for stress, rather than as reporters of war's harsh reality. "If he could pick a company of men best suited for warfare," Pyle reported the doctor as saying, "he'd choose all ex-newsboys. He thinks they would have shifted themselves so early in life that they would have built up an inner strength that would carry them thru battle."[22]

Pyle was not so sure. He knew his own inner strength was ebbing away. In mid-January, as Clark planned yet another amphibious assault, this time to outflank the major German defensive line at Monte Cassino by landing two divisions at Anzio, Ernie passed up a chance to accompany the GIs on a landing craft. His thinking was partly practical: "everybody's stuff had to be pooled," he explained to his wife, "and you can't very well pool a column." But he also remained plagued by a stiff cold, and in truth, he just "didn't want to" witness yet another offensive. He much preferred to stay with the bomber boys, where he could try to shake off his sluggishness, fix the broken cylinder on his typewriter, and reconstruct his "cushion" of columns.[23]

Pyle was not the only reporter who was suffering. Hal Boyle, his columnist colleague, had traipsed all the way north from Salerno, operating mostly as the AP's roving correspondent, charged with recording his experiences with the front-line GIs. In North Africa, Boyle had almost drowned when landing on a Moroccan beach, before retreating with the troops at Kasserine and braving sniper fire in Bizerte. Now, he pined for those relatively carefree days. The Italian fighting was too "tough," he told a colleague. The German fortifications were "unbelievable; nothing like in Tunisia."[24] Then there was the constant shelling. Before leaving the United States in October 1942, Boyle had excitedly pictured himself following in the footsteps of the heroic war correspondents of the past. Now, this particular illusion had been shattered as well. "Nothing takes that Richard Harding Davis complex out of your system," he half-jokingly commented, "like an artillery barrage. You really long for civilian days at home when life was a simple routine of suicides, husband poisonings, elections, paternity suits, and ax murders."[25]

Because the conditions in Italy were so dismal and dangerous, Boyle added, correspondents needed three traits to succeed: "a strong stomach, a weak mind, and plenty of endurance."[26] Many lacked the latter. By November the morale of some reporters was "very low." The press bosses who had toured the front-line understood why. Before Tregaskis was wounded, Barry Faris, the INS editor-in-chief, had joined him on a hair-raising daylong journey to the front and back, sheltering from shells and a strafing. Faris was quick to admit that it was not an experience he ever wanted to repeat.[27]

Despite the danger, most correspondents had no choice on most days but to revisit the battlefield. The war reporter, observed Pyle's roommate Clark Lee, takes his "risks with everyone else, but he doesn't get it in as sustained doses as the front line soldier," for the simple reason that he needed to return periodically to HQ to file his story. "On the other hand," Lee added, "he gets it more frequently, because his job is to go where things are happening."[28] The main problem for those correspondents struggling to cope was that too much was happening in Italy in the early months of 1944.

CHAPTER 12

Anzio and Cassino

"IT'S SURE NOT A SOFT WAR"

Despite the gloom, grime, and gore, Rome seemed tantalizingly by the middle of January 1944. After six weeks and sixteen thousand casualties, the Fifth Army had finally made it through the Bernhard Line. Now, directly ahead lay the Liri Valley, a relatively flat plain that accommodated Highway 6, the main route to the Italian capital, eighty miles away. Only two obstacles blocked the Allies' path, but both were formidable. The Rapido River gushed directly in front of the Fifth Army's new forward positions, its value as a defensive barrier heightened by its steep muddy banks and swollen waters. On either side of the Liri Valley sat a series of forbidding mountains, including one to the right that housed the imposing Monte Cassino abbey, whose peaks were bristling with German guns. Still, Clark was determined to push north toward Rome. In an effort to avoid the destructive power of the Cassino guns, he decided to launch a night crossing of the Rapido River on January 20, using the Thirty-Sixth (Texas National Guard) Division, which had already borne the brunt of the fighting at Salerno and San Pietro.

The GIs set off soon after dark. Although the engineers had cleared paths through the minefields that lay between the Thirty-Sixth and the river, German patrols had re-laid some mines, and the markers delineating the paths were difficult to spot in the dark. Many of the troops came under vicious fire even before they got near the riverbank. On reaching their boats, some found them severely damaged by enemy artillery fire; others dropped them along the marshy paths, as they took cover from incoming shells. The thick fog enveloping the river offered some protection, but it also compounded the confusion. After a couple of hours, less than a hundred men had made it across the Rapido, as the Germans poured down a deadly retaliatory fire.

Dawn revealed the size of the debacle. It also promised to make a bad situation far worse, for the enemy artillery could now see precisely whom to target. But Clark would not be deterred. He pressed his officers "to get tanks across and tank destroyers across [the Rapido] promptly," so that the reinforcements could help expand the precarious bridgehead on the far bank of the river. It proved to be a vain order. The engineers were unable to build bridges substantial enough to accommodate tanks. Although they did construct a few footbridges, the reinforcements that trickled across came too late to make a difference. By January 22, it was clear that the effort to cross the Rapido had failed, and so Clark belatedly ordered the pockets of survivors to make another harrowing journey across the icy river, back to the safety of their own lines.[1]

There, the men found a group of correspondents waiting to record their traumatic experiences, including Cyrus L. Sulzberger of the *New York Times*. Until now, Sulzberger had been more of a front-line dabbler. Rather than spend long periods with the GIs, he had "hitch-hiked" all around the war zones, from reporting on Monty's Eighth Army in Cairo to having virtually everything he wrote about Stalin's Red Army censored in Moscow. Yet what Sulzberger lacked in sustained experience of the fighting, he more than made up for in high-placed connections.

That his "uncle Arthur" published the *New York Times* had certainly done his career at the paper no harm, although his advancement derived from much more than nepotism. Cy Sulzberger had his own happy knack of acquiring friends in high places, which helped to account for his so often seeming to be in the right place at the right time. On his last visit to the American front, in North Africa, Sulzberger was the correspondent closest to the historic juncture between GIs and Tommies in North Africa and had duly grabbed a notable scoop. Almost a year later, he arrived at the Palace of Caserta just in time to find a "big commotion" among the top brass. Clark, he soon discovered, planned to pierce the Gustav Line, and Sulzberger jumped at the chance to head north toward this new battle.[2]

Sulzberger reached the Rapido just in time to witness the carnage of the battlefield and to interview the American survivors. Both appalled him. "It was a noisy, messy, bloody affair," he remembered much later. "For the first time in my experience I heard American GIs muttering to each other of mutiny." Sulzberger avoided referencing muntinous sentiments in his dispatches, knowing full well that the censors had already blocked stories on the dishonorable discharge of men who had left their units without permission.[3] Yet in other ways he pulled no punches. American forces, he wrote, had received "a terrific drubbing." Having endured minefields and "a trap of machine gun crossfire," Sulzberger explained, these troops had been forced to withdraw "by swimming through the raging, icy water." "One unit was cut off and simply stayed, fighting to the last man. There were so many casualties," he elaborated, "that a sergeant of one company had to go back for first aid, recrossing the river by swimming past a blown-up bridge. There was no one left in that area but enlisted men."

Over the past four months, the Texans of the Thirty-Sixth Division had already suffered so much hardship, from Black Monday on the Salerno beachhead to the Purple Heart Valley around San Pietro, but Sulzberger thought the Rapido battle "was about the toughest action of its kind that these troops had yet met." The GIs agreed. "It's sure not a soft war," they told the *Times* man.[4]

Back in Washington, many senior officials applauded the candor of the *Times*' stories, no one more so than the president. On most afternoons Roosevelt visited the office that had recently been converted from a ladies' cloakroom into the grandly titled White House Map Room: a state-of-the-art communications center manned around the clock by army and navy officers. By the end of January, the messages these officers were handing the president told a dark story—and not only of the Rapido debacle.[5]

Clark had launched the river attack with a broader strategic goal in mind. If the Rapido crossing failed to punch a hole through the German defenses around Cassino, he still hoped it would deflect the enemy's attention away from Italy's western coast fifty miles to the north, where two Allied divisions had landed at Anzio on January 22.[6] The Anzio assault had been Churchill's brainchild. The British prime minister saw it as an audacious move to outflank the Gustav Line, cutting the Germans' supply route to Cassino and forcing the enemy to retreat north, beyond Rome. The reality proved very different. Although the Rapido attack had drawn enough Germans south to make the initial Anzio landing an easy walkover, neither event knocked the enemy off balance. On the contrary, the Germans had sufficient troops not just to halt a series of piecemeal Allied attacks on the forbidding terrain around Cassino, but also to contain, and even threaten to eradicate, the Anzio beachhead. As a result, instead of a bold and bloodless breakthrough to Rome, by February the Fifth Army faced not one, but two, costly fiascos.[7]

Roosevelt decided that this was no time to sugarcoat the bad news. Of course, it is always easier for politicians to be candid about a disaster that is the fault of others—in this case, Churchill. But Roosevelt continued to believe that the public needed to be jolted out of its complacency about the ease and inevitability of the war's successful outcome.

On February 11, after meeting with his top military advisers, the president summoned the White House press corps to the Oval Office. In most press conferences, the president ducked and dodged the reporters' questions with such aplomb that many of them simply watched in awe. On this day, he decided to be much more forthright. Asked about the war in Italy, he gave an uncharacteristically blunt response. "It's a very tense situation," he admitted, with "very heavy fighting."[8]

The headlines the next day trumpeted the president's pessimism. Roosevelt "Points to Danger in Italy," declared the *New York Times*. "Roosevelt: Situation Tense in Italy," proclaimed the *Christian Science Monitor*.[9] Near the battlefield, however, the war correspondents suddenly found it difficult to follow the president's clear lead. In recent months they had been allowed, if not encouraged, to accentuate the negative. At Anzio, a variety of factors combined to transform the situation.

"THEY ARE AFRAID THAT THE PUBLIC CANNOT STAND THE SHOCK OF BAD NEWS"

Bigart, Stoneman, and Whitehead had accompanied the initial armada bound for Anzio. A few days earlier, they had each won a place by participating in the customary lottery, and at first, as Stoneman explained, they had experienced the "thrill that you might [have] in a poker game to discover that [you] have drawn high cards." Moments later, however, all the three began "to think things over." "Upon discovering that we are going into a knock-down drag-out battle with nothing but our typewriter," Stoneman elaborated on January 19, "we wonder whether our insurance is paid. Next we wonder why in the devil we ever got into the newspaper business." The word on the grapevine predicted that Anzio would be a really nasty affair: "an area full of mines, heavily covered by all kinds of machine guns and artillery, and defended by good German troops."[10]

In the early hours of January 22, Bigart, Stoneman, and Whitehead waded ashore to an eerie quiet. Fifty miles to the south, the Rapido still ran red with American blood, but the region around Anzio seemed almost deserted. After stumbling ashore in the darkness, Whitehead headed into some woods to wait for dawn to break. As soon as the sun began to burn off the sea mist, he unwrapped his typewriter from its waterproofing, sat on a tree stump, and began pounding out his story. "We walked in behind the German lines today," Whitehead wrote, "with scarcely a shot fired in a most sensational amphibious operation. It was so easy and simply done and caught the Germans so completely by surprise that, as I write this dispatch six hours after the landing, American troops are standing with their mouths open and shaking their heads in amazement."[11]

In the absence of a fierce German reception, the Fifth Army's PR team managed to get Whitehead's dispatch off the beachhead posthaste. It hit the wires that same evening, allowing the AP to beat its rivals and grab a major scoop in all the Sunday papers.[12]

Stoneman, Whitehead, and Bigart remained wary. They knew only too well that in North Africa, Sicily, and Salerno, the German riposte had taken days, if not weeks, to gather momentum. In his second Anzio dispatch, which detailed the landing's "clock-like precision," Whitehead cautioned his readers to be aware "of the danger that is sure to develop when the enemy counterattacks." Two days later Stoneman looked toward the Alban Hills and mused on how close the Allies were to Rome. Then he added his own warning. "Unfortunately," Stoneman conceded, "the intervening ground is full of Germans, and for obvious reasons we are not sticking our necks out."[13]

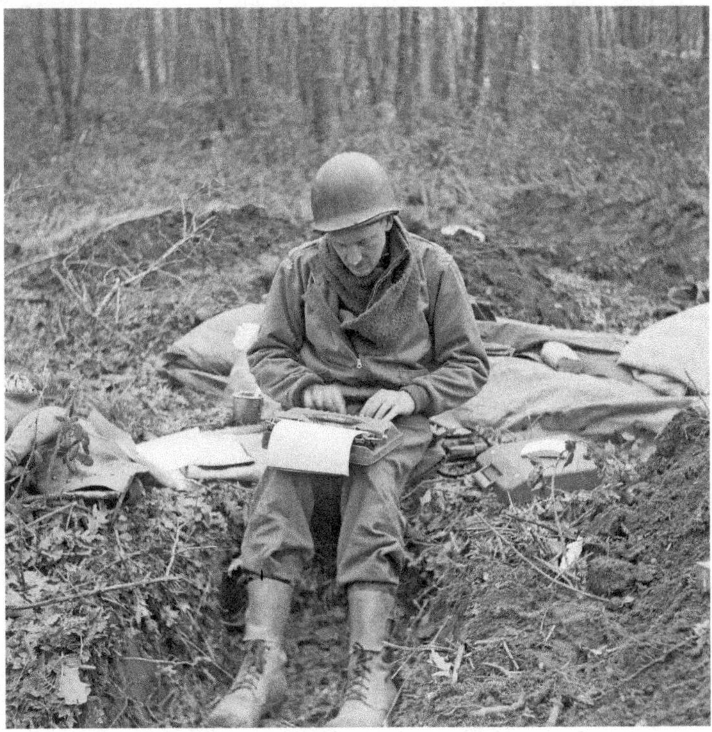

Figure 12.1 Don Whitehead tapping out a story in the Anzio beachhead, January 1944. © PA Photos Limited.

Among the senior Allied commanders, the need to add a cautionary caveat seemed to have gotten lost in the recent command shake-up. Eisenhower had left the theater for good on the last day of 1943, having been handpicked by Roosevelt to head the biggest operation of all: the second front against northern France scheduled for the spring. Field Marshal Henry Maitland Wilson had replaced Ike, but the real power above Clark's Fifth Army resided with General Sir Harold R. L. G. Alexander, who commanded the Fifteenth Army Group.

The Brits Wilson and Alexander did not share Washington's concerns about the public's complacency. In fact, after almost four-and-a-half years of war, they felt that their compatriots back home needed to be told some good news for a change. So after a brief visit to the Anzio bridgehead, on January 26, Alexander reassured reporters that "everything is going wonderfully." A few days later, Wilson's Algiers HQ went even further, hinting to its press corps that the fall of Rome's was imminent.[14]

The correspondents based in Algiers and Naples had little choice but to accept the sanguine steer; the reporters at the beachhead, however, knew that these claims had little grounding in reality. The Allies' problems at Anzio had begun with the limited availability of landing craft, which constrained how many men could be shipped onto the beachhead. From the very beginning, Major General John P. Lucas, the commander on the ground, had been worried that he lacked the troops to sustain a deep penetration inland against any concerted German resistance. He therefore ordered his troops to dig in, rather than push on to capture the key positions of Cisterna and Campoleone, let alone the distant Alban Hills.

Whatever the wisdom of Lucas's decision, the delay gave the Germans a chance to rally. On the night of January 30, the Allies received their first nasty taste of the enemy's strengthening presence. Having waited over a week to gather more troops and armor, Lucas ordered two Ranger battalions to infiltrate the enemy's positions around Cisterna. Their goal was to wreak havoc and pave the way for the main assault a few hours later. Almost immediately, the Rangers marched straight into an unexpectedly large number of Germans. The result was a disaster of the first magnitude. Of the 767 men who went into battle, only six returned. The others "were either killed or captured," resulting, as one scholar has put it, in "a staggering loss rate of 99 percent."[15]

The elite US Army Rangers had until this moment been a major hit with war correspondents. Hal Boyle had spent time with them in Tunisia, lured by their audacious, and successful, bayonet charge on an Italian outpost in the desert. Robert Capa had joined the Rangers, too, shortly after landing at Salerno, enticed by the fact that they "talked like jerks, fought like killers—and once I found them crying like heroes."[16] Now, as their commander sat privately sobbing at the loss of so many of his men, the censors placed the Rangers totally off limits. Not until March 8 did they permit the press to mention what one reporter dubbed the "grim secret." And even then, correspondents could only piece together "the fragmentary picture framed by a few who returned." "Even now," observed the AP dispatch, "it is not known whether they were the victims of a clever German trap or merely a fantastic fluke of war."[17]

The precise cause of the Rangers' fate may have remained murky, but by February few reporters had any doubt about the ultimate source of the beachhead's woes: the Wehrmacht's obvious determination to wipe out Lucas's force.

Each morning, the Anzio correspondents would gather at headquarters, sitting stiffly in "hard-backed chairs, like a class at school." Then Colonel Joe Langevin would walk in and address them in his brisk, efficient manner. Normally, the reporters came away impressed by Langevin's "frank" statements about the problems at the beachhead. Indeed, as one of them recalled after the war, though Langevin always tried to strike "a note of confidence," he never hesitated to break "bad news straight away."[18]

Before long, correspondents did not need Langevin's briefings to realize just how bad the news was. Enemy shelling intensified first. Then the sound of a vicious fight could be heard to the left of the beachhead. The arrows on the briefing-room maps now pointed inward from the crucial positions around Campoleone and Cisterna, suggesting that the Germans were in a position to drive Allied forces back toward the sea. Soon, the correspondents could see it all for themselves. The press headquarters offered them some protection from the incessant shelling, for it "leaned against a squat cliff which ran down the beach." On clear days, the reporters could climb up to the roof and gaze at the entire beachhead, which stretched only seven miles inland and fifteen miles along the beach.[19]

Alarmed by what they saw and heard, the correspondents began to challenge the military's optimistic line. "We never were more frightened than we were last night," Stoneman wrote in a dispatch at the end of January—"a cold, glaring night with the Luftwaffe coming over in steady waves, our guns roaring steadily, and acoustic effects that almost bounced us out of our beds." Bigart agreed. In two stories at the start of February, he told his *New York Herald Tribune* readers of the enemy's "desperate bids to seize the initiative," which resulted in "five days of bitter fighting for Cisterna."[20]

Before long, even the HQ reporters began adopting a downbeat tone. Radio news reports—which seven out of ten Americans rated as their "preferred news source"—made the biggest splash.[21] On February 11, as Roosevelt proffered his gloomy assessments of the battlefield situation, John Charles Daly of CBS broadcast from Naples: "The situation in the beachhead is grim," he reported, "we have been forced to give ground . . . the Germans have massed strong forces against us." Minutes later, Chester Morrison, his NBC rival in Algiers, was even more alarmist, insisting that the struggle at Anzio had become "desperate."[22]

These radio reports alarmed Winston Churchill. The prime minister had envisaged Anzio as a daring gambit that could jumpstart the Allies' efforts, making the Gustav Line untenable and the liberation of Rome inevitable. After three weeks, the best that could be said for the operation was that Allied troops were just about managing to survive. "I had hoped that we were hurling a wildcat onto the shore," Churchill famously remarked, "but all we had got was a stranded whale." Even worse from his perspective, this particular beached mammal threatened to have political claws as sharp as any wildcat, especially since it reminded the prime minister's critics of the disastrous Gallipoli Campaign—the World War I misadventure that had almost destroyed his budding career. Keen to head off a major inquest, Churchill, on February 12, fired off an urgent cable to his top generals. Referring to Morrison's description of a "desperate" struggle on the beachhead, he pressed for a vigorous response to the media critics. "There is also a lot of pessimistic stuff being given out by press correspondents," Churchill explained, before reassuring his commanders that "any measures you may take to prevent the circulation of rumors likely to spread undue despondency and alarm will be supported by me."[23]

Alexander returned to Anzio on February 14, armed with Churchill's message. He immediately called the correspondents to a meeting. Alexander, Bigart noted, "said he had been notified by superiors that stories emanating from the beachhead 'alarmed the people.' He found the reporters guilty," Bigart added, "of an abrupt reversal from over-optimistic accounts during the first week of the invasion to over-pessimistic accounts of the last two weeks." And he planned to impose a severe sanction: they would be denied access to radio facilities for filing stories to Naples until they had mended their ways.[24]

The reporters were outraged. Those in London, Algiers, and at the beachhead lobbied hard for the immediate restoration of radio access at Anzio.[25] Facing this united front, the military relented. But many of the

Figure 12.2 An agitated Alexander (*center*, with his hand behind his head) addresses reporters in the Anzio press room. National Archives 111-SC-188100.

correspondents remained angry, especially when Alexander's subordinates suggested that their boss's action had been a sensible response to the recent overly gloomy newspaper dispatches, which had encouraged the Germans to attack with such vigor.[26]

For Homer Bigart, this claim went too far, and he boldly complained about it in print. Reporters, he insisted, have been "exceedingly careful lest our dispatches give information of military value to the enemy. But the quarrel," Bigart told his readers,

> is not over battlefield security. Apparently there are still some military advisers who feel the British and American public do not yet realize that war involves risks, that the breaks do not always go to the Allies. They are afraid that the public cannot stand the shock of bad news and that it must be broken to them gradually over long periods of time and preferably after some victory.[27]

A few weeks later, Bigart shipped out of the beachhead for a brief rest. But what he found at Caserta angered him so much that he quickly compiled an even more explosive dispatch, turning the tables on those who had blamed the reporters for the problems at Anzio. "It is depressing to return from the Anzio beachhead," he began, "where frontline misery rivals World War [I] Flanders, and find in a city sixty miles behind the lines a complacency and lack of realism worse than that prevailing in New York. . . . At headquarters," he elaborated, "the bad news was always glossed over. If we failed to take a town in one attack we could get it next time, so why worry? At headquarters there was always good food, amusements and security, and every one, of course, was chock full of confidence and quite happy about the situation."[28]

This excoriating attack could not have come at a worse time for those in the US government who were still campaigning for more realistic battlefield reporting. For Bigart's was not an isolated voice. The week before his critical dispatch, two very different figures had offered similar evaluations, both suggesting that Allied officers were in some ways addicted to covering up bad news.

Sergeant Jack Foisie, a correspondent with the army newspaper *Stars and Stripes*, took the first swipe. In a speech at San Francisco's Commonwealth Club, on March 15, Foisie spoke openly about the friendly fire incident at Gela the previous July, claiming that the Allied navy had killed 410 paratroopers from the Eighty-Second Airborne. Of course, many of the reporters present had long known about this incident, and about the War Department's absolute block on publicizing it. The next day, however, an AP correspondent wrote a story about Foisie's speech, and the local censor "erroneously took it that the whole story was inward from the United States." Since articles written in America were normally "cleared with few cuts," the censor passed the story—and suddenly, all hell broke loose. The media, which had long wanted permission to print, immediately called on the Pentagon to come clean. Feeling there was little choice, Henry Stimson, the war secretary, obliged. But his grudging concession citing the "confusion" inherent in a nighttime paratroop operation did little to quell the questions about why the Pentagon had tried to to keep the whole matter secret—questions that inevitably centered on the extent to which the military was censoring war reporting not for legitimate security reasons but to prevent the public from learning about avoidable military mistakes.[29]

Stimson's reluctant admission also failed to head off a partisan political assault on the administration. A little over a week later, Thomas Dewey, the governor of New York and front runner for the Republican presidential nomination, added his voice to the clamor. Too much important news "has been released only after it leaked out and became the subject of widespread gossip," Dewey charged in a radio address. Referring specifically to the

Gela incident, the presidential contender even claimed that the Roosevelt administration "seemed to have embarked on 'a deliberate and dangerous policy of suppression of the news at home.'"[30]

Bigart's savage criticism appeared in the *New York Herald Tribune* on March 27, three days after Dewey's speech. Not only did it remind Americans that news of the Anzio debacle had been restricted, too, when the military cut off all transmissions from the beachhead; it also suggested that the public was being fed a diet of sanguine nonsense by HQ officers who were housed in great comfort at a considerable distance from the fighting.

The public appeared to agree. Analyzing a range of opinion polls, the OWI concluded that the "outstanding finding . . . is a gradual but consistent downward trend in satisfaction with the amount and quality of the information released." By the spring of 1944, only 57 percent of Americans felt that the government was "releasing as much war news as it should," down from 61 percent the previous October. Even worse, only 38 percent of those polled thought that the news being released was accurate; 44 percent believed it made the situation look better than it actually was—a total reversal in the past year.[31]

Senior government officials found these figures deeply troubling, not just because they had received no credit for trying to present a more realistic picture of the war. If, after all the stories of death and destruction in Italy, the public still thought the government was sugarcoating

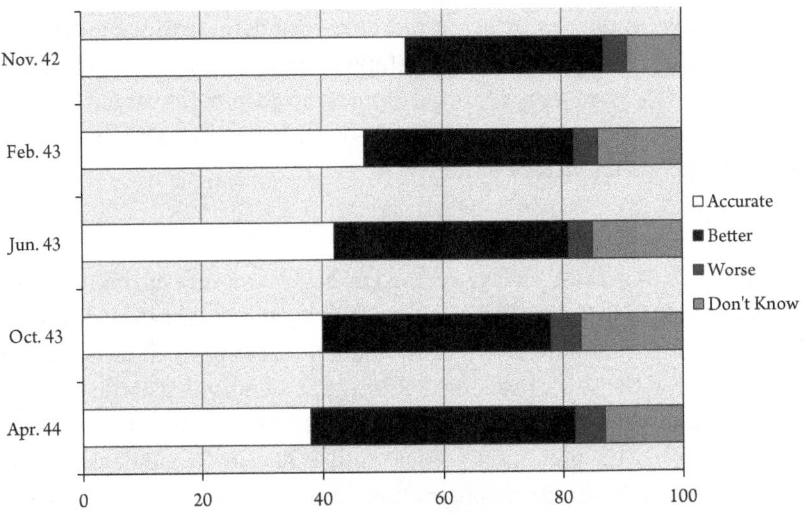

Figure 12.3 Is the news released accurate . . . or does it make the situation look better, worse, than it is? Source: OWI, Surveys Division, "Public Appraisal of War Information," Memo No. 77, May 12, 1944, Entry 164, box 1800, RG44.

the news, then the repercussions could well be grave. Some officials even wondered if Americans might believe the battlefield situation was worse than the media was reporting. If so, how long would they support such a gruesome fight?

Perhaps, these officials concluded, the fickle popular mood was about to enter a dangerous downswing. As winter gave way to spring, a growing number of press commentators thought that the Allies ought to offer Germany assurances of fair postwar treatment; only then, they argued, might the enemy stop undertaking desperate last-ditch fights like those in Italy. Even more ominously, a significant minority of the public also believed that the Allies should consider a negotiated peace in Europe, albeit only if the German army overthrew Hitler first. Indeed, more than 40 percent of Americans seemed to favor this course, a figure that was noticeably higher than at any other time of the war, including the months of setback and defeat during 1942.[32]

If Americans were doubtful about seeing the war through to the bitter end, then the most obvious propaganda solution would be to relax the anti-complacency drive. Instead of letting the media concentrate on its war-is-hell message, the time had arrived, perhaps, to prod reporters to tell a more upbeat story again. Yet recent events had placed major obstacles in the way of this particular course. With Dewey already accusing the government of suppressing bad news, Roosevelt scarcely wanted to hand his rival more ammunition to drive home his attack—precisely what a series of happy front-line dispatches would achieve. Moreover, the war correspondents were already suspicious of being fed over-confident stories by detached officers. The military needed to re-establish its reputation with the press, not provide it with more rose-tinted reports. So despite the mounting signs of domestic unease, the government was stymied. It could do little except wait—and hope for victory in Italy.

Along the Gustav Line, victory seemed as elusive as ever during February and March. Cy Sulzberger hung around, hoping to witness a breakthrough in the fighting. He would often repair to a hilltop from which he had a panoramic view of the static battlefield. From afar, he mused, it almost seemed possible to forget the extent of the carnage, as tiny groups of men moved back and forth up mountain passes, rather like in "a medieval battle." Up close, though, the gruesome nature of modern warfare could not be avoided. On one occasion, the commander of the Thirty-Fourth Division, which had launched the first wave of attacks on Cassino, privately told Sulzberger that "his rifle companies had suffered 65 percent casualties."

What this meant was "American boys lying in the mud," he recalled after the war, "their throats eaten out by ravenous dogs."[33]

Sulzberger predictably kept such gruesome details out of his dispatches; but the combination of his growing knowledge of events on the ground and the censors' relatively light touch helped him to convey a strong sense of the battle's ebb and flow. Sometimes he loyally toed the obvious military line. In reporting the controversial bombing of the Monte Cassino abbey in mid-February, for example, he laid the blame squarely on the Germans, "who had violated all civilized codes by employing the sanctuary for military purposes." When the air force bombed the abbey again a month later, he even hitched a ride on one of the planes, revealing the nerves of the crews and recounting the most powerful support an air arm had ever rendered to a ground offensive.[34]

Safely back on his hilltop perch, Sulzberger started developing a more disturbing narrative. After the first bombing raid on Cassino failed to unseat the Germans, he had few doubts about the ineffectiveness of the second—despite its billing as "the heaviest aerial bombardment in history." "In a sense," Sulzberger told his readers the next day, "the ground forces had to pay the penalty for the luxury of their unprecedented air support," because "such a mass of debris was piled up in the narrow streets" that both the infantry and armor would find it difficult to penetrate the German defenses.[35]

From his lofty vantage point, Sulzberger certainly saw little obvious forward movement as a muddle of units clambered up steep slopes, got stuck among the wreckage, or became victims of enemy guns. And by March 25, he had concluded that the current assault was spent. "It is no exaggeration to state," Sulzberger reported the next day, "that the third major attack on the bastion of the Gustav Line is so far an utter failure."[36]

Few divisions suffered more during these failed battles than the Thirty-Fourth, which had been away from home longer than any other American division: two years, and counting, including doing an initial stint in Northern Ireland, where Ernie Pyle had first encountered it. By early 1944, this lengthy service, together with the terrible conditions in Italy, had clearly taken a toll. When Alexander asked a senior American officer to inspect the Cassino front, he received the disturbing report that "morale was 'becoming progressively worse,' with troops 'so disheartened as to be almost mutinous.'"[37]

Pyle rejoined the Thirty-Fourth a short while later. Like Sulzberger on the Rapido, Ernie never contemplated mentioning the possibility of mutiny in his columns, knowing that it would never get past the censor. Instead, he focused on the fatalism of the troops tempered by a desire to pull together: characteristics that the military was more than happy for a correspondent to stress.[38]

The fatalism came from one of the Thirty-Fourth Division's old-timers, a quiet Westerner named Sergeant Frank "Buck" Eversole, whom Pyle considered his personal hero. A cowboy before the war, Eversole survived through a combination of lottery-like luck and battlefield wisdom—along with a smattering of emotional hardness that immunized him from the loss of so many of the boys in his platoon. As Pyle told his readers in mid-February, even heroes like Eversole were disheartened by the Italian stalemate, but, he added, they were determined to see the job through to the bitter end. The ex-cowboy, he wrote,

> has no hatred for Germans. He kills because he's trying to keep alive himself. . . . 'I'm mighty sick of it,' he says very quietly, 'but there ain't no use to complain. I just figure it this way, that I've been given a job to do and I've got to do it. And if I don't live thru it, there's nothing I can do about it.'

Eversole knew that his chances of survival were slim. Of the 200 men in his company who had originally shipped out in 1942, he was one of only eight remaining. The rest of the troops were replacements for those who had been killed, captured, or wounded in Tunisia and Italy. This attrition rate had clearly exerted a profound impact on the survivors' mindsets and demeanors, as had the endless slugging along the slopes to Cassino. "Of course they changed," Pyle conceded, "they had to." No one could witness such carnage and not come away severely affected. Yet, he stressed, these American boys still "seemed just like ordinary human beings back home," albeit with one crucial difference. "The ties that grow between men who live savagely together," Pyle argued, "relentlessly communing with Death, are ties of great strength. There is a sense of fidelity to each other in a little corps of men who have endured so long, and whose hope in the end can be so small."[39]

Pyle emerged from the carnage in Cassino strangely energized—so much so that he decided that the time had come to brave Anzio. He arrived at the beachhead toward the end of February, when the conditions were particularly frightening. Soldiers crouched all day in sodden trenches, knowing that if they broke cover for a split second, they risked joining the burgeoning casualty lists.[40]

As Pyle soon discovered, many of the correspondents were still furious at the military's efforts to shift the blame for the stalemate onto them. Homer Bigart remained their most vocal leader. Even in the face of Alexander's continued injunctions to "always strike a confident note," the *Herald Tribune* reporter was determined to depict the beachhead's uglier side.[41] Hunched over his Olivetti, slowly but relentlessly tapping out his dispatches with two or three fingers, Bigart placed the Anzio battle in the dark pantheon of recent struggles, insisting it was "uglier" than Troina, "rougher" than Salerno, and "more sanguinary" than San Pietro. In other stories he emphasized the unpalatable realities of front-line life: the difficulty of keeping dry, the danger of trench foot while the winter persisted, and the prospect of malaria as soon as the weather improved.[42]

In many respects, Pyle and Bigart were a study in contrasts: one the joiner and explainer, the other the outsider and iconoclast. In Anzio, however, both men decided that whatever Alexander might think, there was only one story: the grimness of daily existence, where the men's main goal was simply to stay alive. Pyle therefore echoed Bigart's gloomy line. In column after column, Ernie described the vulnerability of everyone at the beachhead, from bakers to the typewriter repairmen. He reported on the terrifying variety of enemy shell sounds, which here, for some reason, gave few clues about the direction they were heading. And he described the crowdedness of the beachhead, where any shell was bound to "land not more than 200 yards from somebody."[43]

Pyle himself only narrowly missed being hit by enemy artillery on two occasions. Then, early one morning in mid-March, he was in bed when he heard the sound of antiaircraft guns. Going to the window to see where the noise was coming from, he suddenly felt a massive blast that threw him into the middle of the room: an entire stick of 500-pound bombs had fallen just outside the correspondents' villa.[44]

Pyle confessed to feeling "pretty jumpy" for the next two days, but he refused to be cowered, even deciding to stay another week just to get his "nerve back." It was a telling phrase.[45] The longer he remained in Anzio, the more he noticed a "look" in the soldiers' eyes when they had spent too long at the front. "It's a look of dullness," he explained to his readers,

> eyes that look without seeing, eyes that see without conveying any image to the mind. It's a look that is the display room for what lies behind it—exhaustion, lack of sleep, tension for too long, weariness that is too great, fear beyond misery, misery to the point of numbness, a look of surpassing indifference to anything anybody can do.

No doubt anticipating the censor's hand quivering above this passage, primed to eviscerate an eloquence that could easily disturb the home front at a sensitive moment in the fighting, Pyle added a crucial caveat. "To me," he concluded, "it's one of the perpetual astonishments of a war life that human beings recover as quickly as they do."[46]

After weeks inside the beachhead, Pyle recognized that his own fragile powers of recovery were starting to wane. In need of medical attention, he finally shipped out of Anzio in late March, bound for London and a well-earned rest. He left behind a war in which there was no end in sight.

RADIO REPORTS

On April 23, Eric Sevareid reported from Anzio to his large CBS audience. "You are hearing this morning," he began,

> the first direct broadcasts ever made from the Fifth Army beachhead, this tiny scallop of Italian coast where we have the enemy on three sides and the sea at our backs; the army's radio men have risked their lives many times to install these facilities . . . for this is like living on a bullseye; I do not believe direct radio reports have ever been made from so exposed a position.[47]

As Sevareid must have known, this last assertion was something of an exaggeration. During the London blitz three-and-a-half years earlier, radio correspondents had famously reported live from highly exposed positions. Sevareid had, in fact, been there at the time, as one of the "Murrow boys," the broadcasting pioneers recruited by Edward R. Murrow, the charismatic head of European news at CBS. Back in September 1940, Murrow had spent night after night on top of the BBC building in London, calmly describing the dramatic scenes for his massive audience as the German bombs fell all around.[48]

Still, amid the fear and squalor of Anzio, Sevareid could perhaps be excused for overlooking Murrow's trailblazing broadcasts. The London blitz, after all, was a long time ago. In terms of radio broadcasting, it had also been a highly unusual event that established no real precedents for covering subsequent battles. The reason was simple. The blitz had unfolded not on some faraway, fast-moving battlefield, but right in the center of one of the world's biggest news hubs. It had therefore eliminated the formidable problems that invariably prevented broadcasters from capturing the sounds of war.

During the 1940s, broadcasting live required connecting a telephone line from a microphone to a shortwave transmitter, and, as the CBS correspondents repeatedly told their superiors, "you could not follow an advancing or retreating army dragging a telephone line along with you." Nor did the army take kindly to the prospect of hauling big, powerful transmitters around fluid battlefronts, especially if a broadcaster was going to use them to blurt out sensitive information live on air. Making a recording was more feasible, but the military only began to test prototypes of the first portable recording machines in early 1943. Besides, radio bosses had so far been resistant to the use of recordings, insisting that their listeners only wanted to hear about events as they actually unfolded.[49]

Because of these constraints, the Murrow boys had been a glamorous exception to the dreary norm. Since the brief heyday of the blitz, radio broadcasters had rarely experienced the excitement of battle. Most had remained stuck near a major military headquarters, jostling for office space, interviews, and circuit access in London, Algiers, or Naples. On a normal day, their job had boiled down to little more than regurgitating official military communiqués or reading someone else's eyewitness account into the microphone. They had only two chances to stand out from the crowd: anchoring one of the weekly *Army Hour* broadcasts, a scripted entertainment extravaganza starring men and women in uniform, or broadcasting a spot-news scoop seconds ahead of their rival.[50]

The opening of the Italian campaign promised more exciting times for the eighteen radio broadcasters assigned to Fifth Army. Their hope derived largely from a new army device: the mobile wire recorder, which weighed less than fifty pounds, had a "built-in play-back and instantaneous erasure feature," and could be easily carried around the battlefield. In August 1943, Colonel Edward M. Kirby, chief of the army's Radio Section, arrived in Algiers to show a couple of these "fancy recording machines" to Joe Phillips, who considered them "wonderful for broadcasters, but absolutely guaranteed to drive censors nuts." Kirby struck a much more upbeat note when unveiling them to the press. Until now, he began, "radio reporters have been anchored to stationary radio transmitters in a war of movement. If they go to the front they cannot broadcast until they return to the transmitters.... As a result radio has encountered for the first time in its history a limit of time and distance." In the future, though, Kirby believed that reporters would be able to head to the front with their new machines, record the sounds of battle, and then broadcast these sounds when they returned to headquarters.[51]

If that was the theory, it proved difficult to translate into practice. For one thing, these machines ran on electricity, which tended to be in extremely short supply near the front—"thus the recorder's mobility was reduced accordingly," observed a Fifth Army PRO. For another, they required a degree of technical expertise, also initially lacking. On one occasion NBC's Merrill Mueller returned to Naples to find that his recording "turned out to be blank." That evening an officer watched him "trying to patch the recorder. The last time I looked," the officer noted, Mueller "was down on the floor trying to distinguish red and green wires by the light of a candle."[52]

As the fighting in Italy dragged on, both the military and media began to solve many of these problems. Over time, correspondents became more "familiar" with their recorders and were able to "iron out more of the 'bugs.'" Near the front, helpful PROs managed to cadge a beat-up old generator that they hooked onto a trailer behind a jeep, giving their recorders an all-important mobile electricity supply. The result was a number of radio reports that brought the home front nearer to the combat action: to field hospitals erected dangerously close to incoming artillery shells; to mobile bath units that allowed grimy GIs "to get their first showers in five or six months"; to mule pack trains who trekked the mountain slopes carrying crucial supplies; and to the front-line military police who prevented "people from straying accidentally into the German lines."[53]

Yet radio had still not quite returned to the battlefield itself. Nor had anyone managed to broadcast live from the front. In a sense, therefore, Eric Sevareid was correct. His April 23 Anzio bulletin was the first direct radio report from such an exposed a position, at least since the London blitz.

The man who made it had not set foot in Europe since those heady, dangerous days back in 1940, and he could scarcely believe how strained media-military relations had become in and around the front. The PROs, Sevareid observed, considered the correspondents "as uncooperative and quite unmanageable. Some of them," he added, "resented the fact that we were continuing our careers and making money at it, and more than one of them advocated enrolling all correspondents directly into the army." The reporters, for their part, increasingly resented the lack of facilities in Italy. Many had also come to loathe Clark's brazen efforts to puff up his own reputation, which reached their apogee after the Fifth Army commander invited thirty-one of them to a meeting on May 9.

Clark's goal that afternoon was straightforward enough. For over an hour he went into great detail about a forthcoming offensive that aimed to break through the Gustav Line at Cassino. After months of "scanty news," he and his senior officers fretted that the press would "magnify early successes" and thereby generate inflated home-front expectations. So they pushed reporters to "stress the magnitude of the task." "This is definitely a slugging match all the way in," Clark stressed. "We must be careful about drawing conclusions that soon after the attack we will take Rome."[54]

While the reporters duly reiterated this downbeat line, the situation on the ground brightened. Polish troops took the honor of capturing the Monte Cassino abbey, which finally fell on May 17. Five days later, the forces inside the Anzio beachhead began the second phase of the attack. It promised to be equally momentous, especially since reporters had already developed a catchy way to frame any success. The Nazis had for months been calling Anzio "our biggest prison camp where the prisoners feed themselves." Now the whole press corps was poised to discuss "the greatest jailbreak in history."[55]

Clark was determined to place his own stamp on the breakout. Whereas Alexander always preferred to label operations as "Allied," Clark lobbied hard for the release of communiqués that would stress the role of his own army. "The joining up of my two Fifth Army forces," he explained to fellow officers, "will be one of the highlights of the Fifth Army's career," and his bridgehead command, he insisted, "is entitled to this story." Clark was also desperate to witness this juncture in person. He told his wife that being there "meant more to me than anything since our success at Salerno." But the reporters, censors, and other officers all believed that his real goal was public glory. Certainly, Clark made sure that the censors abandoned their "damn fool idea" that his presence at Anzio could not be mentioned. When word came through on May 25 that a meeting of the two forces was close, he rounded up twenty-five reporters and photographers and sped to the scene with so much fanfare that even he conceded that the "way some correspondents expressed it may have sounded as though I was looking for publicity."[56]

Clark's brazenness at the meeting of the two Fifth Army forces set the scene for a much bigger dispute between him and Alexander over the coming days. At its heart was the direction and purpose of the next phase of the offensive. Alexander wanted the Anzio troops to drive northeast in order to cut off Highway 6 at the town of Valmontone. This was the only way, Alexander believed, to capture the bulk of enemy troops retreating from the Gustav Line around Cassino. But it clashed with Clark's growing "fixation" on Rome. The American commander saw the Eternal City as the only fitting prize after so many months of sacrifice. He also suspected that Alexander's plan was a ruse to distract the Fifth Army while British troops snuck into the Italian capital and grabbed all the plaudits.[57]

As the offensive began, Clark's beachhead troops duly headed northeast, as Alexander had intended, and by May 25 their path to Valmontone seemed virtually clear. Then Clark intervened. He instructed his lieutenants to break off this advance and redeploy toward the north so that they could head directly for Rome. It became one of the most contentious orders of the American war. Even if the change in direction was not the reason so many German troops managed to escape, it nevertheless proved costly in American lives. Instead of continuing the momentum against a crumbling foe, Clark shifted his forces to attack another formidable German defensive position, at the Velletri gap in the Alban Hills.[58]

Luckily for Clark, Homer Bigart was too close to the action to detect these larger controversies. Nevertheless, the Italian campaign's most iconoclastic correspondent could scarcely avoid noticing their effect. On May 25, Bigart joined the push toward Valmontone, which was progressing according to plan. Then, as Clark thinned out the ranks of this offensive in order to pivot his troops toward Velletri, Homer recorded yet another Italian setback. "Again," he wrote in a dispatch on May 28, "we had forgotten that the enemy is brave, tricky, and resourceful, and recovers quickly from defeat." Bigart himself spent an uncomfortable seven-and-a-half hours "pinned down in Artena by self-propelled guns firing with appalling accuracy from woods just 800 yards from town." When he and his UP companion "finally summoned enough courage to leave at dusk," Bigart reported, "snipers fired at us on the northern outskirts of the town."[59]

The following day Bigart relocated with the bulk of Fifth Army to the new focal point in front of the Alban Hills. As he hastened to tell his readers, it was another familiar story of stalemate and frustration. First, the GIs faced "extensive minefields." Next came the hills that provided enemy commanders with "excellent observation," so that they could pour down their fire on the more vulnerable points of the American advance. "Perhaps," Bigart wondered on May 30,

> we have again underestimated the German's ability to improvise—his quick genius for slapping together remnants and oddments of crushed divisions and producing a capable defensive team. Today our gains were measured not in miles but in yards. We secured, in costly fighting, a point near Campoleone, but progress beyond that was painfully slow. Campoleone is sixteen miles from Rome.[60]

Back at headquarters Eric Sevareid astutely spotted the main reason for this new stalemate: Clark's decision to shift the emphasis of attack, which also called into question the central goal of the whole operation. Sitting in the press camp, Sevareid banged out his story. "When this Italian offensive began," he observed, "official declarations of purpose did not mention Rome, but only the destruction of the German armies in Italy as our goal. There is a question," he continued, "whether the two aims are compatible or mutually exclusive: we shall know as events unfold."[61]

Predictably, the Fifth Army censors ruthlessly cut the offending passage in Sevareid's explosive dispatch, although not before their commanding general had had a chance to read the radio man's analysis. Fuming, Clark immediately called reporters together for a lecture. Referring to "a broadcast" that suggested that the Allies had missed the chance to capture the bulk of the Germans, he reacted with scorn. "That is sheer nonsense," Clark insisted. Pointing to a map with his stick, he tapped on all the other side roads, which, he asserted, the Germans could also use to escape north. Sevareid left the session deeply confused—and more than a little suspicious. "No amateur could prove otherwise," he wrote after the war. "Yet such a capture had been our unquestioned aim. Now the general spoke in a manner that seemed to deny that the idea had ever entered his head. Some of us remained puzzled and skeptical. What had happened that we must now rush straight for Rome?"[62]

Figure 12.4 Mark Clark studies a map just outside Rome, June 4, 1944. National Archives 111-SC-191649.

Even to correspondents familiar with Clark's attention seeking, this particular performance left a bitter aftertaste as they trekked the last miles into the Italian capital. After a hot day on the road, they would slump down on the ground to bang out their stories, their typewriters balanced on their knees, while coughing from the dust stirred up by the jeeps and tanks. On Sunday, June 4, Sevareid remembered sitting "before the microphone at a portable table while shells passed over and the concussion whipped my ears. I could say nothing of consequence," he confessed. "I could only say that Rome was falling and that we were all tired and happy."[63]

Rome finally fell on Monday. Chastened by the continued bursts of sniper fire on the outskirts of the city, many of the reporters prudently drove their jeeps alongside Sherman tanks loaded with triumphant GIs. Then the crowds began to gather. The more cynical GIs wondered how many of these cheering Italians had stood on exactly the same spot to greet Mussolini's troops a few years earlier, but most of them simply enjoyed the accolades. Daniel De Luce, the AP's man on the scene, described the most eye-catching moments: the "smiling, brown-eyed girls" who handed flowers to "dust-covered riflemen" or the "bald clerk, carrying an empty wine-flagon," who showed GIs the marks where the Germans had beaten him.[64]

When they reached the city center, the correspondents set up shop in the Stampa Estera building, where chaos prevailed. No one could find a censor or a PRO. Nor did anyone know how to get dispatches to London or New York. When one reporter mooted a plan to fly copy from Anzio to Algiers, the other members of the press pack recalled all the previous occasions such a Mediterranean lottery had been tried—and had failed—and they predictably reacted in a "frenzied state of fury." Then suddenly, Ken Clark appeared and announced that his boss was about to hold an impromptu press conference outside.

The reporters found the Fifth Army commander in a jaunty mood. "Well, gentlemen," he began, "I didn't really expect to have a press conference here—I just called a little meeting with my corps commanders to discuss the situation. However, I'll be glad to answer your questions." As the correspondents paused to think of a suitable line of inquiry, Clark could not help himself. "This," he declared, "is a great day for the Fifth Army." For Sevareid, such a tactless comment just about summed Clark up. "It was not, apparently, a great day for the world, for the Allies, for all the suffering people who had desperately looked toward the time of peace," he thought with great bitterness. "It was a great day for the Fifth Army." Nearby a colleague muttered acidly: "On this historic occasion I feel like vomiting."[65]

Notwithstanding the reporters' privately expressed anger, Clark was a shrewd enough publicist to ensure that his day of glory received good press. During the last weeks of hard fighting, the Fifth Army commander had periodically paused to remember the fallen troops who had made victory possible. "With God's help," he had declared at a memorial service before leaving Anzio on May 30, "we shall carry on the task which they began." Now, during his impromptu Rome press conference, Clark again took care "to say a word of tribute to the gallant men and women who made the supreme sacrifice that could keep us going." Even the most jaundiced correspondents came away impressed by this particular statement. "The Fifth Army had a long, bloody fight to Rome," reported the *New York Times* account. "This loyalty to the men who could not be there was implicit in every word that General Clark said."[66]

It was a revealing moment. In private, many reporters had come to loathe Clark's publicity stunts: his use of personal photographers, his references to the Fifth—not the Allied—armies, his determination to be at the center of the story, from Naples via Anzio to Rome. Over the past nine months, however, little of this loathing had made it into print, largely because the reporters knew that Clark's censors would cut anything that cast aspersions on their boss. It was not until many of them wrote their memoirs after the war that their true feelings became widely known.[67]

The day after the liberation of Rome, the reporters returned to work in the Stampa Estera building. After living out of makeshift bivouacs and facing the ever-present threat of enemy fire for so long, many appreciated the simple comforts of their new office life. Then at mid-morning, a man dashed in and disturbed the tranquil scene. "Eisenhower has announced the invasion of France!" he exclaimed. "It's official!" According to one eyewitness account, "a concerted groan went up from the pressroom." Putting aside their normal rivalries, the wire service reporters chorused: "Why couldn't they have waited for just one week? We might as well all go home." Some did. Others "struck out for the nearest bar." Those remaining, Sevareid recorded, "looked at one another. One or two shrugged their shoulders and went back to work; most of us sat back, pulled out cigarettes, and dropped our half-written stories about Rome to the floor." They had no chance of getting much play now.[68]

Indeed, the real D-Day—the one everyone had anticipated for so long—would dominate the news agenda for weeks, perhaps months, to come. This was scarcely surprising. The Allies expected the new operation, codenamed Overlord, to become the crucial war-winning campaign. American leaders, in particular, had long viewed France as the only place to engage the Wehrmacht in a decisive battle and pave the way for a victorious march into the heart of Hitler's Reich. Such a campaign would inevitably become *the* major news story of the European war. Instead of the chaos and controversy that had increasingly marked media-military relations in Italy, the generals in charge of Overlord were determined to develop the most efficient and effective news system to date, taking on board all the hard lessons learned during the long months of fighting in the Mediterranean. In every respect, then, this new D-Day promised to be very different from the confusion that had prevailed in Italy.

PART IV

Overlord

CHAPTER 13

Fear Lay Blackly Deep Down

RETURNING WARRIORS

None of the reporters who left the Mediterranean for London during the first months of 1944 could quite erase the memory of Anzio from their minds. In April, Ernie Pyle checked in to London's elegant Dorchester Hotel. Already in a bad way after his recent "flurry of close squeaks," he now found the occasional appearance of Luftwaffe bombers a major ordeal. Indeed, Pyle felt so "allergic to raids" that he even had trouble breathing when the British antiaircraft guns retaliated with a vengeance.[1]

Within weeks, though, London provided a partial antidote to such Anzio-induced jitters. George Hicks of the Blue Network, who had spent time in Italy with Pyle, vividly described in his diary his own reactions after spending months at the battlefront. There was the mounting feeling of "emptiness," caused by "the frightful, meaningless hardship and killing all around." Too much smoking bunged up his sinuses. Too much drinking exacerbated his enervating fatigue. Arriving in London at the start of March, Hicks found it difficult to function. "My memory seemed to go weak," he recalled six weeks later. "My eyes, my senses didn't respond with vividness. It was as tho[ugh] everything had gone dead to the taste—nothing meant anything—and I was walking in padded cotton. Then I caught a cold, lost weight, lost everything."[2]

This lassitude did not last long. Simply being away from the constant dangers of combat was the best tonic. Pyle found the English scenery "fresh and green and beautiful" after Italy, and even London "seemed less dreary than in the fall of 1942." "There was more food," Ernie concluded, "and it was better than it used to be. There were more people in the streets, more shopping, more Sunday strollers in the parks."

There were also a lot more war correspondents, as almost every American news outlet seemed to be sending in reinforcements to cover the upcoming invasion in France. "There were gray men who covered the last war," observed Pyle sardonically, "and men from the Pacific, and there were little girls and big girls and pretty girls, and diplomatic correspondents and magazine contributors and editors and cubs and novelists." The veterans of the Italian campaign, particularly those like Ernie who had no civilian clothes, tended to stand out from the interlopers. "We felt like a little family among all the newcomers," remarked Pyle, a feeling that contributed to the recovery process.

Before long, Ernie began to look and feel better. After a series of leisurely lunches in the US Army mess, he found that his weight had shot up to one hundred and twenty pounds, a gain he considered "practically phenomenal." After a number of alcohol-fueled evenings in the familiar Fleet Street pubs, where practiced raconteurs like Bill Stoneman helped to take some of the sting out of Anzio memories, he also began to recall the quirkier, funnier moments in Italy—though that gory wasteland retained its power to hurt. Pyle was particularly affected by the death of Roderick MacDonald, a reporter for the *Sydney Morning Herald*. The two men had spent weeks together during Ernie's last spell of recuperation, after the North African campaign. Learning that his "handsome, brilliant, engaging" friend had been killed at Cassino, Pyle realized that he remained one of those veterans "who still had strong roots and half our hearts in that cruel battleground."[3]

Not every returning veteran reporter dwelled on war's cruelty, however. For correspondents who had covered the Mediterranean campaign from a distance, Italy, and especially Anzio, offered a series of lessons for the future—lessons about the tenacity of the German enemy, the many pitfalls of amphibious landings, and the importance of getting the balance between censorship and publicity right.

Wes Gallagher was in the vanguard of this group. The tall, loud AP reporter had spent the past few months in Algiers, where he had become the bureau's "hard-hitting leg man," observed one colleague, a "fast, capable writer, [who] has a forthright manner that batters open many doors, normally closed."[4] Because of his bad back injury, Gallagher had avoided the horrors of the front, and it showed in his obsession with the decisions made at headquarters, especially the recent ones made by British generals during the Anzio campaign. Despite the Allies' numerical superiority at the outset, Gallagher insisted, in a story written in London on February 8, they had been too cautious and now found themselves on the defensive for the first time in over a year. Had Eisenhower been in charge of Anzio, Gallagher elaborated in private, disaster would surely have been averted. Harry Butcher, who had to sit through one particularly long tirade on the subject, thought that Wes was a little too partisan on the subject; other members of Eisenhower's staff appreciated having such a formidable booster on their side, no one more so than Joe Phillips.[5]

Phillips also returned to London in February, and he fully agreed with Gallagher's critique of the new command structure in the Mediterranean, telling Butcher that things had gone "to pot" since Ike's departure.[6] Yet Phillips also had more pressing matters on his mind. Having found love in London before heading to North Africa, he planned to marry his sweetheart in the British capital.

This was not the only close relationship Phillips forged during the war. Over the past fourteen months, he and Gallagher had become fast friends. It had all begun inside Gibraltar's large rock, when the two men had made a formidable team that dominated the initial press coverage of the North African invasion. Their friendship had ripened during the Italian campaign, when Gallagher had been a reliable mouthpiece for Phillips's efforts to give the reporting about the fighting a more realistic edge, insisting that these battles "had been worth the cost."[7] Now the extent of their close friendship was about to become public knowledge. On February 13, as Phillips's bride walked down the aisle, Gallagher stood next to the groom. The army PRO had asked the AP reporter to be his best man.[8]

It seemed a highly symbolic moment. For these two major players, at least, the months of covering the Mediterranean war had resulted in a lasting friendship, against all the odds. "By the nature of their business," Gallagher pointed out a few weeks later, "reporters and censors are in constant conflict." But unlike in other commands, he added, the officers under Eisenhower had generally managed to mute this conflict by not only giving correspondents "complete access to information" but also allowing them to "send most of it." Now that Ike was back in London to head the new invasion, Gallagher believed, things looked extremely promising for the biggest operation of the war.[9]

PREPARATIONS

For the veteran correspondents who resumed shuttling back and forth between Fleet Street and Grosvenor Square, the US HQ felt reassuringly familiar. Immaculate guards still saluted smartly when visitors flashed their passes; the elevators still creaked, and harried officers still scurried around. Yet, as Gallagher and his colleagues knew only too well, there were two significant changes from the headquarters they had last visited in October 1942. One was the command's new name: SHAEF, an acronym for Supreme Headquarters Allies Expeditionary Force, which reporters would pound out endlessly on their typewriters, day after day. The other change was in the commander. Eisenhower had left London inexperienced in combat. He had returned as the conqueror of North Africa, Sicily, and the southern part of Italy.

Certainly, Churchill's government no longer eyed Ike as a rookie. Nor did Eisenhower feel he had to prove himself. "His relations with Churchill," observes his biographer, "were such that he could disagree violently with the prime minister over issues without affecting their friendship or mutual respect in any way"—which was fortunate, because the two men soon had much to disagree about, especially over media relations.[10]

The clash on this subject was so problematic because its roots were so deep and its implications so grave. Still scarred by memories of the World War I carnage in the French and Belgian trenches, British leaders had never been enthusiastic about invading Western Europe, and they viewed Operation Overlord, slated for spring 1944, as a highly risky proposition. Not only would Eisenhower have to place five Allied divisions on beaches in Normandy that were prickling with defenses, but he would also have to maintain this foothold against inevitable enemy counterattacks.[11] If the Germans got wind of what the Allies were planning and could concentrate their forces, catastrophe could easily ensue. The issue of censorship was therefore bound up tightly with the potential success of the invasion—and perhaps even the war.[12]

Fretful of the risks, the British military chiefs favored a total clampdown, to the extent of refusing to accredit any correspondents to SHAEF until the very last minute. Churchill fully agreed. It was of the "utmost importance," he insisted, "that a very stringent attitude should be adopted in regard to the communication to press correspondents in this country of any background information about Overlord operations, either before they start, or while they proceed."[13]

Eisenhower was sympathetic to some of Churchill's concerns. Like the British, he had few illusions about the riskiness of the Overlord invasion. According to one SHAEF estimate, the operation "had scant chance of success if the enemy received even forty-eight hours' advance notice, and 'any longer warning spells certain defeat.'"[14] Since security was so crucial, Eisenhower naturally reacted with extreme anger when he learned of any breach. In May, he even sent a general home in disgrace after the man had talked too freely about the possible date of the invasion in Claridge's public dining room. In his diary, Butcher noted the effect such incidents were having on his friend. "The strain is telling on him," Butcher wrote. "He looks older now than at any time since I have been with him."[15]

Still, the commander's own views were subtly different from those of the British. Where Churchill emphasized the suppression of all information, Eisenhower recognized the need to tread a thin line between controlling the reporters and alienating them. The goal, Ike told Churchill in February, was "to discover the best means of keeping the press securely in the dark, while at the same time not appearing to treat them as complete outsiders. Personally," he added, "I should feel disturbed if I thought that I or my public relations staff were held as anything but friends of the press."[16]

In the first months of 1944, political pressures reinforced Eisenhower's predilections. Around the turn of the new year, American PROs had detected a sudden spike in stories—no fewer than thirty-six articles published between December 17 and January 2—questioning the "army's right to withhold the news."[17] Then Anzio reared its ugly head. In February, when Alexander attacked the media's reporting from the beachhead, the reporters in London reacted with fury.[18] A few weeks later, when this controversy became entwined with news of the friendly fire cover-up on Sicily, even some of the military's warmest friends in the media began to criticize the excessive censorship.

Wes Gallagher was among them. Although he was careful to exclude Eisenhower and Phillips from his blast, on March 26 Gallagher wrote a strong attack on the military's overuse of two classes of censorship. "One of these," Gallagher explained, "involves stopping information which 'might give aid or comfort to the enemy' and the other is political." Excesses in both, he argued, meant that when stories inevitably leaked, they were not only "exploited out of all proportion to their original value," but also "created the idea that there are scores of such incidents being hidden by the censorship, fostering distrust of war reports in general."[19]

Many of the PROs sympathized with Gallagher's basic message. They knew from painful experience that overly strict censorship was a bad idea. In the period before the Normandy invasion, they thought it highly dangerous to keep "the greatest group of war correspondents in the world" completely in the dark. Such a "short-sighted policy," declared one, would be the quickest way to encourage bored reporters to dig for trouble.[20] They also realized that the public would demand up-to-date and relatively accurate information once the invasion was underway. Otherwise, it would doubtless start to speculate—or, worse, the media might publish stories based on the enemy's highly exaggerated propaganda broadcasts.

General McClure, who, until mid-April, headed Eisenhower's Publicity and Psychological Warfare Division, found this prospect particularly troubling. "The Allied publics are keyed up to expect a great volume of dramatic news as soon as the 'second front' opens," McClure observed. "If adequate news is not available from official Allied sources, the press and public will certainly make immediate use of news from enemy and neutral sources together with comment and speculation based thereon." And this might in turn spark a home-front panic, especially if a combination of Nazi misinformation and ill-informed guessing suggested that the operation was not going according to plan.[21]

For these reasons, McClure endorsed Eisenhower's plan to accredit correspondents as soon as possible, as the first stage in a process that would turn them into "quasi-staff officers" who could be trusted with highly sensitive information.[22] Yet when McClure started to consider which correspondents could join this select team, Gallagher's censorship critique began to rankle. Perhaps it was the AP man's focus on political censorship, which had been McClure's particular specialty over the past eighteen months. Or perhaps he was simply irritated by Gallagher's brash personality. Whatever the precise cause, McClure decided that it was time to try to exact a degree of revenge.

His chance came in April. Taking a close look at the list of correspondents about to be accredited, McClure pointed to the names of three men who had been so "difficult to manage" that they ought to be struck off altogether. The first was Frederick Kuh, the *Chicago Sun*'s London bureau chief, who had recently appalled SHAEF by writing a highly premature story about the "probable" peace terms for a defeated Germany.[23] The second was Pierre Huss of the INS, who had once been accused of cozying up to Hitler and who McClure believed still lacked the requisite "security-mindedness." Finally, there was Wes Gallagher. While the AP reporter had an impressive record as an Eisenhower booster, McClure saw him as a "troublemaker," who had not only attacked the Allies' strategic decisions at Anzio, but had recently accused the censors of seeking "to stop anything that gives them discomfort." How, McClure reasoned, could such a man be trusted with perhaps the biggest secret of the war?[24]

Since security was so crucial, the almost-paranoid voice of a senior officer might easily have held sway. Significantly, however, McClure had just lost his control over public relations, and his replacement doubted the wisdom of treating correspondents too severely.[25] Eisenhower's new public relations chief believed that "most of them are men [*sic*] of tremendous responsibility." The barring of Kuh, Huss, and particularly Gallagher, he added in a forceful memorandum, "appears to me to be a very dangerous procedure." All three reporters had been accredited before, he pointed out, and were never subsequently reprimanded for violating the censorship rules. "It hardly seems possible to make a water-tight case against any one of them now without arousing very provocative complaint from the American press in general."[26]

Besides, Gallagher continued to display an intense loyalty to the cause. Indeed, at almost the same time that McClure was pressing to exclude him, Gallagher approached Ike's new senior PRO "to report that the story was all over town that a major general had offered bets at a cocktail party on the date of the invasion and had talked too freely." It was yet another indication that Gallagher remained someone SHAEF could trust.[27]

Gallagher's new protector was an unlikely champion of the press. Brigadier General Thomas Jefferson Davis assumed control of a new G-6 section in April, with a remit that included "not only public relations, but press censorship and press communications as well as photographic coverage of forthcoming operations." In private, the stocky, tanned South Carolinian considered his new job "a headache spot." As he told anyone who would listen, he had climbed the military ladder because of his skills in administration, not PR; and he now felt so out of his depth that he mounted a pool ball on his desk showing the number eight. Visitors to his office were invariably greeted with the same corny icebreaker. "I am behind the eight ball," he would quip, "the correspondent is not."[28]

Within weeks, this sense of being at a constant disadvantage would take its toll on Davis's health, contributing to a bad bout of sinusitis that landed him in the hospital during the invasion. Yet Eisenhower had had good reasons for making him the chief PRO. And Davis quickly began to deploy all his skills, honed during years as a staffer, to ensure that the media preparations went into high gear.[29] One of these skills was tact, already displayed when he saved Gallagher's professional skin and soon to prove indispensable when resolving problems with prickly bureau chiefs like Pete Daniell.[30] Another was a canny knowledge of how the military system operated. "He is our man," gushed one newspaperman. "He is the best wangler in the whole damn army. . . . Davis gets for his outfit everything possible, employing any means just short of inviting court martial. He gets things done."[31]

Once SHAEF headquarters moved out of the center of London to a "tented, camouflaged area" near Kingston upon Thames, Davis set about wangling "adequate facilities to make it possible for a tremendous news coverage job to be accomplished right from the start of D-Day."[32] This was the first item on his agenda; the next was to ensure that all the media equipment was deployed in the most efficient manner possible—no easy feat given the unprecedented size and complexity of the invasion.

Fortunately, Davis could rely on a group of highly experienced subordinates. He began by placing Joe Phillips in charge of communications—a smart move, since the Mediterranean veteran, remembering how reporters' stories had remained stuck in Gela and Salerno, soon arranged to have three radios placed on the far end of the Normandy beaches during the initial invasion phase.[33] Davis also recruited several other veteran colonels to do the legwork, including Thor M. Smith. Before the war, Smith had been a promotion manager for the *San Francisco Call-Bulletin*, and he now used all his executive experience to ensure that the myriad organizational and logistical headaches involved were speedily resolved.[34]

The sheer number of correspondents underlay most of the difficulties. SHAEF had accredited more than five hundred of them by late spring, and Davis expected that they would produce upwards of a half million words in the first days after the invasion. Handling such massive volume would require recruiting almost two hundred censors, rather than the sixty or so who had been deployed in North Africa. And this, too, had a knock-on effect, especially when it came to coordination, for no one doubted that the reporters on one part of the front would complain loudly if their censors were stricter than those somewhere else.[35]

What really threatened to make coordination so challenging was the unwieldy command structure beneath Eisenhower and SHAEF. True, it was only an interim set-up, planned for the campaign's first phase. Once a sufficient number of troops had landed in France, Eisenhower would preside over two army groups, the Twenty-First, under Bernard Law Montgomery, and the Twelfth, under Omar Bradley. During the first part of Overlord, however, Monty would be the senior officer under Ike. Bradley's Twelfth Army Group would only be activated after enough American troops had come ashore. Until then, Bradley would merely control the US First Army, which, alongside the British Second Army and the Canadian First Army, would have to report to the arrogant and unpredictable Montgomery.

The potential pitfalls in this interim arrangement were obvious to anyone who had been in North Africa, Sicily, or Italy. Many American media organizations, from the spot-news merchants at the AP to the inveterate isolationists at the *Chicago Tribune*, had long suspected that the British military used every trick in the book to ensure scoops for the British media, including allowing their own reporters to send their dispatches first and timing the release of breaking news to meet Fleet Street deadlines. They had also become wise to Monty's antics, especially his tendency to claim all the credit for the British troops, while belittling the Americans.[36]

Desperate to prevent another bout of inter-Allied headline hogging, Davis and his PRO team spent much of the spring trying to forge a clear, unified system that promised "full equality as regards communications, transport, etc."[37] They also intensified the training program. Censors were issued a 200-page "bible," comprehensive enough to enable them to "handle material on any conceivable topic." They also attended a ten-day "indoctrination course," in which the emphasis was on ensuring that everyone understood that the "bible" contained a single truth—one that was the same for the British and Canadians as well as the Americans.[38]

True to form, Eisenhower and Davis were not preoccupied solely with suppressing information. "As a matter of policy," Ike told reporters in May, "accredited war correspondents should be accorded the greatest possible latitude in the gathering of legitimate news." To facilitate this process, Davis arranged for the reporters in France to be accompanied by twenty-three PR specialists who would help them establish portable press camps, and also brief them on "what they could get and pass through censorship."[39]

These "handpicked" specialists had already been through a rigorous training regime that had begun the previous summer in the States. Recently, they had been organized into a number of cells, each one "consisting of twenty jeeps, trucks, communications facilities, mess teams, orderlies, and equipment deemed necessary for the operation of a press camp in the field." Like the combat units massing for the invasion, these PR cells had colonized their own small corner of England to work on last-minute preparations. Clevedon, on the Bristol Channel, served as their training base, its seaside hotels providing comfortable billets and the surrounding countryside becoming the venue for boot-camp exercises that toughened their bodies and trained their minds, especially in the proper use of all their new equipment.[40]

As London basked in unseasonably warm weather, American media executives worked hard to finalize their own plans. Relatively new to the business of providing live battlefield news, radio had the most to do.

To begin with, the main networks needed to ensure that the transatlantic cables were sufficiently robust to deal with up to eighteen hours of continuous daily service. For the big day itself they also planned to establish an international control panel that would allow them to switch between the invasion and a range of other venues.[41] Although the competition for ratings would remain as fierce as ever, in March CBS and NBC (along with the BBC) reached an agreement to pool their copy so that, for the first time, any radio reporter on the scene of a breaking story would send out his or her words as a "combined" broadcast that could be used by rivals as well. "Special radio units," added an NBC executive, "will go into the combat zones with the troops and pick up the grim noises of war for transmission to the homes of eager listeners here and abroad." If there were no facilities for broadcasting live, these special units could use the new equipment that had been pioneered in Italy. "The ingenious 'wire recorder,'" noted one close observer, "will be on hand in every planned operation, hitting the beaches with the invasion forces."[42]

Newspaper editors, meanwhile, started thinking about their special invasion editions, which they hoped to sell in vast quantities. One of their biggest problems was the scarcity of newsprint. The government had forced editors to scale back their editions by 10 percent in early 1943; this was followed by an additional 25 percent reduction in November, "with a further 50 percent cut seriously threatened for 1944." Now that the invasion was imminent, executives had to think creatively about how to deal with the paper ration. Some considered producing two editions: a normal version that included advertising, and a slimmer "War Extra" without it. Others implored their reporters to tighten their writing. The wire services were particularly sensitive to this need. "News stories on a press wire," explained one senior UP manager, "are like firecrackers. The tighter you roll them the more noise they make when they go off." Even the most famous columnists faced cuts. The Scripps-Howard organization employed a number of big names, including Ernie Pyle and Eleanor Roosevelt, but it had no margin to be indulgent, or even diplomatic. "Eleanor is easiest to cut," decided one editor, "because she never says much."[43]

Just before the big day, embarrassed AP executives had good reason to wish that one of their lowly operatives had said even less than the first lady. The AP's big blunder stemmed from another facet of the wire services' intensive preparations. Determined to leave nothing to chance, both the AP and the UP produced dozens of press releases and news stories in late May, which only needed the green light from Eisenhower's HQ to be released. The UP alone had prepared 20,000 words, going as far as to induce "the censors to pass several dispatches describing the armada, air fleet, etc., giving a lot of details" without specifying dates or locations.[44]

The AP was equally prolific, but perhaps not so careful—and therein lay the problem. At 4:39 p.m. on Saturday, June 3, an AP flash suddenly went out over the wires that Allied forces had landed in France. The culprit was a young teletype operator who had been using a quiet moment to practice hammering out one of the AP's pre-prepared stories. As a harassed PRO complained, because of a simple error, "she practiced on 130 million people." Horrified, SHAEF issued a "kill" order within five minutes, but it was too late. Radio networks had already interrupted their programs. Across the United States, announcers at baseball parks and movie theaters had also broken the "news." Some churches even rang their bells in celebration.[45]

At least one invasion-bound correspondent thought the teletype girl ought to "be banished—perhaps shot."[46] Eisenhower, though, appeared to take it all in his stride, largely because he had even weightier worries on his mind. After the months of preparation, he still had to decide when to launch the assault. He had originally selected June 5, but at practically the same time that the rogue AP story hit the wires, the weather across southern Britain started to change. Instead of sunny skies came the more familiar sight of dense clouds, followed by increasingly strong winds. The forecast for June 5 looked particularly unpromising, so Eisenhower deferred the operation for a day. He also postponed the arrival of the correspondents who would accompany him during the invasion period, sighing wearily "that too much [was] going on here at the moment."[47]

TENSION

This time, the military's summons to the media would be camouflaged as much as possible. As the big day approached, the planners decided that the perennial problem of limited space on the transport ships meant that a mere twenty-eight of the 530 accredited correspondents would be hitting the beaches on D-Day. Yet even this small number worried Davis's security-obsessed PROs, especially those who remembered how the sudden disappearance from London of the big-name reporters in October 1942 had fueled the city's hyperactive rumor mill. "Past experience," noted one, "has shown that the general exodus of well-known writers from Fleet Street spreads immediately as an indication of forthcoming operations of importance."

During the spring, SHAEF's PROs employed various strategies to ensure that the same thing did not happen again. On a number of occasions, they took correspondents out of London on short notice, sending them to far-flung parts of the British Isles in order "to accustom possible enemy observers to their absence without arousing suspicion." They also encouraged invasion-bound reporters to build up a backlog of stories that could be published in the period just before the attack, when they would be quarantined from the outside world.[48]

None of these gambits could dispel the mounting tension, however. On the contrary, they often heightened the reporters' fears. Throughout

May, Pyle met frequently with friends like Stoneman and Whitehead to speculate about when and where the massive Allied blow would fall. "In more pensive moments," he admitted, "we also conjectured our chances of coming through alive." Those who had been at Anzio were not optimistic. Whitehead came down with a bad case of "nerves"; Stoneman increasingly contemplated the awful fact that "thousands of men will not be here one week from today," perhaps including himself. But inevitably it was Pyle who suffered the most, including "terrible periods of depression" that resulted in frequent nightmares. "All the time fear lay blackly deep down upon your consciousness," he recalled a few weeks later. "It bore down on your heart like an all-consuming weight. People would talk to you and you wouldn't hear what they were saying."[49]

Pyle's mood was not helped by a particularly morbid example of the military's thorough planning. Not long before the big day, Davis's PROs invited the assault-wave reporters to a meeting in an ordinary-looking building in South Kensington. There, an officer told them to write their obituaries in case they were needed. It was a somber moment, leavened only by gallows humor. Stoneman, as competitive as ever, waited until his *Chicago Sun* rival had typed out four pages and then stated baldly: just say I was all the places he was—"and usually filed first, too." Pyle, who had long believed he would be killed in action, listed his main achievements, covered his face with his hands for a moment, and then wrote: "And when it becomes necessary to release this information, please inform my syndicate so it can break the news to my wife, rather than informing her direct."[50]

As the days dragged on, some of the journalists resorted to bouts of frenetic activity to dispel dark last-minute thoughts. On May 24, Robert Capa hosted a massive party for his old friend Ernest Hemingway, who had just arrived in town. It was a raucous occasion, with free-flowing booze, and peaches soaked in brandy and drizzled with champagne. The famous author left at four the next morning, driven by a doctor who managed to smash the car into a water tank that he had failed to see in the blackout. The next day Capa hurried to the hospital, commiserating with his friend about his stitches and concussion—while also taking a series of photos of a bandaged Hemingway that appeared in *Life* a few weeks later.[51]

After weeks of waiting, the chosen correspondents received their phone calls just after breakfast on May 29. On the other end of the line a voice chatted amiably for a while, before uttering the ominous words: "I'd like you to come over in an hour, and it would be a good idea to bring along a musette bag. You might go out of town for a day or two."[52]

At the PROs' office the reporters collected their travel visas, blankets, shovels, seasickness pills, medical kits, and K rations. Then they jumped into the jeeps and trucks that took them out of London. After a long drive they ended up in an ultra-secure assembly area, wincing as they tried to regain feeling in their cramped legs. Capa was one of four photographers who made the trip, and he thought the assembly point bore an uncanny resemblance to a concentration camp. Most of his fellow travelers tried their best to smile and joke, as they congregated in small groups to wish each other luck or make hopeful promises to meet up later in a favorite café or bar in Paris.[53]

Pyle, Stoneman, and Whitehead stuck together that first night, sleeping in a cold tent and trying to toughen up after weeks of cushy hotel living. Early the next morning the correspondents headed off to their different units, once again traveling jammed roads in jeeps or buses. Twenty miles from the coast, they entered another exclusion area: no civilians, just thousands of troops, with shaved heads and tough, unsmiling expressions. When they reached the packed ports, a waiting PRO reminded them of the "stringent rules" for D-Day censorship. And then the time came for them to board their ships.

Space on every vessel was at a premium. George Hicks had traveled down from London in a bus containing the bandage-swabbed Hemingway, who had ignored his bad head wound, and a doctor's stern warning that he was not fit enough to go, to witness this historic moment. After the slow drive, Hicks found himself allocated to the USS *Ancon*, which proved to be a stroke of luck since the ship would operate as a command and communications center. Like any good pro, Hicks immediately began to look on the bright side: if he came through the coming days unscathed, he mused, he ought to have little difficulty relaying his broadcasts quickly to London and New York.[54]

Despite the mounting tension, other reporters reached equally heartening conclusions. Don Whitehead was overjoyed to learn that he would be rejoining the First Division, with whom he had endured so much on Sicily a year earlier. He was also pleased to discover he would be teaming up with a grinning John Thompson, whose Sicilian exploits continued to inspire a measure of awe. Although Thompson would not be parachuting into the battle this time, the First's commander had made it abundantly clear that a seaborne landing was not a soft option. "We are ready to help you in any way possible," drawled the genial general. "If an unlucky shell should get you," he added ominously, "we'll do all we can. If you're wounded we'll take care of you. If you're killed we'll bury you. Meantime, we'll feed you and see you get what you want."[55]

If the Fighting First's commanding officer was more candid than most, the prospect of imminent death cast a long shadow on every boat, prompting many on board to sit quietly and write a last letter to a loved one. Luckily, most of the war correspondents were initially so preoccupied with more prosaic professional problems that they did not have time to dwell on this saturnine task. Capa was a case in point. As soon as he had dropped off his kitbag on the USS *Samuel Chase*, he attended a briefing. Since the *Chase* was "a mother ship which carried many assault barges," an officer explained, Capa could pick his own spot to land on the target beach, which went by the codename Omaha. Always the gambler, Capa reveled in the task of guessing which unit had the best prospect. Always the risk taker, he ultimately decided to join the first wave of a company scheduled to attack "Easy Red," on the heart of Omaha beach. Making the choice suddenly concentrated Capa's mind. Minutes later, he slouched off to write his own last letter home, before heading to the mess, where he sat and stared at a large meal that his churned-up stomach had little prospect of digesting.[56]

As darkness fell on June 5, Capa was not the only journalist who was fixated on the grim odds. Pyle and Stoneman had equally morose thoughts. Because of his celebrity status, Pyle had been slated to receive the grandest possible treatment, including a personal invitation from Bradley to travel on his flagship, the USS *Augusta*. Yet Ernie could not be tempted. He decided to rough it with the fighting men crammed into a LST (landing ship, tank), even if it meant wading into the cold sea to board his boat. That night Pyle was tenser than ever. "From a vague anticipatory dread," he wrote a short while afterward, "the invasion now turned into a horrible reality to me."[57]

Stoneman fully agreed. "All we know," he mused from another vantage point along the English Channel, "is that the cream of American and British manhood is to be thrown into the noisiest, riskiest, most lethal contest of high-explosive skill, courage, and stamina in history." As June 6 edged ever closer, it was a thought to chill the bones of even the most hard-bitten war correspondent.[58]

CHAPTER 14

Invasion, 1944

A DISTANT BATTLE

On the USS *Ancon* George Hicks managed to grab a few hours of fitful sleep, only to be woken up by the sound of a massive naval bombardment. Hicks walked to the side of the ship, and looked down at the dozens of landing craft bobbing in the choppy sea. The soldiers in the boats had "white, agonizing faces," Hicks noted privately. "It was horrible to see. My mouth tasted bad. I could hardly straighten up. I was sick and wanted to throw up but I was too tired. All I could think was 'My God, they're going in.'"

Along with a number of other correspondents, Hicks had not been assigned to hit the beaches during the first assault waves. All he could do was to peer toward the horizon as the landing craft faded from view and were replaced by yellow flashes and rising plumes of smoke. He managed one brief chat with the admiral commanding the *Ancon*, who told him "things were going well," albeit with "heavier resistance than expected [in] this area." But he had little sense of the actual conditions five miles away. How fast were troops penetrating inland? What was it like to wade through the water and then run across the beach in the midst of enemy fire? Who among those white, agonized faces had suffered the further agonies of being struck by German bullets, shells, or mines? Inevitably, Hicks's private thoughts became deeply personal. Tightly grasping the ship's rail, he wondered if his "kid brother" had survived his first moments on French soil.[1]

Although Hicks was much closer to the scene than most observers, his experience was a somewhat typical blend of anxiety and distance that was felt by the vast majority of Americans on this fateful day. For the twenty or so US war correspondents who were about to hit the beaches, June 6 would be either a huge relief, as they strolled ashore on Utah beach to relatively little resistance, or a harrowing experience, as they scurried around the corpses strewn across bloody Omaha. For the vast majority of reporters and their home-front audience, D-Day was a distant event, something they could only piece together in vague outlines from the sketchy clues provided by Eisenhower's command.

While a small proportion of American reporters spent a nervy night on the English Channel trying to discern the outlines of the French coast, many more remained in London. For those assigned to SHAEF, their destination on that cool, cloudy morning was the hulking British Ministry Information building in Senate House, a mile or so northwest of Fleet Street. To the novelist Evelyn Waugh, the building was little short of an insult to the London skyline.[2] To reporters suddenly roused from their beds at dawn by a terse telephone message, the smoke-filled and airless offices inside were scarcely more alluring.

The hundred or so who arrived just after dawn found an unprecedented level of security. Once they had been admitted to the conference room, they could only leave to visit the bathroom, and even then, a military policeman or woman had to accompany them. Inside the room were two long tables, on which typewriters, pens, and pencils were lined up neatly for the reporters' use, while on every wall were maps, charts, and photographs, illuminated with state-of-the art indirect lighting. When called to their first briefing, the correspondents headed toward six rows of canvas chairs arranged in front of a raised platform, from which an officer droned on about the censorship regulations. Then a British brigadier entered the room. "Ladies and gentlemen," he declared. "In five seconds Communiqué Number One is being released to the entire world." After a pregnant pause, which only increased the tension in the room, he shouted: "Go!"

The sudden frenzy in the room left some of the bigger journalistic names cold, especially those who had been denied an invasion berth. Martha Gellhorn, Hemingway's wife, was the most conspicuous of these. She had encountered all sorts of problems to get to this point, including seeing her husband grab *Collier's* one combat slot (a position she thought was hers) before failing to get her an air ticket from New York (forcing her to travel across the Atlantic on a freighter packed with dynamite). Never one to hide her emotions, Gellhorn let months of frustration bubble to the surface. As another correspondent noted to himself, she "arrived late, wearing white gloves, and when she discovered that all anyone really knew was Communiqué Number One and that she couldn't leave the room, she wished she hadn't come. 'I want to go out and see the expressions on people's faces,' she moaned."[3]

At another desk sat Ed Murrow, who now had a far less glamorous job than reporting the blitz four years earlier—but one so exhausting that he had little time to ponder the prospect of being somewhere else. "Newspaper and magazine correspondents have maybe two, maybe one deadline a day, or maybe only one a week or month," he remarked wearily, his trademark cigarette dangling from his mouth. "We have one every fifteen minutes." Struggling to keep up with this relentless pressure, Murrow took some solace in the absence of competition, since all the radio stories were pooled. As a result, whenever there was a problem, the London heads of the main networks would adjourn to the press bar across from the radio studio, where they would form a "committee" and hammer out a solution together. Even for America's biggest radio star, security remained supertight. As soon as Murrow moved behind the microphone, a censor sat on his left, primed to flick the red switch if he deviated from the officially sanctioned script.[4]

While Murrow doggedly handled both the unremitting pressure and the censors' demands, Wes Gallagher hurried around the conference room aiming to be the first to get Eisenhower's communiqué on the wire. SHAEF released the invasion story at 9:32 a.m. Less than a minute later Gallagher's initial story was being sent to New York, the first of more than 40,000 words that he and the rest of the AP team would hammer out over the next twenty-fours. It was this first cable that was crucial, however. This was the one that would allow his bosses to claim that they had "scored sensationally on the No. 1 story of our times." And Gallagher was taking no chances. As soon as the censors removed the stop order, he sent his first brief "flash" of the breaking news. He also dispatched another 1,300-word story from Senate House to Fleet Street by courier, taking care to backstop "this delivery by telephoning duplicates over the direct line."[5]

Gallagher's lead reached an AP office desperate to forget the rogue story it had put out the previous Saturday. In the early hours of June 6, its invasion staff was alerted by a series of bulletins from the continent. Although these emanated from a Nazi propaganda agency, the media bosses in London and New York took them seriously enough to put their D-Day operations on high alert. For the AP this meant mobilizing copyeditors, checking communications, and ensuring that couriers were on hand to pick up Gallagher's pouches from Senate House. For other news organizations, it entailed putting their carefully considered production plans into action.[6]

The *New York Times* was typical. Before the German news flash, the *Times*' presses had already run off 140,000 copies of its normal edition, but they still managed to churn out 235,000 special invasion issues—and shifted 50,000 newspapers more than usual. "We . . . sold all we could print," remarked Edwin James, the *Times*' managing editor, before adding ruefully that paper rationing had limited output and therefore sales.[7]

As the big-city newspapers distributed their special invasion editions to street-corner vendors, many Americans turned on their radios. With audiences 80 percent larger than normal, the networks "ruthlessly" scrapped all their commercials. Despite depriving itself of the resulting advertising revenue, NBC made its coverage particularly lavish.[8]

Because of the time difference, it was 3:30 a.m. on the East Coast when the NBC newscaster interrupted normal programming. "In a tense, excited voice," he announced that "we can expect, in a very few seconds, a very important broadcast from the British capital." A short while later, the newscaster read out the contents of Communiqué Number One. Then NBC's prearranged D-Day schedule went into overdrive. In quick succession, listeners were bombarded with a series of reports from an impressive array of venues: an analysis from the New York-based news anchor; a description of "twenty-three square miles of invasion boats" from an eyewitness on the fleet's flagship; Eisenhower's broadcast to the people of occupied Europe; another eyewitness story, this time from a correspondent who had been on a plane that had dropped the first paratroopers behind enemy lines; and so on, as the network shifted between New York, London, and the invasion forces.[9]

Despite this frenzy of activity, the actual content of the first reports tended to be heavy on prayers and light on graphic battlefield details. For most of the day neither the networks nor the newspapers could divulge anything more than the basic fact that Eisenhower had launched the invasion and that the beachhead had not been hurled straight back into the sea. As one analyst at the *Baltimore Sun* observed, there was "no suggestion as to how the troops were faring, no clue to the number of separate landings, no inkling as to the numbers of the fighting men involved in the attacks by land, sea, and air."[10]

Security, or more accurately the need to confuse the Nazis, was the key reason for the lack of detail. During the months of preparation, Allied intelligence had reached an important conclusion: the Germans thought that an invasion was most likely, not in Normandy, but in the Pas de Calais region of France, where the English Channel was at its narrowest. According to Eisenhower, the Germans also believed that the Allies would "make more than one major landing and that the first one w[ould] be diversionary."

To foster both misconceptions SHAEF had developed Operation Fortitude, an elaborate deception plan whose goal was to convince Hitler that the Normandy landings were only a ruse. If successful, Fortitude would pin down key German units far to the north of the Allied beachheads and give Eisenhower and Montgomery vital time to establish an impregnable position on Normandy's Cotentin peninsula.[11] But success depended on denying the Germans key information about the type and quantity of resources that the Allies were pouring ashore in Normandy on June 6. "We must keep the enemy guessing," Eisenhower reminded his senior advisers in late May. "Anything that the press and radio can do to keep the enemy in a state of nervousness" was important.[12]

It was largely for this reason that the first London-datelined reports tended to be cagey about key details. Most importantly, they blurred the crucial fact that the attack had been launched on the Normandy beaches, emphasizing instead the massive air assault taking place farther north, in the Pas de Calais region.[13]

"A POOR SHOW ON THE PART OF THE GERMANS"

Then all of a sudden, George Hicks grabbed his D-Day scoop. It was shortly after 10:30 p.m., and the nighttime darkness had emboldened the outgunned Luftwaffe to launch a raid on the huge Allied armada lying off the Normandy coast. Hicks happened to be recording his D-Day impressions for posterity when the first planes passed overhead. He kept on talking while his recorder picked up the terrifying noises: the uneven throbs of the attacking airplanes' engines, the howling whistles of descending bombs, and the brutal thuds of massive naval guns throwing up defensive fire. It was war reporting in its most vivid form, and Hicks's recording created a major sensation after it was relayed through London to New York in time for the last broadcasts of the day. At 11:30 p.m. all the main US networks interrupted their programs. "So, now," intoned one announcer, "NBC takes you to London for the first eyewitness account of the actual invasion of Europe!"[14]

As listeners gathered around their radios, they could hear Hicks calmly recount the arrival of the German planes, and then the Americans firing back. "Tracers are making an arc right over our bow now," he explained excitedly, "and disappearing into the clouds before they burst.... Looks like we're gonna have a night tonight." As the fight between the ships and the German aircraft continued, Hicks's exhilaration mounted. "They got one," he announced to the sound of cheers in the background, "they got one. A great blotch of fire came smoldering down just off our port side in the sea. Smoke and flame there."[15]

Hicks's scoop set the tone for the next wave of D-Day reports, which were written by correspondents who were nearer to the action and could add more color. On board a destroyer, the AP's Tom Yarbrough got to within a mile and a half of the French coast. "With strong binoculars, standing on the bridge," he recorded in a dispatch published on June 7, "I saw thousands of men and machines tumble safely across beaches bristling with ugly spikes driven into the sands at all angles and topped with mines—beaches smoking from the terrible plastering of bombs and naval shells." Tom Treanor of the *Los Angeles Times* made it even closer. Hitchhiking a ride on a coastguard cutter, he set foot on French soil to find relatively weak German resistance. There were certainly dangers, he observed in a story that appeared on June 8, including mines, shells, and a few large fortifications. But Treanor confirmed that the landing appeared to have been "reasonably soft," the navy guns having silenced German artillery, while all along the beach "men, jeeps, bulldozers, and other equipment were moving around."[16]

Thus, the first media frame was rapidly established: D-Day had been a stunning success, bought at the price of surprisingly few casualties. In another dispatch, Yarbrough wrote that the initial landings had "seemed too easy and too smooth to be true." Beforehand, he added, the soldiers had "come to refer to this thing (the invasion) as the 'bloodbath' and not altogether facetiously. But it was not a bloodbath at all." Other accounts agreed. Richard McMillan of the UP expressed surprise at "the weakness of German defense line. I examined with care the so-called Atlantic Wall along the coast. It constitutes the biggest bluff of the war, for it simply does not exist."[17]

To his immense relief, Bill Stoneman enjoyed an equally easy passage back to the country whose language, culture, and wines he loved. The *Chicago Daily News* man hit Utah beach mid-morning, June 6, still not quite believing that he was about to set foot in France after an absence of four years. The landing, he wrote a few hours later, "has been strangely similar to Salerno": sufficient German shelling and machine-gun fire to force him to dash across the sand, but without the slaughter he had long feared.

As Stoneman began to get his bearings and take stock, his optimism grew apace. After touring the beach, he concluded that "our losses of equipment and of life have been small both in landing and in battle." After chatting with the troops, he decided that the main problems derived not from Germans but from "the stupidity or nervousness of a few foolish small-landing-craft crews who, in contrast to the behavior of the great majority of small boatmen, failed to put their boats far enough into the shore when they saw it was being strafed or shelled. As a result," he concluded ruefully, "trucks went over their depth into the briny, and when high tide came their contents in many cases were washed away."

Stoneman's obvious annoyance stemmed from a familiar gripe: one of the main victims of this fiasco had been the radio he needed to relay his stories back to London. With the equipment meant for his part of the beach at the bottom of the sea, all the months of planning by T. J. Davis and Joe Phillips had been effectively rendered useless. Stoneman therefore had little option other than to hand his copy to one of courier boats returning to Britain and pray that it somehow found his editor.[18]

Stoneman's story, when it finally appeared on the front page a few days later, was revealing. A hardened Italian veteran, Stoneman should have known better than to crow. In quieter, more reflective moments, he remembered from the painful experience at Salerno and Anzio that the hardest part of an amphibious assault was not getting ashore, but staying there. Still, when he began to write he could scarcely seem to help himself. It was not just the dictates of censorship, or the patriotic desire to be part of the military team at such a big moment. It was also the months of pent-up tension followed by euphoria at having survived—similar to what Homer Bigart experienced after he had returned unscathed from a B-17 bombing mission. For all these reasons, as Stoneman sat in a foxhole and began to write, exultant words began to flow.[19]

"The more you think about our landing at the base of the Cherbourg [Cotentin] Peninsula last Tuesday," he wrote in one dispatch, "the more mysterious the whole thing becomes." The threatened minefields had failed to materialize. The German troops had turned out to be mediocre and their artillery had been "ridiculously weak." The Luftwaffe, Stoneman added, which "should have been able to put in 1000 planes against us, has produced two piddling little fighter-bomber raids by four and six planes." "Even compared to Salerno or Anzio," he concluded, "this 'battle of the ages' has been a poor show on the part of the Germans, who presumably are fighting for their lives."[20]

As Ike's PR team began to sift through the early stories, they sensed danger. All through D-Day, as he struggled to get a clear sense of the situation on the beaches, Eisenhower confessed to feeling "so goddarn nervous." Thankfully, on Utah beach and in the British and Canadian sectors the landings seemed to have been relatively successful. Nevertheless, Ike and his team remained alarmed at the "build-up of over-optimism" they were seeing in too many press reports, especially as this mood bore little resemblance to the true situation on Omaha beach.[21]

BLOODY OMAHA

John Thompson and Don Whitehead had discovered that Omaha would be their D-Day destination during the journey across the Channel. On the night before the attack, both reporters had visited Colonel George Taylor in his cabin. Taylor commanded the Sixteenth Regiment of the First Division, and he came straight to the point. "There would be hell to pay on the beaches," he told the correspondents. "His regiment had been given the job of opening the way for tens of thousands of other troops and . . . they had to do it no matter what the cost." "Hell," the colonel added, "we might as well face it. We're playing with lives in this game."

A moment like this was crucial in the career of a war reporter. Unlike everyone else on board, Whitehead and Thompson theoretically had a choice. In the final analysis, there was nothing compelling them to join the deadly game—nothing, that is, except their sense of professional obligation, a duty to the home front, and real personal courage. "Because we were participants," Whitehead wrote later, "—carrying typewriters instead of guns—we had accepted the responsibilities that go with the job of being a frontline correspondent. None of us who have seen men die, who have watched the wounded being carried from the battlefield, who in a small way have shared at times their dangers and hardships can forget that responsibility." So, trying to suppress their deepest fears, Whitehead and Thompson joined the Sixteenth Regiment as it hit the hottest part of Omaha beach.[22]

Within seconds of leaving the landing craft, they realized that this particular game would be far deadlier than Colonel Taylor had predicted.[23] Whitehead jumped out of his landing craft with a lightweight typewriter strapped to his back, "encased in a raincoat for waterproofing." Like many of the soldiers around him, he made it no more than a hundred yards inland before being forced to drop to the ground and begin desperately burrowing into the loose gravel to escape the intense incoming fire. As senior officers dashed up and down the beach exhorting the men to advance, Whitehead tried to follow them, "but at times it was impossible," he recalled later, "because of utter exhaustion."

Pausing for breath, Whitehead noticed the hideous sights all around him. "Wounded men," he told a colleague shortly after, "drenched by cold water, lay in the gravel, some with water washing over their legs, shivering, waiting for stretcher-bearers to take them aboard returning small craft." Everywhere, shell bursts constantly struck the ground, "some so close that they threw black water and dirt over us in showers."[24]

Having somehow survived, Whitehead had to get his dispatch off the beach. Because of the strength of the enemy defenses, the first group of

PR specialists only landed around midday. Amazingly their radios had survived, floated ashore from the landing craft "in waterproof chests." But in the chaos of the first hours, the one meant for Whitehead's part of the beach had been placed aboard a jeep that drove off in the wrong direction and could not be located for twenty-eight hours. Like Stoneman on Utah beach, Whitehead hunted for couriers heading back to Britain, only to find that they simply "didn't exist." As on Sicily, he therefore remained frustratingly incommunicado, despite having just been part of one of the main news stories of the war.[25]

Even when he discovered a way to get his story on to the AP wire, Whitehead struggled to communicate what he had seen. Naturally, he had to write with one eye on what the censors would permit; but another important process was at work. Just as Stoneman's profound relief at surviving the landing had encouraged him to write with a tinge of euphoria, so Whitehead's numbed shock made it difficult for him to reproduce the true horror of what he had witnessed on Omaha beach. Nor did the frightening and frenzied working environment help. After spending much of the morning lying prostate in hastily scrabbled trenches, Whitehead finally hauled himself into a more secure foxhole. By now, he "was ready to drop with fatigue," but he still had to tap out his story, which he did "that afternoon under shellfire that made his typewriter jump on his shaking knees."[26]

Small wonder that Whitehead's first stories were anodyne. In one, he merely described the troops wading ashore to the "rattle of machine guns and the bursting of shells." In another, he revealed that the "Fighting First" had taken on the biggest D-Day job, which entailed dodging underwater obstacles and diving for cover under "murderous fire." Whitehead did admit to witnessing numerous "grisly sights," from dead bodies sprawled everywhere to wounded soldiers lying "at the water's edge with the glazed look of shock waiting until some one could remove them." But he carefully added that "there was no panic. The men even joked and occasionally laughed." As for the battle as a whole, Whitehead concluded that the First Division had proved "that the heralded invincibility of the Atlantic Wall was but a myth. It wasn't easy and it cost lives to prove it, but the Fighting First did it in one epic battle with a magnificent display of sheer courage."[27]

Even on Omaha beach, then, the press coverage failed to burst the overoptimism bubble. But perhaps this was inevitable. Perhaps words were always going to struggle to convey the reality of such a massive and ghastly battle. Don Whitehead certainly thought so. He had been through the trauma of an amphibious landing five times, but all that experience had proved to be more of a hindrance than a help. "I've lost my perspective," he confessed shortly after D-Day. "It's like dreaming the same nightmare over and over again, and when you write you feel that you have written it all before. You can't think of any new or different words to say it with." Tom Treanor, who had briefly scurried ashore on D-Day, put it even more bluntly: "It was too much to describe." [28]

If the print reporters were finding it difficult to convey the reality, then the situation was ripe for other media forms. Radio had already done a better job at conveying the drama, even though George Hicks's blow-by-blow combat report was, for the time being, a one-off. That left photographs—especially those that accompanied the words of the journalists who were working without the pressure of a tight deadline. And this provided Robert Capa with yet another opportunity to burnish his already-legendary reputation.

Capa had boarded a landing craft bound for Omaha shortly after six on D-Day morning. Joining the second wave ashore, he began wading through the cold seawater, pushing past GIs who stumbled and fell. As the shellfire intensified, he hid behind an incoming tank for twenty minutes. Then, realizing that the German artillery were singling out the tanks, he made a dash for the beach and took cover next to a soldier who quipped that he could see his "old mother sitting on the porch" waving his insurance policy. What happened next has gone down in D-Day lore.

"It was very unpleasant there," Capa explained soon after, "and, having nothing else to do, I start[ed] shooting pictures." Within ninety minutes he had run out of film, so he waded back out to sea, toward a returning landing craft loaded with medics. It was scarcely any safer on board. Capa concentrated on changing his film, only to discover that he was covered with feathers: a shell had hit the ship, and the feathers came from the stuffing in the jackets of all the men who had been blown away. It was at this moment that Capa, like Whitehead on the beach, began to succumb to exhaustion—only, in contrast to a print reporter, the creative part of his job was done. His photos had been taken; he had already captured the compelling images of what it had been like on the beach early that fateful overcast morning. All he had to do was to get the film back to London, and then on to New York.[29]

Capa hitched a ride back to England on another ship, and immediately fell asleep. On dry land, confusion reigned. Before the invasion the SHAEF PROs had decided they lacked the "materials, equipment, and help" to establish a single, central darkroom, so they instructed photographers to send their negatives to the London offices of their own organizations for speedy processing.[30] If that was the idea, it took more than a day for Capa

Figure 14.1 American soldiers landing on Omaha Beach, D-Day, Normandy, France, June 6, 1944. Robert Capa. © Center of Photography / Magnum Photos.

to get his film back to the *Life*'s offices in London, where it would have to be developed in a hurry to make the June 19 issue. Because of the rush, a lab technician "put the negatives in the drying cabinet with the heat on high and closed the door." They melted within minutes. Thankfully, eleven of the seventy-two images Capa had taken on the beach could be saved. Many of the surviving pictures had been made blurry by the overheating, but that did not bother the caption writers. "[The] immense excitement of [the] moment," they disingenuously explained, "made Photographer Robert Capa move his camera and blur [his] picture."[31]

Capa was naturally upset when he heard what had happened. The surviving images, he complained, were "nothing compared to the material which . . . got ruined." To soften the blow, *Life* offered Capa a salary of $9,000 a year.[32] It also generously displayed the remaining pictures over seven pages of its major D-Day issue. As the magazine hit the newsstands, it quickly became apparent that the grainy quality of the developed photos actually helped to magnify their impact, giving the battle a vivid, eerie quality. But this was not the only key to their success. Unlike Stoneman, Thompson, or Whitehead, Capa had done his main work during, not after, the battle; as such, the quality of his output was less susceptible to his personal sense of shock, exhaustion, or even exultation. Moreover, because of the longer deadline, *Life*'s New York writers could also place Capa's photos in a sharper perspective, without the intense censorship pressures that print reporters had faced at the start of the invasion.

"Although the first reports of landings indicated little opposition," *Life*'s D-Day issue declared on June 19, "his [Capa's] pictures show how violent the battle was and how strong the German defenses. His best pictures were made when he photographed the floundering American doughboys advancing through the deadly hail of enemy fire to goals on the beaches of Normandy."[33] At long last, then, Americans on the home front had information with which to begin trying to comprehend what had happened on bloody Omaha.

CHAPTER 15

Normandy Stalemate

A ROUTINE WAR

By the morning of June 7, the Germans were gone from Omaha beach, but the carnage remained. From the water's edge up through the steep escarpment, military police had carefully marked out passages that directed the arriving waves of reinforcements through the minefields. Everywhere else betrayed the grim evidence of the desperate battle. In the sea, the sharp edges of defensive obstacles or the overturned remnants of landing craft, tanks, and jeeps protruded through the stiff waves at low tide. The pockmarked sand revealed the areas that had sustained the most shellfire, as did the numerous bodies of the dead that had been lined in neat rows, their faces covered by blankets. More macabre were the bloated corpses that had yet to be given this last little dignity. All around, a curious mishmash of personal belongings, from diaries to shoe polish, socks to Bibles, only added to the disturbing scene, especially when they were scattered again by an occasional shell fired from a German position a couple of miles inland.

Ernie Pyle walked gingerly into the maelstrom early that morning. His first instinct was to make a mental note of all the D-Day destruction, which he duly recounted in one of his inimitable dispatches a few days later. His second impulse was more personal. Pyle clambered up the escarpment in search of his reporter friends, the ones he had bid farewell to a few days ago. Had they survived? About a half mile in land, he saw John Thompson sitting on the edge of a foxhole "dug into the rear slope of a grassy hill." Thompson was easy to spot, his trademark thick beard giving him away from a distance. "You've never seen a beach like it before," the *Tribune* reporter began as soon as Pyle sidled up to his foxhole. "Dead and wounded men were lying so thick you could hardly take a step," Thompson added, relating disturbing details that had been omitted from his D-Day dispatches. "One officer was killed only two feet away from me."

When Ernie met up with the other correspondents he began to understand why they had found it so difficult to report their first impressions. "The boys were unshaved," he noted, as a group of reporters gathered around him, "and their eyes were red. Their muscles were stiff and their bodies ached. They had carried ashore only their typewriters and some K-rations," he explained. "They had gone two days without sleep and then had slept on the ground without blankets, in wet clothes. . . . They were in a sort of daze from the exhaustion and mental turmoil of battle. When anyone asked a question it would take them a few seconds to focus on their thoughts and give an answer."

Pyle found Whitehead in a particularly dazed state. "Get up you lazy so and so," Ernie jokingly shouted into the foxhole in which the aptly nicknamed "beachhead Don" still lay sleeping, a blanket stretched over his body and his sodden socks to one side. When Whitehead finally managed to focus his thoughts, he wondered how he had lived to see another day. "It was really awful," he told Pyle. "For hours there on the beach the shells were so close they were throwing mud and rocks all over you. It was so bad that after a while you didn't care whether you got hit or not." When he heard the full story, Ernie concluded that his buddy really had no "right to be alive at all." Whitehead agreed and even vowed to "slow up a bit"—or at least as much as his sense of duty to the fighting man and loyalty to the AP would permit.[1]

After digesting the appalling anecdotes, Pyle felt no regret that a last-minute change of plan for his boat had denied him the chance to witness the biggest day of the war so far. With the waiting over and his closest friends having made it through alive, his spirits began to revive. "All the haunting premonition, the soul-searching dread, was gone," he recalled a short while later. So was any temptation to recount what had really happened the day before. Pounding out his story, Ernie carefully recorded much of the gory clutter that remained on the beach, but, like his colleagues, he excised the grimmest sights. "It was a lovely day for strolling along the seashore," he wrote in his column. "Men were sleeping on the sand, some of them sleeping forever."[2]

For the correspondents who came through D-Day unscathed, the next week was another ordeal. The fighting was still close, and many of them were unable to get any rest at night unless they got so "tight" on booze that they could no longer "hear the guns and planes." The daylight hours were scarcely more bearable. Back on the beaches the military remained obsessed with getting as many men and as much equipment ashore as possible before the Germans counterattacked, but this meant forgoing the creature comforts that made front-line life tolerable. On June 9 an officer found Capa reading a book underneath an old oak tree; nearby, another group of journalists whiled away the time in an extended "bitch session on army PROs." Besides not getting any mail, their major gripe concerned the lack of transportation. Jeeps were still at a premium, and reporters had to fight hard for a place on one of the tours the army's PR specialists were arranging of the ever-expanding beachhead.[3]

Bill Stoneman went on a couple of these excursions in the week after D-Day, and he was immediately struck by the massive improvements the American army had made since the Mediterranean campaign. "Camouflage is now nearly perfect," he told his readers, "vehicular troops are beautifully dispersed, and discipline in behavior toward citizens could not be better." The censors, however, remained as frustratingly clueless as ever. On June 12, Stoneman encountered the "sorry" sight of a "lonely censor wandering around with the story we had written eighteen hours before, trying to find somebody to tell him whether or not he could allow it to be sent." The hapless man, Stoneman explained, "was at least twenty miles from the place we had delivered the story and still looking for some other censors who were supposed to be capable of censoring the story but who, unfortunately, were ten miles away, nobody knew exactly where."[4]

The next day, a snafu between the army and navy only added to the reporters' frustration. With so much military traffic to handle, the US Navy message centers on the Omaha and Utah beaches briefly stopped accepting press copy, leading to another round of complaints. Robert J. Casey, one of Stoneman's colleagues at the *Chicago Daily News*, joked that his last message had been "corked up in a bottle and tossed into the English Channel." Few others saw the funny side—as Omar Bradley, the US First Army commander, discovered when he held his first press conference on French soil on June 17.[5]

As Bradley reached the end of his briefing, reporters began a barrage of angry complaints about their basic working conditions. Communications, they pointed out, were still erratic, especially the radio links back to London. Food and transportation were hard to come by, and the nightly billets lacked even the most basic comforts. "I've been jailed in every country in Europe," quipped Harold Denny of the *New York Times*, "but this was the first time I've been thrown into a concentration camp by the US Army."

Amid widespread laughter Bradley apologized and asked for understanding. He then moved fast to improve things. Besides launching an investigation into the efficiency of the press communications, he made sure that his First Army reporters had access to seven jeeps and three trucks. Soon thereafter, Bradley established a more permanent press camp in an old chateau, just outside the small town of Vouilly.[6]

Inside the chateau, the First Army PROs kitted out the large living room with army chairs and tables, turning it into a very respectable press room. The reporters slept and ate outside in six-person tents pitched next to a large field in which cows grazed.[7] Pyle shared his with Don Whitehead, whom he now considered his best friend in the press corps. On most nights the two men would join the other reporters in long, convivial conversations, swapping stories and drinking large quantities of the local Calvados, a fiery liquor made from Normandy apples that shared some of the qualities of American moonshine. However bad his hangover, Ernie would get up early the next morning and cook the others bacon and eggs on a small Coleman stove.

The situation at Vouilly was a marked improvement. Pyle and the other veteran correspondents soon set about making their tents more comfortable, using readily available military materiel for more prosaic purposes—sleeping on mattresses made of inflatable boat lifesavers or using ration cans for ashtrays. The only thing Pyle could not abide was the smell inside the chateau, which emanated partly from the food, partly from the cows, and partly from the correspondents themselves. Indeed, as he complained to anyone who would listen, the Château de Vouilly might provide the reporters with basic working facilities and a venue in which to chat and drink with colleagues, but it contained not a single bath or shower.[8]

The unkempt correspondents did, however, enjoy the best communication facilities in Normandy. After Bradley's inquest, they acquired a teleprinter capable of transmitting 10,000 words a day back to England. They were also given access to a 400-watt Press Wireless commercial transmitter that connected them directly to New York, and that could easily handle the current peak demand of 45,000 words a day. The transmitter clearly represented a breach of the SHAEF plan, which stipulated that all copy be routed through London. And it particularly angered the correspondents who were working with the British military, who as yet had no access to a high-speed radio. But the reporters at Vouilly could hardly have been happier. They could now get their stories out quickly—certainly faster than their rivals stationed with the British. They could therefore bask in the knowledge that the outside world was reading about Bradley's exploits, while copy on Montgomery's battles sat in his PR camp waiting to be relayed out.[9]

Buoyed by the thought of beating the British, the correspondents stationed with Bradley's First Army soon settled into a more regular working routine. Each morning they would head out in the jeeps and trucks in search for the front. While Monty's troops became bogged down in front of Caen, the US forces began fanning out to the west to reach the other side of the Cotentin peninsula. This improving strategic situation, especially compared to the stalemate of the British, gave the reporters with the First Army another reason to be cheery—though they also appreciated that this success came at a cost.

The reporters who worked for a wire service found the pace of the work particularly grueling. Because communications were so good, they had little choice, one visiting AP man explained, than "to cover the war exactly the same as a continually breaking news story at home. That meant six or eight trips to the front lines every 24 hours."[10]

As the distance between the next ditch and the press camp grew longer, other reporters worried about the growing prospect of a German ambush. One became so disenchanted with the dangerous commute that he even spilled out his private fears to others in the press camp. "It was unfair for us," he grumbled out loud, "to be shelled on the way home after a hard day's work." He received little sympathy. "Take it up with the Newspaper Guild," an officer gruffly replied, as the other correspondents looked on in amusement.[11]

Whenever fighting erupted in the towns and villages due west of the invasion beaches, conditions immediately became hairier. The battle for St. Sauveur, midway across the base of the Cotentin peninsula, was a case in point. As American troops edged slowly into the town on June 16, Stoneman and Thompson adjourned to a hill about a quarter of a mile away. They watched as the tanks hammered away at houses containing German defenders. When the fighting began to subside, both reporters came off the hill and walked warily into St. Sauveur's battle-torn streets, "ducking stray bullets and occasional shells." In front of them unfolded a scene of utter desolation, most of the town's buildings "battered into oblivion." Many French civilians had remained huddled in the ruins during the fight, terrified by the sounds and sights outside. But, according to Stoneman, when the battle started to die down, they would emerge to "look on with keen curiosity and satisfaction as the Germans get the stuffing kicked out of them."[12]

After St. Sauveur, the relentless American drive pushed on, reaching the west coast of the Cotentin peninsula by Sunday, June 18, and cutting off more than 20,000 German troops positioned in and around Cherbourg to the north. Stoneman took particular pleasure in this little triumph. Exactly four years before, he had been one of the group of reporters who had been forced to evacuate France. Today, he basked in the reversal of fortune. "The historic blitzkrieg of 1940," Stoneman told his readers, "flew right back in the face of the Germans over the weekend when the American Ninth Division turned the Cherbourg [Cotentin] Peninsula into a gigantic mousetrap by striking across its base and cutting off Cherbourg and its environs from the interior of France." To the north, he concluded, "Cherbourg is doomed, and with its fall or capitulation the Allies will have their first principal port in France."[13]

"A THIEVES PARADISE . . . A LOOTER'S HEAVEN"

For the next couple of days a large band of reporters joined the "mad race" toward to Cherbourg. Once again, the weather had turned. A chill wind blew in from the north. The skies became so dark that some correspondents needed flashlights to write during the day. When a massive storm finally struck on June 19, disaster threatened: the artificial harbors that had been constructed around the invasion beaches to facilitate the troop buildup were swept out to sea, making the prompt capture of Cherbourg's port even more vital.[14]

For the reporters trudging north in the wind and rain, the army's PR planning finally began to pay rich dividends. Those accompanying the Ninth Division could scarcely believe it when a group of enlisted men appeared one morning and offered to move their gear to the next camp. When they arrived that night, they even found their kit inside a freshly erected tent that had been furnished with electric lights and tables. "Correspondents who came with the Ninth," noted Pyle approvingly, "could get a meal, a place to write, a jeep for the front, or a courier to the rear—and any time they asked."[15]

Most of them needed all this pampering on the journey north because the storming of Cherbourg would prove to be an ordeal. Desperate not to give the Germans any advantage, senior officers initially ordered a total clampdown on stories about the first thrusts into the city. Stoneman explained the situation. "Censorship, which we are not willing to question at the moment," he wrote on June 23, "has prevented us from telling the full story of the preliminaries to yesterday's attack. All we can say is that they were very interesting."[16]

They certainly were. On the first day of the Cherbourg assault, a group of reporters, including Stoneman, Whitehead, and John O'Reilly of the *New York Herald Tribune*, found a perfect vantage point on a cliff high above the city. "It was one of those rare situations," observed O'Reilly, "where you could look down on a great battle and see even small details." As the attack gathered pace, Stoneman found the vista below particularly compelling. "First came a beautifully executed and aesthetically almost perfect dive-bombing attack by successive groups of Thunderbolts," he reported once the censors had lifted their block.

> From a distance of three-quarters of a mile or so their bombs were deafening. Then our artillery opened up, and great geysers of black and red raised by the bombs gave way to lesser pillars of grey smoke. Then there was an enormous high-pitched symphony of small arms and machine gun fire as our infantry went after the Germans.[17]

As the battle progressed, Stoneman and his band of reporters followed the GIs into the city, meeting up with their friends and rivals coming in from other directions. By now, Robert Capa, Ernie Pyle, Jack Thompson, and Charles Wertenbaker of *Time* had joined the show, which, as they quickly discovered, would be almost as dangerous as the D-Day landings.

Thompson's toughest time came on Friday, June 23. That morning, he had joined a unit that initially inched along a number of back roads, where carefully placed German guns had caused plenty of problems. "The job of collecting news in this sector," he noted later, "ceased abruptly while the Nazi shells pinned our group to the sheltering walls of a peasant home. Then," he explained, "realizing that our shelter was a fine target in itself, we decamped to the rear, having talked ourselves into the need of writing immediately."[18]

Elsewhere, Thompson's colleagues erected their bivouacs in places that promised some protection from the guns, and at night they tried to sleep. Charlie Wertenbaker went to Pyle's tent one evening to catch up on some writing. Pyle believed that Wertenbaker "never seemed nervous," but, as with most reporters, it was all just an act. While Pyle dozed, the *Time* man headed back to his own tent, the one he shared with Capa. There, he "lay awake for two hours, listening to scattered shots." As the sound of shelling intensified, he got so scared that he began to shiver; on two occasions he even contemplated dragging his bedroll into a slit trench. That was how he spent the night. When dawn broke Wertenbaker donned his war correspondent's mask—that typical pose of the hard-bitten veteran, insouciantly puffing on a cigarette, awaiting whatever danger came his way.[19]

For Pyle, daylight provided little comfort. The weather, once again, was cloudy and cold. When Ernie arrived at his unit's command post inside an old church, he detected dangers everywhere. He could see the black smoke billowing up from countless fires across the city, while the shellfire crashes were so close as to be almost deafening. Then a young officer arrived and told Pyle, Capa, and Wertenbaker that he was about to take his company into the heat of this raging battle. "There are probably snipers in some of the houses along the way," he explained, before asking: "Do you want to go with us?" Despite his fears, Pyle took one look at the soldiers milling around, then another glance at Capa and Wertenbaker, who betrayed no emotion. Swallowing hard, Pyle replied, "Sure."

As the group set off slowly in the direction of a series of enemy pillboxes, rain came angling down from the skies, adding to the misery. Even so, for the first time that day, Pyle's anxiety began to ebb. He always hated the waiting before and the brooding after. As soon as the officer gave the order, there was no choice other than to plunge ahead. The scariest moment came when everyone took it in turns to leave the shelter of a high wall and dash across an exposed space. For the rest of the time, the day of battle amounted to little more than a long, energy-sapping wait. Pyle killed time by interviewing his companions, squatting on one knee while a soldier held a helmet over the reporters' notebook to keep it dry. Once again, he considered himself lucky to be a columnist, not a straight-news reporter, for he had no real idea of how the battle was unfolding. "Street fighting," he observed, "is just as confusing as field fighting. One side would bang away for a while, then the other side. Between the sallies there were long lulls, with only stray and isolated shots. Just an occasional soldier was sneaking about, and I didn't see anything of the enemy at all."

Eventually, an American tank appeared. Although it was soon hit by a German shell, it managed to destroy two pillboxes before the crew jumped out to safety. Pyle spent the next hour sheltering in a narrow doorway, while the tankers regaled him with stories of their exploits. Then, at long last, a group of German soldiers appeared in the middle of the street. Pyle had become separated from Capa at the start of the hazardous hike, but he now saw the photographer dash into the street, leapfrog the destroyed tank, and begin taking pictures of the Germans—who, thankfully, held up their arms to signify that they were about to surrender.[20]

After the hard slog came the reward. For Capa, this entailed not only taking a picture of the German commander moments after the entire garrison had surrendered, but also the coining one of the most memorable quotes of the war. The general—almost a caricature of the heel-clicking Prussian—had tried to resist Capa, complaining that he was "tired of this picture-taking." In response, Capa sighed theatrically, before announcing: "I too am tired. I have to take pictures of so many captured generals."[21]

Other rewards were more tangible. As O'Reilly confided to a colleague, they "included not only a great story but also large quantities of cognac, beer, cheese, wine, and rum, originally intended for the use of the Wehrmacht." Indeed, the Germans had used Cherbourg as a major supply center, and, as one group of correspondents told Thor Smith when he visited a few days later, it quickly became "a thieves paradise . . . a looter's heaven." Smith concluded, after a doing spot of investigative work, that the reporters had grabbed a sizeable share of the spoils. They all "rode the gravy train in a big way," he remarked privately. "They were some of the first in, and knew all about what was where."[22]

In print, however, the correspondents largely glossed over this aspect of the battle.[23] Instead, they tried to give a sense of how the American noose had gradually tightened around the port's defenders and what modern street fighting entailed. Pyle was in the vanguard, writing a string of stories in which he focused his readers' attention on the combination of intense anticipation, dread, and fear that filled most of the soldiers who fought in Cherbourg's streets. In one column, he described the grim debris of German defeat that littered a key road, especially "hundreds of carts and guns and dead horses," as well as enemy corpses and "burned-out trucks." In others, he recounted his own stop-start journey with the unit attacking the German strongpoint, including a self-deprecatory passage that explained how, deep down, he had hoped to avoid the whole mission. "Going in to battle with an infantry company," Pyle explained, "is not the way to live to a ripe old age."[24]

A much better way of attaining longevity was simply to lie about being close to the action. According to Lieutenant Colonel John M. Redding, one of the senior PROs in Normandy, this kind of trickery was becoming depressingly familiar. Redding even coined a name for it. A number of unscrupulous reporters, he declared on July 5, were guilty of filing stories with "magic carpet" deadlines: "the occasional practice by individuals," he explained, "of 'capturing' towns and writing eyewitness stories without being anywhere in the area."[25]

Redding was an old pro. Before the war he had been, according to one officer, a "top-notch newspaperman, magazine writer, and author," with a decade of experience with the *Chicago Tribune*, the *Chicago Herald-American*, and the INS. For the past two years he had served as a PRO for the Eighth Air Force and then as an officer attached to Bradley's Twelfth Army Group.[26] Having watched so many reporters risk life and limb to get the closest possible look at the air and ground wars, Redding had little patience for those who filed with "false deadlines." Besides, he worried about the reactions of the reporters who had actually covered the brutal fighting around Cherbourg. So he issued a stern warning at the start of July. Any future "magic carpet deadlines," Redding informed everyone throughout the theater, "will constitute grounds for return of correspondents to London."[27]

For the reporters who had just left Cherbourg the order was a much-needed tonic. Some arrived back at Vouilly looking wasted, including Thompson and Wertenbaker, who both had to persuade a friendly quartermaster to kit them out with new boots, jackets, and pants. Pyle slouched into camp looking as scruffy as ever, but his real problems ran far deeper. Exhausted by the battle, he went into one of those "funks" that knocked him out "two or three times a year." For a while, he could not even face the prospect of sitting at his typewriter: just like Whitehead after Omaha, he feared he had nothing fresh to say. "I've been with the war so long," Pyle confessed to his wife, "that nothing is new to me and it's hard to keep any vitality in your writing. Also I hate the war so and some of the time am so depressed by it all that I feel I can hardly keep going."[28]

Only two things kept Pyle slogging away. One was the stunning success of his columns, which had become such a national phenomenon that his editors would rush to clear their front-pages whenever "Ernie writes something of great distinction." The other was his hope that the war might soon be over. If only the Allies could break out of their Normandy beachhead and sweep east into the rest of Nazi-occupied Western Europe, then he could leave all this ghastliness behind.[29]

INTO THE BOCAGE

Unfortunately, the capture of Cherbourg was unlikely to hasten the German collapse, for the port had been too heavily wrecked and booby-trapped to get it working at full capacity any time soon. Yet this victory in the north did allow the American offensive to shift south, where the German lines would have to be broken before the rest of France could be liberated.

As the weather improved, the Francophiles in the press corps began to enjoy themselves at long last. Always prone to producing purplish prose about the surrounding scenery, Bill Stoneman was particularly enthusiastic. "The most congenital crab in the American second-front army," he wrote in late June, "will admit one thing about this campaign: It is being fought in one of the finest bits of countryside ever bathed by the blood of fighting men," with picturesque farmhouses and grandiose chateaus, ever-present vegetable gardens and "rambling vines of jumbo roses."[30]

When it came to fighting the Germans, however, there turned out to be plenty members of the US Army who disliked the countryside intensely. The reason was always the same: the hedgerow country, known locally as the bocage. As one historian has explained, this country "started about ten miles inland from the Normandy beaches and extended in a wide swath from Caumont on the American left to the western coast of the Cotentin Peninsula." Each small field had been walled in over the centuries by farmers using a combination of earth and hedge to build up structures of between three and fifteen feet. As a defensive position, the bocage could hardly have been much sturdier. Indeed, each hedge provided cover, concealment, and a barrier all in one. And the Germans wasted no time using all three attributes to stall the American offensive before it reached the key town of St. Lô.[31]

The sudden halt came as a depressing shock to everyone in the press corps. Pyle felt it more than most. "This hedge to hedge stuff," he remarked privately on June 30, "is a type of warfare we've never run into before.... One day," he continued, "I'll think I'm getting hardened to dead people, dead young people in vast numbers, and then next day I'll realize I'm not and never could be. I have continually to fight against an inner depression over the ghastliness of it all that almost whips me a good part of the time."[32]

A growing number of soldiers felt the same way. As the battle mutated into an unrelenting slog against the German defenses embedded deep in what everyone soon called those "god-damned hedgerows," combat exhaustion began to mount.[33] The symptoms, according to the army's chief neuropsychiatrist, were dejection and dirtiness, a depressed facial expression sometimes marked by tears, trembling or jerky hands, and "varying degrees of confusion, perhaps to the extent of being mute or staring into space." The censors, however, immediately clamped down hard on this story, convinced that the home front had no stomach for it.[34] So reporters had to find other ways to frame the reality of the bocage battle.

Some used the opportunity to give free rein to their descriptive talents. In the shelter of the hedges, began the *Boston Globe*'s Ira Wolfert, in one of the most striking stories, the sudden silence could feel oppressive. In the pause before the next attack on the next position, he elaborated, the main sound came from the puffs and wheezes of shallow breathing. "Lungs," he noted, "don't work very well when a man is afraid and breath becomes very short." Then, as soon as the time came to dash into the open, there was a sudden sense of exposure even worse than on Cherbourg's menacing streets. "Everybody felt naked standing there," Wolfert recorded. "You felt you were sticking up like a sore thumb waiting to be banged again by a hammer. The hedge across the field seemed like a lifetime away for some fellows," which for some of them was "just what it was": the last moments in an all too short lifetime.[35]

As the terrifying battle dragged on, PROs at both SHAEF and the First Army HQ became increasingly concerned. To be sure, most of the reporters confined their published dispatches to explaining the reasons for the impasse: "fog, rain, and mud," combined with the awkward fact that "the enemy on high ground [is] looking down our throats." But any PRO familiar with the reporters' long, alcohol-fueled conversations at the Vouilly camp knew that much darker thoughts were festering just below the surface. Some correspondents were even privately voicing ideas that, if aired in print, would challenge the fundamental purpose of the war.[36]

Back home, the propagandists had boiled this purpose down to one simple notion: the Allies were fighting to "liberate" a grateful European population from the yoke of Nazi oppression.[37] During the Sicilian and Italian campaigns, the war correspondents—on those occasions when they shifted their gaze from combatants to civilians—had effectively echoed this message, detailing the delighted frenzy of Italians as the GIs drove the defeated Wehrmacht away. By contrast, as the Normandy battle ground down to a deadlock, some of these same reporters were casting a more negative eye on the locals' response to the Allied campaign.

The problems began with food. "The correspondents have to have something to gripe about," remarked one cynical PRO at the start of July, and "now it's the food despite the fact that the whole damned fighting force is still on emergency rations." Taking the situation into their own hands, some of the correspondents created an informal a food pool, and, as the PRO noted privately, "they go scrounging out in the countryside for butter and meat and vegetables.... Normandy," he added, "is the home of Camembert, and that is one thing they have a lot of. Right now, bread is the most prized item."[38]

The senior officers in London took a particularly dim view of this behavior. The Allies, they fervently believed, were meant to be sweeping through occupied Europe freeing an ecstatic population from the terror of Nazi occupation. But perhaps, they fretted, this scrounging by the journalists was a sign that the Allies were becoming little better than the Germans, who had long looted the countryside for all its best produce. That was the first troubling consequence of the reporters' search for food. Even more alarming was a growing sense among the correspondents that the French were a big disappointment. Why, some reporters began to ask openly, were they and the GIs fed such a drab diet when the surrounding Norman countryside was teeming with fresh food? Was this because—some muttered menacingly—"the French in Normandy were hostile to the Allies"?[39]

As such talk proliferated, it began to mesh with an even more disturbing conspiracy theory. Some Francophobe reporters began to hint that the deadly sniping in the bocage might not just be the work of the Germans. Perhaps, they intimated, French riflemen were taking aim at the Allies.

SHAEF considered this scuttlebutt extremely dangerous. Keen to prevent it from gaining traction, in early July a senior PRO held a press conference that, as one internal report put it, "was entirely devoted to the attitude of the French towards the Allies." The briefing officer left no one in any doubt: he categorically "denied the sniper stories and explained the apparent anomaly of the food situation (cheese, butter, milk)." His trenchant remarks had some effect on the assembled London-based reporters, but they were only a start. SHAEF also wanted its war correspondents to stress the warm relationship between the Allies and the French—and this was where Hal Boyle proved his worth.[40]

The AP columnist arrived in France just before American Independence Day. His first destination was a picturesque Norman fishing village, where the whole town had turned out to celebrate the two countries' long, shared history of freedom and liberty, dating back to the eighteenth century. As the July 4 festivities got underway, it was the French kids who, as Boyle hastened to point out, "stole the show." They sang "America, the Beautiful" instead of the "Star-Spangled Banner," having found the latter too difficult to learn. Afterward, a thirteen-year-old boy read a message about the town's "unspeakable happiness" at being liberated from a "terrible enemy" that was so moving that "many black-clad old women and several men wept openly." "At the conclusion of the ceremony," Boyle recorded in words designed to heal the rift that had threatened to emerge in recent days, "the children went to the American cemetery and decked the graves of the new-fallen soldiers with flowers."[41]

For the next two weeks Boyle joined the grueling American advance on St. Lô. At first, even he struggled to find a positive way to write about the carnage. Each day, he would spend countless hours interviewing GIs, too many of whom soon joined the First Army's lengthening casualty list. Then, on July 17, Boyle learned of a standout story that at least contained sufficient redemptive qualities to convince the censors to release it without delay.[42]

Major Thomas D. Howie had led a valiant push that day to capture the last big defensive position around St. Lô. Along the way he had rescued another unit that had been cut off for more than twenty-four hours. But the cost of doing so was high, and Howie had paid with his life. Soon after, the American troops finally pushed the Germans out of St. Lô. Boyle discovered what happened next. "They found the major lying covered in a field where medics were working to save the lives of Americans and Germans just wounded," Boyle wrote in a particularly moving dispatch.

> They lifted his light body on a litter and covered him with his raincoat and hospital blanket. It was a rough battlefield ceremony—but there were no flags available. You don't fly brightly colored flags along a battlefront. They drove the dead major slowly back along the road he had walked upon 36 hours before when he was moving his men up to attack. They drove slowly because the dry road was under enemy artillery fire, and any dust cloud visible to German observers brought down immediate shellfire. When the point was reached where a column was assembling for formal entry into St. Lô the body was transferred to an ambulance.

The division commander wanted Howie's remains to enter the city with this vanguard column. "He died trying to win it," explained another officer, "and if it hadn't been for his bravery and military ability we wouldn't have gotten it so quickly." The cortege discovered that the main church, located in the city center, like almost everything else, had been reduced to rubble. So a group of soldiers lifted Howie's body on to the top of the remaining mound of stone. As wave after wave of GIs entered the town, many heard what had happened. "Some," reported Boyle, "doffed their helmets as they passed. Some knelt."[43]

Many more entered St. Lô with their own safety uppermost in their minds, especially as the German artillery remained a deadly menace. One group of correspondents was particularly cautious. Finding themselves sprawled face down in the dirt, they ruefully "wondered," one of them recalled, "whether the Pulitzer Prize was worth all the trouble."[44]

For the military, taking St. Lô was certainly worth the hard slog. The exhausted GIs were just thankful to be free of the bocage, and, as one reporter noted, they entered town "with all the joy of a band of claustrophobes released from a maze."[45] A restive Bradley, for his part, felt relieved to have a little more elbow room for the next phase of his attack: a massive air strike by the heavy bombers, followed by a concentrated assault on the German defensive line.

As Bradley intensified his preparations for this new offensive, codenamed Cobra, he was gripped with a combination of fear and hope. The Germans remained a tenacious enemy. The bloody bocage had demonstrated this awkward fact, as had Montgomery's recent travails near Caen. Like Bradley, Monty had planned a massive air strike to pave the way for a decisive tank breakthrough, but his assault, launched on July 18, had quickly ground to a halt. Worse, Monty had misleadingly briefed the BBC that his Second Army had broken through the German lines. When it was clear that nothing of the sort had transpired, the journalists felt deceived; some even suggested that the British commander be fired.[46]

Bradley obviously wanted to avoid a similar shambles, so he planned Cobra with care. He pushed for the heavy bombers to drop their loads as close to the Allied lines as possible, which would allow his troops to rush forward to exploit the gap caused by the destruction. He also pressed for the use of small bombs that would kill the enemy without cratering the roads and making them impassable for the tanks. The air force fretted about the risk of friendly fire casualties, but Bradley steeled himself for this possibility. To him, the most important thing was cracking the enemy's defenses.[47]

As the day of the attack approached, Bradley found it impossible to conceal his budding confidence, even from reporters. "Once the crust goes," he told Wertenbaker on one occasion, ". . . we are expected to roll through the stuff easily."[48]

A few evenings later, Bradley appeared at the correspondents' camp in Vouilly and summoned everyone to a shed that served as both a briefing room and movie theater. In the dusk he appeared "almost gaunt," one reporter remembered. Gripping a walking stick "as a schoolmaster might use a pointer," he began jabbing it at the maps his aides had pinned to the wall, his voice growing in confidence by the minute. All he needed, Bradley told the rapt reporters, in his slow Missouri drawl, was "three hours of good flying weather any forenoon" and then "he would break out of Normandy."[49] The weather forecast for Monday, July 24, was not optimal, but Bradley decided to attack anyway. Under cloudy skies he gave Operation Cobra the green light.

CHAPTER 16

Breakout

COBRA

When the first bombers thundered over Normandy on Monday, July 24, John Thompson, peering into the grey clouds, thought they "looked like great flocks of geese heading south." He realized the inexactitude of the simile almost immediately. These were deadly machines, not graceful birds. Lacking the unerring homing device of migratory geese, they were also easily knocked off course—in this case, by dense cloud. "The ceiling," Thompson reported a little too candidly for the air force's liking, "was obviously too low for 'precision' work by the heavies." And so it proved. Only 15 percent of the bombs dropped that day landed on their targets, forcing Bradley to order a second attack at ten o'clock the following morning.[1]

As the sense of anticipation mounted, Harold Denny located an ideal spot to view the second air assault. The *New York Times* reporter watched in awe as 3,000 planes hammered away at a narrow box of land for more than two hours. This, he told his readers, was "the most concentrated air support ever given to American ground forces." "Wave on wave" of planes kept coming, he explained. And "the roar of their exploding bombs" was such that he thought it "impossible that any human being could live through it."

As soon as the bombers had gone, however, Denny was awestruck by a second sight. "The Germans came up out of their holes," he reported, "shaken but still belligerent, and fought stubbornly with machine guns, mortars, and other artillery and even with dug-in tanks." By the end of the day, Denny added, even the most advanced American units had only pushed forward a mile and a half, where they encountered fresher enemy troops who had missed the devastating air bombardment. So much for breaking through the thin German crust.[2]

When Denny awoke the next morning, he found that he had company. In the past couple of weeks the SHEAF PROs had decided that the equipment shortages had eased enough to allow the bigger news organizations to bump up their front-line coverage. No one in the *New York Times*' London office craved the French assignment more than Drew Middleton. Four years earlier, he had ventured around the collapsing French front with Harold Denny, and like many who had suffered through that searing experience, he was anxious to see the Germans get their comeuppance.[3]

Middleton arrived at the First Army HQ on Tuesday, July 25, the day after Bradley had launched Operation Cobra. Checking in at Vouilly, he discovered that Denny was suddenly more optimistic. The thin German crust, Denny believed, was finally poised to crumble.[4]

Two days later Denny and Middleton hit the road with Bradley's First Army. They found it an exhilarating experience. As the enemy's resistance withered away, Denny compared the Americans' rapid forward thrust to the German blitzkrieg he had witnessed four years earlier, arguing that, as much as D-Day, July 27 marked "a visible reversal of history."[5]

Middleton agreed entirely. "Hundreds of American tanks are waddling over the green hills through the tiny villages west and south of St. Lô," he recorded that evening, "rooting out German resistance like gigantic hump-backed hogs in what is surely the most important and skillful armored assault in France since the German breakthrough in the grim May days of 1940." To the hearty approval of his bosses in New York, Middleton placed this battle in an even broader context. In his eyes, it was about the future as much as the past—a rousing future filled with hope for a newly buoyant and potent America. "There is a dash and confidence about our troops," Middleton believed, having just seen them in action for the first time in over a year, "that is like new blood to the French, indeed, to any one has seen a lot in this war. Never had the soldiers of an army taken the field so magnificently equipped not only in weapons and materiel but in sober assurance that they are the masters of the Germans and that the end is near. . . . The flood tide of the New World at war," Middleton concluded with a flourish, "is sweeping over Germany, and even those Germans fighting so fanatically must know it now."[6]

For the top military brass, Cobra's stunning success occasioned a collective sigh of relief. Not only had the shattering armored drive transformed the strategic situation in Normandy, it also took attention away from the victims of friendly fire that Operation Cobra had left in its wake.

The omens for such an outcome had been evident from the outset. After dense cloud had hampered Monday's air attack, officers on the ground had redoubled their efforts to ensure their own troops did not become victims in the second raid the next day. Early on Tuesday morning they handed out mimeographed sketches of the front line, which delineated the areas where the bombs were supposed to fall. Then the men had carefully laid long strips of colored cloth on the ground to mark their positions, and lit colored flares to show the airmen where these lines began.

Ernie Pyle had watched the preparations with interest. Suspecting that the glamor boys in the fast-moving tanks would receive all the plaudits the minute Cobra got moving, he planned to write a series of columns extolling the actions of the infantrymen. The night before he had slept in an orchard, "snugly dug in behind a hedgerow so the [German] 88s could not get me so easily." On Tuesday morning, he had much more to worry about than enemy guns.[7]

When the first Flying Fortresses appeared Pyle cupped his hands over his eyes and gazed up at the sky. At first, he found the sight of so many planes breathtaking. Then the bombs started to fall. "A wall of smoke and dust erected by them grew high into the sky," Pyle noted. "It filtered along the ground back through our orchards. It sifted around us and into our noses. The bright day grew slowly dark from it." After a while, Pyle suddenly detected an ominous pattern to the way the bombs were falling: not in the direction of the Germans, but close to where he stood. Then he noticed with terror that a gentle breeze was blowing the smoke back toward friendly lines. Too slow to find a space in a tin-roofed dugout, he sprinted to a wagon shed, hit the ground hard, and spread himself out "like the cartoons of people flattened by steam rollers." "There is no description of the sound and fury of those bombs," Pyle reported soon afterward, "except to say it was chaos, and a waiting for darkness. The feeling was sensational. The air struck us in hundreds of continuing flutters. Our ears drummed and rang. We could feel little waves of concussion on the chest and in our eyes."[8]

After the last plane had departed, Pyle emerged from his shed without any overt wounds. Even so, the experience had taken a profound toll. He ached all over, as if he had been beaten by a club: the result of tensing his muscles "for too long against anticipated shock." Others had been far less fortunate. Bede Irvin, an AP photographer, had been killed in the attack. So had Lieutenant General Lesley J. McNair, the commander of Army Ground Forces, who happened to be touring the front at the time. As the medics scoured the area, they counted McNair as one of 111 soldiers killed by their own planes; another 490 had been wounded.[9]

The inquest began straight away. Eisenhower flew across the Channel to meet with Bradley; he was seething. "That's a job for the artillery," he pronounced. "I gave them [the bombers] a green light this time. But I promise you it's the last." As the news spread rapidly, other generals were equally appalled, especially when they discovered that a mix-up had meant that the air force had approached from the wrong direction, making a fatal error more likely.[10] Their emotions running high, some officers found it difficult to conceal their "unmistakable" anger in front of the press, giving reporters an obvious opening to hint that something had gone disastrously wrong. As a result, John Thompson was not the only correspondent to question the air force's precision. "Despite exaggerated boasts," declared ABC commentator John Vandercook in a typical comment, "it is no longer a secret that bombs do not always hit what they are intended to hit."[11]

As rumors flew around the Vouilly press camp, Eisenhower recognized the need to act. The story was already seeping out, and without an official comment, the estimates of friendly fire losses might easily inflate by the hour. Besides, Ike vividly recalled Marshall's scorn at the attempted cover up of friendly fire casualties during the parachute jump in Sicily. The policy statement the army chief had issued back in April remained in force. "Unless security reasons are obvious," Marshall had instructed, "consideration should be given to the prompt publication of loss and damage due to accident or misfortune except where that information would be useful to the enemy."[12]

On July 28 Marshall underlined his determination to stick to this policy. "Believe matter should be taken up today in briefing press on operations," he advised in a terse cable, "as an unavoidable hazard of bombing operation of such unprecedented size and intensity." Eisenhower naturally obliged. "Because the dust and smoke kicked up by the bombers preceding them over the target obscured prearranged markings," a senior officer told the assembled correspondents that same afternoon, "heavy bombers and some mediums dropped bombs short of the target and hit elements of American divisions waiting to 'jump off.' . . . However," the officer concluded, "the number of American casualties from our bombing was much less than was thought, the day before."[13]

And that was not the only encouraging news. As the American tanks surged forward, most of the reporters preferred to tell the exciting story of the rapid breakout, rather than dwell on the depressing friendly fire deaths. Even better from Ike's perspective, those reporters who did stop to ponder the whole incident tended to endorse the military's line with surprising gusto. Bill Stoneman was one of them. Back in London for a rest, Stoneman told his readers that "nobody who has watched many 'close support' air bombardments in this war will be surprised, impressed, or shocked" by what had occurred. On the contrary, he explained, "this happens surprisingly often and is regarded by front-line troops, its inevitable victims, as part of the game."[14]

Yet Eisenhower continued to worry. He thought that journalists back in the States might be far less docile than their colleagues based in Britain or France, for they lacked the same battlefield perspective. He also knew that the air force was still angry at being singled out for the friendly fire fiasco. He therefore called on Marshall to do everything possible to ensure that the discussion at home remained "moderate and sensible so that we do not get a ground versus air war started that is completely senseless and harmful."[15]

THE AIR FORCE REVISITED

Eisenhower was wise to worry. For more than two years, the air force had invested so much time and energy claiming that it bombed with surgical precision that any suggestion otherwise tended to throw it into spasms of outrage.[16]

As senior air force officers recoiled from the stories describing how American bombs had fallen on American troops, a deeper set of grievances bubbled to the surface. The air force had entered the war supremely confident. The daylight bombing campaign against key German targets, Arnold, Eaker, Spaatz, and Doolittle had all believed, would be so devastating to the enemy that it would demonstrate the air force's viability as an independent branch of the American military. In recent months, however, these generals had reeled from one setback to another: first, the massive losses over Schweinfurt, then having to switch from bombing German factories to destroying road and rail links in France ahead of D-Day, and now this highly criticized support mission to help the ground forces breakout of Normandy. Too much effort, the air leaders believed, had been spent—perhaps squandered—acting as a mere adjunct of the army.

Few felt this sense of frustration more deeply than those assigned to the Ninth Air Force, which had been created to provide tactical support for ground operations in France. The Ninth had established its first headquarters in Normandy on June 8, and its bases immediately became a magnet for war correspondents.[17] The Ninth soon understood why, and it was not pleased. Before the invasion, London had been awash with ambitious reporters jockeying for the best position on D-Day, almost hypnotically attracted, as one PRO officer observed, by "the lure of the front-page by-line and the established reputation for all time." Then came the bad news that less than 10 percent of them would get an invasion berth. The jockeying immediately became even more intense—and much more creative—and the Ninth Air Force emerged as a major target. As one of its PROs wryly observed, the Ninth's bases became an "expedient [for reporters] to get into France at the earliest possible date, quotas for the ground units having been filled."[18]

The Ninth's conviction that its reporters had scant interest in covering the air force underpinned all the problems that unfolded over the ensuing weeks. The Ninth's PROs were certainly annoyed when their accredited reporters immediately headed off to cover the ground war. Partly in response—or, as reporters saw it, largely in retribution—the Ninth rarely went out of its way to provide them with the all-important amenities: jeeps, briefings, and communications. Many correspondents were particularly upset by the lack of a radio at the press camp, forcing them, as one complained, to rely on a "catch-as-can" courier service to get their copy out of the theater.

As relations between the two sides deteriorated, reporters tried to explain that they were not all headline-hunting cheerleaders for the US Army. Some stressed that they worked for small newspapers with small staffs. For this reason, they pointed out, their bosses expected them "to try to give their readers an overall picture of the war in France rather than primarily report on the air aspect of the struggle."[19] But Colonel Robert Parham, the Ninth's chief PRO, turned a deaf ear. Although he had been a UP bureau chief before the war, Parham was now an unapologetic air force booster. He was also determined to whip the reporters into shape. In one briefing, he told "correspondents attached to the Ninth that 50 percent of their writing should be devoted to the Ninth." At other times, he intimated that a failure to fulfill this ratio would have adverse consequences. "We, at first, were inclined to treat threats made against some of the correspondents here as a joke," remarked Jack Tait, who had been covering the air war for the *New York Herald Tribune* for more than a year. "It seemed inconceivable that one group engaged in this war would consider publicity for itself more precious than giving the United States the story of this war, whether it be the air story, the ground story, or a combination of both."[20]

The matter came to a head on August 18. Without explanation, Parham ordered four correspondents out of France. Stanley Frank of the *New York Post*, Gordon Gammack of the *Des Moines Register*, Lee McCardell of the *Baltimore Sun*, and John Groth, an artist for *Parade*, were nonplussed. Their colleagues were outraged. When pressed, Parham hinted that he had made the decision for administrative reasons, with one eye on the currently available resources, but this made little sense. Why, more than one reporter asked, had Parham suddenly decided to reduce the size of the press camp at a time when the Ninth's activities were being stepped up?[21]

There seemed to be only one explanation. The four reporters had been expelled, concluded Tait in a particularly explosive story, "apparently because their work has not measured up to standards set by publicity-minded Ninth Air Force officers in the higher ranks." "Public relations officers of the Ninth," agreed Frederick Graham in the *New York Times*, "have been using almost as high pressure as Hollywood press agents, stressing over and over that 'we brought you over here, we provide you with jeeps and feed you, and we expect you to write about the Ninth Air Force.'"[22]

Back home, the ousted reporters' bosses stood behind their men. The *Baltimore Sun* was especially emphatic. On August 21, it released details of McCardell's war record, which, it stressed, included stints covering the bombing campaign, the Italian war, and the D-Day assault. "The man has a mastery of his craft," a *Sun* editorial declared two days later. "He has utter devotion to duty. But he has, also, an elevation of spirit which makes his words march and sing."[23]

In Washington, reporters covering the Pentagon beat added to the "considerable stir" over this expulsion. "The charge is made," the Pentagon press pack observed in a pointed round robin, "that four correspondents failed to measure up to the publicity standards set by high-ranking officers of the Ninth Air Force. What are those standards," it asked, "and by whom were they set?"

The War Department wanted to know as well. Early on the morning of August 22, Major General Alexander D. Surles, the War Department's director of public relations, cabled SHAEF requesting an explanation.[24] When none was forthcoming, Parham received his marching orders. Significantly, the four expelled correspondents remained in France, where they continued to report the war.[25]

This embarrassing reversal only confirmed what the Cobra operation had already revealed—namely, that the air force had become one of the main Allied losers since D-Day. Over the coming months, senior air force generals would continue their feverish search for front-page publicity. While some pushed for the release of "colorful dramatic roundup analyses with hitherto unused pictures," others tried to recruit "outstanding" PR men "whose services in this highly complex field will ensure desired results."[26] Ultimately, they faced a difficult, if not impossible, task. As the Allies drove rapidly into the French heartland, media interest in the air war continued to dwindle. For the air force, the only scant consolation was the existence of a startling number of other losers at a time of such spectacular front-line success.

THE TROUBLE WITH SUCCESS

For a year George Patton had often felt like the biggest loser of all. After the slapping incident in Sicily, he had been forced to sit out the Italian campaign. At the start of 1944, he learned that Eisenhower had given him Third Army to command, but Patton viewed this as a mixed blessing. It offered him a chance at redemption, but this chance would only come after the Overlord operation had succeeded and Bradley had stepped up to command the Twelfth Army Group. Until then, Patton would face the indignity of playing decoy—suffering in silence, since Third Army's very existence remained a strict secret, while SHAEF purposely leaked word that Patton commanded "a fictitious First US Army Group, created to convince the Germans that the Allies were planning to invade the Pas de Calais."[27]

At least Patton was supposed to suffer in silence. True to his flamboyant character, in April he again came dangerously close to destroying his career, this time with an unfortunate speech that the media interpreted as a call for "Anglo-American domination of the postwar world." "General Patton," editorialized the *Washington Post*, in a barbed but typical comment, "has progressed from simple assaults on individuals to collective assaults on entire nationalities." Once more, only Eisenhower's belief in Patton's fighting abilities saved him from being sacked, but his old friend left him no doubt that this was his last chance. Ike even sent one of his PROs to tell Patton "personally that there were to be no more public statements by him or any member of his staff."[28]

Duly chastened, Patton arrived in France in the middle of July, not just raring to go, but also desperate to avoid another public slip. With forty-six correspondents already attached to Third Army, this proved to be no easy task. On July 16, when one senior correspondent pressed for a meeting, his chief of staff was blunt: "The presence of the Third Army and the presence of General Patton on the Continent was a secret," the officer reminded the reporter. Moreover, he added, "the Third Army was not operational, and that due to past unfortunate newspaper incidents certain precautions had to be taken which were somewhat distasteful to the Third Army, but were necessary."[29]

That evening, however, Patton's own PRO threw all caution to the wind. At eight o'clock, he summoned a group of reporters to his tent. Dropping his voice, he said he would divulge something that was "absolutely secret," before providing "a rough outline of projected plan 'Cobra.'" Technically, Patton's PRO had done nothing wrong. It had long been standard practice in Eisenhower's command "to place utmost confidence in the newspaper correspondents, to give them every bit of information possible, and to expect them to respect it." The reporters, for their part, never even considered writing up what they had been told, knowing full well that the briefing was strictly for background. But all of this missed the point: Eisenhower had categorically told Patton to keep his "goddamned mouth" shut.[30]

Bradley was keen to remind his old rival of this crucial fact. As soon as he learned from a loose-lipped reporter what the Third Army PRO had done, Bradley called Patton and demanded an explanation. Patton, fearing that his chance of battlefield glory might be over before it had begun, summoned all of his correspondents to an impromptu meeting. His anger barely under control, he told them: "I don't know whether I am more shocked or disgusted at what has happened," before declaring that someone had committed a "military offense." "The only charitable view I can take," Patton continued,

> is that some of you do not realize your tremendous responsibility. If I were to say that as a result of what you have done you will get no information, I would be aborting the press, because the press must know in order to speak and give credit to the men who deserve credit. Therefore, I do not intend to change the policy. I shall continue to trust you, but you must realize that you must not—I repeat—not, NEVER, NEVER, NEVER *talk about anything that you are told unless it is officially told you that you can mention it.*"[31]

It was a critical moment. Third Army finally became operational on August 1, just in time to exploit the big gap in the German defenses that Cobra had cracked open. Over the coming weeks, Patton moved with customary speed: his tanks drove west toward the Brittany ports; then they turned east to try to eradicate German forces in France before heading in the direction of Paris. Yet, in public, Patton enjoyed none of his customary glory. Bradley later wrote bitterly in his memoirs about Patton making "big headlines" as he "blazed through Brittany with armored divisions and motorized infantry."[32] The reality was quite different. For more than two weeks after Third Army's advance, it was Bradley, not Patton, who received all the public's plaudits. Bradley, still keen to deceive the enemy, had decided to keep Patton's presence in France under wraps. Patton, still worried that the Cobra leak had weakened his position with his superiors, not only swallowed this slight but also imposed especially strict limits on what the reporters could write about.[33]

With this veil of secrecy in place, Bradley became the media star. In profile after profile, reporters described his "unruffled calm," his "professorial" appearance, and the crucial fact that "nearly 30 years of intense study of military problems" had now reaped its reward. "An American tidal wave," noted a typical dispatch on August 3, was "pouring across Brittany . . . as Lt. Gen. Omar N. Bradley's armor raced toward Rennes."[34]

Outwardly, Patton did not seem to mind that all the acclaim was going elsewhere. Hurrying around the front, he seemed to be in his element. He was "like a man possessed," observed his biographer, "turning up seemingly everywhere to prod, cajole, exhort, and generally 'rais[e] merry hell.'"[35] Yet deep down, Patton was hurt that he had yet to re-establish his public reputation. "It is well to note," complained his chief of staff on August 15, the day the ban on mentioning the general's presence in France was finally lifted, "that although it was the first time that the Third Army has been announced, it had over-run a very large portion of France, had captured upwards of 35,000 prisoners, and destroyed many German installations and much German equipment."[36]

The time was about come, Patton's staffers believed, to ensure that the world knew who was racing so quickly across the French countryside toward Paris. Yet this would mean forging a more positive relationship with the press, something that proved to be surprisingly difficult.

The sheer pace of the offensive was partly to blame. Patton's Third Army drove forward so quickly that its command post had to be relocated almost every night, leading to what its camp followers joked was "a series of one-night stands."[37] Then, after a short rest, the next morning was often even more taxing. "It is almost impossible to keep up with this front in daylight," revealed Wes Gallagher after one brief trip to the battlefield. "You can follow the trail of battle along the roads across Brittany. It is a trail of burning wreckage of tanks, 88 guns, and horse-drawn vehicles. But you never seem to quite catch up with the front lines."[38]

Although this drive forward was far more exhilarating than the grim stalemates in Italy or Normandy, the grueling game of catch-up nonetheless took a toll. Hal Boyle told his readers that this new phase of the war reminded the officers of "Indian country." "Although American armored columns cut this great block of France away from the main body of the German army," Boyle wrote on August 12, "there still are wandering and pocketed groups ranging from small squads to units of some size still intact and fighting like roving tribes of old."[39]

Throughout August, these retreating German tribes made the dash across France one of the most dangerous moments for reporters in the entire war. Holbrook Bradley of the *Baltimore Sun* became one of the first victims, sent to the hospital by a German mortar round that had gouged his leg.[40] A week later, one close observer noted that, finally, "the law of averages [had] caught up . . . with war correspondents hurrying along the bloody roads toward Paris." Three reporters were killed in the space of a few days, including Tom Treanor of the *Los Angeles Times*. Treanor's death came when "his jeep collided with an American tank on a highway east of Chartres while en route to the battlefront." Treanor was rushed to the hospital and gained consciousness for a time. Ever the deadline-driven pro, he even urged the doctors to "hurry up and get this job over with so I can file my story." Soon afterward the thirty-five-year old veteran of Sicily, Anzio, Cassino, and D-Day succumbed to his wounds, making him the nineteenth correspondent to die in the war to date.[41]

Those who mourned the passing of their colorful and gifted colleague naturally began to calculate their own odds of survival—although, as the escapades of one eminent band of reporters revealed, there was no consensus on whether to gamble or fold.

Ernie Pyle spent the first days of the breakout alongside Bob Capa and Ernest Hemingway, and the three men were a study in contrasts. Hemingway, in a mocking nod to other reporters' tendency to call themselves "the poor man's Pyle," sometimes told everyone within earshot that he was "the rich man's hemorrhoid." Many troops, as Pyle noted with mortification, could scarcely tell the two men apart. Ernie thought this confusion was "because of the first name." It certainly did not derive from a similar attitude toward battlefield danger. "He is very bold," Pyle remarked privately of Hemingway, "and if he doesn't slow down a little he's going to get killed." The PROs agreed. One even instructed Hemingway to shave off his mustache "so that he wouldn't be such a conspicuous target for snipers." It was a pointless order, for being conspicuous never troubled Hemingway. Indeed, rather than writing news, he seemed more intent than ever on making it. One of his biggest moments came on August 3, when many newspapers reported that he and a private had tossed hand grenades into a French house, "and six of Hitler's supermen piled out and surrendered" to the famous author.[42]

Another time, Pyle noted privately, Hemingway and Capa "almost got it." The photographer, Pyle added, was equally brave, but "very wise in the ways of war, and knows pretty well how to take care of himself."[43] Capa

Figure 16.1 Ernest Hemingway (*right*) and Robert Capa (*left*), having braved another day at the front in France, July 30, 1944. In the center is their driver. National Archives 111-SC-192117.

certainly had reason to temper his courage with caution. "Unshaven and dirty," he was starting to tire of the war and even began dreaming of returning to New York in the fall, after seeing Paris one more time. Besides the relentless danger of the fluid front, Capa could never quite shake Omaha beach from his mind, the horror of that morning being compounded by the fact that he had been posted as missing for a while. Characteristically, he tried to laugh it off. "Some people even saw my body floating in the water," he would joke. "I hope if ever my body has to float it will be in whiskey."[44]

If these grim memories sometimes made Capa pause, he still had a strong professional incentive to get as close as possible to the action. Indeed, unlike Hemingway, who retained his best material for a future novel rather than file it with *Collier's*, Capa needed to be at the front.[45] That was where he had shot his best photos in the past. Just as importantly, Capa—like all the war correspondents who worked for a Henry Luce magazine—knew that taking risks offered the best chance of getting into print. Only recently, Frank Scherschel had awed his *Life* editors with a series of derring-do exploits. "Not content with following the armies on the ground," one of them had enthused, "he [Scherschel] got in a low flying artillery observation plane, went up and photographed the battle from the air. Then he went down on the ground and picked out the identical points he saw from the air."[46]

Since *Life* had run a two-page spread of Scherschel's pictures in the August 8 issue, Capa's continued audacity made professional sense. Pyle, by contrast, faced a different set of pressures. As well as an overpowering urge to survive, he had succumbed to yet another series of debilitating ailments. "I believe it was just kind of a 'collapse reaction,'" Pyle wrote home, "after the five days and nights of unnatural tension you're in during an attack." An enforced period of resting, joking, and drinking at Vouilly soon revived his spirits. On returning to the front he immediately discovered that, even without Hemingway around, danger still lurked everywhere. On one particularly fraught day, Ernie was temporarily deafened when a shell landed near him. He headed for a command post, only to find that it had taken a direct hit; the command post he had just left had also been destroyed. Someone then told him about a "nice clean farm house" about half a mile away. He went off in search of it, but when he arrived he discovered that an enemy mortar had wiped it out just twenty minutes before.

Increasingly drained by the peril, Pyle found the victorious sweep through France difficult to write about. "The war is working up to a climax," he remarked privately, ". . . and I have an idea people at home aren't any longer interested in little details of fighting, but only in miles gained and signs of complete enemy collapse."[47]

Pyle was not alone in his professional doubts. Even the correspondents charged with reporting the Allies' spectacular gains struggled, and not just because of the pace of the advance. They also faced the censors' increasingly sharp blue pencils.

As the offensive gathered pace, the senior generals worried that the press might easily, if unwittingly, divulge sensitive information to the Germans. "In fast moving situations in which enemy communications may well be lacking," Eisenhower's command warned subordinates on August 10, "there is [a] grave danger that the cumulative effect of the premature public announcement of the capture of localities will disclose to the enemy the massing of our strength and the broad outlines of our strategic plans." The only solution was to impose strict censorship at the front, but, as the reporters soon complained, this effectively made their jobs impossible.[48]

On August 14, John Thompson and Don Whitehead arrived at Bradley's headquarters. They were acting "as a deputation representing the newspapermen assigned to American forces," they told the general, "to protest against the stop on news which prevented their publicizing the names of towns reached in the American advance." Bradley responded in his most cordial tone. He began by explaining that the fast-moving pace of the battlefield made it crucial to deny information to the enemy. For the past few days, the Allies had been attempting to tighten the noose around the enemy troops near the town of Falaise. "Had the correspondents been permitted to write freely of our movements," Bradley elaborated, "it is possible that the German[s] could have sufficiently G-2d our situation [that is, acquired sufficient intelligence of US positions] to escape easily." For this reason, Bradley refused to relent until the Falaise pocket had been eradicated.[49]

With the front-line correspondents stymied by the censor, their London-based colleagues took control of the Falaise story. In SHAEF headquarters, the briefers carefully handed reporters information that the hypercautious intelligence officers considered of no value to the enemy. As the fighting heated up over the weekend of August 12–13, the briefers became so tight-lipped that their correspondents began to call the battle at Falaise the "silent" offensive. The only information available was the stunning prospect that Allied commanders hoped "to bag" about 100,000 soldiers inside the Falaise pocket. Having so little else to go on, the media fixated on this large, round number, contrasting it with the distance between the Canadian troops who were trying to close the gap in the north and the American units moving up from the south. "Newsmen," one media commentator explained on August 19, "contented themselves with whittling down each day the width of the opening through which the Germans were escaping the trap, and writing dire predictions of what was going to happen to those still inside."[50]

Even with this scanty information, by August 16 the sharper correspondents had spotted the main problem: the Falaise gap remained open, and too many Germans were dashing through it. Therefore, noted Clifton Daniel on page one of the *New York Times*, observers had undertaken a "recount" of likely POWs. A short while ago, Daniel explained, informed eyewitnesses in the field had been "forecasting a bag of possibly 100,000 men of the German Fifth and Seventh Armies. At least half the enemy's remaining armor is now believed to have fled and no more than 50,000 men are now expected to be netted."[51]

In the years to come, this great escape would fuel a bitter controversy. At the time, however, few in the media had much energy to investigate, for the simple reason that too much was happening elsewhere.

On August 15, the Allies launched another invasion of France, this time in the south. The correspondents who had won a place to accompany the first assault found the gloomy weather a major disappointment as they approached the fabled beaches of the French Riviera. Low-hanging clouds, observed Eric Sevareid, made the shoreline "almost indistinguishable from the rippling, iron-colored sea."

Still, the lack of sustained German resistance more than compensated for the poor view. By the end of the first day of fighting, the Allies had put 66,000 men ashore, suffering only four hundred casualties, ninety-five of them killed. For their part, the PROs had brought along a radio transmitter, enabling "the first direct broadcast made from an invasion craft during the European war." NBC seemed to be in the lead to exploit this momentous moment. Its correspondent, Chester Morrison, had won the draw, and shortly after midday he began to speak, slowly and calmly, into the mike. Then, after only ninety seconds, the transmitter's fuse blew, ending this debut experiment in live invasion broadcasting.

By mid-afternoon the PROs had established a little press camp near the vineyards that bordered the bay of St. Tropez. They had also repaired the transmitter, enabling the radio correspondents to speak live from the battlefield for almost a quarter of an hour—a feat not achieved since the Anzio broadcast in April. The reception was impressive, too. According to one proud PRO, Sevareid and Morrison both made "perfect broadcasts," at least in terms of the clarity of transmission to Rome and then New York.[52]

For the newspaper correspondents, perfection had a very different meaning that day. Those who had languished in and around Rome since June 5 while their Normandy-based colleagues stole all the headlines, were getting their long-awaited chance to witness a French fight, and they dashed inland—in a vain search for the enemy. To those who had suffered their share of battlefield agony in the earlier Italian stalemate, the absence of Wehrmacht troops on invasion day provided a different cause for concern. The UP's Reynolds Packard fell into this category. Packard, as one of his colleagues noted, "was inclined to find something ominous in the general quiet that prevailed after the first few hours of the landing. He remembered the calm that hung for a time over Anzio." So did Homer Bigart, whose Anzio experiences had been as searing as anyone's. Yet even Bigart struggled to find something pessimistic to write over the coming days, as the German defenders continued to melt away.[53]

Bigart's first experience on French soil came with the invasion of Ile du Levant, a small, "desolate island" that guarded the approaches to the port of Toulon. This attack, he reported, was "an amphibious operation unusual for its emphasis on stealth rather than overwhelming firepower." The GIs, having daubed their faces with charcoal, stole ashore in rubber boats, and captured the big guns that dominated the area while scarcely firing a shot.

A few days later, Bigart filed another dispatch, this time documenting his experiences on the mainland, where the Germans were the least of everyone's worries. American troops, he wrote, had sped so rapidly around Marseille "that ration trucks have not yet caught up, and the men are subsisting chiefly on cantaloupes and tomatoes stripped from gardens en route. Fortunately," he added, lest anyone think that the GIs were looting those they had liberated, "the country seems rich in melons and vegetables, and the farmers eagerly share their bread and wine."[54]

While this successful operation in the south stole some of the thunder from the Falaise battle, SHAEF's announcement on August 15 that Patton had been in France for the past two weeks became the real headline grabber. All of a sudden, Bradley had reason to be jealous. Fawning reporters—forgetting their past suspicions of Patton's bombastic and belligerent behavior—hastened to frame the entire French campaign around his almost-mythical presence. A widely used AP dispatch set the tone. "Patton," it trumpeted, "is the tactical genius who has driven across Brittany, through Le Mans, and then northward through Alencon and Argentan, completing the southern jaw of the trap on the Nazi Seventh Army."[55]

If Bradley was envious of Patton's sudden media dominance, he could take solace from his own elevation to command the Twelfth Army Group. Eisenhower broke this news in an early-morning press conference on August 15, but with so much "red tape" to be navigated to get the "stuff on the wires and networks" Thor Smith embargoed the release until 1:30 p.m. Patton's PROs, as impatient as ever, could scarcely abide this last little delay. One told reporters in the Third Army press camp what was about to happen, adding the juicy detail that the command shake-up meant that Bradley's Twelfth Army Group would now be on a par with Montgomery's Twenty-First Army Group.[56]

Wes Gallagher happened to be at the Third Army camp when the PROs began blabbing, and he immediately spotted an opportunity. Returning with his story to London later that morning, he stopped at the Senate House building, but rather than seek out a SHAEF censor, he approached someone from the British Ministry of Information. The man immediately noticed the French dateline on the dispatch. Gallagher reassured him that his account was based on a conversation with an American staff officer. Although it was still almost two hours before the release time, the British official was satisfied. He passed Gallagher's copy without informing SHAEF.[57]

It turned out to be a fateful oversight. Other news organizations, convinced that "the Gallagher story was filed and censored overseas," hastened to use it in their own accounts. Within hours, the world had learned far more than the stunning fact that Patton was on the loose. The American press was now reporting that Eisenhower had "taken personal charge of operations in the Battle of France," and that Bradley had been placed "on an equal status" with Montgomery.[58]

Eisenhower was appalled, and deeply angry, especially because Gallagher's dispatch sparked a renewed bout of Anglo-American press bickering. He immediately sanctioned a strong denial. Yes, Ike's briefers explained, two army groups now existed, but that did not mean that Montgomery had been demoted. "It is the same situation," the official added, "as if you had . . . two platoons in the field, in which one of the . . . platoon commanders would command both."[59]

Gallagher's scoop signified the deeper problems that now existed. During the invasion period, the military had found the reporters fairly easy to manage. Although they had griped about the poor communications, rudimentary billets, and clueless censors, the reporters had also shared the battlefield experience, the tense waiting followed by extreme danger—and for this reason they had invariably agreed that almost total censorship was needed.

By mid-August, the shift from stalemate to success had reversed the dynamics of media-military relations. Even the old timers Thompson and Whitehead had complained loudly about the stops placed on covering the Falaise battle. Much to Eisenhower's disgust, Gallagher had joined the band of troublemakers, with a vengeance. "Ike furious with Wes Gallagher story," recorded one senior officer on August 18. "We're going to have to put them under wraps if they can't get more detail and accuracy to a story like that," Eisenhower seethed to his subordinates. "Unless stories are correct," he added, "they will have to be thrown out altogether by the censor."[60]

For the past two years, as the Allies had faced the daunting task of breaking into Nazi-occupied Europe, Eisenhower had worked hard to build a close and positive relationship with the press, based where possible on trust and openness. Now, as Nazi resistance crumbled, he was beginning to contemplate a crackdown. If even Ike was thinking in these terms, the last phase of the war promised to be far from easy.

PART V

Victory

CHAPTER 17

To Germany's Borders

"CHAMPAGNE DREAM"

As August 1944 drew to a close, the entire press corps was afflicted with a single malady. It went by the name of dateline desperation, and its origin could not have been simpler. Every self-respecting war correspondent in France wanted to be the first to file a story with the magic tag, "Paris."

The wire-service reporters and radio broadcasters suffered most from this malady, since their entire professional existence depended on beating rivals to the big news stories. For these correspondents the symptoms were always the same: agitation, excitement, and impatience; the constant badgering of PROs for the latest dope or a fully fueled jeep; and an obsession with hoarding information, which tended to turn the press corps from a collegial band of brothers into a paranoid and anarchic mob. Thor Smith, who observed Ike's reporters with a mixture of amusement and exasperation, described the process: "After a while, the veneer wears off, and they start to heckle each other. . . . Unfortunately," he explained, "every once in a while the PRO finds himself in the middle, having to be an arbitrator, or else the butt of squawks about transportation, communications, censorship, orderlies, and God knows what." For their part, Smith believed, many correspondents were "inclined to cut corners on straight fact[s] when it comes to color reporting, not on hard news stuff. But whenever any of the others catch it, they get an unmerciful ragging. [NBC's Merrill] Mueller, who is inclined to strut it about a bit, is dubbed 'I Was There Mueller.'"[1]

On August 23, it was not Mueller who cut corners, but his CBS rival. That afternoon CBS broadcast one of the most eye-catching I-Was-There stories of the whole war. "The Second Armored Division entered Paris today," announced its war correspondent Charles Collingwood, "after the Parisians had risen as one man to beat down the German troops who had garrisoned the city."[2] As newscasters hastened to tell their listeners, Collingwood's dispatch was a world exclusive: no other news organization had yet reported the liberation of Paris, nor had any other reporter filed with a Paris deadline. Unfortunately, it was also a massive mistake: the French capital remained in German hands, and Collingwood, along with every other Allied reporter, had yet to march triumphantly down its streets. So within hours, CBS sheepishly retracted the story, and then tried to discover exactly what had gone wrong.

Collingwood immediately blamed the military. "When we were briefed by a staff officer on the decision to enter Paris," he explained to his superiors, "we were specifically advised to write our stories before the event so that we could leave them with Communications when we made our dash for Paris. The stories were to be released upon the announcement by SHAEF of our entry into Paris."[3]

As a matter of fact, the reporters had yet to make it out of Rambouillet, a little town thirty miles south of the French capital, which had long been a summer haven for kings and presidents. The PROs arrived there on Wednesday, August 23. Led by John Redding, they discovered an incredibly chaotic mess. "In the main street," recorded one officer, "was every press vehicle in the American armies and the entire international press corps of more than 200 were gathered in the little hotel. . . . Our mission was to take over in Paris," he explained, "but we simply had to take over here and start work right away. The press climbed over us so we went to work with a rush."

After setting up a copy room in the bar of the elegant Hotel Grand Veneur, Redding made his next moves with Collingwood's egregious error fixed firmly in his mind. Collingwood had gone astray, Redding recognized, because of the same old problem: too many reporters chasing insufficient communications. In Collingwood's case, the military had tried to sidestep the problem by getting reporters to file their stories ahead of the time, but the initiative had failed disastrously. Throughout Thursday, as dateline desperation grew, Redding sought an alternative. He was particularly worried that, upon arriving in Paris, many of the reporters would simply seek out an underground French radio network, which they could use to report their eyewitness impressions directly to the home front, bypassing the Allied censors. He therefore issued a clear order: Rambouillet would remain the press base for the duration of the Paris liberation. All reporters would have to return there, both to get their accounts censored and to send them out via official military channels.[4]

The race into the French capital began at dawn on Friday, August 25. For those who remained behind in Rambouillet to tend to routine business, the wait seemed endless. Who would be first back? The mystery was finally solved just after midday. A dust-coated jeep suddenly screeched to a halt in the driveway of Grand Veneur. Don Whitehead climbed out, trying his best to adopt a casual air. "Where have you been Don?" another reporter asked. "Paris," Whitehead confirmed, before dashing inside to pound out his 1,600-word story.[5]

Although Whitehead was the first reporter to return, he had not been the first into the French capital. That honor went to Robert Capa and Charlie Wertenbaker. Riding their luck as ever, they had joined a column headed by Jacques Leclerc, the senior French general charged with liberating the city, and they clocked their time of entry at 9:40 and 20 seconds.[6]

Whitehead had arrived just seventeen minutes later, and he had quite a tale to tell. When they were only two miles from the city center, Whitehead and his driver had ground to a halt. A French captain had explained that they could go no further without written permission from Leclerc or the Free French leader, Charles De Gaulle. "He told three British correspondents who tried to pass that he would shoot," Whitehead recounted afterward. The Brits obediently "turned around," but the AP man was made of sterner stuff. He quickly found an American colonel who said that only Eisenhower or Bradley could issue that order. Grabbing the wheel of the jeep, Whitehead decided to take a chance. The second time the French captain tried to stop him he "just stepped on the gas and drove on in with the column."[7]

The scale of the story justified the risk. Like every other reporter, Whitehead had found "hysterical Parisians" jamming the streets. Trying hard to frame the amazing spectacle in a way that his American readers would understand, he reached for familiar comparisons. "All the emotions suppressed by four years of German domination," he reported, "surged through the people. The streets of the city as we entered were like a combined Mardi Gras, Fourth of July celebration, American Legion convention, and New Year's Eve in Times Square all packed into one."[8]

Desperate to be the first to file, Whitehead had spent less than an hour in Paris before rushing back to Rambouillet. It proved to be the most perilous part of the whole day. "We passed through an open stretch," Whitehead told his colleagues a few hours later, "where there were no troops of any kind yet snipers opened up on us from both sides of the street. We ducked and flattened out in the street, and after fifteen minutes there, I decided it would be no more dangerous to ride back than to lie there exposed, so we got back into the jeep and tore out of town."

In Rambouillet, Whitehead's rivals eyed him with envy, while his colleagues feted his achievement. Whitehead, the AP's top brass noted proudly, had beaten every other reporter by more than three hours—that is, every other reporter who had played by the rules. As the AP soon discovered, three Americans had not.[9]

The reason for this particular round of rule breaking was straightforward enough. Paris on that euphoric Friday was not a place many correspondents wanted to leave in a hurry, not with the biggest party ever in full swing.

Much of the city, to be sure, remained a combat zone, as German snipers took pot shots by day and Hitler ordered a rocket attack that night.[10] Still, even the ongoing danger failed to dampen the city's spirit. Larry LeSueur of CBS estimated that he received "a hundred happy kisses for each 100 meters of progress." For once, John Thompson wondered about the practicality of his trademark whiskers. "This correspondent encountered mass kissing," Thompson told his *Tribune* readers. "His beard, when not waving in the breeze, was pulled, tugged, stroked, or kissed by swarms of women ranging from grandmothers to chic girls. Only once did any woman ask permission to embrace the beard. She hugged the correspondent and then started crying. Perhaps," he joked, "the whiskers tickled her."[11]

By mid-afternoon, the more conscientious reporters had adjourned to a relatively quiet café, where they set up their typewriters and searched for the words to summarize the scenes they had just witnessed. Their wire service and radio colleagues, who faced stiffer deadlines, had no such luxury. Like Whitehead, they had to file immediately. Yet some became so immersed in what one called their "champagne dream" that they decided to forego the dangerous drive back to Rambouillet and took a short cut instead.[12]

James C. McClincy was in the vanguard. The UP reporter had already missed one huge story. He had been slated to cover the assault on June 6, but "his assignment," as a close colleague observed, "was changed somewhat at the last minute without his knowledge and he awakened 'D-Day' morning to find the invasion had started without him."[13] It was the sort of high-handed action that an ambitious correspondent found hard to forget, and this time McClincy was determined not to rank among the losers. Shortly after arriving in the city center, he led a group of reporters to a French underground radio station. As an operator looked for a radio frequency with good reception, the temptation proved too great. McClincy grabbed the microphone. After saying a few pertinent words, he handed the mike to the lipstick-covered Larry LeSueur, who delivered his brief thoughts and then passed it to Paul Manning of the Mutual Network.[14]

While McClincy had a score to settle with the military, LeSueur and Manning were motivated by their own frustrations. As radio reporters, they had enjoyed surprisingly few chances to regale their listeners with combat sounds. Their bosses were largely to blame. Network executives in New York remained leery of the new wire recorder, believing that radio ought to broadcast only live material. As a result, only about 5 percent of the combat sounds captured on the wire recorder since D-Day were actually "heard by the listening audiences in the United States," according to one survey.

Unable to get battlefield recordings on air, the radio reporters had mostly based themselves at press camps, where they remained little more than purveyors of the official communiqués. Now, on this festive Friday, LeSueur and Manning found themselves in the thick of the Paris action, with access to a radio connection straight to New York. Small wonder that they grabbed the unexpected opportunity with scarcely a second thought.[15]

Whatever the reporters' reasons, many of their colleagues were so angry at being scooped that they insisted that the three men be expelled from France forthwith. Redding's reaction, however, was calmer. When McClincy pleaded exhaustion, explaining that he had traveled nonstop for two days, without food, to witness the story, Redding was sympathetic. All three correspondents, his inquest diplomatically concluded, had been operating "under abnormal strain and under abnormal conditions." For this reason, SHAEF decided against a court martial followed by immediate eviction from the theater. Still, the three reporters had breached Redding's clear rules. So SHAEF suspended them for the next sixty days, to the rest of the press corps' intense satisfaction.[16]

On Saturday, August 26, the party in Paris became a little more orderly. Charles De Gaulle appeared at a parade at the Arc de Triomphe at three o'clock, and then at a mass at Notre Dame Cathedral an hour later. As more than a million people lined the city's tree-lined boulevards, the familiar male reporters were not the only ones around to cover the seminal scenes. A group of women reporters wrote a series of highly influential dispatches, too, including Helen Kirkpatrick of the *Chicago Daily News*.[17]

Until now, Kirkpatrick's French experiences had been mixed. After leaving Italy for London, she had been part of a small committee of correspondents that had helped SHAEF with press preparations for the invasion—a "signal honor" for a woman at that time. But for D-Day itself she had drawn the short straw. As Bill Stoneman and Robert Casey were witnessing the fighting first-hand, she remained at the London office of the *Daily News*, reporting the battle by communiqué. She knew that this posting was not merely due to bad luck. Eisenhower's command was again reluctant to allow women reporters anywhere near the fighting. Not until early July did it permit female correspondents to cross the Channel. When they got there, they faced the familiar restrictions that effectively confined them to covering field hospitals. They were also denied access to jeeps and to front-line censors.[18]

Chafing at these restrictions, Kirkpatrick decided to trade on her professional experience. Because she had made her name as a top political reporter, she asked for permission "to cover French administrative activities in the liberated areas." At first, SHAEF officers were skeptical. Many of them viewed her request as a transparent attempt to get close to the fighting. Yet Kirkpatrick was persistent. She also knew Eisenhower well enough to ask for a face-to-face meeting, which he granted on July 8. At a time when German V-1 rockets were peppering London, Kirkpatrick took advantage of Ike's better nature. "It's not safe in England," she almost begged. "Send me to France." Flashing his trademark smile, Eisenhower replied that he had "no objection," a simple statement that quickly got the bureaucratic machinery churning out the necessary paperwork.[19]

Once she was on French soil, Kirkpatrick began interviewing the GIs who had just left the front line for a rest, though she found this angle a little underwhelming with such a dramatic battle unfolding. So she soon headed off in search of Patton's troops, who gave her a story with enough political undertones to justify her presence near the action: the joyful liberation of the towns and cities in Brittany, where, as Kirkpatrick reported, the "people cheered, clapped, and cried and tried to embrace every American." Overcome by the reception, she could scarcely wait for the big day of Paris's liberation to arrive.[20]

At Rambouillet Kirkpatrick broke her toe while getting out of her jeep, but even the sharp pain she suffered over the next days could not dent her joy. "I will never forget the next morning coming up over the hill and there below was Paris," she recalled long after the war. "Our driver was as excited as we were." Inside the city, the crowds were so immense that Kirkpatrick could not get anywhere near the procession planned for the Arc de Triomphe, so she headed to Notre Dame to await the mass. When de Gaulle and his two senior generals arrived, shortly after four o'clock, Kirkpatrick finally had the opportunity to report real combat. A revolver shot rang out, she told her readers back home. Then machine gun fire sprayed the pavement next to where she stood.[21]

When they heard about such exploits, the SHAEF censors were not happy. "A number of women correspondents," one noted, "have succeeded in reaching the vicinity of Paris and are writing stories of which they were not phased in to write." Nevertheless, even the crustiest censor could scarcely complain about what Kirkpatrick had written. "The Germans are still holding out," she concluded in her first dispatch, "but Paris is free. Its freedom is heady and intoxicating."[22]

By Monday, August 28, the last remaining German resistance had been silenced and the revelry had started to subside. Just after 8:30 that morning, Kirkpatrick left her hotel and walked the short distance to Rue de la Paix, where the Paris office of the *Chicago Daily News* had been located before the fall of France. Stepping inside was like going back in time. Four years of dust covered the desks, chairs, and tables. "Piled unopened by the door," she reported, "are June 1940 editions of the *Chicago Daily News*. They arrived after the staff had left as the Germans were entering Paris." In the intervening years, Kirkpatrick happily discovered, the Frenchman who owned the building "had prevented the Germans from requisitioning the office, despite the fact our lease had expired in September 1943 and no rent had been paid since 1940." Now it was time to go back to work. The maid who had last received a *Daily News* paycheck four year earlier suddenly appeared to tidy up. The local telephone company even pledged that the phone would be reconnected the following day. For once, reporting the war by communiqué had, if not an aura of glamor, then at least a warm nostalgic glow.[23]

As Paris settled back into a semblance of normality, it became the Allies' major news hub. A week after the liberation, more than a 150 correspondents remained in town, representing countless news organizations and attached to at least four different Allied commands.[24] Most stayed at the Hotel Scribe, where SHAEF established a new press camp a day after a large group of Germans had hurriedly checked out.[25]

Like the rest of the city, the Scribe held obvious attractions. It was located close to all the main points of interest, for both work and pleasure. Its rooms, Don Whitehead remarked, were "places of luxury," especially to anyone who had spent more than a month roughing it in the field.[26] Capa shared his with Wertenbaker and Walton. It was "a huge, high-ceilinged room," Walton told his bosses in New York, "with a crystal chandelier, and two immense windows opening on an iron balcony that overlooks the Rue Scribe, a teeming mass of press jeeps lined up at the curb with the French standing around curiously to watch the comings and goings and pick up cigarette butts."[27]

As the correspondents settled into their new surroundings, the censors and PROs colonized the hotel's second floor. Here, they organized separate

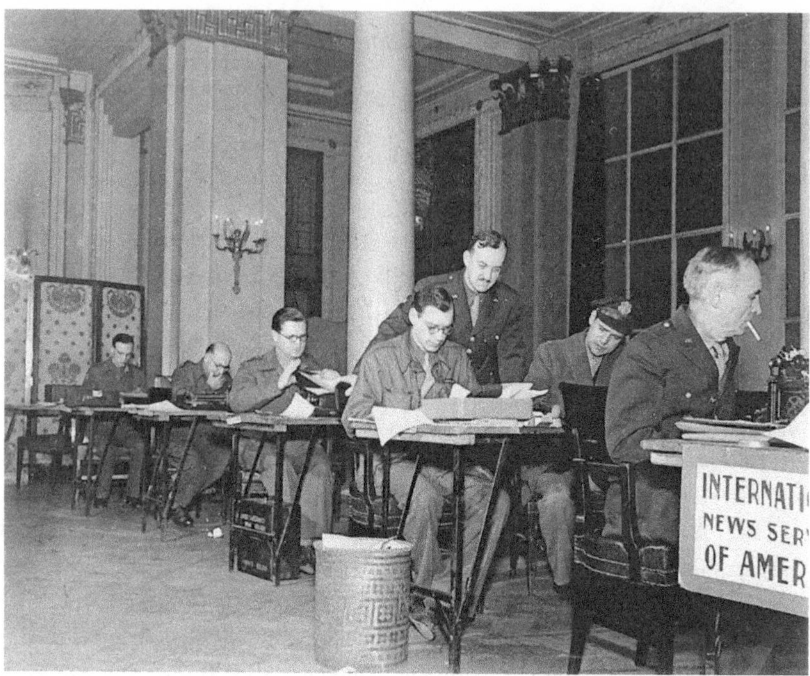

Figure 17.1 Reporters working in the Scribe press room. National Archives 111-SC-204497.

spaces for different needs, from censorship and briefings to photographic production.[28] But however hard they tried, the PROs could find no immediate solution to the fundamental problem of how to get 100,000 words a day from Paris to the United States. The recent battles in the French countryside had devastated "land cables, repeater stations, radio stations, and other facilities," while in Paris radio stations used old and unreliable receivers. Although SHAEF worked hard to repair and update this equipment, it was the middle of October before it could to provide reporters with relatively swift and smooth communications directly to the United States. And even then, "there were many technical faults" and "considerable delays in press transmission."[29]

Unsurprisingly, these glitches angered the reporters with deadline pressures, especially those who had lost the race to report the liberation of the city. Yet this was not the only reason the reporters' mood began to sour. Although the battle for Paris had been won, the war continued to drag on. After the heady experience of liberation weekend, the prospect suddenly loomed of a return to the front. Although the Germans were currently fleeing to their own borders, the reporters who had dashed from Normandy to Paris knew that a fluid fight could be more dangerous than a static one. And what if the Wehrmacht still had enough strength to defend the Reich with vigor? That would mean a third successive winter covering the American war: a third year of cold, rain, and mud. For some the prospect seemed almost unbearable.[30]

Pyle concluded that he could not bear it at all. "Ernie has decided," his editor wrote on August 28, "that having seen Paris he has seen everything, so he plans to start negotiating in a few days for immediate transportation home."[31] His editor seemed more intent on burnishing the legend than telling the truth. A better description would have been that Pyle had seen too much—the carnage on Omaha, the snipers in Cherbourg, the friendly fire at St. Lô, and the artillery shells during the breakout. Even the party in Paris had left him cold. "When I was there," he commented a few months later, "I felt as though I was living in a whorehouse—not physically but spiritually." When the German V-1 rockets started raining down on the first night of liberation, he decided that the end had come for him. "I knew then," he remarked upon reaching New York in late September, "I'd have to get some rest."[32]

"THE GIANT BALLOON OF US OPTIMISM"

Whitehead and Thompson were particularly sad to see Ernie go. On August 24, the day before the liberation, Pyle had sat down with his friends for a long chat. Everyone agreed that they were "homesick." They were also "fed up with the war," Pyle noted privately, "and feeling like . . . [they] couldn't take it any longer." Only Ernie, though, decided to head home. For the others, the "pent-up semi-delirium" of the next few days helped to recharge them, although this was not the only reason they decided to stay. Having been together on bloody Omaha, Whitehead and Thompson wanted to join forces again to cover the Allied assault into Germany. It seemed like the most fitting way to end their grim battlefield journey.[33]

On September 2 Whitehead accompanied the first Allied spearheads penetrating into Belgium. As the American troops "rolled forward 120 air-line miles" in a little over a week, Whitehead reported on a series of new celebrations, as "laughing, cheering, and weeping natives, decked American tanks, trucks, and jeeps with garlands of flowers."[34]

Germany came next. Whitehead watched intently on September 10 as US artillerymen fired their first shots into Hitler's Reich. Three days later, he joined an infantry unit as it approached the famous Siegfried Line, much heralded as the enemy's last major defensive position before the Rhine. As he spoke to the GIs, Whitehead learned that they were amazed by what they had found. "Coming into Germany," he told his readers, "the troops saw what looked like a concrete fortification on a hillside overlooking the route of the advance. But closer inspection showed it was just a house camouflaged to look like a concrete fortification. It was not manned."[35]

After reaching the Siegfried Line, Thompson was equally sanguine. American troops, he reported on September 16, have "smashed thru the main fortifications," while suffering "only a 'handful' of casualties." Convinced that the end was near, Thompson decided that the time had come to sum up "one of the most brilliant campaigns ever waged by any soldiers." Knowing the how much his *Tribune* boss hated the British ally, he quietly omitted them from his account. In just 103 days, he observed, the Americans had broken the back of the once-powerful Wehrmacht. "Hitler," Thompson concluded, "has not yet run up the white flag. But there is no doubt in any one's mind that Germany is doomed, not thru any so-called home front collapse, which became the German alibi after the 1918 defeat, but by having her armies knocked apart and destroyed in battle with the Americans."[36]

This was not the first time Hitler's impending defeat had dominated the headlines: exactly a year earlier, Mussolini's fall had led to a spate of stories predicting an internal collapse inside Germany. Yet clearly this was different. As Thompson pointed out, no one was predicting a domestic revolution. A rapid military defeat seemed much more likely.

Back home, the American public naturally reacted with glee. "The fall of Paris," noted *Time* on September 4, "gave another puff to the giant balloon of US optimism." Across the country, the magazine reported, city and state officials had begun planning in earnest for the day of final victory, with almost everyone acting "on the assumption that the citizenry would get roaring drunk." A few weeks later, as the stories of Germany's imminent doom proliferated, a majority of Americans still seemed primed to party at a moment's notice. According to one opinion poll, more than two-thirds of them believed that the war would be over by Christmas.[37]

Precisely how to end the war dominated the thoughts of all the senior Allied generals during September, although they disagreed on how it could be achieved. After weeks of bad-tempered haggling, Montgomery won the resources, if not the argument. On Sunday, September 17, he launched Operation Market-Garden, an audacious attempt to deploy airborne troops deep inside enemy-held territory in the Netherlands, where they would pave the way for the Allied crossing of the Rhine. The British paratroopers, known as the Red Devils, got the worst job. They were to be dropped the farthest away from Allied lines, at Arnhem; Americans from the Eighty-Second and 101st divisions would land to the south, around Nijmegen and Eindhoven, respectively. Under Montgomery's plan, all three airborne divisions were expected to do the same thing: to secure and hold key bridges over various rivers in those regions until relieved by British armored units pushing from the south.[38]

The small group of London-based reporters who covered this airborne battle included the current and future stars of CBS news. Early on Sunday morning, Ed Murrow clambered into his plane with a colleague who would be handling the portable recording equipment. Murrow began speaking into the recorder's mike as soon as he was above Nazi-occupied Holland. The Germans, he explained, had deluged the countryside, making it look "like the area around the Mississippi in flood time." As the drop site approached, Murrow introduced the nineteen paratroopers in the plane, before counting them off as they jumped. "Every man out," he shouted excitedly. "I can see their 'chutes going down now. Every man clear. They're dropping just beside a little windmill near a church. Hanging there, very gracefully—completely relaxed . . . like nothing so much as . . . dolls hanging beneath a green lampshade."[39]

Murrow returned to Britain with his plane, heading straight for London. From there, CBS quickly aired his vivid descriptions, recognizing that their punch and immediacy overrode normal editorial concerns about using recordings. By this time, Walter Cronkite was heading in the opposite direction. Normally so buoyant and nerveless, today he felt an unfamiliar pang of intense fear.

When the UP received a place on the operation, Cronkite had been the obvious choice. He had been based in Fleet Street ever since the abrupt demise of the Writing Sixty-Ninth eighteen months earlier. In that time he had cemented his reputation as a reporter who would grab any opportunity to take to the skies. At first, though, Cronkite had a tough time on the Market-Garden mission. He hated the terrifying sensation of going to war in a glider—the eerie silence, the sudden plunge to earth, and then the hair-raising feeling as the wheels jammed up through the floor when the craft landed.[40] Landing with the 101st Airborne near Eindhoven, he found the German resistance to be much stronger than expected. Enemy forces had demolished a key bridge, and it took the engineers more than a day to replace it, holding up the land attack for precious hours. Even after the 101st hooked up with the British armored columns, it faced a hard struggle to keep its section of the road—suitably dubbed "Hell's Highway"—open in the face of persistent German attacks.[41]

Little of this darker side of the battle appeared in Cronkite's reports. Once he was safely on the ground, he quickly absorbed the euphoric mood among many of the 101st veterans. Then he tried to get his bearings, before finding a quiet spot to pound out a dispatch on his damaged typewriter. The resulting story, although not quite as "purple" as his famous account of the Wilhelmshaven bombing, nevertheless told a heady tale of triumph. "Thousands of Allied parachutists and glider troops landed behind the German lines in the Netherlands today," Cronkite revealed, and "liberated village after village from enemy troops who fled in panic before them, and, as I write, are pushing on to their first big objective, which they expect to reach by nightfall."[42]

Farther north the battle proved tougher. At Arnhem, the British paratroopers had landed perilously close to two SS panzer divisions, and they immediately faced a major battle simply to survive. Yet no US correspondents had been accredited to cover this battle, and the four-man British press team struggled to get anything out of the beleaguered town. So American editors turned largely to HQ-written stories, which at first were wildly overconfident.[43]

On September 20, as the Red Devils lost their tenuous foothold on the Arnhem bridge, SHAEF remained largely in the dark about the true situation. Instead of playing safe, it allowed correspondents to report that the offensive had so far been "extraordinarily effective." In the next few days, as Montgomery's command received more accurate information from the besieged town, his briefers began to acknowledge that the "situation is serious."[44] Then, on September 26, a day-long "security dimout of news from middle Holland" got everyone worrying. SHAEF imposed it during the period when the British troopers were making a desperate bid to retreat across the Rhine, and the whole press corps recognized its dark portents.[45] Even so, when SHAEF lifted the news ban the next day, the briefing officers at headquarters encouraged the correspondents to put the best possible gloss on what had happened—and, crucially, the newspaper correspondents obeyed, focusing on the large number of British paratroopers who had retreated to safety.[46]

Other media forms were even more phlegmatic. "We should not get too excited about the dramatic battle in Holland," concluded William L. Shirer on CBS. "The overall situation on the western front is so good that Gen. Eisenhower can declare, as he did yesterday, that Germany's military situation is hopeless." Since the news from the American fronts was still rosy, the headline writers were particularly sanguine. "OUR MEN TRIUMPH," declared the *New York Times* on October 4.[47]

"COLD AS ICE"

As he sat in his office at the Pentagon perusing these stories, Major General Alexander D. Surles, the War Department's director of public relations, became alarmed. Surles had spent three years in public relations, a long apprenticeship that had taught him all about the media's dangerous tendency toward excessive optimism, even when the underlying facts warranted greater caution.[48]

On October 4, as headlines continued to trumpet the "triumph" of Allied troops, despite the reality on the ground, Surles wrote a long letter to Eisenhower. "Everyone," he began ". . . with typical American psychology was bowled over, along with the Germans, when your armies streaked across France and no one could have told them that the troops weren't heading for Berlin. This feeling," he continued, "reached its peak when the airborne troops were dropped in Holland," and even the setback there had done little to dispel the heady mood. Surles thought he knew the reason why. "There is always a build-up starting with the correspondent who is slightly optimistic," he explained to Ike, "thence to the rewrite man who further emphasizes the favorable aspect of the story, up to the headline writer who is aiming solely at circulation." As a result, Surles believed, "the public invariably gets overplay on the actual happening. It is therefore highly necessary," he concluded, "for the official announcements and the briefing officers to be factually cold as ice, particularly with so-called breakthroughs."[49]

The man picked to implement this policy offered an interesting insight into Surles's attitude toward media relations. By September, T. J. Davis's continued poor health meant he could no longer continue as head of SHAEF's G-6 section, and Harry Butcher, who had been temporarily filling in, needed to be moved to other tasks. So Eisenhower asked Surles to recommend a replacement and was happy to accept his suggestion. Brigadier General Frank A. Allen was a field officer by trade, which hardly seemed the best background for constructing an open relationship with the press. Allen also had a firm and forbidding manner, which would soon reveal itself in a tendency to give any journalist who disregarded his instructions a "spanking."[50] But perhaps this was part of Surles's design. Perhaps the Pentagon PR chief felt that the Allied PROs had been a little too free in handing out information to the press in recent weeks. Perhaps he believed that the correspondents had then used this information to inflate the bullish bubble that threatened to soar out of control.[51]

When he scoured recent press reports, Surles certainly found plenty of evidence to support these suspicions, most of it coming from one source.

Since re-emerging into the public eye, Patton had not only provided his Third Army reporters with a torrent of battlefield victories, but had also put on a dazzling personal performance that had kept these exploits firmly on the front page. His methods were transparent enough, but highly effective all the same. "When a big show is coming up," one reporter noted admiringly,

> Patton himself strides into the press camp and gives us the lowdown. Chewing a fat cigar and bumming cigarettes when it gives out, Pistol Packin' [Patton] seats himself in front of our war map and briefs us in detail. Then when he's finished he turns around and answers questions for an hour or so, explaining the operation in football terms and salting his comments with phrases which would not do for repetition at Sunday school.

Patton's predictions about what would had happen when Third Army reached Germany's defenses were a case in point. "I hope to go through the Siegfried Line," he told reporters on September 7, "like shit through a goose."[52]

In the following weeks, Patton's crude boast proved unfounded, as neither he nor any other Allied commander found the Siegfried Line easy to penetrate. Crucially, however, the full extent of the battlefield slowdown—and especially the reasons behind it—remained largely shrouded from public view. As Surles recognized, the reporters were partly to blame, but only partly. The military shouldered some of the responsibility, especially when it came to publicizing the shortages of gasoline and equipment. According to one PRO, "It was necessary to cushion this news to the public," to deny sensitive information to the enemy. The censorship guidelines for the reporters were therefore perfectly clear: "No mention or intimation [that] Third Army is unable to attack at this time due to shortage of supplies or that they are assuming defensive positions."[53] And the results were predictable. Whatever the reality of the situation, in the pages of the American newspapers and magazines, Patton continued to roam "up and down the line" at will, his tanks mounting "major assault[s]" against an enemy who always came off worse.[54]

Patton's exceptionally good press had rankled many of his senior colleagues well before the Allied slowdown. In late August, Bradley's command had even gone so far as to offer to help correspondents get into the French capital first if they promised to tell their readers that Patton had not liberated Paris single-handedly.[55] In early September, SHAEF went even further. Seeing that the war correspondents were still obsessed with Patton, Eisenhower's senior advisers tried to shift the media's focus toward the

First Army, commanded by Lieutenant General Courtney H. Hodges. They instructed the briefers "to attract a little more attention to Hodges and Bradley as against Patton's colorful appeal to the press." They also encouraged Hodges to speak to his reporters about upcoming operations, with the aim of bringing the "splendid work of First Army into better play."[56]

Bradley and Eisenhower justified these initiatives in terms of equity: they simply wanted the First Army, which was "the largest American fighting force in Europe," to receive something approaching its fair share of media attention. Yet there was another likely consequence of pushing reporters toward the First Army. If the mere presence of the flamboyant Patton seemed to instill a sprightly optimism in the press corps, then exposure to Hodges was likely to have the reverse effect.

"God gave him a face that always looked pessimistic," Eisenhower once noted, and the tough fighting of recent weeks had scarcely made Hodges's expression any cheerier. When *Life* published a portrait of him in September, Hodges admitted that he looked "a little too sad." When the general began inviting one correspondent a night to dinner, the outcome tended to be far from enlivening, especially since he was suffering from a bad head cold at the time. The published results certainly did nothing to stimulate a new bout of jauntiness. They merely revealed a commander who "is a firm believer in the army's long-established tactical doctrines" and "does his thinking with a cold brain."[57]

While Hodges' demeanor helped to bring down the mood a notch or two, Allen began working on more substantive changes. His main goal was to ensure that the SHAEF PROs gave the correspondents a much more realistic picture of the fighting. "All press guidance from this division has emphasized [the] serious task confronting the Allied Expeditionary Forces," Allen assured Surles on October 14. Then, as the weather turned, Allen stressed the inevitable: the war would not be over by Christmas, he confirmed, and the GIs would have to prepare for another long winter in their foxholes.[58]

At least one reporter appreciated the change of emphasis. After leaving France in late June, Bill Stoneman had watched the campaign unfold from afar. Like millions of Americans, he had followed the tumultuous events of July and August through the daily news stories, and by September had concluded that the war would soon be over. Keen to witness the impending Allied victory firsthand, Stoneman decided to head back to France, making straight for the First Army press camp. From here, he soon learned about the disjuncture between what he had read and the reality on the ground, and he searched for an explanation.

American newspapers, Stoneman complained to fellow reporters, always seemed to lean to the side of "good news," though he believed they might merely be pandering to their readers' wishes. "It would be very helpful and interesting to know," he mused,

> whether the people responsible for selecting and placing war news in our papers are fooling themselves in thinking that the people demand sugarcoated stories. If it is true that the biggest street sales go to the papers with the pleasantest headlines, then the public itself is as much to blame as those who cater to its tastes. In any case, correspondents and the public in general are entitled to demand that the army officers who brief the press shall be realistic and not allow wishfulness or complacency to result in the publication of false impressions.[59]

When he returned to the front, Stoneman was particularly pleased to find that Allen's PROs were now willing to let reporters record more of the battlefield's grim new reality. But the old veteran scarcely needed any encouragement. As the fighting stalled, he simply decided to write about what he saw, with obvious consequences.

"Using fresh crack troops who had last seen service in Russia," Stoneman told his readers in one dispatch, "and employing the greatest mass of artillery they have used against us since Normandy, the Germans have lashed back against the American First Army in a serious and well-organized effort." "Bad weather continues to plague us," he explained a few days later, "and this morning a thick ground mist again put our air force out of action." As the weather completely closed in, the likelihood of additional gains became even more remote. "The high hopes of two weeks ago for a speedy advance to the Rhine," Stoneman stressed in another story, "have been dampened, and in the minds of less optimistic observers, completely washed away by the rain which has fallen almost daily since our penetration of the Siegfried Line."[60]

At the end of September Stoneman encountered Drew Middleton, who had also returned to the front. The two men had covered the fall of France together more than four years earlier, and Middleton respected few people more than the man he called "the Doctor."

"How goes it?" the *New York Times* man asked his old friend. "It doesn't," Stoneman answered gloomily. "We're stuck." In Paris, Middleton had heard that First Army was poised to break through to the Rhine. Stoneman vehemently disagreed. "Wait till you see the country they've got to fight over and the way the Germans are fighting," he explained. "We'll be goddamned lucky if we see the Rhine by spring."[61]

Middleton toured the front the next day. What he saw, combined with Stoneman's prediction that the fighting would continue into 1945, completely overrode all the confident comments he had heard away from the battlefield. It also helped him to frame his first dispatch. "The fickle fortunes of war," Middleton told his readers in a front-page story, "have combined to slow down the comparatively slow advance of the First Army to a point where only a comparatively slow advance toward the Rhine can be expected. . . . The war in the west," he emphasized, "is not going to end in five minutes or even in five weeks. The First Army will get through to the Rhine, but it may see it first through snowflakes."[62]

Before the Rhine came Aachen. Having witnessed the destruction the Germans had wrought on London, Tébourba, and countless other places, Middleton desperately wanted to be on the scene when the Americans captured "the first German city to be taken by an invading army in over a hundred years." He and Stoneman therefore joined a group of GIs as they slowly and cautiously fought their way through rubble-strewn streets and shattered buildings.[63]

As they inched along, both reporters soon realized that they were looking at everything through the eyes of jaded veterans who had seen too much carnage over the past five years. Middleton's war weariness translated into an intense hatred of the enemy. Indeed, when he watched "haggard" German refugees trudge to safety with their last remaining possessions, he wanted to feel compassion. But, as he wrote after the war, his only thoughts centered on what the Germans had inflicted on others since 1940: "the roads of France and Belgium black with frightened, tired people, the gray faces of Londoners leaving their shelters to start another day's work, the Arab woman holding her dead baby outside Medjez-el-Bab after the German fighters had been over."[64]

In print, however, Middleton merely described the plight of enemy civilians, instead of using the opportunity to condemn them for Germany's earlier deeds. Thus his published dispatches generally had a dispassionate tone, as he recounted how "civilians were poking in the midst of rubble that once was their homes. They had been in air raid shelters for weeks and were dirty and half-starved," Middleton explained. "Women, old men, and children salvaged what they could from the wreckage and then began to trudge long miles to refuge outside the dead city. There is no shelter in Aachen."[65]

Stoneman, by contrast, had no qualms about comparing the city's destruction to blitzed Britain, albeit with one significant difference. "This time the blitz technique seems to have achieved its purpose," he wrote, "and it gives you a funny feeling when you realize that it has happened in Germany."[66]

Aachen surrendered a short while later. For Stoneman, the desolation of the city's center offered a salutary warning to every German. "We have no compunction," he explained, "for we are fighting people who once boasted that they would wipe out every city in England." For Middleton, the time spent taking the city provided an equally valuable lesson to the American public that victory remained a fair way off. Aachen's capitulation, he wrote, "has been won at an amazingly low cost" in terms of American casualties. "Yet the Germans," he pointed out, in words that Surles and Allen would have appreciated, "who need time, have won it in the bunkers and the cellars of Aachen." They would doubtless use it, he intimated, to bolster the Siegfried Line and hold up the Allied advance throughout the winter.[67]

Neither Middleton nor Stoneman would stay to watch the next phase of the fight. While Stoneman's bosses called him home to enjoy a long winter break, Middleton decided go back to reporting the war from London and Paris. Like so many of his colleagues, he "felt tired and emotionally spent." More importantly, having watched the war "returning to its origin," he believed that "it was as good a time as any to leave the front." The war had come "full circle," Middleton explained later, and he no longer had any desire to see its horrors up close.[68]

As the fighting remained bogged down along the Siegfried Line, other reporters reached similar conclusions. Even Thompson and Whitehead realized that the time had come to take some stateside leave.

Thompson returned first, looking "a trifle grayer and somewhat aged," according to those who knew him well. "Modern aircraft has its advantages," the *Tribune* man told a colleague, "but it serves to bring a war-weary correspondent from the front lines back into comfortable civilian life with such swiftness that the contrast between the tired men and the sleek, well-fed, and groomed civilians is, at first, a little hard to comprehend."[69]

As Thompson struggled to adjust, Whitehead continued to dwell on the gruesome battles of recent weeks. "There are going to be more Americans killed on the soil of Germany," he told colleagues, "than anywhere else in the war. Our troops are up against the heaviest artillery they have faced. The Germans have concentrated a tremendous defense in depth. It's going to be a slow, hard, house-to-house fight—and we must expect our losses to be heavy."

Whitehead conceded that, personally, he had been lucky. Like Thompson, he had survived Omaha, Cherbourg, St. Lô, Paris, and the Siegfried Line.

So what explained the bandage on his hand? When asked, his response was always the same. It had nothing to do with the six amphibious landings he had made or his daring dash into Paris. It came from a wound sustained opening a bottle of champagne to celebrate his arrival in New York. "I earned my Purple Heart after I got home," Whitehead joked. "I damn nearly cut my finger off."[70]

CHAPTER 18

Blackout in the Bulge

TROUBLEMAKERS

The AP operation Don Whitehead had left behind was in the process of acquiring a toxic reputation with the American military, largely because of the actions of two of its top figures in Europe, Wes Gallagher and Ed Kennedy. Gallagher's major offense had come in mid-August. Eisenhower had been particularly livid with "Wes," one of Bradley's aides noted, for the underhanded way he had published a story suggesting that Montgomery had been demoted. Since then, Gallagher had managed to recover his position somewhat. During the liberation of Paris, the aide added, there had been so "many subsequent slips" that Gallagher's infraction "was soon forgotten."[1] A few weeks later the AP picked Ed Kennedy to become its new Paris bureau chief, and most of the PROs began to view Gallagher in an even more positive light. Gallagher, they noted, might be a little too pushy at times. He might even be tempted to pull a fast trick, as he had by slipping the command shake-up story past an unwitting British censor. But for all his reputation as a "troublemaker," Gallagher had nothing on Kennedy, a man many of the PROs considered volatile, belligerent, and a security risk.

The problems dated back to Italy a year earlier. Joe Phillips had had little time for the man who ran the AP's Naples office. Indeed, Phillips came to believe that the AP under Kennedy had been "extraordinarily aggressive in it's [*sic*] attitude toward the censorship," making "far more complaints with less real basis than any other group." Phillips could marshal plenty of supporting evidence. He could cite the occasion when Kennedy had called for a congressional investigation into censorship in the theater, only to back down the next day and concede that he had "acted hastily and in a fit of anger."[2] Or, he could dig up the time when Kennedy had allegedly broken a strict embargo on an impending offensive in Italy, apparently wiring a story at 11:55 p.m. on the night before the assault that the censors believed "was liable to indicate that an attack was imminent."[3] More recently, Phillips's colleagues in France had yet more proof that the AP man was nothing but trouble. His latest transgression had come when German resistance in the south had started to collapse. Kennedy had borrowed a jeep from the military and, without waiting for permission, had made a bold and dangerous dash for Paris, "slipping between trapped German units."[4]

Kennedy's bosses were delighted when they heard about this escapade. They still considered him their chief point man in Europe, and so as soon as he appeared in the French capital, they named him their new Paris bureau chief. The military responded with disgust. Desperate to delay or even scupper the appointment, the SHAEF PROs appealed to the War Department for help. Kennedy's passage to Paris, Surles informed a senior AP executive, had been "wholly unauthorized." Even worse, Surles added, the AP's announcement of his new job had been premature: the military had yet to allow news bureaus to be officially opened in the French capital. So, Surles mischievously added, the AP's proposed new chief would have to wait before assuming his new duties.[5]

Although annoyed at what he deemed another slight from an officious military establishment, Kennedy quickly saw that the delay would give him a chance to launch a thorough audit of all the AP's war reporting in the theater. Kennedy teamed up with Gallagher for this task, although the two men rarely seemed to pull in the same direction. The strengths that allowed them both to thrive inside the AP—an intense competitive drive and forceful, even domineering, personalities—tended to be a combustible mix whenever they had to work too closely together.

Still, throughout that September both men realized they had little time to bicker, for they had too many pressing problems to resolve. They began with communications. Since radio links between army headquarters and New York were constantly improving, Kennedy and Gallagher decided to let the staffers in the field send their stories straight back to the States whenever possible. Next, they discussed the hardships facing their frontline reporters. Kennedy and Gallagher agreed to allow them "relief as frequently as possible," rotating them to and from Paris—or, in Whitehead's case, all the way back home. Finally, they addressed the growing length of the battlefield. The American section of the front now stretched hundreds of miles, so Kennedy and Gallagher decided to place an additional layer of management between the reporters at the front and Kennedy in Paris. Gallagher would assume this new role. While Kennedy concentrated on producing round-ups of the big picture, Gallagher would be the war reporters' boss, charged with imparting his own sense of competitive energy and drive to every AP correspondent within striking distance of the battlefield.[6]

To undertake the new job, Gallagher left his usual HQ berth for his first sustained period of combat experience. He decided to base himself with the recently formed US Ninth Army, which had from mid-October assumed responsibility for the area just north of Aachen. Gallagher made this decision on the basis of a hunch. Although the Ninth Army was relatively untested, a simple glance at the map suggested that it had been placed in a crucial position. "As the armies came closer to the Rhine," observed Barney Oldfield, the Ninth's PRO, "it was obvious that a gigantic wheeling motion and shift to the north and east would be dictated. This made the Ninth Army the best bet in the early winter of 1944 to be the one which would skirt north of the Ruhr, Germany's industrial heart, and point straight at Berlin."[7]

That was the theory. When Gallagher arrived at the Hôtel du Lévrier in Maastricht, which served as the press camp for the Ninth, he initially found nothing much to report on at all. To the south, the First Army continued to slog its way into Aachen, while making its first bloody steps into the treacherous Huertgen Forest. Near Maastricht, by contrast, Ninth Army troops remained stuck in their foxholes, as the rain continued to lash down, turning the ground into a quagmire that was hardly conducive to a dashing tank-led offensive.

At least the Ninth Army's press base proved comfortable. Oldfield recruited local Dutch cooks and waitresses, whose cuisine and service quickly proved a "great success" with all the reporters. In the lobby lounge, next to Oldfield's office and a teleprinter, those waiting for the rain to stop and the action to begin would spend most of their days playing games of poker. Then, as soon as the chips had been gathered in and the IOUs scrawled out, they would head to the small, private dining hall that Oldfield had turned into a briefing room. For almost a month, the PRO who stood at the front had little to say. To the correspondents' intense frustration, the officer would not even allow them to report that the Ninth and First Armies intended, at some point, to push toward the Roer River dams. The censors had deemed this basic information too sensitive.[8]

At first Wednesday, November 15, appeared to be little different than all the other monotonous days. The rain continued to pour down, making air support impossible and a tank drive unlikely. Then at their daily briefing, the correspondents received stunning news: an attack would begin tomorrow. Eisenhower and Bradley had finally lost patience waiting for the weather to improve. It was vital, they believed, to stop the Germans from consolidating their Siegfried Line positions before winter descended in earnest.[9]

As an excited buzz went around the briefing room, the Ninth's PRO stressed that this attack would "be local with limited objectives, and that a major offensive on the Western front would not come certainly until the Rhine has been reached and bridgeheads had been established across the Rhine." Gallagher and his rivals scarcely noticed this effort to manage expectations. All they knew was that, at long last, they would have some proper battlefield news to report.[10]

Early the next morning Gallagher climbed to the top of a slagheap, which afforded a sweeping view of the flat plain leading to the Roer five miles away. Watching as Allied artillery pounded the enemy's defense line, he noted the impact. "Towns," Gallagher wrote in his dispatch, "just spewed smoke and debris high into the air." When the tanks began to move, the mud often slowed them down to a crawl. "But they kept going," he observed, "with doughboys trudging beside them."

After weeks of boredom and frustration, Gallagher found it impossible to contain himself. He sat down at his typewriter and let the euphoria of the scene take over. "Tired of long weeks of stationary warfare," he wrote, "begrimed GIs in frozen foxholes and mud-caked tanks carried out their promise to make the United States Ninth Army's initial attack against Hitler's west wall a success today by breaking thru the Nazi crust of defenses to take many initial objectives an hour after the assault had started."[11]

Back home, Gallagher's powerful dispatches received big play in numerous newspapers. In Paris, however, instead of being read with interest and admiration, they quickly brought the simmering tensions between him and Ed Kennedy to the surface.

The military had by now given Kennedy the coveted spot of Paris bureau chief, but he quickly found the job as unglamorous as it had been in Algiers or Naples. The AP had been allocated two rooms on the fourth floor of the Scribe, one for an office and another for sleeping. Apart from the heading to the bar and the mess, or attending briefings in an airless ballroom, Kennedy hardly left the AP quarters, and he soon began to feel like a hermit. "I was now completely a Headquarters *wallah*," he complained, "as far removed from the front as though I had been in Chicago."

The job was thankless in other ways, too. Kennedy spent much of each day piecing together news from the various battle fronts, but these

Figure 18.1 Wes Gallagher at the front. © PA Photos Limited.

dispatches tended to go out without a byline—a sharp contrast to the conspicuous success Gallagher was enjoying with the Ninth Army. As Kennedy sat in the Scribe, feeling out of touch and increasingly out of sorts, his anger began to bubble over. He even began to believe that Gallagher was misusing his new position to skew the AP coverage in favor of the exploits of the Ninth Army. "Gallagher has lost balance," Kennedy cabled New York, "[as] regards [the] relative importance of fronts and although he [is] supposed to be in charge [of] all front staffers has not taken this responsibility but think[s] front he is on is only front that counts."[12]

Omar Bradley was, for once, inclined to agree with Kennedy, though he would have viewed his demonization of Gallagher as well wide of the mark.

Like Kennedy, Bradley believed that too many correspondents had begun to identify with the armies they had been allocated to.[13] Unlike Kennedy, Bradley did not blame those reporting from the front. He blamed himself. Not only had he been the one encouraging reporters to spend more time with specific armies, but he had also rejected the creation of a Twelfth Army Group press camp when Gallagher had suggested the "desirability" of such a set-up.[14]

Bradley came to bitterly regret that decision. The most obvious consequence, he had realized by December, was that the media was ignoring his own exploits, although this was not his main concern at the time. Bradley believed that SHAEF was too distant from the fighting to provide timely and accurate battlefield information. As a result, most of the news organizations looked to their correspondents in the field, which tended to result in stories that failed to explain the "coordinated" efforts of the Allied offensive. As one of Bradley's PROs put it, the lack of a Twelfth Army Group press camp created the impression that the Ninth, the First, and the Third "were competing with each other, and not carrying out their portions of an overall plan."[15]

Just about the only thing that unified battlefield stories as November drew to a close was the continued accent on the Allies' limited gains. This, of course, had been Allen's objective since taking over as the SHAEF PRO in September. It also reflected the reality on the ground, where the offensive soon began to grind down into a slow battle of attrition. After the jubilation of his first reports even Gallagher got on message, detailing an advance that had decelerated to such a crawl that it looked likely to end at the Roer not the Rhine. Yet, as he changed tack, Gallagher was not content merely to describe what he was seeing. He also began to investigate it, and, in so doing, he revived his reputation as a major troublemaker.

Gallagher started his investigation into the slowdown by exploring familiar factors: the Germans' greater incentive to resist now that the fight was being waged on their homeland, or the atrocious weather that bogged down tanks and grounded the air force.[16] As he began to dig deeper, Gallagher became convinced that two major shortages—in ammunition and replacement troops—were severely hampering operations. More importantly, after talking to a number of Ninth Army officers, he reached an incendiary conclusion about where the blame lay for this dangerous dearth. "The assertion is made here," Gallagher wrote on Friday, December 15, "that the situation on the western front is due to the short-sighted and optimistic planning in Washington, which led to heavy commitments for the Pacific theater, along with general cuts in munitions and men in the belief that the war would be over this year."[17]

The planners in Washington were furious. Surles even summoned Major General Ray W. Baker, Eisenhower's deputy chief of staff, to an urgent teleprinter conference. Demanding an explanation for the Gallagher dispatch, Surles wanted to know not only who had talked but also why the censor had not blocked it. Baker was defensive. "Gallagher['s] story [is] not based on facts," he replied. "We know of no responsible officer who has stated [that] the situation is due to optimistic planning in War Department."

Regardless of who had leaked the story, Gallagher had nevertheless publicized an important problem. Eisenhower's armies had suffered so badly during the limited offensives of October and November that they desperately needed an infusion of new men. Baker therefore agreed to return to Washington to hammer out the problem. What to do with Gallagher—and with the censor who had passed his stories—remained undecided. Left to their own devices, both Kennedy and SHAEF would have preferred to transfer Gallagher away from the Ninth Army, but before either had a chance to act the situation had been transformed.[18]

"WHEN THERE IS BAD NEWS YOU WON'T RELEASE IT"

The noise provided the first clue that something big was afoot: outside, the distant rumble of artillery and the muffled screams of Nebelwerfer rockets; inside, a jittery, staccato chatter on the overworked teleprinter. At the various army camps over the weekend of December 16–17, the PROs tried their best to appear calm, but nothwithstanding their dry recital of place names, engaged units, and troop movements, the reporters soon realized that a major moment in the war had arrived, though they had little inkling that it was the start of Hitler's last gamble to stave off disaster.[19]

Despite months of defeat and retreat, the Nazi leader had somehow managed to cobble together three armies. His plan was to throw them against lightly defended Allied positions to the south of Aachen in a desperate attempt to relive his greatest victory. Four-and-a-half years earlier, Hitler's Wehrmacht had scythed through thin lines of unsuspecting French troops in the apparently impenetrable Ardennes, paving the way for the dazzling success that had almost won him the war. Now his troops would use the cover of ice, fog, and snow to push through the same terrain; their goal was to destroy twenty-five to thirty Allied divisions, recapture the vital port at Antwerp, and inflict such a heavy defeat on his adversaries that they would be prepared to negotiate a peace.[20]

Well before anyone fully comprehended the scale of the German challenge, the Hôtel du Lévrier erupted into a frenzy of activity. Gallagher made straight for the phones. His first calls were to Hal Boyle and Bill Boni, stationed with the First Army to the south. Gallagher instructed them to cover the first major breakthrough, which had been reported to the east of their press camp in Spa. Next, he got hold of Ken Dixon, who was currently at the front with a division attached to the Ninth Army. He ordered Dixon back to the du Lévrier to hold the fort there. Gallagher wanted to cover this big battle himself.[21]

His redeployments made, Gallagher jumped into a jeep with William Strand of the *Chicago Tribune*. Their destination was the First Division headquarters. Although the "Fighting First" was supposed to be enjoying a rest behind the lines, they learned that it was already being hurried to one of the danger spots near a town called Monschau.

As they sped along the icy roads, the two reporters encountered nothing short of chaos. Rumors were already swirling that German paratroopers had been dropped behind the Allied lines. Military policemen, who were supposed to be directing traffic, appeared baffled when asked for directions. After driving for several hours, Gallagher and Strand finally found the divisional command post, in a cozy two-story house. Inside, everything was quiet, almost businesslike. "What's doing?" the reporters asked. "Nothing much," the intelligence officer replied. "Things are pretty well under control." To two men who had spent the morning on the road, this seemed like dangerous complacency. "But," the two correspondents almost yelled, "what about the attack? Are the Germans going to get thru? We hear there are tanks roaming around everywhere." "O, hell that," the officer responded. "There's nobody coming thru here. This is the First Division."[22]

Perhaps, but Gallagher and Strand were not prepared to take the officer's word for it. After a surprisingly good meal of fried chicken, followed by steaming coffee, the two reporters headed back out on the road, where they would need all the courage they could muster. One colonel told them that if they took a certain road, they would be "corpses within an hour." Undaunted, they went in that direction anyway—and, with a sense of sangfroid that the intelligence officer would have been proud of, discovered that the road was, as Gallagher reported, "as safe as New York's Fifth Ave."[23]

They were not the only ones to take such risks. All along the fluid, fast-moving front, reporters suddenly faced unfamiliar decisions: Where to go? What road to take? To head east toward the sound of gunfire, or west to safety? Their snap answers could mean the difference between not just a good or a bad story, but life or death. And for the first time in two years, they lacked a well-briefed PRO to guide them—for the simple reason that the PROs were as clueless as everyone else.

When left to their own devices, the reporters reacted in a number of ways. Some, like Gallagher, relied on instinct. Others, including his AP colleague, Hal Boyle, depended more on their hard-earned battle experience. On Sunday, December 17, Boyle could not stop thinking about Kasserine Pass, especially how on that first day the Germans had driven so easily through thinly held American lines. When he returned to the First Army press camp in Spa that evening, Boyle was determined to raise the alarm. He found a raucous Christmas party in full swing, as reporters marched around the hotel, drinks in hand and singing loudly. Boyle tried to interrupt the revelry to express his concerns. If Kasserine was any guide, he told everyone he could buttonhole, the hotel was too close to the front and in real danger of being overrun. Many of his colleagues looked at him with amused disdain. The Germans would never get this far, they replied; and besides, no one wanted to leave Spa, a resort town so luxurious it had housed the Kaiser's supreme headquarters in the last war.[24]

The next night, when Boyle returned from an eighteen-hour trip around the fast-collapsing front, he found that "everyone had become panicky and had fled during the day."[25] This included the censors. That Monday, as the retreat gathered pace, no one seemed to have a clear sense of how far the enemy had come or how far it planned to go. And no one wanted the reporters to send out a dispatch that would hand the marauding Germans any additional advantage. The First Army censors therefore imposed a total "blackout" on all news stories from the front. Until further notice, nothing would be passed.[26]

After the demoralizing retreat from Spa, the war correspondents arrived at their new press camp to hear about the new order, and it sent their mood plunging. A pivotal moment in the war was unfolding before their eyes. They were willing to take inordinate risks to report it to an anxious home front. Only now, they had suddenly been thwarted. Any risks they took would be for naught. A "death-white mist" of censorship, as one of them put it, had shrouded the battlefield. Nothing they witnessed, nothing they wrote, would make it back home.[27]

In earlier campaigns, Allied headquarters had normally filled any vacuum resulting from a lack of fresh battlefield copy, but this time the situation was different. Communications, for once, were not the issue. The censors were, and this placed Allen and his PROs in a real bind. They could not overrule front-line censors who had decided that a total blackout was crucial for security reasons. All they could do was to stave off their own information-hungry reporters, who were being pressed by their bosses for stories on one of the biggest battles of the war.

On December 19, Major James Hughes, the SHAEF briefing officer, had the job of confronting the increasingly snarly reporters. He began by sounding suitably contrite. "For a day when such great things are happening," he apologized, "there is distressingly little news." The reporters' response verged on the apoplectic, especially when Hughes started to stonewall their questions. When will the blackout be lifted? Hughes did not know. Does the continuation of the blackout mean that the Germans are still advancing? Hughes could supply no information. Are enemy paratroopers still being dropped behind Allied lines? To no one's surprise, Hughes had not yet been briefed about this.[28]

"Why don't you step down and let us hit General Allen?" one reporter asked aggressively, as everyone's patience ran out. "It is his place to answer these questions." Relieved to end the session, Hughes hurried out of the room to speak to his boss, who made an appearance at the 10 o'clock briefing that night. By now, the mood inside the Scribe had turned ugly. Undeterred, Allen's first instinct was to defend his fellow officers at First Army HQ, insisting that the blackout remained crucial to denying the German generals valuable information.

Few in the room agreed. George Lyon, the OWI representative at SHAEF and a former newspaper editor, broke ranks first. "May I say that SHAEF's policy on this matter is stupid," he declared. "Everybody across hell and 40 acres knows what's going on. The American people are entitled to know what's going on." Drew Middleton jumped in next. "I don't believe that security covers the news of what happened last Sunday," he insisted. "Everybody knows that the Germans are good soldiers, and they certainly know what happened to them." "You complain about complacency on the home front," added Joe Evans of *Newsweek*, "but when there is bad news you won't release it."[29]

For Allen, the hypocrisy charge was only the first of many new problems. Others stemmed from the most fundamental fact of newspaper life: the need to fill column inches every day. Denied official information, some correspondents chose to speculate. James McClincy, having served out his ban for the Paris liberation story, got a measure of revenge by provocatively describing the current battle as the worst Allied setback since Stalingrad two years earlier. A number of his colleagues did something even more alarming: they based their accounts on German communiqués, which were not noted for their understatement or veracity. "German commentators claimed tonight," declared a front-page story in the *New York Times* on

December 22, "that their armies had made a breach sixty miles wide in the center of the Allied front and that the number of prisoners taken had risen to 20,000 troops."[30]

As such stories magnified the scale of defeat, the home-front suffered a spasm of doubt. On Capitol Hill, congressmen found themselves inundated with missives from "worried parents asking for news of their boys fighting on foreign fronts, and particularly those in action around Bastogne and the Belgian bulge." The Roosevelt administration detected a similar mood. One OWI correspondence panel—an early form of focus group—recorded a "general spirit of discouragement, dejection, and disillusionment" across the country. The nation's obvious state of shock, fretted a senior official, "has been almost as devastating in some respects as that surge of national incredulity and numbness which ensued immediately on Pearl Harbor."[31]

As Americans tried to make sense of this unexpected German attack, many of the news organizations decided to direct their attention to the news blackout itself—and by extension, the military's entire media operation. *Time* magazine threatened to publish the most damaging exposé. On the day after Allen's tumultuous press briefing, Ed Lockett, *Time*'s Washington correspondent, began digging. He discovered that the blackout fit an obvious pattern: as with the Gela friendly fire episode and the Patton slapping incident, the military's instinct in a crisis always seemed to be to cover up. Lockett searched for causes. Knee-jerk restriction, he concluded, was "usually the result of stupidity rather than any vicious desire to withhold news," but it was a stupidity that emanated from the very top. "Surles isn't his own boss," Lockett believed. "Sometimes Marshall himself calls Surles in, to get his advice on a public relations matter. Much more often, Surles runs to Marshall when a big thing is at stake."

The more he burrowed, the more Lockett found lower-level officers who were eager to talk. Colonel Bryan Houston, a former Madison Avenue advertising executive, provided one of the most damning indictments. Everyone in the Pentagon, Houston told the *Time* reporter, knew what was happening on the ground—that "we're getting the pants licked off us ... [and] casualties are heavy." But no one under Eisenhower had been willing to trust reporters with this information. "They didn't have enough sense to be frank," Lockett insisted, "up to the point of security."[32]

Surles, on getting wind of Lockett's investigation, immediately sent him an admonitory message. "Give this a lot of thought," the PR chief cautioned the correspondent, "and remember what I say, that the press will be the ones who are red faced over that silly blow up in the end."[33] Significantly, *Time* only partly heeded Surles's advice. It delayed the story until January

1, by which time the worst of the battlefield crisis had passed. Having proclaimed Eisenhower as its "Man of the Year," the magazine also excised some of Lockett's most inflammatory comments, but the outcome was damaging all the same. "Younger officers," *Time* reported, were stating openly "that if the public relations people had played fair and sensibly in the past, had not withheld news which had no real security angle, then in this crisis they could have got prompt cooperation."[34]

Even before *Time*'s attack, the military had decided on a partial retreat from the total blackout order. It began on Wednesday, December 20, when the First Army allowed reporters to state "that the German offensive is mounting in strength."[35] Then, on Thursday, Hughes announced that his briefing sessions, although reduced from three to one a day, would be much more informative. They would reveal key details of how the battle was unfolding, he explained, albeit with a forty-eight-hour time lag to ensure that the reporters did not inadvertently provide any crucial information to the enemy. On Saturday, December 23, Hughes divulged that the time lag was being reduced to thirty-six hours.[36]

WINNERS AND LOSERS

When he looked back on the battle a few weeks later, Wes Gallagher came up with a theory. "For many correspondents on the western front," he concluded, "it was the first time they had been on the losing side of the war, and they cracked up completely, getting nothing in the crucial period." Veterans like himself, Boyle, and Denny had flourished, however. They "had been on the receiving end before," Gallagher believed, "and they profited from the experience." Sometimes, their greater knowledge of the battlefield simply helped them come through relatively unscathed. More often than not, it enabled them to make the right choices, so that they were positioned to get the best stories from the front.[37]

Gallagher's theory had merit. His own reporting blended information gleaned from senior officers with eyewitness accounts of the action from hotspots like Monschau and Malmédy. As soon as the censors eased some of the restrictions, he recorded fighting on "the wooded front along roads which Belgian refugees peddle one way on bicycles and guns and tanks go in the other direction." On another occasion, he reported sitting in a command post "shaking to the thunder of artillery, both outgoing and incoming."[38]

Wherever he traveled, Gallagher enjoyed his biggest run of success since reporting from Gibraltar more than two years earlier: day after day of bylined stories appearing on the front pages of the nation's biggest newspapers. Yet even Gallagher was forced to concede that battlefield smarts could only take reporters so far. As ever, luck also played an important role.

Take Hal Boyle. The veteran of Kasserine used all his battlefield know-how to avoid the worst dangers, but he virtually stumbled onto his biggest scoop of the war. On the first day of the battle, Boyle was driving toward the Belgian town of Malmédy when he spotted "a small group of half-frozen Americans . . . at a moment when two felled trees across the road were all that stood between us and the Germans." On close inspection, Boyle realized that the men were "weeping with rage." Grabbing his notebook, he began a series of impromptu interviews that yielded a horrifying tale. "A German task force," Boyle reported, had "ruthlessly poured machine-gun fire into a group of 150 Americans who had been disarmed and herded into a field." "We had to lie there," recounted one of the survivors, "and listen to German non-coms kill with pistols every one of our wounded men who groaned or tried to move."[39]

Boyle was filled with horror, but he also recognized that he had a major story all to himself. Even his timing was good. He returned to camp just before the First Army censors imposed the total news blackout. Just as importantly, Hodges's command had already heard what had happened from another survivor. Convinced that there was "absolutely no question as to its proof," the First Army PROs wanted "immediate publicity" for what was already being called the Malmédy Massacre. And almost by accident, Boyle had a major front-page scoop to his name.[40]

During the following week, Jack Bell became another of the battle's big winners. The *Chicago Daily News* reporter had only recently joined what he dubbed the "Hardball League" because Bill Stoneman was enjoying his stateside vacation. Although Bell was no novice, having covered the war in Italy, India, and Egypt, he initially found the prospect of filling Stoneman's big shoes intimidating. He also took an instant dislike to the atmosphere in the Scribe, especially when another reporter snootily told him "that all fronts except Germany were mere batting practice."

Bell discovered a more appealing camaraderie as he got nearer to the sound of gunfire. Not long after he arrived in Spa, word spread of the German offensive. Bell sat near Harold Denny, the most seasoned of all the old hands, at a press briefing. The two men exchanged a few words, and decided to join forces. They requisitioned a jeep together the next day, and drove east through the cold, foggy forest. It was the first of a deeply exhausting series of road trips.[41]

Much of Bell's time on the road was spent following the troops charged with relieving Bastogne, a small Belgian town located at a crossroads that was crucial to the German advance. Paratroopers from the 101st Airborne had arrived to defend Bastogne on the evening of Monday, December 18. A day later they came into contact with three divisions from the Fifth Panzer Army. By Thursday, December 21, they were surrounded and facing a desperate battle for survival.[42]

Eisenhower had tasked the Third Army with lifting this vital siege, and Patton wasted little time. His plan was to use three divisions to pry open a corridor into Bastogne, hoping the frozen roads would allow his tanks to move swiftly for the first time since October. As the attack got underway, the news blackout—which had become a big headache for SHAEF—turned into a major boon for Third Army, for it masked the fact that, contrary to Patton's expectations, the relief effort almost stalled.

The reasons were not difficult to discern. Besides frigid temperatures, Patton's tanks had to try to navigate a seemingly endless number of valleys filled with snow, ice, and mud. The correspondents, for their part, found the cold particularly punishing. "My icy cameras hung around my neck," Capa recalled later, "and I could not keep my gloved hand on the frozen shutter for longer than a split second."[43]

Capa, like Bell, accompanied the Fourth Armored Division. The two men had received a tip that this "slashing, wheeling outfit" would be in the vanguard of the attack, but they soon found its progression almost tortuously sluggish. "Slowly the battle went on," Bell remembered afterward. "The Fourth Armored lost tanks and men—but took towns. . . . Still days went on, each longer than yesterday, and no food or ammunition for Bastogne."[44]

Until that town was recaptured every correspondent faced stringent censorship, which meant that the details of the frustrating drive remained unreported. Nor could Americans read about the even more harrowing situation inside Bastogne, although here the problem was compounded by a lack of communication to the outside world.

Fred MacKenzie of the *Buffalo Evening News* was the only reporter stuck in Bastogne. A year earlier, MacKenzie had been a lowly rewrite man, and even now, he was far from a household name. But having tagged along with the temporary commander of the 101st all the way from the Scribe, MacKenzie had the inside Bastogne story all to himself. "I watched the battle rise to climax after climax," he noted afterward. On Christmas Eve, the situation turned particularly ugly. German planes bombed the American positions incessantly, and the shelling was so devastating it seemed to obliterate everything, from the surrounding buildings to his own bedroll. "I was the only war correspondent here," MacKenzie explained after it was all over, "exceedingly lonely and frightened save for the comfort and companionship to be had among the hard-fighting, very busy American soldiers ready to battle the enemy to death."[45]

Finally, late on the afternoon of December 26, the first of Patton's tanks made it through the German ring, opening a lifeline into Bastogne. That night, as the ambulances evacuated a thousand wounded troops, Bell dashed back to the Third Army press camp. He was writing his story when a happy censor shouted, "They've lifted the ban. Just now, 9 o'clock. Guess they want to give the world some good news for a change."[46]

Good news was certainly what the home front received. As they produced their pieces, Bell, Capa, and MacKenzie could not help but contrast the initial heartache with the triumphant end. "It was a costly business," Bell reported on page one of the *Chicago Daily News*. "Jerry was devilishly well-informed about our weaknesses. He hit just where we were spread thinnest. Every division we had in that action was pretty badly beaten, and it took us a lot of time to stop the Nazi tide." Ultimately, however, the GIs won through—a victory, Bell insisted, that showed an impressive "American alertness when aroused to impending doom."[47]

Capa's photos told a similar tale. A five-page spread in *Life*'s January 15 issue revealed a white, frozen landscape that framed an assortment of US soldiers, tanks, and planes, sometimes with their guns ablaze, on other occasions herding large groups of German prisoners. Whatever the detail, each of Capa's pictures contained the same central message: the Americans were driving relentlessly forward to retake Bastogne.[48]

When the siege on that town was lifted, MacKenzie could finally tell his story. For six straight days, the *Buffalo Evening News* ran his exclusive eyewitness reports under the headline the "Hottest Spot in Belgium." Brigadier General Anthony C. McAuliffe, the division's temporary commander, emerged as one of the main heroes in McKenzie's dispatches. McAuliffe had "out-maneuvered the enemy," MacKenzie reported, while his "soldiers fought tanks with grenades, bazookas, and machine-guns, and German dead piled high outside the circle defended by the division."[49]

While MacKenzie was describing the conditions inside Bastogne, the AP broke the most startling soundbite of the whole battle: McAuliffe's response to a German surrender ultimatum. According to the AP story released on December 29, McAuliffe's reply "may rank with John Paul Jones' 'We have just begun to fight!' It was simply: 'Nuts!' "[50]

Patton could not have been more delighted with McAuliffe's blunt rejoinder. On January 1, still exultant at relieving Bastogne, he summoned his reporters for a press conference. When they asked him to place the battle in perspective, Patton reached for another historical comparison. "It was just as important as the Battle of Gettysburg was to the Civil War," he announced. "The credit for seeing that goes to General Bradley."[51]

Ensconced in his "steam-heated" brownstone office in Luxembourg City, Bradley greatly appreciated this shout-out, for the Bulge was threatening to become the lowest point of his career. Indeed, while Patton basked in the glory of having relieved Bastogne, Bradley seemed on the verge of becoming this battle's biggest loser.[52]

Bradley's problems dated back to the middle of December, when Eisenhower had rearranged his command to deal with the crisis. With a bulge protruding deep into Allied lines, Ike decided that it made the most sense to have one army group to the north, and another to the south, of the German advance. Because Montgomery already held the most northerly positions, Ike gave him control here, even though this meant shifting the American First and Ninth Armies to the British commander. Bradley was appalled at the prospect of relenquishing control of these forces to Montgomery. He even threatened to resign, before Ike put him in his place. "Well, Brad," Eisenhower barked, "those are my orders."[53]

For the bereft army group commander, there was, initially, only one small consolation: news of the command shift was censored until early January, when *Time* threatened to publish the explosive story.[54] Then, to make matters much worse, Montgomery chose exactly the same moment to hold a press conference. It turned out to be highly controversial, even by his provocative standards.

"The first thing I did," Monty told reporters about the day he took over from Bradley, "was [to] busy myself in getting the battle area tidy—getting it sorted out. As soon as I saw what was happening I took certain steps myself to ensure that if the Germans got to the Meuse they would certainly not get over that river. And I carried out certain movements so as to provide balanced dispositions."[55]

Bradley felt humiliated. Already upset at losing two armies, he fumed to his aides that Montgomery's statement created the impression that the British had pulled "our 'Chestnuts from the fire.'" Desperate to respond, he hosted his own press conference, in which he vigorously defended his generalship and argued that the main consequence of the Bulge had been expose the Germans to a massive Allied counterattack. "This breakthrough," he suggested, "which appeared so disastrous at first, may be the turning point in the war, shortening rather than prolonging it."[56]

Gallagher watched these developments with intense interest. Back in August, his report about the earlier command shake-up had earned him

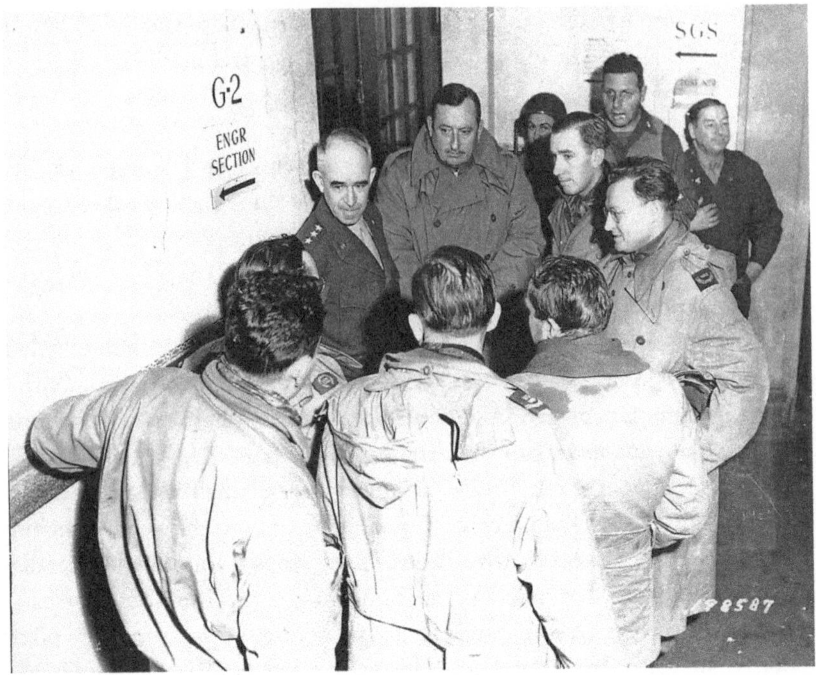

Figure 18.2 Omar Bradley holds an impromptu press conference at his headquarters, January 1945. National Archives 111-SC-198587-A.

a reputation as a booster of the American, as opposed to the Allied, war effort. Now, his reaction was quite different. Gallagher came away from Montgomery's fateful press conference extremely impressed.[57] By contrast, he reached some highly critical conclusions about US commanders.

In private, other seasoned hands, including Drew Middleton, were suggesting that Hodges deserved a large slice of the blame for his erroneous assessment of German strength before the Bulge. In another long investigative piece, Gallagher said the same thing publicly. On January 6, he accused Hodges of "keeping the Ardennes front lightly manned in the hope that the Germans would not attack," adding that "certainly Eisenhower and Bradley both knew about the situation."[58]

By attacking the American generals at a time of setback, Gallagher guaranteed that his story would reverberate way beyond the front. Many of his rivals were critical. One complained that he "somewhat overdraws his picture."[59] Ed Kennedy went much further. On January 8, Kennedy wrote to New York that he wanted Gallagher "relieved from Ninth Army assignment."

Kennedy badly mistimed his move. Gallagher had emerged in recent weeks as one of the biggest winners from the Bulge. As his bosses recognized, he had skillfully shifted his reporters around the battlefield, while producing his own barrage of page-one stories. Although these had ruffled the egos of reporters and officers alike, none had broken the censorship rules. Nor could anyone seriously claim that Gallagher's dispatches threatened American lives.

Gallagher's public criticism, in other words, remained within acceptable bounds. As a result, when his New York bosses heard about Kennedy's plans to relieve him, they immediately came to Wes's rescue. "Gallagher remaining present location," Kennedy sheepishly backtracked on January 9, "where doing usual splendid work in all respects."[60]

This was an important decision in terms of the ongoing coverage of the war. Over the past two years, the AP had been perhaps the premier purveyor of battlefield news. Now that the fighting was poised to head into Germany proper, the AP's two main players in Europe—both known for their ability to stir up trouble—would remain in key positions. They would therefore be able to exert a profound impact on how the home front perceived the last actions of the war, sometimes to the extreme consternation of Eisenhower and his subordinates.

CHAPTER 19

Into the Reich

HIDDEN WAR

Whether they were at the front or the rear, in the midst of combat, or relaxing in a press camp, the war correspondents could never lose sight of the main dictums of their profession. One was the transient nature of news cycles, which meant that even big exclusives could spark a brief flurry of interest and then be quickly forgotten. Because of this evanescence, good reporters were never able rest on their laurels. To be successful, they had to acquire a tough, forward-looking mentality, refusing to complain when the next day's edition contained not even the barest hint of yesterday's scoop

Wes Gallagher received a particularly brutal example of this truism in mid-December. On Friday, the 15th, he had cabled a major story indicting the "short-sighted" Washington planners for the lack of manpower at the front. Then over the weekend Gallagher, like all his fellow reporters, had become totally engrossed in the Battle of the Bulge, and the manpower problem had been pushed off the front pages. For weeks to come, even the most eagle-eyed reader would have found it hard to locate a story on the subject.

But if Gallagher's big scoop had fizzled, the problem he had revealed did not go away. Weeks of furious fighting in frigid temperatures had only heightened the need for replacement troops. The military's response came in various guises. For its part, Washington pushed up the sailing date of five divisions from the United States and reassigned two other divisions to Western Europe.[1] SHAEF, meanwhile, edged toward a much more momentous decision: to use more black troops in combat roles, and perhaps even to integrate volunteer black platoons into white units.[2]

Since Pearl Harbor, black Americans had been waging a dual war—against "fascism abroad and racism, segregation, and discrimination at home"—and it had not been easy. Under pressure from black leaders, the War Department in 1940 had agreed to take black draftees "in numbers approximate to their proportion in the national population, about 10 percent." All of these draftees had been put in all-black, segregated units. Although some black soldiers had found a place in an artillery battalion or a fighter squadron, most of them were restricted to service roles in the Engineer or Quartermaster Corps. Now, in the wake of the German offensive in the Ardennes, Eisenhower was suggesting that more of them would have the chance not just to fight, but to fight alongside white troops. And if they succeeded, the repercussions could be huge.

Indeed, the black GIs bound for the front had the chance to demolish the racist myths about their intellectual and physical abilities. By shedding blood for their country, they could also strengthen their case for being treated as equal citizens. And by fighting effectively alongside white troops, they could further the cause of integration in both the military and other areas of American life.[3]

But first their exploits had to be recorded, which meant overcoming another major dictum of the American media: the idea that some stories were best left hidden, including most of the stories related to race. "The mainstream American press," observe historians Gene Roberts and Hank Klibanoff, "wrote about whites but seldom about Negro Americans or discrimination against them; that was left to the Negro press."[4] Often, white reporters simply ignored black issues. Sometimes, they simply excised black Americans from their stories.

One of the most conspicuous episodes of such brazen editing had come in late 1943, when the main newsreel companies released footage showing Roosevelt and Eisenhower reviewing American troops in North Africa. As one black reporter noted in outraged capitals, "NO NEGRO TROOPS WERE VISIBLE" in the film—an omission that was no accident. "About two weeks later," the reporter explained,

> the All-American newsreel concern, which specializes in all-Negro subjects for distribution in colored houses only . . . acquired cuttings from the same film release showing the deleted phases. It shows clearly that the inspection of the troops by the President in line with all other troops. They all passed in review, and the Negro troops had full equipment, including rifles, along with other troops. In deleting the Negro troops, the guilty newsreel concerns sacrificed

> the best shot of the President and General Eisenhower chatting in the jeep, merely because the colored Americans provided the incidental background to this scene.[5]

Although it was the media that had censored this particular story, the military invariably acted as an enthusiastic co-conspirator in the efforts to hide stories about the exploits of black troops. The War Department's basic policy stemmed from a deep-rooted preference for segregation, which it sought to extend to media relations. This meant trying to ensure that only black reporters working for black newspapers were accredited to black units.[6] This policy reinforced the mainstream media's inclination to ignore stories about black troops, but for some senior officers it was not enough. The mere prospect of black correspondents traveling overseas left them searching the rulebook for restrictions.

In World War I, the War Department had accredited only a single, handpicked black correspondent. This time, Franklin Roosevelt's administration would ultimately allow almost thirty black reporters into the various warzones.[7] But this did not mean that they had an easy time. Some PROs fretted that they were prone to "sensationalism in playing up real or alleged racial discrimination" and would therefore "be looking for all situations which may be publicized as white injustices to Negro soldiers."[8] Those who were accredited, such as Ollie Stewart of the *Baltimore Afro-American*, initially found it difficult to report much of interest. Stewart arrived in Oran with Ernie Pyle in November 1942, but while the columnist quickly found stardom at the front, Stewart spent the vast majority of his time in the rear, covering the work of the black service units.[9]

Getting so little from their own reporters during the Mediterreanean campaigns, black editors repeatedly lobbied Eisenhower's command for more information on black troops. They rarely received much in return. In North Africa, for instance, Eisenhower's HQ calculated that it had commanded 34,000 black troops, 7,200 of whom had performed some type of combat role, from manning antiaircraft guns to providing airbase security. When the black editors approached Ike's command, however, they discovered that his PROs were resistant to publicizing these facts, albeit on practical grounds. "No authentic information available," one of them told Surles in May 1943, "as to the number, type, and conduct of Negro units that came under fire." A few months later, after "Negro papers protest[ed] lack of news of Negro soldiers," the PROs proved equally disobliging, although their reason had changed. "Suggest inadvisable [to] publish information on all Negro units in Sicily," they told Surles on this occasion, "since enemy broadcasters would distort for propaganda weapon."[10]

There was one partial exception to this blanket silence. In an effort to court the black vote in the 1940 presidential campaign, Roosevelt had promised to form black flying units. Soon after his election victory, the president had ordered the creation of the Ninety-Ninth Fighter Squadron, which began its training at the Tuskegee Institute in Alabama.[11] From the outset the military saw value in publicizing the "Tuskegee experiment." Despite the racist attitudes that predominated at the top of the War Department, where War Secretary Henry L. Stimson fully "accepted notions of Negro inferiority," Stimson's publicists were prepared to emphasize certain "stories about Negroes which would reflect favorably upon the army." The black pilot-training program at Tuskegee fit this bill. Some PROs even thought stories about the program might counteract "the inflammatory articles which have appeared at times in the Negro press." At the very least, they believed, it demonstrated "that this Negro outfit has received more thorough training than most Air Force units in the country."[12]

With the military's overt blessing, the black press hastened to tell the Ninety-Ninth's story in all its glory. Ollie Stewart led the way. Having languished during Operation Torch, Stewart dashed to the squadron's base in North Africa, arriving in time to record its "first positive destruction of a German plane."[13] In the months that followed, Stewart and his colleagues found plenty more eye-catching angles, from the pilots' "close brushes with death" to their growing expertise in fighting the Luftwaffe.[14] "In six months of operations," a number of black newspapers proudly proclaimed at the start of 1944, "the 99th Fighter Squadron has flown 236 missions of 1,156 sorties . . . , with the loss of four pilots, two by enemy action."[15]

Unsurprisingly, the mainstream press covered the Ninety-Ninth with much more reserve. Only *Time* seemed genuinely interested in the Tuskegee Airmen. Henry Luce had long been a champion of civil rights, starting, as his biographer observes, "with *Time*'s attacks on lynching in the South in the 1920s and 1930s, and continuing with *Life*'s growing effort to portray African-American life with sensitivity and respect in the 1940s and 1950s."[16] In September 1943, *Time* angered the Ninety-Ninth and its supporters by claiming that the first unofficial reports on the Tuskegee Airmen had rated their combat record as patchy. But when the squadron flew over the Anzio beachhead in January 1944 and racked up twelve kills, *Time* trumpeted these "Sweet Victories." "We have not turned out to be super-duper pilots—but as good as any the US Army turns out," the squadron leader told a *Time* reporter. "That's important. Because we had one handicap: people assumed we were not producing because we were Negroes. Our men have been under a strain because of the civilian attitude. It is remarkable that they kept up their morale. But now that we have produced, things have changed."[17]

Yet real change would come at glacial pace. The *New York Times*' coverage of the Tuskegee airmen was much more typical than *Time*'s; the paper published only two small stories on the Ninety-Ninth in more than a year, both buried deep inside the newspaper.[18] Just as importantly, the reports that did appear in either the black press or Luce's magazines depended largely on the military's willingness to give journalists access to information. And when it came to black issues unrelated to Tuskegee, such access was still not forthcoming.

The activities of the Ninety-Second Infantry Division offer the best illustration. In the late summer of 1944, it became the only black division to experience ground combat in Europe. Yet, as *Time* complained six months later, the censors "never permitted correspondents to tell the whole story of the Ninety-Second." Instead, they merely released two skimpy pieces of information—that the division had been activated in October 1942 and that it had been assigned to the front near Pisa almost two years later. "After that," *Time* noted, "few stories on the Ninety-Second came through."[19]

By the time of the Bulge, therefore, media coverage of black units had already settled into a depressingly familiar pattern. To those in the know, the dramatic events in the Ardennes promised to alter the role of at least some black troops in the segregated American army. To the media, nothing that happened during these tumultuous weeks would prove sufficient to alter the established pattern.

For their part, black newspapers searched for each and every snippet of information on black troops. When they found that some units had taken part in Patton's relief of Bastogne, they rejoiced that these men were no longer "sweat[ing] it out on the bench" but were on the pitch with the rest of the team. When they learned that an artillery unit had been inside Bastogne with the 101st Airborne, they hastened to compile a "list of individual exploits" that included evacuating the wounded, rescuing vehicles, and, at the moment when a German breakthrough seemed possible, destroying classified material.[20]

Predictably, the mainstream press largely ignored these stories. Although some white correspondents at the front occasionally referred to the black units fighting to stem the German tide, the first article devoted purely to the subject was written by the AP's Pentagon correspondent. Based on a War Department briefing, it appeared more than a month after the event. "The 969th Field Artillery Battalion," it began in a cold, factual tone, "with Negro enlisted men manning its 155-mm. howitzers . . . stuck to its guns and helped beat off waves of German attackers at Bastogne. . . . Casualties became heavy," the report concluded, "before the tide turned with the appearance of supply planes and armored forces from the south."[21]

When, soon after, the first newly trained black platoons were integrated into infantry and armored divisions, the army was even more reticent. In March 1945, the wire services got word that at least two American armies were using mixed "negro and white units." SHAEF's response was to issue a press release that did little to clarify the matter. "Negro reinforcements have volunteered for infantry training," it stated. "Upon completion of organization and training the platoons and companies are attached to the various United States combat divisions as additional tactical units."[22]

Like the coverage of the 969th Battalion, it was scarcely stirring stuff, but then that was the point. Neither the mainstream media nor the Pentagon brass saw much value in playing up this dimension of the story. They both preferred it to remain hidden.

"A RUTHLESS EXPEDIENT TO HASTEN HITLER'S DOOM"

In contrast to the noncoverage of black GIs, the media's indifference to the air war was less willful—and for that reason more easily rectified, although not always with the consequences that the air force desired.

For reporters, the main problem with the bombing campaign was its mind-numbing familiarity. Day after day, the air force released similar sets of figures, emphasizing the number of planes sent over Germany and the number of bombs they had dropped, and, for a year now, the destruction of German industry instead of the number of Allied casualties. What reporters needed if they were to switch their gaze back to the air war was an eye-catching new frame. On February 16, 1945, they received one.

The reporter who put the air war back on the front page was the AP's Howard Cowan, a thirty-year-old Oklahoman working under Ed Kennedy in Paris. Since arriving in France, Cowan had succumbed to one of the hazards common to the profession. The married reporter had fallen in love on his travels, necessitating a pained confession to his wife, who had planned to join him in the City of Light.[23]

Apart from his tangled personal life, Cowan, like many other reporters, found working in Paris a strain: the long days, the relentless routines, and the sparring with unhelpful PROs. Nor was Kennedy an easy boss. At the end of January, AP executives lavished a large pay increase on their Paris bureau chief, placing him in "the five figure class" as a reward for his "sustained services, personal sacrifice, and devotion to the cause." Even as they gave him this raise, however, his bosses pointedly instructed Kennedy to desist from sending the "occasional 'funk' messages and letters"—such as the one calling for Gallagher's relief. For reporters working in the AP's cramped offices, the ever-present danger that "one of those Kennedy boomerangs" might redound on their heads only added to their stress.[24]

Unsurprisingly, Cowan longed for a chance to escape to the front. But in mid-February he remained stuck in the Scribe, making the daily rounds of monotonous briefings, jotting down the odd salient detail in his notebook, and then cabling back a story that, if it received any play, rarely carried his byline. The air briefing on Wednesday, February 14, was typical. At noon that day, 311 Flying Fortresses had dropped nearly 1,900 high-explosive bombs and 136,800 incendiaries on the historic city of Dresden, wreaking yet more devastation after two massive RAF attacks had generated a hellish firestorm the night before. Yet that afternoon's briefing session was as bland as ever, as the PRO merely reported that sixteen Allied planes had been lost in attacks on "transportation and industrial targets."[25]

Two days later, Cowan and his colleagues arrived at another briefing session with little hope of receiving anything more substantial. RAF Commodore Colin M. Grierson began by explaining the reasons for the Dresden raid. Then, under questioning from reporters, he insisted that the principal target had been to stop the enemy from "moving military supplies." Had Grierson left matters there, the Dresden raid might have remained as hidden as so many others. But, not for the first time, an air force spokesman added a careless, offhand comment that would cause endless trouble. The Dresden attack, Grierson suggested, had also been aimed at destroying "what morale there is left to have any effect on"—an admission that, though vague, suggested that civilians, not factories, were now a conscious target for the American and British bombers.[26]

Unwittingly, Grierson had given Cowan his lead. On Friday, February 16, the AP man sat down and tapped out a story with a stunning opening. "The Allied Air Commanders," he wrote, "have made the long awaited decision to adopt deliberate terror bombing of the great German population centers as a ruthless expedient to hasten Hitler's doom." Late that afternoon, as everyone began winding down for the weekend, Cowan walked down two floors to the censors' office in the Scribe and handed over his copy. The chief censor told the reporter that he could not possibly pass such an explosive dispatch, but the AP man persisted. After "considerable discussion," and a close check of the guidelines covering the press conference, the censor, reluctantly, changed his mind.

When Cowan's story hit the wires, even his New York bosses were astonished. The AP had gone to great lengths over the years to foster a close and cooperative relationship with the air force, and they feared that this one rogue story would destroy all that hard work. The AP executives in New York therefore cabled Kennedy "asking him for the authority for the Cowan story." After checking with the censors, Kennedy told them that "he was not permitted to give the source"—a suitably ambiguous response that implicitly confirmed the military's decision not to challenge the story. The AP therefore circulated it on February 17.

When air force officers picked up the Sunday morning *Washington Star* on February 18, and saw Cowan's dispatch on page one, they were horrified. As one immediately realized, the story was bound to "bring an avalanche of queries because it contradicts all of our announced policies and purposes in precision bombing." In Paris, the censors at the Scribe swiftly admitted that they had made "an egregious error which is much regretted," but this confession was hardly likely to prevent a major nationwide inquest into what was going on.[27] So senior air force officers moved quickly to refute Cowan's story. "We have never done deliberate terror bombing," they told the press, ". . . we are not doing it now, . . . we will not do it."[28]

Despite this emphatic denial, the air force now encountered a third dictum of the media profession. On some issues, editors might be easily convinced to remain silent. On others, their interest in a story might be all too fleeting. But when their attention is suddenly grabbed by a shocking new angle, a pack mentality can take hold—and they will dig their teeth into a story and not let go.

In the second half of February, many editors were certainly emboldened to search for further stories on "terror bombing."[29] The most striking appeared on February 23. Written by Jerje Granberg, a Swedish journalist, it confirmed what Cowan's Dresden dispatch had suggested—namely, that American bombs rarely hit purely military targets with surgical precision, but rather inflicted terror and death on the civilian population, young and old.

Having lived in Berlin for years, Granberg had already experienced more than 700 air alerts and almost half as many raids, but he considered the American attack on February 3 worse than any of the others. As soon as the bombers appeared, he had dashed to one Berlin's "safest" shelters. "Thousands of people were packed together there," Granberg recounted in a story that hit the front pages of a number of American papers.

> Then the first bombs came. The ground heaved, lights flickered. People scrambled about like frightened animals. . . . Then a heavy bomb crashed through the

> tunnel roof . . . and a wave of cold air, followed by dust, swept over us. In the distance someone yelled for a doctor. The clamor for help was taken up by many voices, which were drowned in the next wave of bombs, more fearful than the first. . . . The all-clear finally came. Above in the railway station there were dead. Hardly any of the crowd . . . paid any attention to the dead. In the square a hurricane of fire raged. Smoke and flames limited visibility to less than 100 yards. I was blinded by smoke and soot.[30]

The article represented a major change in the press coverage of the air war. Newspapers had until this point been leery of using stories emanating from Berlin, aware that even neutral journalists reporting from the Nazi capital were subject to the strictures of Goebbels's propagandists. As the Reich collapsed, however, Granberg fled to safety in Sweden, where he could write the story unhampered by the Nazi censors. The result was particularly inflammatory in the wake of Cowan's dispatch about terror bombing, but it was by no means the last time the media grabbed the chance to reveal what it felt like to be on the receiving end of the massive Allied bombing campaign.

In early March the air force received a striking photograph. It showed two dark gothic spires jagging up into the sky, as the silvery Rhine flowed just to the east. All around lay nothing except gutted buildings and a broken bridge—underscoring both the magnificence of Cologne's Cathedral and the miracle of its survival.

Images had always been crucial to the air force's PR efforts, and when it received this remarkable photograph, its propagandists were naturally tempted to claim that the cathedral's survival had not been an accident. At first, many newspapers dutifully toed the air force line. The *Chicago Daily News* captioned the photograph, "A Picture of Precision Bombing." On the inside pages of other papers, editorial writers argued that Cologne was proof "that our bombers can hit what they want to hit and miss what they want to miss."[31]

Once again, however, the air force publicists discovered that their war had suddenly changed. Gone were the days when they had held an absolute monopoly over information going out to the press. Now, newspapers were not only publishing eyewitness accounts from neutral observers on the receiving end of bombs; they were also sending their own reporters to visit the targets of the intensive air campaign.

Cologne acted as a particularly powerful magnet. Many reporters hurried there simply to grab a valuable dateline—an unappealing motive that sparked an unseemly free-for-all, as a "motley collection of grown men [could be seen] sprinting into the Cologne city limits a few feet, spinning on their heels, and running back. Once they had regained their jeeps," a PRO acidly noted, "they told the drivers to pour on the coal, high-tailing it to the press camps."[32] Not every reporter was so opportunistic, however. Some of the bigger names at least tried to look at the damage the bombers had done to Cologne's "culture, the beauty of its churches, its spacious boulevards, its sprawling industries, and immense railroad yards."[33]

Having returned from their stateside vacations, John Thompson and Don Whitehead fell into this category. The two reporters had begun their latest adventure on the banks the Roer River at the end of February. Because the Germans had opened the dams to flood the area, the operation became another Whitehead special: ducking shells and snipers while making a hazardous boat journey to take a hostile shore. "The moon was very bright," Whitehead recorded, "—too bright—for a night attack."[34] Despite ferocious German gunfire, he and Thompson made it across the river, and were soon pressing fast for the Rhine, as the German resistance crumbled.

Both men were particularly struck by how much had changed since they had had their last taste of battle on German soil. Cologne, Thompson recorded on March 6, "fell, not with the thunder of Aachen, whose defenders fought from house to house almost until the end. It collapsed like a punctured balloon."[35]

If Cologne's fall came with a swift pop, the damage done by three years of Allied air raids had left the city far more devastated than even Aachen had been. Thompson estimated that more than 90 percent of the city had been destroyed and predicted that there was "almost no chance of rehabilitating . . . [its] large industrial structure." "The heart of Cologne," agreed Whitehead, "lay in waste. For block upon block there was nothing but the gutted skeletons of buildings and debris piled many feet high." Cologne Cathedral had survived, but this had been more by luck than design. "Seven times in two years," Whitehead discovered, "the famous cathedral has been hit by bombs and yet it stood, with remarkably little damage to its Gothic beauty."[36]

Shocked by the destruction, Whitehead's boss decided to dig even deeper into this aspect of the story. "The American dash to the Rhine," Gallagher wrote on March 9, "has lifted the lid of German secrecy on the effects of Allied air raids." Cities like Cologne, he concluded, had clearly suffered far more than anyone had imagined. But, he cautioned, the military results had been mixed. Despite the vast devastation, the morale of German civilians had not been broken. Nor had Germany's road and rail networks been decisively cut. Gallagher therefore left the most pertinent question hanging: had all the bombing raids, all the suffering of aircrews and civilians alike, been worth the effort?[37]

It was not a question that he or the rest of the press pack spent any time answering. Their interest as fleeting as ever, the correspondents swiftly moved on to the war's next big story: the crossing of the Rhine, the last remaining obstacle before Berlin.

ACROSS THE RHINE

Howard Cowan, the reporter who had provoked the sudden intense interest in "terror bombing," made it to the front at a curious moment. The Allies' main thrust across the Rhine was scheduled for the latter part of March, when Montgomery would lead an assault anticipated to be almost as big and complex as the Normandy landings. Until then, most American troops concentrated on clearing the Rhine's west bank of the last remnants of German resistance. Apart from the capture of big cities, it made for a dull, shapeless fight. "The battle had not ceased," observed the official historian; "it had only been shattered. The bits here and there, meaningless in the larger picture, were grim and bloody for the troops unlucky enough to run into them."[38]

These were not the type of battles that the correspondents found easy to frame. Partly for this reason, Gallagher took a few days off to help scout a new location for the Ninth Army's press camp. Maastricht was now too far from the action, so he suggested Schloss Rheydt, an ancient castle and tourist attraction northwest of Cologne. The castle yard had enough space for the correspondents' jeeps. And its moat gave added "bounce" to a Press Wireless antenna installed nearby, improving the radio reception back to the United States. As soon as the technicians installed the communications network, Gallagher scored another scoop for the AP. He filed the first dispatch directly from German soil to the United States.[39]

While Gallagher concentrated on communications, further to the south Cowan was enjoying a huge slice of good fortune. On the afternoon of March 7, he found himself the closest reporter to a town called Remagen, where some First Army units came across an astonishing sight. "The Hindenburg Bridge, still standing!" one officer exclaimed.[40] As the GIs began preparing to storm across, the defenders tried to blow up the bridge—but the explosion failed. Within minutes, the first Americans dashed through the smoke and over to the east bank of the Rhine. Then they dug in to secure the unexpected new acquisition against the anticipated German counterattack.[41]

Cowan arrived soon after. "I went across with a Dakota farm boy," he reported with glee, "to get a first-hand story of the heroic doughboys who snatched up a German fumble and raced right across the Rhine for what looms as the greatest American touchdown of the war." In the midst of the action, Cowan found the soldiers too preoccupied to talk, but he did manage to jot down the names of the first officers and men to make it to the Rhine's east bank. Then, like any good wire-service reporter, he scurried back to the press camp so that he could be the first to file.[42]

By now, word of the capture of the bridge had sparked a stampede into Remagen. Any journalist who could grab a ride immediately joined the melee in what Hal Boyle dubbed "the hardest journalistic marathon of the war." Sharing a jeep with John Thompson, Boyle spent fourteen hours traveling 225 miles, waiting impatiently in jams, taking confusing detours, and mending two flat tires along the way. Then after less than half an hour at the scene, the two reporters had to reverse the journey in order to file their stories. "Newspaper men assigned to the First Army," joked Boyle shortly after, "returned to the press camp after a long day of jeeping over muddy roads with enough diluted German real estate on their faces to start a potato farm. The story was so hot, however, they had *no* time to get rid of the accumulated topsoil until they had finished pounding out their accounts."[43]

For everyone except Cowan, the censors provided a valuable service that day. Under orders from intelligence officers worried about a swift German response, they stopped "any reference to First Army crossing the Rhine . . . until sufficient fighting [force] has been built up on far side of River." So instead of grabbing another massive scoop, Cowan had to be content with professional bragging rights. When drinking with colleagues in the evening, he could say that he had been the first across the Rhine and the first to file a story—even if the next day, when the news was finally released, he had to share the front page with his colleagues and rivals.[44]

As Germany's final defeat approached, Eisenhower, though exhausted, could not suppress a growing sense of jubilation. On one occasion, he complimented Patton for the first time since the start of the war, calling him both a good and a lucky general. On another, he stunned everyone at Patton's army headquarters.[45]

"If I have one criticism to make," Eisenhower told the Third Army staff at the end of March, "it is that you are too modest. You don't boast enough about your great achievements. . . . I want you to talk more about yourselves and your great victories." "Call in the reporters and see that they get the right kind of stories," he instructed them. "They'll use them and the folks back home will eat them up."

The liaison officers from the other armies thought Ike must have gone "nuts." "You are already the most blow-harding bastards over here," remarked one after Ike had left the room. "From now on, you'll be completely unbearable." "You and the goddamned Krauts said it," replied a young Third Army captain. "Cocky bastards, that's us."[46]

Cocky they might have been, but the Third Army officers also suffered from a long-standing persecution complex. They recalled all too vividly that Bradley had taken all the plaudits during the first half of August, when Third Army's dash through Brittany and beyond had been shrouded in secrecy. They also believed they had been robbed of the chance to liberate Paris, the glory given to other, undeserving, units as the Third pushed on to Germany's borders. "Publicly," recalled a Third Army officer, "Patton never received credit for this vital role that he played in the ETO war. His great victories were 'released,' often belatedly, but their crucial import and scope were never indicated."[47]

The Bulge had been a notable exception. After the relief of Bastogne no one who read a newspaper could doubt that Patton had played crucial role. Still, the weeks since had been difficult. Eisenhower might have considered Patton a lucky general, but fortune had smiled on other armies during February and the first three weeks of March. In the center of the Allied line, the First Army had liberated Cologne and achieved the striking success at Remagen. To the north, the Ninth Army remained part of Montgomery's Twelfth Army Group. As such, it was poised to participate in the last great set-piece battle of the war: a major Rhine crossing scheduled for the night of March 23–24, which would involve more than a million-and-a-quarter men, including eleven American divisions, as well as a two-division airborne assault. In the meantime, Patton was stuck with the more prosaic task of eradicating the last German position west of the Rhine, in a region known as the Saar-Palatinate.[48]

In private, Patton confessed to feeling "just a little envious" of the First Army's capture of the bridge at Remagen.[49] He, like Bradley, had little tolerance for Montgomery's attempts grab all the headlines for himself. Even worse, both Patton and Bradley feared that Montgomery's big attack would, like Operation Market-Garden in September, suck the air out of every other Allied operation, forcing the First and Third Armies to stand still while Monty's army group swept into the heart of the Reich. So, after the Third Army made another lightning advance, this time to clear the Saar-Palatinate, Bradley and Patton had a quiet word. The upshot was significant: Third Army was given the green light "to take the Rhine on the run."[50]

Patton responded with typical vigor. By the afternoon of March 22, he had just enough boats and bridging equipment alongside the river to make an attack that night. The operation would be risky. Many officers preferred to wait for more equipment to arrive, fearing that if they sent too few troops across the Rhine the Germans could eradicate a flimsy bridgehead. But Patton would brook no delay. Every hour, he insisted, would give the enemy time to dig in. Besides, March 23 would be too late—by then news of any Third Army crossing would be submerged beneath the tidal wade of copy on Montgomery's big battle.[51]

The reporter who accompanied the Third Army across the Rhine that night could hardly believe his luck. Edward D. Ball was, like Cowan before him, an unheralded AP reporter who suddenly had a major story all to himself. "Shortly after 10 o'clock," he recorded, ". . . the first wave moved out of the shadows like pallbearers, carrying their little assault boats with six men on each side." Ball jumped into a boat commanded by a soldier from Portsmouth, Virginia. "Hell," the GI confidently proclaimed, "this Rhine is nothing but a creek."[52]

The soldier's confidence was well placed. Within hours, the Third Army had established its lodgment on the Rhine's east bank. Ball returned to write his major scoop in the middle of the night, scarcely crediting the fact that he was still the only reporter on the scene. When he tried to file his dispatch at seven the next morning, however, Ball encountered the same obstacle that had foiled Cowan two weeks earlier: the censor initially held the story, out of fear that premature release would give the Germans a chance to mobilize a counterattack. "On top of all this," Ball complained as his frustration mounted, "all the guts were slashed out of my copy." Even so, enough remained to dominate the front pages when the censor finally released it. "The United States Third Army stormed across the Rhine at 10:25 last night," Ball began, "without the loss of a single man and without drawing a single shot from the Germans for a good twenty minutes after the crossing was made good."[53]

Ball's story hit the wires just as fifty correspondents were gathering along the northern sector of the Rhine, shrouded in "a thick black haze" laid to obscure Montgomery's attack from the enemy. Neither Ball's scoop nor the impending offensive placed them in a good humor. In fact, everyone was on edge, for no one wanted to die with the end of the war so close. The American reporters were also suspicious. In theory this was an Anglo-American operation, but they had been told that Montgomery would announce Ninth Army's involvement "in due time"—a statement they assumed meant only after British units had been accorded all the glory.[54]

Unhappy at all these professional indignities, Wes Gallagher joined a group of GIs as they marched along moonlit roads to their assembly areas. As the massive artillery barrage intensified, Gallagher dashed across the river in one of the many boats heading for the far shore. Once safely across, he changed his mode of transportation, hitching a ride in Cub spotter plane. The view below filled him with awe at the Allies' organizational power. "The most impressive sight of all," he observed, "as always, was that of the long lines of silent infantry walking across fields and along the roads. The sight always brings a tightness to one's throat.... In the forests," Gallagher continued,

> there came a rumble of tanks and trucks; and on the roads long convoys sprang forth loaded with every conceivable piece of equipment, including thousands of tons of bridging material and huge landing craft on giant trailers. It seemed impossible that this vast assortment could be untangled and moved to the right place at the right time. But most of it got there.[55]

Not for the first time, the media arrangements proved far more chaotic than the combat preparations. When Gallagher and his fellow mud-spattered correspondents returned to the Schloss Rheydt on the morning of March 24, they discovered that the teletype had already "gone dead." Most of them headed for a long lunch, safe in the knowledge that the censors had placed a four o'clock release time on the story, only to learn that SHAEF had suddenly changed its mind. Paris would be releasing the story at noon. This announcement, one observer noted, "caused a great spewing of coffee. Chairs were shoved back and upset with crashes." The reporters ran to their typewriters. The fastest soon dashed to the censor with their copy, among them Gallagher with his eyewitness account. The laggards were destined to be unlucky. Gallagher's dispatch received a big play back home; whereas other reporters, as another witness explained, "disconsolately watched their stories fade and die in the blighting atmosphere of censorship, and cursed the 18-point bylines many a writer from SHAEF Paris was getting in the American papers while the first-hand stories for which they had risked their lives were lying on a PRO's desk."[56]

This press fiasco only added to Patton's elation. For the past two years, he and Monty had vied for troops, materiel, and headlines, as Anglo-American armies had swept across North Africa, Sicily, and Western Europe. Now,

Figure 19.1 Wes Gallagher (*right*) at the Rhine. With him is Gordon Gammack, of the *Des Moines Register Tribune*, one of the four reporters the Ninth Air Force had tried to order out of the theater in August 1944. © PA Photos Limited.

with the last German defensive line breached, Patton had emerged as the clear victor; his army's exploits across the Rhine grabbed the headlines even as Montgomery seized most of the supplies. "Brad, we're across," Patton had yelled down the phone on March 23 to the Twelfth Army Group commander. "And you can tell the world Third Army made it before Monty."[57]

Contributing still further to Patton's delight was Eisenhower's clear instruction to start bragging about his achievements. He even had the perfect platform to do so, for *Time* magazine was planning a major cover story on the man who had surged across Europe so extravagantly, before crossing the Rhine so stealthily. There were only two potential problems: Patton's long history of saying the wrong thing, even at moments of triumph, and the awkward fact that *Time* had attacked him during the slapping incident eighteen months earlier.[58]

The powerful magazine certainly received strange treatment from a general so keen to boast about his record. When *Time* correspondent Sid Olsen arrived at the Third Army HQ, Patton's PRO carefully intercepted him and gave him "hell about some of the previous articles in *Time* long ago." As the interview began, Patton took care to have three senior officers present as witnesses, in case Olsen tried to twist his words.[59] Even when Margaret

Bourke-White showed up to photograph him, Patton could not seem to relax. "Don't show my jowls." he demanded. "And don't show the creases in my neck. . . . This is the only angle at which the little hair I have will show."[60]

Yet with victory so close, Patton ultimately found it impossible to hide his passion for the job at hand. He became particularly expansive when telling Olsen about how and why the Germans would finally quit fighting.[61] The *Time* man left the interview charmed, and the article he wrote could hardly have been more glowing. The enemy "had reason to fear him," *Time* observed. "He had consistently out-slicked them, mauled them, beaten them. The Germans had always put more men and guns opposite Patton's outfits," the report claimed, but to no avail. Patton had always prevailed. For that reason *Time* placed him "in nomination for Public Hero No. 1 of the war in Europe."[62]

For all Patton's charisma, the list for this spot was bound to be crowded. Its final compilation would also have to wait until the guns fell silent—although with so many Allied troops across the Rhine, few doubted that this red-letter day would come soon.

CHAPTER 20

Unconditional Surrender

"THE GOLDEN GRAIL"

The news came through on the radio first. It had long been anticipated, even expected, but it was a big moment nonetheless. Nazi Germany had surrendered unconditionally. The war was over. The long-planned celebrations could finally begin. March 27, 1945, would henceforth be known as VE—Victory in Europe—Day.

Then came the hurried apology. In reality, the Wehrmacht was still fighting a desperate rearguard in the center of Germany, while Hitler remained defiant in his Berlin bunker. The news flash, in other words, had been plain wrong, and not for the first time. Every major event over the past nine months seemed to have been foreshadowed by a premature bulletin of this type, from the AP's June 3 announcement of the invasion of Europe to CBS's August 23 "scoop" on the liberation of Paris.[1]

One expert even found a name for this phenomenon. "The psychologist calls it pre-perception," pronounced Professor Henry E. Garrett of Columbia University after the latest snafu, "which means hearing a thing before it happens because you're expecting it to happen, or want it to happen." The journalist, Garrett believed, was particularly susceptible to this tendency. "He [*sic*] is trained to react to the stimulus of news," Garrett explained. "He's sensitized—or to use a common expression, he's 'hopped up.' His error may be one of momentary impulse rather than considered judgment—but in this day of split-second radio broadcasting of news bulletins that is sufficient time to permit the story to go out on air."[2]

Although media observers were worried about this poor track record, few bought Garrett's explanation. Most detected a far more prosaic reason for the foul-ups: cut-throat competition, especially among wire-service reporters and radio broadcasters. They also saw little chance that this would change. Indeed, since the prime cause was so deeply embedded in the media process, a recurrence seemed almost inevitable.

As the spring sunshine arrived in earnest, Bill Stoneman returned to the front. He had been away for more than six months and was amazed to discover that the war was no longer a fierce stalemated fight to break through fixed German defenses, but a mad dash along the impressive Nazi-built *Autobahnen*. "This is the war that no longer is war," Stoneman proclaimed on April 9,

> it is an Indianapolis auto race or a Kentucky Derby—between Lt. Gen. Patton and Lt. Gen. Hodges and the Russians. It bears no resemblance to the knock-down, dragout business of the last year. There is no Luftwaffe and there are no mines. There is no artillery, and even the silly young men of the highly touted SS (Elite Guard) don't fight properly to defend their towns.[3]

Thompson and Whitehead fully agreed. Thompson began to dateline his stories with the phrase, "On the Road to Berlin," while Whitehead saved this arresting thought for the body of his article. "The victory-flushed First Army," Whitehead reported in a typical story, "continued its sweep toward Berlin today with armored and infantry columns running wild in another 24 hours of spectacular gains." According to the AP man, the main resistance was no longer coming from the Germans; it came in the form of minor practical headaches. "The trouble is," one officer explained, "we can't keep enough maps on the wall to keep up with the advances."[4]

Alongside the euphoria of speeding into the heart of Hitler's Reich came bouts of horror whenever the foundations of the Nazi regime were exposed. Whitehead encountered the slave laborers first. "Along the roads to the front you see them," he reported on April 5, "—walking across fields or in ditches or by the roadside, making their way toward rear areas and away from Germans who held them captive. They plod along in small groups bound for home—or what once was home." Next Whitehead visited an American evacuation hospital that was treating the first freed American POWs, and his revulsion mounted. The "gaunt" GIs described to the reporter their "brutal treatment" by the Germans. The charts at the foot of their beds told him even more: "malnutrition due to starvation," "dysentery."[5]

However terrible the sight of these half-dead prisoners, nothing could prepare the Americans for the scenes they found in Nazi concentration camps. Eisenhower, Bradley, and Patton arrived at Ohrdruf on April 12, and were truly horrified by the gruesome sight of "more than 3,200 naked bodies" lying in "shallow graves, with lice crawling "over the yellow skin of their sharp, bony frames." Patton became physically ill, while Eisenhower found it difficult to control his anger, incredulous that "such cruelty, bestiality, and savagery could really exist in this world." "I made this trip deliberately," Eisenhower wrote to Marshall a few days later, "in order to be in a position to give *first-hand* evidence of these things if ever, in the future, there develops a tendency to charge these allegations merely to 'propaganda.'" To make doubly certain that no one back home would question the extent of the savagery, Ike immediately called for twelve congressional leaders and twelve editors to come and view the camps.[6]

War correspondents accompanied the delegations. Whitehead went to Buchenwald, where, he reported, "decency was torn aside and men died like beasts in one of Germany's worst butcher shops." Stoneman visited the same camp with a group of GIs, who, he realized, had "fought and won without ever knowing precisely why." That soon changed. The American soldiers, Stoneman told his readers, "found 20,000 wretches still wandering or sitting about the barracks, or lying in their bunks, awaiting death from years of brutality and hunger and long neglected diseases. Outside the crematorium," he continued, "they saw a truck loaded with the corpses of men who had died the last day or two, too far gone when we arrived two weeks ago to benefit by treatment. . . . In the basement of the crematorium they gazed wrathfully at hooks on the walls from which prisoners were hanged."[7]

After this brief pause to gaze into the dark heart of the disintegrating Nazi empire, the correspondents continued to look east, where Berlin's capture beckoned. Eisenhower sparked renewed interest in this next big story when he arrived at the Rhine on March 26 and began lavishing praise on the men of Hodges's First Army. "I expect them to lick everybody they come up against," Ike told an impromptu press conference, "and I see no reason why they should stop on the road to Berlin."[8]

Eisenhower's casual remark generated major excitement among the reporters, each of whom yearned to be the first into the Nazi capital. Over the next week the First and Ninth Armies would execute what Ike proudly dubbed the "largest double envelopment in history," trapping more than 300,000 German troops in the Ruhr pocket. But the press paid little attention. As the Ninth Army's PRO complained, "no amount of talk about the importance of snapping shut and destroying the Ruhr, taking with it Germany's war-making capacity, ever dented any war correspondent's consciousness. The Berlin dateline was all that mattered."[9]

Because Eisenhower remained uncertain how far his troops would drive into Germany, he continued to offer tantalizing encouragement to the Berlin obsessives. In a press conference at the end of March, one reporter pointedly asked him: "Who do you think will be into Berlin first, the Russians or us?" Ike began his answer cautiously enough. "Well, I think mileage alone ought to make them do it. After all," he explained, "they are thirty-three miles and we are two hundred and fifty." Yet he did not rule out a sudden sprint into the Nazi capital. "I wouldn't want to make a prediction," he concluded. "They have the shorter race to run, although they are faced by the bulk of the German forces."[10]

Soon after, it appeared that the American troops had made a sudden spurt to narrow the remaining distance. "Paris is wild with excitement tonight," reported Drew Middleton from the Scribe on April 12.

> A special edition of the *France-Soir* carries a report by the radio station "Voice of America" that places American forces fifteen and five-eights miles from Berlin after an airborne landing that had linked up with Lieut. Gen. William H. Simpson's [Ninth Army] forces only seventy-five miles from the Red Army vanguard.[11]

As a matter of fact, Eisenhower had ordered no such airborne assault. The biggest development that day was Roosevelt's death from a stroke. Even so, the news about Americans entering the Nazi capital would not subside. Once the shock of the president's death began to wear off, Drew Pearson even gave the Berlin story a dramatic new twist. "United States army patrols," the muckraking columnist claimed on April 22, "were in Potsdam, adjacent to Berlin, on Friday, April 13, one day after President Roosevelt's death, but were withdrawn 50 miles because of an agreement made at Yalta by the Big Three that the Russians were to occupy Berlin."[12]

This allegation was not only plain wrong but also contradicted the decision that Eisenhower had finally reached. Instead of starting a potentially dangerous race into Berlin, Ike decided to focus on eradicating what remained of the Wehrmacht. Hitler's capital, he remarked privately, "has become, so far as I am concerned, nothing but a geographical location. . . . My purpose is to destroy the enemy's forces and his powers to resist."[13]

Eisenhower asked Walter Bedell Smith, his chief of staff, to hold a press conference on April 21 to explain his stance. The effect could scarcely have been more favorable, at least in the short run. Raising the specter of a "national redoubt" in southern Germany, where Hitler and the die-hard Nazis apparently planned a bitter last stand, Bedell Smith successfully shifted the media's attention away from Berlin. Indeed, many of the reporters at the conference fully bought the notion that the Nazi capital no longer held any real military value. Crucially, those at the front, who knew how the average GI felt, agreed that Ike had made the right call. "While the staff officers were disappointed," wrote Gallagher with the Ninth Army, "the American doughboys and tankmen who had to do the fighting and dying to get to Berlin expressed no regret. Almost to a man, they felt they could do without the final 'glory' of getting to Berlin and the resulting expense in casualties."[14]

After Eisenhower had placed Berlin out of reach, the correspondents had to settle for another symbolic story to mark the effective end of the fighting. They did not have too far to look. From Tunisia to Anzio, any juncture between two armies had sent the reporters into a frenzy, but the next meeting promised to be of a different magnitude altogether. The Soviets had long been a distant, mysterious partner, fighting on their own, with none of the day-to-day mingling that had characterized Anglo-American operations. The GIs' impending encounter with the Red Army was therefore an intensely exciting prospect, especially because it would underline the fact that Hitler's Reich had been conquered from both the east and west.

"The western front has gone Russian wacky," Wes Gallagher reported on April 23, after crossing a northern section of the Elbe River, "seeing Marshal Stalin's troops around every bend, hearing strange voices on the air, and developing rumors 20 to a minute." Further to the south, Bill Stoneman had yet to reach the Elbe, but he remained hopeful of grabbing the climactic scoop. On April 25, he borrowed a bicycle and pushed on ahead of the First Army's most easterly troops, passing "groups of Germans who plodded down the road toward our lines and tried to surrender when they saw our one-man expeditionary force." After hours of pedaling, Stoneman was forced to admit defeat. "Combing the countryside 15 miles beyond our frontlines," he reported, ruefully, that night, we "failed to find the Russians—the golden grail of every war correspondent at this moment."[15]

As Stoneman tapped out his frustrations, an American patrol finally encountered a Red Army unit.[16] The news buzzed around the theater shortly after six o'clock that evening. Within minutes, every war correspondent within touching distance began a mad dash toward the town of Torgau, the site of the American and Soviet meeting. Within the hour, Thor

Smith, based in the SHAEF PRO office in Paris, activated a long-standing plan to round up representatives from the news organizations that did not have any reporters near the scene. Given only thirty minutes' notice, Smith could not locate many of the names on his list, but he did gather enough reporters to justify a plane trip to the Elbe. They arrived at sunset. "It was a bright, crisp moonlight night," Smith recorded, "and it was a weird feeling driving through Germany up toward the 'front,' and realizing that for the first time there was no enemy immediately in front of us. They were Allies . . . stretching all the way to China."[17]

For the next two days, a hastily arranged series of ceremonies and celebrations enveloped Torgau. As the stiff-looking American generals self-consciously shook hands with their Soviet counterparts, jolly soldiers shared food, proclaimed toasts, and consumed alcohol in prodigious quantities.[18]

The resulting stories focused heavily on the revelry. Thompson began by emphasizing the similarity between the American and Soviet troops, both of whom, he believed, exhibited a "combination of easy informality and discipline." Fraternization between the two sides developed rapidly, Thompson added, "aided by generous bottles of fiery vodka"—although the *Tribune* man prudently kept his distance when drunken soldiers began showing off their firearms. Whitehead recorded a more bucolic scene. "Americans and Russians slapped each other on the back," he wrote, "gave each other bear hugs and sat in the warm sunshine drinking champagne and toasting the great occasion."[19]

As soon as the the party began to subside, the sense of euphoria was quickly replaced by the familiar pangs of frustration. Reporters discovered that Eisenhower had placed an absolute embargo on all stories of the meeting. Motivated more by alliance diplomacy than concerns over military security, Ike had ordered that "no news story was to be cleared until after simultaneous announcement of the event by the governments in Washington, London, and Moscow." Throughout April 26 and much of the following day, Thor Smith and his PROs accumulated a large backlog of censored copy, while the correspondents increasingly "stewed around" complaining about the delay. Then, just before five on the afternoon of April 27, a little more than an hour before the joint announcement was scheduled to be made, one news organization broke the story early.[20]

The culprit was the French wire service, Agence France-Presse (AFP). As a SHAEF investigation discovered, someone at the AFP had committed a mistake similar to the one made by its American counterpart just before D-Day. A lowly employee had typed out the story ahead of time, and then handed it to the Colonial News Service, who duly broadcast the news to the world. The BBC and Reuters then magnified the mistake. To the intense anger of all the American correspondents, these two British news organizations both aired the story minutes before the embargo time.

SHAEF's response was telling. Despite their extreme annoyance, Allen's PROs recognized that, with the fighting almost over, "no security" had been breached. So they decided to tread softly. Allen brushed off the AFP's story as an honest mistake. Viewing the BBC's premature release against the backdrop of the long history of Anglo-American rivalry, he considered its infraction to be far worse and so sent the British broadcaster a letter of protest pointing to the "breach of faith in the violation of an agreed embargo time." But he took no further action. He would not suspend or disaccredit anyone, let alone convene a dreaded court martial. What signal this sent to the rest of the resentful press corps only remained to be seen.[21]

"THE FLAGRANT VIOLATION OF A SOLEMN PLEDGE"

Some members of the press corps had been accompanying Eisenhower and his entourage for almost three years, and during that time the relationship had gradually changed. Back in the summer of 1942, Pete Daniell and Drew Middleton had viewed themselves as seasoned veterans, especially compared to the war virgins who staffed the senior positions in the US command. In the intervening years, Ike and his team had survived, even flourished, amid the huge stresses of combat, taking a green army from the shores of North Africa and turning it into a highly efficient military machine that had penetrated the heart of Hitler's Reich. The war correspondents had also acquired more experience, but this had come at a cost. Many were jaded, even exhausted. As the war ground to its end, they also became far less tolerant of their military interlocutors.

In a sense, the two sides had come to resemble an old married couple, bickering loudly over every little disagreement, every imagined slight. Other processes helped to reinforce this tetchiness. Fundamentally, the correspondents no longer had the same incentive to cooperate. They had tolerated the military censorship during times of extreme peril, but bristled once SHAEF began to justify stops on political grounds, their First Amendment instincts rising to the fore.

The working conditions in the Scribe only made the situation worse. In the bar, the reporters could order a cocktail called the "Suffering Bastard." Those who had worked in the hotel for months appreciated the reference. They had come to loathe the incessant, dreary routine. "It's like a big convention," noted one reporter, "that just goes on week after week and month after month, with the nervous strain proportional."[22]

As April turned to May, this strain became almost unbearable. Everyone knew that Germany was expected to surrender in a matter of days. Hitler had just committed suicide in his Berlin bunker. The only real question was whether there was a successor with enough clout to sign a surrender document. Reporters therefore expected the end to come at any moment, but how would they report it? Allen's PROs had established a klaxon system that summoned correspondents to a briefing whenever a story broke. In recent days, the horns had blared out five times, or more, only for the briefing officers to announce a lesser piece of news: the surrender of German troops in the north, or the junction of the First Army with forces pushing from Italy. The tension generated by all this activity, observed one reporter, "reduced the hardiest to a state of jumping jitters."[23]

While the reporters at the Scribe suffered, Eisenhower's headquarters began preparations to make the official surrender announcement. Once again, it had ballooned in size over time, so that, by the spring, there were more than five thousand officers crammed into various buildings in the cathedral city of Reims, eighty miles northeast of Paris.

Despite its vast experience in waging war, SHAEF would find making peace a major challenge. On May 5, Harry Butcher took control of press relations for the big event. He began by arranging for cables, cameras, and klieg lights to be installed in the L-shaped war room. As soon as word came through that General Alfred Jodl would be arriving at Reims, Butcher called Allen and instructed him to bring between fifteen and twenty correspondents to Reims straight away. Within minutes, Thor Smith had rounded up seventeen agency and radio reporters, and was shepherding them to a transport plane.[24]

Ed Kennedy joined the lucky group, although he would soon have reason to rue his good fortune. The problems began on the plane. The inside of a noisy C-47 was a bad place to hold an important briefing. Kennedy could barely hear Allen's words over "the din of the propellers," and, as he explained later, he found the PRO's talk "rather long and rambling."[25] Allen would always insist that his message could not have been clearer. "This story is off the record," he claimed he told the seventeen reporters, "until the respective heads of the Allied governments announce the fact to the world. I therefore pledge each and every one of you on your honor not to communicate the result of this conference or the fact of its existence until it is released by SHAEF." Kennedy's recollection differed. Allen, the AP man claimed later, merely said that "it was important that this be kept secret until the surrender was signed."[26]

Whatever transpired on the plane, Kennedy's impatience grew as soon as the party arrived at the redbrick French technical school that housed Eisenhower's HQ. Thor Smith immediately established an impromptu press camp in one of the classrooms, handing out paper for the reporters to insert into their borrowed typewriters. Allen soon entered and announced a change of plan. The story was so momentous, Allen declared, that SHAEF would release the news from Paris shortly after the surrender had been signed. That would leave the press group stranded at Reims, with no way to get their stories back to their editors. The reporters predictably erupted in fury at this sudden policy change. Only Allen's promise to hold a plane in readiness for a rapid flight back to Paris stilled the incipient insurrection, but the mood in the classroom remained ugly, especially as the clock ticked slowly past midnight.[27]

Then, outside came the sound of familiar voices. A number of newspaper reporters, angry at being excluded from the press party, had traveled to Reims on their own and were standing at the classroom window shouting "taunts" at Allen and his press group. Pete Daniell of the *New York Times* was the most senior of this group of newspaper reporters. Like Kennedy, Daniell had spent much of the war in the thankless role of bureau chief and HQ reporter. Having scarcely tasted battle, he felt particularly aggrieved at the prospect of missing the surrender announcement, although that was not his only beef. Ever since his meeting with Joe Phillips, in September 1942, to decide how many reporters should accompany the North African invasion, Daniell had been involved in discussions with the military over the sensitive matter of media representation at key events. Sometimes—as when choosing who would fly on a bombing mission—he had supported the use of a lottery. On other occasions, he had helped draw up "an order of precedence" that both the military and the media had generally accepted. Now, to his horror, Allen's PROs had cobbled together their own press party, with little consultation—and, more to the point, without a single newspaper representative. Since space was at a premium, Allen had calculated that the papers could all rely on wire-service reports. Daniell begged to differ. "It was unjust," he yelled through the window, "that . . . newspapers should be barred from reporting one of the great news stories in history."[28]

Just after 2:30 in the morning, on Monday, May 7, the waiting finally came to an end. The reporters filed into the room where Jodl and his colleague stood poised to sign the unconditional surrender document. As cameras clicked and bulbs flashed, Kennedy and his competitors jotted down the salient details: the expressions on the Germans' faces, the running order of the event, and Jodl's comments at the end. After it was over, Allen allowed the "illegal" newspaper journalists into the room, so that they could jot down their personal observations about its shape and size and insert this color material into their stories—although this concession scarcely quelled their anger. Helen Kirkpatrick, who had arrived at Reims with Daniell, even took out a tape measure "to prove that there had been space for more than seventeen correspondents."[29]

Meanwhile, the chosen seventeen repaired to the classroom to write their dispatches, still not knowing when they would be released. Once again, Allen appeared with an answer—which, once again, Kennedy did not like. "General Eisenhower," the PRO explained, "is desirous of having the news announced immediately for its possible effect in saving lives, but his hands are tied at a high political level and we can do nothing about it. The release time has been set for 3 p.m., Tuesday [May 8] Paris time."[30] "Well," Thor Smith observed, "by the time the entire event was over, the shouting had died down, and the recrimination sessions were over, it was almost dawn. We piled in a truck, drove to the airfield, and flew back to Paris absolutely punch drunk."[31]

Back at the Scribe, Kennedy could not relax. After a fitful nap, he went for a stroll.[32] Ambling along the Parisian boulevards, he had plenty to mull over. First, there were those recent cases when other news organizations had violated censorship and received no real sanction. More importantly, there was his conviction that this particular story was being stopped for political, not military, reasons. Political censorship had long been a Kennedy bugbear, any mention of which drove him almost to apoplexy, fearing it heralded the "end of all freedom in reporting,"[33] With Allen explaining that political motives accounted for the hold on the surrender news, Kennedy was almost ready to snap.

The final catalyst came when he returned to the Scribe after his walk and discovered that the Germans had already broadcast news of their capitulation. The AP chief bounded down two floors to speak to the censors. "Kennedy ranted to me to the effect that there was no security in the story," one of them noted shortly after, "and that it was being held for no good reason[,] that he was going to 'bust' it if he had to send everyone [*sic*] of his men to the Swiss and Spanish border." Kennedy's recollection was somewhat different. "I considered myself under no further obligation to observe the censorship," the AP man wrote later.[34]

Having made his decision, Kennedy found it surprisingly easy to get his unauthorized story past the censor. He simply asked one of his reporters,

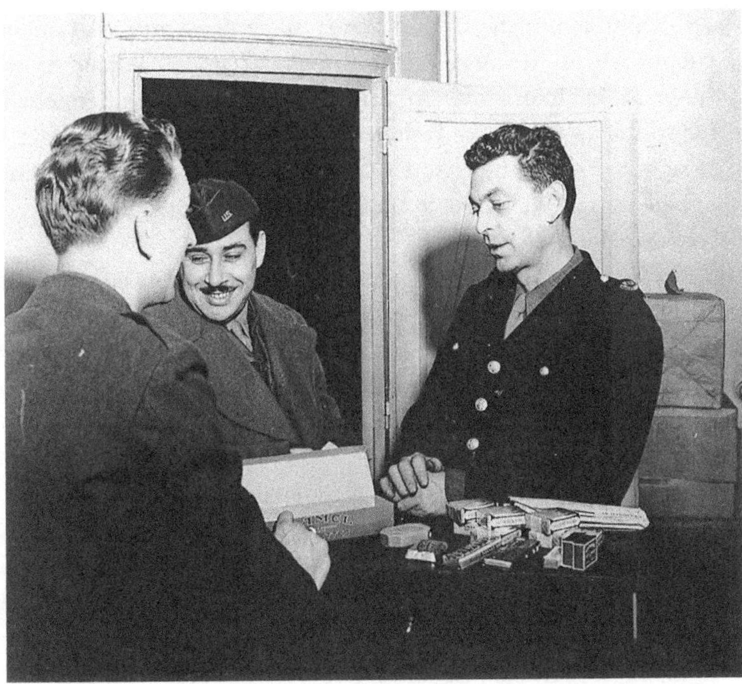

Figure 20.1 Ed Kennedy (*right*) inside the Scribe. National Archives 111-SC-204502.

Morton Gudebrod, to place a call to London. At 3:24 p.m. London time, the AP office near Fleet Street heard "a faint, muffled voice." "This is Paris calling," Gudebrod repeated a few times before handing the phone to Kennedy, who then read his story over the line, until his voice also faded. The AP staffers in London wasted no time. They cabled the story to New York, where the foreign desk held it up for a few minutes "to make certain there was no possibility of error." Confident, the AP released the news to the world. At 3:35 p.m. London time—9:35 a.m. in New York—on Monday, May 7, Kennedy revealed that Germany had surrendered unconditionally.[35]

Almost immediately, Kennedy's story sparked a bewildering array of reactions. Most Americans were jubilant that the European war was finally over, and they hurried to celebrate, remaining mindful that on the other side of the world the fight against Japan still had to be won.

In New York, as a half million revelers gathered in Times Square, the AP hierarchy was ecstatic. To be sure, Kennedy's scoop came at a cost: SHAEF immediately suspended the AP's access to communications throughout the European theater pending an investigation into how it had broken the story early. But across the United States many news organizations were fully supportive of Kennedy's action. Even George Marshall conceded that the press "is almost unanimously taking the line that Kennedy only reported to the people of the United States what was true and what they had the right to know." The next day, Marshall instructed SHAEF to end its blanket ban on the AP's access to communications, although Kennedy and Gudebrod remained suspended.[36]

The response inside the Scribe was quite different. Rather than "martyrize" Kennedy for his courageous opposition to political censorship, his rivals believed he had pulled the fastest of tricks to obtain the biggest of scoops. "For 24 hours," the local head of the INS protested to Eisenhower in a typical comment, "the AP was the only American news agency able to publish the official story of Germany's surrender under a Reims dateline. This meant that, regardless of the flagrant violation of a solemn pledge, the AP was rewarded with a smashing scoop over every other news agency and newspaper in the world while the others were unable to do anything but sit by and watch the AP capture [of] the headlines. The injustice and unfairness of this situation cannot be too strongly emphasized."[37]

Even highly experienced newspaper reporters agreed with this verdict. Drew Middleton had been an AP man when the war started, but he now took the lead against his former employer. "You realize, gentlemen," he told a hastily arranged meeting of his fellow war correspondents, "that you have taken the worst beating of your life. The question is, what are you going to do about it[?]"[38] The answer was a call for SHAEF's ban on the AP to be reinstated. The lifting of this ban, declared Middleton and fifty other reporters, "is a most outrageously unfair treatment of those news agencies and newspapers whose correspondents have respected the confidence placed in them by SHAEF; and who as a result of so doing have suffered the most disgraceful, deliberate, and unethical double cross in the history of journalism."[39]

Allen piled on the pressure the next day. Deeply angered at Kennedy's action, and desperate to shift the press corps' ire away from his own policies, Allen launched a stinging attack. First he accused Kennedy of a "deliberate violation against good faith and . . . security definitely involving the possible loss of American and Allied lives." Then he read a statement from Eisenhower. The supreme commander, Allen announced, "considered the affair the first time in nearly three years that his confidence in the press has been violated."[40]

As opinion turned furiously against their Paris bureau chief, the AP hierarchy in New York changed tack. On May 10, the president of the AP issued a public apology. By that time, the AP executives had also decided to replace Kennedy with Wes Gallagher, who undertook a frantic all-night drive from the Elbe to take up his new post.[41]

Upon arriving at the Scribe, Gallagher was taken aback to find that even the most "mild-mannered" AP staffers were recommending that their new boss "slug" any rival who mentioned Kennedy's name. Gallagher soon understood why. As he walked into the jammed pressroom, Gallagher heard one correspondent mutter, "We just got rid of one AP son of a bitch, and now we've got a bigger one."[42]

Gallagher resisted the urge to slug this critic. But he did not shrink from the bigger challenge he faced. His next move was to get back into his jeep and drive to Reims, where he demanded to see Eisenhower. The two men had been together in Gibraltar at the start of America's war against Germany. They were together in the Reims schoolhouse at its end, as Gallagher brazenly told Ike, "If I'd been Kennedy, I'd have done the same thing—except that I'd have telephoned you first." "I would have thrown you in jail," Eisenhower responded firmly, although, ever the diplomat, Ike immediately called in Bedell Smith and told his chief of staff "that the AP was to be treated like any other [news] organization."

Their business complete, the general invited the reporter to lunch, where they chatted amiably about old times. Gallagher, perhaps remembering the flap over his command-change article the previous summer, even told Ike that he had made the correct decision in handing the First and Ninth Armies to Montgomery at the height of the Bulge. "Eisenhower said he was pleased to hear that," Gallagher recorded. "It vindicated his decision to relieve his longtime friend, General Bradley."[43]

While Gallagher placated Ike, Kennedy continued to suffer. Stuck in his room, unable even to use the Scribe phone to call for room service, he awaited his fate. It came a few days into the new postwar era. Although Allen decided that the evidence against the AP man did not warrant a court martial, he did formally expel him from the theater. Kennedy returned to New York straight away, where the controversy surrounding his final dispatch continued to reverberate. Still seething at the AP's unwillingness to back him, Kennedy left the organization in September, thoroughly disillusioned with his treatment by both the military and media.[44]

DEPARTURES—AND REAPPEARANCES

Kennedy's departure was only the most dramatic sign of a more general redeployment process. Throughout the previous winter, editors had already begun devoting more column inches to the Pacific conflict; a few star reporters, including Ernie Pyle and Homer Bigart, had even headed in that direction. VE Day sparked a much bigger exodus. Thompson and Whitehead, who had spent so much time together the past year, both planned to cover the Pacific War. Neither arrived in time to see any more fighting, but Whitehead did report the atomic test on Bikini atoll in July 1946.[45]

Other reporters stayed in Europe, though their bosses often shifted them from place to place. Gallagher and Middleton were among these. Before the end of 1945 both left Paris for occupied Germany, where they soon confronted the transition from world war to cold war, as former allies became enemies and former enemies turned into friends. For these battlefield veterans, the process raised a set of jarring questions. Could they really learn to hate the Soviet Union, whose troops so many of them had celebrated with that memorable day in Torgau? Could they really forget everything the Germans had done under Hitler—deeds that both Gallagher and Middleton gained chilling new insights into when they covered the Nuremberg trials in 1946?[46]

At least one seasoned hand went through the motions of trying to remain neutral. Between 1946 and 1949, Bill Stoneman took a leave of absence from the *Chicago Daily News* to become an adviser to Trygve Lie, the first secretary general of the new United Nations organization. As Lie got caught in the middle of the growing tension between Washington and Moscow, Stoneman did his best to make the public case for resolving differences through negotiation.[47] But ultimately he never doubted which side he was on. It was not just his instinctive hatred of totalitarianism or even his first-hand experience of Stalinism during the 1930s. Stoneman could never quite forget how World War II had ended for him: not with the triumphant party at Torgau but with a much more sinister event. "I spent VE Day in Prague," he recalled many years later, "where I was captured by the Russians, who were supposed to be our allies. I got away by jumping off a tank on which they were taking me to headquarters for questioning."[48]

Stoneman's innate distrust of the Soviet Union was not unusual. John Thompson, who traveled behind the newly descended Iron Curtain, came away convinced that Stalin was violating diplomatic agreements in Rumania, unleashing a "reign of terror" in Poland, and threatening to use force against Turkey.[49] Middleton spent 1946 and 1947 in the USSR as the *Times*' Moscow correspondent, and he reached a similarly jaundiced view of America's new enemy. Initially, he found reporting extremely difficult, for Stalinist censorship was so strict that he once had an 800-word article reduced to a single eight-word sentence. In the end, he was unable to do any reporting at all, for Stalin's government refused to issue him a new visa after he had left the country for a brief period.[50]

If hating the Soviets proved easy, embracing the Germans was a different matter. Most of the former war correspondents gradually accepted the need to revive the western occupation zones in order to turn this section of Germany into a vital and viable ally against communism. Gallagher's intellectual journey was typical. He began, in 1946, by reporting the high cost of occupying an economically prostrate German zone, in a story that suggested resurrecting it would save the American taxpayer a significant sum. By the middle of 1947, he was pointing out that even the US officials who had previously advocated "a 'hard peace' for Germany have come to the conclusion that an industriously prosperous Germany is essential to Europe."[51] A couple of years later, he was writing a raft of articles that effectively pushed for the rearmament of Western Europe, including western Germany, in order to combat the Soviet menace. But, Gallagher stressed, the German people themselves were the main obstacles to such a policy, for the simple reason that they had changed so much. "Those particularly between the ages of 20 and 40 have had a stomach full of war," he wrote in 1951. "There is scarcely a family that has not lost at least two close relatives in the last war. Virtually all have lost their homes, their money, and their security."[52]

Drew Middleton was far less certain of the new German attitude. He had been too scarred by the war to believe that the Germans could ever change. During his first stint in the American occupation zone, Middleton fretted about the persistence of Nazi sentiment, and wrote approvingly of the US policy of "systematic[ally] wrecking" the German industries that had contributed to Hitler's war production.[53] When he returned in 1948, his attitude toward the Germans had hardly softened. "They were," he wrote, ". . . a people who, although viciously cruel and insanely ambitious in power, were boot-lickers when someone else held the power." That explained their willingness to put on a docile antiwar act under their occupiers, Middleton believed. He refused to buy any of it. As the *New York Times*' chief German correspondent, he wrote a series of dispatches on the prevalence of Nazi sentiment. The stories worried the US occupation authorities, not because they feared a German right-wing revival but because they thought his arguments might delay the creation a new West German state. Yet when these American officials protested, Middleton refused to budge, and his bosses supported him to the hilt.[54]

Although Middleton's continued distrust of the Germans was not shared by most of his colleagues, his actions during the early Cold War did fit a familiar pattern. Wherever they ended up, the World War II correspondents invariably brought with them three pieces of war-related baggage.

One had been evident since the very start of America's war against Nazi Germany: a sense that they were hardened veterans who knew as much, if not more, about the world than those in official positions of power. The second was a propensity to relive the war at every opportunity. Middleton demonstrated the first of these characteristics when he persisted with his stories on German neo-Nazism in the face of government pressure. The second underpinned his negative opinion of the Germans, and it highlighted a third trait he shared with other veterans: a tendency to dwell on one or two moments in the war that were either particularly ugly or particularly glorious, or perhaps both.

Middleton's mind often seemed to go back to the blitz. Years later, he still found it impossible to forget all of those long nights spent sheltering from Luftwaffe bombs that gouged deep holes into his beloved London.[55] Other reporters had their own particular reference points. Whitehead, for example, could never seem to escape Omaha beach. The AP man paid his first visit a year after D-Day, as he was about to leave France for the Pacific. He returned fifteen and then twenty years after the event, writing long articles for numerous newspapers that recounted the main highlights of the Normandy battles. Going back brought some peace, if only because the beach—like the rest of Europe—was starting the process of recovery. "Time and the endless tide," he recorded in June 1945, "mercifully have wiped out most of the signs of death and destruction along this invasion beach hallowed by the deaths of so many American youths."[56]

John Thompson had been with Whitehead on Omaha, and he, too, wrote anniversary recollection articles on the Normandy campaign.[57] But Thompson's main fixation was different again. His thoughts invariably returned to his biggest triumph: that night in July 1943 when he had jumped out of a plane to land in Sicily. Thompson still wore the beard he had grown to fit into the paratroop team, and he retained such a strong attachment to the men he had served with that week, that when the Eighty-Second Airborne was threatened with postwar budget cuts, he came to its defense. He had been proud to jump in 1943, Thompson told more than 1,800 paratroopers four years later. "And if there's another war, I'll tuck my long white beard in my boots and come tottering along with the 82d."[58]

As it happened, neither Thompson nor the Eighty-Second would jump in the next war, but others of this generation would be enticed by the prospect of covering the army again. Homer Bigart, Hal Boyle, and Don Whitehead all hurried to Korea in the summer of 1950, after President Harry Truman sent four American divisions to the peninsula to halt the communist attack. They soon found themselves reporting a messy, bloody retreat, but they refused to cower before military censors who demanded that they excise anything negative from their reports.

Bigart had faced it all before, of course, at Anzio where he had stood up to General Alexander's efforts to sugarcoat news of the battle. He found the initial situation in Korea even worse and was determined to say so. "Many times in World War II," he wrote in July 1950, "this correspondent observed American troops in conditions of adversity, but he never saw anything like the bitterness and bewilderment displayed at the front yesterday when the men received their orders to withdraw." The first Korean battles, Bigart concluded, were "a galling humiliation."[59] Whitehead and Boyle, though not quite so trenchant in their criticism, likewise compared Korea unfavorably to World War II—in Whitehead's case because he had witnessed a retreat in Korea, whereas in Sicily, Italy, and Western Europe, he wrote, "I saw only victorious drives by the Americans."[60]

When the military aggressively opposed these dispatches, the reporters' bosses stood firmly behind their seasoned veterans. The AP brass told Whitehead and Boyle "not to engage in in self-censorship where no authoritative restrictions are imposed." The profession as a whole was even more appreciative. In 1951 it awarded Bigart and Whitehead a Pulitzer Prize for their Korean War reporting, despite their overt criticism of the military command.[61]

By the time of the Vietnam War a decade later, even fewer reporters from the World War II generation could be lured into the combat zone for any length of time. Many of the big names had become, as one historian has put it, "perched at or near the pinnacle of their profession in Washington and New York," including Gallagher, who was now the AP general manager; Middleton, who went to London and then Paris as the *Times*' bureau chief; and Walter Cronkite and Eric Sevareid, who both became fixtures on the CBS evening news.[62]

Once again, Bigart stood out from the crowd. As well as stints covering conflicts in the Middle East and Africa, he not only reported the French war in Indochina during the 1950s, but also returned to Vietnam a decade later, bringing his own brand of anti-authoritarian iconoclasm to a conflict where such an attitude became the norm. Convinced that war could never be reported from the safety of a HQ briefing room, Bigart continued to take risks, though he had never believed in heroics for their own sake, viewing combat as a dirty, unglamorous business. This jaundiced attitude dated back to Bigart's own World War II reference point: the day in February 1943 when he had flown on a bombing mission with the Writing Sixty-Ninth. "After Wilhelmshaven," one writer observed, "he would never find war dapper or debonair." It would always remain a hellish affair, run by officers whose wisdom needed to be challenged.[63]

From his much loftier vantage point, Gallagher agreed. The AP chief had reason to be grateful to the commander of American forces in Vietnam; William Westmoreland had pulled him out of the jeep that had broken his back in Bizerte in May 1943.[64] But Gallagher had never meekly toed the military line, and he had no intention of starting to do so now, despite his personal debt to Westmoreland.

During the 1960s, Gallagher's main innovation was to push his AP writers toward a more analytical approach to the news, digging deeper into issues to produce the type of investigative pieces that had been his signature during the winter of 1944–45. He also showed a great determination to stand behind his reporters, especially when he became convinced that the US military in Vietnam was engaged in a concerted effort to mask the reality on the ground. His correspondents deeply appreciated his firm backing. "The consistently solid home office support that the Saigon bureau received," one of them wrote, "was one of the key elements that helped the AP establish and maintain its status as a superior news agency in Vietnam over the entire decade [of that war.]"[65]

Such actions were highly revealing. Much has been made of the difference between the 1940s and 1960s, contrasting the patriotic team players of the former era with the subversive rule-breakers of the latter. A large part of this change, historians believe, came from a generational shift: the youthful members of a countercultural cohort rebelling against the placid conformity of their elders. Yet, on close inspection, it is clear that influential old-timers like Bigart and Gallagher used the experience and expertise they had acquired during World War II to create an atmosphere that allowed—even encouraged—their juniors to challenge the American military during the Vietnam War. This challenge, to be sure, became much more intense and fundamental than anything that had occurred in World War II; but then, the Vietnam War raised far more troubling issues, while the military in the 1960s undertook a much more concerted effort to manipulate the media.

As the American intervention in Vietnam unraveled, it distorted memories of what had actually happened during the earlier "good war." Although military-media relations hit an all-time low in Vietnam, this did not mean that things had been smooth and easy a generation earlier. Veterans of the Allied bombing campaign, Anzio, or the Bulge, those who had covered Patton or suffered in the Scribe, could vouch for that. The trouble was that Vietnam became the new reference point, shaping and twisting the views of not only the reporters who lived and worked through that turbulent era but also the historians and analysts of the military-media relationship.

Conclusion

"We were all on the same side then," Walter Cronkite wrote of World War II in his memoirs, "and most of us abandoned any thought of impartiality as we reported on the heroism of our boys and the bestiality of the hated Nazis."[1] Cronkite's recollection was typical, and not entirely wrong. Even viewed outside the distorting prism of the Vietnam experience, there can be no denying that the World War II reporters periodically became enthusiastic members of the military team. During the North African landings or the bombing missions over Germany, the lines between journalistic observation and operational participation became especially blurred. The correspondents who jumped with the Eighty-Second Airborne or followed the Fighting First from Troina to the Siegfried Line often felt a particularly close kinship with those units. Ernie Pyle, who spent so much time with so many troops in so many foxholes, invariably looked as disheveled as the infantrymen he wrote about with so much affection. Others made sure that their uniforms were impeccably tailored, with sharply ironed creases. Rare indeed was the reporter who did not don his military garb with pride.

Yet the idea that the media and military were on the same side, the war reporters effectively acting as cheerleaders for the Allied cause, conceals more than it reveals. In any war, correspondents face a complex series of incentives that push them toward different places on a broad spectrum ranging from outright collaboration to subversive troublemaking.[2] Those who are motivated to cooperate recognize that the military wields powerful tools. To get accredited war correspondents must undergo background checks before signing on to official censorship regulations that prohibit them from writing about a long list of subjects. At the front, they not only depend on military transportation to get near the fighting but also on official briefings to place the battles in some sort of perspective. Once their stories are written and censored, they must rely on military communications systems to transmit them to the United States.

While these practical pressures push war reporters toward cooperation, the nature of their job is always in conflict with many basic military concepts. At the core of this clash is the simple maxim: "The essence of successful warfare is secrecy; the essence of successful journalism is publicity." Around the periphery sit a range of additional irritants: the contrast between a military creed based on obedience and a media code focused on questioning authority; the difference between generals laboriously planning an operation that will take place weeks or months in the future and correspondents needing to find something new to write about for each day's deadline.[3]

Compared to subsequent conflicts, the balance sheet during World War II seemed heavily weighted in favor of cooperation. This is the point made by Cronkite—and many others—and it is worth emphasizing. For much of the war, to be sure, few reporters completely bought into the notion of a "bestial" Nazi opponent. Indeed, most of them remained ignorant of the full extent of Hitler's crimes until they entered the heart of the Reich in 1945 and saw the camps at Ohrdruf and Buchenwald. Nevertheless, in stark contrast to the Korean and Vietnam conflicts, the World War II correspondents were in no doubt that they faced a total war in which the goal was clear: to eradicate an enemy that, if not irredeemably evil, at least had clear responsibility for unleashing the cataclysm in 1939 and then had bombed innocent civilians during the 1940 London blitz. The reporters also believed that their own military was waging conventional warfare against uniformed soldiers, not unarmed civilians. Of course, the reality of the Allied bombing campaign was quite different. But the small number of reporters who accompanied Allied bombing missions only saw the explosions from a distance that made it impossible to detect whether or not the bombs had fallen solely on military targets. The reporters who accompanied the army had even fewer doubts. Convinced of the necessity of undertaking a series of highly dangerous amphibious operations, they knew the fearsome Wehrmacht lay in wait. They therefore accepted the need for strict operational security on these missions. It seemed essential to avoid a wholesale slaughter on the beaches.

That these huge, hazardous battles were Allied affairs, waged in close tandem with the British military, further encouraged American reporters to identify with their own military. In North Africa, the US Army initially absorbed important lessons from the more battle-hardened British, including the value of well-appointed press camps and chaperoned visits to the front. Many reporters acknowledged the need for both innovations, especially after experiencing the delays and dangers of the first months of the Tunisian campaign. Increasingly, though, competition between the two allies was the crucial dynamic pushing correspondents toward a stronger relationship with their own side. At first, the American reporters were angered whenever British journalists appeared to grab scoops by breaking news embargoes. Partly in response, they tended to swell with pride when their own side did a better job of beating the Germans on the battlefield. Certainly, there were few US correspondents who did not enjoy Patton's dashes across Sicily and France, especially at a time when the arrogant Montgomery was finding it difficult to break through German defenses.

Still, even with all these incentives to cooperate, the most striking characteristic of the World War II correspondents was their lack of docility. These were not compliant cheerleaders who abandoned all thought of impartiality to trumpet the official line. Nor did they always give the home front an anodyne version of war that conveniently airbrushed out all the gruesome bits. Faced with the possibility of setback at Salerno, or a bloody reversal over Schweinfurt, the correspondents hastened to tell their audiences that the war was not going well. When the fighting bogged down in Italy, Homer Bigart vehemently attacked what he described as the military's efforts to conceal the reality of the situation. When the Allies were finding it difficult to pierce Germany's Siegfried Line, Wes Gallagher produced a number of investigative pieces in which he blamed the Washington planners for the debilitating shortages of men and resources at the front.

Bigart and Gallagher were "troublemakers" in the proudest tradition of American journalism: reporters determined to get at the truth, not to undermine the war effort but to highlight what was wrong in the hope that it would spark change. Others caused the military major headaches for a very modern reason: speed. In the cutthroat world of wire-service journalism, scooping a rival by minutes, even seconds, meant the difference between selling a story to hundreds of newspapers or having it spiked. Radio broadcasting worked on a slightly more leisurely schedule. The main networks relied heavily on the vocal skills and reputations of their increasingly famous correspondents to build and maintain their audience shares, but they, too, were keen to get the big stories out first. Small wonder that some of the most high-profile problems came from the AP's Ed Kennedy, the UP's James McClincy, and CBS's Charles Collingwood, who bent the rules in order to break major stories—and had to deal with the wrath of colleagues and censors alike.

By contrast, the newspaper columnists and weekly magazine correspondents had more time to digest censorship stops and more patience with temporary communications breakdowns. They also tended to be heirs to a literary journalistic tradition that aimed less at unearthing information or scoring beats and more at describing the conditions on the battlefield. These reporters sometimes seemed the most pliable, producing stories that downplayed the war's true horror. Hal Boyle, for instance, tried his best to sugarcoat both the Kasserine disaster in Tunisia and the bocage battles in Normandy. Ernie Pyle likewise packaged certain aspects of front-line life in a palatable narrative. Typical was his description of Omaha beach the day after D-Day, in which he not only excised the blood and gore of the savage battle but also offered his readers a soothing view of the soldiers "sleeping on the sand, some of them sleeping forever."

Despite this tendency to wrap certain elements of warfare in a comfortingly bland blanket, the big-name reporters rarely wrote totally lifeless stories about the dead. On the contrary, they movingly described the numerous GI casualties in so many previously unheard of places, including San Pietro, St. Lô, and Malmédy. Crucially, they did so with the broad agreement of a military hierarchy that went all the way up to the commander-in-chief inside the White House.

The official tolerance of this harder-edged writing stemmed partly from the fact that many of the reporters depicted death as having a clear purpose in this war. They adopted this line not merely because they identified so closely with their own military or feared the censors' blue pencils. They were also motivated by a much more fundamental factor: success. Initially, the reporters defined success simply as America's citizen soldiers learning how to fight a war—how to deal with the discomforts of front-line life, the homesickness and lack of little luxuries, and the challenge of confronting a highly effective enemy that had conquered much of Europe. After the Allied victories in North Africa and Sicily, abetted by Mussolini's dramatic ouster, the reporters' definition of success assumed that Germany's unconditional surrender could not be too far away. Animated by this belief, many reporters infused even the bleakest stories with a redemptive quality. The loss of hundreds of bomber boys in an ill-fated raid, the deaths of the much-loved Captain Waskow and Major Howie, the bloody chaos on Omaha beach or around Bastogne: all these sacrifices, the correspondents stressed, would not be in vain. They were bringing the inevitable day of triumph a step closer.

As the prospect of an Allied victory began to loom large, the military's attitude started to shift. Rather than merely accept that the reporters would write about death, the PROs began actively encouraging them to cover the war's gorier aspects. This was a highly significant move, and it raises an important point that has often been missed. Effective team play is never a one-way process. To keep the media on its side, the military invariably has to make concessions. One of Eisenhower's major strengths during World War II was his recognition of this important fact. From his very first London press conference, in July 1942, through to his attempts to encourage reporters to correct the overoptimistic stories during the first phase of the North African, Sicilian, and Normandy invasions, Ike also tried to facilitate the media's job by making straightforward, practical improvements in censorship and communications .

Eisenhower could rely on an impressive team of his own to carry out this task. Near the front he could turn to the experienced media men Butcher, Phillips, Redding, and Thor Smith, who had switched sides to join the military. In Washington he enjoyed the powerful support of his superiors, especially President Roosevelt, who thought news of the North African offensive would make the home front more committed to the fight against Nazism, and General Marshall, who wanted the exploits of his citizen army publicized. When the American public appeared to be feeling dangerously complacent in 1943, Roosevelt and Marshall both decided to allow more realistic depictions of combat, to instill a realization that victory, though inevitable, remained a long way off. A year later, when most Americans believed that the liberation of Paris foreshadowed a swift end to the European conflict, Major General Surles again encouraged a more downbeat line.

Once the "sphere of legitimate controversy" began encompassing more convincing and accurate depictions of battlefield conditions, reporters like Bigart and Pyle could capture the grittier, gorier side of the war without upsetting too many military officers. But it was Robert Capa who became the biggest beneficiary of the lenient new policy. The famous photographer arrived at the front just as the US government was launching its anticomplacency drive. Suddenly, the censors were willing to release pictures that his editors lauded as "grim and unsentimental," images that showed "it's a tough war."[4]

As the tough fight dragged on, the press corps became seasoned in the ways of war reporting. This has often been depicted as a crucial dynamic in the forging of an effective partnership between the press and the military. The assumption is that the more time reporters spent as part of the military machine, the more they became socialized within its enclosed world, with the result that they adopted an unquestioning attitude. The reality was far more complex.

Experience, to be sure, sometimes did lead inexorably to affection: witness Pyle's fondness for the slogging foot soldiers he memorably dubbed "the-mud-rain-frost-and-wind boys," or Thompson's identification with the paratroopers of the Eighty-Second Airborne. More strikingly, after some of the fiercest battles, even the hard-nosed veterans of journalism could lose a sense of perspective as the euphoria of survival kicked in, and the resulting stories played into the military's hands. Indeed, without prompting from PROs or cuts by the censors, these exhilarated, exhausted survivors—Bigart and Cronkite after Wilhelmshaven or Stoneman and Whitehead on D-Day—painted the big battles with bold, rose-tinted strokes.

Far more often, however, battlefield experience had a negative impact on the media-military relationship. Alongside a growing tetchiness as the American war entered its third year, a number of correspondents increasingly believed they knew best, which made them much less likely to accept the judgment of their military partners. Others suffered from exhaustion, which became an even bigger blight.[5] Reporting the war for any length of time was grueling: day after day of heart-stopping, visceral fear, along with the mud and blood, the harsh noises and vile smells, the hot dust or intense cold. Ernie Pyle, in particular, suffered for his craft. During the long Italian winter of 1943–44, he found it difficult to keep his profound war weariness out of his dispatches, which became increasingly downbeat at a particularly depressing moment of the war. A year later, his exhaustion had an even bigger impact on his output.

After the liberation of Paris, Pyle decided that the time had come to take a stateside break before heading off to the Pacific War. He therefore missed the last six months of the fight against Nazi Germany—as did the millions of Americans who had come to depend on his insights to get a feel for the war in Europe. Although Pyle's absence left the biggest hole, he was not the only reporter to seek refuge from the battlefield. Middleton, Stoneman, Thompson, and Whitehead all left the theater for extended periods. Capa was one of the old hands who stayed on in Paris, but even this photographer—a man who prided himself on getting as close as possible to the action—could barely bring himself to visit the front in the fall of 1944. Like Pyle, he was approaching the limits of his emotional reserves.

Ultimately, neither Capa nor Pyle could stay away from the battlefield for too long. Capa headed to Aachen and then to Bastogne in late 1944, before following American troops into the heart of Germany. He arrived in Leipzig on April 18. As he entered a room in a plush apartment building, he began taking photos of a GI manning a machine gun on the balcony. While he was clicking away, the young soldier suddenly slumped to the floor, felled by a fatal bullet wound to the neck. The shots produced another gruesomely graphic spread in *Life*; but Capa was unable to savor this particular success. That evening he learned that Ernie Pyle had also become a victim of an enemy bullet, on the small island of Ie Shima, off Okinawa.[6]

Pyle, the man who had done more to describe the war to the home front than any other, would not live to see its end. Capa took the news badly. The photographer had always considered the columnist almost immune from death. Ernie, by contrast, had long believed he would be killed in action. Just before he left for the Okinawa invasion, he had told a colleague that "I'm not coming back from this one." He had therefore been pleasantly surprised when the initial assault proved to be an anticlimax. "I've had no narrow escapes," he wrote his editor on April 15, "and feel in much higher spirits than when I left."

Two days later, Pyle decided to visit Ie Shima to take a look at a new tank destroyer. The scene was surprisingly tranquil, until a Japanese machine gun began to fire. Pyle jumped into a ditch for cover. After a short while, he looked up. This time, the machine gunner hit him in the head, killing him instantly.[7]

Ernie's colleagues were stunned. "I am tired and grieved and don't feel like writing anything," began a tribute by one of his closest associates. "They asked me to send in an article about my friend, Ernie Pyle, but Ernie wrote his own story. He wrote it in his blood—there with the foot soldiers whose dangers it was his self-imposed lot to share."[8]

That Ernie's blood had been spilled on a remote and desolate island on the other side of the world was a tragic reminder of the cost of this conflict. It underlines, in the saddest way possible, a crucial fact about all war reporters: whether they join the military team or cause trouble, become household names or see their material published without a byline, they all put their lives on the line every time they visit the front.

Ernie Pyle became one of fifty-four American reporters who made the ultimate sacrifice during World War II. Looking back almost ten years later, a colleague paid these journalists a fitting tribute: "They represented a free press and a free people, and when the chips were down, they were not afraid to die for both."[9]

NOTES

ABBREVIATIONS

AFHRA	Air Force Historical Research Agency
AP	Associated Press
APCA	Associated Press Corporate Archives, New York
BD	Harry Butcher Diary, Principal File: Subject Series, Eisenhower Pre-Presidential Papers, Eisenhower Library
BPR	Bureau of Public Relations
BS: WWII	Walter Bedell Smith: Collection of World War II Documents, Eisenhower Library
CTCA	Chicago Tribune Company Archives
DF	Decimal File
E&P	*Editor & Publisher*
EPPP	Dwight D. Eisenhower Pre-Presidential Papers, Eisenhower Library
NA-UK	National Archives, UK
NYT: AHS	New York Times Company Records: Arthur Hays Sulzberger Papers, New York Public Library
OWI	Office of War Information
RG	Record Group, National Archives II
RP	Franklin D. Roosevelt Papers, Roosevelt Library
SGS	Secretary of the General Staff

INTRODUCTION

1. Gay, *Assignment*, xiii.
2. Prochnau, *Distant War*, 219.
3. Voss, *Reporting*, 185. See also Sterne, *Combat Correspondents*, xi.
4. For the development of this image of the war, see Bodnar, "Good War," 4–5. On the idea that reporters of this era abandoned objectivity to support the war effort, see, for instance, Halberstam, *Powers That Be*, 39–40.
5. Sherry, *Rise*, 132–33; Gay, *Assignment*, 218. See also Adams, *Best War*, 48–51, 66.
6. Tobin, *Pyle's War*, 242–43. See also Collier, *Warcos*, 83; Fussell, *Wartime*, 155–56; Sweeney, *Military and Press*, 99–105; Huebner, *Warrior Image*, 37–43.
7. Knightley, *First Casualty*, 274–76, 330. See also Pratt, "How the Censors Rigged the News," 100, 101–2; Matthews, *Reporting*, 175–78.
8. See, for instance, Braestrup, *Battle Lines*, esp. 27–45, which looks at the media-military relationship in the wake of Vietnam and the almost total news blackout during the invasion of Grenada in 1983—though Braestrup does concede that

there were "plenty of complaints about military secrecy during the war in the European theater."

9. Paul and Kim, *Reporters*; Seib, *Beyond the Front Lines*, 51–64; Casey, *When Soldiers Fall*, 215.
10. Recent books that follow one or more correspondents include Tobin, *Pyle's War*; Brady, *Death in San Pietro*; Brinkley, *Cronkite*; and Gay, *Assignment*. Those that focus on one dimension, include Roeder, *Censored War*, and Maslowski, *Armed with Cameras*, which explore visual images; or Sorel, *Women Who Wrote the War*, and Colman, *Where the Action Was*, which examine the role of female correspondents. For a fuller literature review, see Casey, "War Correspondents."
11. As the esteemed foreign correspondent Helen Kirkpatrick pointed out in a review of Knightley's highly influential book *First Casualty*, this standard work on war correspondents contains no reference to "great reporting like that of Homer Bigart, Don Whitehead, . . . and Bill Stoneman." Kirkpatrick, "Rating the War Correspondents," *Boston Globe*, November 16, 1975. Brief biographical sketches of some of the reporters covered in the pages below—including Bigart, Capa, Cronkite, Gallagher, Middleton, Murrow, and Pyle—can be found in Cook, *American World War II Correspondents*.
12. On the importance of "the personal orientations and beliefs of [foreign] correspondents," see Pollock, *Politics of Crisis Reporting*, xiv, 5–6, 16–17.
13. Gibbs, introduction to *Days of Glory*, vii
14. On Davis, see Hamilton, *Journalism's Roving Eye*, 226. See also Seelye, *War Games*; Stephens, "Shattered Windows."
15. For the changing image of correspondents during and after World War I, see Mander, *Pen and Sword*, 105, 113.
16. Preston, *We Saw Spain Die*; Sperber, *Murrow*.
17. "Lifts Picture Ban on War's Realism," *New York Times*, September 5, 1943.
18. Hallin, *"Uncensored War,"* 116–17.
19. Gallagher, *Back Door to Berlin*, 37.
20. US War Department, *Regulations*.
21. Barnouw, *Golden Web*, 17–19, 58, 74, 80, 128–38; Hosley, *As Good as Any*, 12–13, 29, 43, 59.
22. Gunther, *D-Day*, 20, 34.

CHAPTER 1

1. Hamilton, *Journalism's Roving Eye*, 70, 437–38.
2. Matthews, *Reporting*, 241–48; Pedelty, *War Stories*, 6–8, 29, 72–76; Dell'Orto, *AP Foreign Correspondents*, 147–48.
3. Casey, "Reporting," 117–23.
4. Pace, "Middleton of the *Times* Dies at 76," *New York Times*, January 12, 1990; Biographical Data, Middleton Folder, box 15, NYT: AHS: General File. On Middleton's coverage of the fall of France, see Middleton, *Our Share*, 75–89; Beattie, *Passport to War*, 236–54.
5. Middleton, *Our Share*, 114–19; Middleton, "How London Crowds Acted," *Baltimore Sun*, September 8, 1940.
6. Pace, "Middleton of the *Times* Dies at 76," *New York Times*, January 12, 1990; Stowe, *No Other Road*, 1–3.
7. Sheean, *Thunder and the Sun*, 182; "London Raid Havoc Awes Witness" and "Abbey Is Refuge during 'All Clear,'" *New York Times*, September 9 and 14, 1940.

8. "Battle of London—AP 'Bombed Out,'" *AP Inter-Office*, January 29, 1941, WWII Book Project Folder, AP28, Writings about the AP, Series II, box 14, APCA; Middleton, *Our Share*, 123–33; Middleton, "Describes Bombing of AP Bureau," *Baltimore Sun*, September 26, 1940.
9. Middleton to Sulzberger, February 19, 1948, Middleton Folder, box 51, NYT: AHS.
10. Sevareid, *Not So Wild*, 106–7.
11. Note to Managing Editors, November 18, 1941, AP War Correspondents and Bureaus Folder, AP02A.3, Subject Files, Series III, box 51; "Wagnon, Middleton, Okin to Get Home Leave," *AP Inter-Office*, March 6, 1941, General Information Folder, WWII Book Project Folder, AP28, Writings about the AP, Series II, box 14; both in APCA. On the movement between AP and the *Times*, see Talese, *Kingdom*, 65.
12. Daniell to Sulzberger, September 25, 1939, September 20 and 23, 1940, all in London Bureau Folder, box 198, NYT: AHS; Daniell, "Nazi Bomb Strikes the London Savoy," *New York Times*, November 29, 1940; Stacks, *Scotty*, 61–62.
13. Daniell to Sulzberger, September 20 and 23, 1940, in London Bureau Folder, box 198, NYT: AHS; Daniell, *Civilians*, 18, 308–10.
14. Daniell to Sulzberger, June 19 and 29, 1941, Daniell Folder, box 15, NYT: AHS. For the difficulty of readjusting, see Sheean, *Thunder and the Sun*, 113; Shirer, *Nightmare Years*, 228–29.
15. Daniell, *Civilians*, 13–14.
16. Daniell to James, December 3, 1942, London Bureau Folder, box 198, NYT: AHS.
17. Membership Department to Managing Editors, "Congratulations on Coverage of Greer," September 10, 1941, Beats, 1941 Folder, Series 3: Subject Files, AP 02A.3, box 39, APCA; AP, "British Airmen Helped Repel Attack, Greer's Officers Say," *New York Times*, September 6, 1941.
18. Daniell to Sulzberger, January 20, 1942, London Bureau Folder, box 198, NYT: AHS.
19. Middleton, *Last July*, 85.
20. Belair to McConaughy, "Notes on New York Times Foreign Service," March 26, 1943, Folder 59, Time Dispatches. Belair considered Herbert L. Matthews the *Times*' other preeminent correspondent, but Matthews increasingly prioritized political matters, not the war. See World War II Dispatches, IV Series: NYT, boxes 27 and 28, Matthews Papers.
21. Ambrose, *Supreme Commander*, 47, 56–57, 78–79.
22. Gabel, "Maneuvers of 1941," 75–87, 133–49, 221–54, 282.
23. Pogue, *Supreme Command*, 33
24. Bunelle to Hinton, July 13, 1942, 8th AF PRO Misc. Folder, IRIS No. 225543, reel 7212, AFHRA; BD, July 14 and 15, 1942, I:42–43, box 165.
25. Eisenhower to Herron, June 11, 1943, Herron Folder, box 45, EPPP; BD, January 28, 1943, V: A194, box 166.
26. Butcher, *My Three Years*, 3; BD, July 14 and 15, 1942, I:42–43, box 165. Eisenhower's command followed up by calling on subordinate commands to issue "timely and plentiful" information to the press. Hinton, Memo for Public Relations Officer, 8th Air Force, July 18, 1942, 8th AF PRO Misc. Folder, IRIS No. 225543, reel 7212, AFHRA.
27. Hassett, *Off the Record*, 94.
28. OWI, Intelligence Report, No. 20, July 1, 1942, PSF-OWI, Survey of Intelligence, and, Cantril to Roosevelt, September 14, 1942, OF 857, both in RP; OWI, "How

the War Appears to Be Going: Trends—July to September 1942," September 29, 1942, entry 162, box 1784, and, OWI, "Supplement to Trends in American Opinion since Pearl Harbor: The Fighting Front," August 31, 1942, entry 164, box 1798, both in RG 44.

29. Casey, *Cautious Crusade*, 35, 90–91.
30. *Foreign Relations of the United States: Conference at Washington*, 72.
31. Bland, *Papers of George Catlett Marshall*, 3:27; Matloff and Snell, *Strategic Planning*, 104, 188; Pogue, *Ordeal and Hope*, 304; Stimson Diary, June 17, 1942, 39: 96, Stimson Papers.
32. Larrabee, *Commander in Chief*, 96–100; Bland, *Interviews and Reminiscences*, 108–9.
33. Minutes, Combined Staff Conference, July 22, 1942, and, Roosevelt to Hopkins, Marshall, and King, July 22, 1942, both in Sherwood Collection, box 308, Hopkins Papers. Bland, *Papers of George Catlett Marshall*, 3:276; Sherwood, *Roosevelt and Hopkins*, 602–12; Stoler, "Pacific Front Alternative," 443–45.
34. Pogue, *Ordeal and Hope*, 330, 341. See also Matloff and Snell, *Strategic Planning*, 272; Steele, *First Offensive*, 81–92.
35. BD, July 14 and 16, 1942, I:42, 45, box 165.
36. BD, July 15, August 4 and 27, 1942, I:43, 102, 166, and, September 20, 1942, II:251, all in box 165.
37. Biographical File, Phillips Records; "Phillips, Former Reporter, Newsweek Editor," *New York Times*, February 24, 1977; BD, August 9 and 15, 1942, I:108, 128, box 165.
38. Daniell to Sulzberger, December 23, 1942, London Bureau Folder, box 198, NYT: AHS.
39. BD, September 18, 1942, II:241–42, box 165.
40. BD, September 30, 1942, II:273, box 165. For Phillips views on what constituted "basic coverage," see Phillips to Clark, October 23, 1943, Special Staff Records: PI Section, Fifth Army Folder, box 2261, RG492. Phillips planned to have ten correspondents on the ground by the fourth day of the operation: four around Algeria and six in Oran. See Clark Diary, October 2, 1942, 11:9, box 64, Clark Papers.
41. Eisenhower to Marshall, September 1, 1942, Marshall Folder, box 80, EPPP.
42. "Press: Secret Assignment," *Time*, November 23, 1942; Parris, "Groundwork," 24–26. On the genesis of this deliberate plan of misinformation, see Clark Diary, October 2, 1942, II:9, box 64, Clark Papers.
43. BD, October 10 and 31, 1942, II:307, 357, box 165; AP, "Eisenhower Recalled for Parleys, Says Report Reviving Invasion Talk," *New York Times*, October 30, 1942.
44. For background on the *Daily News*, see Hamilton, *Journalism's Roving Eye*, 156–91. On the paper's early attitudes toward the war, see Schneider, *Should America*, 11.
45. Beckles, "Our Reporters under Blitzkrieg," *Living Age*, January 1941; Helse, "Foreign Correspondent William Stoneman, 83," *Chicago Tribune*, April 15, 1987; Middleton, *Last July*, 30.
46. Stoneman, "Remarks to Seminar on Foreign Correspondence," September 18, 1969, box 1, Stoneman Papers.
47. Stoneman, Diary Notes, September 4, 5, 7, 8, and 13, 1939, box 1, Stoneman Papers; Stoneman, "Nazi Bombers Turn World's Largest City into 'Hellhole,'" *Los Angeles Times*, September 21, 1940.
48. Parris, "Groundwork," 23–34.
49. Daniell to James, October 10, 1942, London Bureau Folder, box 198, NYT: AHS; Schneider, "35 US Newsmen at Newsfronts in Africa with American Army," *E&P*, November 14, 1942.

50. These paragraphs are based on Parris, "Groundwork," 34–35; Gallagher, *Back Door*, 17–24; MacVane, *On the Air*, 113–15; Bennett, *Assignment*, 30.

CHAPTER 2

1. Eisenhower to Marshall, November 7, 1942, Marshall Folder, box 80, EPPP; BD Diary, November 11, 1942, III:G-58, box 165; Gallagher, "No 'Wild Dream'—Eisenhower Had Command of Gibraltar," *Baltimore Sun*, December 22, 1942; Gallagher, *Back Door*, 35; Atkinson, *Army at Dawn*, 59.
2. Gallagher, *Back Door*, 37; BD, November 7, 1942, III:G-11, box 165.
3. Clark Diary, November 7, 1942, II: 78, box 64, Clark Papers; Atkinson, *Army at Dawn*, 62–63; Gallagher, *Back Door*, 37.
4. These paragraphs are based on information in Gallagher Vertical File, APCA. See also "3 AP Writers Off for War Duty in Europe," *E&P*, March 9, 1940; Gallagher, "The US Today," *Baltimore Sun*, February 22, 1942; Pace, "Wes Gallagher," October 13, 1997, *New York Times*.
5. Oldfield, *Never a Shot*, 54, 156; Butcher, *Three Years*, 692.
6. Gallagher, *Back Door*, 37–40.
7. Parris and Russell, prologue to *Springboard*, 8.
8. Schneider, "35 US Newsmen at Newsfronts in Africa with American Army," *E&P*, November 14, 1942; "AEF INVADES AFRICA," *Chicago Tribune*, November 8, 1942.
9. "Disher Marries," *New York Times*, August 4, 1942.
10. Disher, "HMS *Walney*," 101–25; Schneider, "35 US Newsmen at Newsfronts," *E&P*, November 14, 1942. On the *Walney* mission, see "Operation Reservist: Recommendations for Honours and Awards," December 18, 1942, ADM 1/11915, NA-UK; Atkinson, *Army at Dawn*, 69–76.
11. "Operation Reservist: Recommendations for Honours and Awards," December 18, 1942, ADM 1/11915, NA-UK.
12. "UP War Correspondent Given Purple Heart," *Boston Globe*, November 23, 1942. On Disher's wounds, see Morris, *Deadline*, 260.
13. Russell, "Algiers," in Parris and Russell, *Springboard*, 129–52; Middleton, *Our Share*, 187.
14. Russell, "Algiers," in Parris and Russell, *Springboard*, 152-53; HMS *Bulolo* to Phillips, November 10, 1942, and, Le Vien to Phillips, November 13, 1942, both in BD, III:G-42 and G-80-81, box 165; Stoneman and Russell, "How Cornbelt Seized Algiers," *Chicago Daily News*, November 10, 1942; Schneider, "35 US Newsmen at Newsfronts," *E&P*, November 14, 1942.
15. The press contingent of the Western Task Force consisted of "three newsmen and two radiomen." Clark Diary, October 2, 1942, II:9, box 64, Clark Papers.
16. Gay, *Assignment*, 38–40; Boyle to Evans, November 4, 1942, and, AP, "Front Line Press," September 1943, both in box 1, Boyle Papers.
17. Boyle to Evans, November 4, 1942, box 1, Boyle Papers; "13 Innoculations [*sic*] for Not-So-Lucky War Reporter," *E&P*, November 21, 1942.
18. Dave to Stonehouse, November 25, 1942, BPR File, 000.77, Entry 499, box 7, RG165; Atkinson, *Army at Dawn*, 103–4.
19. Atkinson, *Army at Dawn*, 109–11.
20. Boyle to Evans, November 26, 1942, box 1, Boyle Papers; Gallagher, *Back Door*, 43.
21. Boyle to Evans, November 26, 1942, box 1, Boyle Papers; Boyle, "How US Army Smashed French Ashore," *Boston Globe*, November 16, 1942.
22. Blumenson, *Patton Papers*, 2:119.

23. Boyle to Evans, November 4, 1942, box 1, Boyle Papers; Dave to Stonehouse, November 25, 1942, BPR File, 000.77, Entry 499, box 7, RG165
24. Gallagher, "New Headquarters Set Up by Gen. Eisenhower," and, Gallagher, "Record 'Blitz' Seen for Yank African Army," *Chicago Tribune*, November 9 and 10, 1942.
25. BD, November 25, 1942, III:A-4, box 165.
26. Eisenhower to Bedell Smith, November 16, 1942, Smith Folder, box 109, EPPP; Gallagher, *Back Door*, 80–81; Bennett, *Assignment*, 277–78.
27. Patton Diary, October 30 and November 9, 1942, box 2, Patton Papers; Atkinson, *Army at Dawn*, 35–36, 136–37; D'Este, *Patton*, 433–34; Hirshson, *General Patton*, 270–71; Gallagher, *Back Door*, 41–42.
28. Atkinson, *Army at Dawn*, 267–68.
29. On this mission, see Clark Diary, October 17–25, 1942, II:39–56, box 64, Clark Papers.
30. Eisenhower to Marshall, Ref. 272, November 10, 1942, CCS Folder, Principal File: Subject Series, box 130, EPPP; Eisenhower to Marshall, Ref.1033, November 21, 1942, Chief of Staff: D-Day Torch File, box 16, BS: WWII; Gallagher, "US Officers 'Set' Invasion on Spy Tour Landed by Sub," *Christian Science Monitor*, November 12, 1942.
31. BD, January 28, 1943, V:A-195, box 166. Eisenhower passed on Marshall's views to Clark. See Eisenhower to Clark, November 21, 1942, Clark Folder, box 23, EPPP.
32. On the background to the Darlan deal, see Funk, "Negotiating the 'Deal with Darlan," 94–97; Murphy, *Diplomat among Warriors*, 164–71. On the domestic reaction, see Casey, *Cautious Crusade*, 112–16.
33. BD, November 25, 1942, III:A-6, box 165; Atkinson, *Army at Dawn*, 194.
34. BD, November 25, 1942, III:A-4, box 165; Eisenhower to Marshall, Ref.1152, November 22, 1942, Cable Log Folder, box 2, BS: WWII; "US Deal with Darlan to Save 90 Days in Africa Campaign," *Chicago Daily News*, November 19, 1942.
35. Algiers, Ref.817, November 30, 1942, Cable Log Folder, box 2, BS: WWII; Eisenhower to Marshall, December 11, 1942, War Info Office Folder, box 89, Marshall Papers; Eisenhower to Surles, December 11, 1942, Surles Folder, box 113, EPPP; Gallagher, *Back Door*, 79.
36. Eisenhower to Marshall, Ref.1033, November 21, 1942, Chief of Staff: D-Day Torch File, box 16, BS: WWII; BD, December 9 1942, III:A-59, box 165, and, December 12, 1942, IV:A-68-69, box 166.
37. Eisenhower to Marshall, Ref.1033, November 21, 1942, Chief of Staff: D-Day Torch File, box 16, BS: WWII; McClure to Murphy, February 1, 1943, Civil Affairs: PR, WO 204/5425, NA-UK; Gallagher, *Back Door*, 81.

CHAPTER 3

1. Middleton, *Our Share*, 186
2. Middleton, *Our Share*, 182–86, 192–93.
3. Eisenhower to Marshall, November 7, 1942, Marshall Folder, box 80, EPPP.
4. Jordan, *Tunis Diary*, 53; D'Arcy-Dawson, *Tunisian Battle*, 19; Howe, *Northwest Africa*, 20.
5. Middleton, *Our Share*, 198; Russell, "Long Chance," 210–11.
6. BD, November 25, 1942, III:A-4, box 165; Eisenhower to Marshall, Ref.1152, November 22, 1942, Cable Log Folder, box 2, BS: WWII; "US Deal with Darlan to Save 90 Days in Africa Campaign," *Chicago Daily News*, November 19, 1942.

7. AP, "Yank Artillery Destroys Third of Axis Column," and, "Allies Hurling Armor against Bizerte, Tunis," *Chicago Daily News*, November 20, 1942; AP, "Hammer Tunis, Bizerte, Gabes," *Chicago Daily News*, November 21, 1942.
8. These paragraphs are based on Russell, "Long Chance," 206–40. See also Russell, "Germans Rule Air," *Washington Post*, December 5, 1942.
9. Stoneman, "Allies vs. a Tornado of Fire," *Chicago Daily News*, December 5, 1942.
10. D'Arcy-Dawson, *Tunisian Battle*, 27–28; Jordan, *Tunis Diary*, 66, 70, 87.
11. Stoneman, "Entry in a Tunisian Diary," *Chicago Daily News*, December 3, 1942; Jordan, *Tunis Diary*, 61.
12. Foreign News Salaries, August 1, 1941, and, Foreign News Service: Expenses and Revenue, 1919–43, both in Memoranda Folder, Series 3, box 30, Binder Papers.
13. Minutes of Meeting of New York AP Members, November 16, 1942, City File: NY: AP, box 183, Howard Papers.
14. Gramling, *AP*, 489; Cooper, *Associated Press*, 271.
15. Cooper, *Barriers Down*; Cooper, "'GI Joe' Reporting," undated, Series II-WWII Book Projects, General Information, AP28, box 14, APCA.
16. Crawford, *Report*, 138–39; Whitehead, "Saga of Boyle—'Son of Toil,'" *AP World*, Summer 1947, Series II-WWII Book Projects, General Information, AP28, box 14, APCA.
17. Gallagher, *Back Door*, 99, 235; Hamill, *Liebling*, 325–26; Boyle, "Leaves from a Correspondent's Notebook," *Washington Post*, December 27, 1942 and February 3, 1943.
18. Gould to Hackler, March 30, 1943, box 1, Kennedy Papers.
19. "Howard, Publisher, Dead," *New York Times*, November 21, 1964; Trimble, *Handbook*, 77–84. On the UP's early days, see Ault, *News*, 53, 78–79; Morris, *Deadline*, 23–25; Zacher, *Scripps Newspapers*, 19–21.
20. "Howard, Publisher, Dead," *New York Times*, November 21, 1964.
21. Howard to all editors, September 2, 1942, City File: NY: Hawkins, box 185, Howard Papers.
22. "Howard, Publisher, Dead," *New York Times*, November 21, 1964.
23. Baillie to Bickel, December 9 and 28, 1942, City File: NY: UP, Baillie, box 186, and, Howard to Parker, December 19, 1942, City File: Washington DC: Parker, box 188, both in Howard Papers.
24. Except where otherwise indicated, the following paragraphs are based on Tobin, *Pyle's War*, esp., 17, 28, 32–33, 41, 44–45, 51, 54–55, 63.
25. Miller to Carlin, January 12, 1942, Pyle Correspondence, box 9, Stone Papers.
26. See also Sorrells to Stone, March 5, 1941, City File: NY: Sorrells, box 178, Howard Papers. On Pyle's low at this point, see also Nichols, *Ernie's War*, 12.
27. Jack Howard to Parker, October 29, 1942, City File: NY: Jack Howard, box 186, Howard Papers; Tobin, *Pyle's War*, 67.
28. Pyle to Papa and Auntie, August 27, 1942, Pyle Mss., II, Lilly Library.
29. Nichols, *Ernie's War*, 7.
30. Pyle, "No Walkaway in Africa," *Washington Daily News*, January 4, 1943.
31. Jack Howard to Scripps-Howard editors, December 30, 1942, City File: NY: Jack Howard, box 186, Howard Papers.
32. Tobin, *Pyle's War*, 70–71. On the mystery of how the story got through, see also Hohenberg, *Foreign Correspondence*, 355
33. Eisenhower to Marshall, December 14, 1942, Cables OFF (GCM/DDE), box 131, EPPP.

34. Back in Washington, the War Department was not so enthusiastic. A senior officer, pointing out that Pyle's story had "caused widespread and possibly damaging repercussions," believed Eisenhower's "relaxation of censorship" needed to be reassessed. See War Department to Algiers, No. 845, January 7, 1943, BPR File, 000.73, Entry 499, box 17, RG165.
35. Parton, *"Air Force Spoken Here"*, 207.
36. Pyle, "A Faithful Flying Fort Carrying 10 'Dead" Men Drags Itself Home," *Washington Daily News*, January 19, 1943; Tobin, *Pyle's War*, 72–74.
37. Tobin, *Pyle's War*, 77–79.
38. Pyle to Papa and Auntie, January 25, 1943, Pyle MSS.
39. Pyle, "US Soldiers Are Thrust into New Way of Life," and, "Men in Advanced Air Base Dig Holes for Bedrooms," *Washington Daily News*, December 2, 1942 and January 20, 1943
40. Miller to Carlin, February 10, 1943, Pyle Correspondence, box 9, Stone Papers.
41. Tobin, *Pyle's War*, 86–87, 116; Gay, *Assignment*, 109.
42. Pyle, *Here Is Your War*, 220–21,

CHAPTER 4

1. Atkinson, *Army at Dawn*, 346.
2. Atkinson, *Army at Dawn*, 389–90; Middleton, "Americans Retire," *New York Times*, February 19, 1943.
3. Pyle, *Here Is Your War*, 170–82; Ault, "Southern Tunisia," 285; Atkinson, *Army at Dawn*, 350.
4. Gallagher, *Back Door*, 181–82; Stoneman, "Nazi Gunners Wound Writer in His Retreat," *Chicago Daily News*, January 25, 1943; Butcher to Allen, February 18, 1943, Correspondence File, box 2, Butcher Papers.
5. Tobin, *Pyle's War*, 81; Rame, *Road to Tunis*, 253.
6. Pyle, "Four Exclusives Give a Varied Picture of Our Times," *Boston Globe*, February 25, 1943; Pyle, *Here Is Your War*, 175.
7. Tobin, *Pyle's War*, 82.
8. Pyle, "Four Exclusives Give a Varied Picture of Our Times," *Boston Globe*, February 25, 1943 (emphasis added); Pyle, "Our Orderly Retreat Took Curse Off Fact That We Did Scram," *Washington Daily News*, March 5, 1943 (emphasis added).
9. Boyle to Gallagher, February 13, 1943, Correspondence Folder, box 1, Boyle Papers.
10. Boyle, "Retreating Yanks 'Fighting Mad,'" *Boston Globe*, February 19, 1943; Boyle, "Lone US Tank Battles 10 of Foe In a Little Alamo," *New York Herald Tribune*, February 21, 1943.
11. Gunther, *D-Day*, 21.
12. Sommers, "Inside Story of Getting Out News from North Africa Is Army Epic," *E&P*, August 14, 1943; MacVane, *On the Air*, 139; Rame, *Road to Tunis*, 271.
13. Rame, *Road to Tunis*, 205–6. Gunther, *D-Day*, 20.
14. "Kluckhohn, Author, Dies," *New York Times*, October 4, 1970. On his troubles with AFHQ, see Schneider, "Press Misses Historic Juncture in Tunisia," *E&P*, April 10, 1943; Sulzberger to James, April 5, 1943, Kluckhohn Folder, box 37, NYT: AHS. On Kluckohn at the front, see Bennett, *Assignment*, 63, 93, 124. For his own assessment of frontline stress, see Kluckhohn, "Most No. African Writers To Rest in London or US," *E&P*, May 29, 1943.
15. Middleton, "'Together We Can Lick the World,'" *New York Times*, December 27, 1942; Middleton, *Our Share*, 235.
16. Middleton, *Last July*, 102–3.

17. BD, February 20, 1943, V:A-237, box 166; Surles to McClure, February 18, 1943, and, Phillips to Surles, February 19, 1943, BPR File, 000.77, Entry 499, boxes 13 and 15, RG165; "Worst Defeat," *Time*, March 1, 1943.
18. Middleton, "Battle at Sbeïtla," and, "Patrols Probing Allied Lines," *New York Times*, February 18 and 21, 1943.
19. Middleton, *Our Share*, 265; Middleton, "Battle at Sbeïtla," *New York Times*, February 18, 1943.
20. Memo to Morgan, August 24, 1943, Policy re Release of Information to the Press, Chief of Staff, SGS, DF 000.7, box 2, RG331.
21. On McCormick, see Norton-Smith, *The Colonel*, 251–53, 300–301, 375–78; Hamilton, *Journalism's Roving Eye*, 163–64, 184; Williams, "I Worked for McCormick," 348. On the fierce competition among Chicago newspapers, see "Chicago Newspapers Compete in Field of Foreign News," *E&P*, June 12, 1943.
22. "No Favoritism Played by War Censor—McClure," *Chicago Tribune*, December 15, 1942; "Nazi Claim—US-Britain at War on News," *Christian Science Monitor*, December 15, 1942; "African News Speed-Up Controversy Debated," *E&P*, December 19, 1942.
23. Schneider, "Algiers Circuit Starts," and, "'Advanced Echelon' Aided Tunisian Writers, *E&P*, January 9 and May 29, 1943; Gay, *Assignment*, 109.
24. Atkinson, *Army at Dawn*, 258–59; Eisenhower to Patton, April 5, 1943, Patton Folder, box 91, EPPP.
25. BD, February 7 and 10, 1943, V:A-209 and A-211, box 166; Eisenhower to Marshall, February 8, 1943, Cables (CCS) Principal File: Subject Series, box 131, EPPP; Algiers to War, V-9876, February 9, 1943, BPR File, 000.7, Entry 499, box 13, RG165; Middleton, "British Land, Air, Sea Chiefs to Serve under Eisenhower," *New York Times*, February 12, 1943; Atkinson, *Army at Dawn*, 328.
26. BD, March 4, 1943, V:A-265 and A-211, box 166.
27. Eisenhower continued to complain about "damn fool" American censors passing "unwise" stories on this subject. See Eisenhower to Surles, May 17, 1943, Surles Folder, box 113, EPPP.
28. Kluckhohn, "Anglo-US Strain in Tunisia Noted," *New York Times*, March 2, 1943.
29. Kluckhohn, "Anglo-US Strain in Tunisia Noted," *New York Times*, March 2, 1943.
30. Eisenhower to Alexander, March 9, 1943, Alexander Folder, box 3, EPPP.
31. BD, April 17, 1943, V:A-313, box 166; Eisenhower to Bradley, April 16, 1943, Correspondence with Major Historical Figures File, Bradley Papers; Atkinson, *Army at Dawn*, 477–78.
32. McCormick to Thompson, March 2, 1943, and, Thompson to McCormick, March 3, 1943, Thompson Folder, McCormick: Foreign Correspondents—I-62, box 11, CTCA.
33. Harrison, "British-American Comradery Shown Daily in North Africa," *Christian Science Monitor*, March 15, 1943.
34. Atkinson, *Army at Dawn*, 419.

CHAPTER 5

1. Patton Diary, November 24, 1942, box 2, Patton Papers; D'Este, *Patton*, 441, 443–45.
2. D'Este, *Patton*, 289–90; Eisenhower to Patton, March 6, 1943, Patton Folder, box 91, EPPP.
3. UP, "Patton Commands in Mid-Tunisia," *New York Times*, March 19, 1943; Boyle, "Gen. Patton Braves Fire," *Baltimore Sun*, March 26, 1943.

4. Thompson, "Sees Gafsa Fall," *Chicago Tribune*, March 19. 1943; MacVane, *Journey*, 232.
5. Patton to Beatrice, March 30, 1943, Chronological File, box 10, Patton Papers; D'Este, *Patton*, 468; D'Arcy-Dawson, *Tunisian Battle*, 177–78.
6. Kluckhohn, "Returning Americans Find Romantic Gafsa Desolated," *New York Times*, March 19, 1943.
7. Patton Diary, March 21, 30, and 31, 1943, box 2, Patton Papers; Jordan, *Tunis Diary*, 213–15; Atkinson, *Army at Dawn*, 433, 458–59; D'Este, *Patton*, 472–75.
8. Kluckhohn, "Returning Americans Find Romantic Gafsa Desolated," and, "US Wounded Stick to Guns to Beat Off German Thrusts," *New York Times*, March 19 and 25, 1943
9. Sulzberger to James, April 5, 1943, Kluckhohn Folder, box 37, NYT: AHS; Schneider, "Press Misses Historic Juncture in Tunisia," *E&P*, April 10, 1943.
10. Kluckhohn, "'Always Go Forward!'" *New York Times*, April 4, 1943.
11. Jordan, *Tunis Diary*, 214, 216.
12. Boyle, "Patton Braves Nazi Fire," *Washington Post*, March 26, 1943; Boyle, "Americans Hammer Foe with Own Guns," *Los Angeles Times*, March 28, 1943.
13. Anspacher, "How PRO Staff Aided Writers Invading Africa," *E&P*, April 24, 1943.
14. Atkinson, *Army at Dawn*, 194–95.
15. Jordan, *Tunis Diary*, 212; Schneider, "War Coverage Restricted in North Africa, Pacific," *E&P*, March 13, 1943.
16. Pyle, *Here Is Your War*, 223; Schneider, "War Coverage Restricted in North Africa, Pacific," *E&P*, March 13, 1943.
17. Liebling, *Mollie*, 100; LeVien to Commanding General, II Corps, "Press Matters before Junction of 8th Army and II Corps," April 3, 1943, AFHQ File, Capa Papers.
18. Ault, "Southern Tunisia," 312–13; Schneider, "Press Misses Historic Juncture in Tunisia," *E&P*, April 10, 1943; Sulzberger, "Yank Met Tommy with Back Slaps," *New York Times*, April 9, 1943. The photos taken of this meeting were posed after the event. See Wellard, *Man in a Helmet*, 89.
19. Pyle, "Most Correspondents Find Work Thrilling—but Long for Peace," *Washington Daily News*, April 15, 1943; Gallagher, *Back Door*, 104.
20. Stoneman, "Yanks Consolidate Gafsa Gains, " and, Stoneman, "Military Prize in Tunisia Just Worthless Mud, Scrub," *Chicago Daily News*, March 19 and 20, 1943
21. Stoneman, "Beautiful Day in Tunisia Upset," *Chicago Daily News*, April 6, 1943.
22. Stoneman, "Beautiful Day in Tunisia Upset," *Chicago Daily News*, April 6, 1943; White, "War Reporters Strafed Along Tunisian Road," *New York Herald Tribune*, April 7, 1943.
23. Stoneman, "American Forces Edge Forward in Attack in North Sector," *Chicago Daily News*, April 29, 1943.
24. Stoneman, "American Forces on Verge of Taking Ferryville," *Chicago Daily News*, May 6, 1943.
25. Tobin, *Pyle's War*, 90–91.
26. Pyle, *Here Is Your War*, 220–21; "Pyle Tells How Underdogs (Infantry) Won in Tunisia," *Boston Globe*, May 4, 1943; Pyle to Jerry Pyle, April 18, 1943, Pyle MSS.
27. "Pyle Tells How Underdogs (Infantry) Won in Tunisia," "Yank Doughboys' Advance in Tunisia," "First Hot Food in 4 Days Great, Says Ernie Pyle," and, "Yanks in Tunisia Get Brief Rests," *Boston Globe*, May 4, 5, 6, 7, 1943.
28. Tucker, "Edward Kennedy—AP War Correspondent," October 19, 1942, and, Bunelle to Cooper, May 6, 1942, and, JMR to JE, July 8, 1942, all in box 1, Kennedy Papers. On his earlier experiences, see Cochran, *Kennedy's War*, 16–100.

29. Romeiser, *Combat Reporter*, 110, 227n4.
30. Hackler to Kenper, February 18, 1943, and, New York to London, APCD14 240, undated, and, Cooper to Curtis, March 17, 1943, all in box 1, Kennedy Papers; Morton, "Why the Bets are on AP," *AP Inter-Office*, November 1943.
31. Gallagher, *Back Door*, 231–37; Boyle to Kennedy, May 10, 1943, box 1, Boyle Papers. On Westmoreland's rescue action, see Gallagher to Hitt, April 1, 1964, Gallagher Vertical File, APCA.
32. Boyle to Kennedy, May 10, 1943, Correspondence, box 1, Boyle Papers; Algiers (McClure) to War Office, No. T89/W11, May 8, 1943, BPR File, 000.7, Entry 499, box 13, RG165.
33. Boyle, "Yanks Liberated Bizerte Once," and, "American Demands Unconditional Surrender," *Baltimore Sun*, May 10 and 11, 1943.
34. Pyle, *Here Is Your War*, 308–9.
35. Sulzberger to Middleton, May 13, 1943, Middleton Folder, box 51, NYT: AHS; "Drew Middleton Marries," *New York Times*, April 1, 1943.
36. Middleton, "What Sort of World Do Our Soldiers Want?" *New York Times*, May 2, 1943.
37. Middleton, "Hill 609 a Jagged Monument to Yanks Who Made History," *New York Times*, May 6, 1943. His bosses considered this a particularly "fine piece." See Sulzberger to Middleton, May 7, 1943, Middleton Folder, box 51, NYT: AHS.
38. Middleton, "The Story of an American Soldier," *New York Times*, May 30, 1943.
39. OWI, "Public Attitudes Toward a Negotiated Peace and Current Military Strategy," August 18, 1943, Entry 164, box 1802, RG44.
40. OWI, "Intelligence Report," No. 51, November 27, 1942, PSF-OWI, Survey of Intelligence, RP.
41. Katz to Kane, "Government's Information Policy Antagonizes Public and Press," November 17, 1943, Entry 149, box 1710, RG44.
42. OWI, "Trends: Satisfaction with Information," undated, Entry 162, box 1787, and, "War Information Wanted," May 15, 1943, Entry 164, box 1799, both in RG44.
43. BD, May 25, 1943, VI:A-416, box 166. Eisenhower to Surles, May 10, 1943, Surles Folder, box 111; Eisenhower to Marshall, May, 13, 1943, Marshall Folder, box 80, EPPP; Atkinson, *Army at Dawn*, 532.
44. Pyle to Jerry, November 6, 1943, Pyle MSS.
45. Butcher to Allen, May 23, 1943, Correspondence File, box 2, Butcher Papers; Middleton to Eisenhower, August 10, 1943, Middleton Folder, box 82, EPPP.
46. Schneider, "War Staffs in N. Africa to Get Well-Earned Rest," *E&P*, May 15, 1943; Pyle, *Here Is Your War*, 286–87.

CHAPTER 6

1. For a sense of reporting this battle, see Cronkite to Betsy, January 9 and 25, 1943, box 2.325/E454a, Cronkite Papers; Kluger, *The Paper*, 366.
2. Stoneman to Portal, March 27, 1941, PRO's and Press Correspondents' Participation in Operational Flights, AIR 2/5309, NA-UK.
3. Wood to Monks, December 4, 1940, AIR 2/5309.
4. Peirse to Undersecretary of State, May 9, 1941, AIR 2/5309.
5. PS to S of S, June 5, 1941, and, Lawrence to Peake, September 9, 1941, both in AIR 2/5309. For the British bombing campaign at this time, see Hastings, *Bomber Command*, 97–99, 107–9.
6. Stoneman to Robertson, June 5, 1941, AIR 2/5309.

7. Stansgate, ACAS (9), August 14, 1942, AIR 2/5309; Gordon, "Passengers in Military Aircraft," August 12, 1942, 8th AF PRO Misc. Folder, IRIS No.225543, reel 7212, AFHRA.
8. Stansgate, "Operational Flights by Press and Camera Men," September 1, 1942, and, Caines to Air Officer Commanding-in-Chief, September 21, 1942, both in AIR 2/5309.
9. Robertson, Note, October 29, 1942, and December 12, 1942, AIR 2/5309. Craven and Cate, *Army Air Forces*, 2:229–37; Parton, *"Air Force Spoken Here"*, 199; Davis, *Spaatz*, 108–14. For the time being, the Eighth Air Force decided only to allow accredited reporters on training, not operational, flights. See Krum to G-2, 8th AF, September 29, 1942, 8th AF PRO Misc. Folder, IRIS No. 225543, reel 7212, AFHRA.
10. "Raymond Daniell Dead at 68," *New York Times*, April 13, 1969.
11. On the December 16 meeting, see Robertson, Note, December 12, 1942, and, "Conference on Flights for Correspondents in Operational Aircraft," December 16, 1942, both in AIR 2/5309. On the lots and the coin toss, see Daniell to Blow, December 17, 1942, AIR 2/5309; MacDonald, "Fires Rage in City," *New York Times*, January 18, 1943. On MacDonald, see Daniell, *Civilians*, 236.
12. MacDonald, "Fires Rage in City," and, "With Seven Men in a Bomber," *New York Times*, January 18 and February 4, 1943. For background on training, see Blow, PR9, January 9, 1943, and, Robertson to Will, January 10, 1943, both in AIR 2/5309. On the normal drill for this kind of raid, see McKinstry, *Lancaster*, 133–47.
13. Stansgate, "Operational Flights by Air Correspondents," January 28, 1943, AIR 2/5309.
14. "Newspapermen on Berlin Raid," *Newspaper World*, January 23, 1943; Lawrence to Robertson, January 29, 1943, AIR 2/5309.
15. Tania Daniell to Sulzberger, February 1, 1943, London Bureau Folder, box 198, NYT: AHS.
16. Kluger, *The Paper*, 290–305. See also Prochnau, *Distant War*, 136; Talese, *Kingdom and the Power*, 198–99.
17. The following paragraphs are based largely on Kluger, *The Paper*, 363–65. See also, biographical information, box 2, Bigart Papers; Wade, introduction to *Forward Positions*, xix–xx; Prochnau, *Distant War*, 33–34, 136.
18. Prochnau, *Distant War*, 341.
19. Salisbury, foreword to *Forward Positions*, xi.
20. "Agreement Reached on 22 October, 1942, at Meeting of Staff of 8th Air Force and Executive Committee of the Association of American Newspaper Correspondents in London," General (PR Policies and Procedures File), IRIS No.225543, reel 7212, AFHRA.
21. Daniell to Sulzberger, December 23, 1942, London Bureau Folder, box 198, NYT: AHS; McCrary to Ordway, undated, General (PR Policies and Procedures File), IRIS No.225543, reel 7212, AFHRA.
22. Ordway to Redding, January 20, 1943, General (PR Policies and Procedures File), IRIS No.225543, reel 7212, AFHRA.
23. Hamilton, *Writing 69th*, 39–40, 45. Five newsreel cameramen also attended the course.
24. Cronkite to Betsy, February 6, 1943, box 2.325/E454a, Cronkite Papers.
25. Hamilton, *Writing 69th*, 13–24; Daniell, *Civilians*, 207; ETO, HQ, "War Correspondent Missing after Raid," February 27, 1943, Eighth Air Force Press Releases, box 5, Redding Papers. Daniell's wife also believed that Post "was the only

one young enough in our bureau" to be acceptable to the Eighth Air Force, which apparently had more stringent age requirements than the RAF. See Tania Daniell to Sulzberger, February 1, 1943, London Bureau Folder, box 198, NYT: AHS.

26. Cronkite to Betsy, February 6, 1943, box 2.325/E454a, Cronkite Papers.
27. London USSOS to War, No. 7042, February 6, 1943, BPR File, 000.7, Entry 499, box 14, RG165; ETO, HQ, "Newsmen to Fly with Bombers," February 12, 1943, Eighth Air Force Press Releases, box 5, Redding Papers; Cronkite, *Reporter's Life*, 98.
28. Cronkite to Betsy, February 6, 1943, box 2.325/E454a, Cronkite Papers.
29. Bigart, "US Reporters Training to Fly with Bombers," *New York Herald Tribune*, February 9, 1943; Post, "First Group Completes Intensive Course at Eighth Air Force Training Depot," *New York Times*, February 9, 1943. On the survival rate for ditching, see Miller, *Eighth Air Force*, 98–99.
30. Hamilton, *Writing 69th*, 45; Cronkite to Betsy, February 6, 1943, box 2.325/E454a, Cronkite Papers.
31. Laidlaw to Dashiell, May 8, 1951, Cronkite Folder, box 186, Salisbury Papers; Hamilton, *Writing 69th*, 53–55.
32. Reynolds, *Rich Relations*, 289; Cronkite to Betsy, February 19, 1943, box 2.325/E454a, Cronkite Papers.
33. Hamilton, *Writing 69th*, 67; Redding and Leyshon, *Skyways to Berlin*, 44–48.
34. Redding and Leyshon, *Skyways to Berlin*, 46; Miller, *Eighth Air Force*, 116.
35. Hamilton, *Writing 69th*, 67–81.
36. Salisbury to Nordau, February 6, 1943, HES London 1943: Nordau's Dupes Folder, box 185, Salisbury Papers; Salisbury, *Journey*, 192.
37. Salisbury, *Journey*, 192–93.
38. Bigart, "Reporter Rides Fortress in Wilhelmshaven Raid," *New York Herald Tribune*, February 27, 1943.
39. Bigart, "Raid on Wilhelmshaven: A Lesson in Perspective," *New York Herald Tribune*, March 7, 1943.
40. Cronkite to Betsy, March 8, 1943, box 2.325/E454a, Cronkite Papers. Salisbury, *Journey*, 193.
41. Bigart, "Raid on Wilhelmshaven: A Lesson in Perspective," *New York Herald Tribune*, March 7, 1943.
42. Cronkite, "Hell 26,000 Feet Up," February 27, 1943, clipping, Cronkite Folder, box 186, Salisbury Papers; Cronkite, *Reporter's Life*, 99.
43. Salisbury, memo of telephone conversation with Bigart, March 3, 1981, Cronkite Folder, box 186, Salisbury Papers. When Salisbury tried almost forty years later to re-create what had happened for his memoirs, he felt like he was in the Rashomon play "in which each character says a murder in a different light." In this instance, each participant had a different memory of what had happened after the raid. See Salisbury to Cronkite, March 17, 1980, Cronkite Folder, box 186, Salisbury Papers.
44. Bigart, "Reporter Rides Fortress in Wilhelmshaven Raid," *New York Herald Tribune*, February 27, 1943.
45. Cronkite to Betsy, March 8, 1943, box 2.325/E454a, Cronkite Papers.
46. Cronkite to Betsy, March 8, 1943, box 2.325/E454a, Cronkite Papers; "Robert Post Dead, Red Cross Learns," *New York Times*, August 12, 1943. Even then, Post's family refused to accept that he had been killed; as his boss at the *Times* explained, they would "not accept his insurance money and have not permitted a Liberty Ship to be named after him." See Sulzberger to Lawson, November 30, 1943, Darnton Folder, box 15, NYT: AHS.

47. Cronkite to Betsy, March 8, 1943, box 2.325/E454a, Cronkite Papers; ETO, HQ, "War Correspondent Missing after Raid," February 27, 1943, Eighth Air Force Press Releases, box 5, Redding Papers; Salisbury, *Journey for Our Times*, 193–94.
48. See, for example, "OWI Hails Bravery of War Reporters," *New York Times*, April 15, 1943.
49. "Flights by US Writers at Fronts Discouraged," *E&P*, April 3, 1943.
50. "Staffs See Bombing Trips as Futile, Kennedy Says," *E&P*, July 10, 1943.

CHAPTER 7

1. Daniell, "The Team That Harries Hitler," *New York Times*, June 6, 1943.
2. "General Eaker's Press Conference at Widewing," March 24, 1943, Eighth Air Force: Press Conferences Folder, box I:22, Eaker Papers.
3. Craven and Cate, *Army Air Forces*, 2:60–66, 105–7, 282–83; Parton, *"Air Force Spoken Here"*, 158–60, 183, 233–34.
4. Eaker, "Night Bombing," October 8, 1942, Official Diary, box I:10, Spaatz Papers; Parton, *"Air Force Spoken Here"*, 130, 140–41, 190–91, 220–22; Davis, *Spaatz*, 161–64.
5. Allan A. Michie, "What's Holding Up the Air Offensive against Germany?" *Reader's Digest*, February 1943, 21–28; Parmentier to Surles, February 12, 1943, BPR File, 000.7, Entry 499, box 13, RG165.
6. Arnold to Surles, "Contradicting Published Criticisms of AAF Tactics," February 23, 1943, BPR File, 000.7, Entry 499, box 13, RG165.
7. Eaker to Arnold, June 29, 1943, Arnold Correspondence Folder, box 1:17, Eaker Papers; Parton, *"Air Force Spoken Here"*, 191, 243–44.
8. War Department Press Release, "558 Enemy Planes Destroyed in Combat by 6 Air Forces Bombardment Groups," April 16, 1943, BPR File, 000.7, Entry 499, box 17, RG165; War Department, BPR, "Radio Digest," March 25, 1943, Entry 497, box 2, RG165; Bigart, "150 American Bombers Pound Emden," and, "Record Raid Smashes Dortmund," and, "British-Based Air Strength of US Is Doubled," *New York Herald Tribune*, May 16 and 25, and June 11, 1943.
9. Arnold to Eaker, June 29, 1943, Arnold Correspondence Folder, box 1:17, Eaker Papers.
10. Arnold to Eaker, August 10, 1943, Military File, DF 000.7, box 61, Arnold Papers.
11. Parton, *"Air Force Spoken Here,"* 86–87, 102, 239.
12. Parton, *"Air Force Spoken Here,"* 131–32, 199–200; Miller, *Eighth Air Force*, 121.
13. "History of Eight [*sic*] Air Force," undated, IRIS No.225549, reel 7212, AFHRA; Krum to Childers, November 2, 1942, Military, 1942–44, box 7, Redding Papers.
14. Salisbury, *Journey*, 195.
15. Hill to Col. W, April 26, 1943, 8th AF PRO Misc. Folder, IRIS No.225543, reel 7212, AFHRA.
16. Whitney to Lovett, September 25, 1943, Publicity and Press Folder, 000.7, Entry 292-A, box 3, RG18.
17. Luce to Senior Editors of *Time*, October 22, 1943, Time-Life-Fortune Papers, box 1, Billings Papers; Brinkley, *Luce*, 228–29, 240–41.
18. Whitney to Lovett, September 25, 1943, Publicity and Press Folder, 000.7, Entry 292-A, box 3, RG18; Eaker to Walton, June 29, 1943, Eighth Air Force: PR Folder, box I:22, Eaker Papers.
19. USAWW to War, August 21, 1943, BPR File, 000.7, Entry 499, box 17, RG165; "Victory is in the Air," *Time*, August 30, 1943.
20. Brinkley, *Luce*, 282–83.

21. Arnold to Spaatz, September 2, 1942, Personal Diary, box I:8, Spaatz Papers.
22. Courtney to McCrary, September 25, 1943, Publicity and Press Folder, 000.7, Entry 292-A, box 3, RG18.
23. Whitney to Lovett, September 25, 1943, Publicity and Press Folder, 000.7, Entry 292-A, box 3, RG18.
24. "Public Relations Photographic School," 8th AF PRO Misc. Folder, IRIS No.225548, reel 7212, AFHRA.
25. Cronkite to Betsy, February 6, 1943, box 2.325/E454a, Cronkite Papers; Parton, *"Air Force Spoken Here"*, 199–200; Miller, *Eighth Air Force*, 121; Kelly, *McCrary*, 44.
26. McCrary and Scherman, *First of the Many*, 31; Eaker to Westlake, December 5, 1943, Eighth Air Force: PR Folder, box I:22, Eaker Papers.
27. McCrary and Scherman, *First of the Many*, 6, 31–52,
28. "Aerial Photography," undated, Office of Info Services, Entry 5, box 26, RG18; Arnold to Eaker, June 29, 1943, and, Eaker to Arnold, July 10, 1943, both in Eighth Air Force: Arnold Correspondence Folder, box I:17, Eaker Papers; Parton, *"Air Force Spoken Here"*, 244; Maslowski, *Armed with Cameras*, 189–90.
29. Smith to Childers, August 22, 1942, 8th AF PRO Misc. Folder, IRIS No.225543, reel 7212, AFHRA; Redding and Leyshon, *Skyways to Berlin*, 10–11.
30. "Crews Stories of Flying Fortress Raid on Rouen," March 12, 1943, Eighth Air Force Press Releases, box 5, Redding Papers
31. "Jack Mathis—American Bombardier," March 20, 1943, Eighth Air Force Press Releases, box 5, Redding Papers; Miller, *Eighth Air Force*, 123–24.
32. Reynolds, *Rich Relations*, 288.
33. USFOR to War, 8117, March 22, 1943, BPR File, 000.7, Entry 499, box 14, RG165; Redding and Leyshon, *Skyways to Berlin*, 10–11; McCrary and Scherman, *First of the Many*, 85–86.
34. AP, "Vegesack Hero's Brother Hits Bremen in Same Ship," *New York Times*, April 19, 1943.
35. Redding and Leyshon, *Skyways to Berlin*, 12.
36. Morgan, *Man Who Flew*, 98–99, 210–11; *Memphis Belle*: Original Eighth Air Force Movie, https://www.youtube.com/watch?v=4ZO6UtAfxEM, accessed February 2015.
37. Miller, *Eighth Air Force*, 145–46; Morgan, *Man Who Flew*, 98–99, 225, 228.
38. USFOR to London, W-505, W-607, W-608, June 5 and 9, 1943, BPR File, 000.7, Entry 499, box 13, RG165; Eaker to Arnold, June 29, 1943, Arnold Correspondence Folder, box 1:17, Eaker Papers.
39. Morgan, *Man Who Flew*, 220, 224–25, 232–33; Miller, *Eighth Air Force*, 145–46.
40. Krum to A-2, 8th AF, October 9, 1942, 8th AF PRO Misc. Folder, IRIS No.225543, reel 7212, AFHRA; Kozloff, "Wyler's Wars," 459–60; Madsen, *Wyler*, 228.
41. Morgan, *Man Who Flew*, 174–75; Cronkite to Betsy, February 6, 1943, box 2.325/E454a, Cronkite Papers.
42. Madsen, *Wyler*, 234–35; Herman, *Talent for Trouble*, 251.
43. Herman, *Talent for Trouble*, 257.
44. Miller, *Eighth Air Force*, 117–18; Morgan, *Man Who Flew*, 210–12, 244–45; Kozloff, "Wyler's Wars," 459–60; Maslowski, *Armed with Cameras*, 181–84.

CHAPTER 8

1. Kluckhohn, "Eaker Leads Raid," *New York Times*, August 18, 1942; *Memphis Belle*: Original Eighth Air Force Movie; Reynolds, *Rich Relations*, 284.
2. Salisbury, *Journey*, 193, 198–99.

3. Craven and Cate, *Army Air Forces*, 2:666–83.
4. Miller, *Eighth Air Force*, 208.
5. Craven and Cate, *Army Air Forces*, 2:702–4.
6. McCrary and Scherman, *First of the Many*, 218–19; Lyon to Hoyt, undated [October 1943], BPR File, 000.7, Entry 499, box 34, RG165.
7. AP, "60 US 'Forts' Shot Down," *Chicago Tribune*, October 15, 1943.
8. Lyon to Hoyt, undated [October 1943], BPR File, 000.7, Entry 499, box 16, RG165.
9. Roosevelt, *Press Conferences*, October 15, 1943, No. 922, 10–11.
10. 8th Air Force to AGWAR, October 15, 1943, Press Releases and Telegrams: Schweinfurt Folder, IRIS No.1075629, reel 40505, AFHRA; Westlake to Whitney, A-3960, October 16, 1943, BPR File, 000.7, Entry 499, box 16, RG165; "General Arnold's Press Statement," *New York Times*, October 16, 1943.
11. Eaker to Arnold, October 15, 1943, Arnold Correspondence Folder, box 1:17, Eaker Papers; Eaker to Arnold, D-1447, October 19, 1943, BPR File, 000.7, Entry 499, box 15, RG165.
12. "Crescendo," *New York Times*, October 17, 1943.
13. "General Arnold—Press Conference, October 18, 1943," Memo Folder, Personal File, box 23, Clapper Papers; AP, "Gen. Arnold Maintains Bomber Loss Justified," *Los Angeles Times*, October 19, 1943.
14. Merrick to A.C-of-S, A2 HQ, October 19, 1943, Eighth Air Force, Press Releases and Telegrams: Schweinfurt Folder, IRIS No.1075629, reel 40505, AFHRA.
15. Merrick to A.C-of-S, A2 HQ, October 19, 1943, Eighth Air Force, Press Releases and Telegrams: Schweinfurt Folder, IRIS No.1075629, reel 40505, AFHRA; Eaker to Arnold, October 19, 1943, Arnold Correspondence Folder, box 1:17, Eaker Papers; AP, "Deny a Tip-Off Led to Loss of 60 Bombers," *Chicago Tribune*, October 28, 1943.
16. Salisbury, *Journey*, 196, 198–99.
17. Miller, *Eighth Air Force*, 121, citing Andy Rooney of the *Stars and Stripes*.
18. "Larry Rue, Famed Correspondent, Dies," *Chicago Tribune*, July 13, 1965.
19. Rue to McCormick, October 15, 1943, Rue Folder, McCormick: Foreign Correspondents—I-62, box 8, CTCA.
20. Sevareid, *Not So Wild*, 79–80; Calder, *People's War*, 285.
21. Calder, *People's War*, 318–19. Noderer, July 15, 1943, Notebook 2, box 2, XI-231, Noderer Papers.
22. Noderer, October 7, 1943, Notebook 2, box 2, XI-231, Noderer Papers. While this was the experience of newspaper reporters, other media correspondents had a less drab time. *Time*'s William Walton went on a raid over Paris in July; Murrow accompanied the RAF on a trip to Berlin in December. See "Holiday Over Paris," *Time*, August 2, 1943; Sperber, *Murrow*, 230–33.
23. Sterne, *Combat Correspondents*, 55–56.
24. "Sixty Bombers Are Missing," *Time*, October 25, 1943.
25. Whitney to Lovett, September 25, 1943, and, Westlake to Arnold, October 26, 1943, both in Publicity and Press Folder, 000.7, Entry 292-A, box 3, RG18. Lay, "I Saw Regensburg Destroyed," *Saturday Evening Post*, November 6, 1943.
26. Proctor to Arnold, November 16, 1943, and, Arnold to Eaker, undated [November 1943], both in Publicity and Press Folder, 000.7, Entry 292-A, box 2, RG18.
27. Markel to Sulzberger, October 28, 1943, and Surles to Sulzberger, November 15, 1943, and Sulzberger to Surles, November 17, 1943, all in WW2 Folder, box 274, NYT: AHS.

28. Arnold to Eaker, undated [November 1943], Publicity and Press Folder, 000.7, Entry 292-A, box 2, RG18.
29. McCardell, "Eighth Air Force Head Is Gambler Who Plays Cards Close to His Vest," *Baltimore Sun*, November 25, 1943. On McCardell's background and reporting of the air war, see Sterne, *Combat Correspondents*, 38–45, 55–56.
30. Davis, *Spaatz*, 271.
31. Craven and Cate, *Army Air Forces*, 2:689–94.
32. Crane, *Bombs, Cities, Civilians*, 28, 33.
33. Eaker to Arnold, November 7, 1943, BPR File, 000.7, Entry 499, box 15, RG165.
34. Parton, *"Air Force Spoken Here,"* 336–46; Davis, *Spaatz*, 271–78; Miller, *Eighth Air Force*, 243–45; Craven and Cate, *Army Air Forces*, 3:6–7.
35. Miller, *Eighth Air Force*, 245–46; Davis, *Spaatz*, 287–88.
36. Doolittle to Commanding General, VIII Fighter Command, January 19, 1944, Operational File, box 19, Doolittle Papers; Miller, *Eighth Air Force*, 245–49; Craven and Cate, *Army Air Forces*, 3:12–13.
37. Gallagher, *Back Door*, 34–35; BD, November 11, 1942, III:G-55, box 165.
38. "Eighth Air Force Frowns on Word 'Raids' to Describe Air Operations over Europe," *New York Times*, October 21, 1943.
39. Arnold to Spaatz, January 24, 1944, Personal Diary, box I:14, Spaatz Papers; Westlake, Memo for Chief of Air Staff, March 7, 1944, BPR File, 000.7, Entry 499, box 39, RG165. There was also an effort to tighten censorship. "If in doubt," censors were instructed to "consult Operations or Intelligence officers." If these officers could not be reached, they were told to "kill doubtful stuff." See Boyd, "Increased Censorship Facilities," February 14, 1944, Official Diary, box I:17, Spaatz Papers.
40. Davis, *Spaatz*, 323–27. Doolittle, "Relief of Combat Crew Personnel," March 4, 1944, Operational File, box 19, Doolittle Papers. On "Big Week" see also, Craven and Cate, *Army Air Forces*, 3:9–13, 43, 46–47.
41. Tait, "US Flyers Hit Nazi Aircraft Centers," and, "US Air Fleet Blasts German Plane Factories," *New York Herald Tribune*, February 25 and 26, 1944. UP, "Luftwaffe's Fight Savage," *New York Times*, February 23, 1944.
42. "Shabby London," *Boston Globe*, August 10, 1943.
43. Middleton, "Why the British Are Wonderful," *New York Times*, February 28, 1944.
44. Middleton, "Britain Rebuffs Bombing Critics," and, "Bomb Accuracy in Clouds Mastered by 8th Air Force," *New York Times*, February 10, 1944, and December 29, 1943. Middleton to Sulzberger, February 13, 1944, Middleton Folder, box 51, NYT: AHS; Middleton, *Last July*, 122–23.

CHAPTER 9

1. Thompson, "Tribune Writer Flies to Battle," *Chicago Tribune*, July 12, 1943; D'Este, *Bitter Victory*, 240; Atkinson, *Day of Battle*, 39–40, 76.
2. Pyle, "Most Correspondents Find Work Thrilling—but Long for Peace," *Washington Daily News*, April 15, 1943
3. Byrnes to McCormick, May 24, 1943, and the attached biographical sketch, "Thompson: *Chicago Tribune* Reporter," undated, Thompson Folder, McCormick: Foreign Correspondents—I-62, box 11, CTCA.
4. D'Este, *Bitter Victory*, 249; Ridgway, *Soldier*, 66.
5. Thompson, "Tribune Writer Flies to Battle," *Chicago Tribune*, July 12, 1943.
6. Overy, *Bombing War*, 27–28, 52.
7. Thompson, "Tribune Writer Flies to Battle," *Chicago Tribune*, July 12, 1943.

8. Bennett, *Assignment*, 69–76.
9. Atkinson, *Day of Battle*, 76.
10. Bennett, *Assignment*, 72; Thompson, "Tribune Writer Flies to Battle," *Chicago Tribune*, July 12, 1943.
11. Thompson, "Tanks Fought to a Standstill," *Chicago Tribune*, July 16, 1943. For background on the battle, see Biggs, *Gavin*, 37–43.
12. Moroso, "Plans to Expedite Stories from Sicily Fleet Miscued," *E&P*, August 14, 1943.
13. Duncan-Clark to Press Liaison Officer, July 11, 1943, In-Log, Allied Command: AFHQ Sub-Series, box 5, BS: WWII; Middleton, "Air-Borne Force Was First to Attack Sicily," *New York Times*; Morin, "US Troops Seize Two Airdromes on Sicily," *Washington Post*, July 12, 1943.
14. Mrs. Thompson to McCormick, July 23, 1943, Thompson Folder, McCormick: Foreign Correspondents—I-62, box 11, CTCA.
15. Thompson, "Terror by Night," *Chicago Daily News*, July 15, 1943; "Plans Broadcast Tonight," *Chicago Tribune*, July 16, 1943; McCormick to Thompson, July 19, 1943, Thompson Folder, McCormick: Foreign Correspondents—I-62, box 11, CTCA.
16. Schneider, "Sicily News Pool Ends," *E&P*, July 24, 1943.
17. McCormick to Thompson, July 19, 1943, Thompson Folder, McCormick: Foreign Correspondents—I-62, box 11, CTCA.
18. Hutchison, "The Public Relations Report of the Seventh Army," August 30, 1943, Special Staff Records: PI Section, box 2260, RG492; Green, "Sicilian Invasion Wordage Hit 1,400,000 in 13 Days," *E&P*, July 31, 1943; Belden, "Troop Landings at Gela in Sicily," *Life*, July 26, 1943.
19. Atkinson, *Day of Battle*, 79–91; Lucas to Eisenhower, July 21, 1943, Chief of Staff Official Correspondence File, box 15, BS: WWII; Green, "Sicilian Invasion Wordage Hit 1,400,000 in 13 Days," *E&P*, July 31, 1943.
20. Romeiser, *Combat Reporter*, 164–67; Hutchison, "The Public Relations Report of the Seventh Army," August 30, 1943, Special Staff Records: PI Section, box 2260, RG492.
21. Gunther, *D-Day*, 50.
22. AP, "Invasion Secret Kept for a Month Can Now Be Told by Reporters," *Christian Science Monitor*, July 10, 1943; Monchak, "Record Allied Press Corps Covering Invasion of Sicily," *E&P*, July 17, 1943.
23. Gunther, *D-Day*, 20, 34; Phillips to AGWAR, W3895, July 1, 1943, Special Staff Records: PI Section, box 2259, RG492.
24. UP, "All Is Calm at Zero Hour for Invasion," *Chicago Daily News*, July 10, 1943; Bigart, "How Reporters Got the News of Sicily Invasion," *New York Herald Tribune*, July 11, 1943.
25. BD, July 1, 1943, VI:A-513, box 166; July 10, 1943, VII:A-554, box 167; Kirkpatrick, "Island Attacked by Land, Sea, Air," *Chicago Daily News*, July 10, 1943.
26. Korman, "See Toughest Tasks in Sicily Still to Be Met," *Chicago Tribune*, July 11, 1943; Middleton, "Air-Borne Force was First to Attack Sicily," *New York Times*, July 12, 1943; AP, "Cow in Sicily Americanized as Hamburger," *Chicago Daily News*, July 14, 1943.
27. Green, "Sicilian Invasion Wordage Hit 1,400,000 in 13 Days," *E&P*, July 31, 1943.
28. BD, July 10, 1943, VII:A-553, box 167.
29. Gunther, *D-Day*, 20–23, 45–49.
30. Gunther, "How Eisenhower Spent Night of Allied Sicilian Adventure," and, "Eisenhower Visits Sicily," *Baltimore Sun*, July 11 and 13, 1943; Gilling, "2,000 Vessels Used in Attack on Sicily," *New York Times*, July 12, 1943.

31. Monchak, "Record Allied Press Corps Covering Invasion of Sicily," *E&P*, July 17, 1943.
32. Monchak, "Record Allied Press Corps Covering Invasion of Sicily," *E&P*, July 17, 1943; Grogan to Eisenhower for Surles, July 14, 1943, In-Log, Allied Command: AFHQ Sub-Series, box 5, BS: WWII. Munro's scoop was not entirely an accident. To welcome the Canadians to his command, Eisenhower had planned to release news of their invasion exploits first. See Algiers to War, No. W-4448/8977, July 9, 1943, BPR File, 000.7, Entry 499, box 13, RG165.
33. Patton Diary, July 17 and 19 1943, box 2, Patton Papers; Hamilton, *Master of the Battlefield*, 301–7; D'Este, *Bitter Victory*, 321–33; Atkinson, *Day of Battle*, 124, 133.
34. Whitehead, "Palermo Turns Out to Welcome Seventh Army," *New York Times*, July 25, 1943.
35. USFOR to WDBPR, No.4007, July 21, 1943, Special Staff Records: PI Section, AGWAR Cables Folder, box 2258, RG492.
36. Lock to Finbat PR, July 20, 1943, In-Log, Allied Command: AFHQ Sub-Series, box 5, BS: WWII.
37. Hutchison, "The Public Relations Report of the Seventh Army," August 30, 1943, Special Staff Records: PI Section, box 2260, RG492; Daly to Fowler, August 13, 1943, Radio Broadcasts Italy Folder, box 2, Daly Papers; Green, "Sicilian Invasion Wordage Hit 1,400,000 in 13 Days," *E&P*, July 31, 1943.
38. Atkinson, *Day of Battle*, 144–45; Gervasi, *Violent Decade*, 467.
39. BD, July 1, 1943, VI:A-513, box 166.
40. Mowrer, "'Fantastic' Cheers of Sicily Make Comic Opera of War," and, "German Units Cut to Pieces in Attempt to Save Troina," *Chicago Daily News*, July 30 and August 9, 1943.
41. "Whitehead 'Uncorks' Claim to Purple Heart," *E&P*, November 6, 1944. Whitehead, "A War Correspondent's Life," *Washington Post*, January 4, 1942. Romeiser, *Combat Reporter*, xi, 12, 46–47.
42. Romeiser, *Combat Reporter*, 183–88; Whitehead, "Savage Fighting Around Dead Woman's Hill," *Baltimore Sun*, August 7, 1943.
43. Boyle, "Two Divisions Share Seizure of Messina," *Washington Post*, August 18, 1943.
44. Tregaskis, *Invasion Diary*, 89; D'Este, *Patton*, 531–32.
45. Hutchison, "The Public Relations Report of the Seventh Army," August 30, 1943, Special Staff Records: PI Section, box 2260, RG492.
46. Long, "Mistreatment of Patients in Receiving Tents of the 15th and 93rd Evacuation Hospitals," August 16, 1943, Patton Folder, box 91, EPPP.
47. Eisenhower to Marshall, August 24, 1943, Marshall Folder, box 80, EPPP; BD, August 21, 1943, VIII:A-678-79, box 167.
48. Bess to Eisenhower, "Report of an Investigation," August 19, 1943, Patton Folder, box 91, EPPP.
49. Atkinson, *Day of Battle*, 115; D'Este, *Patton*, 525; Pyle, "Bradley Chases Sniper Who Took Pot Shot at Him," and, "Universally Loved, Respected by All, That's Gen. Bradley," undated, XII.25-26, Pyle MSS. Quentin Reynolds, the reporter who quipped that 50,000 GIs wanted to shoot Patton, considered the "unassuming, quiet, and brainy Bradley . . . a great general." See Reynolds, *Curtain Rises*, 223.
50. Tobin, *Pyle's War*, 110; Romeiser, *Combat Reporter*, 206.
51. BD, August 20 and 21, 1943, VIII:A-673, A-678, box 167.
52. BD, September 2, 1943, VIII:A-716, box 167; Ambrose, *Supreme Commander*, 229.

53. BD, September 2, 1943, VIII:A-716, box 167; Eisenhower to Surles, December 14, 1943, Surles Folder, box 113, EPPP; Monchak, "Censorship Backfired on Patton Story," *E&P*, November 27, 1943; Reynolds, *Curtain Rises*, 226–27.
54. BD, September 2, 1943, VIII:A-716, box 167.
55. Stimson to Eisenhower, December 18, 1943, Stimson Folder, box 111, EPPP; Daly, CBS Broadcast, November 23, 1943, Radio Broadcasts Italy Folder, box 2, Daly Papers.
56. Monchak, "Censorship Backfired on Patton Story," *E&P*, November 27, 1943; Drummond, "Patton Tempest Quieted by Eisenhower Frankness," *Christian Science Monitor*, November 27, 1943; Bracker, "Patton Struck Ailing Soldier," *New York Times*, November 24, 1943. On Mueller's unearthing of the story, see Mueller, "Reporter's Notebook," August 15, 1943, box 2, Mueller Papers.
57. Atkinson, *Day of Battle*, 106–10.
58. The figure of 410 fatalities would appear in the press the following March, but Ridgway always disputed this number. See Ridgway to TAG, "Casualties, Sicilian Campaign, CT 504," May 19, 1944, BPR File, 0007, Entry 499, box 36, RG165.
59. Patton Diary, July 13, 1943, box 2, Patton Papers; Atkinson, *Day of Battle*, 112.
60. Although Eisenhower did question the "future effectiveness of this powerful arm of opportunity." See Eisenhower to Marshall, July 29, 1943, Cables Off Folder, Principal File: Subject Series, Cables, box 132, EPPP.
61. Romeiser, *Combat Reporter*, 168; Lockett to Welch, "Army's News Policy," December 21, 1944, Folder 236, Time Dispatches.
62. After the story finally broke in March, Butcher believed it "could have been released months ago but with action developing so fast in the Mediterranean and other problems pressing for attention, this affair was more forgotten than purposely hidden." BD, April 4, 1944, X:A-1179, box 168.

CHAPTER 10

1. Crockett to Cornell Friedman, March 11, 1943, and, Capa to Cornell Friedman, undated [September 1943], and, Capa to Julia and Cornell Friedman, undated [October 1943], all in Capa Papers.
2. The following paragraphs are based on Whelan, *Capa*, 18–59, 80–83, 156–58, 169, 174–76, 183–84; Kershaw, *Blood and Champagne*, 8–22, 28–30, 70, 94–96.
3. He also relished the prospect of being confused with the film director Frank Capra.
4. Capa, *Slightly*, 33.
5. USFOR to PRO, No. 626, December 17, 1942, Cable Log Folder (CoS), box 3, BS: WWII; Algiers to Surles, March, 26, 1943, BPR File, 000.7, Entry 499, box 14, RG165; LeVien to Phillips, "Results of Today's Discussion on Photographic Coverage in this Theater," December 30, 1942, AFHQ File, Capa Papers.
6. Crockett to Cornell Capa, March 11, 1943, Capa Papers.
7. Ulio, "Motion Picture and Still Photography in the Theaters of Operations," June 30, 1942, and, LeVien, "Operating Procedure of the Pictorial Section," September 30, 1942, both in BPR File, 000.77, Entry 499, box 7, RG165.
8. Wright, Memo for the Director, November 23, 1942, BPR File, 000.77, Entry 499, box 7, RG165; AP, "How Gafsa Pictures Reached the Globe," *Boston Globe*, March 23, 1943. LeVien to Mitchell, April 7, 1943, AFHQ File, Capa Papers.
9. LeVien to Phillips, "Comments on Breaking of Picture Pool," February 14, 1943, AFHQ File, Capa Papers. Unlike newspaper stories, which still received a byline while the pooled was in operation, pooled photographs often went out anonymously.

10. "The Beginning of Victory," *Collier's*, June 19, 1943, 12–14.
11. Capa, *Slightly*, 59.
12. Capa to Julia Friedman, undated [July 1943], Capa Papers.
13. Eisenhower to Surles, undated [June 1943], AFHQ File, Capa Papers.
14. Capa, *Slightly*, 58–80; Whelan, *Capa*, 194–96; Capa to Julia Friedman, undated September 16, 1943, Capa Papers; AGWAR to Eisenhower, No.4088, August 3, 1943, and, USFOR to FHPRO, No.4438, August 13, 1943, both in Special Staff Records: PI Section, box 2258, RG492; "The Surrender of Palermo," *Life*, August 23, 1943.
15. Shepley to McConaughy, "Communiqués (Army Angles)," March 26, 1943, folder 59, Times Dispatches.
16. Harsch, "Allied Victories Recall 1918 Pattern," *Christian Science Monitor*, August 7, 1943; Stoneman and Ghali, "Axis Is Licked, Europe Thinks," *Chicago Daily News*, August 9, 1943.
17. OWI, "Current Surveys," No. 13, July 21, 1943, box 1715; OWI, Correspondence Panels Section to Glick, and, "Lack of Realism about the Fighting Fronts—Its Effects," August 30, 1943, box 1710, both in Entry 149, RG44. See also "Prominent Americans See Victory Now Assured," *Boston Globe*, September 9, 1943.
18. Garland and Smyth, *Sicily*, 290–93, 476–78, 482, 523–34. For the government's skepticism about a repeat of 1918, see Marshall, Memo for Hopkins, September 29, 1943, Pentagon Office: Correspondence, Hopkins Folder, box 71, Marshall Papers.
19. Roeder, *Censored War*, 11–12; Board of War Information, "Minutes of Meeting," July 21, 1943, OWI, Records of Historian: Subject File, box 12, RG208.
20. Davis, "Notes on First Day in Office," June 16, 1942, and, Davis, Report to the President, OWI, June 13, 1942 to September 15, 1945, 14–15, both in Subject File: OWI, box 10, Elmer Davis Papers.
21. Roeder, *Censored War*, 11–12; Memo for Director of BPR, Pictorial Branch, September 3, 1943, BPR File, 062.1, Entry 499, box 23, RG165; "Lifts Picture Ban on War's Realism," *New York Times*, September 5, 1943.
22. Atkinson, *Day of Battle*, 190–93; Blumenson, *Salerno to Cassino*, 25–26; Whelan, *Capa*, 200.
23. Reynolds, *Curtain Rises*, 282–83.
24. Blumenson, *Salerno to Cassino*, 55–57; Walker, *From Texas to Rome*, 230–31.
25. Stoneman, "Takeoff for Italian Invasion," *Chicago Daily News*, January 24, 1944; Clark to Phillips, September 10, 1943, Special Staff Records: PI Section, Fifth Army Folder, box 2261, RG492.
26. Reynolds, *Curtain Rises*, 279; Clark to Phillips, September 10, 1943, Special Staff Records: PI Section, Fifth Army Folder, box 2261, RG492.
27. Reynolds, *Curtain Rises*, 318, 332–33; Reynolds, *By Quentin Reynolds*, 302. Gorrell, "Navy Thought Gorell's Stories Were Dynamite," *E&P*, October 24, 1943; Belden, *Still Time to Die*, 291–95.
28. GB to APG, Sepember 3, 1943, box 1, Kennedy Papers; Kennedy, "Panzer Forces Hurled Back in Naples Area by Fifth Army," *Washington Post*, September 12, 1943; Lee, "Bitter Struggle for Italy Seen by Eisenhower," *New York Herald Tribune*, September 13, 1943.
29. Blumenson, *Salerno to Cassino*, 99–112.
30. Shapiro, *They Left the Back Door Open*, 147–50.
31. Atkinson, *Day of Battle*, 202–30; Walker, *From Texas to Rome*, 245–49; 15th Army Group to 5th Army, September 13, 1943, Subject File, Important Messages Folder,

box 63, and, Clark Diary, September 13, 1943, V:24–28, box 64, both in Clark Papers.

32. Packard, "Yanks Deal Germans Heaviest Losses Yet," *Boston Globe*, September 14, 1943.
33. Stoneman, "Newsman Finds Fault with Salerno Operations," *Baltimore Sun*, September 14, 1943; Stoneman, "Allies Strive to Throw Back Nazi Spearhead," *Chicago Tribune*, September 15, 1943.
34. AP, "Violent Salerno Battle Raging," and, UP, "Grim Battle Rages at Salerno," *Los Angeles Times*, September 14, and 15, 1943; Off the Record Briefing, September 13 and 14, 1943, In-Log, Allied Command: AFHQ Sub-Series, box 7, BS: WWII.
35. Packard, "Position Never Desperate at Salerno: Clark," *Chicago Tribune*, September 17, 1943. On Clark's annoyance at these negative reports, see Clark to Eisenhower, September 16, 1943, Clark Folder, box 23, EPPP; Clark Diary, September 16, 1943, V:34–35, box 64, Clark Papers.
36. Morton, "State of Flux Existed during Landing in Italy," *E&P*, November 6, 1943.
37. Tregaskis, *Invasion Diary*, 109–10.
38. Tregaskis, *Invasion Diary*, 109–12; Capa, *Slightly*, 58–80; Morton, "State of Flux Existed during Landing in Italy," *E&P*, November 6, 1943.
39. Capa, *Slightly*, 91; Clark to Phillips, September 19, 1943, Special Staff Records: PI Section, Fifth Army Folder, box 2261, RG492.
40. Ridgway to *Life* editor, November 15, 1943, Capa Papers; Capa, *Slightly*, 95–100.
41. Capa to Cornell Friedman, undated [October 1943], and, *Life* accounts, undated, both in Capa Papers.
42. Clark to Phillips, September 20 and 26, 1943, Special Staff Records: PI Section, Fifth Army Folder, box 2261, RG492.
43. Clark to Phillips, October 11, 1943, and, Bremer to Clark, "Photographers," October 13, 1943, and, Phillips to Clark, October 16, 1943, all in Special Staff Records: PI Section, Fifth Army Folder, box 2261, RG492.
44. Clark to Phillips, September 30, 1943, Special Staff Records: PI Section, Fifth Army Folder, box 2261, RG492.
45. Capa, *Slightly*, 102–3. Atkinson, *Day of Battle*, 237; Moorehead, *Eclipse*, 62.
46. Capa, *Slightly*, 111; Whelan, *Capa*, 201–2.
47. Capa was not pleased, commenting that *Life* had sent "the eternal [infernal?] Bourke-White on our necks." See Capa to Cornell Friedman, undated, Capa Papers.
48. Goldberg, *Bourke-White*, 63, 72, 98, 105, 127–35, 148, 174–76, 184–85, 206–8, 236–48; Bourke-White, *Purple Heart Valley*, 13.
49. Sorel, *Women Who Wrote*, 180–92; Carpenter, *No Woman's World*, 15.
50. Goldberg, *Bourke-White*, 284.
51. "*Life's* Bourke-White Goes Bombing," *Life*, March 1, 1943; Goldberg, *Bourke-White*, 257–69.
52. Eaker, "Women War Correspondents on Operational Flights," March 9 and 16, 1943, 8th AF PRO Misc. Folder, IRIS No.225543, reel 7212, AFHRA.
53. Goldberg, *Bourke-White*, 262–64, 274; Bourke-White to Eisenhower, April 23, 1943, Eisenhower Folder, box 15, Bourke-White Papers.
54. Clark to Phillips, October 11, 1943; Bremer to Clark, "Photographers," October 13, 1943, Special Staff Records: PI Section, Fifth Army Folder, box 2261, RG492; Bourke-White, *Purple Heart Valley*, 17.
55. Phillips to Clark, October 19, 1943, Special Staff Records: PI Section, Fifth Army Folder, box 2261, RG492.

56. Phillips to Clark, October 16 and 19, 1943, Special Staff Records: PI Section, Fifth Army Folder, box 2261, RG492.
57. Grasett to ACOS G-2, July 11, 1944, Press Correspondents File, Chief of Staff, SGS, DF 000.74, box 4, RG331; Phillips to Clark, October 19, 1943, Special Staff Records: PI Section, Fifth Army Folder, box 2261, RG492.
58. Kasper, "Kirkpatrick Interview," April 4, 1990.
59. Bourke-White, *Purple Heart Valley*, 62, 88.
60. Bourke-White for *Life*, "Note to Darkroom," undated, Italy Folder, box 71, Bourke-White Papers.
61. Goldberg, *Bourke-White*, 297–98; Bourke-White, *Purple Heart Valley*, 7, and photos between 8 and 9.
62. "It's a Tough War," *Life*, January 31, 1944.
63. "Artillery and Infantry in Italy," *Life*, February 14, 1944.
64. Capa thought it was "time to get back to civilization." See Capa to Cornell Friedman, December 14, 1943, Capa Papers.

CHAPTER 11

1. Pyle, *Brave Men*, 5–6; Pyle to Jerry, July 11 1943, Pyle MSS.
2. Dickson, G-2 Journal: Algiers to the Elbe, 91, box 1, Dickson Papers.
3. Pyle, *Brave Men*, 48–49, 62–64, 90–91; Clapper to Jerry Pyle, August 16, 1943, Personal File: Foreign Travel, SEA Folder, box 37, Clapper Papers.
4. Miller to Coke, August 18, 1943, Pyle Correspondence Folder, box 9, Stone Papers; Monchak, "Restless Ernie Pyle Checks In," *E&P*, September 11, 1943; "Ernie Pyle," *Life*, November 15, 1943; Miller, *Story*, 280–82.
5. Miller, *Story*, 282–83; Pyle to Jerry, November 6, 1943, Pyle MSS.
6. Pyle, "I Hate to Get Back to the Front, but What Can a Guy Do?", *Washington Daily News*, November 9, 1943. Privately, Pyle admitted that it would be "sad and difficult" to return to the front. See Pyle to Clapper, September 30, 1943, Correspondence Folder, box 51, Clapper Papers.
7. Roy Howard, who had initially been skeptical of Ernie's "low-altitude" output, was by now a full-fledged convert. "Pyle is undoubtedly presenting the wartime activities of the American forces with a technique and a style that is duplicated by no other writer with whose work I am acquainted," he had commented earlier in the year. "He has certainly humanized war coverage to a greater degree than any other contemporaneous American writer and he has done it by making the individual soldier the common denominator of all war activity." See Howard to Wood, February 4, 1943, City File: New York: Wood; box 196, Howard Papers.
8. Pyle to Jerry, November 6, 1943; Pyle to Cavanaugh, November 18, 1943; Pyle MSS; Miller, *Story*, 283. Tobin, *Pyle's War*, 111.
9. Vaughan-Thomas, *Anzio*, 35–36; Atkinson, *Day of Battle*, 372–73; LeVien to Phillips, October 27, 1943, Special Staff Records: PI Section, 5th Army Folder, box 2261, RG492.
10. Pyle to Cavanaugh, November 18, 1943, and, Pyle to Jerry, December 19, 1943, Pyle MSS; Miller, *Story*, 297.
11. Blumenson, *Salerno to Cassino*, 207–8, 226, 311–14; Caddick-Adams, *Monte Cassino*, 31; Atkinson, *Day of Battle*, 260, 279, 299.
12. Pyle to Jerry, January 1, 1944, Pyle MSS.
13. Clark to Phillips, October 1, 1943, Special Staff Records: PI Section, 5th Army Folder, box 2261, RG492; Gay, *Assignment*, 221; Walker, *From Texas to Rome*, 282–83.

14. Brady, *Death in San Pietro*, 184, 195–202, 204; Atkinson, *Day of Battle*, 287–89; Pyle to Jerry, January 27, 1944, Pyle MSS.
15. Pyle, *Brave Men*, 164–66.
16. "Page One Is Different Today," *Washington Daily News*, January 10, 1944; Miller, *Story*, 297–98; Tobin, *Pyle's War*, 137–39.
17. Bigart, "San Pietro a Village of the Dead; Victory Cost Americans Dearly," *New York Herald Tribune*, December 20, 1943; Wade, *Forward Positions*, 28; Whitehead, "Victory Most Costly for Americans Thus Far in Italian Campaign," *New York Times*, December 20, 1943; Gay, *Assignment*, 230–33. So many San Pietro stories emphasized death that the War Department felt under pressure "to estimate the casualties for this particular operation." See Surles to Devers, January 4, 1944, BPR File, 000.7, Entry 499, box 33, RG165.
18. Pyle to Jerry, January 12, 1944, Pyle MSS.
19. Pyle, "Death Comes to Airmen Rather Decently," January 18, 1944, XII.59, Pyle MSS.
20. Tregaskis, *Invasion Diary*, 201–15.
21. Pyle, "Reporter Loses Part of Brain, but He Plans to Return to War Front," December 29, 1943, XII.53, Pyle MSS.
22. Pyle, "Ex-Newsboys Would Make the Best Soldiers, Army Medical Officer Believes," January 13, 1944, XII.57, Pyle MSS.
23. Pyle to Jerry, January 27, 1944, Pyle MSS.
24. Rovner, "Censorship Still Unsatisfactory, Says AP's Boyle," *E&P*, February 26, 1944.
25. Boyle, "Cassino," *AP Inter-Office*, March 1944.
26. Rovner, "Censorship Still Unsatisfactory, Says AP's Boyle," *E&P*, February 26, 1944
27. Thompson, Note, November 21, 1943, Thompson Folder, McCormick: Foreign Correspondents—I-62, box 11, CTCA; Faris, "Tregaskis Takes Faris on a 'Cook's Tour' of Front," *E&P*, November 6, 1943.
28. Lee, "Lee Tells How Writers Spend Day during Lull," *E&P*, November 27, 1943.

CHAPTER 12

1. Blumenson, *Salerno to Cassino*, 322–48; Walker, *From Texas to Rome*, 305–13; Atkinson, *Day of Battle*, 328–30.
2. Sulzberger, *Long Row*, 93, 198, 204–27. On nepotism at the *Times*, see Talese, *Kingdom*, 182, 203.
3. Sulzberger, *Long Row*, 229. On morale and censorship in the Thirty-Fourth Division, see Clark Diary, December 10, 1943, V:163 164, box 64, Clark Papers.
4. Sulzberger, "Americans Swim Rapido River to Escape Germans," *New York Times*, January 25, 1944.
5. Kearns, *No Ordinary Time*, 301–3, 310–11; "FDR's White House Map Room," http://www.fdrlibrary.marist.edu/aboutfdr/maproom.html, accessed February 2015.
6. Clark Diary, January 23, 1944, VI:41, box 65, Clark Papers.
7. D'Este, *Fatal Decision*, 72–79.
8. Roosevelt, *Press Conferences*, February 11, 1944, No. 935, 3. On the mood in these sessions, see Steele, *Propaganda in an Open Society*, 8–13, 112; Winfield, *FDR and the Media*, 29–30; White, *FDR and the Press*, 10–15.
9. "President Sees War Chiefs; Points to Danger in Italy," *New York Times*, February 11, 1944; Harsch, "Roosevelt: Situation Tense in Italy," *Christian Science Monitor*," February 11, 1943.
10. Stoneman, "Takeoff for Italian Invasion," *Chicago Daily News*, January 24, 1943

11. Whitehead, "Anzio," *AP Inter-Office*, March 1944; Whitehead, "Allies 'Just Walked' Ashore on Empty Italian Beaches," *New York Times*, January 23, 1944.
12. Cochran, *Kennedy's War*, 119.
13. Whitehead, "Lack of Opposition When They Hit Shore Left Officers and Soldiers Alike with Great Impression of Anticlimax," *New York Times*, January 25, 1944; Stoneman, "Allies Break German Push below Rome," *Chicago Daily News*, January 27, 1944.
14. Sulzberger, "Allies below Rome Hold Initiative, Says Alexander," and, "No Allied Surprise of Nazis Quit Rome," *New York Times*, January 26 and February 1, 1944. On Alexander and PR, see Nicolson, *Alex*, 241.
15. G-3 Report, January 31 and February 1, 1944, Third Division: Operations File, box 11, Truscott Papers; D'Este, *Fatal Decision*, 160–67; Adleman and Walton, *Rome Fell*, 156–66.
16. Boyle to Gallagher, February 13, 1943, Correspondence Folder, box 1, Boyle Papers; Atkinson, *Army at Dawn*, 331; Capa, *Slightly*, 91.
17. AP, "US Rangers: Tragic Stand in Italy," March 8, 1944; AP, "2 Ranger Battalions Lost Inside Cisterna," *New York Times*, March 9, 1944; Atkinson, *Day of Battle*, 393–94.
18. Vaughan-Thomas, *Anzio*, 91–92, 144. Langevin proved so valuable that the bridgehead commanders were reluctant to let him go. See Clark to Truscott and Truscott to Clark, April 16, 1944, VI Corps Correspondence, box 12, Truscott Papers.
19. Vaughan-Thomas, *Anzio*, 91, 132; Cochran, *Kennedy's War*, 120.
20. Stoneman, "Yanks Cut Nazis Defenses in Push North of Cassino," *Chicago Daily News*, January 31, 1944; Bigart, "Nazis Massing to Hold Allies Near Cisterna," and, "Cisterna Battle in Stalemate after 5 Days of Bitter Fighting," *New York Herald Tribune*, February 3 and 5, 1943.
21. Hosley, *As Good as Any*, 59.
22. Burnham, "Press Treatment of Situation at Bridgehead," undated, PREM 3, 248/5, NA-UK. This British document names the NBC correspondent from Algiers as "Martin." No such correspondent existed. Morrison was NBC's man in Algiers at that time. See Morrison, "Special Feed from Algiers," January 3, 1944, Call: RWA 6903 A4, NBC Radio Archives.
23. Churchill, *Second World War*, 5:383–84, 410–23; D'Este, *Fatal Decision*, 252–53; Churchill to Wilson, February 12, 1944, PREM 3, 248/5.
24. Gervasi, *Violent Decade*, 517; Bigart, "Alexander Explains News Curb," *New York Herald Tribune*, February 19, 1944.
25. Newspaper and Periodical Emergency Council to Grigg, February 17, 1944, PREM 3, 248/5, and, AFHQ to Surles, February 18, 1944, Security & Censorship Italy, WO 106/4073, and, war correspondents to Lucas, February 12, 1944, Press Censorship Correspondence, WO 204/6880, all in NA-UK.
26. "Allies Now Easing News from Italy," *New York Times*, February 27, 1944.
27. Bigart, "Alexander Explains News Curb," *New York Herald Tribune*, February 19, 1944; "5th Army Tightens Censorship," *New York Times*, February 16, 1944.
28. Bigart, "Reporter Says Allies at Anzio Tried Too Much with Too Little," *New York Herald Tribune*, March 27, 1944.
29. Conrad to Marshall, W-13451, March 20, 1944, BPR File, 000.7, Entry 499, box 33, RG165; AP, "410 US Paratroopers, Mistaken for Foe, Killed in Air Battle," *Los Angeles Times*, March 17, 1944; "Stimson Attacks Story of Laxity in Transports' Loss," *Washington Post*, March 24, 1944.
30. "News Suppression by Administration Charged by Dewey," *New York Times*, March 25, 1944.

31. OWI, "Public Appraisal of War Information," Memo No. 77, May 12, 1944, Entry 164, box 1800, RG44.
32. State Department, "Public Attitudes on Foreign Policy: Increasing Demand for a More Positive Statement on Foreign Policy," No.16, March 20, 1944, Foster Files, Entry 568J, box 1, RG59; Cantril to Walker, May 8, 1944, OF 857, RP.
33. Sulzberger, *Long Row*, 229–31.
34. Sulzberger, "200 Germans Flee," and, "3,500 Tons Dropped", *New York Times*, February 16 and March 16, 1944.
35. Sulzberger, "3,500 Tons Dropped," and, "Castle Hill Taken," *New York Times*, March 16 and 17, 1944.
36. Sulzberger, "Allies at Cassino Seize Rail Station," and, "Cassino Push Lags," and, "Allies' Third Drive on Cassino Failure," *New York Times*, March 18, 21, and 26, 1944.
37. Atkinson, *Day of Battle*, 406–7.
38. Pyle to Jerry, February 11, and March 15, 1944, Pyle MSS.
39. Pyle, "Introducing 'My Personal Hero,'" February 21, 1944, XII.70, Pyle MSS; Pyle, *Brave Men*, 193–209.
40. Pyle to Jerry, March 15, 1944, Pyle MSS; D'Este, *Fatal Decision*, 300–301; Vaughan-Thomas, *Anzio*, 191.
41. Bigart, "Reporter Says Allies at Anzio Tried Too Much with Too Little," *New York Herald Tribune*, March 27, 1944; "Alexander Finds Beachhead Firm," *New York Times*, March 10, 1944.
42. Bigart, "Nazis' Thrusts at Beachhead Cracking Up," and, "Anzio Soldiers in Good Health in Spite of Mud," *New York Herald Tribune*, February 20, 1944 and March 21, 1944.
43. Pyle, "D-Day Veterans," and, "It Ain't No Picnic," and, "Under Artillery Fire," and, "Anzio Dugouts," March 28 and 30, 1944, April 6 and 7, 1944; XIII.14–15; XIII.18–19, Pyle, MSS.
44. Pyle to Jerry, March 30, 1944, Pyle MSS. "US Newsmen Four Wounded as Officers Bombed," *Washington Daily News*, March 16, 1944; Tobin, *Pyle's War*, 154–55.
45. Pyle to Cavanaugh, March 24, 1944, Pyle MSS.
46. Pyle, "That Battle Look," April 5, 1944, XIII.18, Pyle MSS. Pyle, *Brave Men*, 285–86.
47. Sevareid, Beachhead Broadcast, April 23, 1944, box I:D3, Sevareid Papers. Two other broadcasters followed Sevareid—Ralph Howard for NBC and Wynford Vaughan-Thomas for BBC—for a show that the three networks pooled. See Special News Feed from Anzio, April 23, 1944, Call: RWB 6920 A2, NBC Radio Archives.
48. Cull, *Selling War*, 101–4; Sperber, *Murrow*, 168.
49. Shirer, *Nightmare Years*, 284–304, 321–22, 457; Kirby and Harris, *Star-Spangled Radio*, 18–20; Barnouw, *Golden Web*, 109; Hosley, *As Good as Any*, 138–39.
50. "Sicily News Aired in 33 Seconds," *Broadcasting*, July 19, 1943; Kirby and Harris, *Star-Spangled Radio*, 26–36; MacVane, *On the Air*, 125–30.
51. Phillips to McCarthy, August 4, 1943, Phillips Folder, box 21, McCarthy Papers; "New Wire Recorders Prove Value in Army Test Abroad," *Broadcasting*, August 23, 1943.
52. Wharfield to Clark, September 24, 1943, and, Clark to Phillips, October 5 and 27, 1943, all in Special Staff Records: PI Section, Fifth Army Folder, box 2261, RG492; Pellegrin, "Nothing Can Escape the Wire Recorder," *Broadcasting*, April 3, 1944.
53. Wharfield to Clark, September 24, 1943, Special Staff Records: PI Section, Fifth Army Folder, box 2261, RG492. Pellegrin, "Nothing Can Escape the Wire Recorder,"

Broadcasting, April 3, 1944; White to Daly, February 4, 1944, Correspondence: General Folder, box 3, Daly Papers.

54. AFHQ to Surles, F-44250, May 11, 1944, Press and Publicity, MR 0000.7 (sec.2), box 46, Map Room Files, RP; "General Clark's Press Conference, May 9, 1944, Subject Files: Messages, box 63, and, Clark Diary, May 9, 1944, VII:59–60, box 65, both in Clark Papers
55. Sevareid, Beachhead Broadcast, May 25, 1944, box I:D3, Sevareid Papers.
56. Clark to Gruenther, May 23 and 24, 1944, Subject Files: Messages, box 63, and, Clark Diary, May 25, 1944, VII:102–3, box 6, and, Clark to Renie, May 26, 1944, Personal Correspondence, box 67, all in Clark Papers.
57. Clark Diary, May 17 and 30, 1944, VII:75, 123–24, box 65, and, Gruenther to Clark and Clark to Gruenther, May 25 and 31, 1944, Subject Files: Messages, box 63, all in Clark Papers.
58. Clark Diary, May 27, 1944, VII:111, box 65, Clark Papers. On this dispute, see D'Este, *Bitter Victory*, 335–37, 352–53; Atkinson, *Day of Battle*, 515–17; Adleman and Walton, *Rome Fell*, 226; Blumenson, *Clark*, 200–201.
59. Bigart, "Nazi Suicide Squads Ambush US Troops Outside Artena," *New York Herald Tribune*, May 29, 1944.
60. Bigart, "Americans Drive on Rome, 16 Miles Off," and, "Battle Rages for Last Line Below Rome," *New York Herald Tribune*, May 30 and 31, 1944.
61. Sevareid, Beachhead Broadcast, May 30, 1944, box I:D3, Sevareid Papers.
62. Sevareid, *Not So Wild*, 400–401.
63. Adleman and Walton, *Rome Fell*, 251–52; Sevareid, *Not So Wild*, 410–11.
64. Adleman and Walton, *Rome Fell*, 263; De Luce, "Eyewitness Story of Rome's Fall," *Los Angeles Times*, June 5, 1944.
65. Clark Diary, June 5, 1944, VII:147–48, box 65; Sevareid, *Not So Wild*, 414.
66. Sedgwick, "Fifth Army's Dead Honored by Clark," and, "Gen. Clark Sees 2 Armies Beaten," *New York Times*, May 31 and June 6, 1944.
67. By that stage Clark faced a number of public attacks. The growing controversy around the Rapido River crossing even led to a congressional investigation in 1946. See Blumenson, *Salerno to Cassino*, 351.
68. Hume, "Invasion Came Too Soon for Italy Press Corps," *E&P*, July 1, 1944; Sevareid, *Not So Wild*, 413–17.

CHAPTER 13

1. Pyle to wife, March 15 and 30, 1944, Pyle MSS; Miller to Carlin, March 2, 1944, Pyle Correspondence, box 9, Stone Papers; Tobin, *Pyle's War*, 157.
2. Hicks, Background Notes, March 2–April 22, 1944, box 4, Hicks Papers.
3. Pyle, *Brave Men*, 315–21; Pyle to wife, April 14, 1944, Pyle MSS; Miller to Cowan, April 21, 1944, Pyle Correspondence, box 9, Stone Papers.
4. Morton, "Why the Bets Are on the AP," *Inter-Office*, November 1943; AJG to Cooper, March 21, 1944, Foreign Bureaus Correspondence: London, AP2.1, box 3, AP Archive.
5. Gallagher, "Great Peril Seen in Allies' Delay at Anzio Beachhead," *Chicago Tribune*, February 9, 1944; BD, February 8, 1944, X:A-1075, box 168.
6. BD, February 8, 1944, X:A-1075, box 168. On Phillips's redeployment, see Astley to Mainwaring, March 7, 1944, Press Censorship Correspondence, WO 204/6880, NA-UK.
7. Gallagher, "Still Far from Rome," *Washington Post*, December 18, 1943.

8. "Colonel J. B. Phillips Marries Mrs. MacLean," February 13, 1944, Phillips, Records; AP, "Col. J. D. Phillips Weds," *New York Times*, February 16, 1944.
9. Gallagher, "Reporters, Military Censors Engage in 'Constant Conflict,'" *Atlanta Constitution*, March 26, 1944.
10. Ambrose, *Eisenhower*, 1:281.
11. As the plan evolved, the Allies would also drop three parachute divisions behind the beaches.
12. McClure to Strong, January 12, 1944, and, Strong to McClure, January 14, 1944, both in Policy re Release of Information to the Press, Chief of Staff, SGS, DF 000.7, box 2, RG331.
13. Ismay to COSSAC, January 14, 1944, and, Churchill to Eisenhower, January 28, 1944, both in Policy re Release of Information to the Press, Chief of Staff, SGS, DF 000.7, box 2, RG331.
14. Atkinson, *Guns at Last Light*, 26.
15. Butcher, *Three Years*, 538–39. On the breach, see Sibert to Bradley, April 19, 1944, Bradley Folder, box 13, EPPP.
16. Eisenhower to Churchill, February 6, 1944, Churchill Folder, box 22, EPPP.
17. Tatum to Director, "Supplementary Press Digest," December 28, 1944, and, LeMonnier to Chief, January 4, 1944, both in Press and News Analyses, BPR: Records of News Division, Entry 350, box 8, RG107.
18. Newspaper and Periodical Emergency Council to Grigg, February 17, 1944, PREM 3, 248/5, NA-UK; BD, February 17, 1944, X:A-1092, box 168.
19. Gallagher, "Reporters, Military Censors Engage in 'Constant Conflict,'" *Atlanta Constitution*, March 26, 1944. On the concern in Eisenhower's command about these stories, see BD, April 4, 1944, XI:A-1179, box 168.
20. SHEAF, PRD, "Minutes of Meeting Held on April 20, 1944," April 24, 1944, Correspondents–Military, box 6, Redding Papers.
21. McClure to Chief of Staff, "Guidance of Press in Initial Stage," April 26, 1944, Press and Radio Releases for Initial Plans of OVERLORD, Chief of Staff, SGS, DF 000.71/5, box 3, RG331. McClure was right to be concerned. "If we don't get spot news from the American-British source," the AP head noted a month later, "if and when there is an invasion, we will, of course, get it from the Germans who do not hold up news for twelve-hour periods." See Cooper to Howard, May 23, 1944, City File-NY-AP, box 179, Howard Papers.
22. Reid, Memo to CoS, "Accrediting of War Correspondents to SHAEF," March 28, 1944, and, Address by Supreme Commander, undated [May 11, 1944], both in Press Correspondents File, SGS, DF 000.74, box 4, RG331; "History of US and SHAEF Press Censorship in ETO, 1942-1945," 83–84, box 2, Merrick Papers.
23. Kuh, "Winant Presents Draft of US Armistice Terms," *Boston Globe*, February 6, 1944; McClure to Chief of Staff, February 11, 1944, and, Surles to Eisenhower, February 11, 1944, Press Release Regarding Peace Terms, both in Chief of Staff, SGS, DF 000.7, box 3, RG331.
24. Davis to Chief of Staff, "War Correspondents concerning Whom Some Question Has Arisen," April 25, 1944, Press Correspondents File, Chief of Staff, SGS, DF 000.74, box 4, RG331.
25. McClure lost public relations in a shake-up implemented on April 13. See Pogue, *Supreme Command*, 84–86; and Crosswell, *Beetle*, 596. Davis had been lined up to take over for almost a month before. See Davis to Bedell Smith, March 15, 1944, box 1, T. J. Davis Papers; Butcher, *Three Years*, 501.

26. SHEAF, PRD, "Minutes of Meeting Held on April 20, 1944," April 24, 1944, and, Davis to Chief of Staff, "War Correspondents concerning Whom Some Question Has Arisen," April 25, 1944, both in Press Correspondents File, Chief of Staff, SGS, DF 000.74, box 4, RG331
27. BD, May 12, 1944, XI:1252, box 168.
28. Davis to Bedell Smith, March 15, 1944, and, Davis to McFarland, May 1, 1944, and, Davis to Roberts, May 10, 1944, all in box 1, T. J. Davis Papers; BD, March 16, 1944, XI:1140, box 168; Pinkley, "Correspondent Corps Is Set for Invasion Coverage," *E&P*, May 27, 1944.
29. Davis to Roberts, July 14, 1944, and, Eisenhower to Davis, July 14, 1944, box 1, T. J. Davis Papers.
30. Daniell to Davis, May 24, 1944, and, Davis to Daniell, May 25, 1944, box 1, T.J. Davis Papers.
31. Pinkley, "Correspondent Corps Is Set for Invasion Coverage," *E&P*, May 27, 1944.
32. Pinkley, "Correspondent Corps Is Set for Invasion Coverage," *E&P*, May 27, 1944.
33. Bedell Smith to Algiers, M-103, February 17, 1944, Cables Log—Out, Allied Command: SHAEF Sub-Series, box 27, BS: WWII; SHAEF, "Press Policy," Operational Memo 24, April 24, 1944, Policy re Release of Information to the Press, Chief of Staff, SGS, DF 000.7, box 2, RG331; "Communication Arrangements for the Press," undated, Press Coverage and Communications in France, Chief of Staff, SGS, DF 000.7/4, box 3, RG331; Phillips to Davis, April 29, 1944, Twelfth Army Group, Stories and Press Releases, and, Twelfth Army Group, "History of Public Relations Office," undated, both in box 5, Redding Papers.
34. Willicombe, "Ex-Call Bulletin Aide Liaison for Gen. 'Ike,'" *San Francisco Call-Bulletin*, January 25, 1944; Smith to MBS, June 16, 1944, box 3, Thor Smith Papers.
35. Pogue, *Supreme Command*, 90.
36. McClure to Chief of Staff, "Interview with SHAEF High Commanders," March 24, 1944, Policy re Release of Information to the Press, Chief of Staff, SGS, DF 000.7, box 2, RG331.
37. McClure to Chief of Staff, "Interview with SHAEF High Commanders," March 24, 1944, and, SHAEF, "Press Policy," Operational Memo 24, April 24, 1944, both in Policy re Release of Information to the Press, Chief of Staff, SGS, DF 000.7, box 2, RG331.
38. "History of US and SHAEF Press Censorship in ETO, 1942-1945," 69, 85–86, box 2, Merrick Papers; Pogue, *Supreme Command*, 91; "Allies' Censorship Works with Speed," *New York Times*, June 14, 1944.
39. Address by Supreme Commander, undated [May 11, 1944], Press Correspondents File, SHAEF, 000.74, box 4, RG331; "History of US and SHAEF Press Censorship in ETO, 1942-1945," 83–84, box 2, Merrick Papers.
40. Twelfth Army Group, "History of Public Relations Office," undated, box 5, Redding Papers; "PROs Trained to Aid Writers on Invasion," *E&P*, June 17, 1944; Oldfield, *Never a Shot*, 39–43.
41. NBC, *H-Hour*, File 644: World War II—Publications, NBC History Files.
42. NBC Release, March 21, 1944, File 648: World War II—NBC War Clinics, NBC History Files; Taishoff, "Nets Pool Facilities to Cover Invasion," *Broadcasting*, May 8, 1944.
43. Huber to Business Managers, January 31, 1944, City File-NY-Huber, box 202, and, Wood to Howard, December 13, 1943, box 196, both in Howard Papers.

44. Hawkins to Howard, June 7, 1944, City File-NY-Hawkins, box 201, Howard Papers; "UP Chiefs Confer on War Coverage," *E&P*, April 28, 1944.
45. AP wire, A199, June 6, 1944, Foreign News Service Folder, AP01.B, Board President MacLean Papers, Series IV, box 20, APCA; Surles-Stimson Conversation, undated [June 4,1944], BPR File, 000.7, Entry 499, box 39, RG165; Smith to MBS, June 3, 1944, box 3, Thor Smith Papers.
46. Hansen, War Diary, June 4, 1944, box 4, Hansen Papers.
47. Ambrose, *D-Day*, 182–83; BD, June 4, 1944, XI:1327, box 168.
48. "Alerting of War Correspondents," undated, box 6, and, "The Assault Force of Correspondents," undated, box 6, and, Twelfth Army Group, "History of Public Relations Office," undated, box 5, all in Redding Papers.
49. Pyle, *Brave Men*, 375–76; "Word from Ernie Pyle," *Boston Globe*, June 11, 1944; Stoneman, "How Spectator Saw Battle Five Days before Invasion," *Chicago Daily News*, June 6, 1944.
50. Oldfied, *Never a Shot*, 65–66.
51. Capa, *Slightly*, 131–32; Whelan, *Capa*, 209–10; Baker, *Hemingway*, 594–55.
52. Whitehead, "News Writers Held 8 Days to Await Invasion," *Chicago Tribune*, June 7, 1944.
53. Whitehead, "A Correspondent's View," 205–6; Capa, *Slightly*, 134. For excellent footage of the correspondents arriving in the assembly camp, see Lieb, *D-Day to Germany*, YouTube video. https://www.youtube.com/watch?v=jkRDe6epeVg, accessed June 2015.
54. Hicks, D-Day Notes, box 4, Hicks Papers.
55. Whitehead, "News Writers Held 8 Days to Await Invasion," *Chicago Tribune*, June 7, 1944; Whitehead, "Normandy," 204–5; Romeiser, *"Beachhead Don,"* 119–20; Miller, *Story*, 329.
56. Capa, *Slightly*, 136–37; Whelan, *Capa*, 210–11.
57. Pyle, *Brave Men*, 379; Miller, *Story*, 329; Tobin, *Pyle's War*, 167–68; Pyle to wife, July 1, 1944, Pyle MSS.
58. Stoneman, "How Spectator Saw Battle Five Days before Invasion," *Chicago Daily News*, June 6, 1944.

CHAPTER 14

1. Hicks, "Background Notes," June 6, 1944, and, Hicks, D-Day Notes, both in box 4, Hicks Papers.
2. Waugh, *Put Out More Flags*, 61.
3. Pinkley, "How Reporters Got First Invasion Tip," *E&P*, June 10, 1944; Graebner, London Cable Unnumbered, June 6, 1944, D-Day Scripts and Broadcasts Folder, box 3, Graebner Papers. On Gellhorn's recent experiences, see Moorehead, *Gellhorn*, 252–57.
4. Johnson to Hulbard, "London Cable 464," June 9, 1944, Folder 168, Time Dispatches; Murrow, "Inside the London Broadcasting Pool," *Broadcasting*, June 20, 1944.
5. Bunelle, "How the AP Scored Sensationally," *AP Inter-Office*, June-July 1944; Nordness, "'Everything Happened at Once on D-Day," *E&P*, June 10, 1944.
6. Bunelle, "How the AP Scored Sensationally," *AP Inter-Office*, June-July 1944.
7. Schuyler, "US Press, Well Prepared, Covers Invasion in Stride," and, "Dailies Rush Extras on Big Invasion," *E&P*, June 10, 1944. By contrast, the *New York World-Telegram* sold 528,000 copies on D-Day, its eighth highest daily circulation total and a dramatic rise over the 350,000 copies it normally sold. See Macneish to

Howard, June 7, and May 17, 1944, City File-NY-Macneish, box 202, Howard Papers.

8. Robertson, "D-Day Gives Radio Greatest Opportunity," and, "Radio Listening for Week of Invasion Well Above Normal," *Broadcasting*, June 12 and 19, 1944.
9. NBC, *H-Hour*, File 644: World War II Publications, NBC History Files.
10. O'Neill, "Allies Invading France, Troops Land in Normandy," *Baltimore Sun*, June 6, 1944; AP, "Allies Invade France," *Chicago Tribune*, June 6, 1944.
11. Hinsley et al., *British Intelligence*, 3:2, 47–49; Butcher, *Three Years*, 554.
12. Eisenhower to Surles, May 31, 1944, Press and Radio Releases for Initial Plans of OVERLORD, Chief of Staff, SGS, DF 000.71/5, box 3, RG331.
13. "Air Blows Center on Pas-de-Calais," *New York Times*, June 6, 1944.
14. Hicks to Summers, January 12, 1945, box 1, and, Hicks, D-Day Notes, box 4, both in Hicks Papers; "Dramatic Hicks Film Record in Demand by All Networks," *Broadcasting*, June 12, 1944.
15. Hicks, D-Day Report, June 6, 1944, Call: RWB 7547 B4, NBC Radio Archives.
16. Yarbrough, "Undefended Lane across Channel Almost Incredible," *Christian Science Monitor*, June 7, 1944; Treanor, "Treanor's Own Invasion Story," *Los Angeles Times*, June 8, 1944.
17. Lasher, "Eyewitness Invasion Stories Fill Nation's Newspapers," *E&P*, June 17, 1944; Whitman, "Not a Nazi in Hour," *Christian Science Monitor*, June 7, 1944; McDonald, "Casualties Held Surprisingly Low," *New York Times*, June 8, 1944.
18. Stoneman, "First Landing in France Was Salerno Again," and, "Germans Ready for Weeks—to Toss in Sponge," *Chicago Daily News*, June 9 and 10, 1944.
19. For a sense of what the censors cut on D-Day, see Heinz, *When We Were One*, 3–7. These cuts were largely of details that were operationally sensitive.
20. Stoneman, "Weak Resistance to Allied Landing a Mystery," *Chicago Daily News*, June 12, 1944.
21. NBC, *H-Hour*, File 644: World War II—Publications, NBC History Files; Butcher, *Three Years*, 575.
22. Whitehead, "Duty to the Doughboys," undated, WWII Book Project: General Info Folder, AP28, Writings about the AP, Series II, box 14, APCA.
23. On Omaha, see Harrison, *Cross-Channel Attack*, 269–335; Weigley, *Eisenhower's Lieutenants*, 78–91; Beevor, *D-Day*, 88–124; Pogue, *Pogue's War*, 83; Salaita, "Embellishing Omaha Beach," 531–34.
24. Whitehead, "A Correspondent's View," 208–9; Whitehead, "Normandy," 212–13; Wertenbaker, *Invasion*, 40–41; Pyle to wife, July 1, 1944, Pyle MSS.
25. Lasher, "Eyewitness Invasion Stories Fill Nation's Newspapers," *E&P*, June 17, 1944; Twelfth Army Group, "History of Public Relations Office," undated, box 5, Redding Papers.
26. Wertenbaker, *Invasion*, 41.
27. Whitehead, "Courage, Skill Win," *Chicago Tribune*, June 10, 1944; Whitehead, "First Division Proved Mettle," *Baltimore Sun*, June 12, 1944. Thompson produced a similar account, see Thompson, "Doughboys Get the Glory for the Allies' Success," *Chicago Tribune*, June 9, 1944.
28. Pyle, *Brave Men*, 389; Tobin, *Pyle's War*, 170–73.
29. Wertenbaker, *Invasion*, 42–43.
30. Butler, "Invasion Pictures Took Long Preparation," *E&P*, November 18, 1944.
31. "Beachheads of Normandy," *Life*, June 19, 1943; Whelan, *Capa*, 213–14; Kershaw, *Blood and Champagne*, 129–30.

32. Capa to Cornell and Julia Friedman, undated [July 1944], Correspondence 1944 Folder, Capa Papers.
33. "Beachheads of Normandy," *Life*, June 19, 1943; Whelan, *Capa*, 213–14; Kershaw, *Blood and Champagne*, 129–30. Editors of other magazines were quick to congratulate Capa for taking the "great Invasion pictures." See Hopkinson to Capa, June 22, 1944, Correspondence Folder, Capa Papers.

CHAPTER 15

1. Pyle, *Brave Men*, 384–91; Pyle to wife, 1 July 1944, Pyle MSS. For the scenes on Omaha, see also, Hamill, *Liebling*, 487–90; Buell, *We Were There*, 14–15, 128–30.
2. Pyle to wife, June 15, 1944, Pyle MSS; Pyle, *Brave Men*, 381; Tobin, *Pyle's War*, 173–79.
3. Pyle to wife, July 1, 1944, Pyle MSS; Hansen, War Diary, June 9, 1944, box 4, Hansen Papers.
4. Stoneman, "New Yank Troops Perform like Veterans in Normandy," and, "Beachhead Too Big for 10-Hour Tour," *Chicago Daily News*, June 13 and 16, 1944.
5. COMNAVEU to SHAEF, June 13, 1944, Chief of Staff, SGS, DF 000.7, box 2, RG331; Casey, "Writer in Good Company On a Visit to Normandy," *Chicago Daily News*, June 19, 1944.
6. Hansen, War Diary, June 13 and 17, 1944, box 4, Hansen Papers; Vulliamy, "Colonel Dupuy's Report on Press Communications," July 8, 1944, Chief of Staff, SGS, DF 000.7/4, box 3, RG331.
7. Hamill, *Liebling*, 874–75; Oldfield, *Never a Shot*, 86–87.
8. Pyle to wife, July 1 and 4, 1944, Pyle MSS.
9. Dupuy, "Investigation of the System of Press Coverage and Communications," July 5, 1944, Chief of Staff, SGS, DF 000.7/4, box 3, RG331; Thompson, "Yanks Chuckle at Claim News Favors Them," *Chicago Tribune*, July 4, 1944.
10. Whitehead, letter, February 12, 1974, WWII Book Project Folder, AP28, Writings about the AP, Series II, box 14, APCA; Stratton, "War Coverage at Peak in Northern France," *E&P*, August 19, 1944.
11. "Four Invasion Writers Figure in the News," *E&P*, July 8, 1944.
12. Thompson, "How Americans Pushed Thru Foe into St. Sauveur," *Chicago Tribune*, June 17, 1944; Stoneman, "Only Rubble Remains of St. Sauveur," *Chicago Daily News*, June 17, 1944.
13. Beattie, *Passport to War*, 236–54; Middleton, *Our Share*, 75–89; Stoneman, "Blitz in Reverse," *Chicago Daily News*, June 19, 1944.
14. Pyle, *Brave Men*, 402–3; Harrison, *Cross-Channel Attack*, 422–23; Atkinson, *Guns at Last Light*, 113–16.
15. Pyle, *Brave Men*, 422.
16. Harrison, *Cross-Channel Attack*, 429; Atkinson, *Guns at Last Light*, 116–17; Stoneman, "Last Big Push for Cherbourg," *Chicago Daily News*, June 23, 1944.
17. Stoneman, "New Blitz by Yanks," *Chicago Daily News*, June 24, 1944.
18. Thompson, "Germans Order Fight to Death for Cherbourg," *Chicago Tribune*, June 24, 1944.
19. Wertenbaker, *Invasion*, 148–49.
20. Pyle, *Brave Men*, 424–32.
21. Atkinson, *Guns at Last Light*, 120.
22. O'Reilly, "Newsmen Had Choice Seats at Cherbourg," *E&P*, July 15, 1944; Thor Smith to MBS, July 5, 1944, box 3, Thor Smith Papers.

23. An exception was the short article by Stoneman, "Carloads of Good Food and Liquor Abandoned by Nazis," *Boston Globe*, June 28, 1944.
24. Pyle, "With Bert Brandt," and, "'With Guns in Their Hands Sneaking Up a Death-Laden City," and, "Waiting Snipers Ambush in Doorways," *Washington Daily News*, June 27, July 13 and 14, 1944.
25. Redding, "False Date Lines," July 5, 1944, Twelfth Army Group, Stories and Press Releases, box 5, Redding Papers.
26. Krum to Childers, November 2, 1942, Military, 1942–44, box 7, Redding Papers.
27. Redding, "False Date Lines," July 5, 1944, Twelfth Army Group, Stories and Press Releases, box 5, Redding Papers.
28. Hansen, War Diary, July 3, 1944, box 4, Hansen Papers; Pyle to wife, July 1 and 4, 1944, Pyle MSS.
29. Sorrells to Editors, June 20, 1944, City File-NY-Sorrells, box 202, Howard Papers; Pyle to wife, July 1 and 4, 1944, Pyle MSS.
30. Stoneman, "Lush Normandy a Fine Place to Fight War, Writer Finds," *Chicago Daily News*, June 24, 1944.
31. Doubler, *Closing with the Enemy*, 34.
32. Tobin, *Pyle's War*, 185; Pyle, *Brave Men*, 397.
33. Gay, *Assignment*, 297.
34. Doubler, *Closing with the Enemy*, 60–61, 242–43; Blumenson, *Breakout and Pursuit*, 175; Barker to Chief of Staff, "Release of Casualty Figures," September 7, 1944; Boehnke, "Casualty Reports," June 28, 1944, both in SHAEF General Staff, G-1 Administrative Section, DF 704, Entry 6, box 34, RG331. For the media's intermittent interest in such casualties, see Huebner, *Warrior Image*, 32–37.
35. Wolfert, "Battle Hazards at St. Lo," *Boston Globe*, July 14, 1944.
36. Thompson, "Yanks Push on along 25 Mile Normandy Line," *Chicago Tribune*, July 11, 1944; Denny, "US Planes and Guns Hammer Foe into Grogginess on Hill Near St. Lo," *New York Times*, July 12, 1944. On the darker comments circulating around the Vouilly press camp, see Twelfth Army Group, "History of Public Relations Office," 10, undated, Military File, box 5, Redding Papers.
37. "OWI and Government Information Policy," May 31, 1944, Entry 106, box 1025, RG44.
38. Thor Smith to MBS, July 5, 1944, box 3, Thor Smith Papers.
39. See, for instance, Noderer, "Normans Wait to See if Yanks Will Ring True," *Chicago Tribune*, June 25, 1944.
40. Dupuy to Bedell Smith, "Unfriendly Gestures by French Population," July 7, 1944, Policy re Release of Information to the Press, Chief of Staff, SGS, DF 000.7, box 2, RG331; SHAEF War Diary, July 9, Allied Command: SHAEF Sub-Series, box 29, BS: WWII.
41. Boyle, "Children of French Village Honor Liberators on Fourth," *Baltimore Sun*, July 5, 1944.
42. SHAEF PRO to Surles, July 29, 1944, Policy re Release of Information to the Press, Chief of Staff, SGS, DF 000.7, box 2, RG331.
43. Boyle, "Major's Body Borne in State through St. Lo," *Baltimore Sun*, July 19, 1944. For Boyle's postwar recollections, see Buell, *We Were There*, 156; Gay, *Assignment*, 305–6.
44. Hamill, *Liebling*, 510.
45. Atkinson, *Guns at Last Light*, 129.
46. Dupuy to Bedell Smith, "Press Relations," July 20, 1944, Policy re Release of Information to the Press, Chief of Staff, SGS, DF 000.7, box 2, RG331; Parsons,

"Allies in France Bogged Down on Entire Front," *New York Herald Tribune*, July 23, 1944. Atkinson, *Guns at Last Light*, 136–38.

47. Davis, *Spaatz*, 464–65; Atkinson, *Guns at Last Light*, 139–40.
48. Hansen, War Diary, July 3, 1944, box 4, Hansen Papers.
49. Hamill, *Liebling*, 885; Whitehead, "Most Decisive Battle of War in Europe," *Baltimore Sun*, July 19, 1964; Casey Diary, July 20, 1944, Works Series, box 9, Casey Papers; "Battle of France: Bradley Breaks Loose," *Time*, August 14, 1944.

CHAPTER 16

1. Thompson, "Yanks and British Gain in Big Attacks in Normandy," *Chicago Tribune*, July 26, 1944; Atkinson, *Guns at Last Light*, 142.
2. Denny, "Germans Shaken by Big Air Blow," *New York Times*, July 26, 1944.
3. Dupuy to Bedell Smith, undated, and, Bull to Bedell Smith, "Travel of Accredited War Correspondents," July 24, 1944, both in Press Correspondents File, SHAEF, 000.74, box 4, RG331; Middleton, *Last July*, 117–28.
4. Denny, "Germans 'Crust' Cracked at Last," *New York Times*, July 27, 1944.
5. Denny, "Foe Reels before Blitzkrieg Mightier Than His in 1940," *New York Times*, July 28, 1944.
6. Middleton, "US Might Strikes Awe in Normandy," *New York Times*, July 28, 1944; Sulzberger to Middleton, July 28, 1944, Middleton Folder, box 51, NYT: AHS.
7. Pyle to wife, July 16 and August 9, 1944, Pyle MSS.
8. Pyle, "Ernie Came Thru Safely," *Washington Daily News*, August 8, 1944; Pyle, *Brave Men*, 460–63.
9. "AP Man Killed at St. Lo 18th US Press Casualty," *E&P*, July 29, 1944.
10. Atkinson, *Guns at Last Light*, 142–43.
11. Hansen, War Diary, July 25, 1944, box 4, Hansen Papers; Patton Diary, July 29, 1944, box 3, Patton Papers; "Bombing of Troops in Error Explained," *New York Times*, July 28, 1944; Westlake to Boyd, WARX-71643, July 27, 1944, BPR File 000.7, Entry 499, box 36, RG165
12. Marshall, WARX-17749, April 2, 1944, BPR File, 000.7, box 33, RG165.
13. Marshall to Eisenhower, W-71972, July 28, 1944, Policy re Release of Information to the Press, Chief of Staff, SGS, DF 000.7, box 2, RG331; "Bombing of Troops in Error Explained," *New York Times*, July 28, 1944.
14. Stoneman, "Yank Bombing Our Own Troops 'One of Those Things,'" *Chicago Daily News*, July 28, 1944; Oldfield, *Never a Shot*, 50; SHAEF to War Department, S-58530, August 27, 1944, BPR File, 000.7, box 37, RG165.
15. Eisenhower to Marshall, S-56316, July 27, 1944, Policy re Release of Information to the Press, Chief of Staff, SGS, DF 000.7, box 2, RG331.
16. Westlake to Boyd and Nuckols, July 27, 1944, BPR File, 000.7, box 36, RG165.
17. Craven and Cate, *Army Air Forces*, 3:547–48.
18. SHAEF to War Department, S-58530, August 27, 1944, BPR File, 000.7, box 37, RG165.
19. Dupuy, "Investigation of the System of Press Coverage and Communications," July 5, 1944, Chief of Staff, SGS, DF 000.7/4, box 3, RG331; AP, "Three War Reporters Ousted by Ninth Air Force in France," *Christian Science Monitor*, August 22, 1944; Graham, "9th Air Force Ousts 4 of Press," *New York Times*, August 22, 1944; Hansen, War Diary, July 25, 1944, box 4, Hansen Papers.
20. AP, "Three War Reporters Ousted by Ninth Air Force in France," *Christian Science Monitor*, August 22, 1944; Graham, "9th Air Force Ousts 4 of Press," *New York*

Times, August 22, 1944; SHAEF to War Department, S-58530, August 27, 1944, BPR File, 000.7, box 37, RG165.

21. Holt, "Arbitrary Recall of Four Correspondents is Protested," *Boston Globe*, August 22, 1944.
22. "Press Agents' War," *Time*, September 4, 1944; AP, "Three War Reporters Ousted by Ninth Air Force in France," *Christian Science Monitor*, August 22, 1944; Graham, "9th Air Force Ousts 4 of Press," *New York Times*, August 22, 1944.
23. "McCardell's Record," and, "Mr Lee McCardell," *Baltimore Sun*, August 22 and 23, 1944.
24. "US Demands Data on '9th' and Press," *New York Times*, August 23, 1944; Surles to SHAEF, August 22, 1944, BPR File, 000.7, box 37, RG165.
25. Spaatz to Surles, August 18, 1944, EX-43889, August 18, 1944, box 35, and, SHAEF to War Department, box 37, both in BPR File, 000.7, RG165; "Change," *Time*, September 18, 1944.
26. Giles to Spaatz, WAR-4206, May 26, 1944, and, Arnold to all Commanding Generals, WARX-39930, May 22, 1944, and, Spaatz to Arnold, U-66608, August 18, 1944, all in BPR File, 000.7, box 35, RG165; Davis, *Spaatz*, 523–24.
27. D'Este, *Patton*, 566–71, 593; Patton Diary, June 6, 1944, box 3, Patton Papers.
28. Marshall to Eisenhower, W-29722, April 29, 1944, Eyes Only Cables, Allied Command: SHAEF Sub-Series, box 27, BS: WWII; Patton Diary, April 26, 30, and May 1, 1944, box 3, Patton Papers; D'Este, *Patton*, 585–91.
29. Gay Diary, July 16, 1944, box 2, Gay Papers; Twelfth Army Group, "History of Public Relations Office," 11, undated, box 5, Redding Papers. For the list of reporters at Third Army's HQ on July 17, see Annex, "Signatures of Correspondents," Subject File: Press, box 53, Patton Papers, although four were missing on this occasion.
30. "Report Incident to Briefing of Newspaper Correspondents," July 18, 1944, Subject File: Press, box 53, Patton Papers; D'Este, *Patton*, 591.
31. Patton Diary, July 17, 1944, box 3, and, "Notes on Meeting between General Patton and the Correspondents, Including the P&PW Officer at 2200," July 17, 1944, Subject File: Press, box 53, both in Patton Papers. Emphasis in the original.
32. Bradley and Blair, *General's Life*, 285.
33. Gay Diary, August 7, 1944, box 2, Gay Papers.
34. "General Bradley: Opportunity Found Him Prepared to Grasp It," *Baltimore Sun*, August 7, 1944; AP, "Yanks' French Pace Sets New Record," *Los Angeles Times*, August 3, 1944.
35. D'Este, *Patton*, 626; Codman, *Drive*, 158–59.
36. Gay Diary, August 15, 1944, box 2, Gay Papers; Patton Diary, August 14, 1944, box 3, Patton Papers.
37. D'Este, *Patton*, 626.
38. AP, "Yanks' French Pace Sets New Record," *Los Angeles Times*, August 3, 1944.
39. Boyle, AP Dispatch, August 12, 1944, Speeches and Writings File, box 2, Boyle Papers.
40. "Newsmen 'Riding High' with Liberation Army," *E&P*, August 12, 1944.
41. "Death and Injury Strike Correspondents in France," *E&P*, August 26, 1944.
42. Pyle to wife, August 9, 1944, Pyle MSS.; Miller, *Story*, 342; "Newsmen 'Riding High' with Liberation Army," *E&P*, August 12, 1944; "Hemingway 'Captures' 6," *New York Times*, August 4, 1944.
43. Pyle to wife, August 9, 1944, Pyle MSS.

44. Capa to Cornell and Julia Friedman, July 19, 1944, and, Capa to Cornell and Edith Friedman, undated [July 1944], both in Correspondence 1944 Folder, Capa Papers.
45. Baker, *Hemingway: Letters*, 560; Baker, *Hemingway*, 600–601.
46. Longwell to Billings, August 7, 1944, Time-Life-Fortune Papers, box 1, Billings Papers.
47. "Newsmen Celebrate 'Side-Door' Invasion," *E&P*, August 19, 1944; Pyle to wife, August 9, 1944, Pyle MSS.
48. SHAEF Forward to 21 Army Group, FWD-12748, August 10, 1944, Policy re Release of Information to the Press, Chief of Staff, SGS, DF 000.7, box 2, RG331.
49. Hansen, War Diary, August 14, 1944, box 4, Hansen Papers.
50. Daniel, "Drive to Alencon," and, "Two Armies on Run," *New York Times*, August 12 and 14, 1944; Stoneman, "News of War Held Too Hot to Be Bared," *Chicago Daily News*, August 12, 1944; "Newsmen Celebrate 'Side-Door' Invasion," *E&P*, August 19, 1944; Censorship Guidance, August 15, 1944, Twelfth Army Group HQ: Publicity and Psychological Warfare Section, Entry 194-A. box 4, RG331.
51. Daniel, "Falaise Gap Is Cut," and, Denny, "Norman Trap Lines 1,000 Miles of Ruin," *New York Times*, August 16, 1944.
52. On the battle, see Atkinson, *Guns at Last Light*, 199. On Sevareid's experience, see Sevareid, *No So Wild*, 430–33. On the transmission problems and their solution, see Caserta to War Department, FX-84884, August 19, 1944, and, CG Rome Area Command to War Department, 4611, August 18, 1944, both in BPR File, 000.7, box 37, RG165; "Radio On-the-Spot Coverage Long Stride Forward," *Broadcasting*, August 28, 1944.
53. "Newsmen Celebrate 'Side-Door' Invasion," *E&P*, August 19, 1944.
54. Bigart, "Indian Style of Warfare Used by Americans Storming Levant," and, "Ration Trucks Outstripped by US Advance," *New York Herald Tribune*, August 17 and 22, 1944.
55. AP, "Patton the Third Army Chief," *New York Times*, August 16, 1944.
56. Smith to MBS, June 16, 1944, box 3, Thor Smith Papers; Memo to Chief of Staff, "Report on Recent Erroneous News Stories on Ground Forces Command," August 18, 1944, Erroneous New Stories File, Chief of Staff, SGS, DF 000.73/5, box 4, RG331.
57. Memo to Chief of Staff, "Report on Recent Erroneous News Stories on Ground Forces Command," August 18, 1944, Erroneous New Stories File, Chief of Staff, SGS, DF 000.73/5, box 4, RG331.
58. Gallagher, "Bradley Heads Army Group," *Stars and Stripes*, August 16, 1944; Surles to Eisenhower, WAR 89064, August 30, 1944, BPR File, 000.7, box 37, RG165.
59. "Transcript of Briefing by Colonel Dupuy," August 15, 1944, Erroneous New Stories File, Chief of Staff, SGS, DF 000.73/5, box 4, RG331; Eisenhower to Marshall, August 19, 1944, Cables Off, Principal File: Subject Series, box 133, EPPP. Eisenhower intended to make the change that Gallagher reported in early September. See Pogue, *Supreme Command*, 261–64.
60. Hansen, War Diary, August 18, 1944, box 4, Hansen Papers.

CHAPTER 17

1. Smith to MBS, August 25, 1944, box 3, Thor Smith Papers.
2. Collingwood, "French Armored Division Sent into Paris by Bradley," *New York Times*, August 24, 1944.

3. "Press 'Frees' Paris, Scores Two-Day Beat," *E&P*, September 2, 1944; "Collingwood Report of Paris Liberation Brings Confusion," *Broadcasting*, August 28, 1944.
4. Quirk to wife, August 23–24, World War II Folder, box 1, Quirk Papers; Oldfield, *Never a Shot*, 107, 109.
5. Boyle, "Lightning Front," *AP Inter-Office*, August-September 1944.
6. "Paris Extra," *F.Y.I.*, August 28, 1944, Capa Papers.
7. Boyle, "Lightning Front," *AP Inter-Office*, August-September 1944.
8. Whitehead, "Paris Laughs, Cheers, and Cries as Allies Enter," *Baltimore Sun*, August 26, 1944.
9. Boyle, "Lightning Front," *AP Inter-Office*, August-September 1944; Bentel, "Six Newsmen Suspended in Paris by Army Censors," *E&P*, September 2, 1944.
10. Atkinson, *Guns at Last Light*, 176–80; Smith to MBS, August 25, 1944, box 3, Thor Smith Papers.
11. Oldfield, *Never a Shot*, 110–11; Thompson, "Token Battle Loses City, but Honor is Saved," *Chicago Tribune*, August 27, 1944.
12. Moynihan, *War Correspondent*, 75; Tobin, *Pyle's War*, 201.
13. Cronkite to Betsy, June 12, 1944, box 2.325/L32, Cronkite Papers.
14. Dupuy to Chief of Staff, "Violation of Regulations by War Correspondents," September 4, 1944, Press Correspondents File, Chief of Staff, SGS, DF 000.74, box 4, RG331; McGincy, "Inside Paris! Fights Rage, Songs Ring Out," *Chicago Daily News*, August 25, 1944.
15. Twelfth Army Group, "History of Public Relations Office," 9, undated, box 5, Redding Papers.
16. Redding, "Paris," 16–17, Manuscript for Publicity Book (Paris-Loire-Bulge), box 57, Redding Papers; Dupuy to Chief of Staff, "Violation of Regulations by War Correspondents," September 4, 1944, and, Eisenhower, "Violation of Regulations," undated, both in Press Correspondents File, Chief of Staff, SGS, DF 000.74, box 4, RG331; Bentel, "War News Tied Up, so Newsmen Make Some," *E&P*, September 9, 1944. Three British correspondents who used this radio were also suspended.
17. Beevor and Cooper, *Paris after the Liberation*, 52–57.
18. Redding to Neville, July 11, 1944, Twelfth Army Group, Stories and Press Releases, box 5, Redding Papers; Sorel, *Women Who Wrote*, 219, 225, 242.
19. Peake to US PO, July 7, 1944, Dupuy to Chief of Staff, July 8, 1944, and, F.T. to Smith, July 9, 1944, and, Strong to Chief of Staff, July 11, 1944, and, Grasett to ACOS G-2, July 11, 1944, all in Press Correspondents File, Chief of Staff, SGS, DF 000.74, box 4, RG331; Kasper, Kirkpatrick Interview, April 4, 1990.
20. "Sleep Knits Up Yank Frayed Nerves," and, "Rennes Wild with Joy at Yank Victory," *Chicago Daily News*, August 18 and 5, 1944.
21. Kasper, Kirkpatrick Interview, April 4, 1990; Sorel, *Women Who Wrote*, 256–57; Kirkpatrick, "On-Spot Story," *Chicago Daily News*, August 28, 1944.
22. Censorship Guidance, August 25, 1944, Twelfth Army Group HQ: Publicity and Psychological Warfare Section, Entry 194-A, box 4, RG331; Kirkpatrick, "On-Spot Story," *Chicago Daily News*, August 28, 1944.
23. Kirkpatrick, "Daily News Reopens Its Paris Office," *Chicago Daily News*, August 29, 1944.
24. Dupuy to Chief of Staff, "Visit to Paris," September 16, 1944, Press Coverage and Communications File, Chief of Staff, SGS, DF 000.7/4, box 3, RG331.
25. Smith to MBS, August 28, 1944, Correspondence Folder, box 3, Thor Smith Papers.

26. Whitehead, "Mantle of Quiet Rests on Paris as Battle Ends," *Los Angeles Times*, August 27, 1944.
27. Paris cable ex-Walton, September 4, 1944, Correspondence 1944 Folder, Capa Papers.
28. Campbell to Merrick, September 16, 1944, Papers on Organization of Detachment, Folder 6, PRD: Press Censorship Branch, Subject File, Entry 86, box 47, RG331.
29. Brown, "Press Communications—Paris," undated, and, Lee to SHAEF FWD, J-13889, September 2, 1944, and, SHAEF to Agwar, S-63304, October 21, 1944, and, Butcher to Allen, February 2, 1945, all in Press Coverage and Communications File, Chief of Staff, SGS, DF 000.7/4, box 3, RG331.
30. Pogue, *Pogue's War*, 201; Moynihan, *War Correspondent*, 78.
31. Stone to Cowan, August 28, 1944, Pyle Correspondence, box 9, Stone Papers.
32. Tobin, *Pyle's War*, 201; Bentel, "So You Just Sit and Look at Ernie Pyle," *E&P*, September 23, 1944.
33. Pyle to wife, August 24, 1944, Pyle MSS. Pyle's editors were also sad to see him go. They believed that his August 1944 columns had "probably been the greatest of all," fully "worth all that Ernie has cost us in money, management, and trouble." See Hawkins to Howard, August 14, 1944, City File-NY-Hawkins, box 201, Howard Papers.
34. Whitehead, "Joyous Belgians Greet Americans," *Baltimore Sun*, September 3, 1944.
35. Whitehead, "World War I Long Toms First Fire on Reich," and, "Fleeing Nazis Spoil Day for Yanks Seeking Fight," *Los Angeles Times*, September 11 and 14, 1944.
36. Thompson, "Break Siegfried Line," and, "103 Days Prove Yank Is Nazi's Master in War," *Chicago Tribune*, September 16 and 24, 1944.
37. OWI, "Current Opinions," December 8, 1944, Entry 149, box 1719 RG44. "Paris," *Life*, September 4, 1944; "Ready for V-Day?" *Time*, September 4, 1944.
38. Atkinson, *Guns at Last Light*, 264.
39. Murrow, "Paratroopers attack Holland," September 17, 1944, Call: RWB 2859-60 B2, NBC Radio Archives.
40. Cronkite, *Reporter's Life*, 109–12; Brinkley, *Cronkite*, 118–19.
41. MacDonald, *Siegfried Line Campaign*, 143–54.
42. Cronkite to Betsy, October 9, 1944, box 2.325/L32, Cronkite Papers; Cronkite, "Sky Troops Fight as They Hit Earth," *New York Times*, September 18, 1944.
43. Ryan, *Bridge Too Far*, 216n, 541n.
44. Middleton, "Allies Hit at Wing," and, Daniel, "Rescuers Slowed," *New York Times*, September 20 and 23, 1944. Ryan, *Bridge Too Far*, 540–41; Pogue, *Supreme Command*, 286.
45. SCAEF to Allen, FWD-15792, September 26, 1944, Policy re Release of Information to the Press, Chief of Staff, SGS, DF 000.7, box 2, RG331; Censorship Guidance, September 27, 1944, Twelfth Army Group HQ: Publicity and Psychological Warfare Section, Entry 194-A, box 4, RG331.
46. AP, "Allies, However, Still Are Pushing to Relieve Men in Trap"; AP, "Survivor of Nine-Day Struggle Reach South Bank of Lower Rhine," *Chicago Daily News*, September 26 and 27, 1944.
47. BPR, "Radio Digest," September 25, 1944, Entry 497, box 4, RG165; Daniel, "Our Men Triumph," *New York Times*, October 4, 1944.
48. Shepley to McConaughy, "Communiqués (Army Angles)," March 26, 1943, folder 59, Times Dispatches. On Surles' career, see McCloy to Stimson, August 1, 1941, BPR Folder, Stimson "Safe File," Entry 99, box 11, RG107.
49. Surles to Eisenhower, October 4, 1944, Surles Folder, box 113, EPPP.

50. Casey, "Burchett," 532; Pinkley to Eisenhower, May 16, 1945, Correspondence File, box 4, Butcher Papers, Eisenhower Library.
51. Eisenhower to Surles, September 6, 1944, Surles Folder, box 113, EPPP; BD Diary, September 12, 1944, XIII:1697, box 169.
52. Ball, "Men, Mud, Machines," *AP Inter-Office*, October–November 1944; "Transcript of Conference between Patton and Third Army Correspondents," September 7, 1944, Subject File: Press, box 53, Patton Papers.
53. Twelfth Army Group, "History of Public Relations Office," 32, undated, box 5, Redding Papers; Censorship Guidance, September 27, 1944, Twelfth Army Group HQ: Publicity and Psychological Warfare Section, Entry 194-A. box 4, RG331.
54. Daniel, "Rescuers Slowed," and, "Patrols in Contact," *New York Times*, September 23 and 24, 1944.
55. Hansen, War Diary, August 26, 1944, box 4, Hansen Papers; UP, "Liberation of Paris Credited to First Army," *New York Herald Tribune*, August 28, 1944.
56. Bedell Smith to Dupuy, September 6, 1944, and, Butcher to Andrews, September 7, 1944, both in Policy re Release of Information to the Press, Chief of Staff, SGS, DF 000.7, box 2, RG331.
57. Atkinson, *Guns at Last Light*, 310–11; Sylvan, Personal Diary, September 15, 16, 18, 22, October 1, 4, 1944, box 1, Sylvan Papers; Thompson, "Hodges of the First," *Chicago Tribune*, December 3, 1944.
58. Allen to Surles, October 14 and 18, 1944, Policy re Release of Information to the Press, Chief of Staff, SGS, DF 000.7, box 2, RG331; Twelfth Army Group, "History of Public Relations Office," 18, undated, box 5, Redding Papers.
59. "Stoneman Hits Over-Optimism in War News," *E&P*, January 12, 1945.
60. Stoneman, "Germans Fight Furiously to Hurl 1st Army Back over West Wall," and, "Mighty German Artillery Attacks Hold Up 1st Army Advance," and, "Bad Weather Stalls Yanks' Rhine Drive," *Chicago Daily News*, September 18, 19, and 26, 1944.
61. Middleton, *Our Share*, 338–40; Middleton, *Last July*, 138.
62. Middleton, "German Stand on the Rhine through Winter Likely," *New York Times*, September 27, 1944.
63. Middleton, "Last Kilometer," 402.
64. Middleton, *Last July*, 142.
65. Middleton, "Hodge Takes City," *New York Times*, October 21, 1944.
66. Stoneman, "Yanks Holding One Third of Aachen," *Chicago Daily News*, October 18, 1944.
67. Middleton, "Hodges Takes City," *New York Times*, October 21, 1944.
68. Middleton, *Our Share*, 359; Middleton, *Last July*, 143.
69. "Front-Line Writers Get Clearer Picture of War," *E&P*, December 16, 1944; Thompson to McCormick, November 17, 1944, Thompson Folder, McCormick: Foreign Correspondents—I-62, box 11, CTCA.
70. "Whitehead 'Uncorks' Claim to Purple Heart," *E&P*, November 6, 1944.

CHAPTER 18

1. Hansen, War Diary, August 29, 1944, box 4, Hansen Papers.
2. Phillips, Memo to Chief of Staff, December 2, 1943, and, Phillips to Surles, December 21, 1943, both in BPR File, 000.7, box 35, RG165; Kennedy to Kenper, November 16, 1943, box 1, Kennedy Papers.
3. Astley to PRO, AFHQ, May 12, 1944, Scott-Bailey to McChystal, May 15, 1944, and, Tupper to Surles, May 21, 1944, all in BPR File, 000.7, box 35, RG165. The

charge that Kennedy had broken a strict news embargo in May 1944 is difficult to verify, and, although this allegation is made in these War Department files, the military took no action against Kennedy.

4. Cochran, *Kennedy's War*, 130–31, 138–39; Hawkins, "Newsmen Are Wildly Greeted on 200-Mile Maquis Journey," *Atlanta Constitution*, August 27, 1944; "Diary of the War," *Baltimore Sun*, August 27, 1944.
5. AP, WD1003AEW, September 8, 1944; Surles to Miller, September 15, box 1, Kennedy Papers.
6. Kennedy to Cooper, October 11, 1944, box 1, Kennedy Papers; Euson, excerpt from letter, March 11, 1975, Series II-WWII Book Projects, Eunson Folder, AP28, box 14, APCA; Cochran, *Kennedy's War*, 142.
7. Oldfield, *Never a Shot*, 151.
8. Oldfield, *Never a Shot*, 144–45, 149–50, 156.
9. "November Offensive: Monty's View," 40-B, Bradley Commentaries, 1956–51, box 42, Hansen Papers; MacDonald, *Siegfried Line*, 390–91.
10. Tupper to Allen, B-20021, November 19, 1944, Policy re Release of Information to the Press, Chief of Staff, SGS, DF 000.7, box 2, RG331.
11. Gallagher, "Eyewitness Story of Attack," *Chicago Tribune*, November 17, 1944.
12. Cochran, *Kennedy's War*, 141; Kennedy to Kenper, January 8, 1944, box 1, Kennedy Papers.
13. Twelfth Army Group, "History of Public Relations Office," 34, undated, box 5, Redding Papers, Truman Library.
14. "Bradley Errs in Failing to Establish Group Press Camp," S-29, Bradley Commentaries, 1956–51, box 42, Hansen Papers.
15. "Bradley Confesses Error on Failure to Establish Press Camp," 21-B, and, "SHAEF Briefings Bad," S-27, both in Bradley Commentaries, 1956–51, box 42, Hansen Papers; Twelfth Army Group, "History of Public Relations Office," 34, undated, box 5, Redding Papers.
16. Gallagher, "Nazis Waging Stand-and-Die War in West," *Washington Post*, November 20, 1944.
17. Gallagher, "Trained Troops Shortages Irks US Generals," *Los Angeles Times*, December 16, 1944.
18. "Teletype Conference between Surles et al and Barker," December 19, 1944, BPR File, 000.7, box 35, RG165.
19. Bell, *Line of Fire*, 113.
20. Cole, *The Ardennes*, 17–18; Parker, *Battle of the Bulge*, 45–56; Vogel, "German and Allied Conduct of the War in the West," 678–83.
21. Gallagher, "Reporting on the Run!" *AP Inter-Office*, January-February 1945.
22. Strand, "Ace Divisions Decide Issue in Battle of Bulge," *Chicago Tribune*, February 14, 1945.
23. Gallagher, "Yanks at Monschau Stop Panzers' Charge," *Boston Globe*, December 20, 1944.
24. "How Newsmen Faced Nazi Breakthrough," *E&P*, January 6, 1945; Atkinson, *Guns at Last Light*, 440; Carpenter, "The Ardennes," 333.
25. "How Newsmen Faced Nazi Breakthrough," *E&P*, January 6, 1945; Atkinson, *Guns at Last Light*, 440–42; Sylvan, Personal Diary, December 18 and 19, 1944, box 1, Sylvan Papers; Redding, "Bulge," 6, Manuscript for Publicity Book (Paris-Loire-Bulge), box 57, Redding Papers.
26. Censorship Guidance, December 22, 1944, Twelfth Army Group HQ: Publicity and Psychological Warfare Section, Entry 194-A. box 4, RG331.

27. "Newsmen Flare Up at Army Blackout," *E&P*, December 23, 1944.
28. SHAEF, Conference Notes, December 18 and 19, 1944, PRD: Executive Branch, Entry 83, box 25, RG331.
29. "Newsmen Flare Up at Army Blackout," *E&P*, December 23, 1944; SHAEF, Conference Notes, December 19, 1944, PRD: Executive Branch, Entry 83, box 25, RG331.
30. McClincy, "Allies Setback Worst since Stalingrad Days," *Chicago Daily News*, December 22, 1944; "60-Mile Gap Torn in Lines, Nazis Say," *New York Times*, December 22, 1944.
31. *Congressional Record*, 1945, 91, pt.10:A336; OWI Correspondence Panels Section to Foster, "Increasing Public Concern about International Affairs," January 23, 1945, Entry 149, box 1709, RG 44; Price, undated, Censorship Folder, box 25, Early Papers.
32. Lockett to Welch, "Army's News Policy," December 21, 1944, Folder 236, Time Dispatches.
33. Lockett to Welch, "Army's News Policy," December 21, 1944, Folder 236, Time Dispatches.
34. "The Old Army Game," *Time*, January 1, 1945.
35. SHAEF, Conference Guidance, December 20, 1944, Folder 15, PRD: Press Censorship Branch, Subject File, Entry 86, box 47, RG331.
36. Allen to Neville, S-71933, December 21, 1944, and, P & PW to Ninth and First Army, PPW-66, December 23, 1944, both in Policy re Release of Information to the Press, Chief of Staff, SGS, DF 000.7, box 2, RG331; SHAEF, Conference Notes, December 20, 1944, PRD: Executive Branch, Entry 83, box 25, RG331.
37. "How Newsmen Faced Nazi Breakthrough," *E&P*, January 6, 1945; Gallagher, "Reporting on the Run!" *AP Inter-Office*, January-February 1945.
38. Gallagher, "Yanks at Monschau Stop Panzers' Charge," *Boston Globe*, December 20, 1944; Gallagher, "Americans Taking, Receiving Biggest Loss," *New York Times*, December 21, 1944; Gallagher, "Prisoners Few, and GIs Aren't Surrendering," *Washington Post*, December 23, 1944.
39. Boyle, *Help, Help!* 71; Boyle, "Disarmed Yanks Are Massacred by Tank Force," *Buffalo Evening News*, December 18, 1944.
40. Sylvan, Personal Diary, December 17, 1944, box 1, Sylvan Papers.
41. Bell, *Line of Fire*, 114–39.
42. McManus, *Alamo*.
43. Capa to Hulburd for Hicks, December 9, 1944, Capa Papers; Capa, *Slightly*, 208–11.
44. Cole, *Ardennes*, 524; Wellard, *Man in a Helmet*, 131.
45. "How Newsmen Faced Nazi Breakthrough," *E&P*, January 6, 1945; MacKenzie, "MacKenzie with Buffalo Colonel during Battle," and, "101st Air-Borne had One Order, 'Hold Bastogne,'" *Buffalo Evening News*, December 30, 1944, and January 2, 1945; MacKenzie, *Men of Bastogne*, vii–viii; 174–77.
46. Bell, *Line of Fire*, 135–40.
47. Bell, "Yanks Bounce Back, Hold All Cards Again," and, "Tankmen Choose Bastogne for Their Own Hit Parade," *Chicago Daily News*, December 29, 1945, and January 4, 1945.
48. "Allies Squeeze the German Bulge," *Life*, January 15, 1945.
49. How Newsmen Faced Nazi Breakthrough," *E&P*, January 6, 1945; MacKenzie, "MacKenzie with Buffalo Colonel during Battle," and, "101st Air-Borne had One Order, 'Hold Bastogne,'" *Buffalo Evening News*, December 30, 1944, and January 2, 1945.

50. AP, "'Nuts!' Retort by McAuliffe," *New York Times*, December 30, 1944.
51. Patton Diary, December 30, 1944, box 3, and, "Conference between Patton and Third Army Correspondents," January 1, 1945, Subject File: Press, box 53, both in Patton Papers.
52. Atkinson, *Guns at Last Light*, 308; Hansen War Diary, January 1, 1945, box 4, Hansen Papers.
53. Ferrell, *Eisenhower Diaries*, 131; Atkinson, *Guns at Last Light*, 448.
54. Allen to Chief of Staff, "Announcement of Change of Command," January 6, 1945, Policy and Infractions of Censorship File, Chief of Staff, SGS, DF 000.73, box 4, RG331; "Estimate of the Situation," *Time*, January 8, 1945.
55. Gallagher, "Teamwork, Yank Skill Credited by Montgomery for Nazi Halt," *Washington Post*, January 8, 1945; Hamilton, *Field Marshal*, 294–306.
56. Hansen War Diary, January 8 and 9, 1945, box 4, Hansen Papers; "Our Risk May Win, Bradley Declares," *New York Times*, January 10, 1945.
57. Gallagher, "Teamwork, Yank Skill Credited by Montgomery for Nazi Halt," *Washington Post*, January 8, 1945.
58. Gallagher, "Called 'Rest Sector'," and, "Who Let Nazis Thru?" *Chicago Tribune*, December 28, 1944, and January 7, 1945. For Middleton's private views, see Stowe, Notebook, December 21, 1944, box 40, Stowe Papers.
59. Pratt, "Bulge Fight Not Victory but 'Repair Job,'" *Boston Globe*, January 14, 1945.
60. Kennedy to Kenper, January 8 and 9, 1944, and, Kenper to Kennedy, January 9, 1945, both in box 1, Kennedy Papers.

CHAPTER 19

1. Pogue, *Supreme Command*, 391–92.
2. For details on the complexities surrounding these decisions, see Colley, *Blood for Dignity*, 44–51; Johnson, "Black Soldiers," 16–19; MacGregor, *Integration*, 51–52.
3. Rollins, "We Made History," 265–67; MacGregor, *Integration*, 17–18, 24–25.
4. Roberts and Klibanoff, *Race Beat*, 5.
5. "Newsreels and the Negro in the War," *New Journal and Guide*, January 15, 1944.
6. Fitzgerald, Memo for Chief PRO, "Negro Correspondents for Attachment to Units on Far Shore," Correspondents-Military, box 6, Redding Papers.
7. Pietila and Spaulding, *Race Goes to War*.
8. Bissell, Memo for the Chief, BPR, May 18, 1942, and, Bissell, Memo for BPR, December 19, 1942, both in BPR File, 000.77, box 7, RG165.
9. Pietila and Spaulding, *Race Goes to War*.
10. Hull, Memo for BPR, May 20, 1943, BPR to Eisenhower, No.148, June 12, 1943, box 13, and Algiers to War, W-5972, July 28, 1943, box 15, all in BPR File, 000.7, Entry 499, RG165.
11. On the establishment of the Ninety-Ninth Squadron, see Sandler, *Segregated Skies*, 13–14; Moye, *Freedom Flyers*, 78–83; Charles River Editors, *Tuskegee Airmen*.
12. Wilson to Chief, Continental Liaison Branch, BPR, "Story on Negro Air Force Squadrons," May 4, 1943, box 13, BPR File, 000.7, Entry 499, RG165. On Stimson's attitudes, see Sitkoff, *Toward Freedom Land*, 77.
13. Stewart, "99th Gets Two Planes," and, "99th Suffers First Losses," *Baltimore Afro-American*, July 3 and 17, 1943.
14. Stewart, "Flying Dawn Patrol with the 99th in Sicily," *Baltimore Afro-American*, August 7, 1943; Young, "Narrow Escape Initiate 99th Pilots in Ghost Club," *New Journal and Guide*, July 24, 1943; Carter, "Jubilant 99th Pilots Down 12 FW Nazis," *Baltimore Afro-American*, February 5, 1944.

15. "99th Flyers Chalk Up Enviable Record," *New York Amsterdam News*, January 8, 1944.
16. Brinkley, *The Publisher*, 420.
17. "Experiment Proved," and, "Sweet Victories," *Time*, September 20, 1943, and February 14, 1944. On the angry response to the September article, see Davis, *American*, 104–5; Sandler, *Segregated Skies*, 47–51.
18. "Negro Heads Selfridge Unit," and, "Negroes Praised as Air Fighters," *New York Times*, October 6, 1943, and June 25, 1944.
19. "Report on the Negro Soldier," *Time*, March 26, 1945. This was not strictly true; newspapers did carry a brief report that the division had gone into action in August 1944. See AP, "Negro Division in Italy," *New York Herald Tribune*, August 28, 1944. At least part of the reason for the lack of news was the conviction among white officers that the division was a poor outfit. See Kesting, "Conspiracy to Discredit," 10; Atkinson, *Day of Battle*, 383.
20. Stewart, "Artillery Unit Helped Hold Bastogne," and, "969th Artillery Bn. Revealed as Bastogne Heroes," *Baltimore Afro-American*, January 13 and February 3, 1945.
21. AP, "Negro Unit at Bastogne," *New York Times*, January 29, 1945.
22. Surles to Allen, WX-56454, March 21, 1945, and, Allen to Surles, S-83013, March 21, 1945, both in Policy and Infractions of Censorship File, Chief of Staff, SGS, DF 000.73, box 4, RG331. These platoons ultimately served in ten army divisions. See Colley, *Blood for Dignity*, 51.
23. Cowan to Lucile, August 28, 1944, copy in box 3, Thor Smith Papers. On Cowan's background, see AP press card, undated, and, Obits, undated, both in Cowan Vertical File, APCA.
24. Cooper to Kennedy, January 31, 1945, box 1, Kennedy Papers.
25. Taylor, *Dresden*, 378, 412.
26. "Excerpts from Conference of Air Commodore C.M. Grierson," February 16, 1945, Policy and Infractions of Censorship File, Chief of Staff, SGS, DF 000.73, box 4, RG331.
27. Smith to Spaatz, WAR-39722, February 18, 1945, Army Air Forces: Office of Information Services: General Subject File, Entry 55, box 30, RG18; Merrick to Dupuy, "Story by Cowan, AP, Re Bombing," February 18, 1945, and, Deputy Chief of Air Staff to Bedell Smith, February 19, 1945, both in Policy and Infractions of Censorship File, Chief of Staff, SGS, DF 000.73, box 4, RG331.
28. Press briefing, undated, Text Folder, Army Air Forces: Office of Information Services: General Subject File, Entry 55, box 30, RG18. For further efforts to dampen the press reaction, see War to Spaatz, February 19, 1945, Official Diary, box I:23, Spaatz Papers; Davis, *Spaatz*, 561–62; Biddle, "Dresden," 440–41.
29. Although the Dresden bombing itself received little play in the American media after Cowan's story. See Sherry, *Rise*, 263.
30. See, for instance, Granberg, "Witness Tells Terror of Yank Bombing," *Chicago Daily News*, February 23, 1945; "6,500,000 in Berlin Pace Siege Chaos," *New York Times*, February 23, 1945; "Germany: Doomed," *Time*, March 5, 1945.
31. "A Picture of Precision Bombing," *Chicago Daily News*, March 12, 1945; "Spared by the Bombers," *Chicago Tribune*, March 19, 1945.
32. Oldfield, *Never a Shot*, 200–201.
33. Thompson, "Win Cologne," *Chicago Tribune*, March 7, 1943.
34. Whitehead, "Moon Was Very Bright," *Baltimore Sun*, February 24, 1945.
35. Thompson, "Win Cologne," *Chicago Tribune*, March 7, 1943.

36. Thompson, "Find Cologne Industry Dead," *Chicago Tribune*; Whitehead, "The Miracle of Cologne," *Baltimore Sun*, March 8, 1945.
37. Gallagher, "Bomb Damage to Reich Assayed," *Los Angeles Times*, March 10, 1945.
38. MacDonald, *Last Offensive*, 297, 173.
39. Oldfield, *Never a Shot*, 205–6; AP, "Press News Now Sent Direct from Germany," *Boston Globe*, March 11, 1945.
40. Dupuy, "Bonn and Remagen," 375.
41. Hechler, *Bridge at Remagen*, 35, 97, 105–7, 114–22; MacDonald, *Last Offensive*, 214–17.
42. Cowan, "Men First Across," *New York Times*, March 9, 1945; "Cowan First Over Bridge as Press Crosses Rhine," *E&P*, March 17, 1945.
43. "Cowan First Over Bridge as Press Crosses Rhine," *E&P*, March 17, 1945.
44. SHAEF Press Censorship Group Rear to Merrick, B-751, March 8, 1945, Policy re Release of Information to the Press, Chief of Staff, SGS, DF 000.7, box 2, RG331; Sylvan and Smith, *Normandy to Victory*, 327.
45. Ambrose, *Eisenhower*, 1:388–89; Atkinson, *Guns at Last Light*, 576; Patton Diary, March 17, 1945, box 3, and, Patton to Beatrice, March 18, Family Papers, box 19, both in Patton Papers.
46. Allen, *Lucky Forward*, 55.
47. Allen, *Lucky Forward*, 80–81, 95. See also Patton Diary, August 24, 1944, box 3, Patton Papers.
48. MacDonald, *Last Offensive*, 296–99, 236.
49. Patton, *War as I Knew It*, 254.
50. Patton Diary, February 2 and 3, 1945, box 3, Patton Papers; Bradley, *Soldier's Story*, 519.
51. MacDonald, *Last Offensive*, 267–68.
52. Ball, "New Rhine Bridgehead Won without Loss of Single Man," *New York Times*, March 24, 1945.
53. Bentel, "Newsmen Sprint to Catch Fast-Moving War Story," *E&P*, March 31, 1945; Ball, "Patton Crosses Rhine in a Daring Drive," *New York Times*, March 24, 1945.
54. Atkinson, *Guns at Last Light*, 558; Oldfield, *Never a Shot*, 212–14.
55. Gallagher, "Eyewitness Story of Vast Assault," *Los Angeles Times*, March 25, 1945. For the battle, see *Conquer*, 243–46.
56. Oldfield, *Never a Shot*, 218–19; Bentel, "Newsmen Sprint to Catch Fast-Moving War Story," *E&P*, March 31, 1945.
57. Atkinson, *Guns at Last Light*, 558.
58. The magazine had called Patton's behavior "unsoldierly." See "Conduct Unbecoming," *Time*, December 6, 1943.
59. Quirk to wife, March 29, 1945, box 1, Quirk Papers; Gay Diary, March 29, 1945, box 2, Gay Papers.
60. Bourke-White, *"Dear Fatherland,"* 22; D'Este, *Patton*, 725–26.
61. Quirk to wife, March 29, 1945, box 1, Quirk Papers. See also Wertenbaker cable, "For Patton Cover," March 31, 1945, Time-Life-Fortune Papers, box 1, Billings Papers.
62. "The Star Halfback," *Time*, April 9, 1945.

CHAPTER 20

1. AP, "Groundless VE Rumors Excite Nation," *Washington Post*, March 29, 1945.
2. "False Flash . . . Pre-Perception," *E&P*, April 7, 1945.
3. Stoneman, "Allies Drive on Reich like Famed Auto Race," *Chicago Daily News*, April 9, 1945.

4. See, for instance, Thompson, "Sidelights on Road to Berlin," *Chicago Tribune*, March 28, 1945; Whitehead, "Nazis in Rout as Yanks Sweep toward Berlin," *Los Angeles Times*, March 28, 1945.
5. Whitehead, "Europe's Freed 'Slaves' Major Yank Problem," *Washington Post*, April 6, 1945; "American Prisoners in German Camps Like Skeletons," *Los Angeles Times*, April 8, 1945.
6. Patton Diary, April 12, 1945, box 3, Patton Papers; Ambrose *Supreme Commander*, 659; Abzug, *Inside the Vicious Heart*, 30, 128–39; Casey, *Cautious Crusade*, 211–12.
7. Whitehead, "Proof of Nazi Horrors Shown to Congressmen," *Los Angeles Times*, April 23, 1945; Stoneman, "GIs Learn What They're Fighting For," *Chicago Daily News*, April 23, 1945. For background on this coverage, see Lipstadt, *Beyond Belief*, 258–60.
8. UP, "Eisenhower Over Rhine," *Los Angeles Times*, March 27, 1945.
9. Atkinson, *Guns at Last Light*, 583–85; Oldfield, *Never a Shot*, 229–30.
10. Butcher, *Three Years*, 788; Rue, "Nazis Whipped on West Front, Ike Declares," *Chicago Tribune*, March 28, 1945.
11. Middleton, "US and Red Armies Drive to Meet," *New York Times*, April 13, 1945.
12. "Charges Reds Force Yanks to Leave Potsdam," *Chicago Tribune*, April 22, 1945.
13. Eisenhower to Marshall, April 15, 1945, Marshall Folder, box 80, EPPP; Pogue, *Supreme Command*, 445–46; Atkinson, *Guns at Last Light*, 577–78.
14. Butcher, *Three Years*, 809; Crosswell, *Beetle*, 900–2; "The Battle for Berlin," and, AP, "Eisenhower Halted Forces at Elbe," *New York Times*, April 21 and May 2, 1945.
15. Gallagher, "9th Army Front Goes Wacky on Russian Rumors," *Los Angeles Times*, April 23, 1945; Stoneman, "Man on Bike Hunts Vainly for Reds," *Chicago Daily News*, April 25, 1945.
16. MacDonald, *Last Offensive*, 447–56.
17. Carpenter, *No Woman's World*, 323–24; Smith to MBS, May 3, 1945, box 3, Thor Smith Papers.
18. Smith to MBS, May 3, 1945, box 3, Thor Smith Papers.
19. Thompson, "Find Friendship a Hazard When Vodka Flows," and, Whitehead, "Tiny Town Rings with Singing," *Chicago Tribune*, April 28 and 27, 1945; Whitehead, "Los Angeles Officer's Story of Meeting," *Los Angeles Times*, April 28, 1945.
20. MacDonald, *Last Offensive*, 447; Smith to MBS, May 3, 1945, box 3, Thor Smith Papers.
21. Allen to Bedell Smith, "Premature Announcement of Link-up, American and Soviet Forces," April 30, 1945, Policy and Infractions of Censorship File, Chief of Staff, SGS, DF 000.73, box 4, RG331.
22. Beevor and Cooper, *Paris after the Liberation*, 73; Atkinson, *Guns at Last Light*, 402; Hill, "SHEAF a Headache to War Reporters," *E&P*, January 12, 1945.
23. White, *Conquerors' Road*, 110; Hill, "Press at SHAEF Has Tense Wait," *New York Times*, May 9, 1945.
24. Butcher, *Three Years*, 824–25, 828–29; Butcher to Early, May 11, 1945, box 4, Butcher Papers.
25. Smith to MBS, May 10, 1945, box 3, Thor Smith Papers; Cochran, *Kennedy's War*, 155–56.
26. Cochran, *Kennedy's War*, 155–56, 164; Allen to Bedell Smith, "Investigation of AP Unauthorized Transmission of News on German Surrender," May 8, 1945, and, Kennedy Statement, May 12, 1945, both in Kennedy Release File, Chief of Staff, SGS, DF 000.73/6, box 4, RG331.
27. Smith to MBS, May 10, 1945, box 3, Thor Smith Papers.

28. Cochran, *Kennedy's War*, 158–59; Daniell, "Fiasco by SHAEF at Reims is Bared," *New York Times*, May 9, 1945.
29. Cochran, *Kennedy's War*, 159–60; White, *Conquerors' Road*, 113–15; Text of Kennedy's Surrender Story, May 7, 1945, box 1, Kennedy Papers; Thor Smith to MBS, May 10, 1945, box 3, Thor Smith Papers.
30. Cochran, *Kennedy's War*, 160–61.
31. Thor Smith to MBS, May 10, 1945, box 3, Thor Smith Papers.
32. Cochran, *Kennedy's War*, 162; Cooper to Members of the Board of Directors, June 14, 1945, WW2 Folder, box 274, NYT: AHS.
33. Kennedy to Kenper, undated, BPR File, 000.7, box 35, RG165.
34. Merrick to Warden, "Conversation with Ed Kennedy, AP, May 7, 1945," Kennedy Release File, Chief of Staff, SGS, DF 000.73/6, box 4, RG331. Cochran, *Kennedy's War*, 163–64.
35. Allen to Bedell Smith, "Investigation of AP Unauthorized Transmission of News on German Surrender," May 8, 1945, Kennedy Release File, Chief of Staff, SGS, DF 000.73/6, box 4, RG331; "Log on Kennedy Unconditional Surrender Story," May 7, 1945, WW2 Folder, box 274, NYT: AHS; "AP Tells the Story of Historic Break," *New York Times*, May 8, 1945. Due to Eastern War Time, the difference between London and New York was six hours.
36. Marshall to Eisenhower, May 8, 1945, Kennedy Release File, Chief of Staff, SGS, DF 000.73/6, box 4, RG331.
37. Kingsbury Smith to Eisenhower, May 9, 1945, Kennedy Release File, Chief of Staff, SGS, DF 000.73/6, box 4, RG331.
38. Barbour and Gallagher, "While the Smoke," 305.
39. Allen to Surles, May 8, 1945, S-87437, Kennedy Release File, Chief of Staff, SGS, DF 000.73/6, box 4, RG331.
40. Thor Smith to MBS, May 14, 1945, box 3, Thor Smith Papers; Hill, "Peace Jeopardized by AP, SHAEF Says," and, "Gen. Allen's Statement on AP 'Beat,'" *New York Times*, May 10, 1945.
41. Kenper to Gallagher, May 10, 1945, box 1, Kennedy Papers.
42. Hightower, "AP," 86; Barbour and Gallagher, "While the Smoke," 296.
43. Barbour and Gallagher, "While the Smoke," 298–99.
44. Cochran, *Kennedy's War*, 173–82. The AP board discussed a letter informing Kennedy that he had been dismissed, but, as an unpublished history of the AP records, "Kennedy said he never received the letter." See Barbour and Gallagher, "While the Smoke," 305.
45. Thompson, "Nazis Eclipsed, 1st Army Heads for Rising Sun," and, "Japs Bomb Hospital Ship," *Chicago Tribune*, June 4 and 29, 1945; Whitehead, "A-Bomb Hits 19 Ships," *Chicago Tribune*, July 1, 1946.
46. Gallagher, "Behind the Scenes at Nuremberg," *AP World*, January 1946.
47. Stoneman, "Remarks to Seminar on Foreign Correspondence," October 2, 1969, box 1, Stoneman Papers; "William Stoneman, 83," *New York Times*, April 14, 1987; Urquhart, "Character Sketches: Trygve Lie," http://www.un.org/apps/news/infocus/trygvie-lie.asp#, accessed January 2016; Stoneman, "US Wise to Accept Red Bid," *Boston Globe*, May 4, 1949.
48. Stoneman, "Talk to St Joseph Michigan Economic Club," December 2, 1969, box 1, Stoneman Papers.
49. Thompson, "Soviets Renege on Word," and, "Russians Move toward Turkey Nerves War," and "Reign of Terror in East Prussia Told in Letters," *Chicago Tribune*, January 3 and 17, and October 1, 1946.

50. Middleton, *Last July*, 149–64.
51. Gallagher, "Germany Rule Costly for US," and, "Hope for Unifying of Germany Wanes," *Los Angeles Times*, April 7, 1946, and July 27, 1947.
52. Gallagher, "Sudden Red Attack in West Could Wipe Out Allies," *Boston Globe*, July 23, 1950; "Rearming of Germany Seen as Necessary Step," *Los Angeles Times*, August 7, 1951; "Europe Called Team with Its Morale Shot," *Chicago Tribune*, January 11, 1951.
53. Middleton, "Rebirth of Nazism Called Possibility," and, "21 Farben Plants Wiped Out by US," and, "Germans Return to Nationalism," *New York Times*, January 14 and 17, and February 25, 1946.
54. Middleton, *Last July*, 163–74. See also Etheridge, *Enemies to Allies*, 58–59.
55. Middleton was so affected by the Battle of Britain and the blitz that he later wrote a historical study of the period, *Sky Suspended*.
56. Whitehead, "Omaha Beach Peaceful—after Year," and, "Newsman Recalls Agony of D-Day Landings in Normandy," *Washington Post*, June 3, 1945, and June 6, 1959; "Most Decisive Battle of War in Europe," *Baltimore Sun*, July 19, 1964. See also Whitehead, "Correspondent's View," 212.
57. See, for example, Thompson, "Europe's D-Day Thru Eyes of Tribune Man," and, "'Omaha Beach'—Tale of Death and Victory," *Chicago Tribune*, January 5 and 6, 1947.
58. Thompson, "Critics Protest Disbanding of Paratroop Unit," and, "Meet at Airborne Division Reunion," *Chicago Tribune*, October 22, 1945, and July 6, 1947.
59. Bigart, "Outnumbered, Outgunned GIs Bitter at Untenable Positions," *Washington Post*, July 9, 1950.
60. Whitehead, "I've Seen Americans in Defeat," *Boston Globe*, July 27, 1950.
61. Casey, *Selling the Korean War*, 57; "Don Whitehead, Pulitzer Winner for Dispatches on Korean War," *New York Times*, January 4, 1981.
62. Prochnau, *Distant War*, 31.
63. Prochnau, *Distant War*, 36.
64. Gallagher to Hitt, April 1, 1964, Gallagher Vertical File, APCA.
65. Gallagher, *Perspective Reporting*, 7–11; Daniel, "Wes Gallagher," DLB 127, 96–97, Gallagher Vertical File, APCA; Hightower, "AP," 77

CONCLUSION

1. Cronkite, *Reporter's Life*, 289. Whitehead was one of many who made a similar point. See Whitehead, "Correspondent's View," 204–5.
2. Or, as Mander has put it, between "respect" and "disdain." See Mander, *Pen and Sword*, 133–34.
3. On this cultural clash, see Pedelty, *War Stories*, 6–8, 29, 72–76; Braestrup, *Battle Lines*, 141; Carruthers, *Media at War*, 5, 15; Van Ginneken, *Understanding Global News*, 65–75.
4. "It's a Tough War," *Life*, January 31, 1944.
5. On this problem, see Desmond, *Tides of War*, 451–52.
6. "Americans Still Died," *Life*, May 14, 1945; Whelan, *Capa*, 235–36; Whelan, *This Is War!*, 253–67.
7. Pyle to Stone, April 15, 1945, Pyle Correspondence, box 10, Stone Papers; Tobin, *Pyle's War*, 238–40.
8. Miller, "Ernie Wrote His Own Story—in Blood," *Washington Daily News*, April 21, 1945.
9. Chenoweth, "52 War Correspondents K.I.A."

BIBLIOGRAPHY

PRIMARY SOURCES

National Archives, College Park, MD

RG18. Army Air Forces
RG44. Office of Government Reports
RG59. State Department
RG107. Office of the Secretary of War
RG165. War Department
RG208. Office of War Information
RG218. Joint Chiefs of Staff
RG319. Army Chief of Staff
RG331. Supreme Headquarters Allied Expeditionary Forces
RG407. Adjutant General's Office
RG492. Mediterranean Theater of Operations, US Army
RG498. Headquarters, European Theater of Operations

National Archives, UK, Kew Gardens, London

ADM. Records of the Admiralty
AIR. Records of the Air Ministry
PREM. Records of the Prime Minister
WO. Records of the War Office

Manuscript Collections: Media

Agronsky, Martin. Library of Congress, Washington DC
Associated Press Archives. New York, NY
Bigart, Homer. Wisconsin Historical Society, Madison
Billings, John Shaw. Time-Life Fortune Papers. South Caroliniana Library, Columbia
Binder, Carroll. Newberry Library, Chicago, IL
Bourke-White, Margaret. Syracuse University, Syracuse, NY
Boyle, Harold V. Wisconsin Historical Society, Madison
Capa, Robert. International Center for Photography. Mana Contemporary, Jersey City, NJ
Casey, Robert J. Newberry Library, Chicago, IL
Clapper, Raymond. Library of Congress, Washington DC
Chicago Tribune Company Records. Cantigny, IL
Cronkite, Walter. University of Texas, Austin
Daly, John C. Wisconsin Historical Society, Madison
Deuel, Wallace R. Library of Congress, Washington DC

Graebner, Walter. Wisconsin Historical Society, Madison
Hicks, George. Wisconsin Historical Society, Madison
Howard, Roy W. Library of Congress, Washington DC
Kennedy, Ed. AP Corporate Archives, New York, NY
Krock, Arthur. Princeton University, Princeton, NJ
Matthews, Herbert L. Columbia University, New York, NY
McCormick, Robert. Wisconsin Historical Society, Madison
McClean, Robert. AP Corporate Archives, New York, NY
Mueller, Merrill. Wisconsin Historical Society, Madison
Mowrer, Edgar A. Library of Congress, Washington DC
NBC History Files. Library of Congress, Washington DC
NBC Radio Collection. Library of Congress, Washington DC
New York Times Company Records. General Records. New York Public Library
New York Times Company Records. Arthur Hays Sulzberger Papers. New York Public Library
Nixon, Robert G. Wisconsin Historical Society, Madison
Noderer, E. R. Chicago Tribune Company Records. Cantigny, IL
Patterson, Joseph Medill. Lake Forest College, IL
Pyle, Ernie. Lilly Library, Indiana University, Bloomington
Reid, Helen Rogers. Library of Congress, Washington DC
Salisbury, Harrison. Columbia University, New York, NY
Sevareid, Eric A. Library of Congress, Washington DC
Shapiro, Henry. Library of Congress, Washington DC
Smith, Howard K. Wisconsin Historical Society, Madison
Stone, Walker. Wisconsin Historical Society, Madison
Stoneman, William. Bentley Historical Library. University of Michigan, Ann Arbor
Stowe, Leland. Wisconsin Historical Society, Madison
Strout, Richard L. Library of Congress, Washington DC
Time Magazine Dispatches. Houghton Library, Harvard University

Manuscript Collections: Military and Government

Army War College Curriculum Archives. Military History Institute, Carlisle, PA
Arnold, Henry H. Library of Congress, Washington DC
Bradley, Omar. Military History Institute, Carlisle, PA
Butcher, Harry C. Eisenhower Presidential Library, Abilene, KS
Clark, Mark W. The Citadel Archives and Museum, Charleston, SC
Davis, Elmer. Library of Congress, Washington DC
Davis, Thomas Jefferson. Eisenhower Presidential Library, Abilene, KS
Devers, Jacob L. Military History Institute, Carlisle, PA
Dickson, Benjamin A. Military History Institute, Carlisle, PA
Doolittle, James H. Library of Congress, Washington DC
Eaker, Ira. Library of Congress, Washington DC
Early, Stephen. Roosevelt Library, Hyde Park, NY
Eighth Air Force. Air Force Historical Research Agency, Maxwell Air Force Base, AL
Eisenhower, Dwight D., Eisenhower Presidential Library, Abilene, KS
Frey, Robert L. Military History Institute, Carlisle, PA
Gavin, James M. Military History Institute, Carlisle, PA
Gay, Hobart R. Military History Institute, Carlisle, PA
Hansen, Chester B. Military History Institute, Carlisle, PA
Hodges, Courtney H. Eisenhower Presidential Library, Abilene, KS

Hopkins, Harry, L. Roosevelt Presidential Library, Hyde Park, NY
Hughes, Everett S. Library of Congress, Washington DC
King, Ernest J. Library of Congress, Washington DC
Knox, Frank. Library of Congress, Washington DC
Lucas, John P. Diary. Marshall Library, Lexington, VA
MacLeish, Archibald. Library of Congress, Washington DC
Marshall, George C. Marshall Library, Lexington, VA
McCarthy, Frank J. Marshall Library, Lexington, VA
Merrick, Richard H., Military History Institute, Carlisle, PA
Morgenthau, Henry, Jr. Roosevelt Presidential Library, Hyde Park, NY
Parks, Floyd L. Military History Institute, Carlisle, PA
Patton, George S. Library of Congress, Washington DC
Phillips, Joseph B. Records. Virginia Military Institute, Lexington, VA
Pleas, Roger B. Military History Institute, Carlisle, PA
Quirk, James T. Truman Presidential Library, Independence, MO
Redding, John M. Truman Presidential Library, Independence, MO
Ridgway, Matthew B. Military History Institute, Carlisle, PA
Roosevelt, Franklin D. Roosevelt Presidential Library, Hyde Park, NY
Silbar, Howard J. Military History Institute, Carlisle, PA
Simpson, William H. Military History Institute, Carlisle, PA
Smith, Thor M. Eisenhower Presidential Library, Abilene, KS
Smith, Walter Bedell. Collection of World War II Documents. Eisenhower Presidential Library, Abilene, KS
Spaatz, Carl. Library of Congress, Washington DC
Sylvan, William. Military History Institute, Carlisle, PA
Truscott, Lucian K. Marshall Library, Lexington, VA

Newspapers and Magazines

Baltimore Afro-American
Balitmore Sun
Boston Globe
Broadcasting
Buffalo Evening News
Chicago Daily News
Chicago Tribune
Christian Science Monitor
Cleveland Press
Collier's
Editor & Publisher
Life
Los Angeles Times
New Journal and Guide
New York Amsterdam News
New York Herald Tribune
New York Times
Newspaper World
Newsweek
San Francisco Call-Bulletin
Time
U.S. News & World Report

Wall Street Journal
Washington Daily News
Washington Post
World's Press News

SECONDARY SOURCES

Books

Abzug, Robert H. *Inside the Vicious Heart: Americans and the Liberation of the Concentration Camps*. Oxford: Oxford University Press, 1985.

Adams, Michael C. C. *The Best War Ever: America and the Second World War*. 2nd ed. Baltimore: Johns Hopkins University Press, 2015.

Adelman, Robert H., and George Walton. *Rome Fell Today*. Boston: Little, Brown, and Co., 1968.

Allen, Robert S. *Lucky Forward: Patton's Third U.S. Army*. New York: Manor Books, 1977.

Ambrose, Stephen E. *D-Day: The Climactic Battle of World War II*. New York: Simon and Schuster, 1994.

———. *Eisenhower*. Vol. 1, *Soldier, General of the Army, President-Elect, 1890-1952*. London: George Allen and Unwin, 1984.

———. *The Supreme Commander: The War Years of Dwight D. Eisenhower*. Jackson: University Press of Mississippi, 1970.

Arnold, Henry H. *Global Mission*. New York: Harper, 1949.

Atkinson, Rick. *An Army at Dawn: The War in North Africa, 1942-1943*. New York: Henry Holt, 2002.

———. *The Day of Battle: The War in Sicily and Italy, 1943-1944*. New York: Henry Holt, 2007.

———. *The Guns at Last Light: That War in Western Europe, 1944-1945*. New York: Henry Holt, 2013.

Ault, Phil. *News Around the Clock: Press Associations in Action*. New York: Dodd, Mead, 1960.

Baker, Carlos. *Ernest Hemingway: A Life Story*. London: Penguin, 1972.

———, ed. *Ernest Hemingway: Selected Letters, 1917-1961*. New York: Charles Scribner's, 1981.

Barnow, Erik. *The Golden Web: A History of Broadcasting in the United States*. Vol. 2: *1933 to 1953*. New York: Oxford University Press, 1968.

Beattie, Edward W. *Passport to War*. London: Peter Davis, 1943.

Beevor, Antony. *D-Day: The Battle for Normandy*. London: Penguin, 2009.

Beevor, Antony, and Artemis Cooper. *Paris after the Liberation, 1944-1949*. Rev. ed. New York: Penguin, 2004.

Belden, Jack. *Still Time to Die*. New York: Harper, 1944.

Bell, Jack. *Line of Fire*. Coral Gables, FL: Glade House, 1948.

Bennett, Lowell. *Assignment to Nowhere: The Battle for Tunisia*. New York: Vanguard Press, 1943.

Berger, Meyer. *The Story of the New York Times, 1941-1951*. New York: Simon and Schuster, 1951.

Biggs, Bradley. *Gavin*. Hamden, CT: Archon Books, 1980.

Bland, Larry I., ed. *George C. Marshall: Interviews and Reminiscences for Forrest C. Pogue*. Lexington, VA: Marshall Research Foundation, 1991.

———. *The Papers of George Catlett Marshall*. Vols. 2–4: *1939-1944*. Baltimore: Johns Hopkins University Press, 1986–1996.

Bliss, Edward, Jr. *In Search of Light: The Broadcasts of Edward R. Murrow, 1938-1961*. London: Macmillan, 1968.

Blumenson, Martin. *Mark Clark*. New York: Congdon and Weed, 1984.

———, ed. *The Patton Papers*. 2 vols. Boston: Houghton Mifflin, 1972–74.

———. *Salerno to Cassino*. Washington, DC: Office of the Chief of Military History, 1969.

Bodnar, John. *The "Good War" in American Memory*. Baltimore: Johns Hopkins University Press, 2010.

Bourke-White, Margaret. *"Dear Fatherland Rest Quietly": A Report on the Collapse of Hitler's "Thousand Years."* New York: Simon and Schuster, 1946.

———. *Purple Heart Valley: A Combat Chronicle of the War in Italy*. New York: Simon and Schuster, 1944.

Boyle, Hal. *Help, Help! Another Day*. New York: Associated Press, 1969.

Bradley, Omar N. *A Soldier's Story*. New York: Modern Library. 1999.

Bradley, Omar N., and Clay Blair. *A General's Life*. New York: Simon and Schuster, 1983.

Brady, Tim. *A Death in San Pietro: The Untold Story of Ernie Pyle, John Huston, and the Fight for Purple Heart Valley*. Boston: Da Capo Press, 2013.

Braestrup, Peter. *Battle Lines*. New York: Priority Press, 1985.

Brinkley, Alan. *The Publisher: Henry Luce and the American Century*. New York: Alfred A. Knopf, 2010.

Brinkley, Douglas. *Cronkite*. New York: Harper Collins, 2012.

Buell, Hal, ed. *We Were There: Normandy*. New York: Tess Press, 2007.

Butcher, Harry C. *My Three Years with Eisenhower: The Personal Diary of Captain Harry C. Butcher, 1942-1945*. New York: Simon and Schuster, 1946.

Calder, Angus. *The People's War: Britain, 1939-1945*. London: Pimlico, 1992.

Caddick-Adams, Peter. *Monte Cassino: Ten Armies in Hell*. London: Arrow, 2013.

Capa, Robert. *Slightly Out of Focus*. New York: Modern Library, 2001.

Carpenter, Iris. *No Woman's World*. Boston: Houghton Mifflin, 1946.

Carruthers, Susan L. *The Media at War: Communication and Conflict in the Twentieth Century*. Palgrave: Basingstoke, 2000.

Casey, Steven. *Cautious Crusade: Franklin D. Roosevelt, American Public Opinion, and the War against Nazi Germany*. New York: Oxford University Press, 2001.

———. *Selling the Korean War: Propaganda, Politics, and Public Opinion*. New York: Oxford University Press, 2008.

———. *When Soldiers Fall: How Americans Have Confronted Combat Casualties, from World War I to Afghanistan*. New York: Oxford University Press, 2014.

Charles River Editors, *The Tuskegee Airmen: The History and Legacy of America's First Black Fighter Pilots in World War II*. [n.p.]: CreateSpace, 2015.

Churchill, Winston S. *The Second World War*. 6 vols. London: Penguin, 1948–1953.

Cochran, Julia Kennedy, ed. *Ed Kennedy's War: V-E Day, Censorship, and the Associated Press*. Baton Rouge: Louisiana State University Press, 2012.

Codman, Charles R. *Drive*. Boston: Atlantic Monthly Press, 1957.

Cole, Hugh M. *Ardennes: The Battle of the Bulge*. Washington, DC: Center of Military History, 1965.

———. *The Lorraine Campaign*. Washington, DC: Historical Division of Department of the Army, 1950.

Colley, David P. *Blood for Dignity: The Story of the First Integrated Combat Unit in the U.S. Army*. New York: St Martin's Press, 2003.

Collier, Richard. *The Warcos: The War Correspondents of World War II*. London: Weidenfeld and Nicolson, 1969.

Colman, Penny. *Where the Action Was: Women War Correspondents in World War II.* New York: Crown, 2002.

Conquer: The Story of the Ninth Army, 1944-1945. Washington, DC: Infantry Journal Press, 1947.

Cook, Jeffrey B., ed. *American World War II Correspondents.* Farmingdon Hills, MI: Gale, 2012.

Cooper, Kent. *Barriers Down: The Story of the News Agency Epoch.* New York: Farrar and Rinehart, 1942.

———. *Kent Cooper and the Associated Press: An Autobiography.* New York: Random House, 1959.

Crane, Conrad C. *Bombs, Cities, Civilians: American Airpower Strategy in World War II.* Lawrence: University Press of Kansas, 1993.

Craven, Wesley Frank, and James Lea Cate. *The Army Air Forces in World War II.* Vols. 2–3. Washington, DC: Office of Air Force History, 1983.

Crawford, Kenneth G. *Report on North Africa.* New York: Farrar and Rinehart, 1943.

Cronkite, Walter. *A Reporter's Life.* New York: Alfred A. Knopf, 2008.

Crosswell, D. K. R. *Beetle: The Life of General Walter Bedell Smith.* Lexington: University of Kentucky Press, 2010.

Cull, Nicholas John. *Selling War: The British Propaganda Campaign against American "Neutrality" in World War II.* New York: Oxford University Press, 1995.

Daniell, Raymond. *Civilians Must Fight.* Garden City, NY: Doubleday, 1941.

D'Arcy-Dawson, John. *Tunisian Battle.* London: Macdonald, 1943.

Davis, Benjamin O., Jr. *American: An Autobiography.* Washington, DC: Smithsonian, 1991.

Davis, Richard G. *Carl A. Spaatz and the Air War in Europe.* Washington, DC: Center for Air Force History, 1993.

Dell'Orto, Giovanna. *AP Foreign Correspondents in Action: World War II to Present.* Cambridge: Cambridge University Press, 2015.

Desmond, Robert W. *Tides of War: World News Reporting, 1931-1945.* Iowa City: University of Iowa Press, 1984.

D'Este, Carlo. *Bitter Victory: The Battle for Sicily, 1943.* Glasgow: Collins, 1988.

———. *Fatal Decision: Anzio and the Battle for Rome.* New York: Harper Perennial, 1992.

———. *Patton: A Genius for War.* New York: Harper Perennial, 1996.

Doubler, Michael M. *Closing with the Enemy: How GIs Fought the War in Europe, 1944–1945.* Lawrence: University Press of Kansas, 1994.

Eisenhower, Dwight D. *Crusade in Europe.* Garden City, NY: Doubleday, 1948.

Etheridge, Brian C. *Enemies to Allies: Cold War Germany and American Memory.* Lexington: University Press of Kentucky, 2016.

Ferrell, Robert H. *The Eisenhower Diaries.* New York: W. W. Norton, 1981.

Funk, Arthur L. *The Politics of TORCH: The Allied Landings and the Algiers Putsch, 1942.* Lawrence: University Press of Kansas, 1974.

Fussell, Paul. *Wartime: Understanding and Behavior in the Second World War.* New York: Oxford University Press, 1989.

Gallagher, Wes. *Back Door to War: The Full Story of the American Coup in North Africa.* Garden City, NY: Doubleday, 1943.

———. *Perspective Reporting versus Credibility, Gullability, and Humbugability.* Lawrence: University of Kansas Press, 1967.

Garland, Albert N., and Howard McGaw Smyth. *Sicily and the Surrender of Italy.* Washington, DC: Office of the Chief of Military History, 1965.

Gavin, James M. *Airborne Warfare.* Washington, DC: Infantry Journal Press, 1947.

Gay, Timothy M. *Assignment to Hell: The War against Nazi Germany with Correspondents Walter Cronkite, Andy Rooney, A. J. Liebling, Homer Bigart, and Hal Boyle.* New York: Nal Caliber, 2012.

Gellhorn, Martha. *The Face of War.* New York: Atlantic Monthly Press, 1988.

Gervasi, Frank. *The Violent Decade.* New York: W. W. Norton, 1989.

Ginneken, Jaap van. *Understanding Global News: A Critical Introduction.* London: Sage, 1998.

Goldberg, Vicki. *Margaret Bourke-White: A Biography.* London: Heinemann, 1987.

Gramling, Oliver. *AP: The Story of News.* London: Kennikat Press, 1969.

Gunther, John. *D-Day.* London: Hamish Hamilton, 1944.

Hallin, Daniel C. *The "Uncensored War": The Media and Vietnam.* Berkeley: University of California Press, 1986.

Hamill, Pete, ed. *A. J. Liebling: World War II Writings.* New York: Library of America, 2008.

Hamilton, Jim. *The Writing 69th.* Marshfield, MA: Green Harbor, 1999.

Hamilton, John Maxwell. *Journalism's Roving Eye: A History of American Foreign Reporting.* Baton Rouge: Louisiana State University Press, 2009.

Hamilton, Nigel. *Monty: The Field Marshal, 1944-1976.* London: Hamish Hamilton, 1986.

———. *Monty: Master of the Battlefield, 1942-1944.* London: Hamish Hamilton, 1983.

Harrison, Gordon A. *Cross-Channel Attack.* Washington, DC: Office of the Chief of Military History, Department of the Army, 1951.

Hassett, William D. *Off the Record with FDR, 1942-1945.* New Brunswick, NJ: Rutgers University Press, 1958.

Hastings, Max. *Bomber Command: The Myths and Realities of the Strategic Bombing Offensive, 1939-1945.* London: Pan Books, 1979.

Hechler, Ken. *The Bridge at Remagen: The Amazing Story of March 7, 1945; the Day the Rhine River Was Crossed.* Rev. ed. Missoula, MN: Pictorial Histories, 1995.

Heinz, W. C. *When We Were One: Stories of World War II.* New York: Da Capo Press, 2002.

Hemingway, Mary Welsh. *How It Was.* New York: Alfred A. Knopf, 1976.

Herman, Jan. *A Talent for Trouble: The Life of Hollywood's Most Acclaimed Director, William Wyler.* New York: G. P. Putnam's Sons, 1995.

Hinsley, F. H., E. E. Thomas, C. F. G. Ransom, and R. C. Knight. *British Intelligence in the Second World War: Its Influence on Strategy and Operations.* Vol. 3, parts 1 and 2. London: HMSO, 1984, 1988.

Hirshson, Stanley P. *General Patton: A Soldier's Life.* New York: HarperCollins, 2002.

Hohenberg, John. *Foreign Correspondence: The Great Reporters and Their Times.* New York: Columbia University Press, 1964.

Hosley, David H. *As Good as Any: Foreign Correspondence on American Radio, 1930–1940.* Westport, CT: Greenwood Press, 1984.

Howe, George F. *Northwest Africa: Seizing the Initiative in the West.* Washington, DC: Office of the Chief of Military History, Department of the Army, 1957.

Huebner, Andrew J. *The Warrior Image: Soldiers in American Culture from the Second World War to the Vietnam Era.* Chapel Hill: University of North Carolina Press, 2008.

Jordan, Philip. *Jordan's Tunis Diary.* London: Collins, 1943.

Kearns, Dorothy Goodwin. *No Ordinary Time. Franklin and Eleanor Roosevelt: The Home Front in World War II.* New York: Simon and Schuster, 1994.

Kelly, Charles K. *Tex McCrary: Wars, Women, Politics; an Adventurous Life across the American Century.* Lanham, MD: Hamilton Books, 2009.

Kershaw, Alex. *Blood and Champagne: The Life and Times of Robert Capa.* London: Pan Books, 2002.

Kirby, Edward M., and Jack W. Harris, *Star-Spangled Radio*. Chicago: Ziff-Davis, 1948.

Kluger, Richard. *The Paper: The Life and Death of the* New York Herald Tribune. New York: Vintage, 1989.

Knightley, Phillip. *The First Casualty: From the Crimea to the Falklands; the War Correspondent as Hero, Propagandist and Myth Maker*. Rev. ed. London: Pan Books, 1989.

Larrabee, Eric. *Commander in Chief: Franklin Delano Roosevelt, His Lieutenants, and Their War*. New York: Harper and Row, 1987.

Liebling, A. J. *Mollie and Other Writings*. New York: Ballantine Books, 1964.

Lipstadt, Deborah E. *Beyond Belief: The American Press and the Coming of the Holocaust, 1933-1945*. New York: Free Press, 1986.

MacDonald, Charles B. *The Battle of the Huertgen Forest*. Philadelphia: Lippincott, 1963.

———. *The Last Offensive*. Washington, DC: Center of Military History, 1993.

———. *The Siegfried Line Campaign*. Washington, DC: Office of the Chief of Military History, Department of the Army, 1963.

MacGregor, Morris J., Jr. *Integration of the Armed Forces, 1940-1965*. Washington, DC: Center of Military History, 1981.

MacKenzie, Fred. *The Men of Bastogne*. New York: David McKay, 1968.

MacVane, John. *Journey into War: War and Diplomacy in North Africa*. New York: Appleton-Century, 1943.

———. *On the Air in World War II*. New York: William Morrow, 1979.

Madsen, Axel. *William Wyler: The Authorized Biography*. New York: Thomas Y. Crowell, 1973.

Mander, Mary S. *Pen and Sword: American War Correspondents, 1898-1975*. Urbana: University of Illinois Press, 2010.

Maslowski, Peter. *Armed with Cameras: The American Military Photographers of World War II*. New York: Free Press, 1993.

Matthews, Joseph J. *Reporting the Wars*. Minneapolis: University of Minnesota Press, 1957.

Matloff, Maurice. *Strategic Planning for Coalition Warfare, 1943-1944*. Washington, DC: Center of Military History, US Army, 1994.

Matloff, Maurice, and Edwin M. Snell. *Strategic Planning for Coalition Warfare, 1941–1942*. Washington, DC: Office of the Chief of Military History, Department of the Army, 1953.

McCrary, John R. ("Tex"), and David E. Scherman. *First of the Many: A Journal of Action with Men of the Eighth Air Force*. London: Robson Books, 1981.

McKinstry, Leo. *Lancaster: The Second World War's Greatest Bomber*. London: John Murray, 2009.

McManus, Joseph C. *Alamo in the Ardennes: The Untold Story of the American Soldiers Who Made the Defense of Bastogne Possible*. Hoboken, NJ: John Wiley & Sons, 2007.

Middleton, Drew. *Our Share of Night: A Personal Narrative of the War Years*. New York: Viking, 1946.

———. *The Sky Suspended*. New York: Longmans, Green, and Co., 1960.

———. *Where Has Last July Gone?* New York: Quadrangle, 1973.

Miller, Donald L. *Eighth Air Force: The American Bomber Crews in Britain*. London: Aurum, 2006.

Miller, Lee G. *The Story of Ernie Pyle*. New York: Viking, 1950.

Moorehead, Alan. *Eclipse*. London: Hamish Hamilton, 1945.

Moorehead, Caroline. *Martha Gellhorn: A Life*. London: Vintage, 2004.

Morgan, Robert. *The Man Who Flew the Memphis Belle: Memoir of a WWII Bomber Pilot.* With Ron Powers. New York: New American Library, 2002.

Morris, Joe A. *Deadline Every Minute: The Story of the United Press.* Garden City, NY: Doubleday, 1957.

Moye, J. Todd. *Freedom Flyers: The Tuskegee Airmen of World War II.* New York: Oxford University Press, 2010.

Moynihan, Michael. *War Correspondent.* London: Leo Cooper, 1994.

Murphy, Robert. *Diplomat among Warriors.* London: Collins, 1964.

Nichols, David, ed. *Ernie's War: The Best of Ernie Pyle's World War II Dispatches.* New York: Random House, 1986.

Nicolson, Nigel. *Alex: The Life of Field Marshal Earl Alexander of Tunis.* New York: Athenaeum, 1973.

Norton-Smith, Richard. *The Colonel: The Life and Legend of Robert R. McCormick, 1880–1955.* Evanston, IL: Northwestern University Press, 1997.

Oldfield, Barney. *Never a Shot in Anger.* Santa Barbara, CA: Capra Press, 1989.

Overy, Richard. *Bombing War: Europe, 1939-1945.* London: Allen Lane, 2013.

Parker, Danny S., ed. *Battle of the Bulge, The German View: Perspectives from Hitler's High Command.* Mechanicsburg, PA: Stackpole, 1999.

Parton, James. *"Air Force Spoken Here": General Ira Eaker and the Command of the Air.* Bethesda, MD: Adler and Adler, 1986.

Patton, George S. *War as I Knew It.* Boston: Houghton Mifflin, 1947.

Paul, Christopher, and James J. Kim. *Reporters on the Battlefield: The Embedded Press System in Historical Context.* Santa Monica, CA: Rand, 2004.

Pedelty, Mark. *War Stories: The Culture of Foreign Correspondents.* New York: Routledge, 1995.

Perisco, Joseph E. *Edward R. Murrow: An American Original.* New York: Da Capo Press, 1997.

Pietila, Antero, and Stacy Spaulding. *Race Goes to War: Ollie Stewart and the Reporting of Black Correspondents in World War II.* Santa Monica, CA: Now and Then, 2015.

Pogue, Forrest C. *George C. Marshall: Ordeal and Hope, 1939-1942.* London: MacGibbon and Kee, 1965.

———. *George C. Marshall: Organizer of Victory, 1943-1945.* New York: Viking Press, 1973.

———. *Pogue's War.* Lexington: University of Kentucky Press, 2001.

———. *The Supreme Command.* Washington, DC: Office of the Chief of Military History, 1954.

Pollock, James Crothers. *The Politics of Crisis Reporting: Learning to be a Foreign Correspondent.* New York: Praeger, 1981.

Preston, Paul. *We Saw Spain Die: Foreign Correspondents in the Spanish Civil War.* London: Constable, 2008.

Prochnau, William. *Once upon a Distant War: David Halberstam, Neil Sheehan, Peter Arnett; Young War Correspondents and Their Early Vietnam Battles.* New York: Vintage Books, 1995.

Pyle, Ernie. *Brave Men.* Lincoln: University of Nebraska Press, 2001.

———. *Here Is Your War.* New York: Pocket Books, 1944.

Rame, David. *Road to Tunis.* New York: Macmillan, 1944.

Redding, John M., and Harold I. Leyshon. *Skyways to Berlin: With the American Flyers in England.* London: Hutchinson, 1944.

Reporting World War II. 2 vols. New York: Library of America, 1995.

Reynolds, David. *In Command of History: Churchill Fighting and Writing World War II*. London: Allen Lane, 2004.

———. *Rich Relations: The American Occupation of Britain, 1942–1945*. London: Harper Collins, 1995.

Reynolds, Quentin. *By Quentin Reynolds*. New York: McGraw-Hill, 1963.

———. *The Curtain Rises*. New York: Random House, 1944.

Ridgway, Matthew B. *Soldier: The Memoirs of Matthew B. Ridgway*. New York: Harper, 1956.

Roberts, Gene, and Hank Klibanoff. *The Race Beat: The Press, the Civil Rights Struggle, and the Awakening of a Nation*. New York: Vintage, 2007.

Roeder, George H. *The Censored War: American Visual Experience during World War II*. New Haven, CT: Yale University Press, 1993.

Romeiser, John B., ed. *"Beachhead Don": Reporting the War from the European Theater, 1942-1945*. New York: Fordham University Press, 2004.

———. *Combat Reporter: Don Whitehead's World War II Diary and Memoirs*. New York: Fordham University Press, 2006.

Roosevelt, Elliott, ed. *FDR: His Personal Letters*. 2 vols. New York: Duell, Sloan and Pearce, 1950.

Roosevelt, Franklin D. *Complete Presidential Press Conferences of Franklin D. Roosevelt*. New York: Da Capo Press, 1972.

Ruppenthal, Roland G. *Logistical Support of the Armies*. 2 vols. Washington, DC: Office of the Chief of Military History, 1953.

Ryan, Cornelius. *A Bridge Too Far*. New York: Touchstone, 1995.

Salisbury, Harrison. *A Journey for Our Times: A Memoir*. New York: Harper and Row, 1983.

Sandler, Stanley. *Segregated Skies: All-Black Combat Squadrons of WWII*. Washington, DC: Smithsonian Institution Press, 1992.

Schaffer, Ronald. *Wings of Judgment: American Bombing in World War II*. New York: Oxford University Press, 1985.

Schneider, James C. *Should America Go to War? The Debate over Foreign Policy in Chicago, 1939-1941*. Chapel Hill: University of North Carolina Press, 1989.

Seelye, John. *War Games: Richard Harding Davis and the New Imperialism*. Amherst: University of Massachusetts Press, 2003.

Seib, Philip. *Beyond the Front Lines: How the News Media Cover a World Shaped by War*. Basingstoke, UK: Palgrave, 2004.

Sevareid, Eric. *Not So Wild a Dream: A Personal Story of Youth and War and the American Faith*. New York: Athenaeum, 1976.

Shapiro, Lionel S. B. *They Left the Back Door Open: A Chronicle of the Allied Campaign in Sicily and Italy*. Toronto: The Ryerson Press, 1944.

Sheean, Vincent. *Between the Thunder and the Sun*. London: Macmillan, 1943.

Sherry, Michael S. *The Rise of American Air Power: The Creation of Armageddon*. New Haven, CT: Yale University Press, 1987.

Sherwood, Robert E. *Roosevelt and Hopkins: An Intimate History*. Rev. ed. New York: Harper and Row, 1950.

Shirer, William. *The Nightmare Years, 1930-1940*. New York: Bantam, 1985.

Sitkoff, Harvard. *Toward Freedom Land: The Long Struggle for Racial Equality in America*. Lexington: University Press of Kentucky, 2010.

Sorel, Nancy Caldwell. *The Women Who Wrote the War: The Riveting Saga of World War II's Daredevil Women Correspondents*. New York: Arcade, 2011.

Sperber, A. M. *Murrow: His Life and Times*. London: Michael Joseph, 1987.

Stacks, John F. *Scotty: James B. Reston and the Rise and Fall of American Journalism.* Boston: Little, Brown, 2003.

Steele, Richard W. *The First Offensive 1942: Roosevelt, Marshall and the Making of American Strategy.* Bloomington: Indiana University Press, 1973.

———. *Propaganda in an Open Society: The Roosevelt Administration and the Media, 1933-1941.* Westport, CT: Greenwood Press, 1985.

Steinbeck, John. *Once There Was a War.* New York: Penguin, 2007.

Sterne, Joseph R. L. *Combat Correspondents: The Baltimore Sun in World War II.* Baltimore: Maryland Historical Society, 2009.

Stoler, Mark A. *The Politics of the Second Front: American Military Planning and Diplomacy in Coalition Warfare, 1941-1943.* Westport, CT: Greenwood Press, 1977.

Sulzberger, C[yrus] L. *A Long Row of Candles: Memoirs and Diaries, 1933-54.* London: Macdonald, 1969.

Sweeney, Michael S. *The Military and the Press: An Uneasy Truce.* Evanston IL: Northwestern University Press, 2006.

———. *Secrets of Victory: The Office of Censorship and the American Press and Radio in World War II.* Chapel Hill: University of North Carolina Press, 2001.

Sylvan, William C., and Francis G. Smith. *Normandy to Victory: The War Diary of General Courtney H. Hodges and the U.S. First Army.* Lexington: University Press of Kentucky, 2008.

Talese, Guy. *The Kingdom and the Power.* New York: World Publishing, 1969.

Taylor, Frederick. *Dresden: Tuesday 13 February 1945.* London: Bloomsbury, 2004.

Thompson, R. W. *Men under Fire.* London: Macdonald, 1946.

Thussu, Daya Kishan, and Des Freedman, eds. *War and the Media: Reporting Conflict 24/7.* London: Sage, 2003.

Tobin, James. *Ernie Pyle's War: America's Eyewitness to World War II.* New York: Free Press, 2006.

Tregaskis, Richard. *Invasion Diary.* Lincoln: University of Nebraska Press, 2004.

Trimble, Vance H., ed. *Scripps-Howard Handbook.* Cincinnati, OH: E. W. Scripps, 1981.

US Congress. *Congressional Record: Proceedings and Debates of the 78th Congress.* Washington, DC: US Government Printing Office, 1944–45.

US State Department. *Foreign Relations of the United States; The Conferences at Washington, 1941–1942, and Casablanca, 1943.* Washington, DC: US Government Printing Office, 1968.

US War Department. *Regulations for Correspondents Accompanying U.S. Army Forces in the Field.* Washington DC, 1941.

Vaughan-Thomas, Wynford. *Anzio.* New York: Holt, Rinehart, and Winston, 1961.

Voss, Frederick S. *Reporting the War: The Journalistic Coverage of World War II.* Washington, DC: Smithsonian, 1994.

Wade, Betsy, ed. *Forward Positions: The War Correspondence of Homer Bigart.* Fayetteville: University of Arkansas Press, 1992.

Walker, Fred L. *From Texas to Rome: A General's Journal.* Dallas, TX: Taylor Publishing, 1969.

Waugh, Evelyn. *Put Out More Flags.* London: Penguin, 2000.

Weigley, Russell F. *Eisenhower's Lieutenants: The Campaign of France and Germany, 1944–1945.* Bloomington: Indiana University Press, 1981.

Weinberg, Gerhard L. *A World at Arms: A Global History of World War II.* Cambridge, UK: Cambridge University Press, 1994.

Wellard, James. *The Man in a Helmet: The Life of General Patton.* London: Eyre and Spottiswoode, 1947.

Wertenbaker, Charles C. *Invasion!* New York: Appleton-Century, 1944.

Whelan, Richard. *Robert Capa: A Biography*. New York: Alfred A. Knopf, 1985.

———. *This Is War! Robert Capa at Work*. New York: ICM/Steidl, 2007.

White, Osmar. *Conquerors' Road: An Eyewitness Report of Germany 1945*. Cambridge: Cambridge University Press, 1996.

White, Graham J. *FDR and the Press*. Chicago: University of Chicago Press, 1979.

Winfield, Betty Houchin. *FDR and the News Media*. New York: Columbia University Press, 1994.

Winkler, Allan M. *The Politics of Propaganda: The Office of War Information*. New Haven, CT: Yale University Press, 1978.

Winton, Harold R. *Corps Commanders of the Bulge: Six Generals and Victory in the Ardennes*. Lawrence: University Press of Kansas, 2007.

Zacher, Dale E. *The Scripps Newspapers Go to War, 1914-1918*. Urbana: University of Illinois Press, 2008.

Zanuck, Darryl F. *Tunis Expedition*. New York: Random House, 1943.

Articles and Chapters in Edited Collections

Ault, Phil. "Southern Tunisia." In *Springboard to Berlin*, edited by John A. Parris and Ned Russell, 283–315. New York: Thomas Crowell, 1943.

Beckles, Gordon. "Our Reporters under Blitzkrieg." *Living Age* (January 1941): 448–52.

Biddle, Tami Davis. "Dresden 1945: Reality, History, and Memory." *Journal of Military History* 72 (2008): 413–49.

Burma, John H. "An Analysis of the Present Negro Press." *Social Forces* 26 (1947/8): 172–80.

Carpenter, Iris. "The Ardennes: As I Saw It." In *Danger Forward: The Story of the First Division in World War II*, edited by H. R. Knickerbocker et al., 333–51. Washington, DC: Society of the First Division, 1947.

Casey, Steven. "Reporting from the Battlefield: Censorship and Journalism." In *The Cambridge History of the Second World War*, edited by Richard J. Bosworth and Joe Maiolo, II: 117–38. Cambridge, UK: Cambridge University Press, 2015.

———. "War Correspondents." In *Oxford Bibliographies in Military History*, edited by Dennis Showalter. New York: Oxford University Press, 2014.

———. "Wilfred Burchett and the United Nations Command's Media Relations during the Korean War." *Journal of Military History* 74 (2010): 523–56.

Curley, Tom, and John Maxwell Hamilton. Introduction to *Ed Kennedy's War: V-E Day, Censorship, and the Associated Press*, edited by Julia Kennedy Cochran, vii–xxii. Baton Rouge: Louisiana State University Press, 2012.

Disher, Leo. "H.M.S. Walney." In *Springboard to Berlin*, edited by John A. Parris and Ned Russell, 91–125. New York: Thomas Crowell, 1943.

Dupuy, R. Ernest. "Bonn and Remagen: As I Saw It." In *Danger Forward: The Story of the First Division in World War II*, edited by H. R. Knickerbocker et al, 370–80. Washington, DC: Society of the First Division, 1947.

Funk, Arthur L. "Negotiating the 'Deal with Darlan.'" *Journal of Contemporary History* 8 (1973): 92–117.

Gibbs, Philip. Introduction to *Days of Glory: The Sketch Book of a Correspondent at the Front*, edited by Frederic Villiers, v–xii. New York: G. H. Doran, 1920.

Johnson, Gerald K. "The Black Soldiers in the Ardennes." *Soldiers* 36 (1981): 16–19.

Kesting, Robert W. "Conspiracy to Discredit the Black Buffaloes: The 92nd Infantry in World War II. *Journal of Negro History* 72 (1987): 1–19.

Kozloff, Sarah. "Wyler's Wars." *Film History: An International Journal* 20 (2008): 456–73.

Lovelace, Alexander G. "The Image of a General: The Wartime Relationship between General George S. Patton Jr. and the American Media." *Journalism History* 40 (2014): 108–20.

Matloff, Maurice. "The 90-Division Gamble." In *Command Decisions*, edited by Kent Roberts Greenfield, 365–81. Washington, DC: Center of Military History, 2000.

Middleton, Drew. "The Last Kilometer: As I Saw It." In *Danger Forward: The Story of the First Division in World War II*, edited by H. R. Knickerbocker et al, 397–403. Washington, DC: Society of the First Division, 1947.

Parris, John A. "The Groundwork." In *Springboard to Berlin*, edited by John A. Parris and Ned Russell, 11–90. New York: Thomas Crowell, 1943.

Parris, John A., and Ned Russell. Prologue to *Springboard to Berlin*, edited by John A. Parris and Ned Russell, 3–10. New York: Thomas Crowell, 1943.

Pratt, Fletcher. "How the Censors Rigged the News." *Harper's* (February 1946): 100, 101–2.

Rollins, Andrea G. "We Made History: Collective Memory and the Legacy of the Tuskegee Airmen," *Journal of Social Issues* 71 (2015): 264–78.

Russell, Ned. "Algiers." In *Springboard to Berlin*, edited by John A. Parris and Ned Russell, 127–55. New York: Thomas Crowell, 1943.

———. "The Long Chance." In *Springboard to Berlin*, edited by John A. Parris and Ned Russell, 199–269. New York: Thomas Crowell, 1943.

Salaita, George D. "Embellishing Omaha Beach." *Journal of Military* History 72 (2008): 531–34.

Salisbury, Harrison. Foreword to *Forward Positions: The War Correspondence of Homer Bigart*, edited by Betsy Wade, xi–xvi. Fayetteville: University of Arkansas Press, 1992.

Schaffer, Ronald. "American Military Ethics in World War II: The Bombing of German Civilians." *Journal of American History* 67 (1980): 318–34.

Stephens, Rodney. "Shattered Windows, German Spies, and Zigzag Trenches: World War I through the Eyes of Richard Harding Davies." *Historian* 65 (2002): 43–73.

Stoler, Mark A. "The 'Pacific-First' Alternative in American World War II Strategy." *International History Review* 2 (1980): 432–52.

Thompson, John. "Tunisia: As I Saw It." In *Danger Forward: The Story of the First Division in World War II*, edited by H. R. Knickerbocker et al, 81–98. Washington, DC: Society of the First Division, 1947.

Vogel, Detlef. "German and Allied Conduct of the War in the West." In *Germany and the Second World War*, edited by Horst Boog, Gerhard Krebs, and Detlef Vogel, 7:459–702. Oxford: Oxford University Press, 2006.

Wade, Betsy. Introduction to *Forward Positions: The War Correspondence of Homer Bigart*, edited by Betsy Wade, xvii–xxv. Fayetteville: University of Arkansas Press, 1992.

Whitehead, Don. "A Correspondent's View of D-Day." In *D-Day 1944*, edited by Theodore A. Wilson, 203–21. Lawrence: University of Kansas Press, 1994.

———. "Normandy: As I Saw It." In *Danger Forward: The Story of the First Division in World War II*, edited by H. R. Knickerbocker et al, 203–19. Washington, DC: Society of the First Division, 1947.

Williams, Greer. "I Worked for McCormick." *The Nation* (October 10, 1942): 348.

Internet Sources

Chenowaeth, Doral. "54 War Correspondents K.I.A. WWII." Accessed January 2016, http://www.54warcorrespondents-kia-30-ww2.com.

"FDR's White House Map Room." Accessed February 2015. http://www.fdrlibrary.marist.edu/aboutfdr/maproom.html, accessed February 2015.

Kasper, Anne S. "Interview with Helen Kirkpatrick Milbank, April 3, 4, and 5, 1990." Washington Press Club Foundation: Women in Journalism, Oral History Project. Accessed February 2015. http://beta.wpcf.org/oralhistory/kirk.html.

Lieb, Jack. *From D-Day to Germany*. National Archives, YouTube video. Accessed June 2015. https://www.youtube.com/watch?v=jkRDe6epeVg.

Memphis Belle: Original Eighth Air Force Movie. Accessed February 2015. https://www.youtube.com/watch?v=4ZO6UtAfxEM.

Urquhart, Brian. "Character Sketches: Trygve Lie." Accessed January 2016. http://www.un.org/apps/news/infocus/trygvie-lie.asp#.VnfnqTbVXzI.

Unpublished Material

Barbour, John, and Wes Gallagher. "While the Smoke Is Still Rising." AP28, Writings About the AP, Series I: Unpublished Writings, box 1, AP Corporate Archives

Gabel, Christopher R. "The U.S. Army GHQ Maneuvers of 1941." PhD thesis. Ohio State University, 1981.

Hightower, John. "AP: The Chief Source of the News—the Decision Makers." AP28, Writings About the AP, Series I: Unpublished Writings, box 3, AP Corporate Archives.

INDEX